SCHOLARLY COMMUNICATION LIBRARIANSHIP
AND OPEN KNOWLEDGE

MARIA BONN, JOSH BOLICK, AND
WILL CROSS, EDITORS

Association of College and Research Libraries
A division of the American Library Association
Chicago, Illinois 2023

The paper used in this publication meets the minimum requirements of american national standard for information sciences–permanence of paper for printed library materials, ansi z39.48-1992. ∞

Library of Congress Control Number: 2023946575

Printed in the United States of America.
27 26 25 24 23 5 4 3 2 1

TABLE OF
CONTENTS

PART III. VOICES FROM THE FIELD: PERSPECTIVES, INTERSECTIONS, AND CASE STUDIES

CONCLUSION: ADDING YOUR VOICE TO THE CONVERSATION

ACCESS IS PRAXIS

Christopher Hollister and Micah Vandegrift

In April of 2018, an energetic hodgepodge of library practitioners, educators, activists, and provocateurs assembled at North Carolina State University's James B. Hunt Jr. Library to participate in a symposium and unconference around the theme of developing an open textbook on scholarly communication. This event, and its ultimate goal of publishing such a work, were the brainchildren of three leaders in the overlapping areas of open education and scholarly communication: Dr. Maria Bonn, Josh Bolick, and Will Cross. The wisdom of their shared vision for this undertaking was supported by a grant from the Institute for Museum and Library Services (LG-72-17-0132-17), and it attracted like-minded professionals from near and far who felt a strong desire to participate in what the authors of this preface would qualify as a pivotal unconference event.

The primary objective of what became known as the OER + Scholarly Communication Unconference (https://lisoer.wordpress.ncsu.edu/symposium/) was for attendees to help Maria, Josh, and Will to articulate, organize, and map what would ultimately become this volume, an open textbook for library and information science (LIS) students, and an open educational resource (OER) for LIS educators to adopt and adapt. During the course of the unconference, the authors of this preface, Christopher Hollister and Micah Vandegrift—henceforth "we" and "us"—along with Dr. Ashley Sands of IMLS, came together in a self-formed breakout group dubbed "Access as Praxis." Our group was charged with the task of aligning the library field's foundational value of access with the development of this open text.

The proclamation inscribed above the central entrance to the Boston Public Library—FREE TO ALL—is a clear expression and demonstration of how unfettered access to information is regarded by librarians as a fundamental professional value; it is an inherent societal good, and it is a right of the citizenry, at least in aspiration. We would argue, however, that for decades the library profession has operated in a manner that runs counter to this core value. In the aggregate, today's libraries are complicit in the creation of a paywalled environment in which publicly funded research is accessible only to those privileged few who can afford it. In addition, we assert that libraries are complicit actors in a stratagem that permits the commercial publishing enterprise to wield monopolistic authority in that paywalled setting. We contend, therefore, that an open access revolution is necessary to break from this recalcitrant system, and we reason that involving a new generation of scholarly communication and allied librarians is critical to that cause. Accordingly, this book—*Scholarly Communication Librarianship and Open Knowledge*—and the related online community and repository the Scholarly Communications Notebook were created were created to engage LIS students in the formative space of their library education, and it was developed as an open text to demonstrate access solutions through professional practice.

The late 2010s granted a spectrum of new lenses through which scholarly communication was viewed. Societal shifts toward equity, diversity, and inclusion became as central to the open conversation as access. The distance between principles and practices of librarianship narrowed even as visibility highlighted distinctions between what we say we believe and what we do. Responding to these, we and our colleagues at the OER + Scholarly Communication Unconference wrestled with the opportunity to clearly express in a resource like this, that *access is what a library is, does, represents, and advances.* Much of the work of increasing equitable access has been born out of the professional literature and industry-shifting ideas of scholarly communication. In the equitable turn, we intend readers to see a political statement, a statement about the future to which we aspire and a statement in an challenge to the industrial, commercial, capitalistic tendencies encroaching on higher education. It is our hope that students, readers, educators, and adaptors of this resource will find and embrace these themes throughout the text and embody them in their work. Access is praxis.

SCHOLCOMM IS RAD

This book was born as a collaboration among three librarians and educators interested in the intersection of scholarly communication (or scholcomm, as it's often abbreviated) librarianship and open education which offers a unique opportunity to expand knowledge of scholarly communication topics in both education and practice. Topics like copyright in teaching and research environments, author's rights, academic publishing, emerging modes of scholarship, scholarly sharing, and impact measurement are central to the work of scholarship and to the libraries that play an important role in scholarly work.

This area of librarianship, as you will read in the text that follows, is vibrant, exciting, and constantly evolving. It can be challenging, exhausting, and frustrating, too. Often, it's all of these things at the same time, which may be the reason many of us find it rewarding. It is an area of specialization, and it impacts and shapes many other aspects of academic librarianship, and in some cases other library fields: public libraries, school libraries, and special libraries and archives. These areas of work and others closely aligned with them have grown rapidly, in every sense, over the course of the twenty-first century. Nearly everyone working in an academic library, in some way or another, is engaging with these topics to a greater or lesser degree. That doesn't mean we all need to be scholarly communication librarians, but it does mean that greater literacy on these topics is helpful, and sometimes necessary, as libraries continue to face significant challenges to serving our basic missions and meeting the needs of our users. Nonetheless, formal graduate training on these issues has lagged behind growth in the field.

Open education is a concept and movement that similarly concerns ownership and access, with a focus on teaching and learning content, such as textbooks, though not limited to that format. Open education (discussed in part II, chapter 3 of this book, "Open Education") is itself an area of scholarly communication work as it deals with open licenses, issues of copyright and fair use, and efforts to reduce or entirely eliminate cost barriers to educational content and success. This area of work has seen enormous growth recently, much of it supported by librarians. In open education, we saw an opportunity: Why not leverage open resources to address the gap in teaching on these timely and critical scholarly communication topics? So an open book on scholarly communication librarianship was conceived, and we set about building it.

The result is a book that has itself evolved over time and reflects hundreds of conversations with valued peers, allies, and critics—often both peers and allies AND critics, which is a good thing. Along the way we got amazing support from the Institute for Museum and Library Services (IMLS), including two grants that have enabled us to conduct research and host a convening to help better grasp relevant needs and improve our varied understandings of them. We found a willing and supportive publisher in ACRL, which surprised us by not even hesitating when we stressed the importance of an open license and free availability. We brought on four widely respected experts on topical areas to edit chapters with the authors of their choosing. We issued an open call for contributed short pieces that you'll find in part III:

"Voices from the Field." Altogether, there are nearly eighty contributors to this book, and we are deeply grateful to them for their generosity in sharing their time, networks, and knowledge to support this project.

Our hope is that this resource will be adopted in library and information studies courses and lead to increased instruction on the issues and practices contained within it. There are a small but growing number of Topics in Scholarly Communication or similarly framed courses for which this book could serve as primary material. There may be more granular courses, such as on library publishing, open education, or data management and curation, for which portions of this book might be suitable. There are also many other courses on any number of topics where there's a connection and an opportunity to grab the portions that may be helpful readings: how open access intersects with collection work, or with the ACRL *Framework for Information Literacy for Higher Education*, for example. We also hope it will serve as a general introduction for the growing number of librarians who are seeking additional knowledge and skills or being tasked with new duties and want an orientation to the field or areas within it. The contributed chapters are informative and engaging and will make interesting reads for practitioners and educators looking to expand their knowledge of important, current topics.

The book consists of three parts. Part I offers definitions of scholarly communication and scholarly communication librarianship and provides an introduction to the social, economic, technological, and policy/legal pressures that underpin and shape scholarly communication work in libraries. These pressures, which have framed ACRL's understanding of scholarly communication for the better part of the past two decades, have unsettled many foundational assumptions and practices in the field, removing core pillars of scholarly communication as it was practiced in the twentieth century. These pressures have also cleared fresh ground, and scholarly communication practitioners have begun to seed the space with values and practices designed to renew and often improve the field. Part II begins with an introduction to "open," the core response to the pressures described in part I. This part offers a general overview of the idea of openness in scholarly communication followed by chapters on different permutations and practices of open, each edited by a recognized expert of these areas with authors of their selection. Amy Buckland edited chapter 2.1, "Open Access." Brianna Marshall edited chapter 2.2, "Open Data." Lillian Hogendoorn edited chapter 2.3, "Open Education." Micah Vandegrift edited chapter 2.4, "Open Science and Infrastructure." Each of them brought on incredible expertise through contributors whom they identified, through both original contributions and repurposing existing openly licensed work, which is something we want to model where possible. Part III consists of twenty-four concise perspectives, intersections, and case studies from practicing librarians and closely related stakeholders, which we hope will stimulate discussion and reflection on theory and implications for practice. In every single case, we're really excited by the editors and authors and the ideas they bring to the whole. Each contribution features light pedagogical apparatuses like suggested further reading, discussion or reflection prompts, and potential activities. It's all available for free and openly licensed with a Creative Commons Attribution Non-Commercial (CC BY-NC) license, so anyone is encouraged to grab whatever parts are useful and to adapt and repurpose and improve them to meet specific course goals and student needs within the confines of the license. If that Creative Commons license is unfamiliar, read on.

One thing we also learned as we developed this book is that a book is inherently static and unable to change at anything close to the rate that our work changes. It's also inherently linear, which our work is not. It's also limited; even though there are roughly eighty great contributors, they don't represent every (contested) perspective, issue, or approach to scholcomm work. That realization led to another IMLS grant, and the development of an online community and repository that we are calling the Scholarly Communication Notebook (SCN), which we hope will become the locus of an active, inclusive, empowered community of practice for teaching scholarly communication to emerging librarians. We consciously modeled the SCN on Robin DeRosa and Rajiv Jhangiani's Open Pedagogy Notebook. Like the OPN, the Scholarly Communication Notebook will host community-designed examples of teaching and doing the work of scholarly communication, examples that we hope will be regularly refreshed by librarians from across the field as well as LIS faculty and students completing coursework on these topics. You can find the SCN at https://www.oercommons. org/hubs/SCN. There's additional information about it on our project site (https://lisoer. wordpress.ncsu.edu/). SCN content that was directly supported by the grant is detailed on the News page of the site, generally with a post for each item (search for "New to the SCN").

This book has been a long time in the making. Since we first started working together, there have been social and political crises and reckonings and a global pandemic that fundamentally changed our lives. Among the contributors to this book, there have been marriages, children born, loved ones lost, career changes, job changes, and many other events large and small that have had an impact upon us in all things. As this book has come together, we have sought to extend grace and understanding to everyone at every point. Many of the crises are ongoing as of 2023, and, of course, this book isn't a matter of life and death. Still, we believe in the work, and we're humbled and grateful to our contributors for sticking with us to the end. While we recognize that the impacts of the last several years are not evenly distributed and that we bear substantial privilege through our identities and circumstances, we also know that this book was developed during one of the most difficult experiences of our lives. Our contributors have generously shared their knowledge and time throughout development. If this book succeeds, they are the source of that success. Where this book is not successful, we bear the responsibility. Critical feedback is fair, and welcome, and will be carefully considered for revision in future editions, so let us know how we can make this work more equitable and useful.

A BRIEF NOTE ABOUT ORDER OF AUTHORSHIP

As with many things in the academy, selecting the order of listed authorship in a work can be both terribly consequential and slightly ridiculous. One the one hand, academic credit is the coin of the realm in higher education. Careers are made by being listed as first author in prestigious venues, and too many "third author" bylines can raise the eyebrows of a tenure committee and do real harm to an emerging scholar. As discussed in several parts of this work, most academic authors simply give away most of the commercially recognized legal rights in their scholarship on the assumption that the real prize is the prestige and impact of appearing in the right venue, which will assure promotion, tenure, major grants, and the other trappings of success. Academic credit matters, often down to the most minute detail.

On the other hand, in cases where many people work together to create something—especially something as large and wide-ranging as a textbook—identifying who contributed *the most* to a book is a bit of a fool's errand. Roughly eighty named authors contributed written materials for this book, and every one of us can point to a mountain of prior work we built upon as well as a legion of uncredited mentors, assistants, friendly readers, project managers, and so forth, without whom our work would have been genuinely impossible. The decision to privilege the three of us as the named authors and editors rather than, for example, our editor Erin (who assembled everything) is enough of a fiction without placing too much weight on whether Josh's name appears before or after Maria's on the cover of the book and where Will fits into all of this.

Nevertheless, someone has to be listed first. Due to the nuances of our particular field and our previous body of work, we're fortunate that deciding whether this will be cited as Bonn et al. (2023), Bolick et al. (2023), or Cross et al. (2023) is mostly (with apologies) an academic decision. In cases where there are real consequences, ethical scholars often grant pride of first authorship to the person with a looming tenure decision or simply to the most junior scholar who would presumably benefit the most from the citation. Strategic groups may instead list the most famous or senior scholar first in the hopes that the big name will get their article in the door and onto the page. Corresponding authors are often important in so-called transformative agreements, in which libraries and publishers negotiate a deal that provides for access to subscribed content and open access to articles produced by researchers at the negotiating institution. Where multiple authors from multiple institutions are involved, the designated corresponding author might determine if an article is open or not, which can further complicate these decisions.

Cheeky (and usually fully tenured) scholars have also decided authorship order based on whimsical methods including flipping a coin, holding a brownie bake-off, staging an arm-wrestling or a free-throw-shooting contest, examining the fluctuation of transatlantic exchange rates, or writing and sharing randomizing computer code included in the article itself.

Ultimately, we decided on the order you see on the cover of this book. Nevertheless, we would like to acknowledge that each one of us made invaluable contributions and could have made a strong case for being listed first. We would also like to recognize that, in addition to the three names you see on the cover, we owe gratitude to many. The Institute for Museum and Library Services (IMLS) provided direct financial support that enabled research into stakeholder perceptions and a gathering in Raleigh, North Carolina, in April 2018 where forty of the brightest minds in scholcomm brainstormed with us. Our grant officer, Ashley Sands, has been wonderful. Our editor, Erin Nevius, has been exceedingly patient, flexible, supportive, and understanding. She expressed enthusiasm from the beginning and readily agreed to the openness of the end result. The source of our ability to provide grace and understanding to our contributors is Erin, who extended the same to us.

Speaking of contributors, we've benefitted immeasurably from the talents and generosity of chapter editors: Amy Buckland, Brianna Marshall, Lillian Hogendoorn, and Micah Vandegrift. They each brought their own unique style and deep understanding to their chapters. The authors they selected to work with, including the authors of open content they chose to repurpose, are among the best of our peers. Amy, Brianna, Lillian, Micah, and other contributors, we're excited for people to read your chapters and to see your work shape collective understanding.

Part III contributors were selected from an incredible set of proposals solicited through an open call and developed in 2020 and 2021. We're thrilled with the resulting pieces and the people and ideas included among them. Again, you all make this work valuable, and we hope readers will reflect on and learn from your contributions. We also owe a great debt to the communities of practice and professional groups that have made this work possible. The landscape would look very different if SPARC and the Open Education Network weren't a part of it, and that's true for this book as well. Thanks to everyone who reviewed a conference proposal or participated in open peer review, who attended a conference session or roundtable, who complicated and challenged our thinking, who provided sounding boards, and who supported us.

Josh would like to thank the many, many people who've supported him and this work. Peter Fritzler and Anne Pemberton planted a seed. Micah Vandegrift hired him with little library experience and gave him real responsibilities and access to his network. Ada Emmett seemed as excited to work with him and he was to work with her. Kevin Smith has been a consistent supporter, as have many other friends and colleagues at KU who are too numerous to name but whom he appreciates deeply. Sarah Cohen and David Ernst nurtured an interest in OER and offered an opportunity to work with the Open Education Network. Heather Joseph has mentored in important and lasting ways, though she may not realize them. He is personally grateful to everyone who contributed to this project in myriad ways, too many to name. Will and Maria are the absolute best collaborators and through our work together over these years have become lasting friends. His dad, Tim, is the best there is. His wife and partner, Dr. Aimee Armande Wilson, believed in and encouraged and supported him at every step, especially when he doubted himself, which, to be transparent, is frequently. Finally, tacos and bicycles—he can't imagine life without you.

Maria would like to thank her family—Nick Bonn, John Wilkin, and Mary Bonn—for their support and willingness to take dinner-table time to discuss things like copyright and research impact from perspectives as varied as a high school student, a seasoned library director, and a nonagenarian leftist. She would also like to thank several years' worth of LIS students at UIUC in her Academic Library and Scholarly Communications classes who bore with early iterations of the content of this book and contributed by asking questions and giving feedback. Most of all, she would like to thank Josh and Will, coeditors and friends, for all they have taught her, for keeping her on her professional toes, and for, yes, endorsing her name appearing first on the cover because of a career situation that is far too complicated for someone in her twenty-fifth year in the profession.

Will would like to thank his friends, mentors, and coconspirators for opening doors, laughing with rather than at him (as is often deserved), and providing ongoing inspiration, support, and direction. Particular gratitude is due to Anne Klinefelter and Lolly Gasaway at UNC Law, Kevin Smith then at Duke, and Greg Raschke at NC State, all of whom helped turn a wayward constitutional law dork into a mostly presentable scholcommie. So many folks, including Mira Waller, Kim Duckett, Phil Edwards, Hilary Davis, Molly Keener, Lisa Macklin, Kris Alpi, Lindsey Gumb, Lillian Hogendoorn, and Micah Vandegrift, have helped him see the field with new eyes, while Peter Jaszi, Prue Adler, Carla Myers, Kyle Courtney, Anne Gilliland, Dave Hansen, and especially Meredith Jacob have kept the law alive in his heart and his work. Maria and Josh have been exceptional partners in crime for the better part of seven years—may it be seventy more. Most of all, Will would like to thank his parents, his brother Patrick, and especially Kimberly and Michael, from brightly which arise all adjectives.

PART I
WHAT IS SCHOLARLY COMMUNICATION?

1

BASICS AND DEFINITIONS

SCHOLCOMM IS...

Josh Bolick with Maria Bonn and Will Cross

et's begin at the beginning with a simple definition. The Association of College and Research Libraries (ACRL) defines scholarly communication as "the system through which research and other scholarly writings are created, evaluated for quality, disseminated to the scholarly community, and preserved for future us."[1] Scholarly communication isn't any single practice, output, format, platform, or stakeholder, but a complex system of these things, all of which are integral to the system. The system includes creation, evaluation, dissemination, and preservation, all important functions that will be explored further in this book and through suggested further reading and discussion questions.

ACRL's definition continues, "The system includes both formal means of communication, such as publication in peer-reviewed journals, and informal channels, such as electronic mailing lists."[2] This understates the incredibly diverse array of scholarly outputs or products. Formal scholarly communication outputs include academic journal articles, monographs, edited volumes and their constituent chapters, conference papers and proceedings, posters, theses and dissertations, grant proposals, and other products that frequently undergo some sort of certification: peer review, editorial selection, committee approval, or a combination of these modes of vetting. These forms are relatively stable, though as you'll gather by the end of this book, there's no shortage of innovation in each of these spaces. This book, whether you're holding a physical printed copy in your hands or are reading electronically on a computer, tablet, or phone, is an example of a formal means of communication. The editors developed the concept, pitched it to an editor, submitted a formal proposal for evaluation by ACRL's New Publications Advisory Board, negotiated rights, signed a contract, and worked closely with ACRL editorial staff through and up to the point of publication.

"Informal channels" are generally more varied and dynamic than the formal means listed above, as there's less of an established vetting process for these formats and the ideas shared through them. Both formal and informal channels, of course, are subject to external evaluation, at least insofar as they can be accessed for evaluation. But the means of informal scholarly communication are more in the control of the researcher than are formal publishing venues. These channels include personal websites and blogs, academic networks and platforms, and other social media; conversations in the hallway at conferences; and indeed, electronic mailing lists and similar online discussion forums, such as Google Groups and

Slack channels. A scholar can express an idea and hit the Send, Publish, Share, or Tweet button, and that idea is transmitted into the ether, where it can be examined, interrogated, critiqued, amplified, or rejected.

Both formal and informal means of scholarly communication serve important purposes, and each carries its own set of risks and rewards. Formal outputs are generally considered of higher academic merit, as they've been through an established vetting process and, hopefully, improved and refined by feedback from reviewers, editors, and other peers with disciplinary expertise. These outputs are the records of academic accomplishment and merit on which scholars build their careers through hiring and promotion, as well as seeking grants, prestigious appointments and editorial positions, and awards. Compiled into a curriculum vitae (Latin: "course of life"), also known as CV or vita, they comprise a researcher's scholarly identity. The perceived value of specific output modes vary across disciplines. For example, journal articles matter in humanities disciplines such as history, philosophy, or literary criticism, but the scholarly monograph, published by a university press with a prestigious reputation within a discipline or subdiscipline, is the pinnacle of humanistic scholarly achievement and frequently a requirement for promotion and tenure. By contrast, many researchers in the physical sciences wouldn't even consider developing a book. The journal article, published in the most prestigious journal possible and achieving a high number of citations, is the coin of the realm and the platform on which careers and academic prominence are built.

The processes behind these outputs are complex, lengthy, and subject to bias and exclusion. Publication cycles can take many months or even years, there are many potential bottlenecks, peer review is more biased and complicated than is generally believed, and editors wield enormous power over what and who gets published. Some aspects of publication are based on pre-internet conditions and have been resistant to change, adhering to practices such as delaying publication of a specific article until an entire issue is ready despite electronic publishing rendering such a delay, and arguably the very concept of volumes and issues, unnecessary and antiquated. These can be difficult conditions to navigate for early career researchers looking for their first job, seeking a grant, or going up for tenure, all of which you could find yourself doing depending on your professional goals.

Informal modes of scholarly communication, on the other hand, are more in the control of the communicating researcher, who determines if and when a blog post or working paper is shared, where, and under what conditions for reuse. They alone (or with chosen collaborators) determine the speed with which they share their ideas. They are entirely in control of content and may accept or reject suggestions and feedback according to their own assessment of its value. Creators are free to determine the best format and representation of their ideas rather than shoehorning truly innovative work into a traditional article or book format. They can iterate toward a more refined version of their work, perhaps as a precursor of formal publication or independent of formal publication. In many cases informal modes have more potential for readership and immediate impact, as they are less likely to have artificial scarcity imposed on them through a paywall or other access restriction, unless of course the scholar imposes those restrictions, which is their prerogative as creator and therefore copyright owner (more on this later). Immediate reactions can give the author a sense of the reception, currency, and potential impact of a project or output long before formal citations could accumulate given the publication cycles outlined above. These strengths are tempered, however, by the lack of formal evaluation, credentialing, and preservation. There's a growing movement toward citing these kinds of outputs, but wide disagreement over their importance and evaluation. A risk-averse early career researcher may have concerns about the impact of these modes on their nascent reputation. Tenure and promotion committees and grant review committees may not understand or appreciate the value of these outputs, which can put the researcher at a disadvantage for hiring, promotion, and funding opportunities.

Every researcher should critically evaluate these risks and rewards and choose the right course for themselves based on their disciplinary and institutional norms, as well as their goals for their work. In practice, formal and informal means of scholarly communication are complementary. They should be understood as a suite of tools and methods available to researchers to communicate their ideas and balance immediacy, impact, and autonomy with credentialing and advancement. A researcher might blog about an early form of an idea and seek feedback by promoting the blog on social media (informal). They might then present that idea at a conference as a working paper or poster, getting more feedback and critique, which informs an article subsequently submitted to a journal of their choosing (formal). After a round of peer review and revision, the article is accepted for publication and eventually published (formal). The author might share a version of this work on a personal web page or blog, through academic and personal social media, and track early measures of impact through a tool like Altmetric (informal) while awaiting the accumulation of citations (formal). Having established themselves as the expert on their idea, they might participate in media interviews (informal) or be invited to give a talk or presentation at a gathering of their peers (formal). In many cases, best possible outcomes can't be achieved through the sole use of formal or informal modes of scholarly communication, but through a savvy deployment of both.

Unfortunately, many researchers are trained on limited portions of the system and practices outlined above. They may take full courses on research methods, but publication norms frequently go entirely unaddressed or insufficiently covered, and the norms themselves warrant scrutiny anyway. Even established scholars who have learned how to adeptly navigate the system may not understand its intricacies and opacities, just as you might drive from one city to another without understanding the electrical and structural engineering of stoplights and bridges respectively. That's where academic librarians have an opportunity to develop and share expertise on these issues from our unique position as both frequent researchers ourselves and significant stakeholders in the scholarly communication system. We connect researchers with resources that inform their own research products, we perform publisher roles at an ever-growing rate, and we acquire those new creations from publishers and content aggregators (or at least we try to, as you will soon see). In other words, librarians have an important role to play in every aspect of the system of scholarly communication, from the creation of new knowledge to its evaluation, dissemination, and preservation. We can innovate for our own research outputs, as well as supporting other stakeholders in their own innovation. Many, many librarians are working in areas of scholarly communication, that will be developed for readers over the course of this book. So what is scholarly communication librarianship?

SCHOLARLY COMMUNICATION AND LIBRARIANSHIP

We would argue that every librarian working in an academic or research library is supporting scholarly communication, a position that we hope to convince you of throughout this book. A huge portion of academic librarian work consists of selecting and curating scholarly outputs, connecting researchers (students, faculty, and staff) with those outputs, and training them in their discovery, selection, evaluation, and appropriate use. Scholarly communication is deeply embedded in information literacy as defined by the ACRL *Framework for Information Literacy for Higher Education*.[3] We teach, consult, and advise on copyright, the ownership of information, and fair use. When that information is ours, as in the resources we create and host, we have an opportunity to openly license it so that our peers and the public can readily discover, access, and use our content and understand their rights to do so. The same is frequently true for special collections and archives, where a great deal of cultural content may be either in the public domain or where the institution controls copyright.

While scholarly communication issues are relevant to all of our jobs, especially in the liaison model,[4] it is the particular province of a growing and vibrant area of librarianship: scholarly communication librarians and librarians who specialize particular subareas of scholarly communication, such as copyright, publishing, open knowledge, open education, data, repositories, and closely related areas. If scholarly communication is "the system through which research and other scholarly writings are created, evaluated for quality, disseminated to the scholarly community, and preserved for future use" and "includes both formal means of communication, such as publication in peer-reviewed journals, and informal channels, such as electronic mailing lists," then scholarly communication librarians are those who directly and overtly support these functions and issues. Because this book is written by and for librarians engaged in scholarly communication work, we frequently refer to that work as "scholcomm" or "scholarly communication" without the "work" or similar modifier. While many librarians are scholarly communicators, in the sense of conducting and sharing the results of research, we are primarily interested in scholarly communication as a professional field of practice, and thus often refer to scholarly communication and scholarly communication library work interchangeably. Here are three librarians working in scholarly communication briefly describing their work in their own words:

> We're alive during an ongoing revolution in the ways people create, share, and build upon information. As a scholarly communication librarian, I'm a subject matter expert and point person for library services which support faculty, staff, and students as they engage with new and emerging forms of scholarly creation and dissemination. Most of my work blends instruction, resource sharing, and advocacy, to support liaison librarian colleagues, advise faculty and staff, and empower creators to share their intellectual work more openly. GVSU is a regional comprehensive university with a strong focus on undergraduate education and on professional graduate programs, so I spend a lot of time talking about open educational resources and copyright issues. For me, the heart of all scholarly communication work is getting people to think more critically about how they create and disseminate information, and then empowering them to take full advantage of the opportunities presented by technology to remove barriers to information.
>
> *Matt Ruen, Scholarly Communications Outreach Coordinator,*
> *Grand Valley State University*

As the scholarly communication librarian, the core of my work is relationship building. Secondarily, consultation, change management, and project management. This role is starting to be referred to as a "functional position" because it requires cross-training in technology and outreach to many different audiences. The web has opened new, flexible ways to create scholarship and share it with others like never before. You become a consultant on campus on the steps and considerations necessary to make those changes as well as a soothsayer around change, which can be scary for those with high stakes in scholarly output. Therefore, there is no successful scholarly communication project or work without strong relationships with faculty, students, administrators, and other librarians being on board. It requires staying up-to-date on policy, scholarship, and practice in the community of practice, then sharing that information with the library. It means helping the library lead radically new initiatives in academia in a local campus environment.

Camille Thomas, Scholarly Communication Librarian,
Florida State University

I support students, faculty, and staff in considering how they create, share, and value scholarly works by exposing them to the full range of options for their scholarship and teaching and encourage them to engage with methods that will increase access to their work. I challenge notions of prestige and critically examine the markers and metrics of quality and impact. Scholarly communication is constantly and quickly evolving and intersects with so many areas of librarianship and higher education, so one of my main roles is to educate about these changes within the libraries and across my institution. This requires continuous learning and close collaboration with colleagues so that we can blend our knowledge to understand how change is unfolding in different disciplines. Much of my time is spent in consultations, teaching, and holding events related to copyright, fair use, open access, open education, and research impact. I also participate in initiatives and conversations about collections, interlibrary loan, promotion and tenure processes, course redesign, and institutional policies on intellectual property and textbook adoptions.

Hillary Miller, Scholarly Communications Librarian,
Virginia Commonwealth University

These short statements are rich with information about how the authors define and approach their work and about what that work consists of in both theoretical and practical senses. In order to analyze and understand them, let's begin by viewing these statements through the lens of the ACRL definition of scholarly communication, with which you're already familiar:

Scholarly communication is the system through which research and other scholarly writings are created, evaluated for quality, disseminated to the scholarly community, and preserved for future use. The system includes both formal means of communication, such as publication in peer-reviewed journals, and informal channels, such as electronic mailing lists.[5]

Creation is a key concept; Matt, Camille, and Hillary each mention the creation of information or scholarly outputs and the status of researchers as creators. Creators are powerful; they have rights and the prerogative to exercise their rights. In the scholarly communication librarianship community, we refer to these rights as "author rights," the ability of authors to have an active role in the post-publication life of their work, a central scholarly communication librarianship concept that will be developed extensively throughout this book. Each of our colleagues moves from creation to sharing. Researchers don't merely create; researchers share their work; they disseminate, Camille says, "like never before." In other words, scholars communicate, and they are frequently educated, supported, and empowered to do so by librarians. Why do researchers disseminate? Hillary discusses impact, value, prestige, metrics, and markers of quality. These are reputational foundations on which scholars build careers. Matt and Camille reference "new and emerging forms" of scholarship, a nod to ACRL's formal and informal means of communication.

It's easy to see how the ACRL definition of scholarly communication is reflected in our colleagues' descriptions of their work, but how do they further explicate and complicate that short definition? What are the broader themes that emerge from a close reading of their statements?

Change is an important motif in their statements. There's evolution and revolution, and change anticipation and management. As Thomas observes, "the scholarly communication landscape has changed rapidly in the last few years, and the pace of change continues to increase."[6] Technology is one of the drivers of this change, as it creates new opportunities and pressures, new modes of conducting or producing scholarship, and new forms of scholarly outputs. New modes and forms have high stakes and implications for evaluation, grant-funding decisions, hiring, promotion and tenure, awards, and appointments to prestigious service positions. Change can be scary, especially for folks with less real and perceived power, and libraries can leverage relationships and expertise to lead change, to create new initiatives to support each other and our stakeholders, to have an impact on our own campuses as well as on higher education. To do this successfully, we must be flexible and dynamic, up-to-date, and cross-trained. We have to be critical, to understand and challenge traditional markers of quality and prestige, to ascertain the holistic value and impact of scholarly contributions. A successful librarian recognizes, as Matt, Camille, and Hillary have, that change is constant and rapid and prepares themselves to deal with and participate in change, even to be drivers of it.

Our friend, colleague, and collaborator on this book, Micah Vandegrift, argues that "scholarly communication is people,"[7] and this is evident in Camille's, Hillary's, and Matt's statements. We support, help, and provide services to different audiences, including students (both graduate and undergraduate), faculty across many disciplines, staff, administration, and our fellow librarians. The change we're collectively participating in requires collaboration, community, and relationships that must be built and nurtured. Scholarly communication doesn't happen in a vacuum; all stakeholders have to be on board, and because we are point people on scholarly communication, our role is to educate and support and to recognize how scholarly communication intersects with and impacts others, within and without the academy, within and without any particular institution, within and without librarianship and individual libraries and librarians.

The content of our work as expressed by Hillary and Matt includes core scholarly communication topics, such as copyright and fair use as they apply to teaching and research, open access (OA) to scholarly literature, measuring the impact of scholarly outputs through metrics, and open educational resources (OER). Each of these concepts will be developed in the course of this book, but for now, suffice it to say that we engage with these and related topics and our constituents through outreach, events, instruction, consultation, advising, and advocacy. We ourselves, and YOU, are consumers and creators of information and knowledge, and we support each other and the advancement of knowledge and practice in our field when we share our work openly and empower peers to reuse and build upon it.

Matt notes that he works at a regional comprehensive university, Grand Valley State University in Allendale, Michigan, and that there are implications that this has on the nature of his scholarly communication work. Indeed, many factors will inform the way scholarly communication topics are handled at a given institution, not least among them their size and prominence. So-called R1 universities, those that the Carnegie Classification of Institutions of Higher Education categorizes as "Doctoral Universities—Very High Research Activity," are highly visible in scholarly communication advocacy. However, they comprise a relatively small portion of the total US system of higher education. The many remaining institutions, from R2: "Doctoral Universities—High Research Activity" to community colleges, are extremely important and make significant research, education, social, and economic contributions to the world. Their libraries and librarians are also engaged in scholarly communication issues and advocacy. The specific form their advocacy and outreach takes may differ, but scholarly communication is core to their missions, and they make important contributions to shifts in the scholarly communication landscape. All institutions are a mix of research and teaching, and the profile of any given institution will suggest ways to approach scholarly communication work in that context, but scholarly communication knowledge and skills are relevant across the board.

This book and the larger project it grows out of, is an expression of the principles and themes discussed above. We have sought to collaborate widely; to highlight the work of peers; to provide open access to the products of our work, including this book; to respond to a dynamic landscape; to identify and fill gaps; to embrace ambiguity and uncertainty; to incorporate diversity, equity, and inclusion; to create; and to share and build upon the work of many colleagues and advocates. This book is an invitation. Reach out, discuss, challenge, contribute, critique, modify, adapt, and extend this work. Customize and personalize it, and then join us in participating in the evolution of scholarly communication. In the remainder of this part of the book, you will learn about some of the economic, social, legal, and technological forces that have shaped and continue to influence scholarly communication work in libraries.

NOTES

1. ACRL Scholarly Communications Committee, *Principles and Strategies for the Reform of Scholarly Communication 1* (Chicago: Association of College and Research Libraries, 2003), https://www.ala.org/acrl/publications/whitepapers/principlesstrategies.
2. ACRL Scholarly Communications Committee, *Principles and Strategies*.
3. Association of College and Research Libraries, *Framework for Information Literacy for Higher Education* (Chicago: Association of College and Research Libraries, 2016), https://www.ala.org/acrl/standards/ilframework.
4. Steve Brantley, Todd A. Bruns, and Kirstin I. Duffin, "Librarians in Transition: Scholarly Communication Support as a Developing Core Competency," *Journal of Electronic Resources Librarianship* 29, no. 3 (2017): 137–50, https://doi.org/10.1080/1941126X.2017.1340718.
5. ACRL Scholarly Communications Committee, *Principles and Strategies*.
6. Wm. Joseph Thomas, "The Structure of Scholarly Communications within Academic Libraries," *Serials Review* 39, no. 3 (2013): 170, https://doi.org/10.1080/00987913.2013.10766387.
7. Micah Vandegrift, "Scholarly Communication Is People: Three Crazy Ideas for LIS to 'Own' Open Access" (presentation, ACRL-NY Symposium on Open Access and the Academic Librarian, Baruch College, New York, NY, December 5, 2014), Figshare, https://doi.org/10.6084/m9.figshare.1273504.v1.

BIBLIOGRAPHY

ACRL Scholarly Communications Committee. *Principles and Strategies for the Reform of Scholarly Communication 1*. Chicago: Association of College and Research Libraries, 2003. https://www.ala.org/acrl/publications/whitepapers/principlesstrategies.

Association of College and Research Libraries. *Framework for Information Literacy for Higher Education*. Chicago: Association of College and Research Libraries, 2016. https://www.ala.org/acrl/standards/ilframework.

Brantley, Steve, Todd A. Bruns, and Kirstin I. Duffin. "Librarians in Transition: Scholarly Communication Support as a Developing Core Competency." *Journal of Electronic Resources Librarianship* 29, no. 3 (2017): 137–50. https://doi.org/10.1080/1941126X.2017.1340718.

Thomas, Wm. Joseph. "The Structure of Scholarly Communications within Academic Libraries." *Serials Review* 39, no. 3 (2013): 167–71. https://doi.org/10.1080/00987913.2013.10766387.

Vandegrift, Micah. "Scholarly Communication Is People: Three Crazy Ideas for LIS to 'Own' Open Access." Presentation, ACRL-NY Symposium on Open Access and the Academic Librarian, Baruch College, New York, NY, December 5, 2014. Figshare. https://doi.org/10.6084/m9.figshare.1273504.v1.

THE ECONOMIC CONTEXT

SCHOLCOMM IS MONEY

Maria Bonn with Will Cross and Josh Bolick

Keywords: publishing, commercial publisher, university press, green and gold open access, article processing charges (APC), institutional repositories (IR)

INTRODUCTION

This chapter introduces the core economic challenge in scholarly communication: the relationship between noncommercial scholarly sharing and for-profit publishers. It discusses economic models for sharing scholarly monographs, academic journals, and educational materials and concludes with an overview of the opportunities for new models and advocacy in the field.

THE SITUATION

Scholars, the librarians who support them, and those of us who are both, are passionately committed to the work of scholarship and to ensuring its impact, both in the moment and over time. Syndey Verba, former director of the Harvard Libraries, when accepting the SPARC innovator award, quotably asserted, "Scholarly communication is a redundancy. There is no scholarship without communication."

At some level, the above is a utopian, communal, and simplified depiction of the culture of scholarly communication. The discourse around scholarly communication, in libraries, and in the disciplinary communities of scholars, is rife with dissatisfaction, concern, and anxiety about whether the scholarly ecosystem sustains and encourages this sort of generous and expansive community. A glance at the American Library Association's SCHOLCOMM e-mail list, a conversation with almost any academic library collection development librarian, or some eavesdropping at a disciplinary conference will quickly surface questions and complaints about issues such as the precarity of authors' rights to use their own work, the difficulties of reaching an audience beyond a narrow set of peers, or the opacity of data and subsequent difficulty of determining the validity of conclusions. That's just the tip of the troubled iceberg peeking out of the scholarly communication waters.

The bright dream of scholarly generosity dimmed by anxious shadows is situated in a complicated economy of innovation, prestige, professional advancement, and, well, money. As is so often the way with economies, that of scholarly communication is driven by a financial market, one populated by many active agents with motives other than supporting the sharing of scholarship as widely as possible with the goal of maximizing its impact. This is not to say that these agents necessarily have bad intentions; many are well-intentioned and passionate about scholarship and its contributions to building a better world. The conviction that market forces and the possibility of profit are the optimal economic underpinnings for distributing scholarship does, however, shape an economy that is often at odds with the goals of scholars and their aspirations for the outcomes of their work.

The conditions that give rise to this disadvantageous market have been widely discussed, and most academic and research librarians can offer a thumbnail version that goes something like the following: Scholars conduct research and produce results with the support of their employing institutions, of government and private funding, and of personal resources. Scholars are motivated to publish the results of their work in order to make meaningful contributions to their disciplines and to ensure advancement in a profession that prioritizes publication through its rewards structures, namely hiring, promotion and tenure, and grant-funding decisions. Particularly in the realm of journal publication, a realm in which many (but not all, as discussed below) scholars largely dwell, the latter half of the twentieth century saw publishing largely owned and operated by private corporations intent on accruing profit to both sustain their work and to reward the investment of their shareholders. Some of these scientific publishers have been remarkably successful in generating that profit. As one observer points out in discussing Elsevier, one of the largest scientific journal publishers:

> The core of Elsevier's operation is in scientific journals, the weekly or monthly publications in which scientists share their results. Despite the narrow audience, scientific publishing is a remarkably big business. With total global revenues of more than £19bn, it weighs in somewhere between the recording and the film industries in size, but it is far more profitable.[1]

Such corporations offer scholars the opportunity to publish under their imprints, generally in exchange for the author assigning a robust set of rights to the publisher. Authors effectively turn ownership of their work over to publishers. Once that ownership has been transferred, publishers are ready, able, and certainly willing to leverage that ownership to their economic advantage by limiting access to those who have paid for it, either through a direct purchase or through an intermediary such as a subscribing library. These barriers to access, commonly known as paywalls,* create an artificial scarcity in which access to financial resources equals access to scholarly resources.

Many participants in and observers of these well-established publishing practices see this exchange as a sort of bargain with the devil. Publishers advocate for their contribution as added value: the value of managing peer review to certify the validity of the work; of editorial development and review to improve the communication of scholarly argument and results; of marketing and promotion so that an interested audience becomes aware of the existence of the work; of distribution in print and electronically, particularly to libraries; and, in some cases, of evaluation to help scholars understand their impact. All this good work requires hands, minds, tools, technology, offices with lights on, and so on, and so on, and all those things come at a cost. In order to cover that cost, their economic logic demands exclusive rights to distribute, to distribute at a price, at a price that can be quite costly.

---

* A 2018 documentary film addresses these economic practices and their consequences in detail: Jason Schmitt, prod. and dir., *Paywall: The Business of Scholarship* (2018), https://paywallthemovie.com/.

THE PROBLEMS IT CAUSES

In sum, then, scholars trade their rights to control the distribution and terms of use of their works to commercial publishers in exchange for publication support and for the prestige the publication venue brings to their professional presence and record. In this journal ecosystem, scholars do not see any direct financial benefit from publication; they are not paid for their articles. It is generally argued that, for scholars, financial return is secondary, coming from increased job security supported by a publication record and from increased visibility in their disciplines—which may lead to financial benefits such as consulting jobs, the interest of funding agencies, recruitment by other institutions, or speakers' fees. The scholarly products are then the property of publishers, which package them into salable commodities: scholarly publications. While the primary consumers of those commodities are scholars, in support of their own research, the primary purchasers of those commodities are most often academic and research libraries. Those libraries are usually funded by institutional dollars, dollars drawn from the same pools of financial resources that supported the initial production of the scholarship.

So, in an exaggerated but not uncommon scenario, we see leading researchers in, for instance, brain research earning salaries from their employing institutions, institutions that also support their laboratories and fund their graduate student assistants. Those researchers are delighted to have their articles accepted in a hypothetical *Journal of Brain Research*, the leading publication venue in the field, and they cheerfully assign an exclusive right to publication to Stroopwaffle Incorporated, the publisher of the journal. Our researchers' libraries are keenly aware that they need to maintain a subscription to *JBR* to support the work of their researchers and to maintain a record of their publication. They are committed to this despite the fact that a subscription comes at a price of about $12,000 a year for print copies or many hundred of thousands of dollars for a bundle of electronic journals that includes *JBR*, as well as the additional burden of a steady record of inflationary increases. The libraries dig deep into their institutional pockets to bring the journal to the very researchers who created its content. While $12,000 may seem costly for a single print volume arriving annually, it pales in comparison to the multimillion dollar cost of access to bundles of electronic journals, access that many researchers have come to see as both necessary and normal.

The complex and seemingly entrenched intersection of scholarly demand for and expectation of access to journal content, library willingness to disintermediate scholars from the cost of publications despite their own declining budgets, and private control of scholarly publications has occasioned a kind of perfect financial storm for academic libraries, known in popular parlance as the serials crisis or the crisis in scholarly communication. Librarians who have long been in the profession might tell you that serials have been in crisis for decades, perhaps raising the question of whether the continued value that libraries provide to their campuses undermines the notion of crisis. That rhetoric aside, the economic impact of the costs of serials acquisitions upon academic libraries is well documented and supported by the anecdotal testimony of scholars from smaller and poorer institutions, institutions that simply cannot afford access to the scholarly literature. As the twenty-first century progresses, scholars at well-resourced institutions have also come up against the limits of access to expensive scholarship. Even the largest and wealthiest universities are having a hard time keeping financial pace with the cost of scholarly resources. Those disadvantaged scholars who wish to remain engaged with the relevant literature have to beg, borrow, and steal access rather than rely on their libraries to support them.

The economic challenges posed by the cost of scholarly journals have been further exacerbated by publisher emphasis on an access model known as the Big Deal in which libraries pay a single price to subscribe to large bundles of journals, defined by the publisher, rather than picking and choosing those journals that their community most needs. This so-called Big Deal warrants further discussion, as it's at the heart of the situation we find ourselves in. Here's an excellent summary from the Scholarly Publishing and Academic Resources Coalition (SPARC):

> Large publishers have marketed bundles of journals at a discount off of aggregated list price since the late 1990's. The value proposition for publishers is a guaranteed revenue stream at a high overall dollar value. The perceived benefit for the institutions has been access to a large volume of journal titles, at a lower per-title price than ala carte purchasing would afford. Over time, however, the actual value of these "big deals" has grown less clear. Publishers have often raised the price of the packages by 5–15%, far outpacing library budgets. This has been justified, in part, by the addition of a growing number of specialized journal titles, launched in quick succession. Libraries have found a growing chunk of their budgets allocated to servicing these big deals, as well as their ability to curate resources and build collections most appropriate for their communities severely hampered.
>
> What was once a no-fuss way to get a significant collection of journals at a discount off of list price has devolved into a restrictive agreement that limits financial and strategic flexibility. The "big deal" has often been compared to a cable or satellite TV package, an apt analogy insofar as the customer cannot choose to pass on content that is of no interest, with initial price breaks quickly giving way to locked-in increases. Much like the millions of consumers who have chosen to "cut the cord", a growing number of libraries are electing to critically appraise these big deals by assessing their collections, the value for money they are receiving from these packages, and how they might more strategically spend their finite collections resources.[2]

To see the growing number of institutions that are making cuts to their content, see SPARC's Big Deal Cancellation Tracking site at https://sparcopen.org/our-work/big-deal-cancellation-tracking/.

THE SCHOLARLY MONOGRAPH AND UNIVERSITY PRESSES

To focus solely on the serials ecosystem does a disservice to the scholarly disciplines that are characterized by long-form book publication. Librarians who work in support of scholarly communication often turn their attention to the ways in which market forces have shaped, some would say distorted, the transmission of scholarship through journal literature. The publishing economy of book cultures is also swept up in the serials crisis. The monograph continues to be an invaluable instrument of scholarly communication—particularly for scholars in the humanities and social sciences who are invested in long-form argumentation and exposition as scholarly modes. Book-centered disciplines, such as those that study literature and history, as well as social sciences like anthropology, sociology, and psychology, to name a few, are often served by university presses and specialized arms of larger academic publishers.

The books that result, commonly referred to as monographs, are, despite digital efficiencies, relatively costly to produce. (Estimates range from $15,140 to $129,909 to produce a single volume. The overall average full cost of producing a book is estimated at $39,892.[3])

High production costs result in high retail prices. If, for instance, you were interested in transhistorical approaches to literary study and wanted a look at *Out of Context: The Uses of Modernist Fiction* by Michaela Bronstein, released by the highly respected Oxford University Press in 2018, you would be asking your library to spend about $78. While tiny compared to the cost of the *Journal of Brain Research*, the number needs to be contextualized with judgment about the likelihood of future use as well as the ongoing cost of maintaining that volume.

Most university presses are not expected to produce a profit. Many receive subsidies or other forms of support (rent-free facilities, network infrastructure, utilities, and so on) from their parent institutions. Those presses are required to cover costs and hope to generate some excess revenue for investment and for operating reserves. If a press fails to do so, it runs the risk of increased scrutiny and oversight by its parent institution, a risk that can extend as far as the threat of closure to prevent institutional liability. For example, after ninety years of operation, Duquesne University Press shut down in 2017 due to budget cuts. The press used to receive an annual subsidy of $300,000 from the university, but according to the university officials, the press was running on a deficit budget, and to sustain its operations, the university had to channel resources from other programs. Such concerns are not limited to the small universities. In 2019, Stanford University announced that it would stop its $1,700,000 annual funding to its press. The press and scholarly communities organized themselves to halt the defunding, but Stanford University Press, which already generated about five million dollars a year in revenue, had to commit to developing a business model that would be entirely self-sustaining.[4]

University press book sales are rarely high volume, even in the best of times. A 2021 article estimates initial print sales for monographs at around 200 copies on average.[5] Occasionally, a university press, though luck or design, acquires a title that will sell at a level that ensures its publisher financial security for some time. In 1976, the University of Chicago Press risked its first fiction publication with Norman MacClean's *A River Runs through It*, a novel about the American West. Sales of that book, and of its film rights for adaptation as a popular 1992 Hollywood movie starring Brad Pitt, continue to support the bottom line of that press, from which you can still buy editions of the book for as much as $35. In 2017, Harvard University Press benefited enormously from the publication of Thomas Picketty's *Capital in the Twenty-First Century*, which spent many months on bestseller lists and outsold its print run several times over. In 2020, perhaps in hopes of recreating this financial magic, Harvard University Press issued a sequel of sorts, Picketty's *Capital and Ideology* for a hardcover list price of $35.95.

Such commercial successes are unicorns of the press world. In fact, many presses pride themselves on prioritizing scholarly value over sales potential, seeing their mission as one of academic service, ensuring a venue for scholarship that might be viewed as niche or arcane, but that is nevertheless an important part of the intellectual record. The work done by university presses to curate and amplify the scholarly record is esteemed by many scholars, particularly in the humanities. This esteem is not often reflected in press funding models.

For a significant part of their history, university presses relied upon academic libraries to acknowledge the value of their work and to sustain it through purchasing books for library collections. In the past, many academic libraries purchased scholarly monographs as a matter of course. Those libraries often placed standing orders for the books published by select university presses, buying the entire press output every year, without review or preapproval. In the present, we see that business models dependent on library purchasing have suffered considerably as libraries have been forced to evaluate their purchasing habits in order to afford access to electronic resources and the high cost of journal subscriptions. By and large, university presses and other small book publishers have struggled to devise effective alternative business models and continue to exist in financial precarity at the same time as they are challenged to develop innovative publishing modes in response to the opportunities offered by digital delivery.

Many libraries still do buy university press books, but less automatically than in the past. Libraries that are shepherding their resources to pay for, for instance, electronic journal subscriptions now forgo such automatic purchases and wait for an active demonstration of demand for books, sometimes described as a just-in-time model of collecting, distinct from the previous just-in-case model. Publishers, uncertain of the market for their books, raise the unit price in hopes of recovering their costs with fewer sales, adding fuel to library reluctance to purchase books when library dollars could be directed to high-demand electronic resources. Higher unit prices also undermine the possibility of course adoption as instructors may be reluctant to require costly materials. The loss of sales to classes further exacerbates the loss of potential revenue. A single instructor dropping a book from required reading might lead to the loss of dozens of sales. Such constraints also make book publishers more selective in accepting titles for publication, with sales potential perhaps outweighing scholarly contribution as the primary criterion for acceptance for publication, a narrowing of publishing opportunity that puts stress on book authors, particularly as regards tenure decisions, and may limit the scholarly reach and potential impact of their work.

AN UNSUSTAINABLE MODEL

The economic implications of the high price of access to scholarship and the monopolistic control of intellectual property asserted by many publishers are not limited to stress on library budgets and scholarly psyches. The resulting implications for access to scholarship reinforce and sometimes deepen the divide between differently resourced scholars and institutions. While libraries at the large research institutions struggle to manage their budgets so as to make ends meet and to provide a comprehensive research collection, for the most part scholars at those institutions continue to reap the benefits of access to that collection. Smaller and less well-funded institutions simply cannot afford to be comprehensive, and their scholars are relatively disadvantaged, uncertain of their ability to have access to the resources that they need to do their work. This inequity in access in turn echoes other cultural inequities. The scholarly rich get richer, metaphorically speaking, relying upon abundant resources to produce more scholarship, confirming the value of investing in a rich collection and thus incentivizing further investment, while scholars with access to more constrained resources struggle to produce work that would validate greater investment in supporting resources. Large research libraries, usually situated at relatively wealthy academic institutions, may shift their purchasing priorities or rely more upon consortial sharing, but scholars at those institutions almost always have access to the materials that they need to do their work, even if sometimes those scholars need to make a special request or wait for delivery. This isn't to say that the situation is simple or rosy at the best resourced institutions. Universal access to all of the scholarly literature doesn't exist, and even the wealthiest institutions are having to make adjustments, including cuts. Those that aren't yet making cus will be soon, because the current economics of scholarly publishing are inherently flawed. This is why Harvard and MIT have demonstrated leadership in open access advocacy and initiatives and why the University of California system suspended its content negotiations with the scholarly publisher Elsevier in 2019. After more than two years, UC renewed its licensing agreement with that publisher, but only when the parties had reached agreement on a clear path to open access for publications from UC scholars. Institutions such as these value a more equitable and sustainable scholarly publishing system, and they address economic challenges as a way of ensuring such a system.

ATTEMPTS TO ADDRESS THOSE PROBLEMS: ENTER OPEN CULTURE

In the latter part of the twentieth century, scholars became increasingly aware of the fraught economics of scholarly publishing. They also became increasingly aware of the communicative possibilities of the internet and the World Wide Web, realizing that sharing their scholarship might not always require a formal publisher, a subscription fee, or even a postage stamp. Many researchers in those disciplines most comfortable with digital technology and networked communication, disciplines like computer science and high-energy physics, began a regular practice of what they generally called "self-archiving," posting versions of their research articles on personal or departmental websites and, eventually, in disciplinary community repositories, with the intent of providing rapid access to research results at no cost to the reader.

GREEN OPEN ACCESS[6]

Self-archiving built upon older practices of disciplinary sharing, such as the distribution of white papers in economics. Economists had a long-established habit of mailing working papers throughout their scholarly community. Such practices relied upon technologies like mimeographs and photocopiers, the labor of departmental secretaries, and the postal services. The widespread adoption of word processing, electronic file sharing, and e-mail made sharing scholarly work, both in process and completed, exponentially more efficient and less costly. Commercial publishers kept a wary eye on self-archiving, concerned about possible threats to their market posed by readily available free versions of the content that they were attempting to sell at a costly markup. At the same time, publishers continued to argue the importance of the value added by their work and to assert that the purchasable product is the true version of scholarly record.

By the turn of the millennium, the popularity and possibilities of self-archiving drove many of the engaged actors to establish a principled and articulated rationale and set of practices for scholars making their research products freely available through the use of the internet. These efforts resulted in a number of declarations and initiatives, notably the Budapest Open Access Initiative in February 2002, the Bethesda Statement on Open Access Publishing in June 2003, and the Berlin Declaration on Open Access to Knowledge in the Sciences and Humanities in October 2003.

The Budapest Open Access Initiative is often cited as the defining event of the open access movement. In the opening sentence of its declaration, BOAI asserts:

> An old tradition and a new technology have converged to make possible an unprecedented public good. The old tradition is the willingness of scientists and scholars to publish the fruits of their research in scholarly journals without payment, for the sake of inquiry and knowledge. The new technology is the internet. The public good they make possible is the world-wide electronic distribution of the peer-reviewed journal literature and completely free and unrestricted access to it by all scientists, scholars, teachers, students, and other curious minds.[7]

The declaration goes on to define open access to scholarly literature as

> free availability on the public internet, permitting any user to read, download, copy, distribute, print, search, or link to the full texts of these articles, crawl them for indexing, pass them as data to software, or use them for any other lawful purpose, without financial, legal, or technical barriers other than those inseparable from gaining access to the internet itself. The only constraint on reproduction and distribution, and the only role for copyright in this domain, should be to give authors control over the integrity of their work and the right to be properly acknowledged and cited.[8]

In the two decades since this declaration, that definition has been discussed, refined, and debated, sometimes with near-religious fervor. Even more attention has been directed to questions of open access in practice, of its economic viability and of the sorts of organizational policy and support and technology services required to realize the aspirations and benefits of open access. Connecting their users with information to the greatest extent possible within their resources and within the law has long been central to the mission of academic libraries. It is natural that as advocacy and demand for open access became prevalent, academic libraries quickly turned their attention to their role in the emerging open access infrastructure. This attention soon became focused, particularly in large research libraries, on institutional repositories. The repositories, or IRs as they became known, were servers and software intended to support scholars in self-archiving their research output. The most prominent early instance of an IR was DSpace at the Massachusetts Institute of Technology. In 2002, MIT, in partnership with Hewlett Packard, openly released its repository software, and other research institutions began building upon it and customizing it for their own use. Also in 2002, the Scholarly Publishing and Academic Resources Coalition (SPARC) released a position paper making *The Case for Institutional Repositories*, essentially an economic argument highlighting the potential for IRs to

> provide a critical component in reforming the system of scholarly communication—a component that expands access to research, reasserts control over scholarship by the academy, increases competition and reduces the monopoly power of journals, and brings economic relief and heightened relevance to the institutions and libraries that support them.[9]

Beyond the very tangible economic incentive of lower costs, *The Case for Institutional Repositories* also points to the potential for increasing the value of their institutions, providing "tangible indicators of a university's quality and to demonstrate the scientific, societal, and economic relevance of its research activities, thus increasing the institution's visibility, status, and public value."[10]

Within a year, the perceived scope of IRs was increasing to what one observer (Clifford Lynch, director for the Coalition of Networked Information) described as

> a set of services that a university offers to the members of its community for the management and dissemination of digital materials created by the institution and its community members. It is most essentially an organizational commitment to the stewardship of these digital materials, including long-term preservation where appropriate, as well as organization and access or distribution.[11]

As the case for IRs gained momentum, a repository became an increasingly important and necessary part of campus infrastructure, and repositories were developed and adopted more widely than just by large research universities. This led to a market demand for software and services that could be supported by a lower level of investment than large platforms like DSpace. One response to this demand came from the Berkeley Electronic Press—Bepress. Bepress was begun by scholars hoping to intervene in the scholarly communication ecosystem by providing low-cost, easily used software for journal publication, thus enabling a more diverse journal marketplace. In partnership with the California Digital Library, Bepress modified its software to support the functions of an institutional repository. That modification became a product called Digital Commons and was widely used as an IR platform by colleges and less well-resourced universities, as well as by a number of larger research institutions that preferred not to develop or host their own platform for their IR. In what many view as an ironic turn, Digital Commons was acquired in 2017 by Reed Elsevier, one of the largest and most profitable commercial publishers, placing control of many IRs in the hands of just those forces that the platform and the IRs it supports were intended to undermine. Nevertheless, more than 500 institutions continue to use Digital Commons as their IR platform. While that is a substantial number, it is only a fraction of the more than 3,000 repositories that now exist worldwide. IRs may not have fundamentally altered the scholarly communication ecosystem, but their growth in two decades has established them as an important force in shaping that ecosystem.*

Institutional repositories are one approach to implementing an open environment for scholarly communication. Through self-archiving on a platform owned or controlled by the academy, scholars can share their work outside of the paywalls built by commercial publishers. Their presence and influence have certainly resulted in some shifts in the economics of scholarly communication. It is, however, important to note that the use of IRs is still largely dependent upon the commitment and action of individual scholars willing and able to take the time and make the effort to deposit their work within the repository. Encouraging such commitment and supporting scholars in making those deposits is a considerable investment for libraries seeking to optimize use of the repository. Self-archiving does, after all, depend upon authors who are motivated to archive. In practice, much "self"-archiving is heavily facilitated and mediated, often by dedicated scholarly communication library staff.

Some academic institutions and some funding agencies that support research have decided that institutional and societal commitment to open access is as important as individual commitment, and these organizations seek to provide other incentives for sharing scholarly work. Around 2008, many institutions of higher education and research turned their attention to formalizing their commitment to open access. In rapid succession, in late 2008 into 2009, Harvard University, Stanford University, the Massachusetts Institute of Technology, and the University of Kansas adopted open access policies expressing their commitment "to disseminating the fruits of… research and scholarship as widely as possible."[12] Similar policies have been adopted by many academic institutions and research organizations. The Registry of Open Access Repository Mandates and Policies (ROARMAP) is

> a searchable international registry charting the growth of open access mandates and policies adopted by universities, research institutions and research funders that require or request their researchers to provide open access to their peer-reviewed research article output by depositing it in an open access repository.[13]

---

* Ample evidence of the presence of IRs can be seen by consulting the Confederation of Open Access Repositories, https://www.coar-repositories.org/, or the Registry of Open Access Repositories, http://roar.eprints.org/.

As of the time of this writing, ROARMAP lists 795 research organizations that have adopted open access policies.

Institutional open access policies, sometimes called mandates, are important signifiers of institutional commitment to open scholarship, and they are meant to encourage scholars to make use of institutional repositories and other open venues. In practice, most institutions stop at encouragement. Many mandates are opt-out, meaning that no one is actually required to make their work openly available, and there are few large-scale efforts to monitor or enforce compliance with open access policies. Even scholars who are fully supportive of the intent of the policy often struggle to make it part of their practice, finding IR deposit one more thing to do on a long list of service, research, and teaching commitments.

As the arguments for open access became persistent and compelling, another sector stepped in to intervene in the economics of scholarly communication: governmental agencies and private foundations took a growing interest in seeing a public return on funding investment, and those entities began to require that the results of funded research be shared in open venues. Those venues might be open access books and journals, or they might be institutional or disciplinary repositories. The record of the results can range from pre-publication drafts to copies of final, peer-reviewed, and publisher-edited articles. There are many flavors of openness, shaped by funding agency policy and by author goals, but funder requirements share a goal of making scholarship and research results available at no cost to the public with the hopes of democratizing access and maximizing impact.

Relatively early examples of funder mandates emerged in the mid-aughts. In Canada in 2007, the Canadian Institutes of Health Research became the first North American funding agency to issue an open access mandate, with the National Institutes of Health in the United States following closely behind. NIH began requesting open availability of the research it funded in 2004 and adopted an open access requirement for all its funding recipients in 2008. By 2013, the United States government established a directive requiring federal agencies "with over $100 million in annual conduct of research and development expenditures" to create, within the next six months, a plan to make the peer-reviewed publications directly arising from federal funding "publicly accessible to search, retrieve, and analyze."[14] While many agencies have addressed this directive, compliance is still a work in progress, subject to the vicissitudes of political and economic change. In 2019, the Government Accountability Office undertook an assessment of agency compliance and concluded:

> The 19 agencies that GAO reviewed have made progress implementing their plans to increase public access to federally funded research results (publications and data), as called for in a 2013 Office of Science and Technology Policy (OSTP) memorandum. However, some agencies have not fully implemented some aspects of their plans, in particular those related to data access and mechanisms to ensure researchers comply with public access requirements.[15]

The most ambitious and sweeping open access funding initiative at the time of this writing has come out of Europe and is known as Plan S (what the S stands for is still an open question). The plan required scientists and researchers who benefit from state-funded research organizations and institutions to publish their work in open repositories or in journals that are available to all by 2021. Plan S generated considerable debate and some consternation among researchers. Proponents of the plan argued, for example:

Funders have every prerogative to put whatever earmarks on the funding that they prefer. When I give my kids $5 for allowance, I am clear that they cannot spend it on candy and ice cream. So, if the funders, who are responsible to policymakers, who are responsible to the good people of the Netherlands, France, Norway, etc., believe that Plan S is necessary, it really doesn't matter what my opinion is as a librarian. I understand the dismay and furor that might cause for researchers, but in an age where transparency is shaking industry after industry to the core, it feels brash and unwise to expect cash to keep flowing into your lab's account without a hint of fiduciary responsibility to the public.[16]

While many welcomed the additional incentive to open their work, others expressed resistance to government dictates about the dissemination of research. Germany, acutely aware of its past under Nazi rule and the potential consequences of governmental control of research, declined to participate in Plan S.

In sum, we see a number of motives for opening scholarship and for moving away from an economic model in which scholarly products are purchasable commodities. Scholars may publish their research results in open access venues or otherwise share their research openly because of a personal conviction or moral imperative. They may do so because of a desire to reach audiences outside paywalls. But they might also do so because "the boss says so," because their employing institutions have directed them to do so as a condition of employment and support. Or scholars may publish and share openly to keep funding flowing in and to remain in the good graces of funding agencies.

Whatever the rationale or belief system is that leads to a desire to publish openly, researchers may still need to confront the cost of such publishing. As we have discussed, the cost of publication, until recent decades, has generally been supported through subscriptions and sales to both libraries and individuals. A shift to open publication necessitates a shift of cost recovery models as well.

One approach to sustainable open access has been to remove the financial necessity for purchases by moving the costs of publication from the reader to the writer, creating a model generally termed an *author-pay model*. Author-pay models are usually supported by article processing charges, commonly known as APCs. As with so many aspects of scholarly communication in a changing ecosystem, APCs are not simple to define or to evaluate. Using article processing charges as a generalized nomenclature immediately raises objections from those who attend to the book-oriented disciplines. Many have adopted the more format-neutral term *publication charge*. Some journals have shifted costs to another locale by charging a submission fee so that some cost is covered before the work of editorial review even begins. This has the advantage of distributing support of open access more generally across interested actors, but it may present a financial barrier that prevents authors from even considering submission fee–charging journals as publication venues.

While APCs are a common feature of the journal publishing landscape, their operationalization is fraught with differences of opinion and debate. In some cases, APCs are not new. Some journals, particularly in the sciences, have a long history of publication charges, often called *page charges*, but not to support open access. Those APCs have been justified as helping to underwrite the high cost of preparing and printing articles that are heavy with images, tables, charts, graphs, and other visual elements, as well as the additional labor needed to ensure the quality and reliability of such elements. Such journals may levy an open access surcharge in addition to the publishing fee, leading interested observers to speculate about what financial need that surcharge is intended to address. In general, publishers are not always transparent about the details of the cost of publication, making it difficult to assess the amount charged an author for open access publication. APCs vary widely. A 2017, the cost of APCs from major publishers, like Wiley, Elsevier, and Taylor & Francis, ranged from about $750 to $3,000 (in today's dollars). PLOS, a nonprofit open access publisher with considerable academic presence, in 2020 charged $1,595 for an article in *PLOS ONE* and $3,000 for publication in *PLOS Medicine*, with several journal-specific price points in between.[17]

For most scholars, these costs are not inconsiderable, making it challenging to put their money where their open access mouths are. Where can authors turn to find the funds to pay APCs? They can certainly reach into their own pockets, but doing so, particularly as a regular practice, could be a considerable financial burden. Authors with sufficient forethought might include publication fees as an expense item in requests for grant funding. They might also turn to their institutions for support or tap annual research funds. Some academic institutions and research organizations have begun to designate and administer funding to support open access publishing, funding managed sometimes by the library and sometimes in other areas of the organization, such as an office for research. These are important sources of funding, but they come with an overhead cost. Authors need to invest the time and energy to apply for the funds, and institutions need to invest in people and processes to manage them.

The most commonly voiced criticism of APCs is that they disadvantage scholars who are less well-funded, particularly those from outside large research institutions and those from developing nations. While locating funding for APCs may place a burden on scholars in some contexts, in others there simply may be no funding to locate, leaving authors with a choice of either using personal funds, which may also be limited or nonexistent, or taking their work to another publication venue.

As the twenty-first century has progressed and the interest in new economic models to support scholarly communication has continued and expanded, a number of academic libraries have turned their attention to another approach to supporting open access publishing, commonly called, with aspiration, *transformative publishing agreements*, *publish and read*, or *read and publish* agreements.

As the University of California Office of Scholarly Communication thoughtfully explains in its toolkit for negotiating with scholarly journal publishers:

> *Transformative open access agreements* has recently come into use as an umbrella term for a type of comprehensive publisher agreement. According to the ESAC Initiative...
>
>> Transformative agreements are those contracts negotiated between institutions (libraries, national and regional consortia) and publishers that transform the business model underlying scholarly journal publishing, moving from one based on toll access (subscription) to one in which publishers are remunerated a fair price for their open access publishing services.
>
> Various flavors of such agreements have evolved in recent years, with a corresponding evolution of terminology:
>
> - **Offsetting agreements**, in which fees for subscriptions and for article publishing offset one another, so that either subscription fees are reduced as publishing fees increase, or article publication charges (APCs) are heavily discounted to account for fees allocated to subscriptions;

- **Read and publish (RAP) agreements**, in which, often, a single fee covers both subscription access and open access publishing for affiliated authors, with the balance tilted toward subscription charges; and

- **Publish and read (PAR) agreements**, in which all or most costs are allocated toward open access publishing at the article level, with read access and perpetual rights to subscription articles included as a benefit of the agreement.[18]

As that toolkit stresses, "This is a fluid and evolving area in which agreement characteristics are subject to ongoing variation, innovation, and negotiation—and additional models continue to be developed."* The earliest advocacy for these transformative agreements was met with some skepticism, but by 2020, several university libraries in the United States had been successful in negotiating these agreements, including the University of California system, Carnegie Mellon University, and the University of North Carolina at Chapel Hill, to name a few. As with all of the processes and principles designed to address the dysfunctional economics of scholarly communication that are discussed here, transformative agreements have been met with as much skepticism as enthusiasm by the scholarly community.†

The most ambitious transformative publishing agreement is known as Projekt DEAL. As the DEAL informational website indicates,

> The German Rectors' Conference was tasked by the Alliance of German Science Organisations to institute Projekt-DEAL to negotiate nationwide transformative "publish and read" agreements with the largest commercial publishers of scholarly journals on behalf of all German academc institutions including universities, universities of applied sciences, research institutions, state and regional libraries.[19]

The first major accomplishment was a country-wide agreement with Wiley, which demonstrated the feasibility of a large-scale transformation and set Germany, as a country, on a path to having the majority of its agreements be transformative agreements. Projekt DEAL's agreement with Wiley was widely lauded as indicative of the potential success of transformative publishing agreements.

In January of 2020, Springer Nature and Projekt DEAL announced that

> the formal contract for the world's largest transformative Open Access (OA) agreement to date has been signed.... The agreement provides OA publishing services and full reading access to Springer Nature journals to scholars and students from across the German research landscape.[20]

The press release detailed that

---

* Lisa Hinchliffe has an excellent and clear explanation of the multiple models for open access: Lisa Hinchliffe, "Seeking Sustainability: Publishing Models for an Open Access Age," *Scholarly Kitchen* (blog), April 7, 2020, https://scholarlykitchen.sspnet.org/2020/04/07/seeking-sustainability-publishing-models-for-an-open-access-age/.

† Ashley Farley and colleagues address six myths of transformative agreements, arguing that "the complexity of TAs obfuscates their true cost and this model's long-term implications remain undetermined": Ashley Farley et al., "Transformative Agreements: Six Myths, Busted," *College and Research Libraries News* 82, no. 7 (July/August 2021): 298, https://doi.org/10.5860/crln.82.7.298.

the Read and Publish, 'transformative', component of the agreement, effective immediately, entitles authors to publish immediately OA in Springer Nature's collection of 1,900 'hybrid' journals and provides participating institutions with permanent access to Springer, Palgrave, Adis and Macmillan journals in the Springer Nature portfolio. The Publish and Read [PAR] fee will be €2,750 [US$2,990 at the time] for each article published and will be paid from central subscription funds.[21]

THE ECONOMICS OF LEARNING MATERIALS

While *scholarly communication* often suggests research results communicated via the scholarly literature, it is important to remember that teaching is also a form of scholarly communication, in which knowledge and information are transmitted from teachers to learners, learners who make up the next generation of scholars. In the late twentieth century, and with increased attention and engagement on into the twenty-first century, as scholars considered the possibilities that the internet affords for the dissemination of scholarship, scholars of all ages also began to explore similar possibilities for the work of education.

The conversation about education quickly became focused on the high cost of textbooks and the benefits of alleviating the cost of education through the development of open educational resources. According to one source, the cost of textbooks has risen at more than three times the rate of inflation for decades,[22] placing a burden on students and their families that is detrimental to the efficacy of education. *Open educational resources* (OER), a term coined by UNESCO in 2002, have arisen in response. OER are

teaching, learning, and research resources that reside in the public domain or have been released under an intellectual property license that permits their free use and re-purposing by others. Open educational resources include full courses, course materials, modules, textbooks, streaming videos, tests, software, and any other tools, materials, or techniques used to support access to knowledge.[23]

Given the commitment of academic librarians to supporting teaching and learning and the value that most libraries place on increasing access, it is not surprising that those librarians have turned their attention to supporting both the creation and use of OER. An increasing number of libraries engage with their faculty in identifying and using authoring tools for OER, in understanding intellectual property rights for material to be included in the OER and in the resulting product, and in identifying and using distribution platforms that will maximize the use and impact of the new work. Libraries also work with faculty to identify existing OER appropriate for their classes, resulting in considerable savings for students.

While much of the work of OER is motivated by intellectual generosity, the economic context for OER is not cashless. Money is still required to pay for staff and technology and other forms of support for the creation and dissemination of OER. As with any area of academic work, this raises financial challenges. At the same time, the obvious and well-documented benefits of OER for students, in terms of both financial savings and access to a rich body of learning materials, have given rise to a number of models for supporting OER. Some institutions have simply identified this work as a priority area for funding and allocated support from their central budgets. In some states, the legislatures have offered funding. OER have also been an attractive area for charitable foundations. The William and Flora Hewlett Foundation, for instance, acting on the belief that "well-designed, customizable, openly licensed materials can engage students and energize educators in ways that enable more responsive teaching and better learning" [24] has, since 2002, awarded more than fourteen million dollars to support the creation and use of OER.[25] Evidence of increased visibility of OER and of a growing imperative to support them was demonstrable in 2018 when, after more than five years of effort by OER advocates, the U.S. federal government allocated five million dollars for an open textbook pilot program.

ECONOMICS AND SCHOLARLY COMMUNICATION LIBRARIANSHIP

The changes in the economic and social scholarly communication ecosystem have created a number of new roles for librarians and information professionals in academic and research libraries. Increasingly, such libraries have a department or office of scholarly communication, managed by a scholarly communication librarian. That scholarly communication librarian is often expected to have expertise in copyright or may have a colleague in the same department with a title such as *copyright librarian*. Since the twenty-first century, there has been an increasing number of positions charged with research data management and services, with titles like *research data librarian* or *data services specialist*. Other flourishing areas of work include repository management and publishing, publishing that may be aligned with university press efforts or that may operate independently from within the library. There is also an increasing number of professional roles with titles such as *OER librarian* or *open education librarian*, jobs that are dedicated to assisting instructors in locating, adapting, and creating OER that meet the needs of their courses and their students.

In addition to creating new areas of work for librarians, all of these changes in modes and models of scholarly communication and the social and cultural shifts that accompany them have been shaped by and are reshaping many long-standing librarian roles. The work of collection development, for instance, which long ago moved away from managing print subscriptions and purchasing print materials, now also has to consider the acquisition of open, online materials. In the past, a purchase initiated the work necessary to make a resource a formal part of a library collection, work such as cataloging and identifying a storage location. New workflows are required to address collecting free resources. Collection development librarians also need to reconsider the most effective use of their funds. Should collection budgets be used to purchase materials with limited access rights or to support the creation and publication of open materials that will be freely available to all? The descriptive work of cataloging and technical services has also taken on new dimensions as that expertise has been applied to the creation of descriptive metadata that includes complex representations of provenance and rights of ownership and use for open scholarship. Subject specialists and departmental liaisons are also increasingly called upon to keep abreast of the changes in practice and attitudes of the disciplines that they serve and to adjust their own practices and attitudes in response.

While the economics of scholarly communication can be, and often are, in flux, evolving and emergent, there are also many indicators that change has taken place and will continue to happen as scholarship and higher education address the ethical and economic imperative for openness. For instance, in the Netherlands, where the Dutch Research Council invests almost one billion euros each year "in curiosity-driven research, research related to societal challenges and research infrastructure"[26] 85 percent of publications resulting from that funding are now open access.[27] In the North American context, in late 2021, the National Academies of Science, Engineering, and Medicine convened a meeting entitled the Presidents' Convening on Open Scholarship.[28] The meeting was attended by more than eighty university presidents, chief research officers, and library directors, an indication of considerable administrative interest in questions of open scholarship and higher education and research. The conversation about the economics of scholarly communication is indeed ongoing, and it is a conversation in which libraries and librarians need to participate.

DISCUSSION QUESTIONS

1. What are some of the possible advantages and disadvantages of
   a. private sector control of scholarly publishing?
   b. academic institutional control of scholarly publishing?
   c. scholarly self-publishing?
2. What are some examples of the way that the economic challenges of scholarly communication vary by academic discipline and specialization?
3. If scholarship is intellectual property, who owns that property? What are some ways of realizing the value of that property?

NOTES

1. Stephen Buryani, "Is the Staggeringly Profitable Business of Scientific Publishing Bad for Science?" *Guardian*, June 27, 2017, https://www.theguardian.com/science/2017/jun/27/profitable-business-scientific-publishing-bad-for-science.
2. SPARC, "Big Deal Cancellation Tracking," under "Overview," https://sparcopen.org/our-work/big-deal-cancellation-tracking/.
3. Nancy L. Maron et al., *The Costs of Publishing Monographs* (New York: Ithaka S+R, 2016), 17, https://doi.org/10.18665/sr.276785.
4. Joseph Nyaingo, February 16, 2020, https://askwonder.com/research/university-press-closures-ylbstagrl (access restricted; requires login).
5. Charles Watkinson, "University Presses and the Impact of COVID19," *Learned Publishing* 34, no. 1 (January 2021): 17–24, https://doi.org/10.1002/leap.1352.
6. For more detail on the variety (and colors) of open access models, see chapter 2.1, "Open Access."
7. Budapest Open Access Initiative, https://www.budapestopenaccessinitiative.org/read/.
8. Budapest Open Access Initiative.
9. Raym Crow, *The Case for Institutional Repositories* (Washington, DC: Scholarly Publishing and Academic Resources Coalition, 2002), 4, https://ils.unc.edu/courses/2014_fall/inls690_109/Readings/Crow2002-CaseforInstitutionalRepositoriesSPARCPaper.pdf.
10. Crow, *Case for Institutional Repositories*, 4.
11. Clifford Lynch, "Institutional Repositories: Essential Infrastructure for Scholarship in the Digital Age," *ARL*, no. 226 (February 2003): 2, https://www.cni.org/wp-content/uploads/2003/02/arl-br-226-Lynch-IRs-2003.pdf.
12. Faculty of Massachusetts Institute of Technology, "MIT Faculty Open Access Policy," March 28, 2009, Scholarly Communications, MIT Libraries, https://libraries.mit.edu/scholarly/mit-open-access/open-access-policy/.
13. Registry of Open Access Repositories Mandates and Policies (ROARMAP), home page, https://roarmap.eprints.org/.
14. John P. Holdren, "Increasing Access to the Results of Federally Funded Scientific Research," memorandum for the heads of executive departments and agencies, February 22, 2013, Executive Office of the President, Office of Science and Technology Policy, 1, 3, https://obamawhitehouse.archives.gov/sites/default/files/microsites/ostp/ostp_public_access_memo_2013.pdf.

15. US Government Accountability Office, "Federal Research: Additional Actions Needed to Improve Public Access to Research Results," GAO-20-81, November 21, 2019, https://www.gao.gov/products/gao-20-81.

16. Rick Anderson and Micah Vandergrift, "Plan S Point–Counterpoint: Discussing the Plan Together" (plenary session, ISMTE North American Conference, Durham, NC, August 1–2, 2019), https://cdn.ymaws.com/www.ismte.org/resource/resmgr/events/2019/na/conference_program_2019.pdf.

17. PLOS, "Publication Fees," https://plos.org/publish/fees/.

18. University of California, "An Introductory Guide to the UC Model Transformative Agreements," in *Negotiating with Scholarly Journal Publishers: A Toolkit from the University of California* (Oakland: University of California Office of Scholarly Communication, 2019), 3–4, https://osc.universityof-california.edu/uc-publisher-relationships/negotiating-with-scholarly-journal-publishers-a-toolkit/an-introductory-guide-to-the-uc-model-transformative-agreement/.

19. DEAL Konsortium, "About DEAL," https://www.projekt-deal.de/about-deal/ (page content changed).

20. Springer Nature Group, "Springer Nature and Germany's Projekt DEAL Finalise World's Largest Transformative Open Access Agreement," news release, January 9, 2020, https://group.springernature.com/gp/group/media/press-releases/archive-2020/springer-nature-projekt-deal/17553230.

21. Springer Nature Group, "Springer Nature and Germany's Projekt DEAL."

22. SPARC, "Open Education," https://sparcopen.org/open-education/.

23. Daniel E. Atkins, John Seely Brown, and Allen L. Hammond, "A Review of the Open Educational Resources (OER) Movement: Achievements, Challenges, and New Opportunities" (report to the William and Flora Hewlett Foundation, February 2007), 4.

24. William and Flora Hewlett Foundation, "Open Education," https://hewlett.org/strategy/open-education/.

25. Hewlett Foundation, "Open Education."

26. NWO (Dutch Research Council), "About NWO," https://www.nwo.nl/en/about-now.

27. NWO (Dutch Research Council), "More Than Eighty Percent of Publications Funded by NWO and ZonMw Open Access," news release, September 7, 2021, https://www.nwo.nl/en/news/more-eighty-percent-publications-funded-nwo-and-zonmw-open-access.

28. "Presidents' Convening on Open Scholarship," draft summary, October 11, 2021, https://facultygov.unc.edu/wp-content/uploads/sites/261/2021/11/PresidentsConvening-OpenScholarship-Summary_draft.pdf.

BIBLIOGRAPHY

Anderson, Rick, and Micah Vandergrift. "Plan S Point–Counterpoint: Discussing the Plan Together." Plenary session, ISMTE North American Conference, Durham, NC, August 1–2, 2019. https://cdn.ymaws.com/www.ismte.org/resource/resmgr/events/2019/na/conference_program_2019.pdf.

Atkins, Daniel E., John Seely Brown, and Allen L. Hammond. "A Review of the Open Educational Resources (OER) Movement: Achievements, Challenges, and New Opportunities." Report to the William and Flora Hewlett Foundation, February 2007.

Budapest Open Access Initiative. https://www.budapestopenaccessinitiative.org/read/.

Buryani, Stephen. "Is the Staggeringly Profitable Business of Scientific Publishing Bad for Science?" *Guardian*, June 27, 2017. https://www.theguardian.com/science/2017/jun/27/profitable-business-scientific-publishing-bad-for-science.

Confederation of Open Access Repositories. Home page. https://www.coar-repositories.org/.

Crow, Raym. *The Case for Institutional Repositories: A SPARC Position Paper.* Washington, DC: Scholarly Publishing and Academic Resources Coalition, 2002. https://ils.unc.edu/courses/2014_fall/inls690_109/Readings/Crow2002-CaseforInstitutionalRepositoriesSPARCPaper.pdf.

DEAL Konsortium. "About DEAL." https://www.projekt-deal.de/about-deal/.

Faculty of Massachusetts Institute of Technology. "MIT Faculty Open Access Policy." March 28, 2009. Scholarly Communications, MIT Libraries. https://libraries.mit.edu/scholarly/mit-open-access/open-access-policy/.

Farley, Ashley, Allison Langham-Putrow, Elisabeth Shook, Leila Belle Sterman, and Megan Wacha. "Transformative Agreements: Six Myths, Busted." *College and Research Libraries News* 82, no. 7 (July/August 2021): 298–301. https://doi.org/10.5860/crln.82.7.298.

Hinchliffe, Lisa. "Seeking Sustainability: Publishing Models for an Open Access Age." *Scholarly Kitchen* (blog), April 7, 2020. https://scholarlykitchen.sspnet.org/2020/04/07/seeking-sustainability-publishing-models-for-an-open-access-age/.

Holdren, John P. "Increasing Access to the Results of Federally Funded Scientific Research." Memorandum for the heads of executive departments and agencies, February 22, 2013. Executive Office of the President, Office of Science and Technology Policy. https://obamawhitehouse.archives.gov/sites/default/files/microsites/ostp/ostp_public_access_memo_2013.pdf.

Lynch, Clifford. "Institutional Repositories: Essential Infrastructure for Scholarship in the Digital Age." *ARL*, no. 226 (February 2003). https://www.cni.org/wp-content/uploads/2003/02/arl-br-226-Lynch-IRs-2003.pdf.

Maron, Nancy L., Christine Mulhern, Daniel Rossman, and Kimberly Schmelzinger. *The Costs of Publishing Monographs: Toward a Transparent Methodology*. New York: Ithaka S+R, 2016. https://doi.org/10.18665/sr.276785.

NOW (Dutch Research Council). "About NOW." https://www.nwo.nl/en/about-now.

———. "More Than Eighty Percent of Publications Funded by NOW and ZonMw Open Access." News release, September 7, 2021. https://www.nwo.nl/en/news/more-eighty-percent-publications-funded-now-and-zonmw-open-access.

Nyaingo, Joseph. "University Press Closures." Ask Wonder, February 16, 2020. https://askwonder.com/research/university-press-closures-ylbstagrl (access restricted; requires login).

PLOS. "Publication Fees." https://plos.org/publish/fees/.

"Presidents' Convening on Open Scholarship." Draft summary, October 11, 2021. https://facultygov.unc.edu/wp-content/uploads/sites/261/2021/11/PresidentsConvening-OpenScholarship-Summary_draft.pdf.

Registry of Open Access Repositories. Home page. http://roar.eprints.org/.

Registry of Open Access Repositories Mandatory Archiving Policies (ROARMAP). Home page. https://roarmap.eprints.org/.

Schmitt, Jason, prod. and dir. *Paywall: The Business of Scholarship*. Film, 2018. https://paywallthemovie.com/.

SPARC. "Big Deal Cancellation Tracking." https://sparcopen.org/our-work/big-deal-cancellation-tracking/.

———. "Open Education." https://sparcopen.org/open-education/.

Springer Nature Group. "Springer Nature and Germany's Projekt DEAL Finalise World's Largest Transformative Open Access Agreement." News release, January 9, 2020. https://group.springernature.com/gp/group/media/press-releases/archive-2020/springer-nature-projekt-deal/17553230.

University of California. "An Introductory Guide to the UC Model Transformative Agreements." In *Negotiating with Scholarly Journal Publishers: A Toolkit from the University of California*. Oakland: University of California Office of Scholarly Communication, 2019. https://osc.universityofcalifornia.edu/uc-publisher-relationships/negotiating-with-scholarly-journal-publishers-a-toolkit/an-introductory-guide-to-the-uc-model-transformative-agreement/.

US Government Accountability Office. "Federal Research: Additional Actions Needed to Improve Public Access to Research Results." GAO-20-81, November 21, 2019. https://www.gao.gov/products/gao-20-81.

Watkinson, Charles. "University Presses and the Impact of COVID19." *Learned Publishing* 34, no. 1 (January 2021): 17–24. https://doi.org/10.1002/leap.1352.

William and Flora Hewlett Foundation. "Open Education." https://hewlett.org/strategy/open-education/.

THE TECHNOLOGICAL CONTEXT:

SCHOLCOMM IS FORMAT

Will Cross with Josh Bolick and Maria Bonn

Keywords: networked communication, digital tools and methods, digital scholarship, scholarly identity, public access, public scholarship

INTRODUCTION

This chapter introduces and complicates the role of digital technologies and networked communication in scholarly communication. It provides an overview of the relationship between technology and the legal, social, and economic issues discussed in this book and identifies new ways of working, connecting, and sharing scholarship.

TECHNOLOGY AS A SHAPING FORCE FOR SCHOLARLY COMMUNICATION

For many researchers, the first exposure to the core issues and challenges in the contemporary practices we call "scholarly communication" may come through an interaction with networked technology. They may wonder why they were not able to download a research article they needed as a student, be inspired by a scholar they are introduced to via social media, or be challenged by questions about evaluation of a digital project on which they are working.

Technology shapes scholarly communication along with much of the rest of modern life. It can be an animating force and, just as often, a roadblock. In the past several decades, the rise of online and networked communication has radically transformed the way everyone—including scholars—communicates. It is hard to overstate the impact that the ability to make copies with no marginal costs or degradation in quality has had on the scholarly enterprise. Similarly, decentralized communication has fundamentally changed the way that relationships are formed, collaboration is done, and information is disseminated across and between communities.

The changes in practice caused by changes in technology have also created some of the most vexing challenges in scholarly communication. In addition to amplifying existing inequalities, the move to using digital tools and methods to conduct research and communicate scholarship has undermined critical components of the balanced copyright system that had underpinned scholarly communication. This has thrown established research, teaching, archiving, and access practices into disarray and precipitated an economic crisis that has been, in many ways, the inciting incident for the field of scholarly communication librarianship.

As we will see in the following chapters, technology is deeply intertwined with all aspects of scholarly communication as both a facilitator of new practices and a confounding force. Economically, changes in technology have facilitated new, inexpensive forms of communication while also empowering for-profit companies to monopolize the traditional outlets for scholarly sharing. The move to digital has unsettled long-standing rules and conventional wisdom around the core legal rights of scholars, publishers, and librarians, necessitating a new body of practice in negotiating for the rights of authors. And social interactions and their implications—from building collaborative networks and conducting citizen science to interrogating social hierarchies and biases—have been completely transformed by networked communication technologies. If scholarly communication is a "system of systems," then technology has been a common variable destabilizing and often short-circuiting all of those systems in a variety of ways.

Fortunately, scholarly communication also benefits from the lessons and practices of early technology exemplars, both academics exploring new options for communicating and activists in the free software and open source movements. While the modern field of scholarly communication librarianship is often dated to benchmarks such as the rise of the serials crisis in the 2000s or a series of foundational documents on openness signed in the same period, computer scientists have been self-archiving in anonymous FTP (file transfer protocol, an early way to transfer files from one computer to another) archives since the 1970s, and some scholars had been exploring open models for sharing decades before that.

One major milestone was the development of arXiv (https://arxiv.org) in the early 1990s by physicist Paul Ginsparg. Designed as a self-archiving platform for online sharing of articles in the fields of mathematics, physics, astronomy, and related STEM disciplines, arXiv quickly emerged as core infrastructure for many fields. As of 2021, roughly 16,000 articles are added per month. Many other fields have followed suit, with more than twenty-six discipline-specific archives built around the Open Science Framework (OSF, https://osf.io), an open source software project that facilitates open collaboration. Information and library science itself has a preprint server in this space, the LIS Scholarship Archive (LISSA, https://lissarchive.org), which offers "a place where anyone can have access to library and information science scholarship, in all its forms."[1]

In addition to these OSF-based preprint servers, which tend to cluster in the sciences, other disciplines have developed similar infrastructure aimed at their own communities. Scholars in the humanities benefit from Humanities Commons (HC, https://hcommons.org), a nonprofit network that enables humanities scholars and practitioners to create a professional profile, discuss common interests, develop new publications, and share their work. Like OSF, HC is an academy-owned and -governed project designed to serve the needs of scholars, writers, researchers, and students as they engage in teaching and research that benefit the larger community.

A third academic sharing network, SSRN (formerly Social Science Research Network), offers similar services for circulating publications throughout the scholarly community at an early stage, permitting the author to incorporate comments into the final version of the paper before its publication in a journal. SSRN was created in 1994 at about the same time as arXiv and grew to serve a wide variety of disciplines from economics and health science to law and public policy. In 2016, however, SSRN was purchased by Elsevier, a notorious for-profit publisher. Shortly after the acquisition, users began to notice papers being removed from SSRN without notice.[2] Data related to papers in SSRN have also been incorporated into other Elsevier products, such as Scopus. Today SSRN remains a valued and highly used resource for many scholars, but also a potential cautionary tale about open resources that can suddenly become commercialized. It's worth noting that Elsevier's acquisition of SSRN prompted the creation of SocArXiv (https://socopen.org) on OSF as a scholar-led alternative.

As with much of modern scholarly communication infrastructure, both HC and OSF come out of the open source community. Open source communities have developed many of the standard tools used today, and many of the philosophical underpinnings of openness as a set of values and practices can be traced to that community as well. The Creative Commons suite of licenses—which will be discussed further in the chapter 2.1 "Open Access" and chapter 2.3.1.1 "What is Open Education?"—were explicitly designed to help address the tension between creators' ability to share digital works globally and copyright regulation.

Whether understood as a transformative opportunity, an existential threat, or an over-hyped source of hot air, technology has been at the center of the ideology and the practices that make up scholarly communication. As we will see, however, the term itself can obscure as much as it reveals about the field.

TECH IS OLD, TECH IS NEW

When we think of technology, we tend to think of the *newest* technology, which is a fast-moving concept. As you read this, you might be thinking of artificial intelligence and machine learning, virtual and augmented reality, blockchain, or 5G cellular networks. In a not very distant future, though, these technologies may seem quaint. They might be so integrated into our lives that we think of them as basic infrastructure and not cutting-edge technology, or they may simply be unsuccessful and abandoned false starts that remain only as a historical curiosity. Whatever eclipses these phenomena will then seem cutting-edge and therefore will define the popular perception of technology. Watch television or film from even a couple of decades ago, such as the 1990s, before the smartphone existed. Those media capture a moment when pagers (aka "beepers") were cool and DVDs were the most advanced way to watch movies at home (followed soon by portable DVD players). Go back another decade, and you'll find great enthusiasm for early cellular phones (huge and expensive, with very short battery lives), personal computers, cassette tapes and players, VHS tapes and players, and video gaming consoles whose games look rudimentary compared to the ones played today. These technologies might look old-fashioned to us, but when they were new, they were as exciting as the newest iPhone, wearable, or advanced computing is today. Before long, the examples of new technology in this chapter and book will be similarly surpassed. The science fiction author, futurist, and, for a short period, academic publishing editor, Sir Arthur C. Clarke, is widely quoted for observing that "Any sufficiently advanced technology is indistinguishable from magic,"[3] the third of his three laws. Imagine what people of the 1950s or before would think of the smartphone, self-driving cars, or hologram concerts. We suspect these technologies would be met with disbelief, shock, or even terror. Similarly, there is every reason to believe that technologies that are new in 100 years would be similarly inconceivable to us, except as magic.*

Note that the examples of now-superseded technology above include both digital and analog technologies. Today, more and more new technology is digital or digitally created, but that hasn't always been the case. Digital technology is largely a development of the mid-twentieth century. Before that, most technology was analog or mechanical. Consider for a moment: the digital revolution that now deeply shapes our lives is well less than a century old. The pace of acceleration from the earliest digital calculators to VR headsets and the ability to stream any audio or visual media from almost anywhere is, for many observers, dizzying. We've

---

* The authors do not believe in magic.

all heard "back in my day" stories from our parents or grandparents and chuckled at them. Someday (sooner than we might like), younger people will be chuckling at us, but the table will turn on them eventually, too.

Technology is far older, however, than post–World War II. The current sense of the word, as "machinery, equipment, etc., developed from the practical application of scientific and technical knowledge" begins, according to the *Oxford English Dictionary*, in the late 19th century, and earlier usage dates back as far as 1612.[4] We can keep regressing to previous technologies: television, talking films, silent films, radio, automobiles, bicycles, photographs, telephone, telegraph, steam engine, cotton gin, printing press, rail, roads, steel, iron, bronze, wheel, stone, and (controlled) fire. Written communication was a new technology at the time of its invention. Stone tools were incredibly important technologies that changed the course of history. Consider how these basic technologies shape your day-to-day life and work! Our lives are suffused with technology, some of it very old; we are surrounded by and enveloped in it in numerous ways, from our births to our deaths.

If you think about the earliest technologies, like the wheel and controlled fire, on to the technologies of the Industrial Revolution and those of the Information Age that we use today, you can see acceleration at work. The amount of time between seismic shifts seems to be getting shorter. This is exemplified by Moore's Law, which stipulates that the number of transistors in a dense integrated circuit doubles roughly every two years.

Some of the technology of the past is deeply embedded in scholarly communication. Indeed, for some people the idea and practice of scholarly communication is deeply tied to ideas about new, and especially digital, technology. Of course, the idea of technology is more complex and varied than a simplistic focus on the digital technologies of the 1990s and 2000s. Our most basic forms of communication, speaking and listening, are facilitated and enhanced by technology in conference presentations and webinars. Twitter is widely used as a conference back channel, where participants share and discuss ideas and events as they happen. Written communication is even more recognizable as embodied in formal channels like articles, books, and conference proceedings. Until the movable type printing press was invented in the fifteenth century, books were rare and expensive, with copies being arduously produced by scribes with ink and quill. The printing press enabled much easier reproduction. For a while, published books and handwritten letters passed among researchers (or natural philosophers) were the available written means of sharing the results of research and knowledge gained through it. In the mid-seventeenth century, the first scholarly journals were created, codifying the model that dominated until the late 1990s and early aughts (i.e., print journals) and to which some disciplines, particularly in the humanities, remain attached. At the most basic level, a print scholarly article is the combined result of two technologies: written communication and printing technology. Similarly, a digital scholarly article is the combined result of written communication, legacies of print technology like formatting and copyediting, and various digital technologies. The internet added networked technology to that static digital file, making it easier to share at nominal cost, to link to it and within it, and to add digital metadata that makes it more discoverable.

It is part of our reality, in both our private and professional lives, to recognize that technology is a shaping force, even if its particular manifestations are transitory and perpetually in flux. As new developments in technology emerge and are widely adopted, they present new possibilities for the conduct of scholarship and the creation and communication of its products. With those possibilities come new challenges.

The widespread adoption of digital technology and the networked means of communication it enables, as well as the rapid improvements in efficiency and effectiveness that ensue, has led to exciting new forms of scholarship, to more visible and widely shared public science, and to the potential for increased reach and broader impact. Scholarship with an online life can reach beyond the borders of campuses and of countries. Scholarship no longer has to live on a researcher's desk, or sometimes on a server under a desk, or, in what used to be the best case, within the walls of the library. Now it flows out of offices, labs, and libraries and can travel the globe with the click of a few keys or the tap of a digital button.

These exciting possibilities, many of which have been and still are being realized, bring with them a new set of social issues that need to be understood and addressed if we are to reap the social benefit that technological developments lead us to believe is possible. The realization that digital files could be copied and shared with no cost and no degradation of quality led many to believe they had entered a new era where scholarship could be freely shared and used by all, or at least by anyone with access to a computer and a network connection. For example, if you are a parent whose child has an unusual disease, in the past you probably had to learn about that disease from whatever materials the medical professionals gave you or the often meager resources at your local public library. If you were lucky, you might have access to a medical library and be able to visit it to do research and read and take notes about things to ask your child's doctors. In a world of online information and scholarship, free of charge, you can research from home or from the doctors' office as you speak with them, making better informed choices and even suggesting new methods for treating your child.

The remainder of this chapter looks at some of the new possibilities created by relatively recent technological developments. These possibilities are particularly important for scholarship and its communication, and they raise important questions for scholars and for the librarians who work with and in support of them. There are new ways to do research, and there are new ways to record and report the results of that research. There are new ways to share research, and there are new ways to support research, particularly through new forms of connection that move out of hallways at conferences, rely on more rapid means than the post office, and create opportunities of personal connection only dreamed of in a pre–digital networked world.

TECHNOLOGY AND NEW TYPES OF SCHOLARLY PRODUCTS

Scholars and researchers are always looking for tools and methods that will help them do their work more efficiently. As they became acquainted with the internet and with computer-supported work, scholars were quick to seize upon new ways to *do* their work, whether it was faster resource discovery or more rapid data analysis. At the same time, scholars came to understand the affordances offered by digital technology and networked delivery for *reporting* their work. They began to imagine, and then create, scholarly products that took full advantage of those affordances to represent their research findings and to share those findings in creative new ways. While early on, this might have been limited to more rapid and extensive delivery of traditional textual products, it wasn't long before scholars turned their attention to incorporating digital practices into the publication and dissemination of scholarship. They explored the possibilities of multimedia delivery and of using hypertext to connect their work to that of others as well as to primary sources, digitally embedding their work in an intellectual and historical context.

The new ways of doing scholarly work and sharing the results of that work are often identified by the umbrella term *digital scholarship*. The concept of digital scholarship (DS) emerged early in the twenty-first century. DS has been described as "discipline-based scholarship produced with digital tools and presented in digital form."[5] It is also considered as a research agenda concerned with the impact of internet and digital technologies that are transforming scholarly practices.[6] Librarians at the University of Washington offer a helpful description of digital scholarship as "often composed of works that are born digital, multimedia, database technology-based, analysis of other born digital material, digital text and images, digital music or art, and data sets." They also note that "this form of scholarly data, presentation and dissemination represents a shift away from publishing the kind of scholarship that we have traditionally collected and preserved in libraries, and is a natural evolution and adaptation of digital technology to scholarship."[7]

Curious and creative scholars have been exploring "multimedia and multimodal" forms of communicating their work for decades. Some point to works like Borges's "Garden of Forking Paths" and Vannevar Bush's "As We May Think" as the earliest modeling, if not realization, of hypertext. Hypertext protocols were developed in the 1960s and fully realized with the advent of the World Wide Web. The use of hypertext allows scholars to link within and out to sources and to provide alternative pathways through an argument. By the mid-1980s, digital innovators were experimenting with the possibilities of electronic publishing. For instance, Bob Stein founded Voyager in 1984, a company that produced some of the earliest multimedia CD-ROM projects. Stein began with the Criterion Collection, classic films on CD-ROM, supported by a rich array of background and supplementary materials.[8]

Many scholars are interested in the ways in which digital delivery can enhance the possibilities for rich illustration of their work, enabling images, sound, video, and embedded data. By the early 1990s, scholars were turning their attention in earnest to these possibilities. Two early and celebrated examples of this kind of multimedia scholarship were developed at the University of Virginia. The Valley of the Shadow, created by Edward Ayers with the support of the Institute for Advanced Technology in the Humanities, is a digital archive that documents the lives of ordinary people in Virginia and Pennsylvania during the American Civil War. As the project site explains it, The Valley of the Shadow is

> more like a library than a single book. There is no "one" story in the Valley Project. Rather, what you'll find are thousands of letters and diaries, census and government records, newspapers and speeches, all of which record different aspects of daily life in these two counties at the time of the Civil War.[9]

At the same time as Ayers was developing the Valley of the Shadow, another UVA scholar, Jerome McGann, was beginning the digital Rossetti Archive to facilitate the scholarly study of Dante Gabriel Rossetti, the painter, designer, writer, and translator. The Rossetti Archive

> provides students and scholars with access to all of DGR's pictorial and textual works and to a large contextual corpus of materials, most drawn from the period when DGR's work first appeared and established its reputation (approximately 1848–1920), but some stretching back to the 14th-century sources of his Italian translations. All documents are encoded for structured search and analysis. The Rossetti Archive aims to include high-quality digital images of every surviving documentary state of DGR's works: all the manuscripts, proofs, and original editions, as well as the drawings, paintings, and designs of various kinds, including his collaborative photographic and craft works. These primary materials are transacted with a substantial body of editorial commentary, notes, and glosses.[10]

Projects like these inspired many scholars to consider how digital technology might be deployed to support, enliven, and strengthen what once would have been straightforward textual presentation and argument. Imagination and inspiration sometimes outpaced the technological realities, and creating and sustaining these works involved considerable investment of time, energy, and other resources. The Rossetti Archive took fifteen years to complete. The Valley of the Shadow lists almost 100 people on its staff page. By the twenty-first century, scholars, the libraries that support them, and funding agencies were all turning their attention to the development of tools that require less investment and expertise, resulting in tools like Scalar, an open source digital publishing tool, to support multimedia-rich digital publications; Omeka, a platform for online exhibits; and Pressbooks, for the rapid creation of both electronic and print books. These tools and their users still require skills, training, and support to be used successfully, but they have lowered the barriers to digital publication for many scholars and increased access for many users.

Recent research, including by one of the creators of this book, has identified growing areas of interest for scholars who want to use technology to enrich both the conduct and the reporting of their research. One of these is the desire to provide evidence in the context of scholarly argument and assertions. If a journal article, for instance, reports on conclusions drawn from survey data, in the past the author may have just summarized the data. Now, free of the space limitations of print and supported by the affordances of digital delivery, the author can attach a downloadable data set or point to an online repository providing access to that data set so a reader can explore the evidence and test the validity of the article's conclusions. Or, to give another example, if historians want to argue that advertisers in historical newspapers influenced journalism, they can include or point to scanned images of newspaper pages to help the reader understand the placement of ads in relation to news stories.

The possibilities for communicating and sharing scholarship have expanded rapidly and widely since the early days of the World Wide Web and even earlier days of the internet. Both scholarly imagination and technology continue to evolve, and tools for digital publishing become ever more functional and full-featured, as well as easier to use. These developments have changed the work of scholarly communication in libraries, but they haven't made it any easier. With new possibilities come new challenges. Digital scholarship and its publication raise questions about accessibility, about intellectual property, about preservation, and about all the ways in which scholars might use and build upon that scholarship. These are the questions that librarians help to address.

TECHNOLOGY AND NEW TYPES OF CONNECTIONS

In addition to new opportunities for sharing information, digital technology has been a key driver for new ways of developing relationships, building collaboration, and establishing connections, both with scholars from other institutions and those beyond the academy. Individual scholars have explored new ways to represent themselves and their body of work, ways that go beyond simply publishing or posting a specific article or project online. They are using technology to build new communities that provide support, connect partners, and welcome new voices and approaches to collaboration and impact. Projects have been launched based on social media connections. Informal support and information make everything easier - from deciding on a graduate program to sharing tips for attending conference sessions or finding a good taco joint near the conference venue. Online communities can also be critical for everything from friendly back-channeling during events to extending whisper networks about toxic or abusive colleagues. It would be hard to imagine accepting a new job, selecting a mentor, or joining a collaboration with a new peer without the benefit of social media. Online identity can be a beacon for attracting fellow travelers and a flashing red light that warns the unwary away from unsupportive or even dangerous colleagues.

At the same time, these new systems can place new burdens on scholars, who must construct and nurture a scholarly identity as they connect in new ways. Some scholars may experience this as extra work, especially when digital social networking requires establishing and learning the ropes of new online platforms. A scholar used to chatting in the hallways at an in-person conference may resist or resent the time it takes to sign up for a Twitter account, learn how to use the interface and follow the vernacular and in-jokes, find a set of people to follow, and periodically check in on the conversation.

Technologically mediated spaces have nontrivial barriers to entry and can also become a distraction and a time suck, blurring the boundaries between professional activities, social interactions, and entertainment. Anyone who has tabbed away from a writing project "just for a minute to check Instagram" and found their afternoon suddenly gone can testify to these challenges. Technically mediated communication can also amplify existing inequalities, exposing personal data for abuse and monetization and exposing scholars themselves to harassment, doxing, and bad-faith decontextualization of their work and their lives. Nevertheless, advances in technology have had a transformative effect for many scholars, empowering new voices and building connections and networks of support and collaboration that would have been inconceivable without these resources.

SCHOLARLY IDENTITY AND RELATIONSHIPS

By situating scholarly communication in new digital spaces, technology has significantly transformed the way scholars interact with each other. Persistent identifiers like ORCID (Open Researcher and Contributor ID, https://orcid.org) provide unique identification and disambiguation for scholars as they move throughout their career, change institutions, and take on new names and titles. These identifiers also offer an automatically updated profile and technical interoperability that can streamline information sharing with peers, publishers, and funding agencies.

Scholars also recognize that, in light of internet services like Google that gather and share data, an online presence is inevitable. The only question is how much agency a scholar chooses to assert in how they are represented online. Whether they create a bespoke website, sign up for professional network services like LinkedIn, or use an academic social media platform like Humanities Commons or a commercial academic social media option like ResearchGate or Academia.edu, the foundation of relationships online is a coherent presence.* From this foundation, scholars can build social and professional networks that establish friendships and connect with professional partners.

---

* While many researchers use commercial academic social media for a variety of purposes, there are critiques of such platforms. See Kathleen Fitzpatrick, "Academia, Not Edu," *Kathleen Fitzpatrick* (blog), October 26, 2015, https://kfitz.info/academia-not-edu/, and Sarah Bond, "Dear Scholars, Delete Your Account at Academia. Edu," *Forbes*, January 23, 2017, https://www.forbes.com/sites/drsarahbond/2017/01/23/dear-scholars-delete-your-account-at-academia-edu/.

COMMUNICATION AND COLLABORATION

Online identity and presence offers an intrinsic set of opportunities but also acts as the foundation for new types of networks and communities of practice. As discussed in chapter 2.4, "Open Science and Infrastructure," open science manifests in a variety of practices, but many of them build on the new opportunities provided by technology to collaborate and connect. The book you are currently reading offers an outstanding case study on communication and collaboration. While your authors work at institutions more than a thousand miles apart, we have developed a partnership, conceptualized and drafted the book, and invited and worked with almost eighty contributors to share their own experiences in the field. None of this would be possible without the digital networked technology that we increasingly take for granted in the academy.

This collaboration began with a series of telephone calls and online meetings and has been driven by recurring calls on videoconferencing platforms. While the authors occasionally meet up at conferences and have benefitted from an IMLS-funded symposium hosted in North Carolina, all stages of authoring from conceptualization to drafting and editing have been done with shared word processing tools provided by Google. Contributors have been recruited through online e-mail discussion groups, social media platforms such as Twitter, and the broader online communities forged in these spaces.

Before the book was released, individual pieces were made available for open peer review online, and some pieces were shared through preprint servers that make research available more quickly but also facilitate new community discussions about the research. Now that the book has been released, tools such as Hypothes.is that permit social annotation are being used to support scholarly communication around the online manuscript but also to facilitate new connections and communities. The book is also linked to the Scholarly Communication Notebook (SCN), a hub on OER Commons that gathers ancillary materials, case studies, and other open learning objects that can make the information in this book actionable for students and instructors as well as practitioners across the field.[11]

NEW PUBLICS

Technological advances have also opened up new ways to connect with people outside the academy. Public engagement can build on the tools and approaches described above with preprints planting a flag and sharing information far beyond the limited paywalls of formal journals. Public annotation and libraries of references provided through tools such as Zotero likewise bridge the gap between the academy and the various publics that exist in the wider world. This textbook is one example of the ability of scholars to use technology to connect with scholars, practitioners, and wider publics.

Open peer review can invite stakeholders from different disciplines and from beyond the academy to respond to scholarship. Public science, including both participatory action through practices such as citizen science and science outreach, has strengthened and extended the power and scope of scientific research and explicitly empowered historically marginalized and delegitimized people and systems of knowledge. From the 1990s-era SETI@home project that used distributed computing to analyze signals in search of extraterrestrial life to more recent examples such as NC State's Fermentology project that explores microbial growth in local communities in order to unlock the science of bread, the work of science is made better by opening it to wider audiences. Funders have taken up this work by increasingly requiring broader impact statements that articulate how research can move beyond the lab in order to support the public good.

While public access to valuable and sometimes essential research and scholarship has definitely increased since the advent of the internet and the technologies that are built upon it, we are not in an information utopia where research and its products are available for all to discover, study, and use. There are still significant legal and economic barriers limiting public access to scholarship and, as a result, limiting the social good that public access might make possible. Those barriers aren't necessarily the same as they were in a primarily print culture, but the motives that drive them *are* much the same. As the communication of scholarship moved online, corporate interests realized that the models of ownership and access, the business models that derived profit from those models, and the laws that ensured their viability were threatened, maybe made irrelevant, by new modes of distribution and access. Eager to protect profits, they moved quickly to retrofit those models to the online world or to create new models equally profit-driven, but now taking into account new threats and possibilities. This is not to say that digital optimists have meekly accepted the reassertion of commercial power. As the law changes or is applied in new ways to protect intellectual property for purposes of profit, or as new ways emerge of extracting that profit from scholarship, there are both individuals and organized bodies of advocates, professionals, and organizations that respond and propose and propagate their own reforms and alternatives in hopes of realizing the greatest social good for the greatest number of people.

DISCUSSION QUESTIONS

1. How has technology changed in your lifetime, and how has it impacted you?
2. What technology have you used as a student, researcher, or librarian? How have you used it, and what were the benefits and challenges of its use?
3. In what ways has scholarly communication been revolutionized by technology, and in what ways is it not revolutionary?
4. How has technology been deployed in harmful ways?
5. Identify three digital tools or platforms that you might consider using in a scholarly or professional way. What are they? What do they do? How are they beneficial? Are there risks to their use?

NOTES

1. LIS Scholarship Archive, home page, https://lissarchive.org.
2. Stephen Henderson, "SSRN postings and copyright," https://prawfsblawg.blogs.com/prawfsblawg/2016/07/ssrn-postings-and-copyright.html.
3. Arthur C. Clarke, "Hazards of Prophecy: The Failure of Imagination," in *Profiles of the Future: An Inquiry into the Limits of the Possible* (New York: Harper and Row, 1962, rev. 1973).
4. *Oxford English Dictionary Online*, s.v. "technology."
5. Edward L. Ayers, "Does Digital Scholarship Have a Future?" *EDUCAUSE Review* 48, no. 4 (July/August 2013): 27, https://er.educause.edu/-/media/files/article-downloads/erm1343.pdf.
6. Wikipedia, s.v. "Digital scholarship," last modified November 6, 2022, https://en.wikipedia.org/wiki/Digital_scholarship.
7. University of Washington, "About Digital Scholarship," University Libraries, https://www.lib.washington.edu/digitalscholarship.
8. Jeremy M. Norman, "Bob Stein and Partners Found The Voyager Company," https://www.historyofinformation.com/detail.php?id=5442.

9. University of Virginia Library, "Guide to the Valley: How to Use the Valley Project," *Valley of the Shadow* website, accessed April 11, 2023, https://valley.lib.virginia.edu/VoS/usingvalley/valleyguide.html.

10. Rosetti Archive, "The Complete Writings and Pictures of Dante Gabriel Rossetti: A Hypermedia Archive," http://www.rossettiarchive.org.

11. OER Commons, "The Scholarly Communication Notebook," https://www.oercommons.org/hubs/SCN.

BIBLIOGRAPHY

Ayers, Edward L. "Does Digital Scholarship Have a Future?" *EDUCAUSE Review* 48, no. 4 (July/August 2013): 24–34. https://er.educause.edu/-/media/files/article-downloads/erm1343.pdf.

Bond, Sarah. "Dear Scholars, Delete Your Account at Academia.Edu." *Forbes*, January 23, 2017. https://www.forbes.com/sites/drsarahbond/2017/01/23/dear-scholars-delete-your-account-at-academia-edu/.

Fitzpatrick, Kathleen. "Academia, Not Edu." *Kathleen Fitzpatrick* (blog), October 26, 2015. https://kfitz.info/academia-not-edu/.

Henderson, Stephen (2016). "SSRN postings and copyright." *PrawfsBlawg* (blog), July 15, 2016. https://prawfsblawg.blogs.com/prawfsblawg/2016/07/ssrn-postings-and-copyright.html.

LIS Scholarship Archive. Home page. https://lissarchive.org.

Norman, Jeremy M. "Bob Stein and Partners Found The Voyager Company." Jeremy Norman's HistoryofInformation.com. https://www.historyofinformation.com/detail.php?id=5442.

OER Commons. "The Scholarly Communication Notebook." https://www.oercommons.org/hubs/SCN.

Rosetti Archive. "The Complete Writings and Pictures of Dante Gabriel Rossetti: A Hypermedia Archive." http://www.rossettiarchive.org.

University of Virginia Library. "Guide to the Valley: How to Use the Valley Project." *Valley of the Shadow* website. Accessed April 11, 2023. https://valley.lib.virginia.edu/VoS/usingvalley/valleyguide.html.

University of Washington. "About Digital Scholarship." University Libraries. https://www.lib.washington.edu/digitalscholarship.

Wikipedia. S.v. "Digital scholarship." Last modified November 6, 2022. https://en.wikipedia.org/wiki/Digital_scholarship.

THE SOCIAL CONTEXT

SCHOLCOMM IS PEOPLE

Josh Bolick with Maria Bonn and Will Cross

Keywords: public good, access/information privilege, research life cycle, bias, DEI, social media

---

INTRODUCTION

This chapter provides a brief examination of the ways that scholarly communication is shaped by social forces and how librarians contribute to those forces. It focuses on three major elements: scholarly communication as a global enterprise, as practice that occurs in social contexts, and as a field that is increasingly done using networked communication tools such as social media services.

While librarianship as an academic discipline is broadly considered a social science, this book is not a sociology text, and the editors and authors are not sociologists. Yet it's impossible to fully understand scholarly communication work in and outside of libraries without discussing the social issues that shape our work. By *social* we mean of or relating to society and the interactions among people, including where those interactions may be heavily mediated by institutions and technology. Humans are inherently social beings and are to large degrees products of our societies and social conditioning. The academy, academic libraries, and disciplinary communities are deeply social environments with complex stakeholder relationships and practices. We all bring our identities, experiences, and social conditioning into our work. We are subject to these social forces and actively contribute to them through our interactions with each other.

While the influence of social issues on scholarly communication is extensive, we will focus on three major elements that we see as fundamental to understanding scholarly communication and the work it entails in academic libraries. First, scholarly communication is a global enterprise with many stakeholders and broad implications. Second, scholarly communication takes place in an inherently social context and is subject to predominant social norms and biases that warrant careful consideration. Third, along with everyone else, researchers are increasingly turning to social media platforms, not only to share events and pictures of pets and food, but also to communicate research results and products and to connect with other users. This chapter is a brief examination of scholarly communication through a social lens in order to understand how it is shaped by social forces and how we contribute to those forces, for better and worse. We hope that this overview is an entry into these complex issues and that you will continue to explore and consider the role of social forces in libraries and scholarly communication.

SCHOLARLY COMMUNICATION AS A GLOBAL ENTERPRISE

While a substantial portion of the most established and influential research institutions, funders, and publishers within the scholarly communication system are presently based in the United States, Canada, and Western Europe, research and research communication are a global phenomenon. This has been the case for hundreds of years, but is increasingly true due to a number of factors. Our ability to communicate across vast distances has increased. Postcolonial nations have established and grown national research infrastructures, often while still contending with their colonial legacies. Networked technology has expanded across the globe, though there are still substantial digital divides both in the US and elsewhere.

There are researchers and research institutions in every country, and much research crosses national borders. Many of the problems that researchers investigate and attempt to address through research are global in scale: medicine and health, environment and climate, education and empowerment, particularly of women and girls, for example. While the majority of the best-known and most powerful academic publishers are based in the US and Western Europe, publishing itself is also distributed throughout the world. Every person isn't a formal researcher, but everyone is impacted by research in myriad ways, so even where research is isolated to a given geographic location, the implications of that research may have an impact on people far beyond that specific locale. Luckily, research (broadly speaking) is not geographically bound. People everywhere stand to benefit from research regardless of where it's conducted, although, as we will discuss, the benefits of research are not evenly distributed. Nonetheless, people around the world are both directly and indirectly involved in the conduct of research and the production of research outputs, or scholarly communication.

SCHOLARLY COMMUNICATION AS PUBLIC GOOD

Let's consider the social imperative for research and the necessity of sharing knowledge gained through research. In one way or another, all research conducted in a university or college context is publicly supported. For public higher education institutions, such as state universities in the US, this is obvious. They are directly taxpayer-supported. A researcher's lab at a state university is really the university's lab, which means it's really the state's lab, and the equipment, material, and tools contained therein are typically the property of the state; often state law governs how these materials can be disposed of or given away. By extension, the lab and its accoutrements belong to the public that supports universities. Arguably, the public that funds research through its tax dollars deserves access to knowledge derived from the research it supports, even as the intellectual property generated in this system is typically not owned by the state or institution. This idea, that publicly supported research should be publicly available, is the foundation of research funder policies requiring public sharing of articles and data derived from funded research, such as the National Institutes of Health (NIH) Public Access Policy and those policies created as a result of the 2013 Office of Science and Technology

Policy (OSTP) memorandum "Increasing Access to the Results of Federally Funded Scientific Research."[1] A White House blog post about the policy memorandum states, "citizens deserve easy access to the results of scientific research their tax dollars have paid for."[2] Funder public access policies are also discussed in chapter 1.2, "The Economic Context," and chapter 1.5, "The Legal and Policy Context," demonstration of how interconnected these forces are.

The argument for public support of private institutions is less obvious, but still clear. For all intents and purposes, research conducted at private institutions is categorically identical to research conducted at public institutions. In other words, research within a discipline is conducted similarly whether it is hosted in a public or private setting. Private institutions, of course, are not directly supported by taxpayers and do not belong to the state. But they do enjoy significant benefits as nonprofit institutions, which is a form of public support. In brief, many societies see public benefit to many kinds of private nonprofit organizations, including those of higher education, and therefore decline to impose taxes on them, which is a de facto public subsidy. Arguably, one of the benefits the public deserves in return is access to knowledge created at those private institutions. A social worker doesn't care that a given intervention was developed by researchers at a public or private institution; the social worker just wants to leverage the best known interventions and information to help their clients, and access to peer-reviewed scholarship may help them do that. Researchers based at private institutions with grants from public funding agencies like the NIH, NSF, and many others are subject to the same compliance measures as researchers based at public institutions. Institutions of higher learning, public and private, as well as funders supporting research through grants, generally share a mission to improve the lives of constituents and to advance knowledge through teaching and research. In short, whether at public or private institutions, researchers in a discipline mostly conduct their research similarly, seek similar funding, create similar outputs, place them in similar venues, and hope for similar impact. It all goes into the same system, and it's all working toward the same ends: increasing human knowledge and solving problems.

While a great number of research articles and other outputs are written by and for researchers, research itself is not produced in a vacuum merely by and for researchers. That is, researchers ask questions and fashion hypotheses because they think other researchers will care and because there's intrinsic value of information and knowledge gained[*] (see also Information Has Value in the ACRL *Information Literacy Framework for Higher Education*).[3] The motivation to research is complex and nuanced, but it's clear that researchers want to know more about the way things work, to expand what is known, and there's limited value to discovery not shared, hence scholarly communication. While what is known is often worked out among experts in peer-reviewed literature, knowledge gained has value beyond the academy, the academy isn't the only home of experts and expertise, and the practical value of knowledge isn't always obvious.

Not everyone, of course, is interested in or capable of engaging with scholarly literature, which is often embedded in disciplinary discourse written for other scholars trained in the language and methods of the discipline rather than the general public. But a sufficient number of people outside of academic contexts are trained (through graduate work, for example) to read and decipher scholarly texts. You or your neighbor or family member may not be interested in or capable of understanding medical literature, but you want your doctor and dentist and other health care professionals to be able to benefit from and apply the relevant research being developed at universities. On the other hand, in a personal or family health emergency, you may desire direct access to health care literature to help guide your questions

---

[*] The selection of research topics and questions is also subjected to other pressures, such as perceived or real editorial preferences for "hot" topics and promotion and tenure influences that distort the pursuit of knowledge.

with health care providers or to read deeply on a diagnosis or treatment. Knowledge is power, and that power can be wielded to advocate for oneself or a loved one, particularly where biases institutionalized in health care institutions and professions may harm marginalized communities. We can also think of many academic disciplines for which there's an applied practice external to higher education: librarians, lawyers, teachers, dieticians, nurses, administrators, entrepreneurs, wellness advocates, coaches, accountants, social workers, engineers, and so on. While often outside of the academy, these professionals benefit from access to scholarly literature and are frequently trained to find and understand it. Unfortunately, in many cases, once they complete their formal education, their access to disciplinary literature largely ceases. It is alarmingly common that practitioners in a position to leverage knowledge gained from research lack access to that research, thus potentially harming the people they serve. As discussed in depth in chapter 1.2, "The Economic Context," chapter and in chapter 2.1, "Open Access," open access (OA) seeks to provide digital access as universally as possible, with as few limitations on reuse as possible. In his excellent and essential book *Open Access*, Peter Suber says, "OA allows us to provide access to everyone who cares to have access, without patronizing guesswork about who really wants it, who really deserves it, and who would really benefit from it." He goes on to say, "The idea is to stop thinking of knowledge as a commodity to meter out to deserving customers, and to start thinking of it as a public good."[4] The thrust of this argument is that there are capable readers outside of traditional research contexts. They contribute to the public good, and their access to research extends the benefits they provide to society and the benefits of the research.

You might be wondering why some people have access to scholarly literature and others do not. Access and the lack of it are further developed in other parts of this book but warrant a brief discussion here. Before the internet made much information remarkably easier to discover and cheaper to obtain, exclusive access was an understandable and reasonable aspect of scholarly publishing. Scholarly articles and books were print-based, and that entailed costs that networked digital distribution does not, such as paper, ink, binding, storage, and shipping. Subscription to journals, either by individual researchers or by their institutional libraries, plus a tradition of circulating copies of articles among researchers and services like interlibrary loan, provided researchers with access to scholarly literature. This was far from a perfect or universal solution, but it was a fact of pre-internet research culture. Subscription-based scholarly publishing business models are based on this reality. Until the internet, there arguably wasn't a better way. By the turn of the twenty-first century, however, the internet created new opportunities for sharing scholarly research. Here's how the Budapest Open Access Initiative (BOAI), which you may recall from chapter 1.2, "The Economic Context," and will encounter elsewhere in this book, put it in early 2002:

> An old tradition and a new technology have converged to make possible an unprecedented public good. The old tradition is the willingness of scientists and scholars to publish the fruits of their research in scholarly journals without payment, for the sake of inquiry and knowledge. The new technology is the internet. The public good they make possible is the world-wide electronic distribution of the peer-reviewed journal literature and completely free and unrestricted access to it by all scientists, scholars, teachers, students, and other curious minds. Removing access barriers to this literature will accelerate research, enrich education, share the learning of the rich with the poor and the poor with the rich, make this literature as useful as it can be, and lay the foundation for uniting humanity in a common intellectual conversation and quest for knowledge.[5]

This statement outlines the preconditions for broader access, which the BOAI goes on to call open access, or OA "Open access refers to scholarly literature that is digital, online, free of charge, and free of most copyright and reuse restrictions."[6] At the most basic level, OA means that anyone with access to the internet may access an open piece of scholarly literature. OA is a response to exclusive access. While enormous strides toward increased access have been made in the twenty years since the BOAI, we remain far from attaining universal OA, which is why innovation and advocacy toward that goal remain of vital importance. OA is much more fully developed in part II of this book, where chapter 2.1 is dedicated to it. For now, know that social, economic, legal, and technological factors contribute to a system of haves and have-nots—those who have access to scholarly literature and those who do not. These are not fixed states. Having access to some of the literature doesn't entail access to all of the literature. Even the most privileged researchers encounter access issues because universal access doesn't exist. Additionally, access privileges are subject to change, such as when a researcher leaves an institution, perhaps by graduating from a degree program or changing jobs, or when an institution changes its research holdings by either adding or reducing subscribed content, which is a routine occurrence. We are all both haves and have-nots, to greater and lesser degrees, in a fluctuating environment. OA seeks to increase the volume of scholarly literature available to anyone with internet access and an interest in reading it.

ACCESS AND THE ACADEMY

Access is desirable and beneficial outside of traditional research contexts, but it's of vital importance within those contexts. Researchers build on existing knowledge by engaging with published research findings, confirming, replicating, altering, challenging, and citing relevant literature. Since access is a precondition to advancing knowledge through research, surely researchers have access to the literature necessary to pursue their programs of research, yes? Unfortunately, in many cases they do not. Let's start at the most privileged and powerful end of the higher educational institutional continuum. A layperson might reasonably assume that well-resourced institutions like Harvard, MIT, Duke, UC Berkeley, and Cambridge enjoy universal access to scholarly literature, but those assumptions would be wrong. In fact, these institutions have been vocal advocates for increasing open access to scholarly literature because they do not have the financial resources to ensure sufficient access and they recognize the benefit of expanded, if not universal, access. The faculties of Harvard, MIT, and Duke, all elite private institutions with substantial fiscal resources, were among the earliest to implement institutional open access policies (more on this later) and establish offices and staffing to advocate for increased access and related practices. At present these universities remain highly visible and influential in international efforts to reform and advance scholarly communication. Lower down, but still high on the privilege spectrum, institutions like Florida State University, the University of North Carolina at Chapel Hill, the University of Michigan, and the University of Kansas, among many more, have also long advocated for reforms in scholarly publishing and increased access to scholarly outputs. Many, many prominent and powerful institutions have canceled or downsized significant journal subscription packages, or so-called Big Deals, because they cannot afford them (see SPARC's Big Deal Cancellation Tracker).[7] These dynamics are present in every powerful national research environment. Recent years have seen national consortia in Sweden, Germany, Norway, the Netherlands, and many other countries at loggerheads with certain publishers over access issues. These are among the wealthiest countries and research infrastructures on Earth, and yet they struggle to access scholarly literature that is fundamental to the pursuit of research. It is not a surprise, then, that less powerful economies and the research and teaching institutions they host, such as those in developing countries, struggle desperately to access research literature. Some institutions in developing countries are unable to subscribe to any toll-access journals and depend entirely on openly available literature supplemented, in some cases, with publisher gestures at access for those who can't afford it, such as Research4Life.[8] While there is a vast difference in access among researchers based in these different circumstances, they share a common problem: insufficient access to scholarly literature (periodical as well as non-periodical literature).

The existence of shadow libraries such as Library Genesis and Sci-Hub is illustrative. Sci-Hub is a shadow library founded in 2011 by a Kazahk graduate student, Alexandra Elbikyan, that hosts tens of millions of scholarly articles online without regard to copyright. You might think of it as Pirate Bay for scholarly articles; much, or most, of the content it hosts and delivers to users at no cost is provided in violation of copyright. In 2017, SciHub was successfully sued for copyright infringement by Elsevier, which was awarded fifteen million dollars in damages, though many believe that the plaintiff is unlikely to ever receive that money.[9] You might think that use of Sci-Hub is focused in developing countries, and indeed there is a great deal of use in those countries. However, in 2016 *Science* reporter John Bohannon demonstrated that developed countries account for a relatively high volume of downloads and that many requests originate in university towns, including in the US.[10] To be clear, much of this activity is illegal, and there have been allegations of phishing and other means of acquiring researcher credentials in order to access papers. That said, Sci-Hub is a symptom of the problem of lack of access. If research articles were universally available, Sci-Hub would be superfluous. That privileged university towns in the US generate a not insignificant volume of requests suggests either that researchers in those locations lack traditional access or that they find the experience of using Sci-Hub superior, perhaps due to a lack of paywalls, login requirements, and multifactor authentication requirements for interlibrary loan requests

As summarized above, research is a global enterprise that is conducted across time, space, culture, disciplines, and institutional types, with implications and benefits that shape our collective knowledge and experiences, whether we are active participants in that enterprise or passive beneficiaries of it. Universal access to scholarly literature doesn't exist, but access is an imperative for both researchers in the academy and practitioners based outside of the academy, where access is far lower but arguably as important. Finally, the public that supports the creation of scholarship, one way or another, ought to benefit from it, both as readers and as indirect beneficiaries of it.

SCHOLARLY COMMUNICATION IN A SOCIAL CONTEXT

Scholarly communication is inherently social in nature and therefore must be examined within its social context. Every stakeholder group consists of people engaging with each other, within their own stakeholder group, and frequently with members of other groups. In other words, we cannot forget that the scholarly communication system is built by and for people. People conceive research questions and ways to study them; they apply for grant funding to conduct the research; the funding applications are reviewed and either approved or rejected by people based on priorities set by people at the funding agency. People conduct the studies, present their findings to peers at academic conferences, write manuscripts reporting on their research, and submit them for publication. People serve in editorial capacities and as peer reviewers. Accepted articles are formatted and copyedited and often distributed by people, though machines are involved in all of these processes. Subsequently, people read the work, cite it, implement or challenge it, and build on it; again, machines increasingly are used in these activities as well, but at the direction of, and in service to, people. Every stage of the research life cycle, which the National Library of Medicine defines as "the process that a researcher takes to complete a project or study from its inception to its completion,"[11] is done by or at the direction of people. These are social activities that often reflect the societies in which this system was designed. Even when it appears as though there's an institutional, corporate, or technological entity influencing the scholarly communication system, that entity is a proxy for the people who it represents, or who designed it, and therefore reflects the biases and assumptions of those people. To put it simply, people aren't neutral, and neither are the institutions, businesses, and technology we create.

Let's consider a couple of examples to illustrate the kinds of biases, and responses to them, at play in systems of scholarly communication.

ON BIAS IN WIKIPEDIA

Paul A. Thomas

While Wikipedia may seem like a digital utopian's dream come true in terms of its size and usage, inequities lie below the surface code. Perhaps the most (in)famous issue is gender. While about 50 percent of the English-speaking world identifies as male, almost 90 percent of Wikipedia's editors identified as male in 2018.[12] This contributor imbalance has resulted in a coverage imbalance. In 2014, only about 15.5 percent of Wikipedia biographies were of women.[13] A number of initiatives have been launched to combat this gap, such as the Women in Red project, which seeks to expand coverage on "women's biographies, women's works, and women's issues,"[14] as well as providing content on those who identify as "non-binary and/or [an]other [gender]."[15] Since Women in Red launched in 2015, conscientious editors have been able to raise the percentage of biographies on Wikipedia that focus on women or nonbinary individuals to over 19 percent.

Another issue that plagues the site is racial bias. Many of the articles on non-white history and culture are underdeveloped; other potential articles do not exist. There are a few reasons for this. For one thing, most Wikipedia editors self-identify as white and are less inclined to write or less knowledgeable about non-white topics, issues, and experiences. Also, Wikipedia requires its articles to cite reliable secondary sources, like books or academic articles, which have historically ignored or minimized the impact of people of color. As with projects that seek to remedy Wikipedia's gender bias, initiatives have also been created to rectify Wikipedia's racial coverage, such as the AfroCrowd project, which aims to improve coverage of Black culture and history on Wikipedia by "giv[ing] people of color opportunities to do more than participate in and consume social media."[16] Since launching in 2016 AfroCrowd has helped steer Wikipedia in a more racially just direction; in 2017 alone, for instance, 367 members of the project edited around 2,500 articles, of which 362 were created from scratch![17]

How is a well-meaning editor supposed to help erase the gender or racial biases of an encyclopedia with over six million articles? While one user out of 41.3 million may not be able to change the world, they can help by organizing large-scale editing operations, such as an edit-a-thon, an event wherein Wikipedia editors collectively edit articles on a specific topic, thereby changing the site's coverage on that topic en masse. The Women in Red project, for example, has hosted numerous edit-a-thons with global participation.[18] While they aren't a magic bullet, edit-a-thons are a tool that Wikipedia editors should heartily embrace to increase equity.

A second example of social context wielding enormous influence over technological tools that are often perceived as neutral or unbiased is discussed at length in Dr. Safiya Umoja Noble's excellent 2018 book, *Algorithms of Oppression: How Search Engines Reinforce Racism*.[19] Noble documents the ways that assumptions and ideology are manifested in search and artificial intelligence tools and the pernicious effects of those manifestations, particularly on women and people of color, especially Black women and girls. She says

Some of the very people who are developing search algorithms and architecture are willing to promote sexist and racist attitudes openly at work and beyond, while we are supposed to believe that these same employees are developing "neutral" or "objective" decision-making tools.[20]

Considering the ever-increasing reliance on commercial web tools as sources of information and -reaching, detrimental, and deeply concerning. "Algorithms are, and will continue to be, contextually relevant and loaded with power," argues Noble.[21]

A scholar of library and information studies, Noble points out that linking and indexing, which are the basis of the web as we understand and experience it, are founded in traditional classification systems such as the Library of Congress.[22] Indeed, while it's somewhat easy to point fingers at some of the most visible and successful companies of our time, our own (library) systems aren't above these biased phenomena. "Ranking [of results] is itself information that also reflects the political, social, and cultural values of the society that search engine companies operate within, a notion that is often obscured in traditional information science studies."[23]

To see how this phenomenon is present in the scholarly communication system, consider that academic institutions and publishing in the United States and Western Europe were built by and for white men of financial means. Harvard University, to choose a prominent example, was founded in 1636 to train clergy in the early American colonies. By the nineteenth century, a secularized Harvard was closely associated with the elite Boston families of early America—not a diverse group in any respect. Harvard admitted its first Black student, Beverly Garnett Williams, in 1847, which prompted riots among students and faculty.[24] Williams died prior to beginning his studies at Harvard, so never actually attended. Richard T. Greener was the first Black student to earn a bachelor's degree from Harvard, over twenty years later, in 1870. It would be nearly 100 years before Martin Kilson became Harvard's first tenured Black professor in 1969.[25] If we similarly consider gender, the first female student was admitted to Harvard in 1920, to the Graduate School of Education, with the Medical School following in 1945, and Law in 1950.[26] Helen Maud Cam became the first woman to be tenured at Harvard in 1948.[27] From its inception, that's 312 years to the first tenured woman, and 333 years to the first tenured Black man. As we write this book, 1948 and 1969 aren't that long ago. To put a finer point on it, in May 2021 the *Chronicle of Higher Education* published a searchable data set of the number of Black women with tenure at US higher education institutions as of fall 2019. Of 1,081 tenured professors at Harvard, only 13 were Black women, 1.2 percent of the total tenured faculty.[28]

Harvard is not uniquely guilty of historical bias against women and people of color within the US academy, of course. Most, if not all, of our academic institutions share this guilt. These biases are widespread in the American college and university system because they are widely present in American society, which was also constructed at its foundation by and for white men of financial means, and because we have yet to eliminate these foundational biases from modern society. Bias is institutionalized in our higher education institutions—in YOUR institution, and in our own. For example, consider the race and gender of the professoriate in the US, which is overwhelmingly white and male.[29] Being of the professoriate, journal editors and editorial boards, as well as peer reviewers, are also disproportionately white and male, so editorial processes and peer review reflect white male biases and norms. Because of the preponderance of whiteness and maleness and the intersection of the two, women and scholars of color are underrepresented in the research literature. Scholarly publishing as a profession is similarly hegemonically white. These issues are amplified in historically male-dominated fields like math, physics, and engineering.[30] Librarianship is not exempt from these forces. Like teaching and nursing, librarianship is historically feminized labor, and women still make up the majority of practitioners. But when we look at the upper leadership of academic libraries, we see that men are overrepresented.[31] We also know that librarianship is overwhelmingly white, despite efforts to address the whiteness of the profession.

Unsurprisingly, systemic and institutional bias in higher education impacts the scholarly communication system. Men are generally overrepresented in academic publishing, benefiting from higher submission and publication rates than women. For example, Day, Corbett, and Boyle reviewed Royal Society of Chemistry data and found

> a gradual trickle-down decrease in this female percentage through the publishing process and each of these female percentages is less than the last: authors of submissions; authors of RSC submissions which are not rejected without peer review; authors of accepted RSC publications; authors of cited articles. The success rate for female authors to progress through each of these publishing stages is lower than that for male authors. There is a decreasing female percentage when progressing through from first authors to corresponding authors to reviewers, reflecting the decreasing female percentage with seniority in Chemistry research.[32]

A 2017 Elsevier report, "Gender in the Global Research Landscape," found that women publish fewer articles than men, though it did not find a meaningful difference in citation rates.[33] On the citation front that sounds good, and assuming the conclusion is correct, it is, but if men generate more articles that are cited at similar rates as those by women, they accumulate more citations across their publication output, reinforcing their gendered advantage.

Race functions in a similar manner. In "Relegated to the Margins: Faculty of Color, the Scholarly Record, and the Necessity of Antiracist Library Disruptions," Inefuku observes, "The inequities in publishing are representative of racial power dynamics in greater society, reflecting and reinscribing White Supremacy over the construction of knowledge."[34] Roberts and colleagues looked at psychology publications from 1974 to 2018 and found a low level of publications that emphasize race, a predominance of white editorship (with an associated dearth of articles concerning race), and the pattern of the race of the author corresponding to the race of most of their study participants. In order to address systemic inequality, they recommend "that journals should consist of diverse editors, reviewers, authors, and participants."[35]

Looking at NIH funding awards, Ginther and colleagues found that Black authors produced fewer publications and citations, were less likely to be coauthors, and had lower cumulative impact factors relative to Asian, Hispanic, and white peers. They specifically note a funding gap between Black and white principal investigators.[36] These gender and race disparities are intersectional; they are amplified, such as for white men or Black women. Because editorial positions, grant awards, publications, and citations are key to hiring and to promotion and tenure decisions, men and white people, particularly white men, advance within the academy at higher rates than their female and non-white peers. Of course, gender and race aren't the only biases exerting influence, and we don't wish to imply that they are by citing these examples. That said, as examples, race and gender illustrate how biases are embedded within scholarly communication with pernicious effect. While significant advances in equity and inclusion have been realized in higher education, much work remains to be done.

Inequities in higher education and scholarly communication as described above are also visible in scholarly communication work in libraries. As the academy and publishing are very white, so is librarianship. There is a real need to critically examine ourselves and our work, to understand its inequitable foundations, and to intentionally and continuously strive to do and be better. Some of our colleagues and organizations are helping us to do that. Pointing out the inequities in scholarly publishing and in libraries and examining the work of scholarly communication roles in academic libraries, Charlotte Roh asks,

> Are we perpetuating the biases and power structures of traditional scholarly publishing? Or are we using library publishing to interrogate, educate, and establish more equitable models of scholarly communication? As librarians, we can be explicit about inequalities in scholarly publishing. We can take action to avoid reproducing them in our unique roles as publishers, scholarly communication experts, and information literacy providers.[37]

Our biases abound, and we bring them to all of our interactions, processes, evaluations, platforms, institutions, and so on, including scholarly communication, often, but not always, in spite of better intentions. Consciousness of our own biases and those within the relevant systems of higher education and publishing is foundational to addressing them and to supporting each other and our constituents who are navigating these opaque and complex systems. Using the metaphor of crossroads, April Hathcock examines the intersections of scholarly communication with democracy, access, and diversity. Hathcock observes,

> In our race to the crossroads of scholarly communication and democracy, it is essential that we engage critically with our professional values—with particular attention to democracy itself, access, and diversity—to ensure that we are building systems that lead to true democracy for all.[38]

The way we do our work matters, and we must be intentional and critical as we undertake it. Noting its over-twenty-year commitment to transforming scholarly communication, in 2019, ACRL released *Open and Equitable Scholarly Communications: Creating a More Inclusive Future*, a research agenda

> designed to provide practical, actionable information for academic librarians; include the perspectives of historically underrepresented communities in order to expand the profession's understanding of research environments and scholarly communication systems; and point librarians and other scholars toward important research questions to investigate.[39]

SPARC has consistently centered equity in recent Open Access Week themes and webinars, such as the 2022 Knowledge Equity Discussion Series.[40]

SCHOLARLY COMMUNICATION AND SOCIAL MEDIA

A couple of decades into the twenty-first century, networked technology is deeply and irrevocably integrated into scholarly communication. Earlier iterations of the World Wide Web were far less interactive than the internet we presently enjoy. So-called Web 1.0 was predominantly read-only except for those with the technical skill and capacity to create and host websites. As technology and platforms developed that enabled users to read and write to the web, more people were empowered to create content and share it with other users, to comment on content and engage in conversations about it. Social media plays a huge role in that landscape, and its impact, both good and bad, can't be overstated. Social media wields enormous influence in society, in our personal and professional lives, in our institutions, and in the ways that scholars collaborate, share their findings, and communicate with each other. The influence of technology on scholarly communication are more fully explored in chapter 1.2, "Technology and Scholarly Communication," but we felt it was important to address the social aspect of these developments within this chapter on social issues, again demonstrating the interwoven nature of these forces.

First, popular social media, those not initially designed for scholarly communication, such as blogging platforms, Facebook, YouTube, Twitter, and Instagram, as well as many others, are often used by researchers and other stakeholders as tools for promoting and discussing research outcomes. For example, publishers, funders, colleges and universities, and related organizations like scholarly societies almost universally maintain social media accounts as a way of sharing information and resources and for communicating with constituents. To take an example from the open education (more about this in part II of this book) advocacy community, the Open Education Network (OEN) maintains accounts on Facebook and Twitter and a YouTube channel, all in addition to a website. It also heavily utilizes Google Docs and related communication tools (Google Groups), plus has developed its own internal community platform, a data dashboard for members with extensive resources and documentation. Most of these tools and platforms are linked together to create a cohesive strategic means of connecting with and providing resources for the communities it supports. There's also Zoom or similar webinar/meeting platforms, e-mail, and the Open Textbook Library,[41] which hosts a growing volume of openly licensed textbooks *and* reviews of those books contributed by scholars. The OEN simply wouldn't be able to engage with and share content among its membership and a broader interested community without these tools, at least not with the degree of participation and engagement enabled by social media and adjacent tools.

Individual researchers, or small collectives of researchers such as a lab or research center, also use these tools for scholarly ends. The popular social media they use can vary by discipline, and uptake is uneven, but many scholars maintain blogs (some with comments enabled), Facebook or Twitter accounts that they use in professional ways or a mixture of personal and professional ways, according to their own preferences and goals as well as the norms of their disciplinary cultures. Research suggests that popular social media use to share publications may result in a citation boost.[42] There are fascinating examples of researchers using YouTube to share information and create engagement opportunities. This is just scratching the surface of how researchers use these tools. A researcher might learn of a conference in their discipline via social media and might network before the conference using hashtags to connect with other attendees and to promote a workshop or panel they're presenting. Video of the presentation may be streamed or recorded and posted for public viewing beyond in-person attendees. The researcher might share the recording on their personal social media accounts. They might link to a copy of the slides or text to share it, perhaps with commenting functions enabled. Perhaps they further develop the ideas presented in the conference presentation into an article. Once the article is accepted and published, they might share it on social media, perhaps using hashtags to help disciplinary colleagues notice it, and might engage in conversations or even debates about their methods and conclusions.

The traditional mode of scholarly communication underlies this—a conference presentation, an article—but social media creates layers of additional sharing and engagement opportunities directly with the authors as well as among a community of peers and folks beyond that peer network. And this is just what's driven by the researcher's savvy use of social media. In reality, there's an expansive network of other actors and organizations also engaged. Academic conferences use social media to promote their event and to discuss aspects of it. They might promote or stream sessions. Attendees use Twitter to create extensive back-channel dialogue, often so rich that nonattenders following the conference hashtag can monitor the conference fairly effectively. Dozens or hundreds or thousands of users might engage in these back-channel discussions. The first time we observed this, we were fascinated by it, unsure whether to pay more attention to the live presentation or the Twitter discussion of it or to try to split interest between the two. It felt like an additional mirror conference, like a second analogous event running in the background.

The discussion of social media above focuses on popular social media rather than academic social media: general platforms that are widely and commonly used by many stakeholders for a variety of purposes. There are also specialized social media platforms for particular activities or user groups. For example, runners and cyclists might use Strava to track, record, and analyze their runs and rides, compare themselves against other users, even compete for fastest times, and earn digital badges. Strava is a social media service for these athletic communities and activities. Similarly, there are social media for researchers and for research sharing and engagement, or academic social media. The two biggest platforms in this arena are Academia. edu and ResearchGate, but there are many others. There are differences between these two platforms, but generally they are what we'd call profile tools. Researchers use them to build and maintain a digital scholarly profile, providing basic information like title and institutional affiliation, as well as to outline research interests, projects, and outputs. In many cases, full text of journal articles or book chapters may be posted (sometimes in violation of publication agreements, as we'll discuss shortly). Broadly speaking, Academia.edu trends toward a humanist user base, and ResearchGate trends toward a scientist user base, with social scientists using either or both depending on their preference and scholarly identity and affinity (social science scholars can identify more as humanists or as scientists and everywhere in between depending on their training and methodology). That said, there are scientists on Academia. edu and humanists on ResearchGate, and many scholars maintain a presence on both. While many researchers globally make use of these platforms, there is a critical discussion of them that is worth considering. As Fitzpatrick observes,

Academia.edu is not an educationally-affiliated organization, but a dot-com, which has raised millions in multiple rounds of venture capital funding. This does not imply anything necessarily negative about the network's model or intent, but it does make clear that there are a limited number of options for the network's future: at some point, it will be required to turn a profit, or it will be sold for parts, or it will shut down.[43]

Echoing and extending Fitzpatrick's critique, Bond adds, "Moving our papers away from Academia.edu is then about taking possession of our work and deciding what we do with it, rather than allowing a private company to use our scholarship for profit."[44] Both of these scholars (notably, humanists) advocate for nonprofit and academy-owned infrastructure, such as MLA Commons/Humanities Commons, to support scholarly sharing.

This use of social web technology for sharing research outputs and enabling collaboration among researchers and others is natural when we consider that the earliest internets were research tools supported by government and universities. As the web became more accessible to more users in the 1990s, more researchers realized its potential in allowing them to share scholarly work and to connect with other researchers. Now we have more tools and applications than those early users might have imagined possible, and they are impacting the research landscape and researchers in myriad ways, including how researchers communicate. Social media isn't the whole of scholarly communication, but a lot of scholarly communication occurs in and flows through social media. Even as there are strong and warranted critiques about our ever-increasingly networked lives, social media is here to stay. Researchers, institutions, and organizations engaged in scholarly communication will use these tools where they see them as aligned with their goals.

CONCLUSION

In this chapter, we've examined some of the broad ways that social factors inform, complicate, and shape scholarly communication and scholarly communication work. We see that scholarly communication is done by many people globally and impacts people everywhere but that access is not equally distributed. Research takes place in a social context and reflects institutionalized and systemic hegemonic culture and biases, often with problematic results. Finally, we examined how social media are changing scholarly communication and researchers' practices. At multiple points, we've seen how social issues intersect and combine with economic issues, technology, and legal and policy dynamics, all of which contribute to scholarly communication work as we experience it. As you read further, here and elsewhere, consider how social factors shape your perceptions and the issues you encounter and how you can contribute to improving the experience of the people you serve and with whom you collaborate.

DISCUSSION QUESTIONS

1. Find a scholarly article that examines bias or social injustice in higher education, libraries, or publishing. What is the issue examined? Are corrective actions suggested? What are they, and who is in a position to implement them? What are the implications for your own work and learning?
2. How can scholarly communication or information professionals advance diversity, equity, and inclusion within our own work?
3. Is access to research a social justice issue? Why or why not?

ACTIVITIES

1. Pick an organization, such as a scholarly publisher, society, journal, or advocacy group, and look into its social media presence. What platforms does fit use? What sort of

content does it post to each? Does it appear to use different platforms for different purposes, or is the same content replicated across them all? Who is its audience? How much engagement does it appear to have (likes, retweets, views, etc.)? How does its social media presence and use advance its purpose or cause? How might it use these tools more effectively?

2. Identify a recent conference related to scholarly communication. What social media did it use? What was the conference hashtag? What can you glean from reviewing tweets using the hashtag? What sort of posts do you observe? How might you engage, or not, in these discussions in the future at a conference you may attend or one you might observe virtually?

NOTES

1. John P. Holdren, "Increasing Access to the Results of Federally Funded Scientific Research," memorandum for the heads of executive departments and agencies, February 22, 2013, Executive Office of the President, Office of Science and Technology Policy, https://obamawhitehouse.archives.gov/sites/default/files/micro-sites/ostp/ostp_public_access_memo_2013.pdf.
2. Michael Stebbins, "Expanding Public Access to the Results of Federally Funded Research," *White House* (blog), February 22, 2013, https://obamawhitehouse.archives.gov/blog/2013/02/22/expanding-public-access-results-federally-funded-research.
3. Association of College and Research Libraries, *Framework for Information Literacy for Higher Education* (Chicago: Association of College and Research Libraries, 2016), https://www.ala.org/acrl/standards/ilframework.
4. Peter Suber, *Open Access* (Cambridge, MA: MIT Press, 2012), 116, https://doi.org/10.7551/mitpress/9286.001.0001.
5. Leslie Chan et al., "Read the Declaration," Budapest Open Access Initiative, February 14, 2002, https://www.budapestopenaccessinitiative.org/read/.
6. Suber, *Open Access*, 4.
7. SPARC, "Big Deal Cancellation Tracking," accessed August 15, 2022, https://sparcopen.org/our-work/big-deal-cancellation-tracking/.
8. Research4Life, home page, https://www.research4life.org/.
9. Quirin Schiermeier, "US Court Grants Elsevier Millions in Damages from Sci-Hub," news release, *Nature*, June 22, 2017, https://doi.org/https://doi.org/10.1038/nature.2017.22196.
10. John Bohannon, "Who's Downloading Pirated Papers? Everyone," *Science* 352, no. 6285 (April 29, 2016): 508–12, https://doi.org/10.1126/science.352.6285.508.
11. National Library of Medicine, "Research Lifecycle," accessed July 24, 2022, https://nnlm.gov/guides/data-glossary/research-lifecycle.
12. Wikipedia, s.v. "List of sovereign states by sex ratio," last updated January 31, 2023, https://en.wikipedia.org/wiki/List_of_countries_by_sex_ratio; Wikimedia, "Community Insights/2018 Report/Contributors," last updated December 9, 2019, https://meta.wikimedia.org/wiki/Community_Insights/2018_Report/Contributors.
13. Wikipedia, s.v. "Wikipedia:WikiProject Women in Red," last updated March 16, 2023, https://en.wikipedia.org/wiki/Wikipedia:WikiProject_Women_in_Red.
14. Wikipedia, s.v. "Women in Red," last updated March 16, 2023, https://en.wikipedia.org/wiki/Women_in_Red.
15. Wikipedia, s.v. "Wikipedia:WikiProject Women in Red."
16. Wikipedia, s.v. "AfroCrowd," last updated March 4, 2023, https://en.wikipedia.org/wiki/AfroCrowd.
17. Wiki Education, "AfroCROWD 2017 Overview," Program and Events Dashboard, https://outreachdashboard.wmflabs.org/campaigns/afrocrowd_2017/overview.
18. Wikipedia, s.v. "Women in Red."
19. Safiya Umoja Noble, *Algorithms of Oppression* (New York: NYU Press, 2018).
20. Noble, *Algorithms of Oppression*, 2.
21. Noble, *Algorithms of Oppression*, 171.
22. Noble, *Algorithms of Oppression*, 143–44.
23. Noble, *Algorithms of Oppression*, 148.

24. Faiz Siddiqui, "The First Black Students Admitted to 15 Prestigious U.S. Universities, and Their Stories," *Complex*, February 16, 2013, https://www.complex.com/pop-culture/2013/02/the-first-black-students-admitted-to-15-prestigious-us-universities-and-their-stories/james-pennington.

25. *Harvard Gazette*, "Martin Kilson, Harvard College's First African American to Be Named Full Professor, Dies at 88," May 1, 2019, https://news.harvard.edu/gazette/story/2019/05/martin-kilson-harvard-colleges-first-african-american-to-be-named-full-professor-dies-at-88/.

26. Colleen Walsh, "Hard-Earned Gains for Women at Harvard," *Harvard Gazette*, April 26, 2012, https://news.harvard.edu/gazette/story/2012/04/hard-earned-gains-for-women-at-harvard/.

27. Harvard University, "The First Tenured Women Professors at Harvard University," Office of the Senior Vice Provost for Faculty Development and Diversity, accessed August 15, 2022, https://faculty.harvard.edu/files/fdd/files/timeline-final_32.pdf.

28. Audrey Williams June and Brian O'Leary, "How Many Black Women Have Tenure on Your Campus? Search Here," *Chronicle of Higher Education*, May 27, 2021, https://www.chronicle.com/article/how-many-black-women-have-tenure-on-your-campus-search-here.

29. National Center for Education Statistics, "Fast Facts: Race/Ethnicity of College Faculty," accessed August 15, 2022, https://nces.ed.gov/fastfacts/display.asp?id=61.

30. See #WomenInSTEM, Twitter, https://twitter.com/hashtag/womeninstem.

31. Kathleen DeLong, "Career Advancement and Writing about Women Librarians: A Literature Review," *Evidence Based Library and Information Practice* 8, no. 1 (2013): 59–75, https://doi.org/10.18438/B8CS4M.

32. A. E. Day, P. Corbett, and J. Boyle. "Is There a Gender Gap in Chemical Sciences Scholarly Communication?" *Chemical Science* 11, no. 8 (January 2020): 2277–2301, https://doi.org/10.1039/c9sc04090k.

33. Elsevier, "Gender in the Global Research Landscape," 2017, https://www.elsevier.com/__data/assets/pdf_file/0008/265661/ElsevierGenderReport_final_for-web.pdf.

34. Harrison W. Inefuku, "Relegated to the Margins: Faculty of Color, the Scholarly Record, and the Necessity of Antiracist Library Disruptions," in *Knowledge Justice: Disrupting Library and Information Studies through Critical Race Theory*, ed. Sofia Y. Leung and Jorge R. López-McKnight (Cambridge, MA: MIT Press, 2021), 197. The book in which this chapter appears is an essential text and highly recommended.

35. Steven O. Roberts et al., "Racial Inequality in Psychological Research: Trends of the Past and Recommendations for the Future," *Perspectives on Psychological Science* 15, no. 6 (2020): 1304, https://doi.org/10.1177/1745691620927709.

36. Donna K. Ginther et al., "Publications as Predictors of Racial and Ethnic Differences in NIH Research Awards," *PLOS ONE* 13, no. 11 (2018): e0205929, https://doi.org/10.1371/journal.pone.0205929.

37. Charlotte Roh, "Library Publishing and Diversity Values: Changing Scholarly Publishing through Policy and Scholarly Communication Education," *College and Research Libraries News* 77, no. 2 (February 2016): 85, https://crln.acrl.org/index.php/crlnews/article/view/9446/10679.

38. April Hathcock, "Racing to the Crossroads of Scholarly Communication and Democracy: But Who Are We Leaving Behind?" *In the Library with the Lead Pipe*, August 22, 2018, http://www.inthelibrarywiththeleadpipe.org/2018/racing-to-the-crossroads-of-scholarly-communication-and-democracy-but-who-are-we-leaving-behind/.

39. Association of College and Research Libraries, *Open and Equitable Scholarly Communications*, prepared by Nancy Maron and Rebecca Kennison with Paul Bracke, Nathan Hall, Isaac Gilman, Kara Malenfant, Charlotte Roh, and Yasmeen Shorish (Chicago: Association of College and Research Libraries, 2019), vii, https://doi.org/10.5860/acrl.1.

40. SPARC, "Announcing SPARC's Knowledge Equity Discussion Series," news release, July 11, 2022, https://sparcopen.org/news/2022/announcing-sparcs-knowledge-equity-discussion-series/.

41. Open Textbook Library, home page, Center for Open Education, University of Minnesota, https://open.umn.edu/opentextbooks.

42. Brandon K. Peoples et al., "Twitter Predicts Citation Rates of Ecological Research," *PLOS ONE* 11, no. 11 (2016): e0166570, https://doi.org/https://doi.org/10.1371/journal.pone.0166570.

43. Kathleen Fitzpatrick, "Academia, Not Edu," *Kathleen Fitzpatrick* (blog). October 26, 2015, https://kfitz.info/academia-not-edu/.

44. Sarah Bond, "Dear Scholars, Delete Your Account at Academia.Edu," Forbes, January 23, 2017, https://www.forbes.com/sites/drsarahbond/2017/01/23/dear-scholars-delete-your-account-at-academia-edu/.

BIBLIOGRAPHY

Association of College and Research Libraries. *Framework for Information Literacy for Higher Education*. Chicago: Association of College and Research Libraries, 2016. https://www.ala.org/acrl/standards/ilframework.

———. *Open and Equitable Scholarly Communications: Creating a More Inclusive Future*. Prepared by Nancy Maron and Rebecca Kennison with Paul Bracke, Nathan Hall, Isaac Gilman, Kara Malenfant, Charlotte Roh, and Yasmeen Shorish. Chicago: Association of College and Research Libraries, 2019. https://doi.org/10.5860/acrl.1.

Bohannon, John. "Who's Downloading Pirated Papers? Everyone." *Science* 352, no. 6285 (April 29, 2016): 508–12. https://www.science.org/doi/10.1126/science.352.6285.508.

Bond, Sarah. "Dear Scholars, Delete Your Account at Academia.Edu." *Forbes*, January 23, 2017. https://www.forbes.com/sites/drsarahbond/2017/01/23/dear-scholars-delete-your-account-at-academia-edu/.

Chan, Leslie, Darius Cuplinskas, Michael Eisen, Fred Friend, Yana Genova, Jean-Claude Guédon, Melissa Hagemann, et al. "Read the Declaration." Budapest Open Access Initiative, February 14, 2002. https://www.budapestopenaccessinitiative.org/read/.

Day, A. E., P. Corbett, and J. Boyle. "Is There a Gender Gap in Chemical Sciences Scholarly Communication?" *Chemical Science* 11, no. 8 (January 2020): 2277–2301. https://doi.org/10.1039/c9sc04090k.

DeLong, Kathleen. "Career Advancement and Writing about Women Librarians: A Literature Review." *Evidence Based Library and Information Practice* 8, no. 1 (2013): 59–75. https://doi.org/10.18438/B8CS4M.

Elsevier. "Gender in the Global Research Landscape." 2017. https://www.elsevier.com/__data/assets/pdf_file/0008/265661/ElsevierGenderReport_final_for-web.pdf.

Fitzpatrick, Kathleen. "Academia, Not Edu." *Kathleen Fitzpatrick* (blog), October 26, 2015. https://kfitz.info/academia-not-edu/.

Ginther, Donna K., Jodi Basner, Unni Jensen, Joshua Schnell, Raynard Kington, and Walter T. Schaffer. "Publications as Predictors of Racial and Ethnic Differences in NIH Research Awards." *PLOS ONE* 13, no. 11 (2018): e0205929. https://doi.org/10.1371/journal.pone.0205929.

Harvard Gazette. "Martin Kilson, Harvard College's First African American to Be Named Full Professor, Dies at 88." May 1, 2019. https://news.harvard.edu/gazette/story/2019/05/martin-kilson-harvard-colleges-first-african-american-to-be-named-full-professor-dies-at-88/.

Harvard University. "The First Tenured Women Professors at Harvard University." Office of the Senior Vice Provost for Faculty Development and Diversity. Accessed August 15, 2022. https://faculty.harvard.edu/files/fdd/files/timeline-final_32.pdf.

Hathcock, April. "Racing to the Crossroads of Scholarly Communication and Democracy: But Who Are We Leaving Behind?" *In the Library with the Lead Pipe*, August 22, 2018. http://www.inthelibrarywiththeleadpipe.org/2018/racing-to-the-crossroads-of-scholarly-communication-and-democracy-but-who-are-we-leaving-behind/.

Holdren, John P. "Increasing Access to the Results of Federally Funded Scientific Research." Memorandum for the heads of executive departments and agencies, February 22, 2013. Executive Office of the President, Office of Science and Technology Policy. https://obamawhitehouse.archives.gov/sites/default/files/microsites/ostp/ostp_public_access_memo_2013.pdf.

Inefuku, Harrison W. "Relegated to the Margins: Faculty of Color, the Scholarly Record, and the Necessity of Antiracist Library Disruptions." In *Knowledge Justice: Disrupting Library and Information Studies through Critical Race Theory*, edited by Sofia Y. Leung and Jorge R. López-McKnight, 197–216. Cambridge, MA: MIT Press, 2021. https://direct.mit.edu/books/oa-edited-volume/5114/chapter/3075324/Relegated-to-the-Margins-Faculty-of-Color-the.

June, Audrey Williams, and Brian O'Leary. "How Many Black Women Have Tenure on Your Campus? Search Here." *Chronicle of Higher Education*, May 27, 2021. https://www.chronicle.com/article/how-many-black-women-have-tenure-on-your-campus-search-here.

National Center for Education Statistics. "Fast Facts: Race/Ethnicity of College Faculty." Accessed August 15, 2022. https://nces.ed.gov/fastfacts/display.asp?id=61.

National Library of Medicine. "Research Lifecycle." Accessed July 24, 2022. https://nnlm.gov/guides/data-glossary/research-lifecycle.

Noble, Safiya Umoja. *Algorithms of Oppression: How Search Engines Reinforce Racism*. New York: NYU Press, 2018.

Open Textbook Library. Home page, Center for Open Education, University of Minnesota, https://open.umn.edu/opentextbooks.

Peoples, Brandon K., Stephen R. Midway, Dana Sackett, Abigail Lynch, and Patrick B. Cooney. "Twitter Predicts Citation Rates of Ecological Research." *PLOS ONE* 11, no. 11 (2016): e0166570. https://doi.org/https://doi.org/10.1371/journal.pone.0166570.

Research4Life. Home page. https://www.research4life.org/.

Roberts, Steven O., Carmelle Bareket-Shavit, Forrest A. Dollins, Peter D. Goldie, and Elizabeth Mortenson. "Racial Inequality in Psychological Research: Trends of the Past and Recommendations for the Future." *Perspectives on Psychological Science* 15, no. 6 (2020): 1295–1309. https://doi.org/10.1177/1745691620927709.

Roh, Charlotte. "Library Publishing and Diversity Values: Changing Scholarly Publishing through Policy and Scholarly Communication Education." *College and Research Libraries News* 77, no. 2 (February 2016): 82–85. https://crln.acrl.org/index.php/crlnews/article/view/9446/10679.

Schiermeier, Quirin. "US Court Grants Elsevier Millions in Damages from Sci-Hub." News release, *Nature*, June 22, 2017. https://doi.org/https://doi.org/10.1038/nature.2017.22196.

Siddiqui, Faiz. "The First Black Students Admitted to 15 Prestigious U.S. Universities, and Their Stories." *Complex*, February 16, 2013. https://www.complex.com/pop-culture/2013/02/the-first-black-students-admitted-to-15-prestigious-us-universities-and-their-stories/james-pennington.

SPARC. "Announcing SPARC's Knowledge Equity Discussion Series." News release, July 11, 2022. https://sparcopen.org/news/2022/announcing-sparcs-knowledge-equity-discussion-series/.

———. "Big Deal Cancellation Tracking." Accessed August 15, 2022. https://sparcopen.org/our-work/big-deal-cancellation-tracking/.

Stebbins, Michael. "Expanding Public Access to the Results of Federally Funded Research." *White House* (blog), February 22, 2013. https://obamawhitehouse.archives.gov/blog/2013/02/22/expanding-public-access-results-federally-funded-research.

Suber, Peter. *Open Access*. Cambridge, MA: MIT Press, 2012. https://doi.org/10.7551/mitpress/9286.001.0001

Walsh, Colleen. "Hard-Earned Gains for Women at Harvard." *Harvard Gazette*, April 26, 2012. https://news.harvard.edu/gazette/story/2012/04/hard-earned-gains-for-women-at-harvard/.

Wiki Education. "AfroCROWD 2017 Overview." Program and Events Dashboard. https://outreachdashboard.wmflabs.org/campaigns/afrocrowd_2017/overview.

Wikimedia. "Community Insights/2018 Report/Contributors." Last updated December 9, 2019. https://meta.wikimedia.org/wiki/Community_Insights/2018_Report/Contributors.

Wikipedia. S.v. "AfroCrowd." Last updated March 4, 2023. https://en.wikipedia.org/wiki/AfroCrowd.

———. S.v. "List of sovereign states by sex ratio." Last updated January 31, 2023. https://en.wikipedia.org/wiki/List_of_countries_by_sex_ratio.

———. S.v. "Wikipedia:WikiProject Women in Red." Last updated March 16, 2023. https://en.wikipedia.org/wiki/Wikipedia:WikiProject_Women_in_Red.

———. S.v. "Women in Red." Last updated March 16, 2023. https://en.wikipedia.org/wiki/Women_in_Red.

THE LEGAL AND POLICY CONTEXT

SCHOLCOMM IS SHARING

Will Cross with Josh Bolick and Maria Bonn

Keywords: copyright, fair use, authors' rights, contracts, licensing

---

INTRODUCTION: COPYRIGHT AND SCHOLARLY COMMUNICATION

This chapter introduces the core legal issues in scholarly communication, including copyright and licensing. It situates those issues in the practice of scholarly sharing and asserting the rights of academic authors.

Scholarly communication is a huge area of practice, but at its heart are a set of fundamental questions about how the law regulates and incentivizes the ways that scholars do their work. The field is animated by questions of authors' rights and sustainable sharing, initially understood primarily in terms of copyright transfer and library licensing. Under the law of most nations, including the US, copyright ownership vests with scholars who create works, but, as discussed in chapter 1.2, "The Economic Context," academic publishing was historically built on transferring those rights to a publisher, who then sold published versions of scholarly works back to the institution's library. This disconnect between the scholars who do the work and the growing number of for-profit corporations that own that work has been one of the earliest and most powerful driving forces for the body of practice that has become known as scholarly communication. While this fundamental tension has been recognized since the beginning of modern practice, it has proved to be a persistent and stubborn problem that remains unresolved after several decades of sustained work.

As the field has developed, however, it has become clear that the legal tensions in scholarly communication actually reflect a series of intellectual and policy knots tangled together. Both copyright law and the traditional approach to publishing where authors surrender their rights reflect a set of assumptions bound to the physical act of copying and printing. As a result, a set of traditional practices emerged in the twentieth century grounded in a mid-century copyright framework and a set of "standard" copyright transfer and licensing practices that more or less aligned with the economic, technical, and social expectations of the academy.

This mid-century compromise could be exclusionary and often exploitative, but it reflected a somewhat sustainable equilibrium between scholars, publishers, funders, and the public that remained relatively stable until a series of changes in the law and policy in the late twentieth century. In many ways, early discussions about scholarly communication reflected an attempt to return to or reset that equilibrium. In recent years, scholarly communication has expanded its view of legal issues, exploring new approaches to ownership, use, and credit. As our conception of what activities constitute scholarly communication and the ways we understand and value the people who are doing scholarly work have evolved, new questions about who should control that work, how it can be used, and how the law can support those practices have taken center stage.

In this chapter we introduce and complicate the traditional approach to copyright and licensing and explore the ways that scholars, activists, and funders have worked to develop new tools and approaches to sustain and transform this approach. We begin with a brief overview of copyright as an evolving system and a set of rules designed to achieve constitutionally mandated outcomes. Much of the day-to-day work of scholarly communication librarianship involves guiding practice in this area, and anyone working in the field, whether or not they have formal legal training, needs to understand the fundamentals for their own work and to guide individual and institutional practices.

Next, we explore the way that this system has been undermined by changes in the law and how other factors have come together to make this system unsustainable by empowering a new set of for-profit actors. In response to this crisis, scholars and political actors have worked to rebalance the legal rules. The most relevant response is the incorporation of scholarly communication work in the libraries armed with expertise in the legal issues introduced in this chapter. These new roles—still rare in 2023 but growing quickly—have opened the door for a host of new practices around rights retention and negotiation. By bringing both formally credentialled legal experts and those who have learned legal issues on the job into the library as a resource for all scholars, the academy has broadened and nuanced the conversation that began with authors' rights. Today, this conversation about law and policy in scholarly communication has expanded to include broad questions about the law of higher education, from recognizing traditional knowledge and honoring student privacy to field-level questions about antitrust and collective action.

BACKGROUND AND HISTORY
COPYRIGHT AND TRADITIONAL PUBLISHING

Copyright law has often been described as a creature of the age of printing. Legal scholars generally date copyright law's origins to the British Statute of Anne in 1710, which transformed what had been the publishers' private law copyright into a public law grant. Early developments in copyright law were also closely linked with debates over publishers' monopoly and what the Statute of Anne called the "encouragement of learning." In the United States, this balance was reflected in the text of the US Constitution, which empowers Congress to "promote the progress of science and the useful arts" by granting authors a limited monopoly on their works. For much of the early history of the United States the law covered only books, maps, and charts, and copyright was only lightly enforced. Indeed, European authors such as Charles Dickens joined local authors such as Mark Twain in criticizing the US as a "pirate nation" that did not sufficiently respect or enforce the copyright of authors. In part, this neglect resulted from a sense that copyright was an obscure issue at the periphery of public life—what Supreme Court Justice Joseph Story called the "metaphysics of the law."[1]

Beginning in the mid-twentieth century, as the US publishing and entertainment industries rose to prominence, copyright law became more central to the lived experiences of average people, including researchers and scholars. Most people in 1950 might be familiar with copyright only in the context of the fine print at the front of a book or in the credits of a television show. Likewise, outside of aggrieved authors like Dickens and Twain, most industries that relied on copyright were primarily concerned with infringement by industrial competitors or large-scale pirates rather than the day-to-day behavior of their customers, even when those customers engaged in unauthorized small-scale duplication and sharing.

This changed with the passage of the 1976 Copyright Act, which removed many of the required steps that must be taken to acquire copyright, sometimes called *formalities*, and codified a set of limitations and exceptions including fair use that made users' rights more explicit. With a single stroke of President Carter's pen, millions of Americans were simultaneously given automatic ownership in every work they wrote, snapped, or recorded and provided them with a new set of guidelines for using materials created by everyone else.

At the same moment that the rise of digital technology in the 1980s and 1990s made creation and copying easy and ubiquitous, every mundane business e-mail, casual instant message, and pithy tweet was endowed with the full suite of copyright protections originally designed for bestselling novels and major Hollywood blockbusters. Copyright policy was also increasingly driven neither by the needs of individual creators nor by the public good that the law was originally designed to serve. Instead the law followed a semantic sleight of hand that focused on "rights holders," the wealthy and powerful administrators and intermediaries such as publishers, record labels, and movie studios that control so many of the most lucrative works under copyright. As discussed in chapter 1.2, "The Economic Context," scholarly publishing mirrored these broad trends toward control by for-profit intermediaries rather than creators or the public, compounded by fundamental changes in the formal workings of the law itself.

COPYRIGHT FUNDAMENTALS

Despite this trend toward corporate control, the fundamental rules under the current Copyright Act are fairly intuitive and align relatively well with much of scholarly activity today. Copyright is automatic, meaning it exists from the moment of creation as long as a work is original to the author, reflects some modicum of the author's creativity, and is fixed in a tangible medium of expression that others can perceive. Lawyers often say that copyright "follows the pen," flowing like ink as an author writes. But we might just as well say that copyright follows the fingers typing on a keyboard or directing the camera for a TikTok video or while broadcasting on a live-streaming platform like Twitch. A published research article or textbook that can be read is "fixed in a tangible medium of expression" and thus potentially eligible for copyright protection. Extemporaneous classroom lectures or sage guidance from an advisor over coffee about selecting a topic for your dissertation are not "fixed" and thus probably not eligible for copyright protection, no matter how inspiring or invaluable they may be.

Copyright also remains nominally an author's right, meaning that the person (or people, when two or more creators work together with an intention to be joint authors and each contributes separately copyrightable content) who creates a work is the presumptive rights holder. As the rights holder, they have the exclusive right to control certain uses of that work as described in Section 106 of the Copyright Act (which is found in Title 17 of the United

States Code, generally abbreviated as 17 U.S.C. §106), including reproduction, creation of derivative works, distribution to the public, public performance, and public display.

This presumption of ownership can be modified in situations where works are created within the scope of the creator's employment responsibilities, either as part of ongoing work or for a specific commissioned project. In these cases, what the law calls "works made for hire" belong to the employer rather than the individual creator. A university website designed by a full-time employee is likely to be work made for hire. A book chapter commissioned by the university for a collective work on the history of the university might be as well, but there must be a written agreement that specifies ownership and meets a set of requirements for commissioned works.

The rules for work made for hire illustrate one tension in copyright as applied to scholarly communication. Under the statute, works "prepared by an employee within the scope of [their] employment" (17 U.S.C. §101) are generally considered to have been made for hire. But that language would seem to describe the way that most academic works are created. After all, most faculty authors (or at least those on the tenure track) research and write journal articles and monographs and prepare their course lectures "within the scope of their employment." They are hired and paid by their institutions to do exactly that.

Historically, the academy exempted many of these works based on a so-called teachers or educators exception. This exception has been recognized in a few early cases such as Sherrill v. Grieves, 57 Wash. L. Rep. 286 (Dist. of Columbia Supreme Court 1929, relying on the notion that faculty works belong to their universities), and Williams v. Weisser, 78 Cal. Rptr. 542 (Ct. App. 1969 considering a copyright claim against a business that published and sold the lecture notes of a professor of anthropology at UCLA). The 1976 Copyright Act, however, did not mention any exception of this kind, and there is significant doubt that whatever exception may have existed prior is still in effect.

Instead, ownership of scholarly works today is generally governed by institutional policies—often called copyright or intellectual property policies—that specify baseline ownership as well as factors, such as unusual institutional support or specifically directed work, that change that baseline. The specifics of these policies can vary widely, and scholars have argued that many of these policies are confusing, poorly drafted, and may even be ineffective in transferring copyright. Nevertheless, they are the defining documents for ownership on campus, and when joining a new institution you would be wise to review your own policy.

A QUICK NOTE ABOUT PLAGIARISM

One area of common confusion is the relationship between copyright—the legal monopoly on certain uses of a work—and ethical issues of attribution and credit. While a good scholar should understand both issues, the law has a lot to say about when permission is needed to make a copy but comparatively little to say about core academic questions such as "Do I need to cite this, and if so, how should I do so?" or "Who should be listed as first author on this work?"

Copyright is a legal issue with a clear set of rules shared across national (and in some cases international) legal systems. Citation practices are primarily ethical and governed by professional norms that can vary significantly across different disciplines. For example, new lawyers are often told "if you weren't born knowing it, you need to cite it." In contrast, scholars in many other fields often follow equally valid but much lighter citation practices, with foot- or endnotes appearing relatively infrequently, if at all. Similarly, questions about how to recognize contributions and authorship can vary substantially across fields. Compare Tanya

Aplin and Lionel Bently's recent coauthored (and highly recommended) monograph *Global Mandatory Fair Use*[2] with a famous 2015 physics article describing a collaborative effort to more precisely describe the mass of the Higgs boson particle, which lists 5,154 coauthors.[3] Both works make significant contributions to their respective fields. Both also acknowledge the many contributors that they built upon in ways that are appropriate in their respective contexts. But each takes a different approach to recognizing those contributions. Neither approach—naming two coauthors or listing more than five thousand—reflects the "right" legal approach because the law simply does not have much of anything to say about citation or credit. In short: copyright violations are a civil or (rarely) criminal breach that can get you sued. Plagiarism is bad manners that can get you fired or drummed out of your professional community. Both must be addressed, but a lawyer (or copyright librarian) can help address only one of them.

LIMITATIONS: DURATION AND THE PUBLIC DOMAIN

Regardless of who owns a particular work, that ownership will last for a very long time. Under the original US Copyright Act of 1790, copyright lasted for a fifteen-year term and authors had the option to renew for a second fifteen-year term if they felt it was worth the time and trouble to do so. Otherwise, the work passed quickly and quietly into the public domain so that other creators could build on the works and society as a whole could benefit.

As time has passed, however, that term has expanded significantly, first with the passage of the Copyright Act of 1831 and then much more regularly and rapidly in the twentieth century. This trend toward expanding the length of copyright protection culminated with the passage of the Copyright Term Extension Act of 1998 (CTEA). Named after former entertainer and congressman Sonny Bono, the CTEA is sometimes sardonically called the Mickey Mouse Protection Act since it was passed after strong lobbying by the Disney Corporation shortly before copyright on Disney's Mickey Mouse character was set to expire.

The Copyright Clause of the US Constitution explicitly requires that copyright last for "limited times," but the courts have been hesitant to second-guess Congressional decisions about what constitutes an appropriate limitation. Many scholars have argued for terms that are aligned with copyright's constitutional purpose of incentivizing the creation of new works. But the Supreme Court declined to overturn the CTEA on those grounds in 2003 as well as in a 2012 companion case, and seems to have no desire to return to the issue, leaving the door open for further extensions, potentially up to and including a proposal from Mary Bono for a "limited" term of "forever less one day."

Today in the US, copyright generally lasts for the life of the author plus 70 years, or for a corporate author 120 years after creation or 95 years after publication, whichever is earlier. This textbook, published in 2023, will be protected for the life of the longest-lived author and then an additional 70 years. Assuming an average lifespan, that means that this text is likely to be in copyright until 2128 or later! Whether or not any information here will still be relevant or useful—or indeed whether human civilization will exist in its current form by the mid-2100s—is a separate question.

Once copyright in a work expires, that work enters the public domain, meaning there are no longer any exclusive copyright limitations on use so the work belongs to everyone (or to no one depending on your point of view). As of this writing in 2023, most works first published in the United States before 1928 are in the public domain. Because each year a new set of works enter the public domain (works from before 1929 will enter the public domain in 2024, works from 1930 in 2025, and so forth), geeky copyright professionals have been known to host New Year's celebrations welcoming the next class of works into the public domain and making new short films, music samples, and memes with the works that are newly freed for anyone to use. For example, in 2022 the Library of Congress hosted the Citizen DJ Project (https://citizen-dj.labs.loc.gov/), supporting remix and use of the more than 10,000 songs that entered the public domain hosted in the library's National Jukebox collection.

As a result of changes to duration and the removal of formalities discussed above, evaluating the copyright status of a particular work can be challenging. As discussed above, works first published in the US before 1928 are generally in the public domain, but there are earlier works—such as those published and registered under the pre-1976 system—that may still be protected, as well as later works that passed into the public domain under a different regime of formalities and remain there today.

As an extreme example, due to some unusual circumstances related to unpublished materials discovered much after the original writing, the diary of John Adams is still under copyright despite the fact that it was written in 1753! Determining the duration of copyright on a specific work can require some detective skills, and large sets of works today have been orphaned, meaning that they are likely in copyright but without a clear rights holder to claim them.

This process of limited protection followed by passage into the public domain is, in many ways, a core value of the copyright system that offers a limited monopoly on expression in order to incentivize more creation with the ultimate aim of stocking a robust public domain for all to use and enjoy. As Justice Breyer wrote for the Supreme Court in a case dealing with resale and lending of imported textbooks,

> copyright law ultimately serves the purpose of enriching the general public through access to creative works.... The statute achieves that end by striking a balance between two subsidiary aims: encouraging and rewarding authors' creations while also enabling others to build on that work.[4]

This societal value built into the public domain can be seen clearly in categories of works that are born directly into the public domain. The public domain automatically includes creations that fall outside of the scope of copyright, like facts and ideas. It also includes materials that are explicitly excluded from copyright, such as works of the federal government, works that have been intentionally dedicated to the public domain by the author or rights holder, and works created by nonhuman robots and animals. The last category received some lighthearted attention in the mid 2010s, when a Celebes crested macaque used equipment left unattended in the jungle by British nature photographer David Slater to take a series of selfies. When the story of the snap-happy macaque went viral, Slater sued several online sites, including Wikimedia Commons, for using the photographs without his permission. A series of countersuits followed, including one from the People for the Ethical Treatment of Animals (PETA) arguing that copyright should belong to the macaque. In the end, the Court of Appeals for the Ninth Circuit rejected all claims, and the so-called "monkey selfies" now reside comfortably in the public domain.[5]

The public domain also includes works that predate copyright, such as the plays of William Shakespeare, which remain an evergreen source for new creations. As of this writing, the Internet Movie Database lists more than 1,632 screenwriting credits for Shakespeare, including recent performances of *King Lear* and *Much Ado about Nothing*, but also remakes and reimaginings such as children's film *Gnomio and Juliet*, teen comedy *Ten Things I Hate about You*, and Gary Busey's *One-Man Hamlet*, a performance by a Busey lookalike presenting "an out-of-control performance, relating the action of Hamlet with the aid of paper dolls and video projections."[6] Entering the public domain is often the real beginning, rather than the end, of the creative life of a book, song, or film.

LIMITATIONS: SCOPE

While copyright today protects much more than the books, maps, and charts named in the original US Act, some materials are so fundamental that they are not eligible for copyright protection at all. Ideas, facts, individual words, and short phrases are the building blocks for all creativity. It is difficult to imagine a sustainable creative culture if a single person or corporation could own the G chord or the special theory of relativity. Similarly, while the color "John Deere green" on a lawn tractor or the phrase "Just Do It" on athletic apparel may qualify for trademark protection that prevents uses that might confuse or deceive a consumer, those things are not eligible for copyright protection.

Works that exist adjacent to these limitations are also unprotected when they can be expressed in only a limited set of ways. A system of bookkeeping or the rules of a contest may not be protected when the idea and expression are merged inseparably together under the "merger doctrine." Likewise, *scènes à faire* (literally "scenes that must be done") that are so common that they are obligatory or customary in a particular genre are not protectable. A fantasy hero's call to action, a spy decoding a secret message, and a charming couple having a meet-cute at a party are stock situations that must be available to all storytellers working in or building on a particular genre. Taken together, copyright offers a limited protection in ways that recognize both the social benefit of short-term monopoly on some expression and the necessity of immediate access to fundamental facts and ideas and eventual access to everything.

For scholars, these limitations on the scope of copyright provide a baseline for ownership and the opportunity to build on work that came before. No scholar can claim copyright in a clever title for an article, a new theory that transforms their field, or the written account of their research methods. This is good news for scholars who want to borrow and build on existing work, and especially critical for efforts to check the reproducibility of existing research by rerunning experiments to see if the same results are reached.

Because copyright does not protect factual information, even when gathering that information required a great deal of labor, much of the research data at the heart of scholarly communication is also not eligible for copyright protection in the United States. A media researcher who documents the number and type of violent images in a television show cannot claim copyright on that factual information. Further, scholars are free to use not only facts and ideas themselves, but also descriptive graphical representations of those facts and ideas. So every chemist is free to use the standard Lewis Structure diagrams that show the bonding between atoms of a molecule. Indeed, many of the charts and graphs included in research outlets are ineligible for copyright protection, although there is a robust business done in some disciplines charging fees for permission to them.

COPYRIGHT EXCEPTIONS

In addition to these limitations on the scope of copyright, copyright law also includes a set of exceptions that are designed to support copyright's public-serving purpose. In order to assure that copyright's limited monopoly does not impede the social values it is designed to support, Congress has carved out a set of systematic and specific exceptions as well as ratifying one significant judge-made exception that looms particularly large today.

Libraries and librarians rely on two major copyright exceptions for day-to-day operations. The first, often called the doctrine of exhaustion or first sale embodied in Section 109, limits the owner's exclusive right to control distribution of a particular copy of a work after its first sale. This means that once a library purchases a physical copy of a particular book, film, or album, the library is free to resell, lend, or weed that copy without permission from the rights holder. The doctrine applies to everyone, so it is also the reason that you are free to loan a PlayStation game to a friend (assuming you own the physical disk), sell vintage records from your parents' vinyl collection to a hipster music collector, or share a printed copy of this textbook with your classmates to save money and trade snarky annotations in the margins.

As anyone knows who has tried to resell a textbook at the end of the semester—especially one paired with a digital access code or online homework system—however, this doctrine has some significant limitations. In particular, it applies only to physical materials that are purchased, leaving digital materials that are acquired through a license under control of the rights holder. Despite a stated invitation to Buy It Now from online retailers like Amazon or iTunes, you do not generally own the digital music, films, or video games you acquire online and thus cannot rely on Section 109 to share or resell any of those materials.

This phenomenon, which legal scholars Aaron Perzanowski and Jason Schultz call "The Buy Now Lie,"[7] has resulted in significant issues for the public. Some cases have been mildly ominous, such as the sudden disappearance of all copies of George Orwell's *1984* purchased for Amazon's Kindle e-reader due to rights issues. Others have been more ridiculous, such as the ham-fisted replacement of all uses of the word *kindle* with *Nook* in versions of Tolstoy's *War and Peace* appearing on Barnes & Noble's Nook e-reader. In all cases, as one author observed, "it is not safe for democracy, or for our cultural posterity, to leave an 'on/off' switch for library books in the hands of corporate publishers."[8] As we will see, this move away from physical ownership to digital licensing has also led to an existential crisis for libraries acquiring and lending e-books and streaming media and for scholarly communication as a whole.

EXCEPTIONS: REPRODUCTION BY LIBRARIES AND ARCHIVES

Libraries also regularly rely on another copyright exception, described in Section 108. This exception reflects the unique role of libraries in the copyright system and provides special abilities and protections for libraries and librarians engaged in core services such as preservation, accessibility, and interlibrary loan. By permitting libraries to make copies for purposes of preservation and to share copies with other libraries, Section 108 provides core policy infrastructure for a distributed system of libraries charged with safeguarding and providing access to our shared cultural record. Section 108 also insulates libraries from liability when patrons make unsupervised use of reproducing equipment located in the library as long as the equipment displays a notice that the making of a copy may be subject to copyright law. If you have ever wondered why your library's photocopiers, scanners, and 3D printers are accompanied by a strange sign filled with legal verbiage, the answer can be found in Section 108(f)(1).

This provision also highlights an important balance struck by the statute as a whole: librarians are generally responsible for providing good information about copyright and responding when they know about potential issues but are not expected to actively monitor use of physical spaces or downstream use for potential violations. In addition to the myriad administrative and privacy issues raised, snooping over the shoulder of a patron using the scanner or doing deep investigation into the uses of materials shared through interlibrary loan would be more likely to create copyright liability for the institution. Librarians are expected to be sources of good copyright information when materials and tools are shared but are emphatically not intended to be the copyright monitors.

EXCEPTIONS: USE IN EDUCATION

Instructors, including faculty, students, and librarians, also rely on another set of copyright exceptions designed to support teaching and learning embodied in Section 110 of the Copyright Act. This exception permits the performance and display of works in educational spaces, both physical and digital.

In particular Section 110(1) permits the performance and display of lawfully acquired work in face-to-face instruction done in a classroom or similar space devoted to instruction. Faculty, librarians, students, and anyone else involved in this sort of education are permitted to screen the films *Black Panther* and *Booksmart* in a course focused on representation in cinema, play Bikini Kill's *Revolution Girl Style Now* and Kendrick Lamar's *To Pimp a Butterfly* in a course on popular protest, or stage an impromptu classroom performance of the Tony Award–winning musical *Hadestown* in a course on literature and mythology without seeking permission.

Section 110(2), also called the TEACH Act, is designed to permit similar use in online instruction, with a crucial difference that has made TEACH almost a dead letter today. While Section 110(1) is widely used by teachers and students at all grade levels (even if they have never read or even heard of the statute), TEACH has not been so successful. Section 110(1) is succinct and clear. TEACH is lengthy, complex, and predicated on a laundry list of laborious technical and administrative requirements. Section 110(1) articulates a concise but robust recognition of the public-serving values of classroom instruction. TEACH is legalistic and cramped, reflecting content lobbyists' anxiety and a middling understanding of digital technology, circa 2002.

The contrast between the open language in 110(1), which remains a powerful engine for teaching and learning today, with the time-bound assumptions and Byzantine requirements that have made TEACH brittle and rarely used reflects a core truth about copyright exceptions. Clear language that centers the values of copyright is resilient and sustainable. Narrow and specific language focused on technical requirements ages like a carton of milk left in the afternoon sun. As we will see, there is no better example of the power—and necessity—of flexible and values-based copyright exceptions for scholarly communication than fair use.

FAIR USE: THE EXCEPTIONAL EXCEPTION

In addition to these specific exceptions where Congress has identified a set of privileged activities done by an identified set of users, scholarly communicators can rely on a different type of exception: fair use. Unlike first sale or library lending under 108, which reflect the technical state of the art and political horse-trading of the US Congress in the 1970s, fair use reflects courts' equitable analysis. It asks, in the words of Second Circuit Judge and fountainhead of much current fair use jurisprudence Pierre Leval, whether a particular use "fulfill[s] the objective of copyright law to stimulate creativity for public illumination."[9] Fair use is almost certainly the most ubiquitous exception today, facilitating everything from the thumbnail images used in search engines to sharing memes on social media.

Fair use dates back at least to the nineteenth-century case of Folsome v. Marsh 9. F.Cas. 342 (C.C.D. Mass. 1841), where a writer and anthologist copied 353 pages from the plaintiff's twelve-volume biography of George Washington in order to produce a separate two-volume work of his own. Considering the issue, Judge Story noted that a "reviewer may fairly cite largely from the original work, if his design be really and truly to use the passages for the purposes of fair and reasonable criticism." On the other hand, Story wrote, in cases like the one at issue, where the use is "not to criticize, but to supersede the use of the original work, and substitute the review for it," fair use should not apply. In order to decide whether a particular use is fair, Story concluded, courts "must often... look to the nature and objects of the selections made, the quantity and value of the materials used, and the degree in which the use may prejudice the sale, or diminish the profits, or supersede the objects, of the original work."

Courts have built on Story's foundation for more than a century and Congress ratified fair use in the 1976 Copyright Act. Section 107 provides that "fair use of a copyrighted work... is not an infringement of copyright." It also enumerates a set of exemplary uses that exist at the heart of the doctrine, including, "criticism, comment, news reporting, teaching (including multiple copies for classroom use), scholarship, or research." In addition to these enumerated uses, the statute makes clear that many other uses may be fair. Under the statute, courts are instructed to consider a set of factors that include (but are not limited to)

1. the purpose and character of the use, including whether such use is of a commercial nature or is for nonprofit educational purposes;
2. the nature of the copyrighted work;
3. the amount and substantiality of the portion used in relation to the copyrighted work as a whole; and
4. the effect of the use upon the potential market for or value of the copyrighted work.

Unlike the specific exceptions discussed above that function like a checklist where all factors must be met, these four factors might better be called four questions or four considerations, since a court would ultimately consider them all holistically rather than mechanically working through each as a binary pass-fail determination.

Many resources suggest thinking of these factors as stones in an old-fashioned set of scales, with each factor tilting the balance toward or away from fair use. In my own analysis, I prefer to think about fair use as somewhat like making soup, with each factor as an ingredient that makes the dish taste better or worse. In this (somewhat whimsical) analogy, the fair use case is ultimately something like a bubbling pot and a court could be imagined taking a large wooden ladle to try a taste before declaring "That's good fair use" with a smile or scrunching up their nose to declare "This fair use claim is terrible!"

Whether you think of fair use as a balancing act, a recipe, or something else altogether, it is important to understand that fair use is a positive right that is clearly supported by over a century of case law and explicit statutory language. While some commenters have attempted to minimize fair use as "simply a defense" or even "nothing more than the right to hire a lawyer," those statements misunderstand and (often intentionally) mischaracterize the doctrine. The Supreme Court has been very clear that fair use is a constitutional safety valve, permitting necessary expression, particularly where a rights holder might not want to grant permission due to neglect, disdain, or especially when a new work engages critically with the original work.

The leading modern case on fair use, Campbell v Acuff-Rose, 510 U.S. 569 (1994), dealt specifically with this issue when it considered a lawsuit over the rap group 2 Live Crew's "lethal parody" of Roy Orbison's classic rock standard "Oh, Pretty Woman." Noting that copyright "must not put manacles upon science," the court held that 2 Live Crew's parodic use was permitted not based just on analysis of economic harm but because of the social value of art that responds to and builds on works that have come before. Particularly given the perceptions of rap music in the early 1990s, it was unsurprising that the socially and musically conservative

Orbison estate denied 2 Live Crew's request to use the song in a way that critiqued the original from the perspective of young Black artists.

This case illustrates the necessity of fair use not just as a tool for reducing economic inefficiency but also as a positive source of engagement and critique that lies at the heart of copyright's historical balance between limited monopoly and promoting new expression. The court recognized this socially valuable function for fair use in this case by describing a new way to analyze claims of fair use. Synthesizing the four statutory factors into a single two-part analysis borrowed from Judge Leval, the court announced that the fair use analysis often ultimately comes down to a question about whether a use is "transformative, altering the original with new expression, meaning, or message."

In cases where the use is transformative and the amount used is appropriate in light of that transformative purpose, courts almost always find fair use. Indeed, in subsequent years it has become clear that scholarly communicators who are critiquing, quoting in order to illustrate an argument, or otherwise using existing works for a transformative purpose can rely on fair use to support these uses that define good scholarly practice. As the nuances of copyright have become more complex and some aspects of the law have become frankly outdated, fair use has been the saving grace for academic uses that align with the core values and practices of the academy.

One example that illustrates the way transformative fair use supports scholarly communication is Bill Graham Archives v. Dorling Kindersley, Ltd., 448 F.3d 605 (2d Cir. 2006). In that case, a scholar sought to include a series of concert posters advertising performances by the rock band the Grateful Dead in a monograph describing the cultural history of the band. The publisher (DK) initially sought permission from the rights holder, Bill Graham Archives, but the parties could not agree on a licensing fee. Nevertheless, DK published the book and, when sued by Bill Graham, claimed fair use. The Second Circuit Court of Appeals agreed, holding that DK's use of the posters "as historical artifacts to document and represent" the cultural history presented in the monograph was transformative and thus fair use. Scholars seeking to borrow and build on works for purposes such as illustration can rely on cases like this to support their own work.

THE DIGITAL MILLENNIUM COPYRIGHT ACT

In many ways we have only scratched the surface of copyright law, with a strong emphasis on the aspects most relevant to creating and sharing scholarly works. One adjacent area that merits a quick look is the Digital Millennium Copyright Act (DMCA), a law implementing two major international treaties related to copyright and digital materials. The DMCA has a tremendous impact on everything we do online. This is particularly true for Section 230 (memorably called "the 26 words that created the internet"), which provides exemption from direct and indirect liability of internet service providers and other intermediaries.

For scholarly communication, however, the most important aspect of the DMCA is likely Section 1201, which limits the circumvention of technological protection measures (TPM) for any purpose, including otherwise lawful access. Even in cases where users are technically able and legally permitted to view a film, play a song, or fix a broken device, they are not permitted to unlock any copy protection required to do those lawful things. Section 1201 gives legal force to technical locks that prohibit consumers from otherwise-lawful activities like unlocking their iPhone to use with a rival carrier, viewing lawfully acquired DVD or Blu-ray discs purchased on an out-of-region player, or even repairing the digital components in their car or tractor. If you've ever had to pay exorbitant fees for a new ink cartridge in your printer, you can thank Section 1201 of the DMCA.

For researchers, educators, and archivists, this anti-circumvention provision has a real cost, locking away much of modern culture behind copy protection and foreclosing many opportunities for hands-on learning with computer code, digital media creation, and engineering. In all of these cases, Congress has made it clear that the law should permit these socially valuable uses, and academics know that their research and teaching requires these uses to be effective. It's harder to do a good job researching digital security deficiencies in public infrastructure if you aren't allowed to look at the source code.

Fortunately, Section 1201 also requires the Librarian of Congress to issue exemptions from this prohibition against circumvention. Exemptions are granted when it is shown that access-control technology has had a substantial adverse effect on the ability of people to make noninfringing uses of copyrighted works. The exemption rules are revised every three years, with existing exemptions expiring and proposals for renewal or new exemptions submitted by the public to the Registrar of Copyrights. After a process of hearings and public comments, the final rule is recommended by the Registrar and issued by the Librarian of Congress.

Exemptions have been granted since the first rulemaking in the year 2000 and have generally included specific exemptions for research and teaching purposes, as using audio-visual works in a university's media studies program and library circumvention on e-books in order to provide accessibility for hearing-impaired patrons through read-aloud services. The most recent set of exemptions were announced in 2021 and included exemptions for software preservation and text and data mining research.

INTERNATIONAL LAW

In addition to the US law that has been the focus of this section, international laws play an important role in the increasingly global body of scholarly communication practices.

Fortunately, these issues are made much less complicated by the Berne Convention, an international agreement governing copyright law. Berne signatories, which include almost every nation in the world, are guaranteed a set of harmonized copyright rules such as automatic protection of copyright and a standardized minimum term as well as a set of exceptions that must be recognized by every nation. In short, Berne assures that the basic outlines of copyright are the same (or at least comparable) around the world and that individuals can generally rely on the specific local nuances of their home country without fear that they will be held accountable for stepping outside the bounds of copyright nuances in a different nation's laws.

While international instruments like Berne often set minimum standards, substantial differences in application remain across individual nations. For example, while Berne requires that copyright be protected for at least the life of the author plus fifty years, the US, as discussed above, has elected to extend the term of copyright for an additional twenty years to life plus seventy. Another difference is that, while the US flatly denies copyright protection for facts and ideas regardless of the so-called "sweat of the brow" required to gather them, many nations do recognize a sui generis (literally "of its own kind") property right that exists to recognize the investment that is made in compiling a database. These database rights are particularly prevalent in the EU and UK and generally last for a shorter period of time and offer more limited protections than standard copyright laws.

Exceptions to copyright can take significantly different forms as well. While almost every nation has specific exceptions for research, teaching, library access, and so on, the specific scope and analysis can differ significantly. Similarly, while fair use has been a critical exception for scholarly communication in the US based on fair use's open, equitable framework, many other nations rely on an analogous but more tightly scoped exception called fair dealing.

These differences have led to some confusion and a fair amount of anxiety about the cross-border potential for open resources. In some cases new international agreements like the Marrakesh VIP Treaty have been adopted to assure that core values like access to published works for persons who are blind, visually impaired, or otherwise print-disabled are respected in all nations. Open creators are also working to harmonize the legal rules for using their materials through shared best practice documents and critically through use of the Creative Commons, as discussed in section 2.1. As we will see below under "Legal Issues for Scholarly Communication Librarianship," the legal rules for scholarly communication today are just as likely to be defined by private law agreements such as licenses and terms of use as they are by the core copyright rules discussed so far.

SCHOLARLY SHARING

In many ways the story of scholarly communication is the story of the academy failing to keep pace with changes in, and the resulting diminution of, copyright law. When an article or monograph was distributed primarily or exclusively as a physical artifact, it often made sense to transfer copyright to the publisher. The publisher could then register the copyright and do the work implicated by copyright, including copying, printing, and distributing at a reasonable price as well as enforcing copyright when infringement occurred. Once libraries acquired physical copies from the publisher, they were permitted under the law to share with scholars and the public at no cost and with minimal barriers through circulation under Section 109 and to make copies for preservation, interlibrary loan, and "private study, scholarship, and research" under Section 108. Because most of the other works created in the academy—lecture notes and syllabi, lab notebooks, interviews, and so forth—were not registered, they were not protected by copyright and could be freely shared based on norms and informal practices.

With the move to automatic copyright protection in the US, however, everything original, fixed, and creative that is made by a scholar is owned by its creator: field notes, slides for classroom instruction, even some raw data. This raised the stakes significantly on materials that had been governed by informal professional understandings and, as discussed in chapter 1.2, "The Economic Context," has led to several copyright land grabs on materials when they were perceived to be valuable.

This move toward automatic ownership also significantly complicated much research, particularly where scholars were investigating more recent cultural materials. Determining the copyright status of a work under a regime that requires registration is fairly straightforward: search the records of registered works, and if a work does not appear, it is likely in the public domain. With automatic protection, however, recent materials are almost certainly protected, and many older materials exist in a morass of mixed copyright status. This has led to a significant and ongoing issue with orphan works, where copyright status is unclear and a resulting gap in access to materials that are in copyright but not commercially available. The so-called Twentieth-Century Black Hole of mid-twentieth-century materials that are under copyright but have no clear rights holder working to provide access and curation has done severe damage to individual scholarly works and to whole fields, with a distressing number of scholars of the twentieth century simply steering their careers away from the black hole and opting to focus on earlier eras in history, literature, and so forth.

Even more significantly, in the absence of exceptions analogous to Section 108 and 109 for digital lending, the rise of digital materials that are licensed rather than purchased has fundamentally altered libraries' and scholars' ability to share their resources widely. Where the careful balance of copyright law made this system sustainable and privileged libraries as essential engines of free expression and cultural growth, this new regime has reduced much of scholarly sharing to a question of contracts and licensing.

CONTRACTS AND AUTHORS' RIGHTS

As discussed in chapter 1.2, "The Economic Context," and chapter 1.3, "Technology and Scholarly Communication," changes in those areas have significantly impacted the way scholarship is made and shared and led directly to what has been called the serials crisis or journal pricing crisis. In response, academic institutions have begun to cultivate new expertise in copyright, contracts, and licensing—often centered in the library—and to encourage more nuanced and empowered action by all scholars.

It is beyond the scope of this chapter to provide a detailed look at contract law. For our purposes it is enough to say that contract law is driven by a significantly different set of values than copyright's commitment to promote the progress of knowledge and learning. Contracts are primarily meant to reflect the intention of the parties and support efficient business operations, mostly eschewing any explicit emphasis on knowledge, access, or public policy. A contract is first and foremost a business document, and large for-profit businesses are very good at crafting those documents to meet narrow business interests and, ultimately, shareholder demands for regular and escalating profits.

As library collections have become dominated by licensed access to digital content rather than physical materials that circulate under the first sale doctrine, collections have become less available, less reliable, and more challenging to use in novel ways since so many licenses explicitly prohibit or implicitly exclude the ability to explore emerging practices such as text and data mining. Library collections have also become much less sustainable. As single purchases that permit unlimited use under copyright have been replaced by carefully negotiated licenses for journal packages, libraries have been forced to develop a much more sophisticated understanding of both business and legal practices. Even as more librarians with more legal knowledge spend more hours negotiating contract terms that support scholarly communication, access has remained limited in ways that would have been inconceivable a generation ago.

A history professor writing in 2003 about the election and presidency of Bill Clinton could pull scholarly monographs from the stacks, VHS recordings of campaign events from nonprint, and newspaper coverage from the archives. Even popular materials primarily intended for nonacademic audiences, like the film *Primary Colors* or Clinton's appearance playing the saxophone on *The Arsenio Hall Show*, were likely available in the library's media center. There was an economic cost when the library initially purchased these resources, and gathering the physical artifacts took time and expertise. But once collected, all of these materials could be expected to be available within the library's collections or through interlibrary loan. Once the materials were gathered, the researcher would be free to review, analyze, and excerpt all of them in scholarly articles and monographs as permitted under the law.

An analogous researcher writing in 2023 on presidents Obama and Trump would find many e-books inaccessible, news stories paywalled, and much popular media available only via consumer-facing platforms like Amazon or Hulu. A huge percentage of these digital resources would be likely to be unavailable at an academic library and not eligible for interlibrary loan. Even if the researcher personally paid for limited, individual access to the e-books, news sites, and streaming media services required to recreate the access available to her 2003-era forebearer, she would find technical locks on textual analysis and scholarly excerpting that she would be forbidden to break by the DMCA, even in cases where copyright law explicitly permitted the use. In many cases, instead of accessing a carefully curated resource in the library, she would be left with a broken hyperlink. A fellow researcher who wanted to check her sources or build on her work in new ways would have to pay for their own access to each resource and face a similar set of limitations on the established, otherwise lawful practices that make up the scholarly enterprise. As we move away from the public-serving law of copyright and toward the business documents that make up licenses, libraries are spending more money in order to provide fewer resources with less access and too many built-in locks and limitations. In cases where materials are not licensed to the library market, there is no recourse at all.

LEGAL LITERACY SUPPORTING AUTHORS RIGHTS

The move toward digital and licensed resources has fundamentally transformed many academic librarians from subject-expert collectors of print materials to copyright and contracts specialists who must understand and be able to negotiate legal terms and conditions for access, preservation, and scholarly use. As legal literacy in libraries has increased and financial pressures have mounted, libraries have also begun to apply this legal expertise upstream by supporting academic authors as they negotiate the terms of publication. After all, authors are the presumptive owners of copyright in the core works of an academic library's collection, and asking scholars to give those rights away only for their institution to purchase access at a premium (if they can afford the license at all) may not be in the best interest of those authors. It is certainly not in the interest of the public and institutions that fund and support them.

As discussed in chapter 1.3, "Technology and Scholarly Communication," if the move to digital delivery has undermined the lending rights of libraries, it has also empowered scholars to share their work in new ways that made the old model of copyright transfer to publishers equally outdated. Scholarly communication activists initially focused on empowering scholarly authors to simply retain their copyright interests in their work. Where the old system required scholars to uncritically surrender all their rights to their own work, a more nuanced approach could help them retain some or all of their rights to share with the public and make their work available to their peers in the field at limited costs and with few restrictions.

This support often focuses on individual negotiations at the point of publication. Scholarly communication librarians can and do offer general guidance on what aspects of a publication agreement might merit closer scrutiny. Scholarly communication librarians also frequently work with authors as they read and negotiate the specific agreements presented after an article or manuscript has been accepted for publication. They have also collectively begun to develop field-level resources like the Sherpa Romeo database of journal copyright policies and authors' addenda that presented specific prewritten language that offered publishers a license to use the author's work rather than transferring copyright at all. Scholars also rely on a set of open licenses that are discussed further in chapter 2.1, "Open Access."

While these questions about ownership that are often presented under the umbrella of "authors' rights" are critical to scholarly communication, they are tangled with many other issues inherent in copyright law. Copyright, particularly in the Anglo-American tradition, often rests on assumptions about commercial use in the marketplace, but the academy has a completely different set of incentives that are often undervalued or simply ignored by copyright.

At a deeper level, copyright's core market orientation privileges, in scholarly communication librarian and lawyer April Hathcock's words, "the development and protection of the published, written word, created by an autonomous and all-powerful male author."[10] This fiction of a unitary (presumptively white and male) creator leaves unprotected or actually robs many creators and communities of traditional knowledge and does not take into account much of the intellectual labor of the academy, from advisors who do not create copyrightable expression to contingent faculty and lab assistants—to say nothing of the librarians and archivists—doing the invisible labor that keeps the academy running. Seemingly every week another scholar announces an amazing discovery of "lost" materials that had been painstakingly preserved, cataloged, and digitized by a team of library professionals. Just as scholarly communication is devoted to empowering scholars to make informed decisions about copyright in and access to their work, the field is also dedicated to recognizing the limitations inherent in the law and finding better ways of recognizing the expertise and labor that goes into this work and the various communities reflected in these materials.

POLITICAL ADVOCACY AND POLICY: ADVOCACY GROUPS

In addition to scholarly communication support on the ground, library organizations and related advocacy groups have worked to effect change at the national and global level. Legislative advocacy has frequently been effective, supporting open access and winning funding and support for open initiatives, including more than forty-seven million dollars as of this writing for the Open Textbook Grant program.[11] Advocacy at the agency level has also been effective, highlighted by the defeat of a proposed merger of textbook publishers Cengage and McGraw-Hill in 2020 after raising antitrust concerns with the Department of Justice.[12]

Legal advocacy has been a particular area of focus, especially in areas of emphasis for libraries and scholarly communication such as copyright and privacy. Professional groups like the American Library Association (ALA) and Association of Research Libraries (ARL), as well as advocacy groups such as SPARC, coordinated activities and amicus briefs to courts considering issues that impact the academy, which have led to substantive changes in the law.

FUNDERS

As discussed in chapter 1.2, "The Economic Context," some of the most significant support for scholarly communication law and policy has come from research funders. The National Institutes of Health (NIH) Public Access Policy is often cited as one of the first, if not the first, open access mandates for a major public funding agency in the United States. As of 2008 the NIH Public Access Policy requires that all funded researchers must submit their published manuscripts to NIH's PubMedCentral, a requirement given teeth by a 2012 commitment to withhold subsequent funds for researchers who are out of compliance.[13]

In 2013 other federal agencies followed suit as directed by a memo from the White House Office of Science and Technology Policy (OSTP). The memo specifically directed all federal agencies with more than $100 million in R&D expenditures to develop plans to make the results of federally funded articles and data freely available to the public—generally within one year of publication.[14] While individual agencies were given broad latitude to develop implementation, this commitment to openness has had a major impact on scholarly communication. Many private funders have also followed suit, requiring open access to research articles, data sets, and other materials generated with grant funds.

In addition, the National Science Foundation (NSF) has led the way on making research more open and impactful by requiring a Broader Impact Statement in proposals for funding. This statement asks researchers to articulate the "potential [for your research] to benefit society and contribute to the achievement of desired society outcomes." (NSF Perspectives on Broader Impacts). The 2022 OSTP Nelson Memo promises to carry this work even further, ensuring free, immediate, and equitable access to federally funded research.[15] As conversations about open knowledge continue to expand from simply removing finance barriers and toward a larger conversation about making scholarly communication an engine for the public good, these conversations about impact are inspiring.

LEGAL ISSUES IN SCHOLARLY COMMUNICATION LIBRARIANSHIP

Legal issues are central to the work of scholarly communication, but most people working in scholarly communication librarianship do not have a Juris Doctor or other formal legal training. Most library schools do not offer any courses in legal issues, and as far as we know none require it. Nevertheless, these issues flow throughout scholarly communication and librarianship. As librarians have skilled up on copyright and related issues and invited formally trained attorneys to join the robust and growing set of respected legal experts who learned on the job, the field of scholarly communication has blossomed. In addition, that legal expertise has been critical for the success of every department in the library. If scholarly communication is increasingly just a different name for modern academic librarianship, then legal issues are a competency for most librarians today. Scholarly communication librarianship includes work that focuses explicitly on answering legal questions and guiding legal practice, but also legally informed work in scholarly communication like scholarly sharing and librarianship writ large, from acquisition and collections to circulation and reference.

CONCLUSION

This chapter has given you a very brief overview of legal issues and the way they fit within the core work of scholarly communication, but there is much more to learn about the topics covered here as well as new issues appearing every day. In addition to the suggested readings listed below, there are a variety of ways to stay up to speed with legal issues in scholarly communication. US primary legal materials such as statutes and cases can be found at major online databases such as FindLaw.com and Justia.com as well as on individual state and federal sites. If the institution where you work or in the area where you live has a law school, there is a team of highly trained law librarians who can help you find materials and resources. The US Copyright Office also has a dedicated YouTube channel with excellent videos and makes available a set of circulars designed to provide up-to-date and authoritative information to a general audience, which can be found at https://copyright.gov/circs/. In addition, copyright scholars often look to several treatises including *Nimmer on Copyright* and *Patry on Copyright*, which present deep analysis on copyright law written by Melville and David Nimmer and by William Patry, respectively. (Lawyers are not known for their creative naming....)

For copyright librarianship, there are excellent books, including Kenneth Crews's highly respected *Copyright Law for Librarians and Educators* and Carrie Russell's *Complete Copyright*. We also highly recommend a framework from copyright librarians Kevin Smith and Lisa Macklin that walks through a set of questions for analyzing copyright issues, available in several places including the University of Kansas' KU ScholarWorks repository at: https://kuscholarworks.ku.edu/handle/1808/22723. You can also find online training from groups like LYRASIS, Creative Commons, and the Library Copyright Institute and well-regarded conferences such as the Miami Copyright Conference. Finally, we have gathered a robust set of open resources in the Scholarly Communication Notebook, a companion to this text. We hope you will review those and add your own materials as you continue to learn about these issues today and throughout your career.

DISCUSSION QUESTIONS

1. Given that copyright is an automatic right, what specific materials do you control copyright in? How many of those did you create with the hope of making money on your work? What type of control and credit are important to you in the different types of work you create?

2. Where in your own life have you encountered fair use? Were you able to decide whether a use was fair yourself, or did someone else, either a gatekeeper or an automatic filter, make the decision for you?

3. What are the advantages and disadvantages of copyright exceptions that are fixed (like Section 110's exception for face-to-face teaching) versus those that are flexible (like fair use)? If you were helping someone make a decision about their own practice, how would you offer guidance for each of these types of exceptions?

4. The chapter focuses on scholarly publication agreements, but everyone who has used e-mail, social media, or streaming platforms with terms of use or service has entered into some sort of legal agreement about sharing their work. How well have you understood these types of agreements? What steps (if any) have you taken to learn more about those agreements and the specific, legally binding terms you are accepting? What support do you wish you had?

5. Copyright is an issue that touches the work of almost every librarian. Think about the specific area of work you are planning to join. What copyright issues are likely to come up in your day-to-day work? What legal issues beyond copyright (privacy in patron records? free expression and book challenges? personal liability if a patron slips on a spill in the building?) would you like to know more about? How would you go about learning more?

6. What nonlegal risks and opportunities might impact your decision to use a work based on a copyright exception, especially if the copyright issue was somewhat unclear, such as with digitizing an orphaned work or relying on fair use in a new context?

NOTES

1.   Folsom v. Marsh, 9. F.Cas. 342 (C.C.D. Mass. 1841)

2. Tanya Aplin and Lionel Bently. "Global Mandatory Fair Use: The Nature and Scope of the Right to Quote Copyright Works." Cambridge Intellectual Property and Information Law. Cambridge: Cambridge University Press, 2020. doi:10.1017/9781108884099.

3. G. Aad et al. "Combined Measurement of the Higgs Boson Mass in pp Collisions at √s=7 and 8 TeV with the ATLAS and CMS Experiments." Phys. Rev. Lett. 114, 191803 https://doi.org/10.1103/PhysRevLett.114.191803

4. Kirtsaeng v. John Wiley & Sons, 136 S. CT. 1979, 1986 (2016).

5. *Naruto v. Slater, et al.,* no. 16-15469 (9th Cir. 23 April 2018).

6. Neil Genzlinger, "If You Want to Make a 'Hamlet,' You Have to Break Some Rules," *New York Times*, March 28, 2016.

7. Aaron Perzanowski and Jason Schultz, "The End of Ownership: Personal Property in the Digital Economy." (2016). MIT Press. https://doi.org/10.7551/mitpress/10524.001.0001.

8. Maria Bustillos, "A Book Is a Book Is a Book—Except When It's an e-Book," *The Nation*, August 30, 2023, https://www.thenation.com/article/culture/internet-archive-lawsuit-libraries-books/.

9   Pierre N. Leval, Toward a Fair Use Standard, Harvard Law Review, Vol. 103, No. 5 (Mar., 1990)

10. April M. Hathcock, "Confining Cultural Expression: How the Historical Principles behind Modern Copyright Law Perpetuate Cultural Exclusion," *American University Journal of Gender, Social Policy and the Law* 25, no. 3 (2017): article 1, https://digitalcommons.wcl.american.edu/cgi/viewcontent.cgi?article=1689&context=jgspl.

11. SPARC, "Open Textbook Pilot Grant Program," https://sparcopen.org/our-work/open-textbook-pilot/.

12. SPARC, "Stopping the Cengage/McGraw-Hill Merger," https://sparcopen.org/our-work/oppose-cengage-mcgraw-hill-merger/.

13. National Institutes of Health, "NIH Public Access Policy Details," https://publicaccess.nih.gov/policy.htm.

14. Obama White House Archives, "Expanding Public Access to the Results of Federally Funded Research," https://obamawhitehouse.archives.gov/blog/2013/02/22/expanding-public-access-results-federally-funded-research.

15. Executive Office of the President, "Ensuring Free, Immediate, and Equitable Access to Federally Funded Research," https://www.whitehouse.gov/wp-content/uploads/2022/08/08-2022-OSTP-Public-Access-Memo.pdf.

BIBLIOGRAPHY

Aad et al. "Combined Measurement of the Higgs Boson Mass in pp Collisions at √s=7 and 8 TeV with the ATLAS and CMS Experiments." Phys. Rev. Lett. 114, 191803 https://doi.org/10.1103/PhysRevLett.114.191803.

Aplin, Tanya, and Lionel Bently. Global Mandatory Fair Use: The Nature and Scope of the Right to Quote Copyright Works. Cambridge Intellectual Property and Information Law. Cambridge: Cambridge University Press, 2020. doi:10.1017/9781108884099.

Bustillos, Maria. "A Book Is a Book Is a Book—Except When It's an e-Book." August 30, 2023. *The Nation*. https://www.thenation.com/article/culture/internet-archive-lawsuit-libraries-books/.

Executive Office of the President. "Ensuring Free, Immediate, and Equitable Access to Federally Funded Research." https://www.whitehouse.gov/wp-content/uploads/2022/08/08-2022-OSTP-Public-Access-Memo.pdf.

Hathcock, April M. "Confining Cultural Expression: How the Historical Principles behind Modern Copyright Law Perpetuate Cultural Exclusion." *American University Journal of Gender, Social Policy and the Law* 25, no. 3 (2017): article 1. https://digitalcommons.wcl.american.edu/cgi/viewcontent.cgi?article=1689&context=jgspl.

Kirtsaeng v. John Wiley & Sons, 136 S. CT. 1979, 1986 (2016).

National Institutes of Health. "NIH Public Access Policy Details." https://publicaccess.nih.gov/policy.htm.

National Science Foundation. "Perspectives on Broader Impacts." https://nsf-gov-resources.nsf.gov/2022-09/Broader_Impacts_0.pdf.

Obama White House Archives. "Expanding Public Access to the Results of Federally Funded Research." https://obamawhitehouse.archives.gov/blog/2013/02/22/expanding-public-access-results-federally-funded-research.

"Pedagogical Apparatus and Callouts: Politics and Law." November 4, 2021. https://docs.google.com/document/d/1s1frZAvCUPlxYIIqjC2WVi-HmWTGRPoleeGUrskrOhg/edit.

SPARC. "Open Textbook Pilot Grant Program." https://sparcopen.org/our-work/open-textbook-pilot/.

——. "Stopping the Cengage/McGraw-Hill Merger." https://sparcopen.org/our-work/oppose-cengage-mcgraw-hill-merger/.

PART II

SCHOLARLY COMMUNICATION AND OPEN CULTURE

2

INTRODUCTION TO OPEN

RESPONSES AND OPPORTUNITIES

Will Cross with Josh Bolick and Maria Bonn

> The opposite of open is not closed; the opposite of open is broken.
>
> —Cable Green[1]

If the foundations of work in scholarly communication are shaped by a set of pressures and challenges, that work today is guided by a related set of opportunities. The North Star for this work is the idea of *openness*. Opening up access to paywalled articles so all researchers and the public can engage with the materials, opening up data sets so peers can reproduce experiments that purport to reveal novel findings, and opening textbooks and other teaching materials to equalize student access all make up the day-to-day work of scholarly communication. In addition to reopening channels that have been closed off by the pressures described in part I, however, scholarly communication is increasingly dedicated to opening up deeper conversations about the core values of academic work. Questions about the public value of research, inequitable systems of prestige, and the precarious nature of adjunct labor are as central to this work as open licenses or article processing charges (APCs).

This robust engagement with concrete practices and shared values is not new. Some of the earliest modern conversations about openness come from the free and open source software (FOSS) community, which recognizes the ambiguity of the English term *free*, which can mean both "at no monetary cost" (*gratis*) and "with little or no restriction" (*libre*). Playing off this distinction, FOSS advocates often argue that free software should be "free as in free speech, not just as in free beer." As we will see in this part, different streams of practice often bring their own lens to openness as a tool for libre and gratis access. Much work around open access, for example, began with powerful advocacy for gratis access, and many funders today, particularly in the US, simply require free public access to read published scholarship rather than libre reuse rights. Open educators, on the other hand, often place a premium on *5R* permissions that make OER not just available without cost but also open to revision and remix.

That said, open educators care very much about reducing costs, and much open education work is devoted to providing affordable resources, even if they are not technically open as the community often uses the term. Likewise, open access advocates are doing pioneering work that goes far beyond gratis access in order to critique practices that center wealthy, English-speaking institutions in the Global North at the expense of scholars around the world. Openness exists along a continuum and must be designed to meet policy goals and enact values. It is not simply a binary on-off switch to be flipped or a box to be checked once the correct license is added or a PDF has been deposited. As open science advocates are fond of saying: access should be "as open as possible, as closed as necessary."

This part begins with a chapter on open access (OA), a body of practices focused on sharing scholarly works such as monographs and journal articles. As an area of the field in full bloom, OA is well-defined and especially ripe for nuanced critique. This chapter provides an overview of OA today and then presents a set of deep dives on legal mechanisms, opportunities to open up publishing, and the role of libraries beyond the traditional academy. This chapter also provides thoughtful discussion about the challenges embedded in OA, from countervailing values such as privacy to systemic issues such as institutional racism and the constraints imposed by late capitalism. As this chapter makes clear, OA comes bundled with a set of cultural and economic baggage that must be unpacked and addressed if it is to live up to its liberatory aspirations.

Next, this part turns to open data. Like OA, the scholarly community's emphasis on research data was driven by a specific set of concerns and has expanded to encompass broader opportunities and challenges. Where many advocates came to OA based on the unsustainable costs of the "serials' crisis," many champions of open data have been driven by a parallel crisis in reproducibility tied to the lack of access to much research data in any form and at any price. As a result, this chapter begins with discussion about how to manage, share, and publish data—work that is well-understood for research articles but still developing in many disciplines when it comes to the data that underlie those articles. It also introduces core practices for making data impactful and for ethical use and sharing of these materials.

One of the most significant turns in scholarly communication has been the recognition that scholarly knowledge is transmitted not only through the established conduits of reporting on research but also through educational materials and practices. The third chapter discusses open education, a body of practice that weaves together at least two central threads: cost savings and pedagogical innovation. This chapter introduces the core concepts and historical context, as well as current issues in the field. Open education today reflects both financial evolution and pedagogical revolution, and this chapter explores those dovetailed values as they are practiced in libraries.

One thing all open advocates can agree on is that openness is not without cost. In response to the "free speech versus free beer" discourse, a third version of "free" has been suggested: "free as in free puppies or kittens." Creating knowledge requires time, expertise, and labor. Sharing knowledge, maximizing its reach, understanding its impact, and preserving it for the historical record can require even more. The final chapter explores open science and infrastructure as a model of integrated and sustainable openness. Open science reflects an emerging synthesis of the various streams of open discussed in this part, but also a recognition that, at its heart, openness is a reaffirmation of the historical values and aspirations of the academy. *Open science*, as the saying goes, is ultimately just another name for good science or science done well, inclusively, and in a way that makes the world better. This chapter introduces core terms and practices and offers a series of recommendations on the variety of ways open science is practiced and infrastructure is made open to support this work.

Open advocates often quote OER pioneer David Wiley's admonition that using an open textbook in the same way we have used a closed resource is like driving an airplane down the highway—it can get you where you're going, but there is an opportunity to do much more.[2] The same is true for open scholarship, data, and infrastructure—openness is both a solution to the problems of the current moment and an invitation to fundamentally transform our work. We hope that this part, taken as a whole, can help orient scholarly communication workers and advocates as they chart their own path through a broad constellation of responses and opportunities.

NOTES

1. Cable Green, "The Obviousness of Open Policy" (keynote address, Open Education Conference, Park City, UT, October 25–27, 2011), YouTube video, 38:56, https://www.youtube.com/watch?v=CU6h-oI6hro&t=2s.
2. David Wiley, "Open Pedagogy: The Importance of Getting In the Air" (2015) https://opencontent.org/blog/archives/3761.

BIBLIOGRAPHY

Green, Cable. "The Obviousness of Open Policy." Keynote address, Open Education Conference, Park City, UT, October 25–27, 2011. YouTube video, 38:56. https://www.youtube.com/watch?v=CU6h-oI6hro&t=2s.

OPEN ACCESS

Amy Buckland

EDITOR'S NOTE

In this chapter, Amy Buckland provides an introduction to the many opportunities and challenges presented by opening access to the scholarly record. She shares both her expertise and her critical perspective, as well as her opinions, opinions that are frank and well-informed, both by research and by considerable professional experience. Throughout her essay she interweaves contributions from notable experts in the field of scholarly communication. These contributions amplify Buckland's perspective and often offer alternatives to that perspective. Each of them should be considered both on its own and as part of Buckland's complete argument. Where these contributions have been previously published, they have been very lightly edited for clarity and style.

She also begins by "assigning" an additional text. Readers should be assured that the current text does not actually have prerequisites. At the same time, the assignment is a good one. Peter Suber's *Open Access* is an extremely useful introduction to the topic, it's free online, openly licensed, highly readable, and available at: https://openaccesseks.mitpress.mit.edu/.

Suber tells us:

> Shifting from ink on paper to digital text suddenly allows us to make perfect copies of our work. Shifting from isolated computers to a globe-spanning network of connected computers suddenly allows us to share perfect copies of our work with a worldwide audience at essentially no cost. About thirty years ago this kind of free global sharing became something new under the sun. Before that, it would have sounded like a quixotic dream.
>
> Digital technologies have created more than one revolution. Let's call this one the access revolution.[1]

Suber's book and the essay that follows here are excellent guides to the origins and consequences, as well as the ongoing work, of that revolution.

INTRODUCTION

First off, put this book down right now and go and read Peter Suber's *Open Access*.[2] Go on, I'll wait. (It is, of course, open access, so excuses are low. Hop to it.)

Good, now that you've done that, welcome back. Let's talk about what open access looks like in practice, and especially what it means for scholarly communication librarians. There are many different stakeholders in the open access community, and they will all have their own angle. In this chapter we will try to work through a number of foundational concepts, learn about some tools, and look at what open access might mean as part of the day-to-day for librarians. Interspersed throughout this chapter you will find short essays meant to present an issue in open access worthy of discussion.

So, what, exactly, is open access?

DEFINITIONS

There are a number of definitions floating around. Since you've already read Suber's book, you'll be familiar with his: "Open access (OA) literature is digital, online, free of charge, and free of most copyright and licensing restrictions."[3] This definition focuses on the delivery mechanism for scholarship and is generally how open access is defined—online, free, and with clear reuse/copyright statements.

UNESCO's definition dives a bit deeper and begins to look at the people involved in scholarly publishing. For UNESCO, open access requires that

> - its content is universally and freely accessible, at no cost to the reader, via the Internet or otherwise;
>
> - the author or copyright owner irrevocably grants to all users, for an unlimited period, the right to use, copy, or distribute the article, on condition that proper attribution is given;
>
> - it is deposited, immediately, in full and in a suitable electronic form, in at least one widely and internationally recognized open access repository committed to open access.[4]

Here we see roles—readers, authors, copyright owners—begin to emerge. The people! This definition is often appreciated as the mention of readers highlights the fact that scholarship is not created simply for the sake of creation—it is meant to be read. UNESCO goes on to add a venue component to its definition, citing an "internationally recognized open access repository." This new component adds a wrinkle that might be seen as a barrier to being deemed OA by UNESCO. Which OA repositories are internationally recognized? If a journal makes all of its work OA through its journal site (not technically a repository, nor, perhaps, internationally recognized), does that mean it doesn't qualify as OA under UNESCO's definition?

There are other concerns with the definitions we often see of OA: what is missing from them. While having scholarship available online, for free, and with some reuse rights is a good start, it's far from truly changing the traditional publishing model. Or, as Samuel Moore puts it: "So unless you define open access in a way that specifically excludes bad actors, any definition of OA will be exploitable by them."[5]

WHAT IS MISSING?

Most definitions are related to the actual technical mechanics of implementing OA—at no point is there a reference to the "why" something this big would even be tackled. This absence has resulted in for-profit publishers, those whose presence in scholarly publishing has cemented a practice where billions of dollars from public institutions is funneled to private shareholders,* co-opting the term *open access* (aka "openwashing") to appear in line with this new practice.

Would including the following concepts in the definition of open access prevent openwashing? Or at least make it more difficult?

Temporality

What if OA required the work be made available permanently? Forever. Not just while the repository has funding or while the traditional publisher sees OA as a great way to increase revenue. To be OA, the scholarship has to be made permanently available. Of course, this is much more difficult to do. For an institution or scholarly society to commit to running its repository in perpetuity is a task too big for many. Doing this scalably and sustainably will require significant investment, collaboration, and vision for the future. For example, Theses Canada, run by Library and Archives Canada (LAC), aims to "acquire and preserve theses and dissertations from participating universities"[6] with a view to making them available for the future (first in print, and now digitally). As the national archive and national library, LAC already has the mandate to preserve content in perpetuity, as well as to collaborate with institutions in Canada, making it easier to build and run an OA service. Other institutions lack a similar mandate and the resourcing to sustain it.

Machine Readability

A definition of open access which included an assurance of machine readability of the scholarship would increase the accessibility of this work by making it available to web-based assistive technologies like screen readers. This would grow readership for content which can often be locked in "flat" PDFs, where the text is an image of the page (either due to older digitization practices or from the access-blocking scripts some publishers have on their sites).

Another aspect of OA making scholarship widely available is the new forms of scholarship which it can support. A number of disciplines, especially digital humanities, have leveraged the availability of the corpus of OA scholarship as the training data for new ways of analyzing texts. The Budapest Open Access Initiative gets into this[7]—more on that below.

Governance/Ownership

As Moore noted in his tweet, if one of the largest and most profitable corporations in the world can claim OA street cred, perhaps the definition should incorporate a component related to the power dynamics present in the scholarly publishing system. Should only non-profit organizations be able to claim they publish OA? What if there was a self-organizing group of researchers who wanted to share their work and license it for complete reuse, and they anonymously posted it in a forum like Reddit? Would that be considered OA?

---

* There is ample documentation of these profits. For example, a 2019 landscape analysis from the Scholarly Publishing and Academic Resources Coalition points out: "Elsevier is not the largest publisher of STM journals in terms of titles (Springer Nature Group publishes about 3,000 titles), but it has the largest journal revenues: Springer Nature Group had 2017 revenues of €1.64/$1.9 (at an exchange rate of 1.16) million, but about 30% of that was books, leaving journal revenues at about $1.333 million, well below Elsevier's estimated $1.8 million": Claudio Aspesi et al., *SPARC Landscape Analysis: The Changing Academic Publishing Industry* (Washington, DC: Scholarly Publishing and Academic Resources Coalition, March 28, 2019_, 10, https://doi.org/10.31229/osf.io/58yhb.

Values

Ultimately a lot of discussions about open access boil down to values. The values of the people and institutions involved in the creation of scholarship. The values of the readers and those who learn and grow from openly accessible scholarship. The values of the publishers facilitating (in many cases) access to new voices, as well as access to a new profit centre within academia for (some of) their shareholders. Is there a way to codify these values in the definition? Can we settle on what those values might even be?

OPEN ACCESS DECLARATIONS

There's the history of open access, and then there's the codification of open access through declarations. To be clear: a number of researchers were already working in open access long before the meetings which spurred these statements ever took place. (arXiv began in 1991 when a group of physics researchers discovered that emailing preprints of articles to each other was a recipe for overloaded inboxes—especially in 1991![8] Imagine!) But at a certain point, the communities saw the benefit of establishing guiding principles and recommendations to move scholarship toward open access.

Budapest Open Access Initiative 2002

The Budapest Open Access Initiative was the first of the *B* declarations in 2002–2003, published on February 14, 2002.[9] BOAI (as it has come to be known) recommends two strategies for achieving open access to scholarship: self-archiving and open access journals. Now think of the state of the internet in 2002. For authors to archive their work on a publicly searchable site was, at the time, a significant boost to access to scholarship. And the creation of a "new generation of journals committed to open access"[10] funded through methods other than traditional subscription fees? All very groundbreaking.

BOAI Twentieth Anniversary

Twenty years later, BOAI was revisited and, through consultation with the community, developed four high-level recommendations.[11] The growth of open access has surfaced issues that weren't foreseen in 2002 when the original drafters sought to make scholarship more available. The new recommendations aim to address these issues by looking at the ecosystem more broadly.

The first recommendation addresses the closed infrastructure currently hosting a significant amount of OA content and recommends a shift to open infrastructure. (Good thing you can learn about this in chapter 2.4, "Open Science and Infrastructure"!) BOAI20 also recommends an overhaul of the entire incentive structure in scholarly publishing to move away from assessment using traditional metrics to one where impact on the public (and accessibility of research) is more prominent. The third and fourth recommendations focus on the money flowing in and around scholarly publishing. While many open access journals resource themselves through article processing charges (APCs), these charges often exclude researchers on financial grounds. And the money currently being used to support OA should further the goals of accessibility and force change within the publishing industry instead of simply paying APCs to traditional publishers.

Berlin Declaration on Open Access to Knowledge in Sciences and Humanities 2003

After BOAI, the folks at the Max Planck Institute developed the Berlin Declaration on Open Access to Knowledge in Sciences and Humanities (aka the Berlin Declaration).[12] This declaration introduced new players to the OA declaration world. Not only did the declaration call on researchers and agencies to make their work OA, it called on "the holders of cultural heritage to support open access by providing their resources on the Internet." Here was a moment where institutions like archives, galleries, libraries, and museums were seen as part of the move to OA by digitizing their collections to facilitate access to them online. If the work of researchers was going to be made openly available online, being able to link directly to the collections researched would surely benefit all involved.

Bethesda Statement on Open Access Publishing 2003

The final of the *B*s, the Bethesda Statement on Open Access Publishing was the first to specifically call on university libraries to support open access through outreach, developing ways for researchers to make their work open and to integrate open access journals into our catalogues.[13] Yes, there was a time when you couldn't find OA journals in library catalogues, or if they were there, you had no idea they were open access.

The Bethesda Statement also calls on journal publishers to "commit to providing an open access option for any research article published in any of the journals they publish." Now if only it had included "without egregious APCs" with its statement....

MYTHS

The arrival of the internet and its ubiquity have thrown a lot of the world into a tizzy (still now, even) in terms of how we work and live. Scholarly communication was not immune to this. Instead of leveraging the arrival of the internet to wildly revolutionize what it means to publish—to share—scholarship, most publishers recreated the printed word online, right down to PDF formatting and the extra charges for colour images. While we have definitely seen advancements recently, many of the myths you will hear about open access come from the fact that the traditional publishing model rendered a previously very closed system more available to new communities, alarming the old guard.

Another issue often conflated in the discussion of open access publishing is that there are bad practices in the scholarly publishing world in general, but we seem to scrutinize the practices only of the OA publishing side. There will always be plagiarism or use without permission. Some folks will leverage the tenure and promotion process to take advantage of early career researchers' need to publish, or create and promote predatory journals which promise quick editorial turnarounds in return for exorbitant fees. There will always be jerks in the world. These myths came about because of the jerks and bad practices in the scholarly publishing world.

Myth: Open Access Publications Are Not Peer-Reviewed

Change is hard. The availability of the internet as a distribution channel forced traditional publishers to change their own distribution concepts. At the same time, some scholarly societies, universities, and libraries saw this as an opportunity to start up online-only journals. The shift to online publishing also meant the shift to managing the editorial process virtually, resulting in quicker publishing time frames. Peer review was present in many of these journals, but because all other aspects of the production were quicker thanks to email and online journal management, the rumour became that they were skipping the peer-review process.

Myth: Open Access Publishing Is Basically a Vanity Press

This myth has two prongs: the fact journals used the internet for distribution, and the fees associated with open access publishing (especially in the early days). "On the internet, nobody knows you're a dog."[14] Similarly, according to this myth, just about anyone could use a hosted WordPress instance and—bing-bang-boom—say they publish a journal. Since publishing no longer relies on printing presses and postage, some barriers to scholarship have been removed—challenging the vetting role of traditional publishers. In the same vein…

Myth: Authors Must Pay to Publish Open Access

Publishing costs money. Despite the claims of some traditional publishers, no one in the OA field ever said it was free (that's another myth you might hear). In the early days of open access, journals were eager to build new funding frameworks to ensure high-quality publications freely accessible to the reader. A framework where the submitting author participates in sharing the cost of the production of their article was a popular funding mechanism. This was interpreted by some as a "pay to publish" route, as though there were no peer review and overall editorial involvement, which is not true. This myth also ignores open publishing without any fee for authors or readers, which exists and is called *platinum* or *diamond open access*, as well as author self-archiving or *green open access*.

Myth: Open Access Publishing Means You Give Up Your Copyright

OH THE IRONY HERE. OA publications typically use Creative Commons licensing, which clearly states the author retains all copyright to their work and simply licenses the publisher to use it in very specific ways (make the work available and be cited as the home of the work are the biggest components of the CC license). Toll-access publishers, on the other hand, often require authors to transfer their copyright to the publisher under the guise of the publisher working to keep your authorship intact and safe. Because…

Myth: Open Access Means Anyone Can Use Your Work

Let's be clear here. Toll access doesn't mean folks can't use your work. It just means that traditional publishers, many of whom tend to be for-profit and thus have significant financial means, are able to litigate against those who use your work without permission, fair use and other exemptions the author and original publication are cited).*

Myth: If You Publish in Open Access Venues, It May Hinder Your Tenure and Promotion Path

Ummmm… well, this one could be true. Sometimes. As previously stated, change is hard, and that goes for universities and how they award tenure and promotions. Typically, this happens through various committees and external reviewers looking at a professor's catalogue

---

* Creative Commons interprets *NonCommercial* thusly: "not primarily intended for or directed towards commercial advantage or monetary compensation." More at Creative Commons Wiki, "NonCommercial interpretation," last updated October 15, 2017, https://wiki.creativecommons.org/wiki/NonCommercial_interpretation. Further, the Second Circuit clarified the interpretation of noncommerciality in the case of Great Minds v. FedEx Office & Print Services, Inc., No. 17-808 (2d Cir. 2018).

of publications. Faculty tend to look for the known-quantity journals as a marker for the value of their work. If they don't have good open options because the OA journals in the field are new or underdeveloped, they may be seen as having less impact, never mind the actual impact of the work. As the success and prominence of OA journals continue to rise, hopefully this concern will lessen and disappear. To read more about a researcher who has received tenure while publishing exclusively open access, check out Erin McKiernan's story.[15] These concerns differ across institutions and disciplines. For example, for academic librarians on the tenure track, publishing exclusively in open journals is viable, and even common, though candidates should always seek to know and understand the policies and perceptions of their own institutions.

Myth: Everything Should Be Open

This is one that some folks in the open access world have been known to support—especially in the early days. But this is a privileged point of view. A lot of scholarship is created based on humans and their lives. The drive toward opening up everything and making it available on the internet has long-term impacts on the people whose information is now openly available. Be it Indigenous oral histories, first-person accounts of violent events, or even location information for unhoused people, not everything should be open.

DIGITIZATION: JUST BECAUSE YOU CAN, DOESN'T MEAN YOU SHOULD[†]

Tara Robertson

I learned this week that Reveal Digital has digitized *On Our Backs* (*OOB*), a lesbian porn magazine that ran from 1984 to 2004. This is a part of the Independent Voices collection that "chronicles the transformative decades of the 60s, 70s and 80s through the lens of an independent alternative press."[16] For a split second I was really excited—porn that was nostalgic for me was online! Then I quickly thought about friends who appeared in this magazine before the internet existed. I am deeply concerned that this kind of exposure could be personally or professionally harmful for them.

While Reveal Digital went through the proper steps to get permission from the copyright holder, there are ethical issues with digitizing collections like this. Consenting to a porn shoot that would be in a queer print magazine is a different thing from consenting to have your porn shoot be available online. I'm disappointed in my profession. Librarians have let down the queer community by digitizing *On Our Backs*.

WHY IS THIS COLLECTION DIFFERENT?

The nature of this content makes it different from digitizing textual content or non-pornographic images. We think about porn differently than other types of content.

† This piece was originally published on the author's blog, https://tararobertson.ca/2016/oob/. Used with permission.

Most of the *OOB* run was published before the internet existed. Consenting to appear in a limited-run print publication is very different from consenting to have one's sexualized image be freely available on the internet. Who in the early 90s could imagine what the internet would look like in 2016?

In talking to some queer pornographers, I've learned that some of their former models are now elementary school teachers, clergy, professors, child care workers, lawyers, mechanics, health care professionals, bus drivers, and librarians. We live and work in a society that is homophobic and not sex-positive. Librarians have an ethical obligation to steward this content with care for both the object and for the people involved in producing it.

HOW COULD THIS BE DIFFERENT?

Reveal Digital does not have a clear takedown policy on its website. A takedown policy describes the mechanism for someone to request that digital content be taken off a website or digital collection. Hathi's Trust's takedown policy is a good example of a policy around copyright. When I spoke to Peggy Glahn, program director for Reveal Digital, she explained there isn't a formal takedown policy. Someone could contact the rights holder (the magazine publisher, the photographer, or the person who owns the copyright to the content) and have them make the takedown request to Reveal Digital. Even for librarians it's sometimes tricky to track down the copyright holder of a magazine that's not being published anymore. By being stewards of this digital content, I believe that Reveal Digital has an ethical obligation to make this process clearer.

I noticed that not all issues are available online. Peggy Glahn said that Reveal Digital digitized *OOB* from copies held by the Sallie Bingham Center for Women's History and Culture at Duke University and Charles Deering McCormick Library of Special Collections at Northwestern University but is still missing many of the later issues. More issues should not be digitized until formal ethical guidelines have been written. This process should include consultation with people who appeared in *OOB*.

There are ways to improve access to the content through metadata initiatives. I'm really, really excited by Bobby Noble and Lisa Sloniowski's proposed project exploring linked data in relation to Derrida and feminism.[17] I've loved hearing how Lisa's project has shifted from a physical or digital archive of feminist porn to a linked data project documenting the various relationships between different people. I think the current iteration avoids dodgy ethics while exploring new ways of thinking about the content and people through linked data. Another example of this is Sarah Mann's index of the first ten years of *OOB* for the Canadian Gay and Lesbian Archive.*

We need to have an in-depth discussion about the ethics of digitization in libraries. The "Zine Librarians Code of Ethics" is the best discussion of these issues that I've read.[18]

---

* Sarah Mann's index of the first 10 years of OOB for the Canadian Gay and Lesbian Archive is available at: https://web.archive.org/web/20160324054743/http://www.clga.ca/on-our-backs.

There are two ideas that are relevant to my concerns are about consent and balancing interests between access to the collection and respect for individuals:

Whenever Possible, It Is Important to Give Creators the Right of Refusal if They Do Not Wish Their Work to Be Highly Visible

Because of the often highly personal content of zines, creators may object to having their material being publicly accessible. Zinesters (especially those who created zines before the internet era) typically create their work without thought to their work ending up in institutions or being read by large numbers of people. To some, exposure to a wider audience is exciting, but others may find it unwelcome. For example, a zinester who wrote about questioning their sexuality as a young person in a zine distributed to their friends may object to having that material available to patrons in a library, or a particular zinester, as a countercultural creator, may object to having their zine in a government or academic institution.

Consent is a key feminist and legal concept. Digitizing a feminist porn publication without consideration for the right to be forgotten is unethical.

The "Zine Librarians Code of Ethics" does a great job of articulating the tension that sometimes exists between making content available and the safety and privacy of the content creators:

> To echo our preamble, zines are "often weird, ephemeral, magical, dangerous, and emotional." Dangerous to whom, one might ask? It likely depends on whom one asks, but in the age of the Internet, at least one prospectively endangered population are zinesters themselves. Librarians and archivists should consider that making zines discoverable on the Web or in local catalogs and databases could have impacts on creators—anything from mild embarrassment to the divulging of dangerous personal information.[19]

Zine Librarians and Archivists Should Strive to Make Zines as Discoverable as Possible While Also Respecting the Safety and Privacy of Their Creators

I've heard similar concerns with lack of care by universities when digitizing traditional Indigenous knowledge without adequate consultation, policies, or understanding of cultural protocols. I want to learn more about Indigenous intellectual property, especially in Canada. It's been a few years since I've looked at Mukurtu, a digital collection platform that was built in collaboration with Indigenous groups to reflect and support cultural protocols. Perhaps queers and other marginalized groups can learn from Indigenous communities about how to create culturally appropriate digital collections.

Librarians need to take more care with the ethical issues that go far beyond simple copyright clearances when digitizing and putting content online.

WHY DO I CARE?

With all that is going on in libraries, and especially academic libraries, why on earth should you care about open access? Simply: it aligns with a lot of the reasons you may be looking to work in libraries.

OPEN ACCESS ENSURES PUBLIC ACCESS TO INFORMATION

Librarians make information available to their communities. Open access seeks to make information available to the world. Dismantling fee barriers and building accessible platforms (the digital divide is still very real and always worth working on) is solid library work. Imagine what might have happened had medical research always been openly available. Would Ebola have torn through West Africa in 2014 had research on the topic been openly available? (Hint: maybe not.[20]) A number of publishers did react to the arrival of COVID-19 by removing paywalls for a certain amount of time. So, not all bad.

PUBLIC LIBRARIES AND OPEN ACCESS

Gillian Byrne

In August 2020, Lisa Hinchliffe, professor and coordinator for information literacy and instruction at the University of Illinois-Urbana Champaign, posed on Twitter:

> Who are the leading public librarians in the open access movement/community?

> FYI, I don't mean academic librarians at public institutions. I mean those working in public libraries.

> I was asked and I didn't have an answer so want to fill this gap in my knowledge![21]

As a librarian who has moved over to public libraries from academic libraries, I followed the thread that developed on the topic with interest.

One of the barriers illustrated in the thread was training. Discovering open access material has challenges and is ever changing. It requires subject knowledge to discover preprint archives. Sophisticated search techniques are needed to explore tools like PubMed. Even Google Scholar, which indexes many institutional repositories and open access resources, can be frustrating when a researcher is faced with many paywalled dead ends. It was also noted that patrons visiting public libraries traditionally exhibit a wider range of research and computer skills than university students, staff, and faculty and may also be less interested in undertaking research than in finding a solution: "When I've been working public library reference, the patrons most likely to come for health info want health ANSWERS not health SOURCES."[22]

The second major theme explored in the Twitter thread was whether open access is a priority for public libraries. Public libraries often differentiate their mandates from those of academic libraries by referring complex research questions to nearby institutions. Public library websites and resources focus more on monographs, streaming services, and homework help than on scholarly research—particularly involving periodicals. Research inquiries—particularly outside genealogy and local history—make up a small percentage of reference service at public libraries. There is another fundamental difference: academic libraries are involved in the production of open access—through open access funding and institutional repositories—as well as consumption. If public libraries don't have the inherent research production and support mandate of academic libraries, it would seem to follow that open access is a lesser priority.

There's a sentence that's often repeated in the discourse around open access: Publicly funded research should be publicly accessible. This is reflected in open access mandates of government agencies, from the National Science Foundation in the US to the "Tri-Agency" federal granting agencies in Canada. The preamble of the "Tri-Agency Open Access Policy on Publications" states:

> Societal advancement is made possible through widespread and barrier-free access to cutting-edge research and knowledge, enabling researchers, scholars, clinicians, policymakers, private sector and not-for-profit organizations and the *public* to use and build on this knowledge.[23] [emphasis mine]

Those involved in open access are aware that producing open materials doesn't instantaneously lead to increased awareness and use of those materials. Advocacy is vital to the adoption of open access. If, as the Tri-Agencies suggest, barrier-free and timely access to research is vital to societal advancement, is there a role for public libraries in providing that access?

Despite the very real barriers, I would argue that yes, there is a role. While in-depth research inquiries generally make up a small part of the work in public libraries, there are use cases that suggest that better awareness and use of open access resources would benefit the communities public libraries serve.

There's quite a bit of research on the rise of the gig economy in North America, but less well covered is the breadth of the current freelance landscape. In the 2019 Statistics Canada paper, *Measuring the Gig Economy in Canada Using Administrative Data*,[24] demonstrates that over 5 percent of workers in natural and applied sciences and related occupations were self-employed.[25] Freelance and self-employed workers in knowledge sectors are likely to be unaffiliated with a university and yet still have complex research needs. In addition, the last ten or so years have shown a rapid increase in community-led and community-based research, as well as citizen science.[26] Scientific databases in particular are increasingly out of reach of public library collections budgets; supporting community efforts to participate in research requires access to a research collection. Some libraries have created programs and partnerships to broaden access to research materials for the community. These are inventive and valuable partnerships; however, they can have limitations based on the e-resource licenses involved. Advocating for open access removes licensing barriers to providing support for community research.

A second use case is closer to home for many public libraries—What are the research needs of the municipality, and how are they being served? A municipality can have research needs beyond traditional municipal documents such as zoning bylaws. Toronto Public Library has an agreement to provide corporate research services to municipal departments. Inquiries come from numerous municipal areas, from planning and transportation to the Toronto Zoo. Providing research services to stakeholders can be beneficial to the library's profile, and including open access sources when fulfilling research requests makes for a better service. A city zoo employee looking for information on polar bears and climate change modeling can be provided with preprints in EcoEvoRxiv (https://ecoevorxiv.org/) and postprints from institutional and subject repositories as well as paywalled resources the library may have licensed.

The growth of residencies in public libraries is a use case where I see opportunities for advocacy in the consumption and production of open access resources. Traditional writers-in-residence models have been successful in public libraries and have resulted in expanding the model to other subject areas, such makers-in-residence, historians-in-residence, and environmentalists-in-residence. Residence models offer opportunities for community experts to provide programs and information in exchange for a stipend and in some cases a space in which to work on their own projects. Many times these experts wish to work with the public library in order to give back and to broaden general awareness on issues. This makes them likely partners for open access efforts. Can their work with the library be better supported through access to open access materials? Can awareness about the importance of open access be woven into programming and outcomes?

With the rise of austerity, many public libraries have seen their mandate broadened while their resources have been constricted. Advocating that public libraries add another expertise to the growing list, especially one well served by the academic sector, should be done with caution and an eye to sustainability. Public library workers could investigate if there are programs or services that naturally align with open access, like residencies, or if there are simple enhancements that can be implemented to improve access to materials, such as installing Unpaywall and promoting it on public access terminals. After all, public libraries do have a mandate in advocating for equitable access, in promoting literacy, and for providing resources to enable citizens to participate in society. And if open access is about serving the public good, as claimed in the Budapest Open Access Initiative, who better to help fulfill that vision than public libraries and public library workers?

WHY CARE? THERE ARE JOBS?

There have always been jobs tackling scholarly communication in academic libraries, and that continues despite the emergence of roles specifically titled "scholarly communication librarian." No matter where you sit, it can be argued that you are part of the scholarly communication support offered at the institution. Some roles may be more obvious than others (see table 2.1).

TABLE 2.1
Library departmental roles in OA

Department	Obvious Role	Less Obvious	Oh, Really?
Collections	Manage collection budgets and negotiate open access options with traditional publishers	Directly invest in open initiatives with collections budgets	Establish practices leveraging copyright exceptions for faculty course readings
Public Services	Promote OA resources to users	Help faculty share their research	Teach students about the scholarly publishing process and help them question the entire system
Systems/Digital Scholarship	Host the open scholarship tools scholars may wish to use	Build/develop tools to support scholarship at your institution	Push for the inclusion of new forms of scholarship—non-text-based, for example—in tenure and promotion at your institution by developing mechanisms for evaluation and preservation of this new scholarship
Administration (Special note for administrators: Open access initiatives that are not properly resourced are pointless. Vision statements don't magically deliver results, but enough staff certainly could. If this article[a] resonates with you, please keep reading.)	Advocate for open access to university leadership by pushing for policy/strategic support for it	Authorize nuking big deals	Position the library as the experts in the knowledge mobilization field and empower your staff to build their work from that vision

a. Dorothea Salo, "How to Scuttle a Scholarly Communication Initiative," *Journal of Librarianship and Scholarly Communication* 1, no. 4 (2013): eP1075, https://doi.org/10.7710/2162-3309.1075.

One caveat on the job front: often, and perhaps currently in many institutions, scholarly communication jobs focusing on open access often have what Dorothea Salo calls the "C-word" in their title: *coordinator*.[27] The problem with this term isn't so much that coordinating initiatives is something below impossible for scholarly communication folks in libraries, it's that as often as not, there's nothing actually to coordinate. No budget. No dedicated staff. No IT resources. No established service. "Coordinate" all too often means "try to establish a beachhead by begging your new colleagues to vouchsafe you a few minutes of their time now and then, knowing that their supervisors won't tell them to and you have no authority whatever to demand anything of them."[28]

So, yes, one reason some readers might care is that there are jobs, jobs in academic and research libraries and in related professions that support the work of scholarship and its communication. There may not be as many jobs as there are candidates, but scholarly communication is a robust area of librarianship and being well informed about topics in scholarly communication is a definite advantage in applying for many roles in libraries.

WHY CARE? YOU LIKE TO CHALLENGE SYSTEMS

Building the future of open access involves challenging current systems and processes—from how knowledge is created and shared to who can participate, both as authors and as readers.

Challenge Who Gets to Participate

The current scholarly publishing world overwhelmingly uses English, which makes up almost 88 percent of the literature in Neylon and Kramer's study,[29] but only 15 percent of the world are English speakers.[30] Even though much of scholarly publishing is reporting on the publicly funded research done by publicly funded scholars, only institutions with subscriptions to the journal are able to learn from this publicly funded knowledge. These subscriptions are priced to ensure maximum profits for the traditional publisher (remember: authors, peer reviewers, and often editors work for the journal for free), something that can be achieved only by charging readers for access.

Challenge What Scholarship Looks Like

Scholarly publishing, like all publishing, was built in an analog world where print containers dictated a number of the current ways we still operate. But what if we truly took advantage of the move to digital publishing to present scholarship in new ways and break free of the journal/book binary? And, more to the point, how could libraries support access to and preservation of these new forms of scholarship?

Challenge Power and Wealth

As mentioned before, the economic model in scholarly publishing pulls everything from publicly funded institutions—time, collections budgets, and especially labour (and salaries)[31]—to benefit the stockholders of corporate publishers. Libraries have been complicit in this model since the beginning, and that is no longer acceptable. What started off as a radical concept has been co-opted (openwashed) by traditional publishers, and we now see calls for those in the open access movement to begin working together with traditional publishers to find a happy medium. As Ghamandi points out, more polarization and challenges to the ecosystem would yield a more just and equal way of sharing knowledge.[32]

OPEN ACCESS AND CAPITALISM

Charlotte Roh

When Trump was elected in 2016, I began to tell people: "I had thought that the problems in America were like mold on cheese. You cut off the mold, and the rest is fine. But this makes me realize that the problems in America are like mold on bread, and the whole loaf has to be thrown out."

I felt stupid for having realized this so late in my life, even though, like many in the United States, I experienced an education that romanticized Christopher Columbus, Junipero Serra, Theodore Roosevelt, and the whole damn history and present of this current empire. This education, or lack thereof, hurt me in so many ways that I am still discovering them now. In my career in academic publishing, as a Korean American first-generation immigrant working in a prestige creative industry, the model minority myth got me in the door but also kept me underpaid, unpromoted, and underappreciated until my departure into librarianship.

For many BIPOC library workers, librarianship can be a kind of cognitive dissonance. On the one hand, the ALA Spectrum Scholarship has been in place since 1998, demonstrating over twenty years of support for diversity in librarianship. On the other hand, the demographics of librarianship remain decidedly the same, the unshifting statistics a sign of the revolving door of representation. It is important to remember that libraries, though possessing high ideals and doing good work, have been complicit in the injustices perpetuated by the discriminatory laws and ways of doing things.* We pat ourselves on the back for the good we do while leaving the rest untaught, a sideways apology that does little to remediate the structures that may still remain.

Similarly, the open access movement, which owes itself to so much unacknowledged feminized and BIPOC library labor,[33] finds itself arguing in circles about who will pay for what, how will things be authenticated, metrics, and promotion and tenure. When I entered the open access arena, the main topic of conversation seemed to be the *color* of open access (i.e. green archiving or gold publishing, discussed further below), which to me was a baffling and obvious misdirection. Why and how did it matter when or where something was made open access? How was this the argument? It was Arianna Becerril-García, professor in the School of Political and Social Sciences at the Autonomous University of the State of Mexico (UAEM) and the executive director of Redalyc, who clarified things for me: science produced and published in Latin America has been always open access, journals supported by (public) universities and research institutions—government-funded.[34]

---

* I was certainly not taught the history of library segregation in my classes as described in Cheryl Knott's book *Not Free, Not for All: Public Libraries in the Age of Jim Crow* (Amherst, MA: University of Massachusetts Press, 2015).

Let me repeat that again: academic publishing in this part of the Global South has always been open access. The model has existed and still exists, without all the billions of dollars of infrastructure that seem to be necessary according to publishing pundits. The problem is not how we pay for scholarly publishing; the problem is how those in commercial scholarly publishing (namely corporations) will continue to get paid.*

Of course, publishers have since solved that problem by co-opting open access as another revenue stream, expanding their services, and targeting customers who are not as knowledgeable about the scholarly communication ecosystem. As an example, in April 2018, I was slated to speak at the California Academic Research Libraries (CARL) conference. I was told the week of the event that Elsevier was the official sponsor of my plenary and was sent the introductory paragraph that follows:

> Elsevier would like to thank the CARL committee members for the opportunity to support their development in leadership education. Elsevier's Research Intelligence solutions answer the most pressing challenges researchers and research managers face, with innovative solutions that improve an institution's and individual's ability to establish, execute and evaluate research strategy and performance. We work in collaborative partnership to meet your specific needs using SciVal tools, the Pure system, rich data assets, and custom Analytical Services. Our solution supports the three primary pillars of strategic research management workflow by providing reliable data and information to facilitate better decision making. We look forward to learning more about you and how we can work together to address your research management needs.

And then, the day of the conference, the following paragraph was read as an introduction instead:

> Elsevier would like to thank the CARL members for this opportunity to support their development and advocacy of the library community. As a global information analytics company, Elsevier is strongly interested in supporting library programs that provide educational and innovative forums that will serve to strengthen research and scholarly communities. We hope you were able to attend the two sessions led by Linda Galloway, customer consultant from Elsevier, and also a recent librarian. The topics were "Responsible Use of Metrics: The Library Can Help," and "Librarians' Role in Research Performance Analytics." If you missed it or have any questions, feel free to look for Linda or any member of the team.

---

* Arianna Becerril-García went on to make the point that in Latin America, "The tradition of scholarly publishing has not been outsourced to commercial publishers, nor supported by charging authors, ever. I would really like to understand how could the north has let [*sic*] some companies grow in such a way that universities can't control the scholarly publishing enterprise?… We cannot just focus our discussions on how companies of the north will continue being profitable. The APC model brings a risk of widening the gap among researchers of different regions in a global scientific conversation, as well as the risk of breaking the open nature of the scientific communication system of Latin America." Arianna Becerril-García, self-introduction, transcript of livestream, Envisioning a World beyond APCs/BPCs International Symposium, Lawrence, KS, November 17, 2016, https://kuscholarworks.ku.edu/bitstream/handle/1808/22153/KUOASymp16LivestreamTranscript.pdf.

These two introductions targeted different audiences and offered different products. The first, for educational leaders, focuses on research management workflow, data, and decision-making. The second, for rank-and-file librarians, focuses on education and the library and has a more personal touch—connecting conference attendees to the Elsevier rep (a recent librarian!) by name. We should not be surprised, of course, that Elsevier has targeted marketing text for different revenue streams. But I was nonetheless surprised because I so rarely see those varying messages and had forgotten that we as librarians are not the only or most important customers in the Elsevier portfolio. I should have known better, as I have been told on several occasions by Elsevier representatives, that as a publicly traded company, Elsevier is responsible to its shareholders—that is, not librarians, not the academic community, and not the public. This is most vividly demonstrated in Elsevier's involvement in the arms trade, a history that I will never stop bringing up because it is such a potent example of how academic publishing—in fact, academia itself—is grounded in colonialist structures and capitalist values.[35]

This means that the open access movement, as we (or rather I) currently engage with it in the Western context, is also grounded in colonialist structures and capitalist values. We are complicit in reinforcing the dominant and destructive narrative as to what is authoritative, what is valuable, and what is worthy in academic scholarship. We prioritize both the English language and the scholarly text, excluding and marginalizing so many forms of communication and thought. By prioritizing digital open access, we are complicit in all the issues wrapped up in technology, from algorithmic bias to inequities in labor to the environmental impact of e-waste and server farms.

The list of things that have been shown to be problematic in Western academic publishing encompass all of its structures of value: impact factor, citation, altmetrics, editorial and peer review, unpaid labor, indexing and metadata, plagiarism, and more recently, diversity and representation. These all seem like fixable problems, and to the credit of those working in the scholarly communication space, there have been calls to fix them—calls for more transparency, more representation, more human-centered metrics, and more education around these issues. But these issues ignore that we don't want to fix the machine that is actually a cage. We want to break it and climb out to a future that actually exists and communicate our scholarship with each other to be heard, cited, and revolutionized.

WHAT IS OA? HOW DO WE DO IT? WHO DOES IT?

SCHOLARLY PUBLISHING 101

Let's take a minute to learn more about the scholarly publishing process. This section will focus on the process for journal publishing. Monograph publishing is a wildly different beast in almost every way from the creation to the editorial involvement to the marketing of the final publication to help it reach its readership. This will be a high-level sketch of the process since journals use a number of different workflows.

Scholarly journals showcase research done in a specific field. Originally, they were attached to scholarly societies as a way to share research done by members, but now they are more likely owned by a large private holding company (many are very profitable for reasons we'll get into below).

When it comes to journal publishing it is important to remember that for academics, this process is directly tied to their success within the academy thanks to tenure and promotion requirements. (More on this below.) The first scholarly journals in the Western world all arrived in 1665–1666.[36] And though life and research have significantly changed over the past 350 years, journals have not evolved significantly. (They continue to present new research and discoveries, and the bulk of those who are published are men.[37])

SUBMISSION PROCESS

Once an author submits a manuscript, it is typically reviewed by an editor to make sure the work falls within the scope of the journal and meets whatever quality standards the journal has. (Note: One major issue with the quality standards is around language of publication. English is generally considered the lingua franca of research in the Western world, leaving many researchers writing up the results of their work in a second language. How much work is rejected by editors because of related grammar concerns?) If a manuscript is not rejected at this point—called *desk reject*—then it is assigned peer reviewers.

Peer reviewers are experts in the field of the manuscript who will read the manuscript and offer feedback to both the editor and the author. Standard peer review is a double-blind process where all author-identifiers are stripped from the manuscript for the peer reviewers, and the reviews are similarly de-identified for the author. Only the editorial crew know the names. This often poses issues, however, especially in smaller fields, as you can identify a researcher by their research. Perhaps you heard them speak at a conference recently or know of their work because you've cited it in yours—all to say, it's rare that the reviews are truly blind to those involved. In response to the not-so-blind issue, and to grow more transparency within the system, some journals have begun using open peer review. In this process authors and reviewers are named to each other.

Journals typically provide guidance to reviewers to focus on the methodology (Is this sound science?) and the currency (Is this adding something new to the field?) in their reviews. These reviews are meant to support the author in improving the manuscript, but sometimes they come off as an airing of grievances (see every meme referring to "reviewer 2").

Reviewers are asked to make a recommendation for the manuscript: accept (often with minor revisions like restructuring a paragraph), revise and resubmit (the author addresses issues raised by the reviewers and sends it back around for another read), or reject (nope, this isn't up to the journal standards). The revise and resubmit process can have multiple rounds, which affects the length of time between the date the author submitted the manuscript and when it finally appears in print, assuming it is ultimately accepted. But this is all done to ensure the highest quality work is published, so folks roll with it.

PRODUCTION/PUBLICATION PROCESS
Copyright

Once a manuscript is accepted (finally!), the author still has some administrative tasks to complete. In traditional publishing, one of the first is to transfer their copyright to the publisher through a copyright transfer agreement. Now, copyright is jurisdictional; each country has different areas covered when it talks about copyright, but one of the best ways to think about copyright is that it is in fact a bundle of rights, not a single monolithic entity. This is discussed in detail in chapter 1.5, "The Legal and Policy Context." Traditional publishers request the author's copyright in order to reproduce the work (in the journal), to distribute copies of the work (through publishing), and to prepare derivative works of based on the original (this can mean a variety of things, including translations, but also inclusion in a future anthology by the publisher). These agreements often use words like *exclusive* and *irrevocable*. When authors transfer their copyright to a traditional publisher, they give up their rights to do any of those things, including host a version of the article on their lab website, or even email a PDF of the article to students in their classes, unless those rights are specifically articulated in the contract. In essence, the author has given the publisher their work for free, and the publisher can now sell access to it and exercise control over it.

You've likely caught on by now that open access publishers probably have a different tactic when it comes to copyright transfer. Many (though still not all) allow authors to use Creative Commons licenses (discussed below and in 2.3 Open Education) or have simple publishing agreements which are nonexclusive and grant the journal first publication rights as well as an acknowledgement of its initial publication in the journal and the right to distribute it *nonexclusively* through publishing. Can an author post a version of the article on their website? Yup. Can they email to students? You bet. Can they share the work with the world without access barriers? A big YES.

Fees

Here's where for-profit publishers start harping about the fees for open access journals (often called APCs or "article processing charges") and why obviously the traditional way is better since in those scenarios authors don't pay (except when they do; there's a long history of author-facing fees that existed before open access and still exist to a lesser extent, such as page charges for colour images and so forth). Worth noting: almost all traditional publishers now have an entire sector of their business which publishes open access journals charging author fees. These companies make billions of dollars, so if anyone was in a position to waive the fees it would be, well, them.

Publishing costs money. Though some on the internet will tell you that AI and various gig workers can do absolutely everything these days, journals are run by people who do everything from manage the web servers to copyediting to layout to rights management. Open access journals have many of these roles which are not supported through the same revenue models of traditional publishers (library subscriptions), so they have sought out other ways to raise funds—typically through charging authors a publication fee.

Production

Once all the administrative side is taken care of, the journal's copy editors and layout editors work with the manuscript to get it ready for publication. While publishing frequency varies significantly, many journals have adopted a rolling publication schedule, meaning that articles are published when they have been copy-edited and laid out and not held for a certain issue or volume. This is great for authors as it is likely the manuscript has been with the publisher for a good chunk of time (sometimes years!), so getting it online—and citable—as soon as it's ready is better than waiting for the next issue.

tl;dr

- Author submits manuscript to journal.
- Journal sends to some folks to read it and share their thoughts.

- Journal can accept, request revisions, or reject it.
- If manuscript is accepted, author may have to transfer copyright to the publisher and/or may have to pay some fees to cover the publishing.
- Journal publishes article.
- Everyone celebrates.

BUT WHAT ARE PREPRINTS?

Preprints are in the news a lot in 2023, especially thanks to the pandemic. They have long been used in the physics, math, and the biomedical sciences as a way to share new research as soon as an author writes up the work. Though authors may feel there are ninety-two versions of their work, in the publishing world the focus is on three: preprint, post-print/author accepted manuscript, and publisher final/version of record. A preprint of an article is the finished manuscript prior to peer review. The post-print/author accepted manuscript (AAM) is the manuscript after all reviews, with all changes made by the author, as accepted for publication. And the publisher final or sometimes version of record is the version once the AAM is copy-edited and laid out for publication. (Curious about the difference between the preprint and the publisher final? Spoiler alert: Klein and colleagues' research shows that "the text contents of the scientific papers generally changed very little from their pre-print to final published versions."[38])

Disciplines with a preprint culture leveraged the arrival of the internet to share their work even further by creating repositories for their work, like arXiv (founded in 1991). As this work is shared prior to formal peer review done by a journal, it can be a way for a researcher to stake a claim to an idea (preventing the dreaded "scoop" of someone getting published sooner—see more about the tenure and promotion system below) and invite feedback from their community. Authors can then go on to publish the work in a journal (assuming the journal or publisher doesn't prohibit the submission of preprints, which some traditional publishers do) and begin the process described above.

Preprint repositories have proliferated over the past decade and are seen as a viable publishing mechanism in some fields. Granting agencies have slowly begun accepting preprints as part of an author's scholarly record. Reporters have begun looking at preprint servers as a spot for breaking research during the COVID pandemic. Though the research is not formally peer reviewed, it is the quickest way to make scholarship relevant to the current global health crisis available to the international community.

THE ROLE OF THE TENURE AND PROMOTION SYSTEM IN SCHOLARLY PUBLISHING

The publishing process is the proving ground for many tenure-track academics, much more so than teaching courses and mentoring students. This is partially because publishing is an easily quantified component of a rather nebulous process and because it is a long-standing structure around which universities have built many legacy requirements. Essentially, researchers need to publish to prove their value to other researchers in order to continue to be funded to do their research (so they can publish to prove their value to others…).

This results in statements such as "It doesn't matter if the public can't read my research, so long as my tenure review committee has access" and "The chair of my department publishes in *Journal X*, so best for me to be found there too" and (my personal favourite) "I need to publish four articles this year, or one in *Nature*." And this is where the concept of an impact factor for journals continues to enjoy traction. Impact factors are meant to show the impact of a journal title within a field by quantifying the number of citations of articles in the journal over the previous two year period. It's one of the many quantifications for impact which can be gamed (if you publish an article that is controversial, you'll get a lot of citations too, though not necessarily in a positive way) yet still very popular when it comes to determining the impact of a researcher's scholarship.

Open access journals tend to be newer, so there's less legacy "My supervisor published in this journal, so I should too," and often impact factors are lower because many journals are still in their first decade of production. But! There are researchers who have focused their careers on publishing solely in open access venues (as mentioned above, Erin McKiernan is a great example).[39]

FLAVOURS OF OPEN/COLOUR

As open access concepts were being codified, a number of terms were adopted, one of the main ones being a colour-coding system for different flavours of open access. Originally there were two colours: green and gold. You'll still hear these terms mentioned, and often framed incorrectly, so to be clear, see table 2.2.

TABLE 2.2
Colours of OA.

Colour	Description
Green	This route makes scholarship openly available through deposit in a repository or a website.
Gold	This route makes scholarship available through publishing in an open access journal.
Bronze	Articles are temporarily available openly on the publisher site, and reuse rights and copyright terms are unclear.
Diamond/Platinum	These are open journals which have no author processing charges.
Hybrid (not a colour, I know)	These are toll-access journals which have some open access articles for authors who choose to pay the APC.

HOW DO WE MAKE WORK OPEN?

While it would be wonderful if every researcher shared their work openly through repositories or open access journals, making it discoverable and accessible to all with internet access, we are not there yet. YET. In the meantime a number of mechanisms have been established to help facilitate making research open to the world.

Typically, toll-access publishers make their titles available to subscribers. The largest chunk of subscription dollars comes from academic libraries that pay the publishers for access to their corpus of articles. Though this model may feel familiarly like other subscription services we have in our lives—like movie and music streaming services—there is one key difference: the creator of the content being sold is not remunerated for their work. Scholarly publishers almost never pay the authors for their work (and when they do, it's often in the form of wee royalty cheques). They also don't pay the peer reviewers, and often the editors are doing this as part of the service component of their tenure and promotion process as well. Then the publisher sells this content back to the institutions, which have been paying the salaries of the authors, reviewers, and editors, via library subscriptions. To add insult to this injury, the agreements often come with significant yearly increases in subscription costs, increases above inflation and well above the increase in library collections budgets. This rise in costs has been termed the "serials crisis" and has been an area of concern for libraries for over twenty years. The cost of journals is significant to the support of open access for very pragmatic reasons: if we all agree that publishing costs money for the actual labour of the staff involved in the process, then adding the costs to support open access journals to the ever-increasing subscriptions at the library makes for an untenable future.

In a bid to move the needle toward open while managing costs, a number of new models have been developed—though still with the publisher protecting its bottom line.

TRANSFORMATIVE AGREEMENTS

Transformative agreements are meant to move the journal-publishing model toward full open access. This model uses subscription fees to fund some open access work at the publisher but does not radically change the business structure. The publisher will still have toll-access content; it merely uses the fees paid in this model to defray APCs or to defray the expected revenue it loses from making articles open. An oft-used example of this model is called "read-and-publish." With a read-and-publish agreement, the authors at the subscribing university are able to publish openly with that publisher with a discounted or waived APC, and members of the university community are able to read subscribed content from the publisher. There are a number of problems with this model,[40] not the least of which is that it is unlikely it will actually transform the business model for traditional publishers, as they continue to make profits in line with Apple and Google.

SUBSCRIPTION DISCOUNTS

To defend against cries of double-dipping (where the library both pays the APC for authors AND the subscription cost for the content), publishers may offer discounts on APCs for authors from subscribing institutions or a number of free APCs for each subscription period. While this can be beneficial for the institution, the management of these programs often falls to the subscribing library. Raising awareness of the discounts, ensuring the opportunity is used by researchers, and, in the case of the APC waivers, letting researchers know when they have been exhausted for the year (and dealing with their disappointment) is all extra work for the scholarly communication and collections librarians.

RIGHTS RETENTION STRATEGIES

In some cases, institutions have established policies that their researchers may not be allowed to transfer their copyright to the publisher, or must retain sufficient rights to enable open sharing, and that they must make the author's accepted manuscript openly available in order to continue working at and receiving funding from the institution. This can be effective, as the researcher must share their work as a condition of employment and thus must consider where they publish their work to be able to meet this condition. Recently members of cOAlition S, a consortium of national research agencies and funders from twelve European countries, have adopted this strategy.[41] Authors at these institutions are not allowed to transfer their full copyright to the publisher and must license the AAM with a Creative Commons license. In another model, faculties at a growing number of institutions have adopted institutional rights-retention open access policies, or Harvard-style open access policies, because Harvard was the first institution to establish such a policy. In these policies, the faculty, usually through faculty governance, agree to grant their university a nonexclusive, irrevocable license to share their work. The Coalition of Open Access Policy Institutions, or COAPI, supports the development and implementation of faculty open access policies in North America.[42]

Creative Commons Licenses

Creative Commons is an organization founded in 2001 which has developed a number of licenses creators can use for their work. These licenses are legal devices which make clear to the public which rights the creator is retaining and which are waived in favour of making work openly available. Many open access publishers have adopted CC licenses instead of copyright transfer agreements, allowing authors to retain their intellectual property. Toll publishers have begun to adopt CC licenses when they publish open work or have developed their own branded licenses that look and feel like CC, but are most certainly not. (And even when they do adopt actual CC licenses, they do so in such confusing ways that many authors are unsure what they can actually do with the work they created. Josh Bolick read through all the legalese and published information for librarians to navigate some confusing wording to actually make work more open![43])

WHAT PUTS THE "OPEN" INTO "OPEN ACCESS"? CREATIVE COMMONS LICENSES, FAIR USE, AND RESEARCH IN THE TWENTY-FIRST CENTURY

Meredith Jacob

Open access publishing is one of the key innovations of the last twenty years in scholarly communication, but there is a broad family of activities that can fall under the umbrella of the open access label. Often faculty and staff rely on librarians for guidance about scholarly publishing options, copyright, and research methods, so it is useful for librarians to understand the landscape of open access, its relationship to the copyright law system, the use of Creative Commons licenses, and the ways that different choices affect the research landscape.

Throughout the teaching and research life cycle, librarians are key advisors to faculty, students, and staff about how to access, use, and disseminate research. When conducting research, faculty turn to librarians to get access to articles and to conduct large-scale search and computational research. When new research is being published, librarians answer questions about publishing agreements and compliance with funder open access policies. And when that research is incorporated into open educational resources, librarians are on the team that helps answer questions about Creative Commons licensing, copyright, and citation.

WHAT MAKES SOMETHING OPEN ACCESS?

The core goal of the open access (OA) movement is to increase the ability of researchers and the public to benefit from the knowledge generated by global research efforts. As the OA movement began gaining momentum in 2002–2004, the ability to access and read articles was the primary goal of most advocates. Over the next nearly twenty years, that landscape has evolved with the development of computational research techniques, rise of platformization, and the use of AI and other analytic techniques to guide reading, and as a result, what comprises meaningful access has changed.

OA policies can vary based on who owns the copyright to the articles, who can access the articles to read, what conditions are required for access, and what activities other than standard reading can be done.

- **Ownership**—Copyright can be transferred to the publisher or can be retained by the author. Different versions may have different use permissions and conditions—for example, the submitted version versus accepted version versus final published version.

- **Access**—Are the articles available online for full worldwide access (including findability at the publisher's site, non-geolocked access)?

- **Activities**—Is a sign-in or other agreement to terms of service required for access? (Can users download articles in bulk? Are there limitations on automated research on articles?) Are there contractual limits to the ability to exercise existing limitations and exceptions in copyright law, such as fair use or fair dealing?

- **Licensing**—Is the public given an open license (such as a Creative Commons license) to use the article without copyright restrictions?

WHY DO THESE QUESTIONS MATTER?

When a student or a researcher clicks on a paywalled article, the first frustration they encounter is the inability to read the article. But individually reading articles is only one (shrinking) part of what researchers, librarians, professors, and the public may want or need to do with an article.

When an article is posted for free, online, all of the baseline all-rights-reserved copyright restrictions can still apply to the article. Additionally, the user may have agreed to terms and conditions for access that further assert limitations on their ability to use the article or share it with others.

In contrast, articles licensed under a Creative Commons (CC) license give to the licensee (the user or reader) the ability to exercise all the rights under copyright law as long as they comply with the license terms. Additionally, the CC licenses do not affect any of the underlying freedoms granted to users under their national law copyright system—fair use in the United States; fair dealing in Canada, the UK, and some others; and specific exceptions for research and study in many civil law countries.

WHAT ARE THE CREATIVE COMMONS LICENSES, AND WHAT DO YOU MEAN BY "LICENSE TERMS"?

The Creative Commons licenses are standard open copyright licenses. Like traditional one-to-one copyright licenses, they work within the established framework of copyright law to structure the transaction where a licensor (the author or copyright owner) gives the licensee (the user, researcher, etc.) the legal ability to do some or all of the things controlled by copyright law (like distribute, make copies, display, or make new derivative works). In standard copyright licensing, licenses are negotiated between individuals or companies. In contrast, Creative Commons licenses are from one entity (the author or owner) to any member of the public, as long as they meet the terms of the license. When an author uses a CC license they are saying to the world, "You can do anything you want with this work, as long as you meet the terms of the license."

The Creative Commons licenses exist in six types that are defined by four different combinable license terms. The least restrictive license is the Creative Commons Attribution License (CC BY). Other licenses can add more restrictive terms, but all licenses retain the attribution requirement.

Those license terms and the acronyms that are used for each are:

BY—Attribution

This license term is shared by all the Creative Commons licenses and requires that any user of the material who needs permission under copyright law provide attribution to the original work and author.[44]

SA—ShareAlike

The ShareAlike license term requires that any derivative works based on the original work must be licensed under the same license as that parent work. This means the specific parent license and not any Creative Commons license of the new author's choosing.[45]

NC—NonCommercial

The NonCommercial license term requires that any uses of the work are not primarily intended for or directed toward commercial advantage or monetary compensation. The evaluation of noncommercial depends upon the use, not the user. So, for example, uses at not-for-profit institutions or educational institutions are not necessarily always either commercial or noncommercial. Rather, it depends on what is being done. The interpretation of what is or is not a commercial use varies significantly by country and community of practice.[46]

ND—NoDerivatives

The No Derivatives license term prohibits the distribution of derivative works based on the original work. The ND license language contains specific technological exceptions to allow, for example, for images to be resized and for format shifting to occur.[47]

Public Domain Dedication (CC-O) and Public Domain Marker

There are two more Creative Commons "licenses" aside from the six primary licenses that use the terms described above. The CC-O (zero) license is a dedication to the public domain, and thus the creators associated with a CC-O licensed item have waived all their rights to the work worldwide under copyright law, thus essentially placing it in the public domain. The CC-PD or Public Domain Marker is used to indicate that an item is believed to be in the public domain. While both CC-O and CC-PD indicate work in the public domain, they differ in an important way. CC-O is used to place work that belongs to the licensor, or rights holder, in the public domain by waiving their rights. CC-PD is used to indicate that work is already in the public domain, such as a collection of late nineteenth-century photography in an archive.

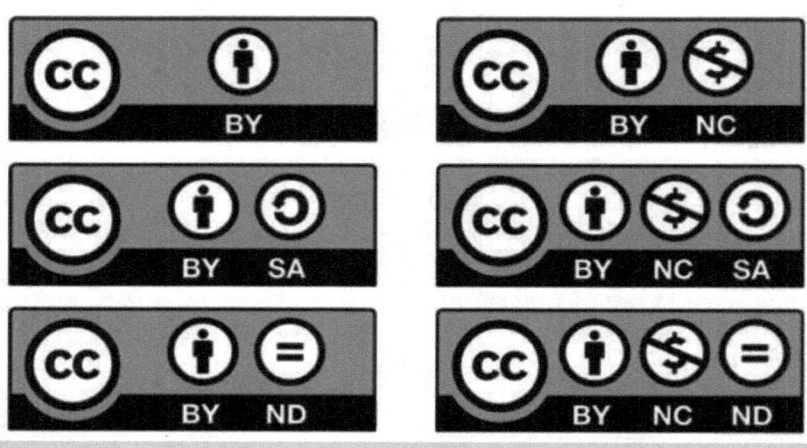

HOW DO CREATIVE COMMONS LICENSES INTERACT WITH OTHER LIMITATIONS AND EXCEPTIONS TO COPYRIGHT IN RESEARCH AND EDUCATION?

As noted above, the Creative Commons licenses work within the existing copyright law system, rather than instead or outside of it. In every national law system, there are a set of limitations and exceptions to copyright law. There is a structure of limitations that lays out what the public can do with copyrighted materials in certain circumstances or for certain purposes. In many common law countries, like the UK, Canada, and the United States, these exceptions may be broader, such as fair dealing or fair use. In other countries, including the majority of civil law countries, these exceptions are often more specific, with individual exceptions for quotation, private study, education, parody, and so on.

The Creative Commons licenses make clear that they do not preempt or overrule any limitations or exceptions to copyright laws that already exist in each national law jurisdiction. So, for example, the user in the United States can fully rely on fair use to allow them to do things that would not otherwise be permitted by the license terms. For example, if a user wanted to, they could create a parody built on a work that was licensed under CC BY-ND, assuming that parody was permitted by fair use. So they didn't need the permission of the license and are not bound by the no derivatives term.

In the context of scholarly communication and teaching, some activities that users will want to conduct are commonly permitted by copyright law, while other research techniques are permitted by the structure of copyright law in some countries, but not others. Every country has a quotation right, enabling the core academic practices referencing and citing preexisting work. In contrast, text and data mining for research, also called nonconsumptive research, can be conducted under existing limitations to exceptions to copyright law in some countries, including the US. In other countries, however, this is not the case, and open licenses may be required to grant researchers in those jurisdictions the ability to do this sort of scholarship.

When a scholar writes an article about twentieth-century visual art, they may rely on fair use for the inclusion of images and quotations, then publish that article under either a CC BY license or and all-rights-reserved copyright. A later scholar might be permitted to do data mining research to evaluate how often artists from the Global South were discussed in scholarship, and whether they need the open license is determined by whether they are in a jurisdiction that has fair use or another limitation and exception to copyright law that permits text and data mining for research, or if they have to rely on the permissions granted by the author in the form of the CC license.

Beyond scholarly communication, research articles, and the images, graphs, and data within them, are also an important input into open educational resources (OER—discussed in chapter 2.3, "Open Education"). The OER community works to release textbooks and other teaching and learning materials under Creative Commons licenses to improve access to education, give professors and teachers more control over pedagogy, and allow for materials to be updated, remixed, and redistributed. While fair use and other user's rights permit many inclusions into OER, it is also important to make scholarly research as available as possible as an input into OER by advocating for open licenses whenever possible.

WHAT DOES THIS MEAN FOR THE FUTURE OF RESEARCH AND TEACHING?

Because the ability to meaningfully interact with scholarly literature goes beyond merely reading single articles online, the ownership, permissions, and access terms for scholarly articles matter. When authors sign publishing agreements and when librarians and library leadership agree to journal licensing deals, they should consider the full range of ways that articles may be used. Open access strategies that include open licensing ensure that new content is available for the widest possible use, while still relying on robust limitations and exceptions to copyright for material that is not available under an open license.

APC Funds

As mentioned above, one of the ways that open access journals fund their operations is through charging article processing charges (APCs). These costs, however, can be paid through a number of different avenues. Many funding agencies allow APCs as legitimate expenses out of grants, as part of knowledge mobilization (a very neoliberal term for "sharing your research") for the grant. University faculties and departments may have dedicated funding to support open publishing, and sometimes the university research office may also have a fund. In most cases where institutional funds are available for APCs, it is through the library and often carved out of the library budget or jointly funded by libraries and a research office.

Managing an APC fund requires significant investment in labour, regardless of where the actual money comes from. And how that money is distributed can be complicated. Say you've been allocated $100,000 to support APCs for your university for the year. If APCs are currently hovering at about $1,000 (that's a cheap one—*Nature* currently has an APC of US $11,000+[48]), do you fund 100 researchers fully, 200 researchers at 50 percent, or a combo of 100 percent for early career researchers (who are less likely to have grant funding) and less for more established researchers? And what do you do with the researcher who has been accepted to *Nature*? Give him 10 percent of the APC even though this is the premier journal in his field and without more he won't be able to publish?

Partnerships

Funding open access requires significant management at the institutional level. Partnership models were developed by a number of OA publishers to ease this management. Through these partnerships, all work is OA with APCs. Essentially the publisher determines the amount of money it needs to operate each year, and institutions agree to partner and fund to cover the costs. The true costs of OA publishing are in flux, with a push to look at it in a more holistic sense than simply a cost-per-article transaction.[49]

An example of the membership model is the Open Library of the Humanities (OLH), which publishes both journals and monographs with zero author fees. Its Library Partnership Subsidy model sees partners share the cost of fully open access publishing. OLH also helps currently toll-access journals flip to OA by supporting the transition editorially and technically.

WHO DOES OA?

There are a number of players in the open access world. Authors are the core of the scholarly publishing system, and more of them are challenging the legacy processes of the system.

Funders—Increasingly we are seeing funding agencies adopt open access requirements for all funded research. The site Sherpa Juliet (a project of Jisc in the UK) hosts a list of research funder policies.[50] Ensuring funded research is another way for funding agencies to evaluate the impact of their funding, and work that is more openly available may be cited more.[51]

Governments—In countries where most universities are public institutions, governments can play a leading role in making work open by signing transformative agreements. (The Netherlands has a significant list.[52])

Institutions—Research and academic institutions often fund APCs for their community in some way, but they, and specifically academic libraries, also offer a number of OA-related services. Many academic libraries manage research repositories for those who want to make their work available through self-archiving. Library-based publishing supports OA by supporting actual journal publishing. (Support can be anything from hosting the software for journal production all the way to an established OA press with full editorial and production capabilities.) Libraries also offer services to help authors meet the funding agency requirements for open access, resulting in library staff who are well versed in both the legalese of funding agency contracts and the myriad services available to researchers to meet those requirements. The Library Publishing Coalition (LPC) has a number of great resources.[53]

Scholarly societies—The genesis of much of scholarly publishing came out of scholarly societies, where members of the society would share their research with other members through publishing in the society's journal. Though many societies have shifted to conferences as a significant revenue source, journal subscriptions (often included as part of society memberships) still remain key to funding the operations of the society. The prospect of making the journal OA and no longer a bonus of membership is often hard for societies to even consider.

UNBUNDLE WITH CARE: CAPACITATING OPEN ACCESS ONE TASK AT A TIME

Marcel LaFlamme

There's a strand of open culture, enabled by the information and communication technologies with which it is intertwined, that emphasizes disaggregation: unlocking potential by turning wholes into parts. Think of SPARC urging authors to regard copyright for their scholarly works as a bundle of rights, some of which they may wish to retain.[54] Think of the libraries challenging the once-dominant model of the Big Deal, canceling high-dollar packages with commercial publishers in favor of a smaller spend on the titles they actually want. Indeed, think about the logic of open educational resources like this one, which can be used as a complete textbook but are also designed to be chopped up and reassembled to meet the particular needs of teachers and students.

Of course, there is a dark side to this appetite for unbundling. The media scholar Gary Hall has warned about the "Uberification of the university,"[55] as platforms and services hawked by the private sector exacerbate long-term trends away from secure employment to increasingly position workers at knowledge institutions—including librarians—as freelancers perpetually on the lookout for the next gig. It is, as Hall points out, one thing when institutions that frustrate us are being disrupted and another when those forces of disruption arrive at our doorstep. In this section, though, I want to suggest that a selective, mission-driven unbundling of the scholarly communication services provided by academic libraries can capacitate and sustain open scholarship. I am writing from the vantage point of a scholar-publisher, having served for four years as the managing editor of *Cultural Anthropology*, a prominent society-owned journal that flipped to open access in 2014. In reflecting on the diverse, piecemeal forms of support from libraries that the journal received along the way, I hope to make the case for unbundling with care—embracing flexibility and modularity in the delivery of services while defending the uniquely integrative role of the library within the broader scholarly communication system.

By the early years of the twenty-first century, anthropologists were actively discussing open access publishing models: the creation of the now-defunct website OpenAccessAnthropology.org in 2006 marked an early effort to establish a hub for advocacy within the discipline. The 2007 decision by the American Anthropological Association (AAA) to partner with the commercial publisher Wiley-Blackwell was seen by many as a step backward for open access, but in 2012 the AAA agreed to allow one of its twenty-plus sections to ungate its journal as a kind of demonstration project. At that time the Society for Cultural Anthropology (SCA) was the only section of the larger association to put forward a proposal. So in the months between that proposal's approval and the publication of *Cultural Anthropology*'s first open-access issue, an organization with the equivalent of one full-time staff position had to figure out how to become a publisher in its own right.

Now, there's a variant of this story in which libraries would swoop in to save the day. But that isn't what happened—at least, not exactly. *Cultural Anthropology*'s editors at the time, who were based at Duke University, had reached out to their library system about securing institutional support for the journal even before the move to open access was in view. The Duke University Libraries had agreed to host the instance of Open Journal Systems (OJS) that *Cultural Anthropology* was using to manage submissions and reviews, as well as to play a role in preserving the short-form and supplemental content that the SCA was publishing alongside its journal. Once the journal itself needed a new point of distribution, a logical option would have been to fold it into Duke's existing library publishing program. But the SCA had just made a significant investment in a custom content management system for its widely admired website. Rather than go the standard library publishing route, then, the SCA asked Duke to continue capacitating its activities in the background while the society retrofitted its website with the features needed to serve as a home for the journal itself.

The launch of an open access *Cultural Anthropology* in February 2014 was hailed as a success and a bellwether. Yet a core feature of the journal's editorial structure would soon put pressure on the organization of its production processes. Since the journal's inception, its editorship has rotated every four years, an arrangement thought to discourage parochialism and promote an influx of new ideas. While a rotating editorship has intellectual advantages, it complicates the formation of lasting library partnerships if a journal's affiliation with the library's parent institution is taken to be a precondition. Thus, when a new editorial collective based at Rice University took the reins of *Cultural Anthropology* in 2015, the Duke University Libraries would have been well within their rights to discontinue the hosting and preservation services that they were providing. The fact that Duke continued to provide those services—not on the basis of the editors' e-mail addresses but on the basis of the libraries' support for scholar-led open access— planted the seed for other partnerships to follow.

When I was hired as managing editor, the Rice collective charged me with realizing its vision for a new section of the journal known as Sound + Vision, which would feature articles with embedded audio and video materials. I knew that whatever technical solution we adopted would need to ensure durable access to the media objects that we would be, in effect, admitting to the scholarly record. A friend pointed me toward the open source media management system Avalon, which was developed by the libraries at Indiana University Bloomington and Northwestern University. Indiana, in particular, is well known for its commitment to collecting ethnographic recordings, and so I approached its library system about the idea of building Avalon into our journal's production processes—a new use case for the tool—and hosting media content on our behalf. The partnership was supposed to include a modest amount of funding for Avalon development from the AAA, which was sadly rescinded when Wiley announced plans to develop a parallel product. Despite this setback, Indiana has continued to host audio and video materials for *Cultural Anthropology* free of charge (again, despite the absence of any formal connection to the journal).

By 2018, the SCA's bespoke content management system was beginning to show its age, and a new editorial team distributed across three institutions began to plan for its successor. Rather than searching for a single all-purpose platform, we decided to integrate a reader-facing instance of OJS with a content management system called Craft; thanks to a unifying set of design elements and a federated search tool, the two halves of the site still feel like one platform to most visitors. Yet what we underestimated was the complexity of ingesting legacy content into these new systems, and it was here that library support again played a crucial role. *Cultural Anthropology* had, for years, offered curated collections of previously published articles, which are accompanied by original content that highlights connections between articles from the journal's back files. OJS, at the time, lacked the functionality to assemble such collections. But through funding provided by the library at the College of William and Mary, where one of the journal's current editors teaches, a Categories feature was developed and added to the latest version of OJS. This one-time investment not only secured ongoing access to digital content that might otherwise have disappeared, but also made this new feature available to the thousands of other publications that use OJS.

Looking back, then, what commonalities can be seen across the forms of library support that *Cultural Anthropology* has received since its transition to open access? I would describe them as partial and modular, taking on specific tasks rather than trying to offer comprehensive solutions. The mechanisms for accomplishing these tasks vary, with a mixture of cash and in-kind support as well as more intangible exchanges of expertise and encouragement. The duration of these commitments can be open-ended, but they carry no ironclad guarantee of permanence; instead, both journal and library acknowledge the constraints on each other and agree, if needed, to wind things down in a way that doesn't cause harm. What animates these arrangements is a willingness to define the library's stakeholders expansively and to think beyond one-size-fits-all service delivery, to meet scholar-led publications where they are rather than trying to reengineer them. At the heart of these encounters is an ethical vision of interdependence that eschews coercion and control.

If you are drawn to a practice of scholarly communication librarianship that embraces what I have described here as unbundling with care, my advice would be to start by taking stock of the services that your library could provide to open access publications and then assess the effort that it would take to deliver them on a modular basis. Be clear-eyed about the time and energy that will go into understanding a publication's needs and getting its systems to talk to yours. Familiarize yourself with the growing body of scholarship on microwork—Mary Gray and Siddharth Suri's 2019 book *Ghost Work* is a good place to start[56]—to make sure that this service model also provides you with the credit and fulfillment that you deserve. Don't be shy about setting boundaries, up to and including a policy on the nature and scope of partnerships that your library is in a position to entertain. But do try to think creatively about what capacitating open access means, even when the ask is more obscure or less transformational than the one you might have wished for.

A couple of caveats, in closing. First, all three of the libraries whose support for *Cultural Anthropology* I discuss above are at US-based R1 or R2 institutions.* While libraries at such institutions surely have an important role to play in capacitating open access, I believe that scholar-led publications would be less beholden to the internal politics of a small number of patrons and, critically, more accountable to the lived realities of the vast majority of teachers and students if they were able to leverage a broader base of institutional support. To be clear, unbundling with care does not mean that every library can or should seek to capacitate open access in the same way; further research is needed on how to tap into the distinctive strengths of libraries at teaching-focused institutions, non-US institutions, and so on in a responsible and equitable way.

Finally, the approach to capacitating open access that I have sketched with reference to *Cultural Anthropology* is a basically dyadic one, which presumes a single publication and a single library. I have seen firsthand that there is value in this approach. But I also want to underscore the value of collective action, where publications band together to benefit from economies of scale and where libraries support portfolios of such publications rather than providing a different widget to each individual title. If there is one strand of open culture that emphasizes disaggregation, then there is another that concerns itself with the constitution of new collectivities. Anthropology has, to date, been less successful than other fields in harnessing the potential of this second strand. But, to the extent that it manages to do so in the future, libraries will be key accomplices.

FURTHER READING

Mangiafico, Paolo, and Kevin L. Smith. "Reason, Risk, and Reward: Models for Libraries and Other Stakeholders in an Evolving Scholarly Publishing Ecosystem." *Cultural Anthropology* 29, no. 2 (2014): 216–35. https://doi.org/10.14506/ca29.2.03.

Stapleton, Suzanne C. "A Team Approach: Library Publishing Partnerships with Scholarly Societies." *Journal of Librarianship and Scholarly Communication* 7, no. 1 (2019): eP2326. https://doi.org/10.7710/2162-3309.2326.

---

*   The Carnegie Classification of Institutions of Higher Education categorizes doctorate-granting universities in the United States with very high research activity as R1 and high research activity as R2. Typically, such institutions are also among the best resourced.

A NOTE ON PREDATORY PUBLISHERS

There's another player in the open access world, and you'll hear the term quite often: predatory publishers. As with any other field, there are bad actors. Predatory publishers are publishers with deceptive practices, which claim to be supporting open access but really just want to get the article processing charges. At one point there was an attempt to create a list of these bad actors that researchers could consult prior to making submission decisions. The existence of any good/bad list will always be subject to manipulation and bias: after all, what I might think is predatory might be normal for the next person.

Signs of a predatory journal include

- mail-merged cold-calling emails which appear in research inboxes asking them to submit a manuscript (though how this differs from "special issues" of traditional publishers, where researchers are invited to submit their work, is fuzzy)
- promises of blisteringly fast turnaround times ("Send us your manuscript and, if accepted, it will be published next week.")
- unclear peer-review standards
- a slick website with no real scholarly content but a lot of search engine optimization
- an editorial board with names of well-known researchers who have not actually been invited to be part of the editorial board (You'll know this only if you do some checking.)

Scholarly communication librarians spend a lot of time talking about predatory publishers with researchers, and not nearly enough time evaluating the practices of traditional publishers.

THE UNDECIDABLE NATURE OF PREDATORY PUBLISHING†

Samuel Moore

The term *predatory publisher* reveals a limit of language—or rather it asks too much of language. It seeks a binary separation between *predatory* and *non-predatory* where no such separation can exist, ultimately illustrating more about the motivations and hidden biases of the accuser than the supposedly predatory journal at hand. We therefore need another way to conceptualise the practices that *predatory publishing* seeks to describe.

The limitations of the term are on display in a preprint circulated by Severin and colleagues titled "Who Reviews for Predatory Journals? A Study on Reviewer Characteristics."[57] The study used a review tracking service called Publons to identify researchers who have declared to have reviewed for journals the authors consider to be predatory. They conclude: "The profiles of scholars who review for predatory journals tend to resemble those scholars who publish their research in these outlets: they tend to be young and inexperienced researchers who are affiliated with institutions in developing regions."[58]

† This piece was originally published on the author's blog, https://www.samuelmoore.org/2020/03/12/the-undecidable-nature-of-predatory-publishing/. Used with permission.

According to the analysis, predatory journals both publish the work and rely on the reviewing expertise of the same groups of inexperienced researchers based in developing regions. This leads the authors to conclude that a possible explanation is that "predatory journals have become an integral part of the workflow for many scholars in low- and lower-middle income countries."[59] The kinds of people publishing in these journals are demographically similar to those reviewing for them.

The authors base their definition of *predatory* on Cabell's Predatory Reports, a proprietary database containing journals identified as "potentially not following scientific publication standards or expectations on quality, peer reviewing, or proper metrics."[60] The authors make it clear that predation is not a "simple binary phenomenon" and that some classified journals may exist in a "grey zone" between predatory and legitimate. As with much humanities and social science research, when something isn't a binary, then it is often conceived as a spectrum.

But the problem with the authors' strategy is that their analysis is still conducted on a binary between predatory and non-predatory, rather than a spectrum of questionable practices. Because of course, if the authors were to analyse journals along this spectrum, then they would have to move outside the list provided by Cabell's toward all journals too. We only have to look at websites like Retraction Watch or various sting articles to know that bad practice occurs across all forms of publishing, not just those identified by Cabell's, the now-defunct Beall's list, or whoever else may have a financial or ideological interest in accusations of predation. We may also consider the extractive nature of publisher profiteering to be a similar kind of bad practice that impacts on the quality of the research published.

I'm not in any way questioning the authors' motivations with this study (and they recognise some of these concerns in a *Nature* story about the article), but rather highlighting that the study of bad publishing practice cannot be conducted according to whether or not a journal is predatory. This is especially important as the journals that are identified as predatory are most often those from outside the Global North. There are always colonial and racial overtones to the analysis of predatory publishers that—consciously or not—separate them from the "trustworthy" outlets in Europe and North America, when, in fact, any study of trustworthiness in publishing should not be limited to publishers already identified as predatory.

So the term *predatory publisher* is an aporia: the moment you define an organisation as predatory is the moment the term collapses and reveals the motivation to decide in advance which publishers are good and which are bad (often according to geographical boundaries). But this issue cannot be decided in advance—it is undecidable and so is continually open to interpretation and shifting context. Either publishing is always-already a predatory practice, or we have to find a different way of analysing trustworthiness.

OA IN PRACTICE

You'll notice that a lot of the conversation around open access revolves around the technology used to make this work available. The arrival of new dissemination venues, like the internet, required publishers to adopt new publishing infrastructure. Concurrently, researchers eager to share their research also developed tools and web spaces to make this a reality. While initially spaces like arXiv were created to host open content, as publishing evolved, the integration of peer review, new dissemination possibilities, and the production of publications via the web also grew. Posada and Chen give us a snapshot of what they call the "academic knowledge production process."[61]

Within the section that Posada and Chen identify as the "traditional publisher role" is where we have seen an explosion in tools. In keeping with the concepts around open access, many of these tools are open source, and funded or supported through academic labour and institutions (see table 2.3).

TABLE 2.3
Tools for OA

Tool	Created By	Used By	Why It's Important
Author Addendum[a]	Scholarly Publishing and Academic Resources Coalition (really just SPARC)	Authors	The addendum supports authors in retaining their rights to their research. Upon acceptance of an article, authors return this addendum with the publication agreement sent by the traditional publisher, requesting to retain certain rights to their publication (such as making the work available in an open access repository). It's a simple fillable PDF making clear the rights for the publisher and for the author.
Sherpa Romeo[b]	Jisc (Joint Information Systems Committee, a UK-based non-profit created to support higher education initiatives)	Authors, librarians, publishers	Sherpa Romeo is a database of publication policies to support authors in understanding their ability to make work open in various journals. Librarians recommend the database to researchers before they submit their work to a journal to enable them to better understand if the journal is compatible with their desire to make their work open (or their funding agency requirements!). Sherpa Romeo encourages librarians and publishers to submit information on journals to keep the database up-to-date. A number of crowd-sourcing[c] efforts have happened over the years to increase the coverage of the database, to make it a truly robust and international tool.

a. SPARC, "Author Rights: Using the SPARC Author Addendum," accessed June 5, 2022, https://sparcopen.org/our-work/author-rights/brochure-html/.
b. Jisc, "Welcome to Sherpa Romeo," accessed July 8, 2022, https://v2.sherpa.ac.uk/romeo/.
c. Lise Brin, "Creating More Visibility for Canadian Journals' Self-Archiving Policies: An Open Access Week 2020 Crowdsourcing Project," *Canadian Association of Research Libraries* (blog), October 15, 2020, https://www.carl-abrc.ca/news/sherpa-romeo-self-archiving-policies-crowdsourcing-project/.

TABLE 2.3
Tools for OA

Tool	Created By	Used By	Why It's Important
Think. Check. Submit.	The Association of Learned and Professional Society Publishers (ALPSP), Association of University Presses (AUP), Committee on Publication Ethics (COPE), Directory of Open Access Journals (DOAJ), ISSN International Centre, Ligue des Bibliothèques Européennes de Recherche – Association of European Research Libraries (LIBER), OAPEN Foundation, Open Access Scholarly Publisher's Association (OASPA), International Association of STM Publishers (STM), and UKSG.	Authors, institutions	Think. Check. Submit. helps researchers identify trusted journals and publishers for their research. Through a range of tools and practical resources, this international cross-sector initiative aims to educate researchers, promote integrity, and build trust in credible research and publications.
Unsub[d]	OurResearch, a non-profit created by Heather Piwowar and Jason Priem, two researchers eager to make scholarship more open and available.	publishers, authors, librarians	Unsub's goal is to "make toll-access publishing financially unsustainable"[e] by pulling together usage data for various library holdings to allow libraries to evaluate if their big package from a traditional publisher is actually worth the cost. The service costs a small amount each year and shows libraries what content in a journal package is already openly available through other means (repositories, OA journals).
Open Journal Systems (OJS)[f]	Public Knowledge Project (PKP), now based at Simon Fraser University, Canada	Publishers, authors, librarians	OJS software helps researchers, libraries, and institutions to spin up their own journals. The software helps the front-facing publication of the scholarly content, as well as the entire production life cycle including peer review. OJS software has been around for 20 years, is used by over 25,000 journals worldwide,[g] and is in constant development as it has a very engaged user community. A number of academic libraries host OJS journals and support the production of open access research by managing the infrastructure and the updates to the software, while members of faculty and students take care of the content and editorial side of journal publishing.

d. Unsub, home page, accessed May 23, 2022, https://unsub.org/.

e. OurResearch, "Our Projects," under "Unsub," https://ourresearch.org/projects#unsub.

f. Public Knowledge Project, home page, Simon Fraser University, accessed May 23, 2022, https://pkp.sfu.ca/.

g. Public Knowledge Project, "Open Journal Systems," Simon Fraser University, https://pkp.sfu.ca/ojs/.

TABLE 2.3
Tools for OA

Tool	Created By	Used By	Why It's Important
Sci-Hub	Alexandra Elbakyan, a programmer from Kazakhstan, who wanted to solve the problem of "closed access to research literature"[h]	Researchers worldwide	Sci-Hub is a shadow library of the large databases of research held by traditional publishers. According to the copyright regimes of most countries, it is illegal due to the unauthorized redistribution of protected works. Why are we talking about it? Because it makes research easily findable—so much so that even researchers at institutions that pay for a number of huge journal packages prefer to use Sci-Hub instead of logging in through various publisher portals to run the same query.[i] It's important for those of us in scholarly communication to know about tools—even the illegal ones—as researchers do use them to access information. Sometimes it may seem as though the traditional publishers do all they can to make it difficult to access the content libraries subscribe to. The search capabilities of these databases are varied and not always intuitive. Authentication is often an issue, with some databases requiring users to have a database-specific log-in instead of just authenticating against the university's existing system. Sci-Hub is also important to the dialogue around open access to scholarship. The commodification of scholarship is a topic that academia has been wrestling with for a long time—and here is a tool that ignores the rules to make research available. What could we learn from Alexandra Elbakyan? Is this civil disobedience? Is this criminal? We certainly know what some traditional publishers think about even mentioning Sci-Hub (hint: they are not fans[j]), but research has been done on what libraries can learn about the creation of crowd-sourced collections.[k]

h. Sci-Hub, "Alexandra Elbakyan," accessed July 8, 2022, https://sci-hub.ru/alexandra.

i. John Bohannon, "Who's Downloading Pirated Papers? Everyone," *Science* 352, no. 6285 (April 29, 2016): 508–12, https://doi.org/10.1126/science.352.6285.508.

j. Scott Jaschik, "Supporting Sci-Hub vs. Explaining Sci-Hub," Inside Higher Ed, August 8, 2016, https://www.insidehighered.com/news/2016/08/08/letter-publishers-group-adds-debate-over-sci-hub-and-librarians-who-study-it.

k. Carolyn Caffrey and Gabriel J. Gardner, "Fast and Furious (at Publishers): The Motivations behind Crowdsourced Research Sharing," *College and Research Libraries* 78, no. 2 (February 2017): 131–49, https://doi.org/10.5860/crl.78.2.131.

A note about the tools that libraries use—whether it's to support publishing or to make a collection available to their community: privacy matters. In this age of digital surveillance, it is important that academic libraries reconcile the data they collect with their actual uses. Even Google Analytics, a tool that many of us use to track page hits, can disclose information that our users don't wish to share. Why is this important to open access? Open access is about access to information free of as many barriers as possible—including surveillance analytics.

OPEN ACCESS AND PRIVACY

Dorothea Salo

Information privacy is a core library value; full freedom to read and learn depends on not being surveilled while doing so. Unfortunately, the present-day web has incorporated many forms of information surveillance. Open access journals, as part of the web, must consciously resist troubling forms of end-user surveillance while still providing feedback to editors and authors about their readership.

Authors working as tenure-track or tenured professors need to demonstrate the impact of their research to advance in their careers. Traditionally, this has been done via citation counting that feeds into various bibliometrics measures; while bibliometrics measures can be (and often are) inappropriately deployed, they remain important to many tenure and promotion cases. More recently, "altmetrics" platforms have surveyed social media and post-publication peer-review platforms to measure attention.

The reasonable desire to measure readership and impact, however, can cross the line into unethical surveillance of journal readers, especially when combined with common privacy-destroying web-tracking technologies. The most common readership-measurement platform on the web is Google Analytics. Unfortunately, Google Analytics tracks the specific reading behavior of any user logged into any Google property and may attempt to reidentify users who are not logged in to Google in order to fatten Google's data dossiers on individuals. Google Analytics surveillance can be lessened through tweaking its configuration, but not eliminated; moreover, Google has repeatedly been caught lying about the type and amount of user surveillance it performs and should therefore not be trusted.

Privacy on the web is also an area of active global regulation, relevant because open access journals enjoy global readership. The European Union's (EU) General Data Protection Regulation (GDPR) govern systematic collection of personal and behavioral data from EU citizens, for example.[62] In the United States, the California Consumer Privacy Act[63] adopts a GDPR-ish approach to privacy; legislation may close its several known loopholes. In short, not only ethics but law requires open access journal platforms and editorial boards to build in reader privacy.

Best practice, honed by many decades of physical-library processes, is to count uses without associating any use with specific users, much less sharing use information with the ever-more-voracious web of surveillance. Self-hosted analytics platforms such as Matomo (formerly Piwik) facilitate privacy-aware usage metrics, but use of appropriate technologies must be coupled with good data-governance practices such as prompt deletion of raw logs.

CONCLUSION

The theory and operationalization of open access have evolved in many wonderful (Lookit—it's really happening! Some research is open!) and worrisome (What do you mean Elsevier claims to be one of the largest OA publishers in the world?[64]) ways since it was labelled decades ago. Even over the course of pulling together the content for this chapter, we have seen how traditional foundations are being rebuilt and improved.[65]

This evolution of the concepts of open access, open science, open educational resources—all of it—is a reflection of how research and scholarship are changing and how they can better share data, information, and knowledge with the public. Open infrastructure will be key to how we make all of this possible moving forward, and we need to focus on that as part of our core work in libraries. And to be sure, we must not replicate the misspent focus of our early years, when those in open access argued about which flavour or colour of openness was the best, wasting a lot of time and energy. When it comes to infrastructure to support our open work, we must focus on sustainability and scalability, and, most importantly, on the people who do the work in the open world. Infrastructure is people[66]—let us stop abstracting the agency of the people involved in open out of the system.

DISCUSSION QUESTIONS

1. How would you define open access, and what are the limitations of your definition?
2. Partner with a friend, colleague, or classmate and practice responding to one of the myths described early in this chapter. Imagine a researcher states a myth as a concern about making their work open access; how would you respond?
3. Tara Robertson discusses a scenario where open access could be harmful. What are circumstances where open access should be approached with caution? How would you approach a discussion with a researcher expressing real concerns?
4. How does open access align with your professional goals and interests?
5. Would you make your own work open access? How? Why or why not?

NOTES

1. Peter Suber, "What Is Open Access?" chapter 1 in *Open Access* (Cambridge, MA: MIT Press, 2012), https://doi.org/10.7551/mitpress/9286.001.0001.
2. MIT Press, "Open Access," accessed July 12, 2020, https://openaccesseks.mitpress.mit.edu/.
3. Suber, "What Is Open Access?"
4. UNESCO, "What Is Open Access?" UNESCO Open Access Publications, accessed May 23, 2022, https://en.unesco.org/open-access/what-open-access.
5. 'Samuel Moore on Twitter: "So unless you define open access in a way that specifically excludes bad actors, any definition of OA will be exploitable by them." Twitter, accessed May 7, 2022, https://twitter.com/samoore_/status/1380078724079624194. [Tweet deleted.]
6. Library and Archives Canada, "Theses Canada," last modified August 29, 2022, https://library-archives.canada.ca/eng/services/services-libraries/theses/pages/theses-canada.aspx.
7. Budapest Open Access Initiative, "Read the Declaration," February 14, 2002, https://www.budapestopenaccessinitiative.org/read/.
8. Cornell University, "About ArXiv," accessed June 6, 2022, https://arxiv.org/about.
9. Budapest Open Access Initiative, "Read the Declaration."
10. Budapest Open Access Initiative, "Read the Declaration."
11. Budapest Open Access Initiative, "The Budapest Open Access Initiative: 20th Anniversary Recommendations," accessed May 22, 2022, https://www.budapestopenaccessinitiative.org/boai20/.

12. Max-Planck-Gesellschaft, "Berlin Declaration," Open Access, accessed July 13, 2020, https://openaccess.mpg.de/Berlin-Declaration.

13. Bethesda Statement on Open Access Publishing, accessed July 13, 2020, https://dash.harvard.edu/handle/1/4725199.

14. Peter Steiner, "On the Internet, Nobody Knows You're a Dog," *New Yorker*, July 5, 1993, 61, Wayback Machine, https://web.archive.org/web/20051029045942/http://www.unc.edu/depts/jomc/academics/dri/idog.html.

15. SPARC, "Openness as a Career Asset: Erin McKiernan," accessed May 8, 2022, https://sparcopen.org/impact-story/erin-mckiernan/.

16. Independent Voices, "About This Collection," https://web.archive.org/web/20160324082838/http://voices.revealdigital.com/.

17. Lisa Sloniowski, "Theorizing the Library," Archive/Counterarchive Working Paper Series, 2019, https://counterarchive.ca/working-papers-series-lisa-sloniowski-theorizing-library.

18. ZineLibraries.info, *Zine Librarians Code of Ethics* (Durham, NC: ZineLibraries.info, November 2015), https://www.zinelibraries.info/code-of-ethics/.

19. *ZineLibraries.info, Code of Ethics, 16.*

20. Bernice Dahn, Vera Mussah, and Cameron Nutt, "Yes, We Were Warned About Ebola," *New York Times*, April 7, 2015, https://www.nytimes.com/2015/04/08/opinion/yes-we-were-warned-about-ebola.html.

21. Lisa Janicke Hinchliffe (@lisalibrarian), Twitter, August 8, 2020, 1:11 p.m., https://twitter.com/lisalibrarian/status/1292146429046272001.

22. Jessamyn West (@jessamyn), "That said, when I've been working public library reference, the patrons most likely to come for health info want health ANSWERS not health SOURCES (like tax stuff… ," Twitter, August 8, 2020, 2:35 p.m., https://twitter.com/jessamyn/status/1292167887793401859.

23. Government of Canada, "Tri-Agency Open Access Policy on Publications," last modified March 10, 2023, https://science.gc.ca/site/science/en/interagency-research-funding/policies-and-guidelines/open-access/tri-agency-open-access-policy-publications?OpenDocument.

24. Sung-Hee Jeon, Huju Liu, and Yuri Ostrovsky, *Measuring the Gig Economy in Canada Using Administrative Data* (Ottawa, ON: Statistics Canada, December 16, 2019), https://www150.statcan.gc.ca/n1/en/pub/11f0019m/11f0019m2019025-eng.pdf?st=Mfy9a-7D.

25. Jeon, Liu, and Ostrovsky, *Measuring the Gig Economy*, table 4, "Occupational Distribution of Gig Workers in 2016 and the Shares of Gig Workers among All Workers," 21.

26. Andrea Wiggins and John Wilbanks, "The Rise of Citizen Science in Health and Biomedica Research," *American Journal of Bioethics* 19, no. 8 (2019): 3–14, https://doi.org/10.1080/15265161.2019.1619859.

27. Library Loon, "The C-Word," *Gavia Libraria* (blog), December 15, 2011, https://gavialib.com/2011/12/the-c-word/.

28. Library Loon, "C-Word."

29. Cameron Neylon and Bianca Kramer, "Language Diversity in Scholarly Publishing," *COKI* (blog), June 21, 2022, https://openknowledge.community/language-diversity/.

30. Wikipedia, s.v. "List of countries by English-speaking population," last updated June 20, 2022, https://en.wikipedia.org/w/index.php?title=List_of_countries_by_English-speaking_population&oldid=1094522853.

31. Samuel Moore, "Why Open Science Is Primarily a Labour Issue," *Samuel Moore* (blog), June 18, 2022, https://www.samuelmoore.org/2022/06/18/why-open-science-is-primarily-a-labour-issue/.

32. Dave Ghamandi, "A Plea for Polarization: Or Why We Shouldn't Center Comfort and Peace before Justice," blog post, Humanities Commons, April 5, 2022, https://doi.org/10.17613/mvjx-hg49.

33. American Library Association, "Diversity Counts 2009–2010 Update," table series A: "2009–2010 American Community Survey Estimates Applied to Institute for Museum and Library Services and National Center for Education Statistics Data," https://www.ala.org/aboutala/sites/ala.org.aboutala/files/content/diversity/diversitycounts/diversitycountstables2012.pdf.

34. Arianna Becerril-García, self-introduction, transcript of livestream, Envisioning a World beyond APCs/BPCs International Symposium, Lawrence, KS, November 17, 2016, https://kuscholarworks.ku.edu/bitstream/handle/1808/22153/KUOASymp16LivestreamTranscript.pdf.

35. Richard Smith, "Reed-Elsevier's hypocrisy in selling arms and health," *Journal of the Royal Society of Medicine* 100, no. 3 (2007):114-5. doi: 10.1177/014107680710000302. PMID: 17339299; PMCID: PMC1809159.

36. Alan Singleton, "The first scientific journal," *Learned Publishing* 27, no. 1 (2014): 2-4. https://doi.org/10.1087/20140101

37. Vincent Larivière et al., "Bibliometrics: Global Gender Disparities in Science," *Nature* 504, no. 7479 (2013): 211–213, https://doi.org/10.1038/504211a.

38. Martin Klein et al., "Comparing Published Scientific Journal Articles to Their Pre-print Versions," *International Journal on Digital Libraries* 20, no. 4 (December 2019): 335-350, https://doi.org/10.1007/s00799-018-0234-1.

39. Erin C. McKiernan, "About," Erin C. McKiernan website, https://emckiernan.wordpress.com/home/.

40. Ashley Farley et al., "Transformative Agreements: Six Myths, Busted," *College and Research Libraries News* 82, no. 7 (July–August 2021): 298–301, https://doi.org/10.5860/crln.82.7.298.

41. Klein et al., "Comparing Published Scientific Journal Articles."

42. SPARC, "Coalition of Open Access Policy Institutions (COAPI)," https://sparcopen.org/coapi/.

43. Josh Bolick, "Leveraging Elsevier's Creative Commons License Requirement to Undermine Embargo," *Journal of Copyright in Education and Librarianship* 2, no. 2 (2018), https://doi.org/10.17161/jcel.v2i2.7415.

44. Creative Commons, "About the Licenses," https://creativecommons.org/licenses/.

45. Creative Commons, "About the Licenses."

46. Creative Commons, "About the Licenses."

47. Creative Commons, "About the Licenses."

48. Holly Else, "Nature Journals Reveal Terms of Landmark Open-Access Option," *Nature* 588, no. 7836 (November 24, 2020): 19–20, https://doi.org/10.1038/d41586-020-03324-y.

49. Martin Paul Eve, "The Problems of Unit Costs per Article," Martin Paul Eve website, September 19, 2019, https://eve.gd/2019/09/19/the-problems-of-unit-costs-per-article/.

50. Jisc, "Research Funders' Open Access Policies," Sherpa Juliet, accessed May 16, 2022, https://v2.sherpa.ac.uk/juliet/.

51. Allison Langham-Putrow, Caitlin Bakker, and Amy Riegelman, "Is the Open Access Citation Advantage Real? A Systematic Review of the Citation of Open Access and Subscription-Based Articles," *PLOS ONE* 16, no. 6 (June 23, 2021): e0253129, https://doi.org/10.1371/journal.pone.0253129.

52. Open Access.nl, "Publisher Deals," accessed May 16, 2022, https://www.openaccess.nl/en/in-the-netherlands/publisher-deals.

53. Library Publishing Coalition, "Resources." https://librarypublishing.org/resources/.

54. SPARC, "An Introduction to Copyright Resources for Authors," https://!sparcopen.org/our-work/author-rights/introduction-to-copyright-resources/.

55. Gary Hall, *The Uberification of the University* (Minneapolis: University of Minnesota Press, 2016).

56. Mary L. Gray and Siddharth Suri, *Ghost Work* (Boston: Houghton Mifflin Harcourt, 2019).

57. Anna Severin et al., "Who Reviews for Predatory Journals? A Study on Reviewer Characteristics," preprint, bioRxiv, March 11, 2020, https://www.biorxiv.org/content/10.1101/2020.03.09.983155v1.

58. Severin et al., "Who Reviews?" 12.

59. Severin et al., "Who Reviews?" 8.

60. Severin et al., "Who Reviews?" 4.

61. George Chen and Alejandro Posada and George Chen, "Inequality in Knowledge Production: The Integration of Academic Infrastructure by Big Publishers" (presentation, ELPUB 2018: International Conference on Electronic Publishing, Toronto, ON, June 22–24, 2018), fig. 4, p. 6, https://doi.org/10.4000/proceedings.elpub.2018.30.

62. GDPR.eu, "What is GDPR, the EU's new data protection law?," https://gdpr.eu/what-is-gdpr/.

63. State of California Department of Justice, "California Consumer Privacy Act (CCPA)," https://oag.ca.gov/privacy/ccpa.

64. Elsevier, "Open Access," accessed July 12, 2022, https://www.elsevier.com/open-access.

65. Dominique Babini (@dominiquebabini), "In the past, our guides for #openaccess were the 3B (Budapest, Bethesda, Berlin declarations) Now, our guides are the UNESCO Open Science Recommendations,…" Twitter, June 10, 2022, 4:51 p.m., https://twitter.com/dominiquebabini/status/1535364145960321025.

66. Dorothea Salo, "Thank You! (And Save a Cow Today!)," slide 43 in "Save the Cows! Cyberinfrastructure for the Rest of Us," SlideShare, March 11, 2009, https://www.slideshare.net/cavlec/save-the-cows-data-curation-for-the-rest-of-us-1533252/43-Thank_youand_save_a_cow.

BIBLIOGRAPHY

American Library Association. "Diversity Counts 2009–2010 Update." Table series A: "2009–2010 American Community Survey Estimates Applied to Institute for Museum and Library Services and National Center for Education Statistics Data." https://www.ala.org/aboutala/sites/ala.org.aboutala/files/content/diversity/diversitycounts/diversitycountstables2012.pdf.

Aspesi, Claudio, Nicole Starr Allen, Raym Crow, Shawn Daugherty, Heather Joseph, Joseph McArthur, and Nick Shockey. *SPARC Landscape Analysis: The Changing Academic Publishing Industry—Implications for Academic Institutions.* Washington, DC: Scholarly Publishing and Academic Resources Coalition, March 28, 2019. https://doi.org/10.31229/osf.io/58yhb.

Babini, Dominique (@dominiquebabini). "In the past, our guides for #openaccess were the 3B (Budapest, Bethesda, Berlin declarations) Now, our guides are the UNESCO Open Science Recommendations…." Twitter, June 10, 2022, 4:51 p.m. https://twitter.com/dominiquebabini/status/1535364145960321025.

Becerril-García, Arianna. Self-introduction. Transcript of livestream, Envisioning a World beyond APCs/BPCs International Symposium, November 17, 2016, Lawrence, KS. https://kuscholarworks.ku.edu/bitstream/handle/1808/22153/KUOASymp16LivestreamTranscript.pdf.

Bethesda Statement on Open Access Publishing. Accessed July 13, 2020. https://dash.harvard.edu/handle/1/4725199.

Bohannon, John. "Who's Downloading Pirated Papers? Everyone." *Science* 352, no. 6285 (April 29, 2016): 508–12. https://doi.org/10.1126/science.352.6285.508.

Bolick, Josh. "Leveraging Elsevier's Creative Commons License Requirement to Undermine Embargo." *Journal of Copyright in Education and Librarianship* 2, no. 2 (2018). https://doi.org/10.17161/jcel.v2i2.7415.

Brin, Lise. "Creating More Visibility for Canadian Journals' Self-Archiving Policies: An Open Access Week 2020 Crowdsourcing Project." *Canadian Association of Research Libraries* (blog), October 15, 2020. https://www.carl-abrc.ca/news/sherpa-romeo-self-archiving-policies-crowdsourcing-project/.

Budapest Open Access Initiative. "The Budapest Open Access Initiative: 20th Anniversary Recommendations." Accessed May 22, 2022. https://www.budapestopenaccessinitiative.org/boai20/.

———. "Read the Declaration." February 14, 2002. https://www.budapestopenaccessinitiative.org/read/.

Caffrey, Carolyn, and Gabriel J. Gardner. "Fast and Furious (at Publishers): The Motivations behind Crowdsourced Research Sharing." *College and Research Libraries* 78, no. 2 (February 2017): 131–49. https://doi.org/10.5860/crl.78.2.131.

Cornell University. "About ArXiv." Accessed June 6, 2022. https://arxiv.org/about.

Creative Commons. "About the Licenses." https://creativecommons.org/licenses/.

Creative Commons Wiki. "NonCommercial Interpretation." Last updated October 15, 2017. https://wiki.creativecommons.org/wiki/NonCommercial_interpretation.

Dahn, Bernice, Vera Mussah, and Cameron Nutt. "Yes, We Were Warned About Ebola." *New York Times*, April 7, 2015. https://www.nytimes.com/2015/04/08/opinion/yes-we-were-warned-about-ebola.html.

EcoEvoRxiv. Home page. https://ecoevorxiv.org/.

Else, Holly. "Nature Journals Reveal Terms of Landmark Open-Access Option." *Nature* 588, no. 7836 (November 24, 2020): 19–20. https://doi.org/10.1038/d41586-020-03324-y.

Elsevier. "Open Access." Accessed July 12, 2022. https://www.elsevier.com/open-access.

Eve, Martin Paul. "The Problems of Unit Costs per Article." Martin Paul Eve website, September 19, 2019. https://eve.gd/2019/09/19/the-problems-of-unit-costs-per-article/.

Farley, Ashley, Allison Langham-Putrow, Elisabeth Shook, Leila Belle Sterman, and Megan Wacha. "Transformative Agreements: Six Myths, Busted." *College and Research Libraries News* 82, no. 7 (July–August 2021): 298–301. https://doi.org/10.5860/crln.82.7.298.

Ghamandi, Dave. "A Plea for Polarization: Or Why We Shouldn't Center Comfort and Peace before Justice." Blog post. Humanities Commons, April 5, 2022. https://doi.org/10.17613/mvjx-hg49.

GDPR.eu. "What is GDPR, the EU's new data protection law?" https://gdpr.eu/what-is-gdpr/.

Government of Canada. "Tri-Agency Open Access Policy on Publications." Last modified March 10, 2023. https://science.gc.ca/site/science/en/interagency-research-funding/policies-and-guidelines/open-access/tri-agency-open-access-policy-publications?OpenDocument.

Gray, Mary L., and Siddharth Suri. *Ghost Work: How to Stop Silicon Valley from Building a New Global Underclass.* Boston: Houghton Mifflin Harcourt, 2019.

Hall, Gary. *The Uberification of the University.* Minneapolis: University of Minnesota Press, 2016.

Hinchliffe, Lisa Janicke (@lisalibrarian). "Who are the leading public librarians in the open access movement/community? FYI, I don't mean academic librarians at public institutions. I mean those working …." Twitter, August 8, 2020, 1:11 p.m. https://twitter.com/lisalibrarian/status/1292146429046272001.

Independent Voices. "About This Collection." https://web.archive.org/web/20160324082838/http://voices.revealdigital.com/.

Jaschik, Scott. "Supporting Sci-Hub vs. Explaining Sci-Hub." Inside Higher Ed, August 8, 2016. https://www.insidehighered.com/news/2016/08/08/letter-publishers-group-adds-debate-over-sci-hub-and-librarians-who-study-it.

Jeon, Sung-Hee, Huju Liu, and Yuri Ostrovsky. *Measuring the Gig Economy in Canada Using Administrative Data.* Ottawa, ON: Statistics Canada, December 16, 2019. https://www150.statcan.gc.ca/n1/en/pub/11f0019m/11f0019m2019025-eng.pdf?st=Mfy9a-7D.

Jisc. "Research Funders' Open Access Policies." Sherpa Juliet. Accessed May 16, 2022. https://v2.sherpa.ac.uk/juliet/.

———. "Welcome to Sherpa Romeo." Accessed July 8, 2022. https://v2.sherpa.ac.uk/romeo/.

Klein, Martin, Peter Broadwell, Sharon E. Farb, and Todd Grappone. "Comparing Published Scientific Journal Articles to Their Pre-print Versions." *International Journal on Digital Libraries* 20, no. 4 (December 2019): 335–50. https://doi.org/10.1007/s00799-018-0234-1.

Knott, Cheryl. *Not Free, Not for All: Public Libraries in the Age of Jim Crow.* Amherst, MA: University of Massachusetts Press, 2015.

Langham-Putrow, Allison, Caitlin Bakker, and Amy Riegelman. "Is the Open Access Citation Advantage Real? A Systematic Review of the Citation of Open Access and Subscription-Based Articles." *PLOS ONE* 16, no. 6 (June 23, 2021): e0253129. https://doi.org/10.1371/journal.pone.0253129.

Larivière, Vincent, Chaoqun Ni, Yves Gingras, Blaise Cronin, and Cassidy R. Sugimoto. "Bibliometrics: Global Gender Disparities in Science." *Nature* 504, no. 7479 (2013): 211–13. https://doi.org/10.1038/504211a.

Library and Archives Canada. "Theses Canada." Last modified August 29, 2022. https://library-archives.canada.ca/eng/services/services-libraries/theses/pages/theses-canada.aspx.

Library Loon. "The C-Word." *Gavia Libraria* (blog), December 15, 2011. https://gavialib.com/2011/12/the-c-word/.

Library Publishing Coalition. "Resources." https://librarypublishing.org/resources/.

Max-Planck-Gesellschaft. "Berlin Declaration." Open Access. Accessed July 13, 2020. https://openaccess.mpg.de/Berlin-Declaration.

McKiernan, Erin C. "About." Erin C. McKiernan website. https://emckiernan.wordpress.com/home/.

MIT Press. "Open Access." Accessed July 12, 2020. https://mitpress.mit.edu/books/open-access (page discontinued).

Moore, Samuel (@samoore_). "[So unless you define open access in a way that specifically excludes bad actors, any definition of OA will be exploitable by them.]." Twitter, accessed 7 May 2022, https://twitter.com/samoore_/status/1380078724079624194. [Tweet deleted]

Moore, Samuel. "Why Open Science Is Primarily a Labour Issue." *Samuel Moore* (blog), June 18, 2022. https://www.samuelmoore.org/2022/06/18/why-open-science-is-primarily-a-labour-issue/.

Neylon, Cameron, and Bianca Kramer. "Language Diversity in Scholarly Publishing." *COKI* (blog), June 21, 2022. https://openknowledge.community/language-diversity/.

Open Access.nl. "Publisher Deals." Accessed May 16, 2022. https://www.openaccess.nl/en/in-the-netherlands/publisher-deals.

OurResearch. "Our Projects," under "Unsub." https://ourresearch.org/projects#unsub.

Posada, Alejandro, and George Chen. "Inequality in Knowledge Production: The Integration of Academic Infrastructure by Big Publishers." Presentation, ELPUB 2018: International Conference on Electronic Publishing, Toronto, ON, June 22–24, 2018. https://doi.org/10.4000/proceedings.elpub.2018.30.

Public Knowledge Project. Home page. Simon Fraser University. Accessed May 23, 2022. https://pkp.sfu.ca/.

———. "Open Journal Systems." Simon Fraser University. https://pkp.sfu.ca/ojs/.

Salo, Dorothea. "How to Scuttle a Scholarly Communication Initiative." *Journal of Librarianship and Scholarly Communication* 1, no. 4 (2013): eP1075. https://doi.org/10.7710/2162-3309.1075.

———. "Thank You! (And Save a Cow Today!)." Slide 43 in "Save the Cows! Cyberinfrastructure for the Rest of Us." SlideShare, March 11, 2009. https://www.slideshare.net/cavlec/save-the-cows-data-curation-for-the-rest-of-us-1533252/43-Thank_youand_save_a_cow.

Sci-Hub. "Alexandra Elbakyan." Accessed July 8, 2022. https://sci-hub.ru/alexandra.

———. Home page. https://sci-hub.ru/.

Severin, Anna, Michaela Strinzel, Matthias Egger, Marc Domingo, and Tiago Barros. "Who Reviews for Predatory Journals? A Study on Reviewer Characteristics." Preprint. bioRxiv, March 11, 2020. https://www.biorxiv.org/content/10.1101/2020.03.09.983155v1.

Singleton, Alan. "The first scientific journal." *Learned Publishing* 27, no. 1 (2014): 2-4. https://doi.org/10.1087/20140101.

Sloniowski, Lisa. "Theorizing the Library." Archive/Counterarchive Working Paper Series. 2019. https://counterarchive.ca/working-papers-series-lisa-sloniowski-theorizing-library.

Smith, Richard. "Reed-Elsevier's hypocrisy in selling arms and health." *Journal of the Royal Society of Medicine* 100, no. 3 (2007): 114-5. doi: 10.1177/014107680710000302. PMID: 17339299; PMCID: PMC1809159.

SPARC. "Author Rights: Using the SPARC Author Addendum." Accessed June 5, 2022. https://sparcopen.org/our-work/author-rights/brochure-html/.

———. "An Introduction to Copyright Resources for Authors." https://sparcopen.org/our-work/author-rights/introduction-to-copyright-resources/.

———. "Coalition of Open Access Policy Institutions (COAPI)." https://sparcopen.org/coapi/.

———. "Openness as a Career Asset: Erin McKiernan." Accessed May 8, 2022. https://sparcopen.org/impact-story/erin-mckiernan/.

State of California Department of Justice. "California Consumer Privacy Act (CCPA)." https://oag.ca.gov/privacy/ccpa.

Steiner, Peter. "On the Internet, Nobody Knows You're a Dog." *New Yorker*, July 5, 1993, 61. Wayback Machine. https://web.archive.org/web/20051029045942/http://www.unc.edu/depts/jomc/academics/dri/idog.html.

Suber, Peter. *Open Access*. Cambridge, MA: MIT Press, 2012. https://doi.org/10.7551/mitpress/9286.001.0001.

UNESCO. "What Is Open Access?" UNESCO Open Access Publications. Accessed May 23, 2022. https://en.unesco.org/open-access/what-open-access.

Unsub. Home page. Accessed May 23, 2022. https://unsub.org/.

West, Jessamyn (@jessamyn). "That said, when I've been working public library reference, the patrons most likely to come for health info want health ANSWERS not health SOURCES (like tax stuff…)." Twitter, August 8, 2020, 2:35 p.m. https://twitter.com/jessamyn/status/1292167887793401859.

Wiggins, Andrea, and John Wilbanks. "The Rise of Citizen Science in Health and Biomedical Research." *American Journal of Bioethics* 19, no. 8 (2019): 3–14. https://doi.org/10.1080/15265161.2019.1619859.

Wikipedia. S.v. "List of countries by English-speaking population." Last updated June 20, 2022. https://en.wikipedia.org/w/index.php?title=List_of_countries_by_English-speaking_population&oldid=1094522853.

ZineLibraries.info. *Zine Librarians Code of Ethics*. Durham, NC: ZineLibraries.info, November 2015. https://www.zinelibraries.info/code-of-ethics/.

OPEN DATA

edited by Brianna Marshall

INTRODUCTION TO OPEN DATA

Cameron Cook

INTRODUCTION

Open data is one component of the larger ecosystem of openness in academia and research that collectively seeks to produce more widely accessible and reproducible research. Within this ecosystem, open data is one of the important building blocks of open science, which is a broader movement of opening up the scientific research process. Open science seeks to facilitate transparency in research and improve the reproducibility (ability to obtain the same results using the same inputs and methods from a study), replicability (ability to obtain the same results with the study's methods but different inputs), and rigor (meaning the adherence to the scientific method and best practices) of research studies. The third section in this chapter, "Supporting Reproducible Research," will dive deeper into these concepts.

How does open data work in this ecosystem and help to facilitate transparency? Open data—alongside open access to publications, open source code, and open protocols or workflows—allows for other researchers and members of the public to review how studies were developed, how data was collected and processed, what analyses were done, and how conclusions were drawn. This allows researchers and the validity of their findings to be held to greater accountability by both peers and the public. Open data extends the potential viability and utility of existing data sets, enabling new discoveries. With access to existing data, anyone can build upon the study and then combine it with their own unique data or disciplinary methods to answer new research questions.

This chapter will provide a practical background on open data for an early career information professional or anyone new to providing data services. It will serve as a high-level introductory primer and provide the necessary terms and definitions, background context, ethical frameworks, and introductions to applied best practices and critical topics.

To start, in this section, we'll lay the groundwork for understanding open data in the academic context and provide the necessary information for engaging more deeply with the following sections focused on data management and sharing, reproducibility, and ethics. In this introduction you will learn to

- define *what* open data is;
- understand the *context* of incentives and pressures of open research data in practice; and
- understand the *skills* needed for the common data professional *roles*.

Subsequent sections in this chapter build on these goals by introducing both the necessary theoretical and applied building blocks for understanding open data as an information professional new to this area.

Section 2.2.2, "Managing, Sharing, and Publishing Data," introduces research data management practices and covers how to share data openly. Section 2.2.3, "Supporting Reproducible Research," will define key terminology and concepts for engaging with reproducibility, followed by outlining five potential ways to support researchers directly in making their research reproducible. The fourth and final section in chapter 2.2, "Open Data," is section 2.2.4, "Ethics of Open Data"; it will introduce the critical ethical frameworks and guiding principles of sharing data and explore their applications through three case studies that illustrate these frameworks in action, which will help a new information professional understand the common debates and critical issues faced in daily practice.

DEFINING OPEN DATA

WHAT IS DATA?

To understand open data, let's start by defining *data*, or in the context of this section, *research data*. While the exact definition of research data may vary depending on your specific context, generally it can be defined as the factual information underlying research findings and necessary for reproducing and validating those findings.[1] To many of us, *data* can have a connotation that implies numbers and figures such as statistics, measurements, or observations from the field. However, across disciplines, *data* can be understood more broadly to also include things like digital images (both born-digital and digitized from a primary material), audio recordings, videos, born-digital text (which may include literature, publications, citations, social media data or websites, etc.), interviews, transcripts, and more. It is important for an information professional to note that research data can be conceptualized more inclusively and also take non-digital forms such as physical samples of a specimen, physical or archival materials such as letters and diaries, and many other primary materials. However, in this section we will be focusing on digital research data.

WHAT IS OPEN DATA?

With our definition of *data* in mind, what then makes research data open? Per the Open Knowledge Foundation, *open data* is data "can be freely accessed, used, modified and shared by anyone for any purpose subject only, at most, to requirements to provide attribution and/or share-alike."[2]

To put this another way, open research data is data with the least possible limitations on future reuse attached to it. You can read the full formal definition and its list of requirements through the foundation's website,[3] but the Open Data Handbook also highlights the most critical aspects of the definition and expands on them. Per the handbook, open data must have the following features:

- *Availability and access*—The data must be available as a whole data set and at no more than a reasonable reproduction cost, preferably by downloading over the internet. The data must also be available in a convenient and modifiable form.[4]
- *Reuse and redistribution*—The data must be provided under terms that permit reuse and redistribution, including intermixing with other data sets.[5]
- *Universal participation*—Everyone must be able to use, reuse and redistribute—there should be no discrimination against fields of endeavor* or against persons or groups. For example, noncommercial restrictions that would prevent commercial use, or restrictions of use to certain purposes (e.g., only in education), are not allowed.[6]

For a data practitioner, these parameters can serve as guidelines when assisting researchers with data sharing and help ensure you are adhering to the guiding definition of openness when possible.

While the phrase *open research data* is most frequently used in the context of scientific data, any discipline can openly share the data underlying their publications (though the definition of data may be more varied in humanities or social sciences disciplines, as mentioned above). In turn, any discipline can also benefit from open data. This is increasingly true as research becomes more interdisciplinary and use of computational and data-intensive methodologies expands across disciplines.

Of course, open data as a concept does not exist only within academic institutions. You may also hear *open data* used in other contexts. Government agencies and many other organizations share data from funding, special projects, or studies as a way to increase transparency and accountability, much as in research.

MAKING DATA OPEN

Section 2.2.2, "Managing, Sharing and Publishing Data," will provide detailed steps and considerations for sharing research data, but let's briefly talk about some of the foundational components and best practices for putting the definition above into practice, including adherence to *technical openness*, and *legal openness* and following the *FAIR Principles*.

Technical Openness

As it sounds, technical openness is about ensuring that the technical aspects of a data set enable ease of access and use by others. As noted in the "availability and access" feature of the definition above, this includes selecting a sharing mechanism that makes the data available for download via the internet as well as sharing the data as a complete data set. It also notes that the data must be in a convenient and modifiable form, which entails that the data set be prepared in a way that enables machine-readability and interoperability with other data sets and across platforms.[7]

Machine-readable means that a computer is able to read and process the data without human interaction. It is important that data can be interpreted and processed by a computer, rather than being structured for ease of human readability and interpretation.

---

* A field of endeavor can be understood as an activity or purpose (e.g., for commercial, research, or educational purposes), as the provided examples illustrate.

For example, a spreadsheet should be structured to enable parsing by a computer rather than for processing by a human through color-coding, comments, or other visual cues. Preferencing human readability can make the data hard to understand or require lots of time to prepare the data before use. Machine readability ensures that data is easy and ready to use for others.

Interoperability means that the data can be used across systems, platforms, or products.[8] Data should be shared in widely used, nonproprietary file formats. In other words, data should be in a format that is not owned or restricted (often by a commercial entity), and the format should be usable across multiple softwares and operating platforms. Using open formats and ensuring the interoperability of your data will help minimize the potential technical barriers to its reuse.

Examples of proprietary formats include Microsoft Excel (.xslx) or Word (.docx); comparable nonproprietary options include comma-separated values (.csv) and plain text files (.txt).

Legal Openness

Now that our data is available in an open format, we can enable its continued future reuse by attaching an open license, which defines the legal terms under which a data set is made available.[9] As noted in the definition shared above, to be considered open, data must be licensed under terms that enable universal reuse and redistribution.

It is considered best practice to always apply a license to data and to apply the least restrictive license possible in order to avoid limiting the reuse potential or redistribution of the data. Per the definition we covered earlier, *at most* a license may require attribution (meaning requiring that the original data set and its creator be cited in subsequent uses) and share-alike (meaning requiring that subsequent iterations or uses apply the original license and not place further restriction on the data).

For further clarification on the definition of *open* or the conditions that open licenses and open works must satisfy, the Open Knowledge Foundation provides in-depth guidance on its website as well as in its Open Data Handbook (see "Further Resources Mentioned" below). Section 2.2.2, "Managing, Sharing, and Publishing Data," will also discuss licensing options that conform to best practices.

The FAIR Principles

The *FAIR Principles*, first published in 2016, serve as actionable guidelines for best practices that will ensure the usability and sustainability of data sets over time. The four principles are *Findability, Accessibility, Interoperability, and Reusability* (creating the acronym *FAIR*).

The principles focus on machine actionability, meaning "the capacity of computational systems to find, access, interoperate, and reuse data with none or minimal human intervention."[10] The authors of the principles also note that the principles "define characteristics that contemporary data resources, tools, vocabularies, and infrastructures should exhibit to assist discovery and reuse by third-parties,"[11] so the principles are meant to be applicable broadly not only to data but also to repositories, metadata, and tools. As a data professional, you might find these principles useful when helping researchers select a repository, or they could be used as guidelines for best practices when developing the functionality and infrastructure of a local data repository. The full principles, their guidelines, and full definitions for each guideline can be found on the FAIR Principles website.[12]

CONTEXT OF INCENTIVES AND PRESSURES

WHY MAKE DATA OPEN?

The beginning of this section noted that open data helps increase transparency and reproducibility of research. However, there are a number of additional motivations and benefits for making data open. At the core of all of them, however, is the notion that data is a valuable asset with immense opportunity as a scholarly building block.

As already noted above, subsequent sections will expand on this idea and provide deeper guidance on the driving principles for sharing open data responsibly. Section 2.2.2, "Managing, Sharing, and Publishing Data," will reframe the benefits of open data from a researcher's perspective and explore the ethical and legal circumstances under which data shouldn't be shared. Section 2.2.4, "Ethics of Open Data," will introduce important frameworks for making responsible, informed choices as a data professional in working with an open data repository, supporting researchers in making data open, or conducting your own research.

Data as a Valuable Asset

Data is a valuable asset—one through which discoveries are made, upon which scholarship is built, and which many industries will share only through strict agreements due to potential value and risk inherent in the data. However, it is not just scientific advancement that makes data valuable. Data is also valuable because it can be *expensive* and *resource-intensive*, *irreproducible*, and *unethical to re-collect*.

Expensive—Research data can be expensive to collect—both financially and in terms of staff time and resources. Some research may also utilize unique or costly instruments and methods that may be prohibitively expensive for other researchers or institutions. These expensive or large-scale instruments can also require intensive cyberinfrastructure investment for the academic institution to be able to effectively store and manage the produced data. Sharing data from these instruments or methods openly can provide access to researchers across institutions and locations, and in general, sharing data helps reduce the burden of resources needed to conduct some aspects of research.

Resource-intensive—Some research data can take large amounts of a researcher's time and labor to not only collect, but also clean, process, and analyze. As an example, digitized or transcribed text from a historical document may need a lot of human intervention to clean and prepare the text data for effective use and analysis. Sharing resource-intensive data ensures that other researchers are able to make the best use of the staff, time, and workflows they have to accelerate their research.

Irreproducible—Observational data—data collected in real time through observation, sensors, or other instruments—are often not reproducible. Examples of this may be data collected by a researcher in the field, longitudinal studies of weather patterns in a specific area, or the health outcomes of a particular population. This data benefits greatly from being shared as it is unique, one-time data that cannot be recaptured.

Unethical to re-collect—In research there is sometimes a moral imperative to limit the re-collection of data. For example, needing to reproduce nonhuman primate or other animal studies can introduce cruel redundancies. Sharing data collected from animal protocols can limit the need to reproduce these data-collection activities. Or in the case of public health crises, sharing data can limit the impact and spread of a disease by enabling researchers to collaborate quickly to speed health research and fuel discovery of treatments. You may have watched data sharing in this context unfold in real time during the COVID-19 pandemic.

Data as a Scholarly Building Block

You may often hear that reproducibility is the bedrock of science. Reproducibility of studies is a critical component of scientific rigor, and for work to be reproducible, the data underlying a study must be accessible and available. Having access to underlying data enables peer review by other researchers who can then verify the methods, data collection, analysis, and findings for validity outside of the traditional publishing process. This process is important for being able to verify research results, identify errors, or spot falsification in the research process.

Another important consideration for data as a scholarly building block is that data can have value beyond the scope of its original collection and beyond the collectors' original intent. This is especially true as technology, methods, and computational possibilities advance—some tests or analyses that were not possible when data was collected may be possible in the future. This allows researchers to build on prior work and fuels new discoveries.

Finally, it's also important to remember that research data produced by taxpayer-funded projects should be seen as a public good. Providing access, and particularly public and open access, to research data ensures that funded research outputs are available to those who helped pay for them. This can also be critical for people who rely on access to emerging research that would otherwise be barred by journal paywalls or embargo periods, for example, patients who want to make informed decisions on crucial but emerging health treatments.

When Data Shouldn't Be Open

While making data open has benefits to both researchers and the public, this fact does not necessitate that all research data should be shared openly. Some research data is highly sensitive and could cause unintended harm if available to others, even if that harm is beyond the researcher's original intent. This potential for harm can stem from a few things: the content of the data itself, the potential use cases for the data, or unintended consequences of the way data was structured, collected, or interpreted.

It is important for researchers and data professionals providing research support to think about their data holistically and to engage thoughtfully with the power structures and dynamics at play when planning for data collection and use. What blind spots, unintentional exploitations, or unequal relationships may occur given the researchers' identities, cultural framing, or access to resources at a university? Some questions to ask might include

- How is the data or research structured?
- What personal worldviews or biases are being imposed through that structure?
- Who does this research serve? Who benefits from it?
- Do the plans for data collection, use, and sharing center the community involved with the study?
- When else can data cause harm?
- if data provides identifiable information for at-risk populations that someone could use to locate or exploit those populations
- if data identifies endangered species of flora or fauna, including information that could be used to locate or harvest those species
- if data is collected or constructed in a way that fundamentally misrepresents or misclassifies communities, ideas, or information
- if data violates oral or written data-sharing agreements with communities participating in the research

Section 2.2.2, "Managing, Sharing, and Publishing Data," will provide concrete examples of common types of sensitive data and explore how to approach sharing them, and section

2.2.4, "Ethics of Open Data," will provide frameworks to help you think through these cases. For now, just know that while there are good reasons for data to be open, there are also good reasons to be thoughtful and critical and to protect data when the conditions warrant.

OPEN DATA AND FUNDER REQUIREMENTS

So far we've covered how to define *open data*, motivations for sharing data, and some associated ethical implications. However, one of the major puzzle pieces for understanding the backdrop of open data in academia is becoming familiar with funding agency requirements. These requirements have been a driving force for increasing the practice of data sharing in the research context and as such often also inform a large part of data professionals' day-to-day roles and responsibilities. As we dive into more detail below, it is important to note that this section focuses on funding agency and publisher requirements specifically within the United States. Other countries or governing bodies around the globe have their own unique policies and incentives regarding research data access and sharing, which we encourage you to look into.

In 2013, the White House Office of Science and Technology Policy released a memo that directed agencies to detail plans "to make the published results of federally funded research freely available to the public within one year of publication and requiring researchers to better account for and manage the digital data resulting from federally funded scientific research."[13] This memo mainly affected the largest funding agencies, which you may recognize as common sponsors of academic research, such as the National Science Foundation (NSF), the National Institutes of Health (NIH), the Department of Energy, and others. Agencies were then required to set individual guidance for implementation of these plans, most of which were released in 2015.

As part of the aim of better accounting and management of data, agencies laid out requirements for data management plans (DMPs) to be included in the proposal process. DMP components frequently differ between agencies and sometimes even within an agency's centers or directorates. However, they are typically two-page documents that request concrete detailing of the plans for handling, storing, and sharing research data during a project. Updated and improved DMP guidance continues to be released by agencies over time; for example, in 2020 the NIH released a new data management and sharing policy to take effect in 2023.[14]

As noted earlier, agency requirements impact the daily responsibilities of many data professionals. Common activities might include assisting researchers with navigating individual agency requirements, reviewing their DMPs for compliance with said requirements as well as with data management best practices, and connecting researchers with campus resources to help implement their plans. Many data professionals may also work with their institution's research data services, which frequently offer DMP consultations, give access to tools that provide templates or guidance for drafting DMPs (such as DMPtool[15]), or offer institutionally hosted data repositories that can help researchers fulfill the public access components of their agency's guidelines. There are likely other offices and units within an institution that also support data management and grant compliance, such as offices of research, pre-award and post-award services, and so on. Maintaining communication with and collaborating with those units can be useful and is becoming more common as a way to improve compliance and repository workflows and ensure more thoughtful data sharing.

Increasingly, scholarly journals are also requiring that the research data underlying accepted publications be made openly available via a data repository. For example, PLOS has a data availability policy that applies to all of its journals.[16] The policy requires "authors to make all data necessary to replicate their study's findings publicly available without restriction at the time of publication"[17] and includes guidance on definitions, limitations on sharing, types of acceptable data repositories, data citation, and much more. Much like agency guidance, each publisher's individual guidance and approved repositories may vary, and researchers may request your help in identifying data repositories that comply with their specific publisher's public access policies.

Funder Requirements in Practice

Section 2.2.2., "Managing, Sharing, and Publishing Data," will provide further details on the process and methods for sharing data, but first we want to note some of the challenges and opportunities that you may encounter in the application of these mandates in your on-the-ground experience working with researchers as a data professional.

DMPS: REVIEW, MONITORING, AND INFRASTRUCTURE

DMPs have faced some friction between the intentions of and the actual implementation of the mandates. While they are meant to serve as a practical and valuable planning exercise for the long-term stewardship and sharing of the data produced by the funded project, for many researchers, they may largely feel like just another task to complete in the proposal process. For many years there has been little clarity in regard to agency standards for assessing submitted DMPs, a lack of agency-provided rubrics, and widely varied quality of provided example DMPs (if they are even available). This has made it difficult for researchers to understand funding agency expectations for DMPs, which in turn makes it more difficult for them to craft their own DMPs for a proposal.

For a number of agencies, monitoring and review of DMPs is currently largely implemented through the inclusion of researcher-provided DMP updates in the post-award reporting requirements. However, there is little evidence of consequences for noncompliance with submitted DMPs, though many data librarians are beginning to hear of cases anecdotally. At this time, most documentation of any potential consequences for noncompliance seems to be focused on impacting the researcher's subsequent awards. For example, in NSF's guide *Proposal and Award Policies and Procedures*, a researcher's compliance with their DMP on a former NSF project is one of the criteria upon which a PI's or co-PI's past work may be assessed during the proposal review.

Machine-actionable DMPs (also called maDMPs—standardized DMPs that allow the exchange of information electronically) have been suggested as a way to improve the current infrastructure and better facilitate the exchange of information between important stakeholders during DMP creation, review, and oversight.[18] Services like DMPTool and DMPonline as well as professional organizations are working to enable the realization of machine-actionable DMPs. However, the infrastructure and coordination required to make them operational mean that broad adoption may be a number of years down the road. (Information on machine-actionable DMPs can be found under "Further Resources Mentioned" at the end of this section.)

As a new data professional, you have a number of resources available to assist you with getting started in understanding and reviewing DMPs. You can get familiar with agency requirements and suggested best practices by examining your local research data services' websites and DataONE Modules or by reviewing DMPTool's resources.[19] You can also use the DART Project rubric to understand how to help researchers craft effective DMPs.[20]

DATA REPOSITORIES AND DMPS

As mentioned earlier, section 2.2.2, "Managing, Sharing, and Publishing Data," will introduce data repositories in depth, but it is worth briefly noting here some of the current challenges with DMPs, public access requirements, and repositories in the data-sharing landscape.

The sharing and archiving of research data presents some challenges that are not experienced when sharing publications. Whereas journal articles and other publications have largely shared standards and formats, research data sets have greater variations in file sizes, storage needs, and file formats, as well as unique or disciplinary metadata. They can require variation in access control for sensitive material and may lack preexisting shared standards. This can cause unique preservation and access challenges for data professionals when we assist researchers, especially those with really large or potentially sensitive data sets. Data professionals who support their local institutional repository may feel these challenges more acutely as they continue to develop and mature their services.

With the advent of the public access requirements, many funding agencies either identified preexisting repositories or built new repositories and portals to support compliance for the publication-sharing aspect of the mandate. However, at the time of original guidance release, no comparable infrastructure solutions were provided or identified to support research data sharing. Lack of formal guidance from agencies, as well as a widely varied ecosystem of repository platforms that provide many options for researchers, can make identifying an ideal place to share data difficult for researchers, who may not have a commonly used repository-of-choice within their disciplines. This multitude of options also presents a challenge for creating coordinated search and discovery across repositories and introduces the potential for disparate quality as deposit policies and curatorial review differ per repository.

While specific requirements for what constitutes compliant data sharing and archiving are still ill-defined as of the writing of this section, we have seen continued efforts from funding agencies to provide clarity. In 2019, the NIH and Figshare, a generalist repository, partnered to pilot a data repository solution for NIH-funded researchers.[21] This pilot demonstrates that one agency understands of the desire for explicit direction for researchers. However, the pilot repository instance is no longer active and is now archived. In another example, in September 2020, the Directorate for Biological Sciences of the NSF released updated guidelines on selecting repositories that details the following:

> Where they exist, PIs are expected to make use of recognized, accessible, community-accepted repositories that conform to appropriate national and international standards for such facilities. DMPs that rely on self-publication on personal or lab websites in lieu of available public repositories may be considered unsatisfactory.[22]

While this updated guidance still leaves room for individual interpretation and selection of a compliant public access repository, it helps narrow the choices and clearly rules out self-hosted self-publication venues as noncompliant. We may see more detailed guidance in the future—in 2020, the Office of Science and Technology Policy released two requests for information on desirable data repository characteristics and increasing access to federally funded research,[23] to which many data professionals responded through their institutions or professional organizations.

While there are some practical challenges, there are also many opportunities for data professionals to have a hand in shaping the future of open data. There are opportunities to help at broader levels—for examples, by joining data professional organizations—which can be a way to contribute to direct change in policies and standards as well as helping to continue building community around these topics. At the local level, many academic institutions are eager to build out their research infrastructure to support their campus's compliance with public access mandates. Data professionals currently have the really exciting opportunity to have a direct hand in shaping their local services and policies as the data-sharing landscape continues to evolve. Building relationships with units on your campus such as IT, the research office, ethics review boards, or other research support units can be very fruitful for developing support and services for data sharing at your institution.

RESEARCHER CHALLENGES AND DISCIPLINARY DIFFERENCES

Researchers across disciplines work with different data types, have different workflows, and experience different pressures and incentives. As a result, researchers also tend to approach open data with varying attitudes and experiences. As a data professional, it's important for you to understand both the attitudes and the interests of the researchers you support so that your outreach efforts and services make the greatest impact. The discussion below explores some of the challenges and disciplinary differences that impact researchers' attitudes toward data sharing.

Supporting Researchers across Disciplines

It's not necessary for you as a data professional to be a disciplinary expert in order to help a researcher with sharing their data. However, becoming familiar with the differences in the frequently used data types across disciplines can help you understand the different constraints, risks, and legal implications researchers in those disciplines encounter. This context can also give you a framework and toolkit for approaching or supporting individual departments and researchers with data sharing.

Disciplinary Data Differences

Disciplines often produce or use different data types due to differences in their respective methodologies, instruments, and unique research questions. Examples of common data types for different domains include the following:
- *Natural and physical sciences*—Data from observations and field studies, physical specimens, laboratory instruments, geospatial data, or computer modeling and simulations.
- *Social sciences*—Survey data, focus groups, interviews, economic indicators, demographics, geospatial data, and so on.
- *Arts and humanities*—Text (from literature, from primary documents, scraped from a website, or others), primary sources, images, geospatial data, video, and so on.[24]

These delineations should be taken as an example; often, researchers may use all of these data types regardless of their discipline (and that is increasingly common with interdisciplinary and collaborative research). However, as noted above, understanding the general differences can help you understand the most common barriers and needs among different disciplines.

For example, certain data types are inherently more fraught with issues of ethics, privacy, and intellectual property. Researchers in disciplines that frequently work with human subjects, such as the medical sciences or social sciences, have more risk due to the potential for identification or other harm to the research participants. The 2015 DataONE study noted that researchers from medical and health sciences, education, and psychology showed less inclination and willingness to share data, likely due to the potential risk to their human subjects' the data posed.[25] As a result, data on human subjects is subject to more ethics oversight regarding data collection and sharing as well as more regulation regarding the technical and security requirements for storage of and access to the data. For researchers in disciplines that frequently work with industry partners, external collaborators, or data providers, copyright or other intellectual property issues can also arise—especially if the other party requires a binding legal agreement regarding specific requirements for the storage, access, or public sharing of the data being shared between the project partners (typically called *data use agreements*).

While researchers who frequently work with these data types may be familiar with these challenges, data professionals often serve as translators when connecting them with local campus resources and as advocates when helping bring attention to their data-sharing needs and solutions at the institutional level.

There can also be cultural differences among disciplines in their attitudes toward open data and data sharing, though it should be noted that each campus, along with its departments and faculty, is unique, so these cultural attitudes may not be shared broadly. For example, over the past decade, STEM disciplines have experienced more formal policy changes and direct pressures applied to their data-sharing practices through the funding agency public access requirements and journal publisher requirements. There has also been a broader cultural shift toward greater emphasis on reproducibility in the general scientific community, so you may find that many of these disciplines are better primed for or attuned to these conversations. Even within STEM, however, certain disciplines (such as genomics or physics) may have longer histories of sharing than others or may tend toward more collaborative research practices, so they may also be more comfortable with data sharing.[26]

Regardless of the discipline you are working with, it can be helpful to become familiar with the data-sharing cultures and expectations within it. Looking into the reward structures and incentives within that discipline, its most common data challenges, and any institution-level or department-level data policies can help you adjust the way you approach researchers and conduct outreach.

DATA SHARING IN PRACTICE

Since 2011, the DataONE Usability and Assessment Working Group has studied the data-sharing attitudes and practices of researchers through three separate surveys. While the 2015 installment of the study saw an increase in the self-reported data-sharing practices from the initial 2011 survey,[27] the 2020 study seems to indicate a continued hesitancy to fully embrace open data practices. The study found that while a majority of researchers expressed willingness to share and reuse others' data, there is less readiness when it comes to sharing full data without restrictions.[28] The study also found that

> less than half of respondents (44.5%) said they would be willing to share all of their data with no restrictions. Around half of respondents (56.4%) said that they would be willing to share data if they could place some conditions on access.[29]

Similarly, a worldwide Elsevier study of 1,162 researchers found that while many were willing to share (64%),[30] in practice "one third of the researchers did not publish their data at all"[31] and "less than 15% of researchers publish their data in a repository."[32]

BARRIERS TO SHARING DATA

So, what barriers or hindrances may exist that make it difficult for a researcher to share data even if they recognize the value of doing so? While researchers may be personally invested in sharing data when possible, oftentimes they face very real constraints in their daily work. One such reason the DataONE study suggests is the issue of resource constraints, such as a lack of the time and funding necessary to properly prepare data for sharing.[33] Preparing data to ensure its reusability and sustainability into the future can be very time-intensive at the end of a project, especially when the necessary data management practices, staffing, and any associated costs were not taken into account at the outset. So researchers may find themselves lacking the time, personnel, or funds to prepare and deposit data.

Some researchers also work with data that is more sensitive and as a result may have legal concerns about sharing proprietary data and violating intellectual property or ethical concerns about research participants' privacy and consent, all of which pose direct challenges to being able to share the data openly.[34] Sharing data impacted by legal or ethical restrictions can require further planning at the outset of a project. For example, researchers may need to work with their campus's research and legal offices to obtain the appropriate rights and formal data use agreements from data providers or research partners. Researchers working with human subject data—that is, data collected from or about human research participants—will have the further requirement to work with their local ethics review boards, often called institutional review boards (IRBs), to have their methods, protocols, and consent processes approved prior to beginning their research. At the end of a project, human subject data and other sensitive data can also require more time and resources to properly prepare for access by others, such as appropriately de-identifying data prior to sharing. Sometimes sharing the data may not even be possible due to restrictive or unclear language in the study's original consent forms or an inability to satisfactorily de-identify the data. Some researchers may also have ethical concerns about the potential misuse and misinterpretation of their data.[35]

Finally, it is important to note that many researchers currently work within a system that does not always incentivize sharing data directly. The current reward system for most researchers frequently prioritizes the output of publications, and research data is not always similarly recognized as a scholarly contribution to be rewarded. As a result, sharing data is harder to prioritize, especially given the constraints mentioned above that many researchers have to work within. Given the importance of formal publishing for career advancement as well, some researchers may also feel reluctant to share data without publishing using it first, which can sometimes come from fear of another researcher scooping their work prior to having an opportunity to publish it. As mentioned earlier, publishers are increasingly requiring that data underlying accepted publications be shared in a repository prior to publishing a researcher's work. Over time, we hope that this will prove to be an effective tool for shifting researchers' practices, as tying data sharing directly to the publishing process begins to improve the reward and incentive impediments.

SKILLS AND ROLES
IMPLICATIONS FOR LIBRARIES AND INFORMATION PROFESSIONALS

As we have noted throughout this section, open data policies and practices are continuing to emerge and change. This dynamic landscape is also reflected in the diversity of data support structures, staffing, and services seen across academic institutions. Some institutions have mature data programs with robust services along with a support staff of a few to a dozen generalist and specialized data roles. However, other institutions may have a single librarian who may balance data support alongside other duties or may contribute partial efforts to local research data or repository services. This range of environments coupled with emerging best practices and external drivers of change means that it's common for data professionals to have to navigate complex tensions between available resources, internal politics, and stakeholder relationships to support researchers and grow their data support services. It can also mean that they often find themselves navigating roles that require a balance between more concrete technical and management skills along with broader, non–technically focused leadership and interpersonal communication skills.

Daily work itself varies greatly and can run the gamut of activities such as taking a consultation with a researcher in their lab or office, meeting with diverse campus stakeholders or partner services to coordinate data support efforts or advocate for resources, teaching a hands-on workshop, presenting or tabling for your services at a campus event, strategically planning new services, and joining leadership roles in national or local organizations to advance best practices for the profession. Depending on the exact scope of a role, data professionals may also find themselves juggling a number of competing priorities among activities like ensuring daily operational support for services they manage, developing new services or projects, and performing high-level strategic program planning and administrative duties. This is often challenging for data professionals, but especially for those who may find themselves as the sole provider of these efforts at an institution. Establishing ongoing commitment and resources from your institution can be critical for combatting this often progress-inhibiting competition of priorities and allows the development of research data units with deep expertise and curated services.

The ability to develop partnerships with other campus units can also be extremely fruitful for generating further buy-in and commitment from your institution. Depending on your institution, there may be a number of research support units that have mission overlap with the library that could be leveraged to deliver more centralized and robust data services. These might be units such as statistical consulting units, departmental or specialized disciplinary data archives, centralized or departmental IT services, high-performance or high-throughput computing groups, or data science initiatives. It may be useful for you to get to know your local environment in more detail through some stakeholder relationship building or a needs analysis to see what services might be the most effective for your local researchers, might fill important gaps, or might leverage each unit's strengths to the most benefit.

So given the diverse environments and responsibilities of data professional roles, what skills are critical for early career individuals to develop? A 2020 study of 180 data professional positions noted that "the most common research data activities mentioned [in the position descriptions] were general data management ($n = 154$, 86%), data repository ($n = 122$, 68%), data curation ($n = 101$, 56%), data discovery ($n = 97$, 54%) and data documentation ($n = 96$, 53%[)]" and also noted that different forms of data analysis were frequently mentioned.[36] While these activities are in actuality quite broad and can have their own pockets of specialization, they provide a good base of competencies that early career data professionals can aim to gain familiarity with. As a result, learning about common repository platforms and researcher workflows, gaining efficiency in languages such as Python or R, learning popular quantitative and qualitative analysis and visualization tools, and becoming conversant in general data management practices are examples of technical and application-focused skills that serve these mentioned responsibilities and many data professionals well. While gaining experience with all of these activities can be useful generally, it can also be beneficial to gain deeper expertise in some of these areas depending on the type of role you are interested in. For students and emerging data professionals, joining professional organizations, such as the Research Data Access and Preservation Association (RDAP), the Research Data Alliance (RDA), or specific interest groups and sections—the Digital Scholarship Section of ACRL, for example—is a great way to stay aware of emerging trends and tools in which you may want to gain further proficiency. To help you guide your skill development, it can also be helpful to keep an inventory of job descriptions you are interested in and then use their specific requirements and qualifications as a guide for which technical skills you wish to gain.

As for nontechnical skills, project management is another critical skill and set of tools that data professionals will want to familiarize themselves with, especially given the range of responsibilities in many data professional roles. As mentioned previously, leadership skills such as strategic planning, stakeholder mapping, and learning to understand political and social landscapes are often useful, especially for those who may be leading the data services efforts on their campuses. In one study, data professionals indicated that the top five skills were "Developing relationships with researchers, faculty, etc.," "Oral communication and presentation skills," "Teamwork and interpersonal skills," "Written communication skills," and "One-on-one consultation or instruction."[37] Another study of competencies and duties for data librarians found that "almost half of the sample job ads require[d] potential applicants to possess excellent interpersonal and communications skills to collaborate and coordinate with stakeholders and partners, provide reference and research assistance, and manage the development and management of RDS [(research data services)]."[38] A study analyzing job listings found that research assistance, outreach, and critical thinking and problem solving were listed highly among more technical skill sets.[39] And a recent commentary also argues that these nontechnical skills are actually critical to the setup, sustainability, and success of data services for libraries.[40] The editors of this book add that interpersonal skills have been frequently raised in discussions with many stakeholders across the scholarly communication library field as important to scholarly communication work. These skills can be difficult to teach, but important to develop for almost any role.

ROLES FOR INFORMATION PROFESSIONALS

As mentioned, data professional roles are diverse and vary widely depending on the institution, the structure and resources of the library, and the needs of the user community. There continues to be little consistency between job duties and titles for data information professionals across institutions. The study of 180 data professional positions, found that 35 percent did not use the title *librarian*, "instead using terms such as specialist, consultant, informationist, curator, coordinator, and analyst."[41] Federer's 2018 study found that of eighty-one respondents who self-reported research data–related duties, "the only titles reported by more than one respondent were 'data services librarian' (*n* = 5) and 'librarian' (*n* = 2)."[42] The study reported that though there was little exact title overlap, there was overlap in terms used among the varied titles, including *librarian*, *data services*, *research data*, *informationist*, *data management*, *manager*, and *director*.[43]

Federer's study also notes that respondents' jobs often fell into two categories: *data generalists* (also sometimes called *functional specialists*) and *subject specialists*. As you dive into the differences of these categories below, it is useful to note that the subject specialists group in the study "considered a smaller number of [data] tasks to be important to their work," while the data generalists "tended to rate a larger number of tasks as more highly important to their work" and "reported spending most of their time on data-related work."[44] Below you'll find more detail about the types of titles, duties, and background needed for roles that fall in these categories.

Functional Specialists/Data Generalists

As noted above, the role of functional specialist or data generalist has diverse titles. *Data services librarian* is perhaps most common.[45] However, you might encounter other titles, such as *research data management librarian, data curation librarian, digital scholarship* or *digital humanities librarian, repository librarian/manager, scholarly communication librarian, data and information specialist, data steward*, and more.[46] These roles tend to work across all disciplines and serve an institution broadly; they also generally do not require deep subject knowledge. In libraries, these are often called *functional specialists* or *functional liaisons* as they focus on a broad area of library support (or function) that is applicable across research domains.

Often these roles will specialize in research data management, scholarly communication, or support for specific technical services such as a campus data repository. These roles might report directly to or give a significant portion of their time to established research data services units. Common activities for these roles include providing instruction and consultations to researchers on research data management topics such as data sharing, reproducibility, or even data analysis and visualization. Roles that support a data repository might work with researchers directly to curate and prepare their data sets for deposit while others might be responsible for the day-to-day management and development of the repository. In some cases, functional specialists may also have departmental liaison responsibilities.

Subject Librarians

Subject librarians have extensive subject expertise that they bring to their work and traditionally provide broad engagement, instruction, and research support to their assigned departments or domains. Familiarity with functional areas like data management or scholarly communication is being considered increasingly important to subject librarian roles.[47] This is especially true in science- and engineering-related roles as the size and complexity of their data sets increase and federal funding agency requirements continue to put the most pressure on these domains.

Like the roles mentioned above, these librarians may give portions of their time to established research data services units or teams, but these duties are often balanced alongside departmental instruction and engagement responsibilities as well. Subject librarians often have a wide net of connections and deep relationships with their engagement areas that can be beneficial to leverage for data services' outreach efforts. Subject librarians with knowledge of domain-specific research workflows and metadata standards are also often better positioned than their functional counterparts to provide intermediate- and expert-level data management instruction to researchers and are able to bring their domain knowledge to data set curation for repositories.

Some subject specialists may be responsible for supporting smaller subject, departmental, or specialized research libraries. Due to the nature of supporting these specific communities, these information professionals may provide blended subject expertise and functional expertise for their patrons.

Specialized and Emerging Data Information Professional Roles

There are also data information professionals outside of traditional academic and research library roles. For example, as libraries and IT continue to partner to provide research data support on campuses, there are beginning to be more research data support roles within IT units. These are often IT positions that have a special focus on building out centralized IT support for research data, research computing, and storage infrastructure. These positions are typically partnered or aligned with campus libraries, research data services groups, and other campus services. This type of hybrid role might be called something like *research data life cycle manager* or *research and consulting lead*.

CONCLUSION

Open research data is critical for transparency and reproducibility in scholarship, is able to fuel future discoveries, and maximizes the value of taxpayer investment in research. Researchers and academic institutions continue to face more stringent regulation and requirements from funding agencies and publishers in efforts to expand public access to this valuable resource, which is the context within which many data professionals operate and provide services. This fact makes the current landscape of supporting open data in academic libraries both exciting and challenging. Infrastructure, guidance, practices, and data professional roles themselves are still developing, which also means there is immense opportunity for data professionals to both contribute to and influence this development.

Data professionals are especially well positioned to support open data as it leverages preexisting skills within the information profession. First, libraries are viewed as vital support centers on campuses—unlike some campus services, libraries often serve entire campuses or domain areas, regardless of a researcher's funding, departmental affiliation, or other resources. This is critical as individual researchers may have varying access to expertise and services for data support, as access to such services can depend on departmental affiliations on some campuses. Some data services are also built on cost-recovery models, which can be a further obstacle for researchers in obtaining the help they need.

Second, from a library practitioner standpoint, supporting open research data fits naturally within both traditional and emerging roles within libraries. Information professionals have long provided services for more traditional scholarly outputs across the research life cycle. Supporting researchers in managing, stewarding, and preserving a data set simply adds a new facet to our traditional research and preservation services. On top of this, many of the prerequisite data management practices that enable effective open data are skill sets that already reside within the librarian's and information professional's toolkit. Skills such as information organization, description, and preservation of both digital and physical formats are part and parcel of our work with our other collections and also directly impact the long-term usability of open data. More traditional librarian skill sets, such as outreach and instruction, can be used to spread awareness and teach data-sharing best practices. Finally, libraries often serve as the locus of collaboration on a campus, often being bridge builders and gap fillers among the various campus entities and services. This positions data professionals well to help researchers navigate decentralized support environments and find collaborators or assistance, and to develop new unique data support services.

DISCUSSION QUESTIONS

1. Have you used open data in your own research for school or work?
   a. Where did that data come from?
   b. How did it help your work?
   c. Were you aware that it was open?
   d. Did you have difficulties in accessing it or using it?

2. Locate your institution's research data or scholarly communication support.
    a. Who is involved in the service, and what are their titles?
    b. What services and resources does the service offer?
    c. What information does it provide on sharing data?
3. This introduction speaks to the myriad interpersonal skills that data information professionals need. How might you begin developing these skills or be able to speak to these skills in a job interview?

NOTES

1. See the following for examples of various definitions: Office of Management and Budget, *OMB Circular A-110, Uniform Administrative Requirements for Grants and Agreements with Institutions of Higher Education, Hospitals, and Other Non-profit Organizations* (Washington, DC: Executive Office of the President, Office of Management and Budget, 1999), §215.36, "Intangible Property," (d)(2)(i), p. 58; institutional policies; organizations such as University of Edinburgh Research Data Service, "Research Data Management," November 13, 2019, https://www.ed.ac.uk/information-services/research-support/research-data-service/research-data-management; Australian National Data Service, ANDS, "What Is Research Data?" 2020, https://www.ands.org.au/guides/what-is-research-data; National Endowment for the Humanities, Office of Digital Humanities, "Data Management Plans for NEH Office of Digital Humanities, Proposals and Awards," executive summary, https://www.neh.gov/sites/default/files/2018-06/data_management_plans_2018.pdf; and many more.
2. Daniel Dietrich et al., Glossary, s.v. "Open Data," Open Data Handbook, https://opendatahandbook.org/glossary/en/terms/open-data/.
3. Open Knowledge Foundation, "Open Definition: Defining Open in Open Data, Open Content and Open Knowledge," version 2.1, https://opendefinition.org/od/2.1/en/.
4. Dietrich et al., "How to Open Up Data."
5. Dietrich et al., "How to Open Up Data."
6. Dietrich et al., "How to Open Up Data."
7. Dietrich et al., "How to Open Up Data."
8. Dietrich et al., "How to Open Up Data."
9. Dietrich et al., "How to Open Up Data."
10. GO FAIR, "FAIR Principles," accessed July 9, 2020, https://www.go-fair.org/fair-principles/.
11. Mark D. Wilkinson et al., "The FAIR Guiding Principles for Scientific Data Management and Stewardship," *Scientific Data* 3 (2016): article 160018, p. 4. https://doi.org/10.1038/sdata.2016.18.
12. GO FAIR, "FAIR Principles."
13. Michael Stebbins, "Expanding Public Access to the Results of Federally Funded Research," *White House* (blog), February 22, 2013, website archive, https://obamawhitehouse.archives.gov/blog/2013/02/22/expanding-public-access-results-federally-funded-research.
14. National Institutes of Health, "Final NIH Policy for Data Management and Sharing," NOT-OD-21-013, October 29, 2020, https://grants.nih.gov/grants/guide/notice-files/NOT-OD-21-013.html.
15. DMPTool, home page, https://dmptool.org/.
16. *PLOS ONE*, "Data Availability," 2019, https://journals.plos.org/plosone/s/data-availability.
17. *PLOS ONE*, "Data Availability."
18. Tomasz Miksa et al., "Ten Principles for Machine-Actionable Data Management Plans," *PLOS Computational Biology* 15, no. 3 (2019): e1006750, https://doi.org/10.1371/journal.pcbi.1006750.
19. DataONE Community Engagement and Outreach Working Group, "3. Data Management Planning," Data Management Skillbuilding Hub, 2016, https://dataoneorg.github.io/Education/lessons/03_planning/index.html; DMPTool, "Data Management General Guidance," https://dmptool.org/general_guidance.
20. Amanda Whitmire et al., "Rubric and Related Files," OSF, last updated December 21, 2017, https://doi.org/10.17605/OSF.IO/QH6AD.
21. National Institutes of Health Office of Data Science Strategy, "Generalist Repository Ecosystem Initiative," September 18, 2020, https://datascience.nih.gov/data-ecosystem/exploring-a-generalist-repository-for-nih-funded-data.
22. National Science Foundation Directorate for Biological Sciences, "Updated Information about the Data Management Plan Required for All Proposals," September 2020, p. 1, https://www.nsf.gov/bio/pubs/BIODMP_Guidance.pdf.
23. Office of Science and Technology Policy, "Request for Public Comment on Draft Desirable Characteristics of Repositories for Managing and Sharing Data Resulting from

Federally Funded Research," *Federal Register* 85, no. 12 (January 17, 2020): 3085, https://www.federalregister.gov/documents/2020/01/17/2020-00689/request-for-public-comment-on-draft-desirable-characteristics-of-repositories-for-managing-and; Office of Science and Technology Policy, "Request for Information: Public Access to Peer-Reviewed Scholarly Publications, Data and Code Resulting from Federally Funded Research," *Federal Register* 85, no. 44 (March 5, 2020): 9488, https://www.federalregister.gov/documents/2020/02/19/2020-03189/request-for-information-public-access-to-peer-reviewed-scholarly-publications-data-and-code.

24. Elaine Russo Martin et al., eds., "Module 2: Types, Formats, and Stages of Data," New England Collaborative Data Management Curriculum, Lamar Soutter Library, UMass Chan Medical School, https://library.umassmed.edu/resources/necdmc/index.

25. Carol Tenopir et al., "Changes in Data Sharing and Data Reuse Practices and Perceptions among Scientists Worldwide," *PLOS ONE* 10, no. 8 (2015): e013482, https://doi.org/10.1371/journal.pone.0134826.

26. Stephane Berghmans et al., *Open Data* (Elsevier, 2017) 21, 35, https://www.elsevier.com/__data/assets/pdf_file/0004/281920/Open-data-report.pdf.

27. Tenopir et al., "Changes in Data Sharing," 8.

28. Carol Tenopir et al., "Data Sharing, Management, Use, and Reuse: Practices and Perceptions of Scientists Worldwide," *PLOS ONE* 15, no. 3 (2020): e0229003, pp. 14–15, https://doi.org/10.1371/journal.pone.0229003.

29. Tenopir et al., "Data Sharing Worldwide," 15.

30. Berghmans et al., *Open Data*, 21.

31. Berghmans et al., *Open Data*, 20.

32. Berghmans et al., *Open Data*, 20.

33. Carol Tenopir et al., "Data Sharing by Scientists: Practices and Perceptions," *PLOS ONE* 6, no. 6 (2011): e21101, p. 16, https://doi.org/10.1371/journal.pone.0021101.

34. Tenopir et al., "Data Sharing by Scientists," 2, 16; Berghmans et al., *Open Data*, 22, 39.

35. Tenopir et al., "Data Sharing Worldwide," 16; Berghmans et al., *Open Data*, 22, 39.

36. Joanna Thielen and Amy Neeser, "Making Job Postings More Equitable: Evidence Based Recommendations from an Analysis of Data Professionals Job Postings between 2013–2018," *Evidence Based Library and Information Practice* 15, no. 3 (2020): 114, https://doi.org/10.18438/eblip29674.

37. Lisa Federer, "Defining Data Librarianship: A Survey of Competencies, Skills, and Training," *Journal of the Medical Library Association* 106, no. 3 (July 2018): 297, https://doi.org/10.5195/jmla.2018.306.

38. Marian Ramos Eclevia et al., "What Makes a Data Librarian? An Analysis of Job Descriptions and Specifications for Data Librarian," *Qualitative and Quantitative Methods in Libraries* 8, no. 3 (2019): 279, 282, https://www.qqml-journal.net/index.php/qqml/article/view/541.

39. Hammad Rauf Khan and Yunfei Du, "What Is a Data Librarian? A Content Analysis of Job Advertisements for Data Librarians in the United States Academic Libraries," paper, July 31, 2018, p. 6, https://digital.library.unt.edu/ark:/67531/metadc1225772/.

40. Margaret Henderson, "Why You Need Soft and Non-technical Skills for Successful Data Librarianship," *Journal of eScience Librarianship* 9, no. 1 (2020): e1183, p. 2, https://doi.org/10.7191/jeslib.2020.1183.

41. Thielen and Neeser, "Making Job Postings More Equitable," 109.

42. Federer, "Defining Data Librarianship," 296.

43. Federer, "Defining Data Librarianship," 296.

44. Federer, "Defining Data Librarianship," 297–98.

45. Federer, "Defining Data Librarianship," 296; Ramos Eclevia et al., "What Makes a Data Librarian?" 278; Khan and Du, "What Is a Data Librarian?" 5.

46. Ramos Eclevia et al., "What Makes a Data Librarian?" 278; Khan and Du, "What Is a Data Librarian?" 65.

47. Steve Brantley, Todd A. Bruns, and Kirstin I. Duffin, "Librarians in Transition: Scholarly Communication Support as a Developing Core Competency," *Journal of Electronic Resources Librarianship* 29, no. 3 (2017): 137–50, https://doi.org/10.1080/1941126X.2017.1340718.

BIBLIOGRAPHY

Berghmans, Stephane, Helena Cousijn, Gemma Deakin, Ingeborg Meijer, Adrian Mulligan, Andrew Plume, Alex Rushforth, et al. *Open Data: The Research Perspective*. Elsevier, 2017. https://www.elsevier.com/__data/assets/pdf_file/0004/281920/Open-data-report.pdf.

Brantley, Steve, Todd A. Bruns, and Kirstin I. Duffin. "Librarians in Transition: Scholarly Communication Support as a Developing Core Competency." *Journal of Electronic Resources Librarianship* 29, no. 3 (2017): 137–50. https://doi.org/10.1080/1941126X.2017.1340718.

DataONE Community Engagement and Outreach Working Group. "3. Data Management Planning." Data Management Skillbuilding Hub, 2016. https://dataoneorg.github.io/Education/lessons/03_planning/index.

Dietrich, Daniel, Jonathan Gray, Tim McNamara, Antti Poikola, Rufus Pollock, Julian Tait, Ton Zijlstra et al. *Open Data Handbook* home page. https://opendatahandbook.org/.

DMPTool. "Data Management General Guidance." https://dmptool.org/general_guidance.

———. Home page. https://dmptool.org/.

Federer, Lisa. "Defining Data Librarianship: A Survey of Competencies, Skills, and Training." *Journal of the Medical Library Association* 106, no. 3 (July 2018): 294–303. https://doi.org/10.5195/jmla.2018.306.

GO FAIR. "FAIR Principles." Accessed July 9, 2020. https://www.go-fair.org/fair-principles/.

Henderson, Margaret. "Why You Need Soft and Non-technical Skills for Successful Data Librarianship." *Journal of eScience Librarianship* 9, no. 1 (2020): e1183. https://doi.org/10.7191/jeslib.2020.1183.

Khan, Hammad Rauf, and Yunfei Du. "What Is a Data Librarian? A Content Analysis of Job Advertisements for Data Librarians in the United States Academic Libraries." Paper, July 31, 2018. https://digital.library.unt.edu/ark:/67531/metadc1225772/.

Martin, Elaine Russo, Julie Goldman, Donna M. Kafel, and Andrew T. Creamer, eds. "Module 2: Types, Formats, and Stages of Data." New England Collaborative Data Management Curriculum, Lamar Soutter Library, UMass Chan Medical School. https://library.umassmed.edu/resources/necdmc/index.

Miksa, Tomasz, Stephanie Simms, Daniel Mietchen, and Sarah Jones. "Ten Principles for Machine-Actionable Data Management Plans." *PLOS Computational Biology* 15, no. 3 (2019): e1006750. https://doi.org/10.1371/journal.pcbi.1006750.

National Institutes of Health. "Final NIH Policy for Data Management and Sharing." NOT-OD-21-013. October 29, 2020. https://grants.nih.gov/grants/guide/notice-files/NOT-OD-21-013.html.

National Institutes of Health Office of Data Science Strategy. "Generalist Repository Ecosystem Initiative." September 18, 2020. https://datascience.nih.gov/data-ecosystem/exploring-a-generalist-repository-for-nih-funded-data.

National Science Foundation Directorate for Biological Sciences. "Updated Information about the Data Management Plan Required for All Proposals." September 2020. https://www.nsf.gov/bio/pubs/BIODMP_Guidance.pdf.

Office of Management and Budget. *OMB Circular A-110, Uniform Administrative Requirements for Grants and Agreements with Institutions of Higher Education, Hospitals, and Other Non-profit Organizations.* Washington, DC: Executive Office of the President, Office of Management and Budget, 2006. https://www.whitehouse.gov/wp-content/uploads/legacy_drupal_files/omb/circulars/A110/2cfr215-0.pdf.

Office of Science and Technology Policy. "Request for Information: Public Access to Peer-Reviewed Scholarly Publications, Data and Code Resulting from Federally Funded Research." *Federal Register* 85, no. 44 (March 5, 2020): 9488. https://www.federalregister.gov/documents/2020/02/19/2020-03189/request-for-information-public-access-to-peer-reviewed-scholarly-publications-data-and-code.

———. "Request for Public Comment on Draft Desirable Characteristics of Repositories for Managing and Sharing Data Resulting from Federally Funded Research." *Federal Register* 85, no. 12 (January 17, 2020): 3085. https://www.federalregister.gov/documents/2020/01/17/2020-00689/request-for-public-comment-on-draft-desirable-characteristics-of-repositories-for-managing-and.

Open Knowledge Foundation. "Open Definition: Defining Open in Open Data, Open Content and Open Knowledge," version 2.1. https://opendefinition.org/od/2.1/en/.

PLOS ONE. "Data Availability." 2019. https://journals.plos.org/plosone/s/data-availability.

Ramos Eclevia, Marian, John Christopher L. T. Fredeluces, Roselle S. Maestro, and Carlos L. Eclevia Jr. "What Makes a Data Librarian? An Analysis of Job Descriptions and Specifications for Data Librarian." *Qualitative and Quantitative Methods in Libraries* 8, no. 3 (2019): 273–90. https://www.qqml-journal.net/index.php/qqml/article/view/541.

Stebbins, Michael. "Expanding Public Access to the Results of Federally Funded Research." *White House* (blog), February 22, 2013. Website archive. https://obamawhitehouse.archives.gov/blog/2013/02/22/expanding-public-access-results-federally-funded-research.

Tenopir, Carol, Suzie Allard, Kimberly Douglass, Arsev Umur Aydinoglu, Lei Wu, Eleanor Read, Maribeth Manoff, and Mike Frame. "Data Sharing by Scientists: Practices and Perceptions." *PLOS ONE* 6, no. 6 (2011): e21101. https://doi.org/10.1371/journal.pone.0021101.

Tenopir, Carol, Elizabeth D. Dalton, Suzie Allard, Mike Frame, Ivanka Pjesivac, Ben Birch, Danielle Pollock, and Kristina Dorsett. "Changes in Data Sharing and Data Reuse Practices and Perceptions among Scientists Worldwide." *PLOS ONE* 10, no. 8 (2015): e013482. https://doi.org/10.1371/journal.pone.0134826.

Tenopir, Carol, Natalie M. Rice, Suzie Allard, Lynn Baird, Josh Borycz, Lisa Christian, Bruce Grant, et al. "Data Sharing, Management, Use, and Reuse: Practices and Perceptions of Scientists Worldwide." *PLOS ONE* 15, no. 3 (2020): e0229003. https://doi.org/10.1371/journal.pone.0229003.

Thielen, Joanna, and Amy Neeser. "Making Job Postings More Equitable: Evidence Based Recommendations from an Analysis of Data Professionals Job Postings between 2013–2018." *Evidence Based Library and Information Practice* 15, no. 3 (2020): 103–56. https://doi.org/10.18438/eblip29674.

Whitmire, Amanda, Jake Carlson, Brian Westra, Patricia Hswe, and Susan Wells Parham. "Rubric and Related Files." OSF. Last updated December 21, 2017. https://doi.org/10.17605/OSF.IO/QH6AD.

Wilkinson, Mark D., Michel Dumontier, IJsbrand Jan Aalbersberg, Gabrielle Appleton, Myles Axton, Arie Baak, Niklas Blomberg, et al. "The FAIR Guiding Principles for Scientific Data Management and Stewardship." *Scientific Data* 3 (2016): article 160018. https://doi.org/10.1038/sdata.2016.18.

MANAGING, SHARING, AND PUBLISHING DATA

Susan Ivey, Sophia Lafferty-Hess, Peace Ossom-Williamson, and Katie Barrick

INTRODUCTION

Research data management (RDM) is a set of foundational practices and decisions regarding the maintenance and care of data produced during a research project. RDM can help ensure the stability, accessibility, and transparency of research materials and increases impact of research through data citation and reuse. The growing interest in RDM was partly driven by public interest in greater research transparency. As noted in section 2.2.1, "Introduction to Open Data," this interest is reflected by an uptick in action taken by policymakers and federal grant-funding agencies, a driver for information professionals' continued involvement in RDM. The first part of this section covers best practices for managing data so they can be understood and used, and the second part addresses sharing research data.

So why is data management important?

RESEARCH DATA MANAGEMENT

DATA SET STABILITY AND LOSS

At any point in the research cycle, there is always a chance of accidental data loss or destruction. Data loss or destruction occurs in a variety of ways ranging from software or computer failure to theft of hard drives and computers, lab members leaving and taking data with them, and even natural disasters. If steps are not taken to store, back up, and secure data, the consequences may be severe. Not only are data lost, but labor and time investments as well, which can set a project back. Not all data can be replaced.

RESEARCH ACCESSIBILITY, TRANSPARENCY, AND IMPACT

While levels of accessibility differ between disciplines, data management and data sharing help enable greater trust in research (see section 2.2.1, "Introduction to Open Data"). Other researchers can use those data to replicate or build on the original research. They can help expand a layperson's or disciplinary newcomer's understanding of a particular project beyond the published article and results. Sharing the details of a study's methodology and analyses allows greater transparency and replicability or the achievement of consistent results within studies that seek to answer the same scientific question.[1] Good data management can support sharing these research outputs in a manner that the data can be reused, which reduces some of the costs of data collection.

BEST PRACTICES FOR RDM

Methods and data types vary across disciplines, and individual research projects can involve multiple data types as well. This can make planning and managing research data a challenge. The following general best practices focus on making robust directions and documentation available that will enable researchers to effectively work with, reproduce, and reuse theirs and others' data. Some steps are universal, while others are specific to the particular type of research being performed. Steps prior to and during research are described here.

Planning Ahead

Before beginning research, it is best practice to write a *protocol*—a study plan that details the purpose of the research, the data that will be collected or compiled, the variables that will be measured and tested, the tests that will be run, how data will be prepared, and how outliers will be dealt with. Protocols should be shared as transparently as possible prior to beginning research by writing and sharing protocols (through systems like Protocols.io or PROSPERO[2]) and creating a *data management plan* (DMP). In a DMP, the plans for collecting, storing, organizing, documenting, and sharing research data are described. A DMP lays the groundwork for beginning to document research methods thoroughly for future reporting when writing articles, preparing presentations, or sharing other research outputs. Using a DMP will also provide a vehicle for starting to talk and make decisions about areas to plan for, including where and how to store data and methods, consistency in file naming and versioning, and establishment of a schedule for updating documentation.[*]

Consistency

RDM is an active and ongoing activity throughout research. Once steps have been put into place, it is important to regularly engage in quality control and documentation. Researchers should provide accurate and detailed description of data and how they were collected from the start. Some tools, such as electronic lab notebooks (ELNs), have built-in ways to effectively document research methods, including data collection and description, which avoids manual steps. Other tools, such as Stata, R, and OpenRefine, that are used in data cleaning and analysis allow you to build "research pipelines" that define the exact actions that were performed. Research pipelines are discussed in more detail in section 2.2.3, "Supporting Reproducible Research." Researchers can also use manual documentation, including data dictionaries and README files, to consistently record relevant metadata.

Researchers should also make a copy of the original raw data prior to taking any steps, leaving the original file or files untouched. It is also useful to engage in versioning to take snapshots of the process of change that occurred. This can be done by saving a new file with a descriptive file name and version number each time a new step is taken in order to preserve and revisit what came before. These data files should be described as to what changes were

---

[*] For an example protocol, see https://doi.org/10.7910/DVN/23835/KA20IB. For an example DMP, see https://doi.org/10.5281/zenodo.1240420.

made and the software used to process them, and these files can be made available through sharing during and after research.

Transparency

When writing about the research that was conducted, researchers should refer to standard guidelines for reporting what was done, like those listed on Equator Network[3] These guidelines include things like the inclusion and exclusion criteria that were used, what data types were analyzed, the tests that were run, how outliers were handled, and what other interpretations and decisions were made, among many other methodological details that are not strictly about data. You can use repositories for sharing more detailed methodology and data. The "Sharing and Publishing Data" section below provides more information about data sharing.

Verifying Reproducibility

When beginning to engage in these practices, the best way to determine if they were done effectively is to see if a researcher can reproduce the research methods as reported and end up with the same results. Having an individual who was not involved in the original research try to replicate the research methods using the files and documentation that would be made available upon completion is a good way to confirm that the descriptions provided are clearly usable to someone who was not originally part of the study. If this can be done, the documentation is likely sufficient. Section 2.2.3 will discuss reproducibility in more detail.

RDM FOR QUALITATIVE AND HUMANITIES RESEARCH[†]

While scholars doing qualitative and humanist work do not always think of their objects of analysis as data, the objects of study and evidence available for analysis has expanded in these fields just as it has in quantitative fields. In other words, qualitative researchers and humanist scholars, too, are facing a data deluge.[4] And with that data deluge comes the concomitant need for data management. Most strategies for data management will be similar across fields, as described throughout this section. However, librarians supporting data management in qualitative and humanist fields should bear in mind the following additional challenges:

- Humanists may not consider their work *data*, preferring instead terms such as *evidence*, *citations*, or *primary sources*.[5] Reaching out actively to these research communities using the academic jargon specific to the discipline you are interacting with will increase your credibility and help researchers understand the value you bring to their projects.
- Researchers in qualitative and humanist fields may not only lack specific technical skills useful to managing research data, but they also may be anxious at being asked to develop or expand this skill set. As with reaching out to researchers in any field, developing relationships and searching for the simplest solutions to a researcher's problem will be important.
- Arts and humanities researchers often face barriers to managing and sharing data due to intellectual property issues, while qualitative researchers need to consider the privacy of their human subjects; for more on these issues, see section 2.2.1, "Introduction to Open Data."

---

† Thank you to Gabriele Hayden for contributing the "RDM for Qualitative and Humanities Research" content in this section.

SHARING AND PUBLISHING DATA

Sharing data can be defined most simply as making data available to others. However, sharing data ranges from providing a copy of as-is files to a researcher who requests them to publishing a well-described, curated data set in an open source format through a reputable data repository. In this chapter, the focus is primarily on sharing by *publishing data*. Sharing data involves extensive preplanning along with a commitment toward good data preparation, description, and quality control; these actions are resource- and time-intensive, but they have many benefits (see figure 2.1).

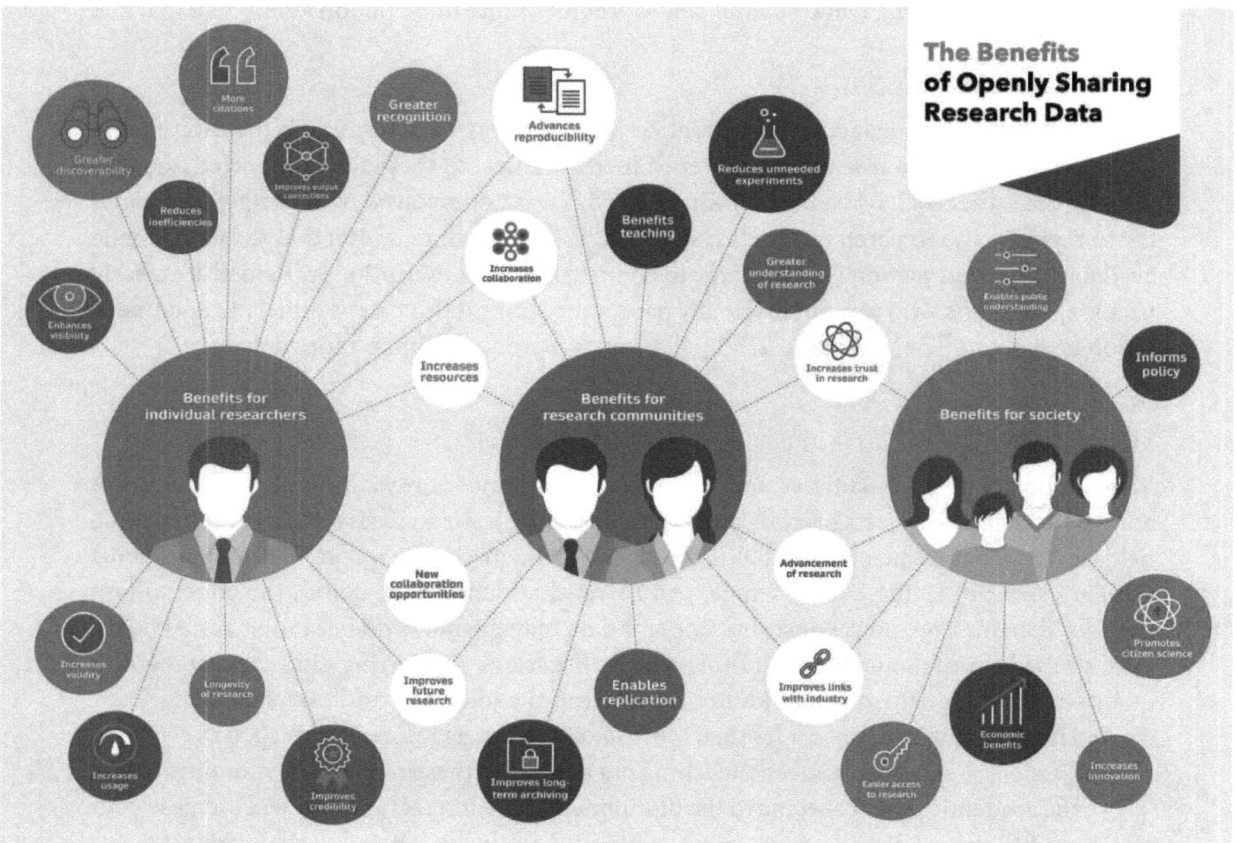

Figure 2.1

The benefits of openly sharing research data. Image adapted from Scientific Data and Mathias Astell, "Benefits of Open Research Data Infographic," Figshare, July 11, 2017, https://doi.org/10.6084/m9.figshare.5179006.v3. CC-BY 4.0, https://creativecommons.org/licenses/by/4.0/.

BENEFITS TO THE RESEARCHER

Complies with mandates—As mentioned in part I, federal granting agencies like the National Science Foundation have decided that the data that are gathered under grants from these agencies are public data because they come from public investment. Therefore, incorporating the tasks necessary for sharing data can help researchers comply with these and other external mandates. Many scholarly associations and research journals are requiring data be shared publicly. Some examples of this include the joint statement for transparency in research coauthored by the editors-in-chief of several leading science journals[6] and the following statement from the American Political Science Association's *Guide to Professional Ethics*:

> Data access: Researchers making evidence-based knowledge claims should reference the data they used to make those claims. If these are data they themselves generated or collected, researchers should provide access to those data or explain why they cannot.
>
> Production transparency: Researchers providing access to data they themselves generated or collected, should offer a full account of the procedures used to collect or generate the data.[7]

Increases data reuse and impact—Sharing data immediately confirms ownership and provides researchers with a persistent link and time stamp of when the data set has been made available, which can be used if others make a claim to be authors or creators of a data set. Therefore, researchers can make data available as early as it is ready, switching from being "'scooped' to being 'credited,'"[8] and those data that have been shared can be used or reused in ways unimagined by the original researcher. Reuse and citation can enhance the reputation and recognition of the originating researcher because most data-sharing repositories publish data in a way that allows for measuring impact (e.g., number of views and downloads, persistent unique identifiers, and metadata). It has also been found that research studies published with accompanying data, particularly links to data deposited in repositories, have greater instances of citations than those published without the underlying data.[9] In some cases, published and well-cited data sets that have undergone quality control review can be seen as a research output in their own right, separate from any publication. Therefore, some researchers have chosen to cultivate, write grants for, and publish data sets for that particular purpose, rather than as underlying a research study. At present, there is limited recognition of this sort of publication from most promotion and tenure committees at US institutions of higher education, but this situation may change as publishing data is increasingly recognized as part of the research process due to aforementioned mandates and publisher requirements.

Allows for quality control—Somewhat less discussed is the impact of the published data on the researcher and the implications on their conclusions in their published articles. The aim of science is to progress toward innovation and solutions. Therefore, sharing data and making it available as immediately as possible allows for earlier recognition of errors in data entry, analysis, or other areas of data use and reduces the risk of harmful conclusions being implemented. This may protect the researcher from reputation damage later on.

BENEFITS TO OTHERS

One multifaceted benefit of sharing data is its implications for future use. Data that can be reused ensure maximum use of expended resources, improve the progression of science, and prevent data loss.

Ensures future access—Many researchers have experienced the phenomenon of requesting another researcher's data, for either reproducibility purposes or for building upon their research, and being told that the data cannot be found because they were saved somewhere forgotten years prior or that the data cannot be accessed because they are stored on files from proprietary software that is no longer available or on devices that cannot be read (e.g., floppy disks, CDs, and punched cards). Many *data repositories* include curation services, preventing data loss and ensuring future access.

Improves reproducibility and progression of research—Researchers without the resources to collect data can contribute to the progression of research by accessing and analyzing open data. Increased data availability also furthers the progression toward open science and research reproducibility because it allows for research methods and the underlying data to be verified by others, and it also allows others to replicate studies that have been performed. Likewise, researchers can more quickly build upon what has come before due to more immediate access to the data, and analysts at government agencies and institutions can make more informed decisions using available data. Since many publishers do not consider published data to be a previous publication of research, data can even be published during the research process, rather than waiting to accompany the research article, making access occur even sooner. Furthermore, *linked data*, or data that can be connected or pooled, allow for greater statistical research power and generalizability.

Limits the expenditure of resources and human investment—Sharing and preserving data along with sufficient documentation means that researchers—including the original researcher who produced the data—can access them in the future. This practice minimizes the time investment and potential risk for research participants (human or animal) and other resources expended each time data are collected, rather than repeating the data collection process.

The following sections provide information that can help with the selection of data-sharing platforms, which data should be shared (including human participant protections and copyright and ownership), how to prepare data for sharing, when data will be shared (e.g., during research, after publication, or after an embargo), and with whom (e.g., limiting access through system functionality and data use agreements).

DECIDING WHICH DATA TO SHARE

Data—Researchers must determine how many and which data to share. Do they need to share all of the raw data generated in a project? Only the analysis data sets? Only the data underlying a particular publication? Requirements from journals or funders may impact these decisions, and standard practice can vary by discipline. Researchers will also need to make assessments about what data are most useful or required for reuse and reproducibility and weigh other practical considerations, such as size and cost.

Code—In addition to sharing data, sharing software and other types of code is an important step for reproducibility. Code repositories, such as GitHub, and code-sharing platforms and tools, such as Jupyter Notebook, Code Ocean, or ReproZip, are popular choices.[10] Some general repositories, including Zenodo and Figshare, integrate with GitHub to allow for code sharing and citation, as they assign persistent identifiers to a specific release or version of the code.[11]

Lab notebooks and workflows—Open lab notebooks allow researchers to share and publish their research, including data, in real time on the open web. Researchers share their data and methods, whether successful or not, for anyone to see. The goal is to save time for other researchers, to uncover potential mistakes, and to advance science more quickly. Openlabnotebooks.org is a free resource for researchers around the world to create and share an open lab notebook.[12] Other platforms, such as the Open Science Framework (OSF), also allow for the open sharing of work processes and workflows where files may be made immediately available for public view and access.[13]

PLATFORMS FOR DATA SHARING

Researchers utilize a variety of systems, platforms, and methods in order to share their data. This section will provide context about the current environment of data sharing. The first three methods—*data repositories, data papers and data journals*, and *open data portals*—are considered best practice for data sharing, as these methods tend to enforce overall curation including data organization, description, and licensing, which ensure that data are in their most reusable form. These systems also promote discoverability on the open web. Other methods described below that are no longer considered best practices for data sharing include web pages, supplemental material alongside publications, and available by request.

Data repositories—Often considered the gold standard for research data sharing, data repositories can provide storage, preservation, description, and access to data sets and metadata that describes the data set and its data files, thus aiding researchers in meeting the increasingly cited and required FAIR data principles.[14] There are many types of data repositories, including discipline-specific, general repositories that accept data regardless of the discipline, institutional repositories, and membership-based repositories that require a membership to deposit or access data. Researchers are generally advised to utilize discipline data repositories if one exists in their field for highest impact and visibility of their data, but general data repositories, institutional data repositories, and membership-based repositories can be valuable options as well.

It is important to understand that not all repositories are created equal, though, and a researcher must do their due diligence to determine if the repository they choose is the most appropriate, offers required features, and is trustworthy. One should consider things such as long-term sustainability plans, preservation policies, license options, embargo ability, file size and data set size limits, and robust metadata for increased findability and reusability. Datacite's Registry of Research Data Repositories (https://www.re3data.org) and FAIRsharing (https://fairsharing.org) are global registries of research data repositories that cover research data repositories from different academic disciplines and provide researchers, funders, journals, and academic institutions with a tool to search, compare, and evaluate thousands of repositories.

It is worth noting that there is a lot of current activity around assessment, evaluation, and certification of data repositories. US federal agencies, journal publishers, and other international entities are grappling with how to evaluate, and thus require or recommend, data repositories that are suitable for publicly funded and open data, and this work is expected to continue to impact the data-sharing landscape for the foreseeable future.

Data papers and data journals—*Data papers*, which are a fairly new type of publication, describe a data set by providing information about the context and content of the data package. Rather than analyzing the data, the purpose of a data paper is to promote data reuse. The actual data themselves are generally deposited into a data repository, and the two are linked via citations with a unique identifier (e.g., DOI). Data papers describe the data much more robustly than does the metadata that describes the data set in a repository, as they can provide more description and context. Data papers can be found in *data journals*, which are publications that contain only data papers. Methodology or data sections of standard publications may also refer to the underlying data and provide contextual information about the data set, although normally not as comprehensively as information found within a data paper.

Open data portals—Functioning like a catalog, open data portals contain metadata records describing and linking to open data, thus facilitating discovery and reuse of open data. Some examples include the National Institute of Mental Health Data Archive (NDA), the Indiana Spatial Data Portal (ISDP), the US government's Data.gov, and the European Union Open Data Portal (EU ODP).[15] DataPortals.org provides a comprehensive list of open data portals, which is curated by government agencies, nongovernmental agencies, and international organizations and is run by the Open Knowledge Foundation.[16]

Websites—Some researchers choose to share their data on a personal, project, or institutional web page. While sharing data on a web page or via a social or professional networking profile can help increase visibility of a researcher's work, it does not meet best practices for long-term preservation or sustainability of data.[17] It also would not fulfill funder or journal mandates for data sharing due to the lack of long-term preservation of the data themselves and of the web page. If researchers wish to share data on a web page, it is best if they do so *in addition* to depositing the data set into a data repository, linking to the persistent identifier of the data set.

Supplementary material alongside an article—The practice of sharing data as supplementary data to a journal article has been occurring for a number of years. As funding agencies and journal publishers increase their focus on reusability and reproducibility of data, though, sharing data as supplementary material no longer meets the data-sharing requirements of most funding agencies and journal publishers. Supplementary materials are not persistently available and have limited standardization in the file formats used and in their organization.[18]

Available by request—Another method of sharing data is when the researcher or a member of the research or project team grants access to data upon request, thus giving the researcher control of when those data are shared and with whom. This method, however, is one of the least open methods of sharing data and is not viewed as sufficient by funding agencies or journal publishers, as these requests are rarely fulfilled, particularly as an article ages.[19]

DATA CURATION

At the foundation of making data open are the RDM best practices explored in the first part of this section, which researchers will ideally implement during the active phase of a project. These set the stage for effective sharing; however, in most cases researchers in collaboration with information professionals will need to further prepare or *curate* data, documentation, and other associated materials to make them openly available in a structure and format that facilitates reproducibility and reuse. Below are a selection of key curation activities. For an even more comprehensive list, see the Data Curation Network's "Definitions of Data Curation Activities."[20]

Quality assurance—Data are complex digital objects that often go through multiple iterations as they are collected, processed, and analyzed. This research process can result in errors, missing information, or structural issues. Researchers and data curators have an opportunity to identify and address any quality assurance issues prior to publishing the data to ensure data accuracy and integrity. While these quality assurance checks will vary across data types and disciplines, some common issues include the coding of missing values, out-of-range values, structures that do not support portability or harmonization with other data sets, incorrect embedded metadata, and the potential inadvertent deductive disclosure of sensitive information.

Documentation and metadata—When preparing data for sharing, researchers should include documentation to explain the content of the data themselves and the context of the study. In some fields they may use structured metadata standards that support interoperability; other researchers might use unstructured files such as README files. Documentation practices vary but the presence of some form of documentation or metadata is essential for others to understand and effectively use the data.

File formats—During the course of a research project, data may be generated and analyzed using proprietary systems or equipment. While it is understandable to work within a format that is ideal for data gathering and analysis, in some cases these formats may limit access by others in the future. When possible, researchers should consider using or converting files to open, standard file formats to allow for broader and longer-term access and to support interoperability.

Associated code, programs, and other materials—To reach the goal of more reproducible research requires sharing not only data but also associated code files, software programs, and any other files necessary to verify and reproduce the outputs from a study. What is needed to prepare a complete reproducible package again varies, but at a minimum one should include code files used to process and analyze the files, documentation on software and dependencies, and detailed instructions for reproducing the results. More computationally advanced methods also exist that package the computing environment within containers. See section 2.2.3, "Supporting Reproducible Research," to learn more.

TECHNICAL INFRASTRUCTURE FOR DATA SHARING

Publishing data in a repository allows researchers to take advantage of system functionalities that support making data easier to find, discover, access, cite, and preserve for the long term. In conjunction with curation actions described above and coupled with the legal and ethical best practices, these systems provide the technical infrastructure needed for realizing the FAIR principles and making data open.

Persistent unique identifiers—Repositories assign persistent identifiers to data sets to enable ongoing access and discovery. There are various types of identifiers, such as digital object identifiers (DOIs), handles, and Archival Resource Keys (ARKs). A persistent identifier ensures a link will continue to resolve to the digital object landing page even as infrastructure and URLs change or data sets are removed.

Metadata—Repositories enable discovery through metadata that describes a data set. Different repositories will use different metadata standards for description depending upon their community standards and disciplinary norms. General or institutional repositories often use domain-agnostic metadata standards such as Dublin Core or DataCite, which support the minimum fields needed for discovery, citation, and interoperability among systems.[21]

Citations—Through the use of standardized metadata and persistent identifiers, repositories provide the necessary information for the creation of data citations. Repositories may also provide structured citations that can be exported for ease of use. It is best practice for researchers to include data citations for any data set they reuse and include them in the reference list of their article—this facilitates tracking impact and reuse of data sets and helps elevate data sets as scholarly objects. The *Joint Declaration of Data Citation Principles* outlines the primary purpose, function, and attributes of data citations.[22]

Licensing and terms of use—Repositories support the use of standardized licenses or terms of use to communicate reuse requirements to others. Increasingly, researchers are using Creative Commons licenses for this purpose.[23] However, an underlying assumption of Creative Commons is that the person assigning the license maintains copyright for those materials, which for data is not always clear. For this reason and in the spirit of openness, some repositories and open data advocates encourage assigning a *CC0 Public Domain Waiver* or the Open Data Commons Public Domain Dedication and License, which releases data into the public domain without restrictions on reuse.

Preservation—The technical infrastructure behind repositories should ideally provide depositors with some assurances that data will be safely stored, backed up, and monitored to ensure ongoing access. When selecting a repository, considerations surrounding preservation plans and policies will help researchers make data openly available not only today but also into the future. Repositories can demonstrate their trustworthiness through certifications, audits, and transparency in policies and procedures.

Embargoes—Embargoes are a request or requirement that data continue to be restricted for a specified period of time, and these can be placed for various reasons. It is currently common practice for a researcher to limit or completely restrict access to their data in order to allow time for completing and publishing their own work; however, there are benefits to making data immediately open. The most notable benefit is the ability of the data creator to claim prior ownership if there is a dispute or plagiarism concern. In the case of secondary research or commissioned research, restrictions may have been placed by the data owner or the company from which the request for research was commissioned. It is recommended that embargoes be avoided or limited to the length of time necessary to protect privacy and confidentiality and comply with research requirements.

Versioning—The majority of data-, code-, and file-sharing platforms allow for *versioning*, which provides data creators with the ability to make updates to the shared data. Using versioning, researchers can publish their data sooner and make updates by re-uploading the newer version of the data. Versioning may also be used to correct errors identified after publishing a final data set. The data citation in a data repository is changed to reflect the new version number. Therefore, previous files and data sets are still available, and each version can be tracked for provenance purposes.

ETHICAL AND LEGAL CONSIDERATIONS OF DATA SHARING

One of the first steps in ethical data sharing is understanding any potential limitations. There can be various reasons why data either cannot be shared or would need to have certain restrictions on access and use placed on them. While RDM greatly enables sharing data and open data, it is important to think critically about potential privacy and access concerns.

Sensitive and Restricted Data

Researchers have an ethical obligation to ensure they are not disclosing information that should be protected, including sensitive and restricted data. In many cases, these data come from human subjects. When dealing with data from human subjects, there is a potential for harm if data were disclosed or permission for data sharing was not granted during informed consent. Other examples of sensitive data include export-controlled data and geographic information concerning the location of endangered species or archeological sites. These data may be made available in other ways, including by request (as mentioned above) or via a protected environment—as is available virtually through the ICPSR virtual data enclave and physically in the US Census Bureau's Federal Statistical Research Data Centers.[24] (See additional information in section 2.2.4, "Ethics of Open Data.") Two specific types of sensitive or restricted data are

- *Personally identifiable information (PII) or protected health information (PHI)*—PII is defined as any information that can be used to trace or reasonably infer an individual's identity by direct or indirect identifiers. Types of PII data include, but are not limited to, names, social security numbers, street or e-mail addresses, biometric identifiers, place and date of birth, race, and religion. The National Institute of Standards and Technology (NIST) published a guide to protecting PII in 2010 that details additional types.[25] Protections for PII are detailed below under the regulation and policy section. Protected health information (PHI) is information in a medical record that can be used to identify individuals and typically generated or disclosed during health care service.

- *At-risk data* refers to data that if exposed, could potentially put subjects in harm's way. Biodiversity data is an example of at-risk data. Although imperiled animal and plant species are protected by the Endangered Species Act of 1973 in the United States and other laws elsewhere, publishing data on them openly may leave them vulnerable to poaching and environmental degradation. Consider the case of the succulent stealers: In 2015, a couple in Spain pieced together various sources of public data, including data from scientific journals, to track down locations of endangered succulents to poach and to resell.[26] Sharing biodiversity data carries risk and the solutions are not clear cut. Some members of the scientific community believe location data should be restricted, while others believe there is benefit in sharing this information. Tulloch and colleagues developed a decision tree aimed at assessing the risks and benefits of sharing biodiversity data; it may help librarians and researchers discuss data-sharing options.[27]

Most protected and at-risk data are regulated by regulations, policies, and rules designed to protect said data from theft, fraud, or exploitation. Table 2.4, while not an exhaustive list, highlights a few major pieces of legislation.

TABLE 2.4
Major laws intended to shield protected and at-risk data.

Policy	Year	Protections	Resources
United States: Health Insurance Portability and Accountability Act (HIPAA)	1996	Protects protected health information (PHI), information in a medical record that can be used to identify individuals and typically generated or disclosed during health care service	"Research," US Department of Health and Human Services, https://www.hhs.gov/hipaa/for-professionals/special-topics/research/index.html
United States: Genetic Information Nondiscrimination Act (GINA)	2008	Protects individuals from discrimination in both employment and health insurance on the basis of their genetic information	122 Stat. 881 Genetic Information Nondiscrimination Act of 2008, https://www.govinfo.gov/app/details/STATUTE-122/STATUTE-122-Pg881 "Genetic Discrimination," National Human Genome Research Institute, https://www.genome.gov/about-genomics/policy-issues/Genetic-Discrimination
United States: Family Educational Rights and Privacy Act (FERPA)	1974	Protects the privacy of and governs access to student education records	"Privacy and Data Sharing," US Department of Education, https://studentprivacy.ed.gov/privacy-and-data-sharing
European Union: General Data Protection Regulation (GDPR)	2016	Aims to provide control to individuals over their own personal data and defines six personal data principles	"Principles Relating to Processing of Personal Data," https://gdpr.eu/article-5-how-to-process-personal-data/ European Commission: EU data protection rules, https://ec.europa.eu/info/law/law-topic/data-protection/eu-data-protection-rules_en GDPR.eu
United Kingdom: Data Protection Act	2018	The UK's implementation of GDPR	"Data Protection Act 2018," https://www.legislation.gov.uk/ukpga/2018/12/section/1

SECONDARY AND PROPRIETARY DATA

When researchers are using secondary data, they also are responsible for doing their due diligence to ensure they have the rights to share. Data may be proprietary, may have restrictions on redistribution, or terms of use may be unclear. *Proprietary data* refers to collected or generated information that is controlled by a company or other organization and restricted in how it can be accessed or used. The restrictions are often documented in contracts or other legal documents. Proprietary data privacy concerns typically come into play when a research project includes private sector organizations as partners or funders, which is common in pharmaceutical and biotechnology research. Proprietary data may be accessible through terms of use or data use agreements (more on these below) wherein restricted or nonpublic data can be shared with registered users. Researchers should share secondary data only when there are no legal barriers in place.

COPYRIGHT AND OWNERSHIP

Within the United States, there are questions surrounding whether certain types of data can be protected by copyright. While the specifics of this legal discussion are beyond the scope of this section, current precedent states that facts cannot be copyrighted and that there must be some aspect of creativity to copyright a work. Therefore, while applying copyright to data is ambiguous, even with primary data, researchers need to understand who *owns* the data. Does an institution claim ownership? A funder? What are the agreements with collaborators regarding ownership? And given these agreements, are there any expectations regarding sharing? These are all important questions to answer prior to ethically sharing data. Researchers should share primary data only when there are no barriers in place due to copyright or ownership.

STRATEGIES FOR ADDRESSING PRIVACY CONCERNS

There is no one-size-fits-all approach for addressing data privacy. Nevertheless, here we discuss a few strategies for mitigating these concerns. It is important to acknowledge that a combination of several strategies should be considered as you work with researchers on how they should handle sensitive data and that this list is not exhaustive.

Data collection instruments and documentation are often among the first materials created for a research project. When creating these materials, we need to keep what we've learned about sensitive data in mind. There are several topics to consider:

Consent Form Language

Researchers may inadvertently limit their ability to share and publish research data from human subjects before they've even started data collection. Overly restrictive language, such as, "All records will be kept private," or, "The study data will be shared only with institutional researchers" can prompt sharing and publishing issues. How will records be kept private? Which records? Which institution and what researchers? Striking a balance between participant confidentiality and data-sharing best practices is critical. Fortunately, there are several resources for librarians and researchers to discuss when drafting or reviewing consent language:

- ICPSR's "Recommended Informed Consent Language for Data Sharing," https://www.icpsr.umich.edu/web/pages/datamanagement/confidentiality/conf-language.html
- TalkBank's "IRB Approval," https://talkbank.org/share/irb/

- Qualitative Data Repository's "Informed Consent," https://qdr.syr.edu/guidance/human-participants/informed-consent
- UK Data Service's "Consent for Data Sharing," https://www.ukdataservice.ac.uk/manage-data/legal-ethical/consent-data-sharing/consent-forms

Identifying Information

As previously discussed, exposing human subjects' data such as PII may endanger research participants by opening their information to theft, fraud, or exploitation. There are many steps a researcher can take to mitigate risk and protect participants.

Developing plans for storage, backup, and sharing that aim to protect PII and ensure confidentiality should occur in the early stages of a research project. Data collection should be monitored and finalized, or cleaned data need to be reviewed for direct or indirect identifiers. Taking it one step further, consider how a research data set could be used when combined with public information such as voting records or recreational genealogical databases. De-identification and anonymization are not technically perfect, as recent studies have noted how research participants can be traced through a variety of methods: Sweeney (1997),[28] Homer and colleagues (2008),[29] Narayana and Shmatikov (2008),[30] Sweeney, Abu, and Winn (2013),[31] and Rocher, Hendrickx, and de Montjoye (2019).[32] The best way to protect these data is to not collect them in the first place if possible, or to keep identifying information to a minimum.

Access

As discussed earlier, sharing sensitive data may be difficult, but it is not impossible. There are several options for researchers harboring concerns about data privacy and sensitive data:

- *Repositories with limited access options*—Some data repositories, commonly serving the health sciences, offer restricted access for data sets. These options may require users to first register for access to microdata, which can be used to send automated access requests to authors or to track usage of the data.
- *Embargos*—Some open data repositories allow authors to select embargo periods for their data sets. A data set that is under embargo means, that while it has been submitted to a repository, it is not available for download and use right away.
- *Data use agreements (DUAs)*—DUAs established permitted users and uses of a data set. DUAs should be specific to individual data sets to prevent misuse and unauthorized access. DUAs typically contain language that prohibit users from attempting reidentification or contact with subjects, as well as language that prohibits data use outside of an explicitly described project. Terms may vary across data sets, repositories, and institutions.

RDM SERVICES

The landscape of RDM services has evolved with the expanding needs of researchers, publisher and funder data mandates, and institutional policies. Many institutions have developed robust RDM services such as the University of Minnesota Research Data Services team, the University of California, Berkeley, Research Data Management Program, and the Cornell University Libraries Research Data Management Service Group.[33] To support institutional efforts to formalize and grow RDM services, a number of institutional collaborations like The Data Curation Network, professional organizations, and national conferences have emerged as resources for service support and professional development.[34]

As previously discussed in section 2.2.1, "Introduction to Open Data," RDM service models in research institutions vary in terms of support, maturity, offerings, and capacity. Here's a practitioner spotlight on Lisa Johnston, research data management/curation lead and codirector of the University Digital Conservancy at the University of Minnesota Libraries, discussing how she got started in data management work and built services and a network to inform them:

> My career started trending toward data librarianship in 2008 when I was asked to serve on a new library group for "E-Science and Data Services" that was charged to address how the collaborative and digital nature of data management, sharing and publishing was influencing research needs at our large university. My focus was on user-needs assessment and education and by performing surveys and holding focus groups with hundreds of faculty and students, the library was able to take an early front seat in understanding and addressing researcher data management needs on our campus. In the absence of a formal campus-wide group looking at data issues, in 2013 I started the university's first "informal Community of Practice for Research Data Management" and to my surprise nearly 50 people wanted to attend our kick-off event! Many years later, our University has a much more unified approach and now I spend a lot of my time working across campus, collaborating with individuals outside the library from units such as information technology (IT), office of research, and supercomputing, as well as cross-institutionally, addressing data curation challenges collaboratively with my colleagues from other universities in the Data Curation Network. The data problem space is vast and there are enough challenges for us all—so collaboration at every level is key. The best way to get started is to attend campus events (or hold your own!) and seek out individual conversations to ask people about their challenges and how they are addressing them. If your experiences are anything like my own—those same people may be ones who you partner with for years to come!

The following services are increasingly common offerings in academic libraries and may serve as inspiration for the services that you can offer to researchers.

CONSULTATIONS

Research consultations are familiar to information professionals, especially subject or liaison librarians working with faculty and students within specific disciplines. RDM consultations can be viewed as an extension of traditional library research consultations. RDM consultations may range from helping research teams choose an electronic lab notebook or advising on sustainable data formats for storage and preservation to reviewing publisher data-sharing policies when a manuscript is ready for submission. Consultations are a growing area of service, especially in assisting researchers with grant applications by helping draft DMPs.[35]

SUPPORT FOR DMPS

Support for DMPs can encompass several types of services and tools. For instance, several research support teams offer help in the review of DMPs. Such review may assist with ensuring language regarding data sharing is not too restrictive or if adequate storage or backup plans are documented. Similarly, some research libraries promote DMPTool, an online tool that assists users with the development of DMPs by utilizing plan templates for many major funding agencies such as the National Endowment for the Humanities, the National Science Foundation, and the National Institutes of Health. Additional support may take the form of keeping abreast of funding agencies' changing requirements and expectations for grant recipients and communicating updates to relevant users. Integrating examples of funder requirements into communications or educational outreach can be useful for not only supporting researchers, but also building working relationships between researchers and support services.

Workshops and Instruction

Research data services may also include educational outreach such as workshop facilitation and instruction. Instructional sessions and workshops are highly customizable types of outreach, and so the logistics, content, and delivery of RDM workshops and instruction can vary across institutions depending on the size or type of institution, the audience, and researcher needs. However, as DMPs are required by all major federal funding agencies, research data service providers often find it most beneficial to target graduate students and early-career researchers new to data management foundations and concepts.

Educational outreach also benefits information professionals by establishing relationships with faculty, graduate students, and other service providers on campus. Fostering these relationships can lead to further collaboration, partnerships, and expansion of services. As mentioned in section 2.2.1, "Introduction to Open Data," potential campus partners that may be interested in collaboration could include campus IT, research computing, instructional support centers, and individual departments or colleges.

Scoping educational outreach for the audience in mind is key. For example, a health sciences librarian may choose to develop a workshop series heavily focused on working with institutional review boards and data privacy. Their colleagues in other disciplines may choose to focus content on the basics—file naming, organization, and backup, for example—for a class of undergraduate students completely new to RDM. Consider what is most appropriate for the target population.

Being Embedded on a Research Team

Another research data service involves a data librarian being embedded as a long-term member of a research team. These roles can incorporate traditional librarian concepts of information retrieval, management, and organization, albeit with a data management focus. Duties of an embedded data librarian may include standardizing data collection language and creating data dictionaries, assisting with search strategy development and execution, and organization of relevant research materials.[36] However, partnerships can extend beyond traditional skills. Information professionals can leverage their skill sets to better organize generated or collected data files, integrate metadata schemata to facilitate data discovery, and assist with writing.

A case study by Wang and Fong found that being successfully embedded with a research team required an awareness of "emerging professional practices" and gaining a "deeper understanding of your users' evolving data needs."[37] The study suggests involvement with appropriate professional organizations such as the International Association for Social Science Information Service and Technology (IASSIST) or the Research Data Access and Preservation Association (RDAP), and interest groups within the Association of College and Research Libraries (ACRL) is important in the familiarization process as such organizations provide spaces for peer-to-peer engagement and sharing of experiences. Subject librarians may have an advantage with regard to awareness of professional practices due to knowledge and expertise with a given discipline.[38] While the Wang and Fong case study examines the dual embedment of a data librarian and earth sciences librarian, a data librarian operating as the only information professional on a research team should consider consulting with the appropriate subject librarian for more information on a given discipline's research and data trends.

Curation

With recent funder mandates and publisher requirements encouraging data sharing, researchers must make decisions and take action to prepare their data adequately for sharing. Some of these services and programs may be hosted by individual departments like university libraries or information technology, or they may be launched as a collaborative or joint responsibility. As an emerging service in academic libraries, data curation is another opportunity for information professionals to exercise their knowledge and experience in data management.

The involvement of information professionals in data curation varies like any other service within an institution. Generally, professionals can expect curatorial duties to include data validation, file transformation, the creation of documentation, the assignment of a DOI to a data set, and so forth (see "Data Curation" above). Similarly, the timing of curatorial work may differ between programs and services. Information professionals may be asked to curate data as they are collected (see "Being Embedded on a Research Team" above), but they increasingly are assigned to curate data sets submitted to institutional repositories after data sets are considered complete.

Best Practices versus Reality

In a perfect world, data collection does not begin until after a protocol or DMP is finalized and shared, infrastructure is agreed upon and set up, and the research team is trained in data management policies and procedures. The DMP would include a file-naming system and folder structure, a chosen metadata schema, and a clear budget detailing expected costs for storage, security, and plans for sharing. The data's documentation would be robust: data collection is described sufficiently and includes pristine samples of any collection instruments. Data analysis and transformation are detailed, down to the version number of any software used. All files and their interdependencies are listed, and all variables are defined in a data dictionary. Files are stored securely, backed up in several places, and then shared publicly if possible in an appropriate repository.

In reality, the key to RDM is understanding the fundamentals and best practices, then adapting them to one's circumstances and the needs of the researchers. Some investments are required when setting up a data management workflow. Time, labor, and funder requirements will primarily decide what best practices are practical, applicable, and most efficient.

CONCLUSION

Clearly, data management and sharing involve complex and context-specific decision-making, keeping in mind current and future use as well as funding agency and journal mandates. Researchers must decide how to manage data they are generating and using, as well as where they will share the data and how they will prepare them for sharing. Ethical dimensions must also be considered—sensitive and restricted data may never be shared openly or may be made available only decades after risk of harm has subsided. These complexities may seem daunting to researchers and impact their willingness to share. As openness becomes more of an expectation in academia, norms and incentives for data sharing will also need to shift accordingly to build a broader culture that supports data sharing. While the benefits are numerous, barriers both technological and cultural still exist. Researchers should consult with others, such as librarians or other information professionals, when more expertise is needed for overcoming barriers and engaging in good data-sharing practices.

ADDITIONAL RESOURCES

Arnold, Becky, Louise Bowler, Sarah Gibson, Patricia Herterich, Rosie Higman, Anna Krystalli, Alexander Morley, Martin O'Reilly, and Kirstie Whitaker. *The Turing Way: A Handbook for Reproducible Data Science*, version 0.0.4. Zenodo, March 25, 2019. https://doi.org/10.5281/zenodo.3233986.

Briney, Kristin A., Heather Coates, and Abigail Goben. "Foundational Practices of Research Data Management." *Research Ideas and Outcomes* 6 (2020): e56508. https://doi.org/10.3897/rio.6.e56508.

Cornell University Research Data Management Service Group. "Guide to Writing 'Readme' Style Metadata." Accessed April 30, 2020. https://data.research.cornell.edu/content/readme.

Data Curation Network. "Data Primers." GitHub. Accessed April 30, 2020. https://github.com/DataCurationNetwork/data-primers.

DMPTool. Home page. https://dmptool.org/.

FAIRsharing.org. Home page. Accessed April 30, 2020. https://fairsharing.org/.

Information Commissioner's Office. "Data Protection Impact Assessments." Last modified 2020. https://ico.org.uk/for-organisations/guide-to-data-protection/guide-to-the-general-data-protection-regulation-gdpr/accountability-and-governance/data-protection-impact-assessments/.

Library of Congress. "Recommended Formats Statement." Accessed April 30, 2020. https://www.loc.gov/preservation/resources/rfs/.

Markowetz, Florian. "Five Selfish Reasons to Work Reproducibly." *Genome Biology* 16 (2015): article 274. https://doi.org/10.1186/s13059-015-0850-7.

McGeever, Mags, Angus Whyte, and Laura Molloy. "Five Things You Need to Know about RDM and the Law: DCC Checklist on Legal Aspects of RDM." Digital Curation Centre, September 2015. https://www.dcc.ac.uk/guidance/how-guides/rdm-law.

McKiernan, Erin C., Philip E. Bourne, C. Titus Brown, Stuart Buck, Amye Kenall, Jennifer Lin, Damon McDougall, et al. "Point of View: How Open Science Helps Researchers Succeed." *eLife* 5 (2016): e16800. https://doi.org/10.7554/eLife.16800.

National Digital Stewardship Alliance. "Levels of Digital Preservation," version 2.0. Last modified 2019. https://ndsa.org//publications/levels-of-digital-preservation/.

Research Data Alliance. "Metadata Standards Directory." Accessed April 30, 2020. http://rd-alliance.github.io/metadata-directory/standards/.

Re3data.org: Registry of Research Data Repositories. Home page. Accessed April 30, 2020. https://doi.org/10.17616/R3D.

Riley, Jenn. *Understanding Metadata: What Is Metadata, and What Is It For? A Primer*. Baltimore, MD: NISO, 2017. https://www.niso.org/publications/understanding-metadata-2017.

DISCUSSION QUESTIONS

1. Have you ever used open data? If so, were there restrictions on use, and how easy or difficult was it to access and use the data?

2. When should data be shared in the research and publication life cycle?
3. What do you see as some of the barriers for sharing data? How can these barriers be overcome?

NOTES

1. National Academies of Sciences, Engineering, and Medicine, *Reproducibility and Replicability in Science* (Washington, DC: National Academies Press, 2019), https://doi.org/10.17226/25303.
2. Protocols.io, home page, https://www.protocols.io/; National Institute for Health Research, PROSPERO, https://www.crd.york.ac.uk/PROSPERO/.
3. Equator Network, home page, https://www.equator-network.org/.
4. Christine L. Borgman, *Big Data, Little Data, No Data* (Cambridge, MA: MIT Press, 2015), https://mitpress.mit.edu/9780262529914/big-data-little-data-no-data/.
5. Miriam Posner, "Humanities Data: A Necessary Contradiction," *Miriam Posner's Blog*, June 25, 2015, https://miriamposner.com/blog/humanities-data-a-necessary-contradiction/.
6. Jeremy Berg et al., "Joint Statement on EPA Proposed Rule and Public Availability of Data," *Science* 360, no. 6388 (2018): eaau0116, https://doi.org/10.1126/science.aau0116.
7. American Political Science Association, *A Guide to Professional Ethics in Political Science*, 2nd ed. (Washington DC: American Political Science Association, 2012), 9–10.
8. Mathias Astell, "Benefits of Data Sharing for You," *Research Data Community* (blog), SpringerNature, December 1, 2017, https://researchdata.springernature.com/posts/28549-benefits-of-data-sharing-for-you.
9. Heather A. Piwowar and Todd J. Vision, "Data Reuse and the Open Data Citation Advantage." *PeerJ*, no. 1 (2013): e175, https://doi.org/10.7717/peerj.175; Giovanni Colavizza et al., "The Citation Advantage of Linking Publications to Research Data," *PLOS ONE* 15, no. 4 (2020): e0230416, https://doi.org/10.1371/journal.pone.0230416; Garret Christensen et al., "A Study of the Impact of Data Sharing on Article Citations Using Journal Policies as a Natural Experiment," *PLOS ONE* 14, no. 12 (2019); e0225883, https://doi.org/10.1371/journal.pone.0225883.
10. GitHub, home page, accessed July 21, 2020, https://github.com/; Jupyter, home page, accessed July 21, 2020, https://jupyter.org/; Code Ocean, home page, accessed July 21, 2020, https://codeocean.com/; ReproZip, home page, accessed July 21, 2020, https://www.reprozip.org/.
11. Zenodo, home page, accessed July 21, 2020, https://zenodo.org/; Figshare, home page, accessed July 21, 2020, https://figshare.com/.
12. Openlabnotebooks.org, home page, accessed July 21, 2020, https://openlabnotebooks.org/.
13. OSF, home page, accessed July 21, 2020, https://osf.io/.
14. Mark D. Wilkinson et al., "The FAIR Guiding Principles for Scientific Data Management and Stewardship." *Scientific Data* 3 (March 2016): article 160018, https://doi.org/10.1038/sdata.2016.18
15. National Institute of Mental Health, "NIMH Data Archive," accessed July 21, 2020, https://nda.nih.gov/; Indiana University, "Indiana Spatial Data Portal," University Information Technology Services, accessed July 21, 2020, https://gis.iu.edu/; Data.gov, home page, accessed July 21, 2020, https://www.data.gov/; European Commission, "EU Open Data Portal," accessed July 21, 2020, https://data.europa.eu/euodp/en/home.
16. DataPortals.org, home page, accessed July 21, 2020, https://dataportals.org/; Open Knowledge Foundation, home page, accessed July 21, 2020, https://okfn.org/.
17. Erzsébet Tóth-Czifra, "One More Word about ResearchGate/Academia.edu and Why Using These Platforms Will Never Be Equal to Proper Self-Archiving," *DARIAH Open* (blog), May 31, 2020, upd. June 5, 2020, https://dariahopen.hypotheses.org/878.
18. Diana Kwon, "The Push to Replace Journal Supplements with Repositories," *Scientist*, August 19, 2019, website archive, https://web.archive.org/web/20190829200838/https://www.the-scientist.com/news-opinion/the-push-to-replace-journal-supplements-with-repositories--66296; Carlos Santos, Judith Blake, and David J. States, "Supplementary Data Need to Be Kept in Public Repositories," *Nature* 438, no. 7069 (2005): 738–738, https://doi.org/10.1038/438738a.
19. Timothy H. Vines et al., "The Availability of Research Data Declines Rapidly with Article Age," *Current Biology* 24, no. 1 (2014): 94–97, https://doi.org/10.1016/j.cub.2013.11.014.
20. Lisa R. Johnston et al., "Data Curation Activities," Data Curation Network, University of Minnesota Digital Conservancy, 2016, https://datacurationnetwork.org/data-curation-activities/.
21. Dublin Core Metadata Initiative, "Dublin Core," accessed April 27, 2020, https://dublincore.org/specifications/dublin-core/; DataCite, "DataCite Metadata Schema," accessed April 27, 2020, https://schema.datacite.org/.
22. Data Citation Synthesis Group, *Joint Declaration of Data Citation Principles*, ed. M. Martone (San Diego: FORCE11, 2014), https://doi.org/10.25490/a97f-egyk.

23. Creative Commons, "Share Your Work," accessed July 21, 2020, https://creativecommons.org/share-your-work/.
24. ICPSR, "Data Enclaves," accessed July 21, 2020, https://www.icpsr.umich.edu/web/pages/ICPSR/access/restricted/enclave.html; US Census Bureau, "Federal Statistical Research Data Centers," accessed July 21, 2020, https://www.census.gov/fsrdc.
25. Erika McCallister, Tim Grance, and Karen Scarfone, *Guide to Protecting the Confidentiality of Personally Identifiable Information (PII)*, NIST Special Publication 800-122 (Gaithersburg, MD: National Institute of Standards and Technology, April 2010), https://doi.org/10.6028/NIST.SP.800-122.
26. Adam Welz, "Unnatural Surveillance: How Online Data Is Putting Species at Risk," *YaleEnvironment360* (blog), September 6, 2017, https://e360.yale.edu/features/unnatural-surveillance-how-online-data-is-putting-species-at-risk.
27. Ayesha I. T. Tulloch et al., "A Decision Tree for Assessing the Risks and Benefits of Publishing Biodiversity Data," *Nature Ecology and Evolution* 2, no. 8 (August 2018): 1209–17, https://doi.org/10.1038/s41559-018-0608-1.
28. Latanya Sweeney, "Weaving Technology and Policy Together to Maintain Confidentiality," *The Journal of Law, Medicine & Ethics*, 25(2–3 (1997): 98–110, https://doi.org/10.1111/j.1748-720X.1997.tb01885.x.
29. Nils Homer et al, "Resolving Individuals Contributing Trace Amounts of DNA to Highly Complex Mixtures Using High-Density SNP Genotyping Microarrays," *PLOS Genetics 4*, no. 8(August 2008): e1000167, https://doi.org/10.1371/journal.pgen.1000167.
30. Arvind Narayanan and Vitaly Shmatikov, "Robust De-anonymization of Large Sparse Datasets," *2008 IEEE Symposium on Security and Privacy,* Spring 2008, Oakland, CA, USA, 2008, pp. 111-125, doi: 10.1109/SP.2008.33.
31. Latanya Sweeney, Akua Abu, and Julia Winn, "Identifying Participants in the Personal Genome Project by Name," April 29, 2013, http://dx.doi.org/10.2139/ssrn.2257732.
32. Luc Rocher, Julien M. Hendrickx, and Yves-Alexandre de Montjoye, "Estimating the success of re-identifications in incomplete datasets using generative models," *Nature Communications 10*, 3069 (2019), https://doi.org/10.1038/s41467-019-10933-3.
33. University of Minnesota Libraries, "Research Data Services," https://www.lib.umn.edu/services/data; University of California, Berkeley, "Research Data Management Program," https://researchdata.berkeley.edu/; Cornell University Libraries, "Research Data Management Service Group, https://data.research.cornell.edu/.
34. Data Curation Network, "Partner Institutions," accessed September 24, 2020, https://datacurationnetwork.org/about/partners/.
35. Carol Tenopir et al., *Research Data Services in Academic Libraries*, white paper (Middletown, CT: Choice, 2019), https://www.choice360.org/content/2-librarianship/5-whitepaper/tenopir-white-paper-2019/tenopir_121019_rds.pdf.
36. Victoria Goode and Blair Anton, "Welch Informationist Collaboration with the Johns Hopkins Medicine Department of Radiology," *Journal of eScience Librarianship* 2, no. 1 (2013): 16–19, https://doi.org/10.7191/jeslib.2013.1033; Sally Gore, "A Librarian by Any Other Name: The Role of the Informationist on a Clinical Research Team," *Journal of eScience Librarianship* 2, no. 1 (2013): 20–24, https://doi.org/10.7191/jeslib.2013.1041.
37. Minglu Wang and Bonnie L. Fong, "Embedded Data Librarianship: A Case Study of Providing Data Management Support for a Science Department," *Science and Technology Libraries* 34, no. 3 (July 3, 2015): 228-240, https://doi.org/10.1080/0194262X.2015.1085348.
38. Jeremy Garritano and Jake Carlson, "A Subject Librarian's Guide to Collaborating on e-Science Projects," *Issues in Science and Technology Librarianship*, no. 57 (Spring 2009), https://docs.lib.purdue.edu/lib_research/140.

BIBLIOGRAPHY

American Political Science Association. *A Guide to Professional Ethics in Political Science*, 2nd ed. Washington DC: American Political Science Association, 2012.
Astell, Mathias, "Benefits of Data Sharing for You." *Research Data Community* (blog), SpringerNature, December 1, 2017. https://researchdata.springernature.com/posts/28549-benefits-of-data-sharing-for-you.
Berg, Jeremy, Philip Campbell, Veronique Kiermer, Natasha Raikhel, and Deborah Sweet. "Joint Statement on EPA Proposed Rule and Public Availability of Data." *Science* 360, no. 6388 (2018): eaau0116. https://doi.org/10.1126/science.aau0116.
Borgman, Christine L. *Big Data, Little Data, No Data: Scholarship in the Networked World*. Cambridge, MA: MIT Press, 2015. https://mitpress.mit.edu/9780262529914/big-data-little-data-no-data/.

Christensen, Garret, Allan Dafoe, Edward Miguel, Don A. Moore, and Andrew K. Rose. "A Study of the Impact of Data Sharing on Article Citations Using Journal Policies as a Natural Experiment." *PLOS ONE* 14, no. 12 (2019): e0225883. https://doi.org/10.1371/journal.pone.0225883.

Code Ocean. Home page. Accessed July 21, 2020. https://codeocean.com/.

Colavizza, Giovanni, Iain Hrynaszkiewicz, Isla Staden, Kirstie Whitaker, and Barbara McGillivray. "The Citation Advantage of Linking Publications to Research Data." PLOS ONE 15, no. 4 (2020): e0230416. https://doi.org/10.1371/journal.pone.0230416.

Cornell University Libraries. "Research Data Management Service Group." https://data.research.cornell.edu/.

Creative Commons. "Share Your Work." Accessed July 21, 2020. https://creativecommons.org/share-your-work/.

Data Citation Synthesis Group. *Joint Declaration of Data Citation Principles*. Edited by M. Martone. San Diego: FORCE11, 2014. https://doi.org/10.25490/a97f-egyk.

DataCite. "DataCite Metadata Schema." Accessed April 27, 2020. https://schema.datacite.org/.

Data Curation Network. "Partner Institutions." Accessed September 24, 2020. https://datacurationnetwork.org/about/partners/.

Data.gov. Home page. Accessed July 21, 2020. https://www.data.gov/.

DataPortals.org. Home page. Accessed July 21, 2020. https://dataportals.org/.

Dublin Core Metadata Initiative. "Dublin Core." Accessed April 27, 2020. https://dublincore.org/specifications/dublin-core/.

Equator Network. Home page. https://www.equator-network.org/.

European Commission. "EU Data Protection Rules." Accessed September 24, 2020. https://ec.europa.eu/info/law/law-topic/data-protection/eu-data-protection-rules_en.

———. "EU Open Data Portal." Accessed July 21, 2020. https://data.europa.eu/euodp/en/home.

Family Educational Rights and Privacy Act (FERPA). Title 34 Code of Federal Regulations. Pt. 99. 2020.

Figshare. Home page. Accessed July 21, 2020. https://figshare.com/.

Garritano, Jeremy, and Jake Carlson. "A Subject Librarian's Guide to Collaborating on e-Science Projects." *Issues in Science and Technology Librarianship*, no. 57 (Spring 2009). https://docs.lib.purdue.edu/lib_research/140.

General Data Protection Regulation (GDPR). "Complete Guide to GDPR Compliance." https://gdpr.eu/.

———. "Principles Relating Processing of Personal Data." Article 5 of GDPR. https://gdpr.eu/article-5-how-to-process-personal-data/.

Genetic Information Nondiscrimination Act of 2008, Public Law 110-233, U.S. Statutes at Large 122 (2008): 881–922. https://www.govinfo.gov/app/details/STATUTE-122/STATUTE-122-Pg881.

GitHub. Home page. Accessed July 21, 2020. https://github.com/.

Goode, Victoria, and Blair Anton. "Welch Informationist Collaboration with the Johns Hopkins Medicine Department of Radiology." *Journal of eScience Librarianship* 2, no. 1 (2013): 16–19. https://doi.org/10.7191/jeslib.2013.1033.

Gore, Sally. "A Librarian by Any Other Name: The Role of the Informationist on a Clinical Research Team." *Journal of eScience Librarianship* 2, no. 1 (2013): 20–24. https://doi.org/10.7191/jeslib.2013.1041.

Homer Nils, Szabolcs Szelinger, Margot Redman, David Duggan, Waibhav Tembe, Jill Muehling, John V. Pearson, Dietrich A. Stephan, Stanley F. Nelson, and David W. Craig. "Resolving Individuals Contributing Trace Amounts of DNA to Highly Complex Mixtures Using High-Density SNP Genotyping Microarrays." *PLOS Genetics* 4, no. 8 (August 2008): e1000167. https://doi.org/10.1371/journal.pgen.1000167.

ICPSR. "Data Enclaves." Accessed July 21, 2020. https://www.icpsr.umich.edu/icpsrweb/content/ICPSR/access/restricted/enclave.html.

———. "Recommended Informed Consent Language for Data Sharing." Accessed September 24, 2020. https://www.icpsr.umich.edu/web/pages/datamanagement/confidentiality/conf-language.html.

Indiana University. "Indiana Spatial Data Portal." University Information Technology Services. Accessed July 21, 2020. https://gis.iu.edu/.

Johnston, Lisa R., Jake Carlson, Cynthia Hudson-Vitale, Heidi Imker, Wendy Kozlowski, Robert Olendorf, and Claire Stewart. "Definitions of Data Curation Activities Used by the Data Curation Network." Data Curation Network, University of Minnesota Digital Conservancy, 2016. https://datacurationnetwork.org/data-curation-activities/.

Jupyter. Home page. Accessed July 21, 2020. https://jupyter.org/.

Kwon, Diana. "The Push to Replace Journal Supplements with Repositories." *Scientist*, August 19, 2019. Website archive. https://web.archive.org/web/20190829200838/https://www.the-scientist.com/news-opinion/the-push-to-replace-journal-supplements-with-repositories--66296.

McCallister, Erika, Tim Grance, and Karen Scarfone. *Guide to Protecting the Confidentiality of Personally Identifiable Information (PII): Recommendations of the National Institute of Standards and Technology*. NIST Special Publication 800-122. Gaithersburg, MD: National Institute of Standards and Technology, April 2010. https://doi.org/10.6028/NIST.SP.800-122.

Narayanan, Arvind, and Vitaly Shmatikov. "Robust De-anonymization of Large Sparse Datasets." *2008 IEEE Symposium on Security and Privacy (Spring 2008)*, Oakland, CA, USA, 2008, pp. 111-125. doi: 10.1109/SP.2008.33.

National Academies of Sciences, Engineering, and Medicine. *Reproducibility and Replicability in Science.* Washington, DC: National Academies Press, 2019. https://doi.org/10.17226/25303.

National Human Genome Research Institute. "Genetic Discrimination." Accessed September 24, 2020. https://www.genome.gov/about-genomics/policy-issues/Genetic-Discrimination.

National Institute for Health Research. PROSPERO. https://www.crd.york.ac.uk/PROSPERO/.

National Institute of Mental Health. "NIMH Data Archive." Accessed July 21, 2020. https://nda.nih.gov/.

Open Knowledge Foundation. Home page. Accessed July 21, 2020. https://okfn.org/.

Openlabnotebooks.org. Home page. Accessed July 21, 2020. https://openlabnotebooks.org/.

OSF. Home page. Accessed July 21, 2020. https://osf.io/.

Piwowar, Heather A., and Todd J. Vision. "Data Reuse and the Open Data Citation Advantage." *PeerJ*, no. 1 (2013): e175. https://doi.org/10.7717/peerj.175.

Posner, Miriam. "Humanities Data: A Necessary Contradiction." *Miriam Posner's Blog*, June 25, 2015. https://miriamposner.com/blog/humanities-data-a-necessary-contradiction/.

Protocols.io. Home page. https://www.protocols.io/.

Qualitative Data Repository. "Informed Consent." Accessed September 24, 2020. https://qdr.syr.edu/guidance/human-participants/informed-consent.

ReproZip. Home page. Accessed July 21, 2020. https://www.reprozip.org/.

Rocher, Luc, Julien M. Hendrickx, and Yves-Alexandre de Montjoye. "Estimating the success of re-identifications in incomplete datasets using generative models." *Nature Communications 10*, 3069 (2019). https://doi.org/10.1038/s41467-019-10933-3.

Santos, Carlos, Judith Blake, and David J. States. "Supplementary Data Need to Be Kept in Public Repositories." *Nature* 438, no. 7069 (2005): 738–738. https://doi.org/10.1038/438738a.

Scientific Data and Mathias Astell. "Benefits of Open Research Data Infographic." Figshare, July 11, 2017. https://doi.org/10.6084/m9.figshare.5179006.v3.

Sweeney, Latanya. "Weaving Technology and Policy Together to Maintain Confidentiality." *The Journal of Law, Medicine & Ethics*, 25(2–3 (1997): 98–110. https://doi.org/10.1111/j.1748-720X.1997.tb01885.x.

Sweeney, Latanya, Akua Abu, and Julia Winn. "Identifying Participants in the Personal Genome Project by Name." April 29, 2013. http://dx.doi.org/10.2139/ssrn.2257732.

TalkBank. "IRB Approval." Accessed September 24, 2020. https://talkbank.org/share/irb/.

Tenopir, Carol, Jordan Kaufman, Robert Sandusky, and Danielle Pollock. *Research Data Services in Academic Libraries: Where Are We Today?* White paper. Middletown, CT: Choice, 2019. http://www.choice360.org/content/2-librarianship/5-whitepaper/tenopir-white-paper-2019/tenopir_121019_rds.pdf.

Tóth-Czifra, Erzsébet. "One More Word about ResearchGate/Academia.edu and Why Using These Platforms Will Never Be Equal to Proper Self-Archiving." *DARIAH Open* (blog), May 31, 2020, upd. June 5, 2020. https://dariahopen.hypotheses.org/878.

Tulloch, Ayesha I. T., Nancy Auerbach, Stephanie Avery-Gomm, Elisa Bayraktarov, Nathalie Butt, Chris R. Dickman, Glenn Ehmke, et al. "A Decision Tree for Assessing the Risks and Benefits of Publishing Biodiversity Data." *Nature Ecology and Evolution* 2, no. 8 (August 2018): 1209–17. https://doi.org/10.1038/s41559-018-0608-1.

UK Data Service. "Consent for Data Sharing." Accessed September 24, 2020. https://ukdataservice.ac.uk/learning-hub/research-data-management/ethical-issues/consent-for-data-sharing/.

University of California, Berkeley. "Research Data Management Program." https://researchdata.berkeley.edu/.

University of Minnesota Libraries. "Research Data Services." https://www.lib.umn.edu/services/data.

US Census Bureau. "Federal Statistical Research Data Centers." Accessed July 21, 2020. https://www.census.gov/fsrdc.

US Department of Education. "Privacy and Data Sharing." Accessed September 24, 2020. https://studentprivacy.ed.gov/privacy-and-data-sharing.

US Department of Health and Human Services. "Research." Accessed September 24, 2020. https://www.hhs.gov/hipaa/for-professionals/special-topics/research/index.html.

Vines, Timothy. H., Arianne Y. K. Albert, Rose L. Andrew, Florence Débarre, Dan G. Bock, Michelle T. Franklin, Kimberly J. Gilbert, et al. "The Availability of Research Data Declines Rapidly with Article Age." *Current Biology* 24, no. 1 (2014): 94–97. https://doi.org/10.1016/j.cub.2013.11.014.

Wang, Minglu, and Bonnie L. Fong. "Embedded Data Librarianship: A Case Study of Providing Data Management Support for a Science Department." *Science and Technology Libraries* 34, no. 3 (July 3, 2015): 228–40. https://doi.org/10.1080/0194262X.2015.1085348.

Welz, Adam. "Unnatural Surveillance: How Online Data Is Putting Species at Risk." *YaleEnvironment360* (blog), September 6, 2017. https://e360.yale.edu/features/unnatural-surveillance-how-online-data-is-putting-species-at-risk.

Wilkinson, Mark D., Michel Dumontier, IJsbrand Jan Aalbersberg, Gabrielle Appleton, Myles Axton, Arie Baak, Niklas Blomberg, et al. "The FAIR Guiding Principles for Scientific Data Management and Stewardship." *Scientific Data* 3 (March 2016): article 160018, https://doi.org/10.1038/sdata.2016.18.

Zenodo. Home page. Accessed July 21, 2020. https://zenodo.org/.

SUPPORTING REPRODUCIBLE RESEARCH

Gabriele Hayden, Tisha Mentnech, Vicky Rampin, and Franklin Sayre

INTRODUCTION

Claims are more likely to be credible—or found wanting—when they can be reviewed, critiqued, extended, and reproduced by others. All phases of the research process provide opportunities for assessing and improving the reliability and efficacy of scientific research.

—National Academies of Sciences, Engineering, and Medicine[1]

In the last decade there has been growing concern that many research studies are not reproducible. This has led to declarations that we are experiencing a "reproducibility crisis" and questions about the veracity of studies used for decision-making in everything from public policy to patient care. Studies looking at the reproducibility of disciplines have occurred in psychology, biology, biomedicine, neuroscience, drug development, chemistry, climate science, economics, and education, and in no field were the majority of findings found to be reproducible.

Reproducibility is considered a fundamental characteristic of research and is a multifaceted concept that broadly refers to the ability of researchers to get the same results when repeating an analysis. There have been many proposed definitions of reproducibility and the related concept of replicability. Here we adopt the definitions proposed in 2015 by Bollen and Kaplin. *Reproducibility* is the ability to take the original methods and data and get the same results. *Replicability* entails the same methods but involves collecting new data and getting substantially the same results. (Because new data is collected, you wouldn't expect exactly the same results.)[2] While this chapter deals primarily with reproducibility, many of the recommendations for improving reproducibility will also make replication easier.

In theory, all published and especially peer-reviewed research should be reproducible. After all, reproducibility doesn't involve anything more than redoing what was originally done, using the original methods and data. In actuality the story is usually more complicated. Experimental and qualitative research increasingly involves large teams, computational tools, and vast amounts of data. Research in fields that do not use experiments will often have some elements that cannot be reproduced.[3] At the same time, scholarly communication has stayed more or less the same for centuries: authors write short narrative reports describing their research, often with strict space limits, which are then peer-reviewed by others who may or may not have access to the underlying research materials, and finally publish in traditional journals. The underlying data is often carefully guarded and methods are described in abstract terms with critical details left out, thus complicating reproducibility.

This book discusses many of the problems with traditional publishing and the advantages of adopting more open practices. The previous section discussed research data management (RDM) and data sharing and how those practices ensure that the study's underlying data can be found, understood, and used. Reproducibility requires that we go further and share as much detail as possible as transparently as possible. Reproducibility thus provides one of the strongest justifications for open scholarly communication practices such as data and code sharing, transparent methods reporting, and open publishing models and metrics. *Reproducibility requires that we adopt open and transparent methods, not just as an abstract good but as a fundamental part of research practice.*

Many of these areas are core aspects of academic librarianship and entail the expertise of librarians and other information professionals. They relate to the packaging of scholarship: how research is described and shared with others, how research is cited, and how impact is measured. The role of information professionals in supporting reproducibility is being increasingly recognized both within librarianship and by researchers, funders, and institutions. Stodden and colleagues highlighted the role librarians could play in "supporting a culture change toward reproducible …research" including using academic libraries' rich connections with departments to support and manage digital scholarly output.[4] In 2017 Vicky Rampin (then Vicky Steeves) described the new field of reproducibility librarianship,[5] and the National Institutes of Health advisory committee recommended that they "lead efforts to support and catalyze open science, data sharing, and research reproducibility."[6] A conference about how librarians can support reproducibility that was organized by several of the authors of this chapter in 2020 drew almost 200 attendees and presenters from around the world.[7]

Librarians aren't the only stakeholders engaged with this topic. Reproducibility is a complex and rapidly changing topic with new studies, guidelines, policies, organizations, and technologies being announced regularly. As discussed in the previous section, reproducibility is also highly discipline-specific; in some areas it has received significant attention, and institutions such as journals and funders have started putting in place measures to address concerns. In other areas researchers are just starting to think through how to make their work more reproducible.

Providing a comprehensive guide to all these issues is beyond the scope of this section. Instead, we focus on five ways librarians can support reproducible research. These ideas are immediately actionable, build on existing services and expertise, and if widely implemented would have a major impact. These ideas are

1. Help researchers find and use reporting guidelines in order to improve reporting and transparency.
2. Promote and support preregistration of studies in order to improve evaluation of research.
3. Support researchers in creating computational pipelines in order to improve methods.
4. Preserve computational environments in order to improve sustainability.
5. Educate researchers about alternative and new scholarly metrics in order to shift incentives.

These aren't the only ways librarians and other information professionals can support reproducibility, and at the end of this section we briefly explore broader roles. We also provide an extensive guide to basic definitions, tools, and resources.

FIVE BIG IDEAS FOR SUPPORTING REPRODUCIBLE RESEARCH

HELP RESEARCHERS FIND AND USE REPORTING GUIDELINES

Many recommendations for improving reproducibility focus on improvising the reporting of a study's methodology, analysis, and results. Traditionally, methods sections have been short descriptions of what the researcher did, with how that was communicated left almost entirely up to the author. Intentionally or unintentionally, details were often left out or described with too little detail to be reproducible by a reviewer or reader. This has become an even greater problem as research has grown more complex and reliant on more people and tools.

Reporting guidelines are detailed lists of what researchers need to report and at what level of detail in order for readers to fully understand, evaluate, and reproduce a study. These guidelines promote transparent and accurate reporting by helping researchers think about what they need to report, either in the text of their article or by publishing data, code, or supplemental files. Many journals now require that authors follow reporting guidelines when submitting an article.

There are different reporting guidelines for different study designs because each design requires authors to report different things. Guidelines are usually created by groups of researchers who look at what needs to be reported for a methodology to be understood and then publish a consensus paper in a major journal that outlines how the guideline was developed and what it requires. The best resource for finding reporting guidelines is the EQUATOR Network (https://www.equator-network.org/reporting-guidelines/), an international collaboration of groups seeking to improve reporting by creating, publishing, and promoting guidelines. The EQUATOR Network also collects these guidelines into a single resource with many of the most important guidelines hosted on its website. Many professional societies also offer discipline-specific guidelines; for example, the American Medical Association and the American Psychological Association include reporting guidelines as part of their style guides.[8]

Many of the best known guidelines are for qualitative methodologies such as randomized controlled trials (RCTs), but a good example of a guideline for qualitative studies is the "Standards for Reporting Qualitative Research: A Synthesis of Recommendations," or SRQR.[9] The SRQR is "a list of 21 items that we consider essential for complete, transparent reporting of qualitative research."[10] As you can see from table 2.5, guidelines simply list information that should be included.

Librarians can help promote reporting guidelines by teaching researchers about them and promoting them on research guides, in workshops, and during consultations. Researchers often don't know about these guidelines until they are preparing a manuscript for submission and are happy to have a template for thinking about what they will need to report when they are writing up their research. Guidelines can also help new researchers evaluate other articles and think through what they need to do when designing their own studies.

Health science librarians have a long history of promoting, using, and creating reporting guidelines due to their work with systematic reviews and the PRISMA (Preferred Reporting Items for Systematic Reviews and Meta-analyses) checklist.[11] The PRISMA checklist sets out elements that need to be reported in a systematic review for others to understand how the research was conducted. PRISMA has always asked researchers to report on aspects of their search strategy, but recently PRISMA-S has been published, an extension to the PRISMA Statement with specific elements required for understanding and reproducing.[12]

TABLE 2.5

"Standards for Reporting Qualitative Research: A Synthesis of Recommendations," or SRQR, Methods section. See full table at https://journals.lww.com/academicmedicine/_layouts/15/oaks.journals/ImageView.aspx?k=academicmedicine:2014:09000:00021&i=T1-21&year=2014&issue=09000&article=00021&type=Fulltext.

No.	Topic	Item
S6	Researcher characteristics and reflexivity	Researchers' characteristics that may influence the research, including personal attributes, qualifications/experience, relationship with participants, assumptions, and/or presuppositions; potential or actual interaction between researchers' characteristics and the research questions, approach, methods, results, and/or transferability
S7	Context	Setting/site and salient contextual factors; rationale*
S8	Sampling strategy	How and why research participants, documents, or events were selected; criteria for deciding when no further sampling was necessary (e.g., sampling saturation); rationale*
S9	Ethical issues pertaining to human subjects	Documentation of approval by an appropriate ethics review board and participant consent, or explanation for lack thereof; other confidentiality and data security issues
S10	Data collection methods	Types of data collected; details of data collection procedures including (as appropriate) start and stop dates of data collection and analysis, iterative process, triangulation of sources/methods, and modification of procedures in response to evolving study findings; rationale*
S11	Data collection instruments and technologies	Description of instruments (e.g., interview guides, questionnaires) and devices (e.g., audio recorders) used for data collection; if/how the instrument(s) changed over the course of the study
S12	Units of study	Number and relevant characteristics of participants, documents, or events included in the study; level of participation (could be reported in results)
S13	Data processing	Methods for processing data prior to and during analysis, including transcription, data entry, data management and security, verification of data integrity, data coding, and anonymization/deidentification of excerpts
S14	Data analysis	Process by which inferences, themes, etc., were identified and developed, including the researchers involved in data analysis; usually references a specific paradigm or approach; rationale*
S15	Techniques to enhance trustworthiness	Techniques to enhance trustworthiness and credibility of data analysis (e.g., member checking, audit trail, triangulation); rationale*

*   The rationale should briefly discuss the justification for choosing that theory, approach, method, or technique rather than other options available, the assumptions and limitations implicit in those choices, and how those choices influence study conclusions and transferability. As appropriate, the rationale for several items might be discussed together.

PROMOTE AND SUPPORT PREREGISTRATIONS AND REGISTERED REPORTS

Preregistration is when authors explicitly and publicly share or publish their study hypothesis and design in a journal or online repository before they begin their research. This is very different from the traditional model where the hypothesis and design are carefully guarded until publication out of fear of being scooped, though some repositories allow preregistrations to be embargoed (i.e., not made fully public for a limited period of time).

Preregistration helps limit bias by reducing opportunities for authors to change their methodology after collecting data in order to get a positive result, also known as HARKing (hypothesizing after results are known). Authors can still make changes to their plan after registration, but because it was already reported they would need to explain and justify those changes on publication. Preregistration also provides a framework for a research project and places an emphasis on transparency in planning and methodology from the start of the project. The Center for Open Science (COS) publicizes and offers model workflows for preregistration. More information on preregistration and preregistration templates can be found on the OSF Preregistration page (https://www.cos.io/initiatives/prereg).

For decades, preregistration has been common and even mandated for some RCTs that are federally funded, and registrations are publicly available at ClinicalTrials.gov. Preregistration is also common for systematic reviews and publicly available in PROS-PERO, a UK-based international prospective register of systematic reviews, and within some journals.

Registered reports are a new publication type that wraps a preregistration into a journal article. These registered reports are peer-reviewed before data collection and are accepted in principle; that is, the journal agrees to publish the final results of the study on the strength of the proposed methods and regardless of the outcome. This has benefits for both individual research groups and the field as a whole. It helps reduce positive results bias, a type of publication bias in which only positive results are published, thus systematically biasing the published literature toward novel results that may not be reproducible. It incentivizes researchers to share their methodology in order to get valuable feedback before data collection and a guaranteed publication once the registered report is in principle accepted. More information can be found on the COS Registered Reports page (https://www.cos.io/initiatives/registered-reports).

Library and information professionals can support and educate researchers about the benefits of preregistration and registered reports and how they promote transparency in research, as well as walk them through the available templates and tools. Library and information professionals are involved in supporting all areas of the research enterprise. Promoting and providing information on preregistrations and registered reports is another way to actively support transparency and reproducible research in scholarly communication.

HELP RESEARCHERS CREATE PIPELINES FOR COMPUTATIONAL REPRODUCIBILITY

A number of drivers of irreproducibility relate to issues with study design and analysis.[*] In the introduction we discussed reproducibility and how it requires transparent open methods and data. Section 2.2.2, on RDM, explored how to manage and share research data so it can be understood, used, and shared. Here we extend these concepts to discuss computational reproducibility and specifically how computational pipelines can support more open and transparent methods.

---

[*] Study design and statistical analysis are highly dependent on the discipline and method used and require disciplinary and methodological expertise. Issues related to study design and analysis are usually harder for librarians and information professionals to directly help address unless they have specific disciplinary and methodological expertise and are embedded on a project. There are some methodologies, such as systematic reviews, that librarians can directly support, but in many other cases it's not appropriate. Here we focus on ways that all LIS professionals can support better methods.

A computational pipeline is "an interdependent set of programs with manipulable parameters, including program version and input data, which output some usable result."[13] For instance, an analysis script in a programming language like Python or R that takes some data as the input and produces an output could be considered a computational pipeline. Another example could be a server website application from a digital humanities project that takes a database and displays a map for a GIS analysis. The goal of computational pipelines is to take any manual or isolated steps and turn them into holistic automated processes that can be documented, audited, and rerun.

Data processing with OpenRefine is a good example of a well-documented computational pipeline.[14] OpenRefine is an open source tool that allows users to load in data in many formats (e.g., CSV, TSV, HTML, etc.), transform and process it quickly and accurately, and then export it. It keeps track of the processing steps that you use *in the order you run them* as a JSON file.[15] JSON is a machine- and human-readable text format that others can use to re-create the pipeline *exactly*. You can see an example of this in figure 2.2, where the left side shows in plain language the steps in order, and the right side shows the JSON version of the same workflow. If you give someone else this JSON file and your raw data, they will be able to reproduce your pipeline exactly.

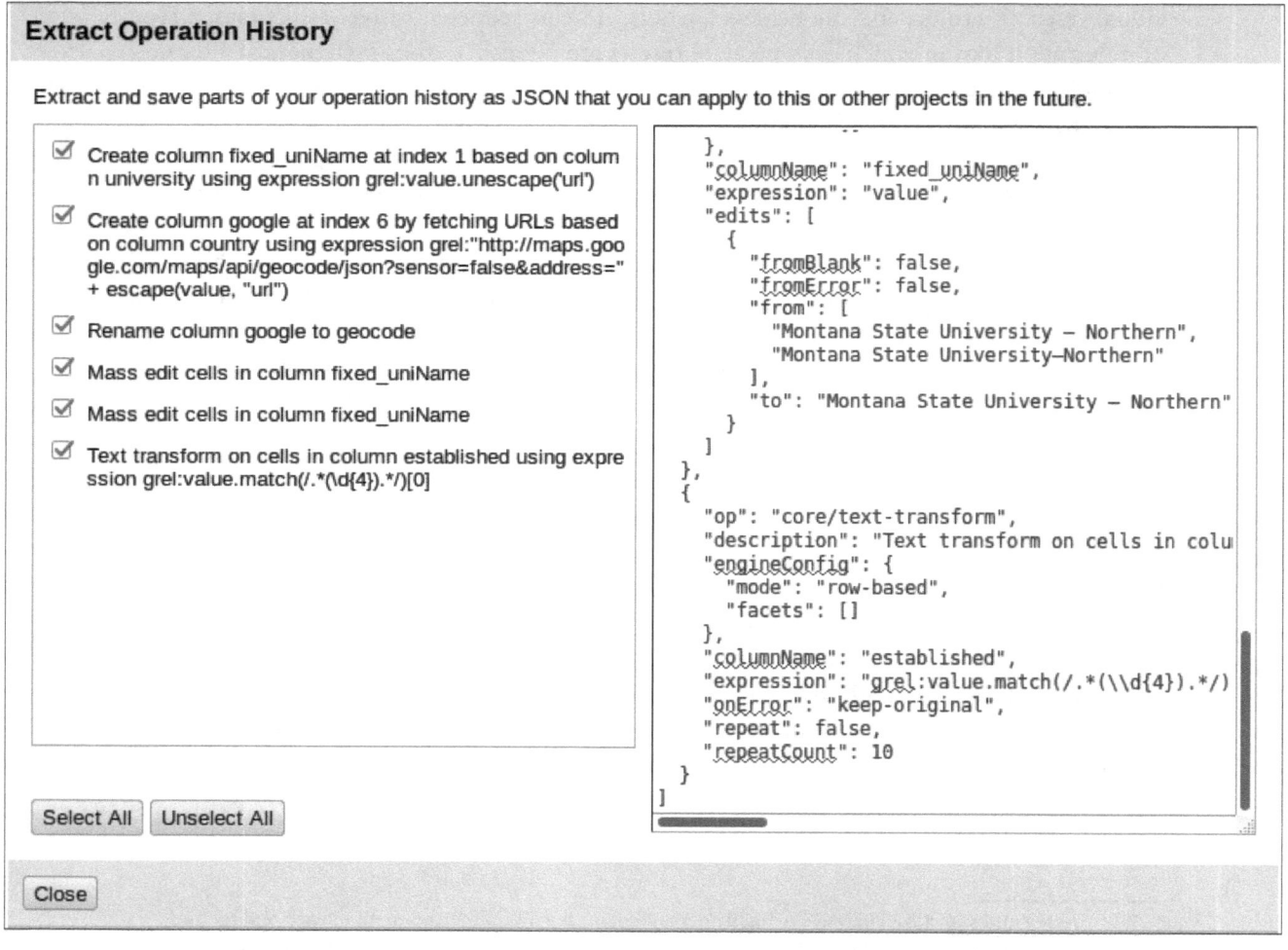

Figure 2.2

Screenshot of OpenRefine's operation history.

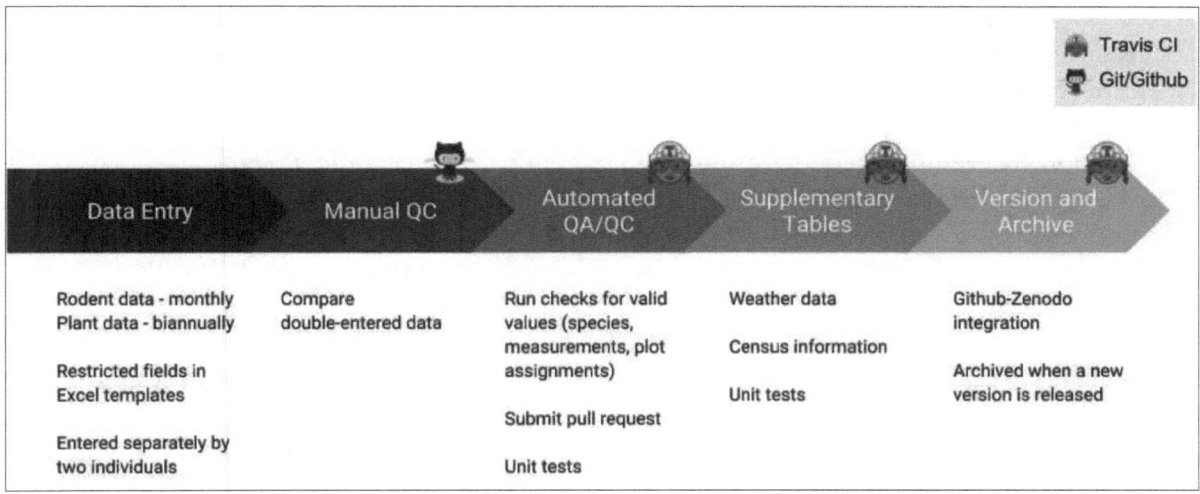

Figure 2.3
Data workflow from Glenda M. Yenni et al., "Developing a Modern Data Workflow for Evolving Data," preprint, BioRxiv, July 24, 2018, p. 5, https://doi.org/10.1101/344804 is used under CC-BY 4.0.

OpenRefine is one of the most reproducible data-processing tools available because of this ability to export, reuse, and share a full pipeline. Given that OpenRefine's pipeline steps are outlined in JSON, they can be easily version controlled so we can see how the pipeline changes over time in ways that potentially affect the research output. This information provides more context for the readers and reviewers.

Computational pipelines can also be more complex when they involve additional computations, such as performing a calculation or creating a visualization.

These computations add complexities to pipelines in terms of software and sometimes even hardware dependencies, as, for example, when the pipeline runs on high-performance computing systems. A great example of a more complex computational pipeline comes from Yenni and colleagues, who describe transitioning their lab from manual data processing (see figure 2.3) to a more automated computational pipeline.[16] Their stated motivations were to

> 1) perform quality assurance and control; 2) import, restructure, version, and archive data; 3) rapidly publish new data in ways that ensure appropriate credit to all contributors; and 4) automate most steps in the data pipeline to reduce the time and effort required by researchers. The workflow uses two tools from software development, version control and continuous integration to create a modern data management system that automates the pipeline.[17]

Yenni and colleagues wanted to eliminate potential spots for human error, as well as create a reproducible, well-documented computational pipeline that others can use.[18] This speaks to one of the goals of computational reproducibility: at the end of a project, make a *research compendium* or a *reproducible bundle* of the pipeline.[19] This is a package that contains all of the things necessary to reproduce your work, from data and code to the computational environment:

> Research compendia are an increasingly used form of publication, which packages not only the research paper's text and figures, but also all data and software for better reproducibility.[20]

Computational pipelines enable *computational reproducibility*, which is the ability to rerun a pipeline using the original computational environment and dependencies, facilitated through the use of research compedia. This is harder than expected, as it requires using the precise version of the software originally used with the exact parameters and input data, and occasionally even particular hardware configurations.[21] The terms *data reproducibility* or *code reproducibility* are also used to describe similar goals but fall short because to reproduce others' work, it's necessary to have not only the data and code, but also the entire *computational* setting in which the research takes place. Without this computational setting, code may fail unexpectedly or may produce subtly different results.

For example, Gronenschild and colleagues found significant differences in the results of neuroscience analyses when using the analysis software FreeSurfer in different types of computational settings (e.g., one running Mac OSX 10.5 and 10.6, an HP versus an Apple workstation, and with two different versions of FreeSurfer).[22] What we are actually trying to keep reproducible is the entire analysis pipeline, hence the name *computational reproducibility*. And of course, there are often multiple pipelines for a given project—for the data preparation, data analysis, data visualizations, and so on. So when we talk about something being computationally reproducible (or not, or reproducible to a varying degree), we're usually talking about one of those pipelines, not any particular object within them (such as data or code).

The ideal situation is to package these computational pipelines into a research compendium that can later be rerun to verify research claims (by a peer reviewer, for instance), build upon it for complementary use cases, and teach newcomers valuable methodologies using real-world research. Sandve and colleagues discuss some basic steps toward computational reproducibility that center on creating computational pipelines.[23] It's worth noting here that computational reproducibility relies on following RDM best practices, just with a few extra steps (the computational part!). If the work can be rerun but not understood, there's limited utility to it. Following the RDM best practices will make sure that your work is rerunnable and understandable not only by machines, but also humans. Creating research compendia that include the computational pipeline is the next step for full computational reproducibility.

Computational Reproducibility in Primarily Non-computational Fields

As computation and interdisciplinary work become widespread in fields that are still dominated by non-computational work, several issues arise. First, it becomes increasingly important that scholars who do not themselves use computational methods understand and value openness and computational reproducibility in order to engage with and assess the work of their colleagues. Second, the computational work practiced in primarily non-computational fields offers many of the same challenges to computational reproducibility, such as using proprietary software, building one-off programs that soon become orphaned or unsupported, or depending on graphical interfaces whose computational dependencies are challenging to document and archive.

Digital humanists are scholars trained in the humanities who study digital artifacts or who use computational methods to study topics traditional to the humanities. They offer one example of scholars who often have colleagues who practice non-computational work. In the past, prominent practitioners sometimes used this fact to lend obscurantist weight to their work, as when Franco Moretti described literary data that he did not share or make open as factual and "independent of interpretation."[24] Even when transparency and computational reproducibility are valued, as they increasingly are, digital humanities projects often involve using or building programs with graphical user interfaces or other elements that do not lend themselves easily to the project of reproducibility. These programs can be proprietary, one-off, or not supported over the long term by the research group that created them. Even when they are open source, the complexity of their technology stack (the programs used to build them) makes them more challenging to reproduce than statistical analyses or visualizations built in R or Python.

A number of solutions have been proposed to address the challenges of hard-to-reproduce and hard-to-archive computational work. One solution used for archiving digital exhibits is web archiving technology. For example, many institutions use Archive-It for static websites and Webrecorder for interactive websites.[25] However, these capture only images or video of the sites rather than the sites themselves. Another promising avenue is the use of ReproZip-Web,[26] an extension of ReproZip (discussed below), to archive the software and code that creates digital journalism and other interactive data visualization websites.[27]

Qualitative social science researchers are another category of researchers whose work sometimes resists classical definitions of reproducibility and whose computational work faces reproducibility challenges. Many of the programs for coding qualitative data and managing media formats such as photos and video are proprietary. For qualitative social scientists, open source programs for qualitative coding such as Taguette and QCoder can simplify data sharing.[28]

PRESERVE COMPUTATIONAL ENVIRONMENTS TO ENSURE SUSTAINABLE REUSE OF RESEARCH

In section 2.2.2, you learned about RDM and data sharing, and above we discussed how computational pipelines can be used to ensure different research workflows can be made reproducible and shareable. While software and data preservation are critical to ensure reproducibility, we also need to preserve the actual computational environment in which the research takes place (much as we need the environment for computational reproducibility!). Many modern research practices (and pipelines) rely on unique toolkits, and the output from these tools often depend on the actual software in which the research happens.[29] Because of this, researchers need to be able to interact with research pipelines in their original computational environment to faithfully reproduce the work: "There is a very clear need to preserve not only digital objects, but reliable access to these objects, which means adopting one or more approaches toward software preservation."[30]

This work is done by those involved in software preservation, a subfield of digital preservation concerned with selecting, accessioning, ingesting, describing, accessing, and archiving of software and associated contextual files (e.g., documentation). This is different from preserving source code: human-readable, uncompiled, plain-text files (e.g., script.py). *Software* refers to compiled code, such as an operating system, or an application (e.g., a file with an .exe extension for Windows programs). Software preservation spans many types of professional activities, ranging from large-scale downloading and archiving of software to in-depth software curation and emulation efforts for specific pieces of software or hardware.[31] Hong and colleagues describe several techniques for software preservation:

- Technical preservation (techno-centric)—Preserve original hardware and software in same state
- Emulation (data-centric)—Emulate original hardware and operating environment, keeping software in same state

- Migration (functionality-centric)—Update software as required to maintain same functionality, porting/transferring before platform obsolescence

- Cultivation (process-centric)—Keep software 'alive' by moving to more open development model bringing on board additional contributors and spreading knowledge of process

- Hibernation (knowledge-centric)—Preserve the knowledge of how to resuscitate/recreate the exact functionality of the software at a later date[32]

Hong and colleagues also outline the considerations for each strategy as it relates to research software in service of reproducibility and archiving of the scholarly record.[33] The authors highlight technical preservation and emulation as ways to continue to access research materials in the long term for reproducibility, and migration, cultivation, and hibernation as the most applicable strategies to promote software reuse.

One general digital preservation tool widely used for reproducible research efforts is BagIt.[34] BagIt is a specification for hierarchical file system conventions. It was designed for export of content normally kept in database structures that are likely to degrade or lose support, as well as to be shipped around to different storage locations. A *bag* in the BagIt terminology has a *payload* and *tags*, which are metadata that describes the storage and transfer of the bag.[35] This specification is widely used by computational reproducibility tools as a means of structuring the research compendia that can be exported out of the platform. Digital archivists use this format for storing data and code for the long term for manual curation processes. Exporting research compendia as bags is attractive because the format integrates well with archival repositories and version control systems, it has the ability to reference external data (e.g., external to the bag), it includes awareness of provenance, it is flexible, and it is readable by humans (see figure 2.4).[36]

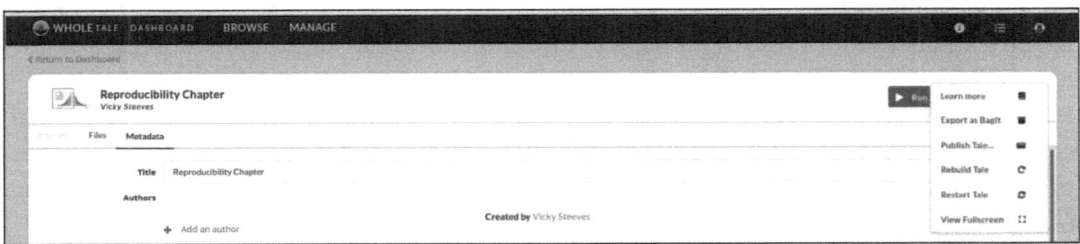

Figure 2.4
Whole Tale (described in appendix B), for instance, allows users to export their tale as a bag.

One project geared specifically toward software preservation taking active steps to be useful for reproducibility use cases is the Emulation-as-a-Service Infrastructure (EaaSI) project.[37] This project seeks to scale up access to Emulation-as-a-Service (EaaS), which is a tool that spins up emulated computational environments whenever a user wants.[38] EaaS uses configuration templates (stored in XML—which is also easily versioned and shared) to assemble emulated hardware and data as specified by the user. This is done either manually, through a web form, or automatically, by importing it from another tool (e.g., ReproZip bundles, Docker and Singularity containers). The user is presented with a virtual computing environment that mimics the behavior of a physical machine. This can be used as a virtual reading room for users who want to interact with legacy materials using the original software, but it also can be used to reproduce legacy research no matter what operating system, no matter how far in the future.[39]

Software preservation is directly tied to the ability to reproduce research in the long term, as well as being a valuable activity for preserving an important cultural artifact. However, "successfully collecting, preserving, and providing access to software as a research object will likely require significant policy and procedural development for research libraries."[40] The costs associated with staff and resources, as well as legal and social challenges, make software preservation a difficult endeavor. However, it's critically important in ensuring the sustainability of research created today, yesterday, and tomorrow.

EDUCATE RESEARCHERS ABOUT CITATION PRACTICES TO CHANGE INCENTIVES

Challenges to reproducibility and replicability persist in part because the pressures of publication, promotion, and tenure are often in direct conflict with best practices for reproducibility. Researchers are encouraged to publish novel and surprising results in high-impact journals and to keep data and other artifacts for themselves in order to maximize its potential future utility. This incentivizes poor and opaque research practices. These incentives exist not only at the individual level but also in the business models of large, interlocking institutions. They are bound up with university prestige and rankings, journal conventions and journal ranking systems, and department- and university-level tenure criteria. At the level of the individual actor (a researcher) or even at the level of the individual institution (a university or journal), the pressure to follow existing conventions is immense.

Despite institutional and cultural challenges, changing how research is incentivized to promote reproducible and transparent practices is one of the best ways to help fix the reproducibility crisis.[41] Researchers across a broad range of disciplines are advocating for the practice of reproducible research within their own fields and making practices of reproducible research part of their research agenda. Advocates often argue for discipline-specific reproducibility and are often responding to discipline-specific incentives that favor reproducibility.[42] For example, social psychology became invested in reproducible research as a result of a crisis of legitimacy in the discipline.[43] A decade later the push for reproducible research in psychology has begun to spread to the social sciences generally.[44] Biomedical research faces a complex set of competing incentives, but ultimately the demand for drugs, treatments, and medical devices that work helps drive support for reproducibility among funders and government agencies.[45]

Many of these researchers advocate for broadening what is considered a legitimate output of research to include things like openly shared code and data, preprints, and new types of publications like registered reports. As researchers in individual disciplines slowly change the consensus within their field regarding what counts as research outputs, this in turn changes criteria for tenure and promotion within that field. Change can also come from the top down. The decision of major granting organizations like the National Science Foundation (NSF) to begin requiring data management plans (DMPs) in 2010 raised both the awareness and the practice of sharing data as well.[46] It also helped drive the development of important infrastructure, such as data repositories. The position of research data management librarian exists in part due to the institutional need for someone to support faculty and principal investigators (PIs) writing DMPs for grants, and the recent move in libraries to support reproducibility similarly responds to demand for this support from funders.[47] Thus, for example, when the National Institutes of Health launched new grant application instructions regarding rigor and reproducibility in 2015, the library faculty at the Spencer S. Eccles Health Sciences Library at the University of Utah responded by hosting a conference and symposium.[48] This is one example of the ways changes in the research environment shape changes in libraries that support researchers.

As librarians we have some ability to advocate for incremental change by increasing awareness and helping make reproducible practices easier in all the ways discussed in this section and throughout this book.[49] One way librarians can support changes to incentives is in the areas we already support: educators and providers of scholarly metrics. We often educate students and faculty on how scholarly metrics work and provide metrics to faculty committees responsible for promotion and tenure. We can use these opportunities to talk about the problems with existing metrics and offer alternatives. When asked to put together a collection of metrics for a tenure, grant, or promotion package, we can include nontraditional outputs such as data sets, code, and registered reports.

For instance, the Office of Scholarly Communication at Texas A&M University Libraries offers one particularly successful model of scholarly communication outreach. Director Bruce Herbert, himself a senior tenured professor of geology and geophysics, meets with faculty before they go up for tenure, helping them develop and communicate metrics appropriate to their field. For example, he helped one faculty member, a renowned poet, earn tenure by helping him document the presence of his poetry on syllabi of universities across the world using the Open Syllabus Project.[50] Librarians with less seniority can nevertheless offer valuable resources to researchers, whether through LibGuides and other web-based materials or through one-on-one consultations.[51]

HOW ELSE LIBRARIES CAN SUPPORT REPRODUCIBILITY

As discussed in this section, improving reproducibility requires broad changes to how research is incentivized, conducted, and communicated. We've focused on five high-impact, immediately actionable interventions that build on the work information professionals already do. However, there are many other ways we can positively impact reproducibility.

Table 2.6 outlines some of these interventions and includes citations of articles and other resources that discuss them further. The themes and interventions in this section are adapted from Sayre and Reigeman, who outline a broad array of interventions and supports that librarians can provide to help improve reproducibility.[52] You may recognize the themes from the interventions outlined above.

Among these interventions you will find roles for functional specialists, disciplinary liaisons, subject experts working within libraries, and anyone else who supports research and scholarly communication. The breadth of expertise required and disciplinary differences mean that any work done in these areas likely needs to involve collaboration between subject specialists, liaisons, and other specialized experts. Supporting reproducible research also requires institutional, national, and international infrastructure that librarians and information professionals are part of developing and supporting.

TABLE 2.6

Library services contributing to reproducibility. Adapted from Franklin Sayre and Amy Riegelman, "Replicable Services for Reproducible Research: A Model for Academic Libraries," *College and Research Libraries* 80, no. 2 (March 2019): 265.

Theme	Intervention
Supporting Reproducible Methods	Support for research methodologies with which LIS professionals have expertise, such as digital humanities, bibliometrics, and GIS.[a]
	Adoption of reproducible practices and transparency in our own research and work practice.
	Support for building computational pipelines for data processing, analysis, and visualization.[b]
	Support for systematic reviews and extending systematic review services to new disciplines outside the health sciences in order to improve researchers' understanding of previous research on a topic.[c]
	Support for active research data management and help for researchers in managing their research data before and during the research process. Work with quality assurance offices, and training for new lab members on best practices during the research process itself.
Improving Reporting and Dissemination	Connection of researchers to methodological and statistical support units on campus.
	Help for researchers in finding and using guidelines and checklists (e.g., PRISMA, etc.) to improve methods reporting.
	Help for researchers in understanding preregistration and finding repositories for preregistration.[d]
	Provision of open access publishing services in order to increase publication of null results and reduce the effects of adverse incentives.
	Encouragement of replications through support, programming (e.g., reproducibility hackathon,[e] poster session featuring replication studies of graduate students), and institutional open access publishing.

a. Allison Campbell-Jensen, "Award-Winning Changemaker," *Continuum* (blog), University of Minnesota Libraries, September 30, 2020, https://www.continuum.umn.edu/2020/09/award-winning-changemaker/.

b. Ana Trisovic et al., "Advancing Computational Reproducibility in the Dataverse Data Repository Platform," in *P-RECS '20: Proceedings of the 3rd International Workshop on Practical Reproducible Evaluation of Computer Systems* (New York: ACM, 2020), 15–20, https://doi.org/10.1145/3391800.3398173; Daniel Nüst and Matthias Hinz, "Containerit: Generating Dockerfiles for Reproducible Research with R," *Journal of Open Source Software* 4, no. 40 (August 21, 2019): 1603, https://doi.org/10.21105/joss.01603; Reem Almugbel et al., "Reproducible Bioconductor Workflows Using Browser-Based Interactive Notebooks and Containers," *Journal of the American Medical Informatics Association* 25, no. 1 (January 2018): 4–12, https://doi.org/10.1093/jamia/ocx120; David L. Donoho, "An Invitation to Reproducible Computational Research," *Biostatistics* 11, no. 3 (July 2010): 385–88, https://doi.org/10.1093/biostatistics/kxq028; Carl Boettiger, "An Introduction to Docker for Reproducible Research," *ACM SIGOPS Operating Systems Review* 49, no. 1 (January 2015): 71–79, https://doi.org/10.1145/2723872.2723882.

c. Melissa L. Rethlefsen et al., "Librarian Co-authors Correlated with Higher Quality Reported Search Strategies in General Internal Medicine Systematic Reviews," *Journal of Clinical Epidemiology* 68, no. 6 (June 2015): 617–26, https://doi.org/10.1016/j.jclinepi.2014.11.025; Jonathan B. Koffel and Melissa L. Rethlefsen, "Reproducibility of Search Strategies Is Poor in Systematic Reviews Published in High-Impact Pediatrics, Cardiology and Surgery Journals: A Cross-Sectional Study," ed. Brett D Thombs, *PLOS ONE* 11, no. 9 (September 26, 2016): e0163309, https://doi.org/10.1371/journal.pone.0163309.

d. Amy Riegelman, "A Primer on Preregistration (& Why I Think It Should Be a Submission Track in LIS Journals)" (presentation, Librarians Building Momentum for Reproducibility, virtual conference, January 28, 2020), https://osf.io/w4dfh/.

e. Kristina Hettne et al., "ReprohackNL 2019: How Libraries Can Promote Research Reproducibility through Community Engagement," *IASSIST Quarterly* 44, no. 1–2 (2020): 1–10, https://doi.org/10.29173/iq977.

TABLE 2.6

Library services contributing to reproducibility. Adapted from Franklin Sayre and Amy Riegelman, "Replicable Services for Reproducible Research: A Model for Academic Libraries," *College and Research Libraries* 80, no. 2 (March 2019): 265.

Theme	Intervention
Supporting Sustainable Reuse of Research (Data, Code, Environment)	Support for data curation (see section 2.2.2).
	Support for data/code/methods sharing, including educating researchers, running institutional data repositories, and helping define standards for citation and sharing.
	Support for preserving computational environments.
Changing How Research Is Evaluated (Diversifying Peer Review)	Education for researchers about new forms of peer review and publication, such as preprints, open peer review, and registered reports.
	Education for researchers about the benefits of preregistrations.
	Provision of support and repositories for preregistrations.
	Support for preprints and help for researchers in finding appropriate venues for depositing preprints, understanding journal guidelines (e.g., Sherpa Romeo) regarding copyright, and negotiating with journals.
Changing the Incentives that Drive the Scholarly Ecosystem (Rewarding Open and Reproducible Practices)	Help in creating citation standards for data, code, research materials, etc.
	Teaching for faculty, researchers, and students about how different citation metrics work and the costs and benefits of each, as well as the longevity of scholar identity (e.g., ORCID).
	Provision of citation data to tenure and promotion committees; providing citation data for data, code, software, and materials to tenure and promotion committees and advocating for changes to academic incentives.

Definitions of reproducible research often imply that *research* means experiments that can be repeated or structured as a computational pipeline of software, code, and data that can be rerun. Yet for many disciplines, research involves something other than a controlled, repeatable computation or experiment.[53] It could instead be the study of primary source documents, the interpretation of texts or works of art, the coding and analysis of interviews, or the documentation of events in time, from the eruption of Mount Vesuvius to the migration of a bird species during a particular year. As this last example suggests, even within STEM, research can be descriptive, exploratory, or documentary. Scholars argue about whether the concept of reproducibility should be applied to this work.[54] However, there is broad agreement that openness or transparency with regard to methodology and data can allow research to be open to scrutiny and can make some elements of research processes and protocols reproducible.

Open methodologies—While not all research involves controlled experiments, all research does require a methodology—a series of steps that an experienced researcher takes to develop an argument or explore a claim. And while a qualitative researcher or humanities scholar generally does not think in terms of computational pipelines and research protocols, their work may involve protocols and computation. Even if scholarship is either not fully reproducible or makes claims that do not fit within a paradigm of reproducibility, its data (objects of study and evidentiary claims) should be shared and its methodology should be as transparent as possible. As we have emphasized throughout this section, openness—sharing as much as possible about the sources and methodology of research work—is what allows research to be questioned, verified, tested, or repeated. It is what allows work to enter the scholarly conversation.[55]

Understanding methodology and data and how they should be communicated is field-specific. Qualitative social scientists have engaged in long-standing scholarly conversations about research methodology and quality in qualitative and mixed-methods research that predate but importantly inform the push for reproducible research in these fields. Some important concepts include generalizability, reliability, rigor, and validity (see the entries for each of these terms in Lewis-Beck and colleagues).[56] Other tools for increasing the credibility of qualitative research include audit trails, decision trials, and reporting guidelines.[57] Recent scholarly interest in preregistration for qualitative research has built on this existing work, and OSF has recently made available a preregistration form for qualitative research.[58] Finally, as qualitative research archived in repositories has begun to be reused, scholars have begun to refine their understanding of how methodologies should be documented in order to better allow for reuse.[59]

Scholars of literature and culture do not often use the language of methodology to describe their work, preferring instead to talk about the theories that inform particular works of scholarship. As humanist scholars have moved toward interdisciplinary and digital work that uses methodologies drawn from other disciplines, however, it becomes essential to share methodologies, since readers can no longer be assumed to have been trained in the same unspoken but shared methodological practices.[60] Recent work on improving the reproducibility of systematic search terms offers one useful model for documenting archival research practices in the humanities.[61]

Open data—Data sharing is essential to transparency, openness, and any form of reproducibility. For more details, see "RDM for Qualitative and Humanities Research" in section 2.2.2, "Managing, Sharing, and Publishing Data."

CONCLUSION

This chapter has outlined five interventions LIS professionals can implement to support rigor and reproducibility. They range from relatively traditional—helping researchers find guidelines and publish preregistrations—to highly technical, such as helping preserve computational environments. Also outlined are a range of other services that can impact rigor and reproducibility. All these interventions will improve the openness of the scholarly communication landscape generally.

One of the best ways librarians can get involved in reproducibility is to adopt open, transparent, and reproducible practices in our own work. We can learn about and use tools like Markdown, R, Git, and Docker to make our own work more reproducible while also making it more efficient.[62] This is usually the best way to learn about these tools so we can later help researchers employ them for their own work. When LIS professionals conduct research, we can and should preregister studies, follow reporting guidelines, use computational pipelines, and ensure that the computational environments of our own research are preserved, shared, and sustainable. We can also adopt incentives within our own communities that encourage the scholarly communication landscape we want to see by encouraging the sharing and citation of data, code, and other nontraditional publications. By doing so we learn about these processes, model their use, and can speak authentically about the value of open and reproducible scholarship.

Appendix A: Glossary: Definitions of Reproducibility Concepts

- Reproducibility
  "the ability of a researcher to duplicate the results of a prior study using the same materials and procedures as were used by the original investigator"[63]
- Reproducibility can have varying definitions depending on the discipline that defines it. Several sources explore the different ways reproducibility can be defined and applied.[64]
- Types of reproducibility
  - *Empirical reproducibility*—Traditional scientific notion of experimental researchers capturing descriptive information about (non-computational) aspects of their research protocols and methods

  - *Computational reproducibility*—The computational details and other information necessary for others to replicate the findings[65]
- Additional definitions of reproducibility
  - *Methods reproducibility*—The ability to implement, as exactly as possible, the experimental and computational procedures, with the same data and tools, to obtain the same results

  - *Results reproducibility* (aka replicability)—The production of corroborating results in a new study, having followed the same experimental methods

  - *Robustness*—The stability of experimental conclusions to variations in either baseline assumptions or experimental procedures

  - *Generalizability* (aka transportability)—The persistence of an effect in settings different from and outside of an experimental framework

  - *Inferential reproducibility*—The making of knowledge claims of similar strength from a study replication or reanalysis[66]
- Replicability
  "the ability of a researcher to duplicate the results of a prior study if the same procedures are followed but new data are collected"[67]
- Transparency
  Transparency is reflected by clear and open communication about the methods and procedures used to obtain the research results and is foundational to reproducibility and replicability.[68]
- Rigor
  Rigor is the strict application of the scientific method to ensure unbiased and well-controlled experimental design, methodology, analysis, interpretation and reporting of results.
- Repeatability
  The measurement can be obtained by the same team using the same measurement procedure, the same measuring system, under the same operating conditions, in the same location on multiple trials. For computational experiments, this means that a researcher can reliably repeat their own computation.[69]

- Research misconduct
Research misconduct is the "fabrication, falsification, or plagiarism in proposing, performing, or reviewing research, or in reporting research results."[70]
- Questionable research practices (QRPs)
Research practices that may give "false impressions about the replicability of empirical results and misleading evidence about the size of an effect"[71]
Types of QRP could be
- P-hacking

  "Occurs when researchers collect or select data or statistical analyses until nonsignificant results become significant"[72]

- HARKing

  HARKing is defined as "presenting a post hoc hypothesis (i.e., one based on or informed by one's results) in one's research report as if it were, in fact, an a priori hypotheses."[73]

- Preregistration
Registering a research project or study before the study is conducted. Registrations typically include the hypothesis, study methods, and the research protocol.[74]
- Registered reports
"Registered Reports is a publishing format used by over 250 journals that emphasizes the importance of the research question and the quality of methodology by conducting peer review prior to data collection. High quality protocols are then provisionally accepted for publication if the authors follow through with the registered methodology. This format is designed to reward best practices in adhering to the hypothetico-deductive model of the scientific method. It eliminates a variety of questionable research practices, including low statistical power, selective reporting of results, and publication bias, while allowing complete flexibility to report serendipitous findings."[75]

Appendix B: Tools for Computational Reproducibility

This section outlines some open, scholar-led software projects that are aimed at helping researchers make their work computationally reproducible. While there are proprietary tools for computational reproducibility, they are not widely available, and this resource focuses on openly available tools as a matter of ethics. The options discussed here are all free and open source grassroots initiatives from scholars who are deeply invested in openness and reproducible research. Nuest and colleagues provide a wider survey of tools for computational reproducibility geared toward publishing computational research, which is inclusive of proprietary software as well as some open platforms described below.[76]

There are four classes of computational reproducibility tools that will be discussed in this section:

1. *Containers*—Lightweight, portable virtual operating systems
2. *Web-based integrated development environments (IDEs)*—Which provide code editing and execution and often have additional features for reproducibility
3. *Web-based replay systems*—Support for computational replay of materials that are hosted in a different place from the system
4. *Packaging systems*—Software that automatically captures dependencies and computational environments used at time of executing a computational pipeline

CONTAINERS

The research community has been increasingly using and sharing containers in service of reproducibility. Containers are a popular way to create virtual operating systems, like sandboxes, separate from the physical infrastructure and native operating system.[77] Two popular container systems, Singularity and Docker, are especially popular for research reproducibility.[78]

Docker was made to "pack, ship and run any application as a lightweight container," specifically with the advantage of working in most computational environments.[79] It is widely used in software development to deploy software in the cloud as well as to ensure a common development environment among programmers. Several other tools described below rely on Docker in the backend to remain reproducible.

Singularity was made for high-performance computing (HPC) work because of security considerations that both allow users full flexibility within the container and keep them from accessing parts of the HPC environment that administrators do not want users to access. Starting a Singularity container swaps out the host operating system environment for one the user controls without having root access and allows the user to run that application in its native environment.[80] Singularity containers can then be shared to allow others to work in the same computational environment.

Containers, however, are best used for short-term reproducibility. There are several problems with their use for long-term sustainability. Containers have no idea of provenance or the computational pipeline used—a container with code and data can be rendered virtually useless if not accompanied by extensive documentation about its inputs and workflow steps. In addition, learning how to use containers is also difficult, as it is not always practical for researchers to create and use containers in their daily workflow.

WEB-BASED INTEGRATED DEVELOPMENT ENVIRONMENTS (IDES)

An integrated development environment (IDE) provides features for authoring, compiling, executing, and debugging code, as well as helpful functions like code completion, built-in support for version control, and syntax highlighting.[81] These are especially helpful for new programmers who benefit from the visual cues and prompts. IDEs can be either desktop or web-based applications.

The scholarly community has taken advantage of both containers and web-based IDEs to create a new type of this application geared for reproducible research. These systems often provide access to a coding environment in browser, such as Jupyter notebooks or RStudio,[82] or their own IDE, and allow users to either export their work as a *research compendium* or allow sharing of these environments to bolster reproducibility.

> an NSF-funded Data Infrastructure Building Block (DIBBS) initiative to build a scalable, open source, web-based, multi-user platform for reproducible research enabling the creation, publication, and execution of tales—executable research objects that capture data, code, and the complete software environment used to produce research findings.[83]

The website defines a tale as "an executable research object that combines data (references), code (computational methods), computational environment, and narrative (traditional science story)"—which we know is also called a research compendium (see figure 2.5).[84]

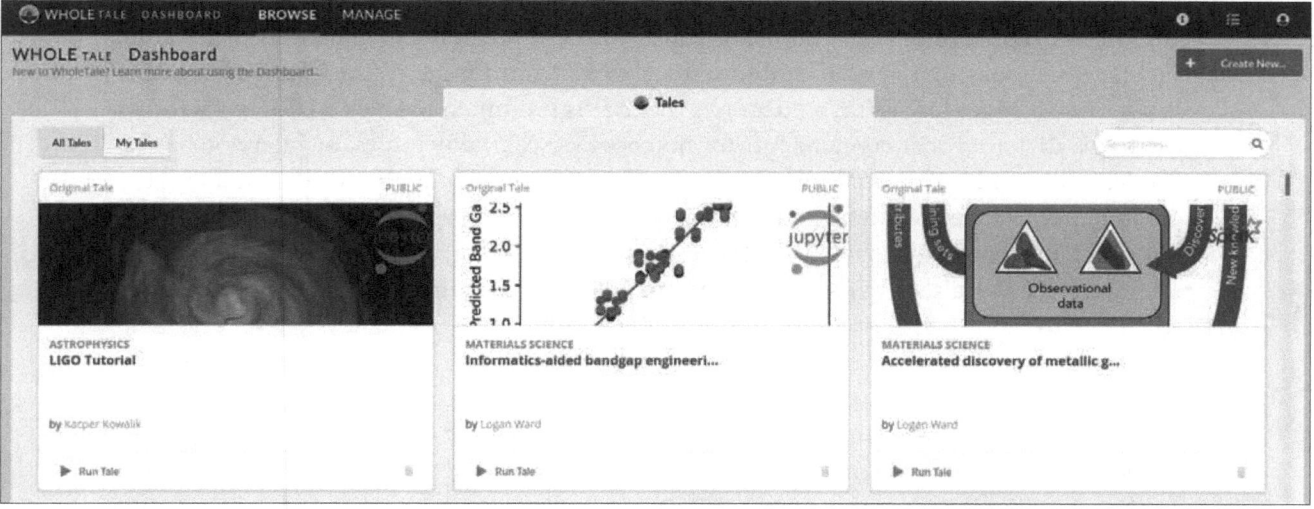

Figure 2.5

A beta version of the Whole Tale system is available at https://dashboard.wholetale.org.

When working in Whole Tale, the users have the option to choose a type of environment from a list of options: RStudio, Jupyter Notebooks, OpenRefine 2.8, Jupyter Notebooks with Spark, and JupyterLab.[85] Once within those environments, users can work as if they were on their local computer—importing and installing new libraries, adding data, and even running high-performance computing jobs. Whole Tale will keep track of the version of any software dependencies and relevant environmental variables. Once a tale is complete, it can be published to a repository like Dataverse,[86] with descriptive metadata and a research compendium that can later be rerun in Whole Tale for reproducibility.[87]

However, the web-based IDEs for reproducibility *require* that researchers work within a specific online platform, and that can be untenable for those who need to be able to, for instance, work offline or work across multiple types of environments for collaboration or compliance purposes. Most, if not all, of the proprietary tools that are marketed for computational reproducibility fall in this category of web-based IDEs.

WEB-BASED REPLAY SYSTEMS

Given that researchers are hard-pressed to change their workflows and tools, *web-based replay systems* were created. These are applications that take a link to research materials hosted elsewhere, build the computational environment in-browser, and display to the user some method of interacting with the materials, such as an instance of JupyterLab. This offloads the responsibility for hosting materials to platforms devoted to that and allows the researchers to have flexibility in how they work.

Web-based replay systems allow any user to interact with reproducible compendia in a sandbox, allowing users to modify input data or parameters, or even code, and re-execute it. They often ask the user to follow some structure for either the input or the directory structure in order to work properly and use container systems in the backend to recreate the research compendia for researchers.

There are two large-scale projects that allow for computational replay of research. One of those is Binder (see Figure 2.6), from Project Jupyter.[88] Binder uses repo2Docker to reproduce the computational environment of research hosted on Git hosting platforms (e.g. GitLab, GitHub) or repositories (e.g. Zenodo, Dataverse).[89] Users can replay materials in RStudio, Jupyter notebooks, JupyterLab, and Julia notebooks from Binder. When navigating to the Binder home page (https://mybinder.org), the user is prompted to enter a URL or DOI that leads to a directory that contains Jupyter notebooks, RMarkdown files, or Julia notebooks. Binder will then look through the directory of files for something that will tell it about the computational dependencies, like a requirements.txt file for a Python project or a Dockerfile. The user will then see the materials in the original computational environment, in the original interface.[90] Binder also provides a reusable link to this page with the live materials to others who want to reproduce the work.

REANA is another example of a computational replay system, based in high-energy physics (HEP).[91] Made by a team at CERN (the European Organization for Nuclear Research), REANA has the goal of helping researchers "structure their input data, analysis code, containerised environments and computational workflows so that the analysis can be instantiated and run on remote compute clouds."[92] REANA relies heavily on the usage of the Common Workflow Language, "an open standard for describing analysis workflows and tools in a way that makes them portable and scalable across a variety of software and hardware environments."[93] This, in combination with the multiple container systems available on REANA, allow for computational replay of HEP workflows. This idea and process could, however, be generalized for other domains as well.

PACKAGING SYSTEMS

The final category of computational reproducibility tools we'll cover are *packaging systems*. Packaging systems are desktop or server-based tools that automatically capture dependencies

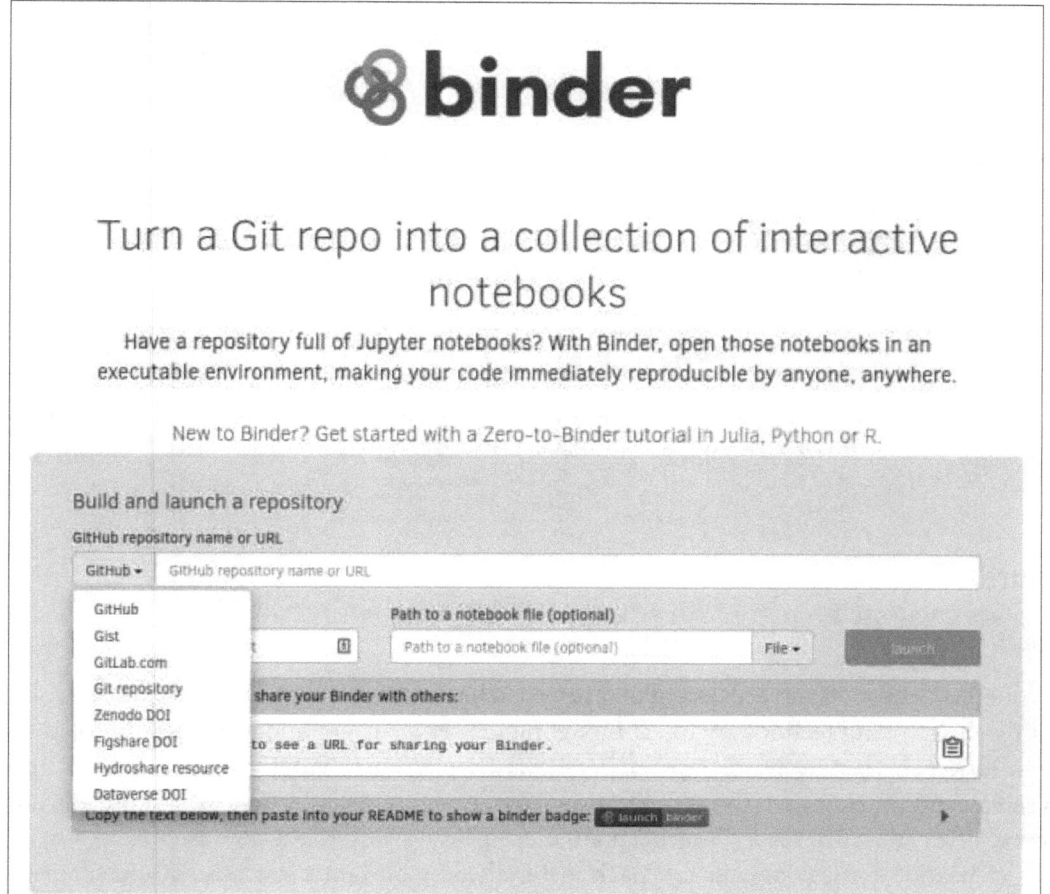

Figure 2.6
Binder, a tool for reproducing the computational environment of research hosted on Git hosting platforms, is available at https://mybinder.org.

and computational environments at time of executing a computational pipeline. The draw with packaging systems is the flexibility—you don't have to go into a project thinking about reproducibility to be able to use a packaging tool to create a record of the computational environment. As long as your pipeline runs, the packaging tool will work.

One example is ReproZip.[94] ReproZip works by running at the same time as a computational pipeline, tracing all the steps and dependencies while the pipeline runs as normal. Then it packages together input files, output files, parameters, environmental variables, executable code, and steps into a portable, generalized format: the RPZ (.rpz), or the ReproZip bundle (see figure 2.7). These bundles are small (size of the bundles really depends on the size of input and output data), portable (can be deposited into a repository or e-mailed!), and self-contained (everything needed to reproduce the pipeline is there!).[95]

ReproZip bundles can be replayed locally on any operating system (using ReproUnzip) or in-browser (using ReproServer). These tools will take a ReproZip bundle and automatically unpack it, setting up all the dependencies and workflow steps for users so they can reproduce the contents in the original computational environment. ReproUnzip operates on the plug-in model so users can choose which unpacker they can use to reproduce the work, for example Docker or Vagrant. However, this can be expanded to include any container or virtual machine systems in the future, because the extensive metadata ReproZip captures.[96]

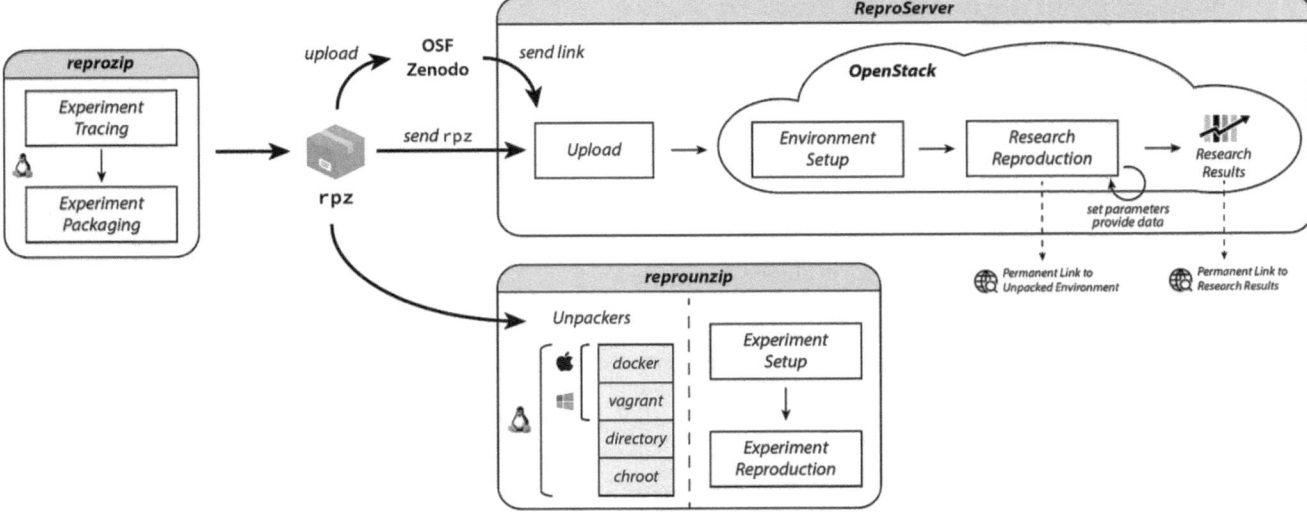

Figure 2.7
ReproZip ecosystem, created by Fernando Chirigati. Used with permission.

ReproZip also has an ecosystem of other open tools: ReproZip-Web (combines ReproZip with web archiving technology to capture complex server-client applications), reprozip-ju-pyter (a ReproZip plug-in for Jupyter notebooks, see example videos), ReproUnzip (a tool to replay and interact with the computational pipelines archived in ReproZip bundles), and ReproServer (a way to replay ReproZip bundles in-browser).[97] Right now, ReproZip, Repro-Zip-Web, and reprozip-jupyter can pack materials only on Linux (because of the extensive information captured and the fact that the OS needs to be recreated at will from ReproZip bundles), but users can install any of the other tools above on any operating system.

However, installing ReproUnzip and another piece of software can be a big ask for some researchers. To that end, ReproServer was created, which allows users to either upload a ReproZip bundle (.rpz) or provide a link to one and then reproduce and interact with the contents of the RPZ file in-browser, drastically reducing the number of steps and complexity. What's more, ReproServer integrates with repositories, such that users can create links like this—https://server.reprozip.org/osf.io/<5 character OSF link>—to immediately begin reproducing the work or send to reviewers or collaborators for their input. ReproServer also provides a permanent URL to the unpacked environment and the results of rerunning the pipeline in the RPZ file.[98]

SUMMARY

Different reproducibility tools will work for different researchers and workflows. For instance, when processing and analyzing research materials, many people tend to use containers or web-based IDEs because the rapid-prototyping capabilities are useful for the more exploratory and error-prone processing step. One key reason why they are especially useful in the analysis step is because they can also be ported to be compatible with web-based replay systems, which are useful in publishing your work.

When the work is done and nearing publication, people tend to prepare, structure, or export their research for web-based replay systems. These are useful because of the near-instant replay of computational research for reviewers of publications or presentations, members of promotion committees, or any interested party. This brings a wider accessibility to the reproducible work, which helps for post-publication review.

Lastly, packaging tools are the most sustainable for long-term reproducibility, especially when combined with emulation technology. Packaging tools are provenance-aware (e.g., they know the order in which research pipelines run), automatically capture dependencies, automatically write in-depth technical and administrative metadata, and are interoperable (in that they are built to work with a variety of other tools). These traits make them the most reliable for preservation and access purposes.

This appendix was meant to guide an understanding of the wider landscape of computational reproducibility tools. These four key classes of tools (containers, web-based IDEs, web-based replay systems, and packaging systems) and the examples discussed here reflect community-based efforts to scaffold the understandability and usability of their research, teaching, and learning. These tools can be used to both make one's own work reproducible and help a designated community make their work more reproducible and sustainable in the long term.

COI: Vicky Rampin contributes to the ReproZip project.

Appendix C: Examples of Computational Reproducibility

This appendix will showcase some examples of how the software described in this chapter has been used to make research reproducible. Further examples can be found in the open book *The Practice of Reproducible Research*, which comprises case studies and workflows for reproducibility across various disciplines.[99]

The first example of computationally reproducible research comes from a machine-learning researcher, Logan Ward, using Whole Tale to promote reuse of their materials. Their tale is meant to allow others to reproduce the materials in a "2016 paper …on using machine learning to predict the properties of materials…. The notebooks within this tale recreate the validation tests from the paper and how the models were used to discover new materials."[100] Users who want to reuse this tale will have to either: (a) create an account on WholeTale and copy it to their workspace to interact with it, or (b) download the tale to their local computer and try to get it running with containers.

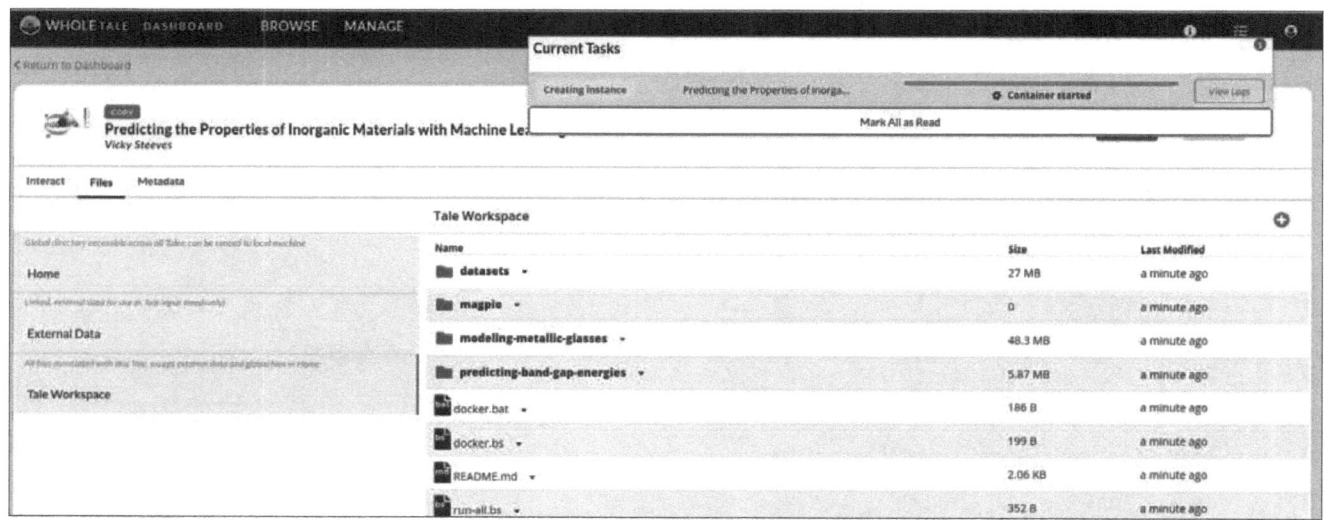

Figure 2.8
Rerunning the Ward tale in my Whole Tale account successfully.

The next example is from the biological sciences, where Lewis and colleagues used the *eLife* journal's reproducible document stack (RDS) to provide an interactive version of their paper (figure 2.9) to allow others to directly rerun the code with original data that was used for analysis and visualizations.[101] The *eLife* RDS is based on Stencila,[102] a tool meant to introduce reproducibility features (such as updating dependencies in real time between code cells as you change data or code) to everyday research tools (like Jupyter notebooks) and Docker to keep the original computing environment. The code and data are then linked and can be downloaded and explored by readers in real time, augmenting their reading experience and allowing for open post-publication peer review.

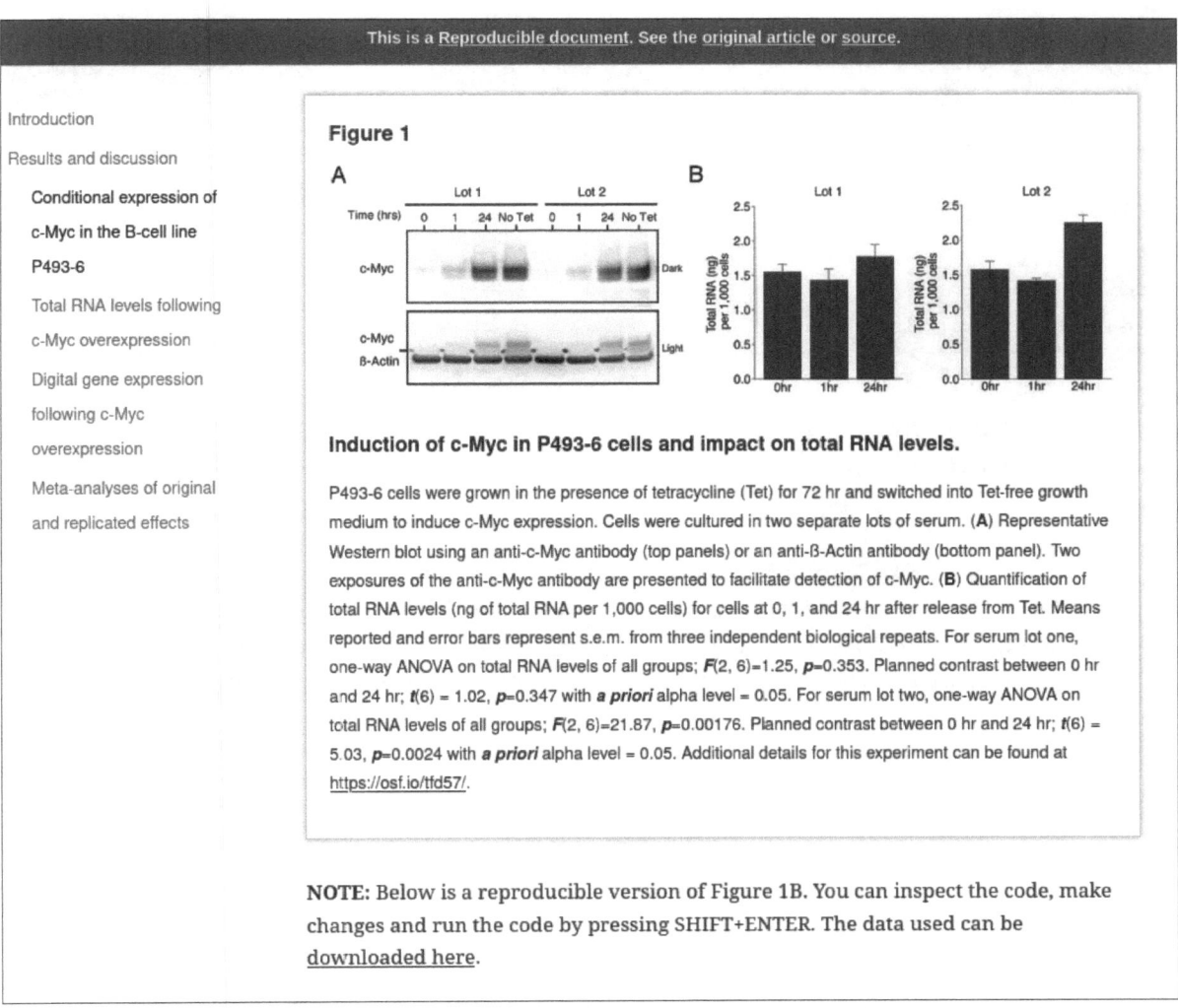

Figure 2.9

A screenshot of the interactive paper L. Michelle Lewis et al., "Replication Study: Transcriptional Amplification in Tumor Cells with Elevated c-Myc," eLife 7 (2018): e30274, https://doi.org/10.7554/eLife.30274 is used under CC BY 4.0.

Another example comes from digital humanities, where Nick Wolf made the materials available for his 2015 Heaney Lecture, "National School System and the Irish Language."[103] Look for the published essay "The National-School System and the Irish Language in the Nineteenth Century."[104] Wolf used ReproZip to make a reproducible research compendium of the R scripts that he wrote to analyze and visualize historical education data from Ireland.

Wolf was able to package his research with two commands: reprozip trace R Rscript NationalSchools_Wolf_2016.R and reprozip pack national-schools.rpz. The RPZ bundle was then uploaded to the Open Science Framework,[105] where it can be either downloaded by secondary users for local interaction or unpacked with ReproServer in-browser for quick reproduction and inspection (see figure 2.10).

Figure 2.10

A screenshot of unpacking Wolf's RPZ bundle with ReproServer: https://server.reprozip.org/reproduce/osf.io/wfvqr. The results can be found at https://server.reprozip.org/results/fyjog.

The next example comes from earth science and mammalogy, using Jupyter notebooks with Binder for reproducibility. This notebook, Analyzing Whale Tracks" by Dr. Roberto De Almeida (see figure 2.11), looks at ocean data to track the trajectories of migrating whales. He wanted to see if whales could benefit from the ocean currents when migrating across the world.[106]

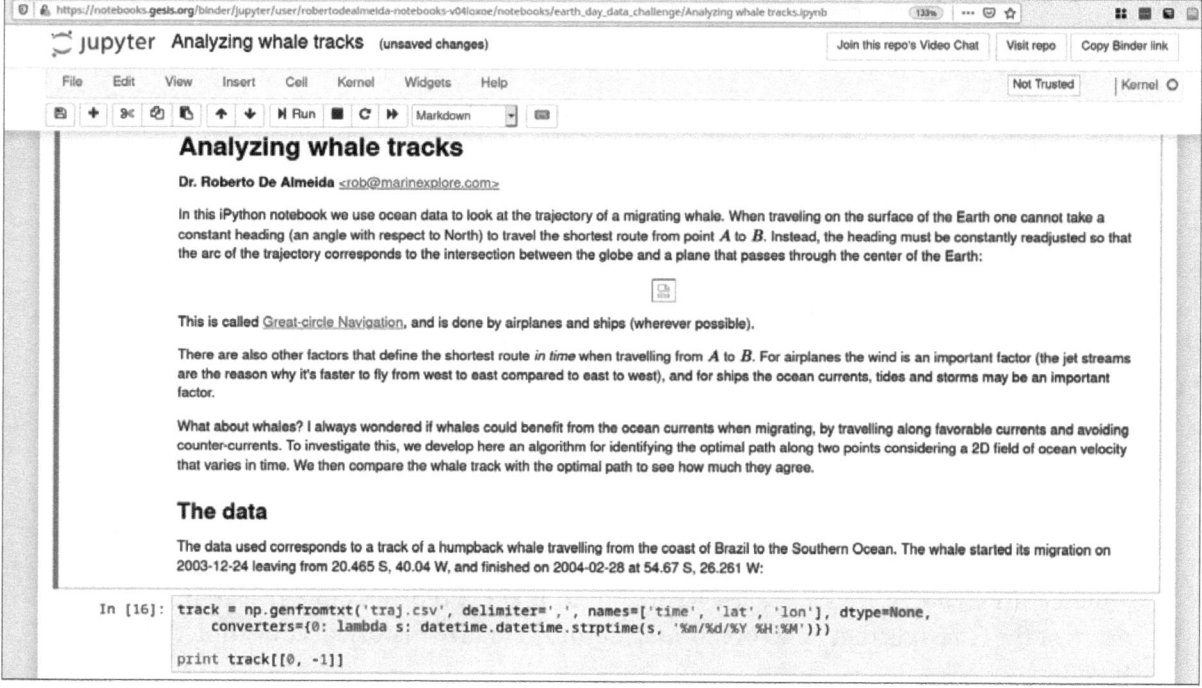

Figure 2.11

A screenshot of the "Analyzing Whale Tracks" Jupyter notebook running in Binder: https://nbviewer.org/github/robertodealmeida/notebooks/blob/master/earth_day_data_challenge/Analyzing%20whale%20tracks.ipynb.

People can interact with the GitHub repository of Jupyter notebooks locally by installing Jupyter notebooks and all the requisite dependencies (e.g., the correct Python version and the correct Python library versions). They can also interact with the notebooks in Binder, to allow for simpler reproducibility in-browser. Users can interact with the notebooks with the same flexibility as if it were their local computer, re-executing and editing code, adding their own data, importing and exporting files, and so on. These sandboxes do not persist, but instead offer a great way to instantly replay research during the reading or reviewing process.

The final example comes from high-energy physics, where the REANA team created an example reproducible analysis pipeline of ATLAS data (see figure 2.12).[107] The workflow that they made reproducible with REANA emulates a "Beyond Standard Model (BSM) search as performed in collider particle physics."[108] This involves reading in observed data, fitting it against a statistical model, and computing the upper limit on the signal strength of the BSM project (the main output).

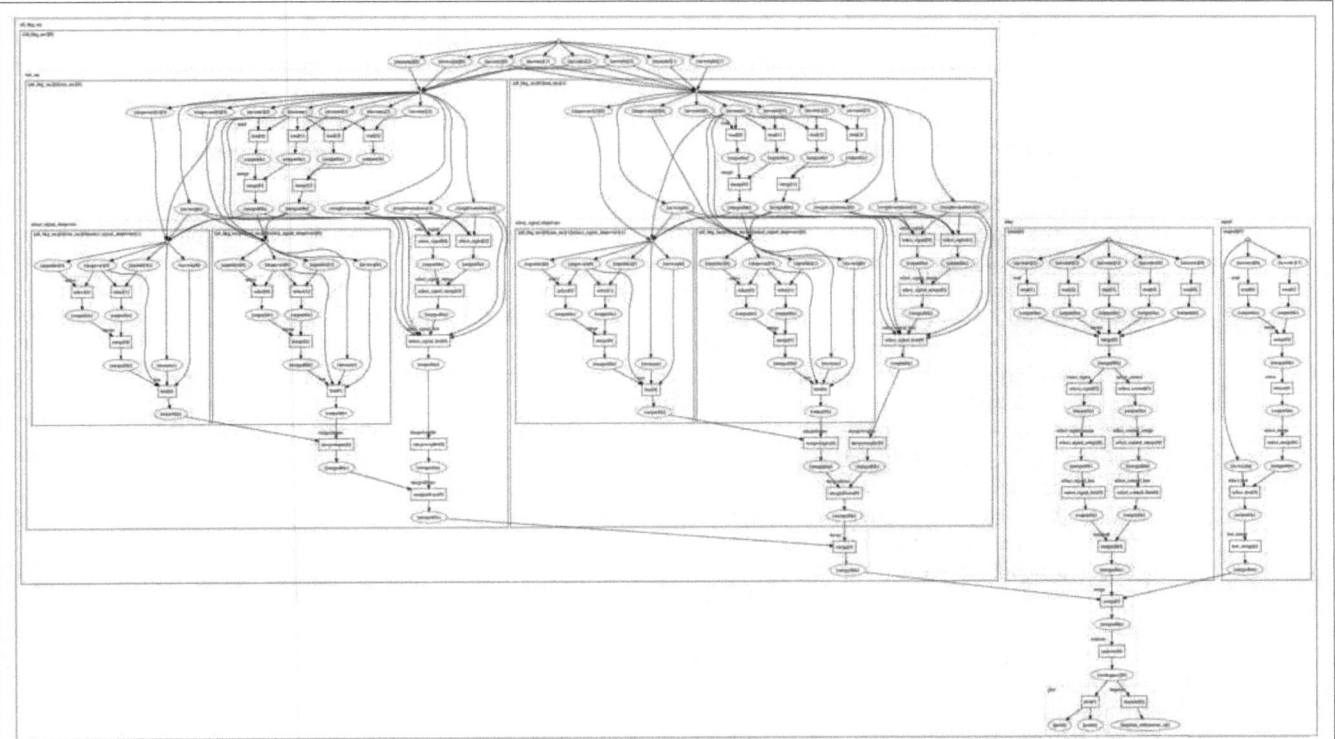

Figure 2.12
The workflow that was made reproducible with REANA. I would not want to manually recreate that! Used under the MIT License.

To create their reproducible analysis pipeline, they have to create

"runnable recipes" addressing (1) where is the input data, (2) what software was used to analyse the data, (3) which computing environments were used to run the software and (4) which computational workflow steps were taken to run the analysis. This will permit instantiation of the analysis on the computational cloud and run the analysis to obtain (5) output results.[109]

The authors then put together a reana.yml file that configures the analysis structure with the correct computational pipeline steps, inputs, parameters, dependencies, and code. It can then be deployed to a REANA server, one of which is hosted by CERN for use. This one is hard to reproduce without domain knowledge, or at least serious computational know-how.

Different reproducibility tools offer different functionality, which appeals to disciplines with varying norms. These examples offer some examples of how a few disciplines have used reproducibility tools to allow others to verify, extend, and interact with their work. By walking the walk, the authors above have provided great examples to follow in terms of making research reproducibly accessible to all.

NOTES

1. National Academies of Sciences, Engineering, and Medicine, *Open Science by Design* (Washington, DC: National Academies Press, 2018), 107, https://doi.org/10.17226/25116.
2. Kenneth Bollen et al., *Social, Behavioral, and Economic Sciences Perspectives on Robust and Reliable Science* (Alexandria, VA: National Science Foundation, May 2015), 3–4, https://www.nsf.gov/sbe/AC_Materials/SBE_Robust_and_Reliable_Research_Report.pdf.
3. Sabina Leonelli, "Rethinking Reproducibility as a Criterion for Research Quality," in *Including a Symposium on Mary Morgan: Curiosity, Imagination, and Surprise*, Research in the History of Economic Thought and Methodology, vol. 36B, ed. Luca Fiorito, Scott Scheall, and Carlos Eduardo Suprinyak (Bingley, UK: Emerald Publishing, 2018), 129–46, https://doi.org/10.1108/S0743-41542018000036B009.
4. Victoria Stodden et al., comps. and eds., "Setting the Default to Reproducible" (developed by participants in ICERM workshop "Reproducibility in Computational and Experimental Mathematics," Providence, RI, December 14, 2012), 5, https://stodden.net/icerm_report.pdf.
5. Vicky Steeves, "Reproducibility Librarianship," *Collaborative Librarianship* 9, no. 2 (2017): article 4, https://digitalcommons.du.edu/collaborativelibrarianship/vol9/iss2/4.
6. National Institutes of Health Advisory Committee to the Director. (2015). National Library of Medicine Working Group Final Report (NLM-06112015-ACD; p. 17). National Institutes of Health. https://acd.od.nih.gov/documents/reports/Report-NLM-06112015-ACD.pdf.
7. Franklin Sayre et al., Librarians Building Momentum for Reproducibility, virtual conference, January 29, 2020, https://vickysteeves.gitlab.io/librarians-reproducibility/.
8. American Medical Association, *AMA Manual of Style*, 11th ed. (New York: Oxford University Press, 2020); American Psychological Association, "Journal Article Reporting Standards (JARS)," APA Style, accessed November 24, 2020, https://apastyle.apa.org/jars.
9. Bridget C. O'Brien et al., "Standards for Reporting Qualitative Research: A Synthesis of Recommendations," *Academic Medicine* 89, no. 9 (September 2014): 1245–51, https://doi.org/10.1097/ACM.0000000000000388.
10. O'Brien, Bridget C. PhD; Harris, Ilene B. PhD; Beckman, Thomas J. MD; Reed, Darcy A. MD, MPH; Cook, David A. MD, MHPE. Standards for Reporting Qualitative Research: A Synthesis of Recommendations. Academic Medicine 89(9):p 1245-1251, September 2014. | DOI: 10.1097/ACM.0000000000000388
11. David Moher et al., "Preferred Reporting Items for Systematic Reviews and Meta-analyses: The PRISMA Statement," *PLOS Medicine* 6, no. 7 (2009): e1000097, https://doi.org/10.1371/journal.pmed.1000097.
12. Melissa L. Rethlefsen et al., "PRISMA-S: An Extension to the PRISMA Statement for Reporting Literature Searches in Systematic Reviews," *Systematic Reviews* 10, no. 1 (January 26, 2021): article 39, https://doi.org/10.1186/s13643-020-01542-z.
13. Raoni Lourenço, Juliana Freire, and Dennis Shasha, "BugDoc: Algorithms to Debug Computational Processes," in *SIGMOD '20: Proceedings of the 2020 ACM SIGMOD International Conference on Management of Data* (New York: Association for Computing Machinery, 2020), 463-478, https://doi.org/10.1145/3318464.3389763.
14. OpenRefine, home page, https://openrefine.org/.
15. Wikipedia, s.v. "JSON," last updated March 22, 2023, https://en.wikipedia.org/wiki/JSON.
16. Glenda M. Yenni et al., "Developing a Modern Data Workflow for Evolving Data," preprint, BioRxiv, July 24, 2018, https://doi.org/10.1101/344804.
17. Yenni et al., "Developing a Modern Data Workflow," 1
18. Yenni et al., "Developing a Modern Data Workflow."
19. Research Compendium, home page, https://research-compendium.science/; Daniel Nüst, Carl Boettiger, and Ben Marwick, "How to Read a Research Compendium," ArXiv:1806.09525 [Cs], June 11, 2018, https://doi.org/10.48550/arXiv.1806.09525.
20. Nüst, Boettiger, and Marwick, "How to Read a Research Compendium."

21. Victoria Stodden, "Resolving Irreproducibility in Empirical and Computational Research," Institute of Mathematical Statistics, November 17, 2013, https://imstat.org/2013/11/17/resolving-irreproducibility-in-empirical-and-computational-research/.

22. Ed H. B. M. Gronenschild et al., "The Effects of FreeSurfer Version, Workstation Type, and Macintosh Operating System Version on Anatomical Volume and Cortical Thickness Measurements," *PLOS ONE* 7, no. 6 (2012): e38234, https://doi.org/10.1371/journal.pone.0038234.

23. Geir Kjetil Sandve et al., "Ten Simple Rules for Reproducible Computational Research," *PLOS Computational Biology* 9, no. 10 (October 24, 2013): e1003285, https://doi.org/10.1371/journal.pcbi.1003285.

24. Katherine Bode, "The Equivalence of 'Close' and 'Distant' Reading; or, Toward a New Object for Data-Rich Literary History," *Modern Language Quarterly* 78, no. 1 (March 1, 2017): 77–106, https://doi.org/10.1215/00267929-3699787; Franco Moretti, *Graphs, Maps, Trees* (London: Verso, 2005).

25. Archive-It, home page, https://archive-it.org/; Webrecorder, home page, https://webrecorder.net/.

26. Saving Data Journalism, home page, https://savingjournalism.reprozip.org/.

27. Katherine Boss et al., "Saving Data Journalism: Using ReproZip-Web to Capture Dynamic Websites for Future Reuse" (presentation, Librarians Building Momentum for Reproducibility, virtual conference, January 28, 2020), slides: https://osf.io/nr9d8/, YouTube video, 13:16, https://youtu.be/xLdFaDL2VWc.

28. Taguette, home page, https://www.taguette.org/; Qcoder, GitHub, https://github.com/ropenscilabs/qcoder; Beth M. Duckles and Vicky Steeves, "Qualitative Research Using Open Tools" (presentation, CSV,conf,v4, Portland, Oregon, May 2019), slides: https://doi.org/10.5281/zenodo.2673016, YouTube video, 17:51: https://youtu.be/DwCunW19wcQ.

29. Mateusz Pawlik et al., "A Link Is Not Enough—Reproducibility of Data," *Datenbank-Spektrum* 19, no. 2 (2019): 107–15, https://doi.org/10.1007/s13222-019-00317-8.

30. Michel Castagné, "Consider the Source: The Value of Source Code to Digital Preservation Strategies," *School of Information Student Research Journal* (San José State University) 2, no. 2 (January 2013): article 5, p. 2, https://doi.org/10.31979/2575-2499.020205.

31. Digital Preservation Coalition, Insert Coin to Continue: A Briefing Day on Software Preservation (London, May 7, 2019), https://www.dpconline.org/events/past-events/software-preservation.

32. Neil Chue Hong et al., *Sustainability and Preservation Framework* (Edinburgh, UK: Software Sustainability Institute, December 7, 2010), https://www.software.ac.uk/sustainability-and-preservation-framework.

33. Hong et al., *Sustainability and Preservation Framework*.

34. J. Kunze et al., "The BagIt File Packaging Format (V1.0)," RFC Editor, October 2018, https://tools.ietf.org/html/rfc8493.

35. Kunze et al., "BagIt File Packaging Format."

36. Kyle Chard et al., "Application of BagIt-Serialized Research Object Bundles for Packaging and Re-execution of Computational Analyses," in *2019 15th International Conference on 3Science* (San Diego: IEEE, 2019), 514–21, https://doi.org/10.1109/eScience.2019.00068.

37. Educopia Institute, "Scaling Emulation as a Service Infrastructure (EaaSI) (subcontract)," 2017–2020, https://educopia.org/emulation-as-a-service-eaasi/.

38. Klaus Rechert et al., "bwFLA—A Functional Approach to Digital Preservation," *PIK— Praxis der Informationsverarbeitung und Kommunikation* 35, no. 4 (November 2012): 259–67, https://doi.org/10.1515/pik-2012-0044.

39. Julia Kim and Don Mennerich, "Jeremy Blake's Time-Based Paintings: A Case Study," *Electronic Media Review* 4 (2015–2016), https://resources.culturalheritage.org/emg-review/volume-4-2015-2016/kim/.

40. Chassanoff, A., & Altman, M. (2020). Curation as "Interoperability With the Future": Preserving Scholarly Research Software in Academic Libraries. Journal of the Association for Information Science and Technology, 71(3), 325–337. https://doi.org/10.1002/asi.24244

41. Brian A. Nosek, Jeffrey R. Spies, and Matt Motyl, "Scientific Utopia: II. Restructuring Incentives and Practices to Promote Truth over Publishability," *Perspectives on Psychological Science* 7, no. 6 (November 2012): 615–31, https://doi.org/10.1177/1745691612459058; Jere D. Odell, Heather L. Coates, and Kristi L. Palmer, "Rewarding Open Access Scholarship in Promotion and Tenure: Driving Institutional Change," *College and Research Libraries News* 77, no. 7 (2016): 322–25, https://doi.org/10.7912/C2R60B.

42. For an overview of some issues in the hard sciences, see National Academies of Sciences, Engineering, and Medicine, *Reproducibility and Replicability in Science* (Washington, DC: National Academies Press, 2019), https://doi.org/10.17226/25303.

43. Open Science Collaboration, "Estimating the Reproducibility of Psychological Science," *Science* 349, no. 6251 (August 28, 2015): aac4716, https://doi.org/10.1126/science.aac4716; Makel and Plucker, *Toward a More Perfect Psychology*.

44. Garret Christensen, Jeremy Freese, and Edward Miguel, *Transparent and Reproducible Social Science Research* (Oakland: University of California Press, 2019), https://www.ucpress.edu/book/9780520296954/transparent-and-reproducible-social-science-research.

45. Dorothy Bishop et al., *Reproducibility and Reliability of Biomedical Research*, symposium report (London: Academy of Medical Sciences, October 2015), https://acmedsci.ac.uk/policy/policy-projects/reproducibility-and-reliability-of-biomedical-research.

46. National Science Foundation, "Scientists Seeking NSF Funding Will Soon Be Required to Submit Data Management Plans," news release 10-077, May 10, 2010, https://www.nsf.gov/news/news_summ.jsp?cntn_id=116928.

47. Steeves, "Reproducibility Librarianship"; Cynthia R. H. Vitale, "Is Research Reproducibility the New Data Management for Libraries?" *Bulletin of the Association for Information Science and Technology* 42, no. 3 (2016): 38–41, https://asistdl.onlinelibrary.wiley.com/doi/full/10.1002/bul2.2016.1720420313.

48. Melissa L. Rethlefsen, Mellanye J. Lackey, and Shirley Zhao, "Building Capacity to Encourage Research Reproducibility and #MakeResearchTrue," *Journal of the Medical Library Association* 106, no. 1 (January 12, 2018): 113–19, https://doi.org/10.5195/jmla.2018.273.

49. Franklin Sayre and Amy Riegelman, "Replicable Services for Reproducible Research: A Model for Academic Libraries," *College and Research Libraries* 80, no. 2 (March 2019): 260.

50. Open Syllabus Explorer, home page, https://opensyllabus.org/. See also Bruce Herbert, Sarah Potvin, and Tina Budzise-Weaver, "Best Practices for the Use of Scholarly Impact Metrics," working paper, February 10, 2016, https://oaktrust.library.tamu.edu/handle/1969.1/156054.

51. Steven Braun, "Supporting Research Impact Metrics in Academic Libraries: A Case Study," *portal: Libraries and the Academy* 17, no. 1 (January 2017): 111–27, https://doi.org/10.1353/pla.2017.0007; Rebecca B. French and Jody Condit Fagan, "The Visibility of Authority Records, Researcher Identifiers, Academic Social Networking Profiles, and Related Faculty Publications in Search Engine Results," *Journal of Web Librarianship* 13, no. 2 (2019): 156–97, https://doi.org/10.1080/19322909.2019.1591324; Björn Brembs, Katherine Button, and Marcus Munafò, "Deep Impact: Unintended Consequences of Journal Rank," *Frontiers in Human Neuroscience* 7 (2013), https://doi.org/10.3389/fnhum.2013.00291; Amy M. Suiter and Heather Lea Moulaison, "Supporting Scholars: An Analysis of Academic Library Websites' Documentation on Metrics and Impact," *Journal of Academic Librarianship* 41, no. 6 (November 2015): 814–20, https://doi.org/10.1016/j.acalib.2015.09.004.

52. Sayre and Riegelman, "Replicable Services."

53. For an interesting theoretical examination of repetition and translation in literary theory and their relationship to the concept of reproducibility, see Ladina Bezzola Lambert, "Repetition with a Difference: Reproducibility in Literature Studies," in *Reproducibility: Principles, Problems, Practices, and Prospects*, ed. Harald Atmanspacher and Sabine Maasen (Hoboken, NJ: John Wiley & Sons, 2016), 491–509, https://doi.org/10.1002/9781118865064.ch23.

54. Herman Aguinis and Angelo M. Solarino, "Transparency and Replicability in Qualitative Research: The Case of Interviews with Elite Informants," *Strategic Management Journal* 40, no. 8 (August 2019): 1291–1315, https://doi.org/10.1002/smj.3015; Leonelli, "Rethinking Reproducibility"; Rik Peels and Lex Bouter, "Humanities Need a Replication Drive Too," *Nature* 558, no. 7710 (June 21, 2018): 372–372, https://doi.org/10.1038/d41586-018-05454-w; Bart Penders, J. Britt Holbrook, and Sarah de Rijcke, "Rinse and Repeat: Understanding the Value of Replication across Different Ways of Knowing," *Publications* 7, no. 3 (September 2019): 52, https://doi.org/10.3390/publications7030052; Michael G. Pratt, Sarah Kaplan, and Richard Whittington, "The Tumult over Transparency: Decoupling Transparency from Replication in Establishing Trustworthy Qualitative Research," *Administrative Science Quarterly* 65, no. 1 (March 1, 2020): 1–19, https://doi.org/10.1177/0001839219887663; Sarah de Rijcke and Bart Penders, "Resist Calls for Replicability in the Humanities," *Nature* 560, no. 7716 (August 1, 2018): 29, https://doi.org/10.1038/d41586-018-05845-z.

55. Christine L. Borgman, *Big Data, Little Data, No Data* (Cambridge, MA: MIT Press, 2015), https://mitpress.mit.edu/9780262529914/big-data-little-data-no-data/.

56. Michael S. Lewis-Beck, et al, The SAGE Encyclopedia of Social Science Research Methods (2004) https://doi.org/10.4135/9781412950589

57. See citations in Tamarinde L. Haven et al., "Preregistering Qualitative Research: A Delphi Study," SocArXiv, last edited November 9, 2020, https://doi.org/10.31235/osf.io/pz9jr.

58. David Thomas Mellor et al., "Templates of OSF Registration Forms," OSF, October 31, 2016, https://osf.io/zab38/. The qualitative preregistration form is based on the work of Haven et al., "Preregistering Qualitative Research."

59. Sebastian Karcher and Nicholas Weber, "Annotation for Transparent Inquiry: Transparent Data and Analysis for Qualitative Research," *IASSIST Quarterly* 43, no. 2 (2019): 1–9, https://doi.org/10.29173/iq959; Aguinis and Solarino, "Transparency and Replicability."

60. Bode, "Equivalence of 'Close' and 'Distant' Reading"; James O'Sullivan, "The Humanities Have a 'Reproducibility' Problem," *Talking Humanities* (blog), July 9, 2019, https://talkinghumanities.blogs.sas.ac.uk/2019/07/09/the-humanities-have-a-reproducibility-problem/.

61. Paul Fehrmann, "Reproducibility of Computer Searches in Systematic Reviews: Checklist Items Used to Assess Computer Search Reports" (presentation, Librarians Building Momentum for Reproducibility, online conference, January 28, 2023), YouTube video, 6:01, posted February 3, 2020, https://www.youtube.com/watch?v=HqYv7IhQ4GU.

62. Heidi Tebbe and Danica Madison Lewis, "What's Sauce for the Goose Is Sauce for the Gander: Reproducible Practice in Library Work," OSF, February 3, 2020, https://osf.io/3xuj2/.

63. Bollen et al., *Social, Behavioral, and Economic Sciences Perspectives*, 3.

64. Lorena A. Barba, "Terminologies for Reproducible Research," ArXiv:1802.03311 [Cs], February 9, 2018, http://arxiv.org/abs/1802.03311; Steven N. Goodman, Danielle Fanelli, and John P. A. Ioannidis, "What Does Research Reproducibility Mean?" *Science Translational Medicine* 8, no. 341 (June 1, 2016): 341ps12, https://doi.org/10.1126/scitranslmed.aaf5027; Stodden, "Resolving Irreproducibility."

65. Stodden, "Resolving Irreproducibility."

66. Goodman, Fanelli, and Ioannidis, "What Does Research Reproducibility Mean?"

67. Bollen, et al., *Social, Behavioral, and Economic Sciences Perspectives*, 4.

68. E. Miguel et al., "Promoting Transparency in Social Science Research," *Science* 343, no. 6166 (2014): 30–31, https://doi.org/10.1126/science.1245317.

69. Association for Computing Machinery, "Artifact Review and Badging—Version 1.0 (Not Current)," last updated August 24, 2020, https://www.acm.org/publications/policies/artifact-review-badging.

70. National Institutes of Health, "Research Misconduct—Definitions," November 29, 2018, https://grants.nih.gov/policy/research_integrity/definitions.htm.

71. Ulrich Schimmack, "Questionable Research Practices: Definition, Detection, and Recommendations for Better Practices," *Replicability-Index* (blog), January 24, 2015, https://replicationindex.com/2015/01/24/qrps/.

72. Megan L. Head et al., "The Extent and Consequences of P-Hacking in Science," *PLOS Biology* 13, no. 3 (March 13, 2015), https://journals.plos.org/plosbiology/article?id=10.1371/journal.pbio.1002106.

73. Norbert L. Kerr, "HARKing: Hypothesizing after the Results Are Known," *Personality and Social Psychology Review*, 2, no. 3 (1998): 196-217, https://doi.org/10.1207/s15327957pspr0203_4.

74. Center for Open Science, "Preregistration," https://www.cos.io/initiatives/prereg; Brian A. Nosek et al. "The Preregistration Revolution." *Proceedings of the National Academy of Sciences* 115, no. 11 (March 13, 2018): 2600–2606, https://doi.org/10.1073/pnas.1708274114; Association for Psychological Science, "Registered Replication Reports," https://www.psychologicalscience.org/publications/replication.

75. Center for Open Science, "Registered Reports," https://www.cos.io/initiatives/registered-reports.

76. Nüst, D., Sochat, V., Marwick, B., Eglen, S. J., Head, T., Hirst, T., & Evans, B. D. (2020). Ten simple rules for writing Dockerfiles for reproducible data science. PLOS Computational Biology, 16(11), e1008316. https://doi.org/10.1371/journal.pcbi.1008316

77. Scott Hogg, "Software Containers: Used More Frequently Than Most Realize," *Network World*, May 26, 2014, https://www.networkworld.com/article/2226996/software-containers--used-more-frequently-than-most-realize.html.

78. Sylabs.io. "Singularity," accessed August 13, 2020, https://sylabs.io/; Docker, home page, accessed August 13, 2020, https://www.docker.com/.

79. Docker, home page.

80. Sylabs.io, "Singularity."

81. Margaret Rouse, "What Does Integrated Development Environment Mean?" Techopedia, January 11, 2017, http://www.techopedia.com/definition/26860/integrated-development-environment-ide.

82. Jupyter, home page, https://jupyter.org/; Posit, "RStudio IDE," https://posit.co/downloads/.

83. Whole Tale, home page, 2019, https://wholetale.org/.

84. Whole Tale, home page.

85. Apache Spark, home page, https://spark.apache.org/; JupyterLab Doumentation, https://jupyterlab.readthedocs.io/en/stable/.

86. Dataverse, home page, https://dataverse.org/.

87. Chard et al., "Application of BagIt."

88. Binder, home page, https://mybinder.org/; Jupyter home page, https://jupyter.org/.

89. repo2Docker, GitHub, https://github.com/jupyterhub/repo2docker; Project Jupyter et al., "Binder 2.0—Reproducible, Interactive, Sharable Environments for Science at Scale," *Proceedings of the 17th Python in Science Conference*, July 15, 2018, 113–20, https://doi.org/10.25080/Majora-4af1f417-011.

90. Project Jupyter et al., "Binder 2.0."

91. REANA, home page, accessed August 13, 2020, https://reanahub.io/.

92. REANA, home page.

93. Peter Amstutz et al., "Common Workflow Language, v1.0," Figshare, July 8, 2016, https://doi.org/10.6084/M9.FIGSHARE.3115156.V2.

94. ReproZip, home page, https://www.reprozip.org/.

95. Fernando Chirigati et al., "ReproZip: Computational Reproducibility with Ease," in *Proceedings of the 2016 International Conference on Management of Data, SIGMOD '16* (New York: Association for Computing Machinery, 2016), 2085–88, https://doi.org/10.1145/2882903.2899401.

96. Chirigati et al., "ReproZip."

97. ReproZip Web, "ReproZip Web's Documentation, https://reprozip-web.readthedocs.io/en/latest/; Reprozip-Jupyter 1.2, home page, https://pypi.org/project/reprozip-jupyter/; VIDA-NYU, "ReproZip Jupyter Extension," example videos, YouTube video, 0:51, https://www.youtube.com/watch?v=Y8YmGVYH-hS8&list=PLjgZ3v4gFxpWb277AEyjsVerB6nViGTVL; ReproZip, "Using *Reprounzip*," https://docs.reprozip.org/en/1.0.x/unpacking.html; ReproServer, home page, https://server.reprozip.org/.

98. Vicky Steeves, Rémi Rampin, and Fernando Chirigati, "Reproducibility, Preservation, and Access to Research with ReproZip and ReproServer," *IASSIST Quarterly* 44, no. 1–2 (June 29, 2020): 1–11, https://doi.org/10.29173/iq969.

99. Justin Kitzes, Daniel Turek, and Fatima Deniz, eds., *The Practice of Reproducible Research* (Oakland, CA: University of California Press, 2018).

100. Logan Ward, "Predicting the Properties of Inorganic Materials with Machine Learning," Whole Tale dashboard, https://dashboard.wholetale.org/run/59fc7f9d60221d000163c37b?token=aJgFSGxFQUSUg-PV6vkerjk7pfowAAOFyhW0NKiE3rx8k9LSbxzugxp8U3XRrB1ev.

101. L. Michelle Lewis et al., "Replication Study: Transcriptional Amplification in Tumor Cells with Elevated c-Myc," *eLife* 7 (2018): e30274, https://doi.org/10.7554/eLife.30274.

102. Stencila, home page, https://stenci.la/.

103. Nicholas Wolf, "National School System and the Irish Language Heaney Lecture 2015," April 12, 2016, https://doi.org/10.17605/OSF.IO/PGK8V.

104. Nicholas Wolf, "The National-School System and the Irish Language in the Nineteenth Century," in *Schools and Schooling, 1650–2000*, ed. James Kelly and Susan Hegarty (Dublin: Four Courts Press, 2017), 208, https://www.fourcourtspress.ie/books/2017/schools-and-schooling/.

105. Nicholas Wolf, "National School System and the Irish Language Heaney Lecture 2015," OSF, https://osf.io/wfvqr.

106. Rob De Almeida, "Analyzing Whale Tracks," EarthPy, September 23, 2013, http://earthpy.org/analyzing-whale-tracks.html.

107. Diego Rodriguez et al., Reanahub/Reana-Demo-Bsm-Search, Python (2018; repr., REANA, 2020), https://github.com/reanahub/reana-demo-bsm-search.

108. https://github.com/reanahub/reana-demo-bsm-search

109. Rodriguez et al., Reanahub/Reana-Demo-Bsm-Search.

BIBLIOGRAPHY

Aguinis, Herman, and Angelo M. Solarino. "Transparency and Replicability in Qualitative Research: The Case of Interviews with Elite Informants." *Strategic Management Journal* 40, no. 8 (August 2019): 1291–1315. https://doi.org/10.1002/smj.3015.

Almugbel, Reem, Ling-Hong Hung, Jiaming Hu, Abeer Almutairy, Nicole Ortogero, Yashaswi Tamta, and Ka Yee Yeung. "Reproducible Bioconductor Workflows Using Browser-Based Interactive Notebooks and Containers." *Journal of the American Medical Informatics Association* 25, no. 1 (January 2018): 4–12. https://doi.org/10.1093/jamia/ocx120.

American Medical Association. *AMA Manual of Style: A Guide for Authors and Editors*, 11th ed. New York: Oxford University Press, 2020.

American Psychological Association. "Journal Article Reporting Standards (JARS)." APA Style. Accessed November 24, 2020. https://apastyle.apa.org/jars.

Amstutz, Peter, Michael R. Crusoe, Nebojša Tijanić, Brad Chapman, John Chilton, Michael Heuer, Andrey Kartashov, et al. "Common Workflow Language, v1.0." Figshare, July 8, 2016. https://doi.org/10.6084/M9.FIGSHARE.3115156.V2.

Apache Spark. Home page. https://spark.apache.org/.

Archive-It. Home page. https://archive-it.org/.

Association for Computing Machinery. "Artifact Review and Badging—Version 1.0 (Not Current)." Last updated August 24, 2020. https://www.acm.org/publications/policies/artifact-review-badging.

Association for Psychological Science. "Registered Replication Reports." https://www.psychologicalscience.org/publications/replication.

Barba, Lorena A. "Terminologies for Reproducible Research." ArXiv:1802.03311 [Cs], February 9, 2018. http://arxiv.org/abs/1802.03311.

Binder. Home page. https://mybinder.org/.

Bishop, Dorothy, Doreen Cantrell, Peter Johnson, Shitij Kapur, Malcom Macleod, Caroline Savage, Jim Smith, et al. *Reproducibility and Reliability of Biomedical Research: Improving Research Practice.* Symposium report. London: Academy of Medical Sciences, October 2015. https://acmedsci.ac.uk/policy/policy-projects/reproducibility-and-reliability-of-biomedical-research.

Bode, Katherine. "The Equivalence of 'Close' and 'Distant' Reading; or, Toward a New Object for Data-Rich Literary History." *Modern Language Quarterly* 78, no. 1 (March 1, 2017): 77–106. https://doi.org/10.1215/00267929-3699787.

Boettiger, Carl. "An Introduction to Docker for Reproducible Research." *ACM SIGOPS Operating Systems Review* 49, no. 1 (January 2015): 71–79. https://doi.org/10.1145/2723872.2723882.

Bollen, Kenneth, John T. Cacioppo, Robert M. Kaplan, Jon A. Krosnick, and James L. Olds. *Social, Behavioral, and Economic Sciences Perspectives on Robust and Reliable Science: Report of the Subcommittee on Replicability in Science, Advisory Committee to the National Science Foundation Directorate for Social, Behavioral, and Economic Sciences.* Alexandria, VA: National Science Foundation, May 2015. https://www.nsf.gov/sbe/AC_Materials/SBE_Robust_and_Reliable_Research_Report.pdf.

Borgman, Christine L. *Big Data, Little Data, No Data: Scholarship in the Networked World.* Cambridge, MA: MIT Press, 2015. https://mitpress.mit.edu/9780262529914/big-data-little-data-no-data/.

Boss, Katherine, Vicky Steeves, Fernando Chirigati, Rémi Rampin, and Brian Hoffman. "Saving Data Journalism: Using ReproZip-Web to Capture Dynamic Websites for Future Reuse." Presentation, Librarians Building Momentum for Reproducibility, virtual conference, January 28, 2020. Slides: https://osf.io/nr9d8/. YouTube video, 13:16, https://youtu.be/xLdFaDL2VWc.

Braun, Steven. "Supporting Research Impact Metrics in Academic Libraries: A Case Study." *portal: Libraries and the Academy* 17, no. 1 (January 2017): 111–27. https://doi.org/10.1353/pla.2017.0007.

Brembs, Björn, Katherine Button, and Marcus Munafò. "Deep Impact: Unintended Consequences of Journal Rank." *Frontiers in Human Neuroscience* 7 (2013). https://doi.org/10.3389/fnhum.2013.00291.

Campbell-Jensen, Allison. "Award-Winning Changemaker." *Continuum* (blog), University of Minnesota Libraries, September 30, 2020. https://www.continuum.umn.edu/2020/09/award-winning-changemaker/.

Castagné, Michel. "Consider the Source: The Value of Source Code to Digital Preservation Strategies." *School of Information Student Research Journal* (San José State University) 2, no. 2 (January 2013): article 5. https://doi.org/10.31979/2575-2499.020205.

Center for Open Science. "Preregistration." https://www.cos.io/initiatives/prereg.

———. "Registered Reports." https://www.cos.io/initiatives/registered-reports.

Chard, Kyle, Niall Gaffney, Matthew B. Jones, Kacper Kowalik, Bertram Ludascher, Timothy McPhillips, Jarek Nabrzyski, et al. "Application of BagIt-Serialized Research Object Bundles for Packaging and Re-execution of Computational Analyses." In *2019 15th International Conference on EScience*, 514–21. San Diego: IEEE, 2019. https://doi.org/10.1109/eScience.2019.00068.

Chassanoff, Alexandra, and Micah Altman. "Curation as 'Interoperability with the Future': Preserving Scholarly Research Software in Academic Libraries." *Journal of the Association for Information Science and Technology* 71, no. 3 (2020): 325–37. https://doi.org/10.1002/asi.24244.

Chirigati, Fernando, Rémi Rampin, Dennis Shasha, and Juliana Freire. "ReproZip: Computational Reproducibility with Ease." In *Proceedings of the 2016 International Conference on Management of Data*, 2085–2088. SIGMOD '16. New York: Association for Computing Machinery, 2016. https://doi.org/10.1145/2882903.2899401.

Christensen, Garret, Jeremy Freese, and Edward Miguel. *Transparent and Reproducible Social Science Research: How to Do Open Science.* Oakland: University of California Press, 2019. https://www.ucpress.edu/book/9780520296954/transparent-and-reproducible-social-science-research.

Cochrane, Euan, Rechert, Klaus, Anderson, Seth, Meyerson, Jessica, and Ethan Gates. (2019) 'Towards a Universal Virtual Interactor (UVI) for Digital Objects.' Proceedings of the 16th International Conference on Digital Preservation iPRES 2019. Available at https://ipres2019.org/static/pdf/iPres2019_paper_128.pdf. DOI:10.17605/OSF.IO/AZEWJ.

Dataverse Project. Home page. https://dataverse.org/.

De Almeida, Rob. "Analyzing Whale Tracks." EarthPy, September 23, 2013. http://earthpy.org/analyzing-whale-tracks.html.

de Rijcke, Sarah, and Bart Penders. "Resist Calls for Replicability in the Humanities." *Nature* 560, no. 7716 (August 1, 2018): 29. https://doi.org/10.1038/d41586-018-05845-z.

Digital Preservation Coalition. Insert Coin to Continue: A Briefing Day on Software Preservation, London, May 7, 2019. https://www.dpconline.org/events/past-events/software-preservation.

Docker. Home page. Accessed August 13, 2020. https://www.docker.com/.

Donoho, David L. "An Invitation to Reproducible Computational Research." *Biostatistics* 11, no. 3 (July 2010): 385–88. https://doi.org/10.1093/biostatistics/kxq028.

Duckles, Beth M., and Vicky Steeves. "Qualitative Research Using Open Tools." Presentation, CSV,conf,v4, [Portland, Oregon], May 2019. Slides: https://doi.org/10.5281/zenodo.2673016. YouTube video, 17:51: https://youtu.be/DwCunW19wcQ.

Educopia Institute. "Scaling Emulation as a Service Infrastructure (EaaSI) (subcontract). 2017–2020. https://educopia.org/emulation-as-a-service-eaasi/.

Evans, Julia. *How Containers Work*. Wizard Zines. 2021. https://wizardzines.com/zines/containers/.

Fehrmann, Paul. "Reproducibility of Computer Searches in Systematic Reviews: Checklist Items Used to Assess Computer Search Reports." Presentation, Librarians Building Momentum for Reproducibility, online conference, January 28, 2023. YouTube video, 6:01, posted February 3, 2020. https://www.youtube.com/watch?v=HqYv7IhQ4GU.

French, Rebecca B., and Jody Condit Fagan. "The Visibility of Authority Records, Researcher Identifiers, Academic Social Networking Profiles, and Related Faculty Publications in Search Engine Results." *Journal of Web Librarianship* 13, no. 2 (2019): 156–97. https://doi.org/10.1080/19322909.2019.1591324.

Goodman, Steven N., Danielle Fanelli, and John P. A. Ioannidis. "What Does Research Reproducibility Mean?" *Science Translational Medicine* 8, no. 341 (June 1, 2016): 341ps12. https://doi.org/10.1126/scitranslmed.aaf5027.

Gronenschild, Ed H. B. M., Petra Habets, Heidi I. L. Jacobs, Ron Mengelers, Nico Rozendaal, Jim van Os, and Machteld Marcelis. "The Effects of FreeSurfer Version, Workstation Type, and Macintosh Operating System Version on Anatomical Volume and Cortical Thickness Measurements." *PLOS ONE* 7, no. 6 (2012)): e38234. https://doi.org/10.1371/journal.pone.0038234.

Haven, Tamarinde L., Timothy M. Errington, Kristian Gleditsch, Leonie van Grootel, Alan M. Jacobs, Florian Kern, Rafael Piñeiro, et al. "Preregistering Qualitative Research: A Delphi Study." SocArXiv. Last edited November 9, 2020. https://doi.org/10.31235/osf.io/pz9jr.

Head, Megan L., Luke Holman, Rob Lanfear, Andrew T. Kahn, and Michael D. Jennions. "The Extent and Consequences of P-Hacking in Science." *PLOS Biology* 13, no. 3 (March 13, 2015). https://journals.plos.org/plosbiology/article?id=10.1371/journal.pbio.1002106.

Herbert, Bruce, Sarah Potvin, and Tina Budzise-Weaver. "Best Practices for the Use of Scholarly Impact Metrics." Working paper, February 10, 2016. https://oaktrust.library.tamu.edu/handle/1969.1/156054.

Hettne, Kristina, Ricarda Proppert, Linda Nab, L. Paloma Rojas-Saunero, and Daniela Gawehns. "ReprohackNL 2019: How Libraries Can Promote Research Reproducibility through Community Engagement." *IASSIST Quarterly* 44, no. 1–2 (2020): 1–10. https://doi.org/10.29173/iq977.

Hogg, Scott. "Software Containers: Used More Frequently Than Most Realize." *Network World*, May 26, 2014. https://www.networkworld.com/article/2226996/software-containers--used-more-frequently-than-most-realize.html.

Hong, Neil Chue, Steve Crouch, Simon Hettrick, Tim Parkinson, and Matt Shreeve. *Sustainability and Preservation Framework*. Edinburgh, UK: Software Sustainability Institute, December 7, 2010. https://www.software.ac.uk/sustainability-and-preservation-framework.

Jupyter. Home page. https://jupyter.org/.

JupyterLab Documentation. https://jupyterlab.readthedocs.io/en/stable/.

Jupyter Project, Matthias Bussonnier, Jessica Forde, Jeremy Freeman, Brian Granger, Tim Head, Chris Holdgraf, et al. "Binder 2.0—Reproducible, Interactive, Sharable Environments for Science at Scale." Proceedings of the 17th Python in Science Conference, July 15, 2018, 113–20. https://doi.org/10.25080/Majora-4af1f417-011.

Karcher, Sebastian, and Nicholas Weber. "Annotation for Transparent Inquiry: Transparent Data and Analysis for Qualitative Research." *IASSIST Quarterly* 43, no. 2 (2019): 1–9. https://doi.org/10.29173/iq959.

Kerr, Norbert L. "HARKing: Hypothesizing after the Results Are Known." *Personality and Social Psychology Review* 2, no. 3 (1998): 196–217. https://doi.org/10.1207/s15327957pspr0203_4.

Kim, Julia, and Don Mennerich. "Jeremy Blake's Time-Based Paintings: A Case Study." *Electronic Media Review* 4 (2015–2016). https://resources.culturalheritage.org/emg-review/volume-4-2015-2016/kim/.

Kitzes, Justin, Daniel Turek, and Fatima Deniz, eds. *The Basic Reproducible Workflow Template: The Practice of Reproducible Research*. Oakland: University of California Press, 2018. http://www.practicereproducibleresearch.org/

Koffel, Jonathan B., and Melissa L. Rethlefsen. "Reproducibility of Search Strategies Is Poor in Systematic Reviews Published in High-Impact Pediatrics, Cardiology and Surgery Journals: A Cross-sectional Study." Edited by Brett D Thombs. *PLOS ONE* 11, no. 9 (September 26, 2016): e0163309. https://doi.org/10.1371/journal.pone.0163309.

Kunze, J., J. Littman, E. Madden, J. Scancella, and C. Adams. "The BagIt File Packaging Format (V1.0)," RFC Editor, October 2018. https://tools.ietf.org/html/rfc8493.

Lambert, Ladina Bezzola. "Repetition with a Difference: Reproducibility in Literature Studies." In *Reproducibility: Principles, Problems, Practices, and Prospects*, edited by Harald Atmanspacher and Sabine Maasen, 491–509. Hoboken, NJ: John Wiley & Sons, 2016. https://doi.org/10.1002/9781118865064.ch23.

Leonelli, Sabina. "Rethinking Reproducibility as a Criterion for Research Quality." In *Including a Symposium on Mary Morgan: Curiosity, Imagination, and Surprise*, Research in the History of Economic Thought and Methodology, vol. 36B, edited by Luca Fiorito, Scott Scheall, and Carlos Eduardo Suprinyak, 129–46. Bingley, UK: Emerald Publishing, 2018. https://doi.org/10.1108/S0743-41542018000036B009.

Lewis, L. Michelle, Meredith C. Edwards, Zachary R. Meyers, C. Conover Talbot Jr., Haiping Hao, David Blum, and Reproducibility Project: Cancer Biology. "Replication Study: Transcriptional Amplification in Tumor Cells with Elevated c-Myc." *eLife* 7 (2018): e30274. https://doi.org/10.7554/eLife.30274.

Michael S. Lewis-Beck, et al, The SAGE Encyclopedia of Social Science Research Methods (2004) https://doi.org/10.4135/9781412950589

Lourenço, Raoni, Juliana Freire, and Dennis Shasha. "BugDoc: Algorithms to Debug Computational Processes." In *SIGMOD '20: Proceedings of the 2020 ACM SIGMOD International Conference on Management of Data*, 463–78. New York: Association for Computing Machinery, 2020. https://doi.org/10.1145/3318464.3389763.

Makel, Matthew C., and Jonathan A. Plucker. *Toward a More Perfect Psychology: Improving Trust, Accuracy, and Transparency in Research*. Washington, DC: American Psychological Association, 2017. https://doi.org/10.1037/0000033-000.

Mellor, David Thomas, Alexander C. DeHaven, Nicole Pfeiffer, Olivia Lowery, and Mark Call. "Templates of OSF Registration Forms." OSF, October 31, 2016. https://osf.io/zab38/.

Miguel, E., C. Camerer, K. Casey, J. Cohen, K. M. Esterling, A. Gerber, R. Glennerster, et al. "Promoting Transparency in Social Science Research." *Science* 343, no. 6166 (2014): 30–31. https://doi.org/10.1126/science.1245317.

Moher, David, Alessandro Liberati, Jennifer Tetzlaff, Douglas G. Altman, and PRISMA Group. "Preferred Reporting Items for Systematic Reviews and Meta-analyses: The PRISMA Statement." *PLOS Medicine* 6, no. 7 (2009): e1000097. https://doi.org/10.1371/journal.pmed.1000097.

Moretti, Franco. *Graphs, Maps, Trees: Abstract Models for a Literary Theory*. London: Verso, 2005.

National Academies of Sciences, Engineering, and Medicine. *Open Science by Design: Realizing a Vision for 21st Century Research*. Washington, DC: National Academies Press, 2018. https://doi.org/10.17226/25116.

National Academies of Sciences, Engineering, and Medicine. *Reproducibility and Replicability in Science*. Washington, DC: National Academies Press, 2019. https://doi.org/10.17226/25303.

National Institutes of Health. "Research Misconduct—Definitions." November 29, 2018. https://grants.nih.gov/policy/research_integrity/definitions.htm.

National Science Foundation. "Scientists Seeking NSF Funding Will Soon Be Required to Submit Data Management Plans." News release 10-077, May 10, 2010. https://www.nsf.gov/news/news_summ.jsp?cntn_id=116928.

Nosek, Brian A., Charles R. Ebersole, Alexander C. DeHaven, and David T. Mellor. "The Preregistration Revolution." *Proceedings of the National Academy of Sciences* 115, no. 11 (March 13, 2018): 2600–06. https://doi.org/10.1073/pnas.1708274114.

Nosek, Brian A., Jeffrey R. Spies, and Matt Motyl. "Scientific Utopia: II. Restructuring Incentives and Practices to Promote Truth over Publishability." *Perspectives on Psychological Science* 7, no. 6 (November 2012): 615–31. https://doi.org/10.1177/1745691612459058.

Nüst, D., Sochat, V., Marwick, B., Eglen, S. J., Head, T., Hirst, T., & Evans, B. D. (2020). Ten simple rules for writing Dockerfiles for reproducible data science. PLOS Computational Biology, 16(11), e1008316. https://doi.org/10.1371/journal.pcbi.1008316

Nüst, Daniel, Carl Boettiger, and Ben Marwick. "How to Read a Research Compendium." ArXiv:1806.09525 [Cs], June 11, 2018. https://doi.org/10.48550/arXiv.1806.09525.

Nüst, Daniel, and Matthias Hinz. "Containerit: Generating Dockerfiles for Reproducible Research with R." *Journal of Open Source Software* 4, no. 40 (August 21, 2019): 1603. https://doi.org/10.21105/joss.01603.

O'Brien, Bridget C., Ilene B. Harris, Thomas J. Beckman, Darcy A. Reed, and David A. Cook. "Standards for Reporting Qualitative Research: A Synthesis of Recommendations." *Academic Medicine* 89, no. 9 (September 2014): 1245–51. https://doi.org/10.1097/ACM.0000000000000388.

Odell, Jere D., Heather L. Coates, and Kristi L. Palmer. "Rewarding Open Access Scholarship in Promotion and Tenure: Driving Institutional Change." *College and Research Libraries News* 77, no. 7 (2016): 322–25. https://doi.org/10.7912/C2R60B.

OpenRefine. Home page. https://openrefine.org/.

Open Science Collaboration. "Estimating the Reproducibility of Psychological Science." *Science* 349, no. 6251 (August 28, 2015): aac4716. https://doi.org/10.1126/science.aac4716.

Open Syllabus Explorer. Home page. https://opensyllabus.org/.

O'Sullivan, James. "The Humanities Have a 'Reproducibility' Problem." *Talking Humanities* (blog), July 9, 2019. https://talkinghumanities.blogs.sas.ac.uk/2019/07/09/the-humanities-have-a-reproducibility-problem/.

Pawlik, Mateusz, Thomas Hütter, Daniel Kocher, Willi Mann, and Nikolaus Augsten. "A Link Is Not Enough—Reproducibility of Data." *Datenbank-Spektrum* 19, no. 2 (2019): 107–15. https://doi.org/10.1007/s13222-019-00317-8.

Peels, Rik, and Lex Bouter. "Humanities Need a Replication Drive Too." *Nature* 558, no. 7710 (June 21, 2018): 372–372. https://doi.org/10.1038/d41586-018-05454-w.

Penders, Bart, J. Britt Holbrook, and Sarah de Rijcke. "Rinse and Repeat: Understanding the Value of Replication across Different Ways of Knowing." *Publications* 7, no. 3 (September 2019): 52. https://doi.org/10.3390/publications7030052.

Posit. "RStudio IDE." https://posit.co/downloads/.

Pratt, Michael G., Sarah Kaplan, and Richard Whittington. "The Tumult over Transparency: Decoupling Transparency from Replication in Establishing Trustworthy Qualitative Research." *Administrative Science Quarterly* 65, no. 1 (March 1, 2020): 1–19. https://doi.org/10.1177/0001839219887663.

Qcoder. GitHub. https://github.com/ropenscilabs/qcoder.

REANA. Home page. Accessed August 13, 2020. https://reanahub.io/.

Rechert, Klaus, Isgandar Valizada, Dirk von Suchodoletz, and Johann Latocha. "bwFLA—A Functional Approach to Digital Preservation." *PIK—Praxis der Informationsverarbeitung und Kommunikation* 35, no. 4 (November 2012): 259–67. https://doi.org/10.1515/pik-2012-0044.

Repo2docker. GitHub. https://github.com/jupyterhub/repo2docker.

ReproServer. Home page. https://server.reprozip.org/.

ReproZip. Home page. https://www.reprozip.org/.

———. "Using *Reprounzip*." https://docs.reprozip.org/en/1.0.x/unpacking.html; https://server.reprozip.org/.

ReproZip-Jupyter 1.2. Home page. https://pypi.org/project/reprozip-jupyter/.

ReproZip Web. "ReproZip Web's Documentation." https://reprozip-web.readthedocs.io/en/latest/.

Research Compedium. Home page. https://research-compendium.science/.

Rethlefsen, Melissa L., Ann M. Farrell, Leah C. Osterhaus Trzasko, and Tara J. Brigham. "Librarian Co-authors Correlated with Higher Quality Reported Search Strategies in General Internal Medicine Systematic Reviews." *Journal of Clinical Epidemiology* 68, no. 6 (June 2015): 617–26. https://doi.org/10.1016/j.jclinepi.2014.11.025.

Rethlefsen, Melissa L., Shona Kirtley, Siw Waffenschmidt, Ana Patricia Ayala, David Moher, Matthew J. Page, Jonathan B. Koffel, and PRISMA-S Group. "PRISMA-S: An Extension to the PRISMA Statement for Reporting Literature Searches in Systematic Reviews." *Systematic Reviews* 10, no. 1 (January 26. 2021): article 39. https://doi.org/10.1186/s13643-020-01542-z.

Rethlefsen, Melissa L., Mellanye J. Lackey, and Shirley Zhao. "Building Capacity to Encourage Research Reproducibility and #MakeResearchTrue." *Journal of the Medical Library Association* 106, no. 1 (January 12, 2018): 113–19. https://doi.org/10.5195/jmla.2018.273.

Riegelman, Amy. "A Primer on Preregistration (& Why I Think It Should Be a Submission Track in LIS Journals)." Presentation, Librarians Building Momentum for Reproducibility, virtual conference, January 28, 2020. https://osf.io/w4dfh/.

Rodriguez, Diego, Lukas Heinrich, Maciulaitis Rokas, Tibor Simko, and Jan Okraska. Reanahub/Reana-Demo-Bsm-Search. Python. 2018. Reprint, REANA, 2020. https://github.com/reanahub/reana-demo-bsm-search.

Rouse, Margaret. "What Does Integrated Development Environment Mean?" Techopedia, January 11, 2017. http://www.techopedia.com/definition/26860/integrated-development-environment-ide.

Sandve, Geir Kjetil, Anton Nekrutenko, James Taylor, and Eivind Hovig. "Ten Simple Rules for Reproducible Computational Research." *PLOS Computational Biology* 9, no. 10 (October 24, 2013): e1003285. https://doi.org/10.1371/journal.pcbi.1003285.

Saving Data Journalism. Home page. https://savingjournalism.reprozip.org/.

Sayre, Franklin, and Amy Riegelman. "Replicable Services for Reproducible Research: A Model for Academic Libraries." *College and Research Libraries* 80, no. 2 (March 2019): 260–72.

———. "Reproducibility Bibliography." Accessed September 30, 2020. https://reproducibility.dash.umn.edu/.

Sayre, Franklin, Amy Riegelman, Shirley Zhao, Vicky Steeves, and Tisha Mentnech. Librarians Building Momentum for Reproducibility, virtual conference, January 28, 2020. https://vickysteeves.gitlab.io/librarians-reproducibility/.

Schimmack, Ulrich. "Questionable Research Practices: Definition, Detection, and Recommendations for Better Practices." *Replicability-Index* (blog), January 24, 2015. https://replicationindex.com/2015/01/24/qrps/.

Steeves, Vicky. "Reproducibility Librarianship." *Collaborative Librarianship* 9, no. 2 (2017): article 4. https://digitalcommons.du.edu/collaborativelibrarianship/vol9/iss2/4.

Steeves, Vicky, Rémi Rampin, and Fernando Chirigati. "Reproducibility, Preservation, and Access to Research with ReproZip and ReproServer." *IASSIST Quarterly* 44, no. 1–2 (June 29, 2020): 1–11. https://doi.org/10.29173/iq969.

Stencila. Home page. https://stenci.la/.

Stodden, Victoria. "Resolving Irreproducibility in Empirical and Computational Research." Institute of Mathematical Statistics, November 17, 2013. https://imstat.org/2013/11/17/resolving-irreproducibility-in-empirical-and-computational-research/.

Stodden, Victoria, David Bailey, Bill Rider, Jonathan Borwein, William Stein, and Randall LeVeque, comps. and eds. "Setting the Default to Reproducible." Developed by participants in ICERM workshop Reproducibility in Computational and Experimental Mathematics, Providence, RI, December 14, 2012. https://stodden. net/icerm_report.pdf.

Suiter, Amy M., and Heather Lea Moulaison. "Supporting Scholars: An Analysis of Academic Library Websites' Documentation on Metrics and Impact." *Journal of Academic Librarianship* 41, no. 6 (November 2015): 814–20. https://doi.org/10.1016/j.acalib.2015.09.004.

Sylabs.io. "Singularity." Accessed August 13, 2020. https://sylabs.io/.

Taguette. Home page. https://www.taguette.org/.

Tebbe, Heidi, and Danica Madison Lewis. "What's Sauce for the Goose Is Sauce for the Gander: Reproducible Practice in Library Work." OSF, February 3, 2020. https://osf.io/3xuj2/.

Trisovic, Ana, Philip Durbin, Tania Schlatter, Gustavo Durand, Sonia Barbosa, Danny Brooke, and Mercè Crosas. "Advancing Computational Reproducibility in the Dataverse Data Repository Platform." In *P-RECS '20: Proceedings of the 3rd International Workshop on Practical Reproducible Evaluation of Computer Systems*, 15–20. New York: ACM, 2020. https://doi.org/10.1145/3391800.3398173.

VIDA-NYU. "ReproZip Jupyter Extension." Example videos. YouTube video, 0:51. https://www.youtube.com/ watch?v=Y8YmGVYHhS8&list=PLjgZ3v4gFxpWb277AEyjsVerB6nViGTVL.

Vitale, Cynthia R. H. "Is Research Reproducibility the New Data Management for Libraries?" *Bulletin of the Association for Information Science and Technology* 42, no. 3 (2016): 38–41. https://asistdl.onlinelibrary. wiley.com/doi/full/10.1002/bul2.2016.1720420313.

Ward, Logan. "Predicting the Properties of Inorganic Materials with Machine Learning." Whole Tale dashboard. https://dashboard.wholetale.org/run/59fc7f9d60221d000163c37b?token=aJgFSGxFQUSUgPV-6vkerjk7pfowAAOFyhW0NKiE3rx8k9LSbxzugxp8U3XRrB1ev.

Webrecorder. Home page. https://webrecorder.net/.

Whole Tale. Home page. 2019. https://wholetale.org/.

Wikipedia. S.v. "JSON." Last updated March 22, 2023. https://en.wikipedia.org/wiki/JSON.

Wolf, Nicholas. "National School System and the Irish Language Heaney Lecture 2015." April 12, 2016. https:// doi.org/10.17605/OSF.IO/PGK8V.

———. "National School System and the Irish Language Heaney Lecture 2015." OSF. https://osf.io/wfvqr.

———. "The National-School System and the Irish Language in the Nineteenth Century." In *Schools and Schooling, 1650–2000*, edited by James Kelly and Susan Hegarty, 208. Dublin: Four Courts Press, 2017. https://www.fourcourtspress.ie/books/2017/schools-and-schooling/.

Yenni, Glenda M., Erica M. Christensen, Ellen K. Bledsoe, Sarah R. Supp, Renata M. Diaz, Ethan P. White, and S. K. Morgan Ernest. "Developing a Modern Data Workflow for Evolving Data." Preprint. BioRxiv, July 24, 2018. https://doi.org/10.1101/344804.

ETHICS OF OPEN DATA

Brandon Locke and Nic Weber

INTRODUCTION

This chapter addresses emergent ethical issues in producing, using, curating, and providing services for open data. Our goal is to provide an introduction to how ethical topics in open data manifest in practical dilemmas for scholarly communication and some approaches to understanding and working through them. We begin with a brief overview of what can be thought of as three basic theories of ethics that intersect with dilemmas in openness, accountability, transparency, and fairness in data: virtue, consequential, and non-consequential ethics. We then map these *kinds* of ethics to the practical questions that arise in provisioning infrastructures, providing services, and supporting sustainable research in science and scholarship that depends upon open access to data. Throughout, we attempt to offer concrete examples of potential ethical dilemmas facing scholarly communication with respect to open data and try to make clear what kinds of ethical positions are helpful to practitioners. In doing so, we hope to both clarify the ethical questions facing librarians doing practical work to support open data access and to situate current debates in the field with respect to these three kinds of ethics.

OPEN DATA AND ETHICS: A BRIEF OVERVIEW

Ethics can be practically framed as "the study of the general nature of morals and of the specific moral judgments or choices to be made by people."[1] This definition situates ethics as a matter of individual choice, but of course the choices we make as individuals have broad impacts on the communities we are part of, serve, and wish to see flourish. That is, ethics is often practically framed as the result of individual choices and actions, but ethics also encompasses the implicit and explicit values of an institution, community of practice, or even group of researchers. The relationship between individual choice and collective action is particularly relevant for scholarly communication, where curators, librarians, and policymakers collaboratively work to provide regular and unfettered access to resources needed to conduct research, develop guidelines or regulations that govern ethical behavior, and practically implement standards that encode or formalize these rules. It is important to acknowledge at the beginning of this chapter that morals and judgments, whether individual or collective, don't arise from the ether—they are grounded in beliefs about what is right, just, or serves the greater good given an alternative set of choices. The ethical dilemmas faced by a community of practitioners are often about deciding what is right, how justice is enacted and preserved, or what choices we make to produce the greatest good for the communities on whose behalf we work.

Broadly speaking, ethics are often broken down into an answer to three questions about *how* to make the "right" or correct choice:

1. Virtue ethics: *What action best exemplifies a high moral character?*[2]
2. Consequential (or teleological) ethics: *What action best achieves desired consequences?*[3]
3. Non-consequential (or deontological) ethics: *What action best adheres to established rules?*[4]

In the following subsections we explain how these questions can be reframed and made specific to the context of scholarly communication and open data.

VIRTUE ETHICS

Virtue ethics focus on the moral character of the action or policy. An approach to open data through a virtue ethics standpoint may say, "Broader access to more information is inherently good for the scholarly community. How can we provide access to our research materials to the most people possible?" While this perspective remains amenable to personal interpretations and understandings, there are a few different aspects one may pursue.

For example, consider data access and reuse justice: Do some instances of data sharing privilege particular people or groups, or does anyone who is interested have free and equal access?

When data is published freely online, anyone with sufficient technology and internet access is free to view and evaluate the data that was produced in the course of research or other data collection processes. When data is not published openly online, some may gain access to data through paywalls, or professional networks, but many others would not. Gate-keeping in this manner, even when unintentional, means that the data would be used only by people with personal connections, or people who have the time and knowledge to make a request. Open licensing, as one alternative, could allow individuals interested in the data to not have to seek out explicit permission to use or modify the data, which likewise removes a barrier to usage that is often more difficult for people without a connection to the creator or an impressive institutional affiliation. Further embrace of open research methods, such as nonproprietary formats, clear documentation, open source software, and open code minimizes barriers to data access and adheres to principles of virtue ethics that seek fair and just access and use to all potential users.

Some questions faced by those working under a virtue ethics umbrella in scholarly communication include

- What is the just and fair way to provide access to data?
- What are the rights of human participants, and what are their reasonable expectations for being notified about the use of their personally identifiable information?
- What are the moral obligations of researchers in sharing data as a common pool of resource that can be expediently reused?

CONSEQUENTIAL (TELEOLOGICAL) ETHICS

Consequential ethics is often framed around utilitarian notions of how the greatest net benefit can be achieved through individual and collective action. A consequential approach to open data would weigh the potential benefits of making data available against the potential harms of doing so. There are many arguments for greater openness providing the greatest good from the creation and curation of data, but data openness may also bring potential harm.

Scholarly Research Data

In academia, many argue that open data derives benefits for the creator of the data, for the health of a scholarly community, and for the efficient and fair reuse of data.[5] Creators of open data see greater scholarship impact metrics, such as increased citations and downloads on research articles and associated data sets, on open access materials than on paywalled or privately held research materials.[6] The scholarly community benefits by encouraging reproducibility and allowing other scholars to critique or verify results of empirical studies. Other researchers benefit from open data by having a greater number of resources to build upon in effectively designing and conducting research.

Government, Nonprofit, and Corporate Data

There are also many benefits to data openness outside the academy. Government agencies (local, state, and federal level), NGOs, and corporations often make some amount of data open and available to the public to encourage transparency and economic, social, and political innovations. The citizens, patrons, and partners of these organizations also value open data because it can be used (at least in theory) to hold organizations accountable for the work they're doing and develop trust with stakeholders.[7] Another benefit of these types of open data is that the data collected can be used by community members, including businesses and nonprofits, enabling more organizations and individuals to glean insights into the area without the expense, time, and (in some cases) intrusiveness of collecting the data on their own.[8] In this context, open data can benefit the community or communities that are being represented, the organizations that are making the data available, and the public at large.

Increasing Benefits and Minimizing Harms

From one perspective, the more open and accessible the data is, the more potential benefit it could bring. In other words, data licensed under CC-BY or similar schemes would enable the largest potential reuse possibilities, without deterring uses that may be commercial or mandating that any users use the same open license. Putting data into the public domain, or using a CC-0 license could garner even greater impact among user communities, though it may ultimately be detrimental to the data set's creator by potentially reducing citations.

However, any harm caused by the data's release would negate the benefits derived from making data openly accessible and available. This harm may be enacted through a number of different ways—personally identifying information may be improperly disclosed, or data that highlights a particular marginalized community could allow people to further marginalize that community. Individuals may also feel negatively about the process if they are not properly informed of the data collection or if they see the data reused in ways that they did not expect or approve of. These harms are not evenly distributed across society and largely exacerbate existing inequality and injustice.

Thus, a consequentialist's approach to open data would weigh likely and potential benefits and harms, trying to determine which modes of access create the greatest overall good given the consequences that can be predicted.

Some questions posed by a consequentialist view of ethics are

- How do we create the greatest utility from data? How can research investments be maximized in terms of credit and benefit that accrue to those that are the subjects of data and those that are the stakeholders of the results (e.g., the general public)?
- What steps (e.g., de-identification and anonymization, licensing, metadata and documentation) can be taken to minimize harm while still maximizing benefits?

- Which standards enable the efficient and effective reuse of data? How should curators or scholarly communication librarians advocate for and promote the use of open formats, encodings, and even analytic software to promote efficient reuse?

NON-CONSEQUENTIAL (DEONTOLOGICAL) ETHICS

Non-consequential, or deontological, ethics usually frames morality around adherence to norms, laws, or other authority structures (e.g., compliance with rules established by scholarly societies, codes of ethics). There are many established layers of laws, rules, and best practices concerning the sharing of research data. These stem from laws protecting privacy and intellectual property, funder mandates, institutional rules, and best practices dictated by the scholarly community. Some of these may limit the information you can collect and share, while others may require that you share things openly (though exceptions are usually built into public access requirements).

Privacy Laws

When it comes to human subjects, the ways data is collected and shared may be limited by broad federal laws in the locations where subjects live. One of the best known among these is the US Health Insurance Portability and Accountability Act (HIPAA), which has a Privacy Rule that outlines individuals' rights to control the collection and sharing of their health information.[9] Another impactful law is the European Union's General Data Protection Regulation (GDPR), which requires anyone who handles human subject data to design systems with privacy in mind and requires informed consent and privacy rights to individuals.[10] At the current moment, several other countries and a few US states are considering legislation modeled after GDPR, potentially greatly broadening overarching human subject protections.

Open Access Mandates

When research is funded by a governmental or private entity, funding bodies may have rules mandating that research outputs, including research data, be made publicly available. In 2013, the White House Office of Science and Technology Policy mandated that all federal granting agencies develop a plan to make research publicly available within twelve months of publication.[11] As a result, federal agencies include requirements for data sharing in their terms and conditions documentation. Likewise, many private funding agencies may also require that research materials be published openly and will include details in grant documentation.

Institutional Review Boards

If work is being conducted at or in collaboration with a college or university and constitutes human subjects research, research plans (including what data is and is not made publicly available) are subject to the institutional review board (IRB) of the institution, which can approve, require modifications, or disapprove research based on the potential for harms.

Although IRB approval is sometimes misunderstood as the be-all and end-all of research ethics, that is simply not true. While they are an important part of an ethics review, IRB reviews may differ greatly on different campuses, and many historical cases of research malfeasance have been approved by IRB. In addition, IRBs have a fairly narrow scope and do not generally cover data collection that doesn't include interactions with human subjects, such as public records, remote sensing, or information accessible on personal blogs or social media. Research that uses these types of sources, particularly blogs and social media, can clearly have a negative impact on the safety, well-being, and privacy of people included (see Case 2). Many professional organizations also have best practices and guidelines for data sharing and privacy protections within the relevant research domain, which may offer guidelines that are better suited for the research than IRB or may cover ethics in areas broader than the IRB scope.

Limitations of Existing Laws and Norms

It is important to note that there are many other potential harms that fall beyond these different sets of established rules. No set of laws, rules, and norms could cover all potential harms, and researchers and data curators should participate in further processes regarding the potential benefits and harms an open data set could cause. These processes should best be created in conversation with the community or communities that are most represented or impacted by the data set, as well as with other scholars or ethicists.

Some questions asked from a non-consequentialist perspective of open data ethics include
- How do data management practices conform with requirements from funding agencies?
- What laws and regulations (local or national) govern the sharing of data? What role should curators play in enforcing and upholding these rules?

SYNTHESIS OF DIFFERENT ETHICAL PERSPECTIVES ON OPEN DATA

What makes ethics interesting and difficult in the context of open data, and scholarly communication more generally, is that the choices between one ethical perspective and another are often about differences in *degree* rather than *kind*. In other words, ethical choices related to open data are about balancing virtue, utility, and rule conformance. As practitioners, we rarely have the liberty to make a wholesale choice between, say, utility and virtue. Instead, we are forced to weigh trade-offs between, for example, how much utility can be achieved in providing access to data without compromising things like the privacy rights and expectations of research participants. An example of how these three ethical schools intersect is made clear in questions such as
- What licenses or clauses in data regulations [non-consequential] can guarantee data is maximally beneficial for reuse [consequential], and how should they be enacted fairly [virtue]?
- Who deserves access, why, and under what circumstances? This includes both the *duties* of those collecting, curating, or managing access to data and the *rights* of individuals who have collected data and critically those who are the subjects of data collection and the norms and *expectations* of public scholarship, civic governance, and so on.

These choices are context-dependent and largely a matter of the institutional setting in which practitioners find themselves.

CASE STUDIES

In the remainder of this chapter we explore specific cases or topics in open data and attempt to unpack the normative assumptions behind actors who may be involved. For each case reviewed, we first describe the topic, the stakeholders, and the type of data that is involved. We then attempt to explain ethical trade-offs made and how these impact access, privacy, intellectual property, or even data quality.

CASE 1: ALICE GOFFMAN'S "ON THE RUN" ETHNOGRAPHY

Some of the most sensitive data generated in the course of empirical research comes from the close study with and of people in their built environments. Observational work that takes seriously the notion of ethnomethodology is, for example, often rooted in practices of reflexivity and participant engagement that places the researcher as a steward of private (personal) information. Increasingly, calls for transparency across the spectrum of qualitative scholarship[12] encourage the open sharing of instruments and data used to generate novel findings when research is conducted with and through participant observation.

In this setting, Alice Goffman's book *On the Run: Fugitive Life in an American City'* (2015) became a crucible for numerous ethical controversies in contemporary qualitative research, ethnography, and sociology.[13] The data collected for Goffman's book came from over six years of intensive field work in which Goffman not only observed, but also lived in a neighborhood of Philadelphia where she befriended a group of black men eking out a living among unjust systems of oppression and lack of social or economic mobility. The book is, regardless of the controversy surrounding its production, an incredible commentary on the vicious cycle that perpetually ensnares young black men in the USA's criminal justice system. As part of her fieldwork, Goffman attended bail hearings and court dates and observed the harassment of her subjects by police officers as they went about navigating life in a Philadelphia neighborhood.

Where Goffman came under ethical fire in academia was for her positionality in relation to crimes that she observed and arguably participated in. *On the Run* details a number of episodes in which a crime may have been committed, and many argued that Goffman crossed a line from simply "participant observation" with her subjects and became implicit in actions that were criminal.[14] The documentary evidence of these controversial events were recorded in Goffman's ethnographic field notes, which—after publication—became highly sought after by scholars (as well as law enforcement) looking to substantiate claims that seemed, on their face, difficult to square with official records of crimes, hospitalizations, and reported locations of her research participants. In both anthropology and sociology, ethnographic field notes are rarely shared between researchers or made publicly available for secondary analysis.[15] Controversially, Goffman destroyed all of her field notes upon completing the project. The destruction of this data was justified as a way to protect participants and shut a door to future criminal investigations.

Ethics at Stake

Part of what has made the controversy of Goffman's work so intense and salient for scholarly communication comes from the notion that a researcher places themselves as the final arbiter in determining what should be done with information collected during the course of a research project. While IRBs are often helpful at initially determining risk and credentialing researchers for the ethical management of data, IRBs are not, solely, responsible for the continued management and safeguarding of sensitive information when a research project ends. In fact, some IRBs encourage researchers to destroy data to minimize institutional risk upon the end of a sanctioned data collection and analysis period.[16]

Critics of Goffman's destruction of her empirical data do so through a consequentialist framework—arguing that, instead of adhering to principles of transparency and research accountability, she violated her ethical duty to provide evidence that could support claims made in her book. In a normative ethical framework there are many additional questions about the alternative decisions that were available to Goffman. For example, working with data curators she might have, instead of destroying these field notes, created a dark archive of her research field notes that would embargo access for an extended period of time (e.g., twenty-five years or beyond). Doing so would allow scholars in the future to access her work after the legal statute of limitations expired. In taking this route, Goffman would have been making a trade-off that had consequential ethics (achieving the best outcome for ensuring the validity of her findings) and virtue ethics (which would have privileged the protection of her research participants). But doing so requires trust that such an archive could readily be protected from law enforcement's inquiry and that there were sufficient long-term preservation policies in place to ensure that a substantial amount of effort in curating this data could be sustained over time. There are, in fact, few examples of how this dark archive proposal may have been practically achieved. In the USA (where Goffman is located), there is only one data repository solely dedicated to the curation of qualitative research data (the Qualitative Data Repository), which has been in operation only since 2014. One can hardly fault Goffman for not being up to speed on alternative choices available and in some sense adhering to the best practices recommended by an IRB.

For information professionals, the ethical choices available for managing and preserving data may seem clear and straightforward—but practically speaking the ability to identify and pick out institutional mechanisms that can preserve one's data remains a challenge. In Goffman's case there was a disciplinary legacy, IRB policies, and research positionality that impacted ethical decisions around data access. Each of these factors influenced a decision to destroy data that could and might have been otherwise preserved and made accessible into the future.

CASE 2: FACEBOOK EMOTIONAL CONTAGION STUDY

The second case study of open data ethics that we explore in this chapter is related to the collection of human subject data. It raises questions as to whether this data should ethically be open and free for research use. In 2014 researchers at Facebook conducted a study in which they manipulated the news feeds of 700,000 users of the online social networking platform.[17] The goal of this work was to understand the impact of post contents on the users' reported well-being (in social psychology the concept of well-being relates to their moment-to-moment emotional experiences and overall life satisfaction). The authors of this study were, in some sense, trying to refute early studies of social comparison—which holds that the emotional tone of news posts correlates inversely with an end user's feelings of well-being. That is, if a news post is positive, then a user will report negative well-being (e.g., the feeling of being alone together), and negative posts invoke feelings of compassion and solidarity (e.g., misery loves company). The study demonstrates that even with positive news the end user can experience negative and positive emotions—that the relationship between post sentiment and end user well-being does not correlate as simply (either directly or inversely) as has been previously reported. This study is unique, however, in that the authors are not depending upon self-reports but instead mining social media logs of users to infer their sentiment and well-being.[18] The controversial nature of this mining is well reported, but what sparked outrage was the finding that invoking negative feelings (that is, the researchers injected negative emotional content into a user feed), can cause a Facebook user to experience acute levels of low well-being. This means that, in a sense, the Facebook researchers were invoking negative well-being in users for the sake of conducting their research. Research interventions that cause harm to participants are often very closely regulated by an IRB, and strict controls are supposed to be in place for such procedural research. However, it was unclear whether or not these researchers had taken such steps. In post-publication reporting, there were numerous conflicting reports about whether or not IRB clearance had been obtained, how the interventions were controlled, and what, if any, outreach to harmed participants occurred.[19]

In an interview after publication, the editor of the article—when asked about its contribution to well-being studies—stated, "I think it's an open ethical question. It's ethically okay from the regulations perspective, but ethics are kind of social decisions."[20] Indeed, the Common Rule—which governs medical and behavioral research—states that not only should research participants be informed of the studies they are participating in (and Facebook users were not informed of their participation), but also that researchers should take care not to actively knowingly cause harm if it does not outweigh the significance of the findings of the research (broadly construed) (Federal Regulation 45 CFR 46 "Protection of Human Subjects").

Ethically, what is at stake in the post hoc analysis of the Facebook emotional contagion study is a confluence of all three ethical positions. From a Facebook user's perspective, the purposeful manipulation of how posts are promoted and displayed to their social network violates assumed virtue of the platform; users have a common and justified assumption that their personal posts are treated fairly by the service provider. When that assumption is manipulated for research purposes, it would seem to violate both an implicit norm (that they are treated equally on the platform) and an explicit norm (the Common Rule that governs ethical behavioral research). When both of these norms are violated, then ethically the data shouldn't be considered purely open, but that users and their data was co-opted and manipulated to meet a narrow research purpose.[21] From a consequentialist perspective, this study could be ethical if the collected data—whether publicly available or not—resulted in findings that were highly valuable to a research phenomenon. But many have argued that the co-opting and manipulation of users taints the research findings—and that interpretations that might be gleaned are therefore of little value when relationships between service providers, users, and researchers are contested.[22] Finally, it remains, as we stated earlier, unclear from multiple ethical viewpoints whether or not this research conformed with ethical obligations of informed consent. Surely, users who agree to terms of service agreements that are lengthy and do not clearly explain the reuse of their personal data are unaware that they may be, unwittingly, enrolled in social experiments. These ethical issues are complex in the context of social media platforms, user expectations, and research data collection. Where norms are assumed and contexts of good will are violated, it's hard to argue that data, even when accessible, is reasonably open for researchers to ethically use. That the experimental conditions require the manipulation of users on the Facebook platform further throws into doubt whether or not the findings can and should be trusted.

CASE 3: FUTURE OF PRIVACY FORUM'S CITY OF SEATTLE OPEN DATA RISK ASSESSMENT

Context

While this section is primarily focused on scholarly research in the university, it can also be helpful to examine other open data contexts. The city of Seattle in Washington launched its Open Data Program in 2010 and stepped up its intentional publishing of open data in 2016 with an executive order making all city data "open by preference."[23] This executive order set the expectation that all city departments will make their data accessible to the public after taking steps to protect the privacy of those represented in the data.

From fall 2016 through summer 2017, the Future of Privacy Forum (FPF), a data privacy advocacy group, conducted an in-depth privacy and risk assessment in collaboration with the city and published an extensive report in January 2018.[24] The report uses a blend of virtue, non-consequential, and some consequential ethics, along with practical technologies and processes, to offer rich opportunities to understand the kinds of risks associated with open data, demonstrate risk-mitigation techniques and methods to balance both access and privacy, and model the type of ongoing assessment of risks that are necessary for researchers and data curators.

Data Harms

The report found that there are three main harms that may arise from the sharing of open data: re-identification, low data quality and lack of equity, and loss of public trust.

Re-identification is when data scrubbed of identifying traits such as names or addresses can still be used to determine the identity of a person. This can occur through the use of other additional data sets or through a combination of data points that are unique to a specific individual. Preventing re-identification can be difficult, particularly as data brokers provide more data and stronger re-identification tools are developed. Data providers should regularly conduct audits and tests to see if re-identification is possible when appropriate.

Low data quality and lack of equity are flaws in the data collection or design that can lead to inaccurate, unintended, or unjust outcomes due to the use of open data by governments and other organizations. The report notes that organizations increasingly rely on public data and that data is often consumed and repurposed, meaning that errors and biases may have both immediate and long-term effects. Data quality and equity harm can be reduced only through regular, in-depth assessments of published data.

Public trust can be damaged when individuals feel their privacy has been violated or that community expectations are disregarded or otherwise unmet. This can lead to lower participation or false data out of fear of harm caused by a lack of privacy or other protections. Public trust can be protected through clear communication to individuals affected about how data will be collected and shared and what steps are taken to protect privacy.

Practices and Process

The Future of Privacy Forum report investigated and scored a wide range of factors in the way the city of Seattle handled its open data pipeline across six domains: privacy leadership and program management, benefit-risk assessment, de-identification tools and strategies, data quality, equity and fairness, and transparency and public engagement. In doing so, it raised a number of details worth highlighting.

Post-publication Review

The report gave the city credit for having a fully documented and implemented pre-publication benefit-risk assessment at the time of the review but found that these assessments weren't regularly reviewed after publication and that the city didn't have any implemented procedures that would trigger reassessment.

Training

People within different departments of the city have some privacy governance responsibilities, in addition to open data and privacy programs in the IT department. There was also broad training, even for nontechnical employees, to help them identify and understand privacy policies and potential failures. The report noted that this training makes data more likely to be protected throughout the full life cycle of collection, use, release, and disposal.

Social Equity

The city has an established Race and Social Justice Initiative program dedicated to eliminating racial disparities in Seattle,[25] and the report noted that the Open Data Program has committed to releasing open data sets that help with promoting positive RSJI outcomes. While the report does not detail how these programs may work together, it is essential to keep in mind that marginalized communities face greater risks from open data privacy breaches and algorithmic decision-making.[26] The inclusion of programs like this, or other experts or specialists can greatly mitigate data harms.

Outreach and Feedback

The report notes that there is a significant amount of community outreach, including social media, public hackathons, presentations to community groups, and community design workshops, many of which were hosted by local community groups, businesses, and academic institutions. In addition to fostering awareness and use of the available data, this outreach also helps to identify errors or gaps in the data set. The report did also note that the city has not expended much effort to provide notification to the community about data collection or the possibility of the data being released openly, outside of a Privacy Statement.

Benefit-Risk Analysis

The city has used a benefit-risk analysis to determine if and how data sets should be shared. This assessment isn't available in the report, but FPF recommended the city conduct the assessment yearly for each data set and provided an example for future use. Using five-point scales of Very Low Likelihood to Very High Likelihood of occurrence and Very Low Impact to Very High Impact of foreseeable risks, the model benefit-risk analysis provided by the FPF asks that the city

- evaluate the information the data set contains
  - evaluate any data that may be identifiable, including limiting indirect identifiers, sensitive attributes, and data that is difficult to de-identify
  - consider how linkable the information in the data set is to others
  - consider how the data was obtained to determine accuracy and if publishing would violate any trust
- evaluate the benefits associated with releasing the data set
  - determine which communities will likely use the data and the likelihood and impact of foreseeable benefits
- evaluate the risks associated with releasing the data set
  - consider the foreseeable privacy risks of the data set, including the impact of re-identification and false re-identification on individuals and the city
  - consider the foreseeable risks regarding the data quality and equity, including how it may reinforce biases, adverse or discriminatory impacts, and unequal distribution of harm
  - determine if public trust would be harmed due to public backlash, individuals' or communities' shock or surprise about being included, chilling effect on business or communities, or the revealing of nonpublic information about an agency's operations

The scores are then tabulated for each data set to determine if it should be open, have limited access, be screened further by the city, or should not be published. Finally, countervailing factors that may justify releasing a data set openly regardless of privacy risk are evaluated and taken into consideration.

The Future of Privacy Forum report and risk assessment methodology provide an excellent model for the types of evaluations and assessments open data providers must routinely perform in order to protect the privacy of human subjects and reduce the potential for inequitable outcomes from their work. While there are certainly differences in terms of accountability, legal requirements, and data production and publication between civic data and scholarly research data, this process serves as a model for anyone participating in the collection and curation of open data.

EMERGING ISSUES IN OPEN DATA ETHICS

In the concluding part of this section we point to future directions and emerging issues related to the curation, use, and library services around open data. We mention briefly two areas where increased access to data poses challenges to ethical data use: privacy and data responsibility.

PRIVACY

One of the inherent tensions in data access is protecting privacy and providing unfettered opportunities for meaningful reuse. A number of privacy-preserving techniques for releasing data are beginning to see real-world implementations. For example, census data collected by the USA provides some of the most valuable demographic open data used by researchers. The 2020 Census will be accessible to researchers through the use of a privacy preservation technique called *differential privacy*—which allows researchers to compute against data without actually obtaining or storing data on local machines.[27] This is the first and by far the broadest implementation of differential privacy for open data, and time will tell if this is an effective method for protecting sensitive data from harmful reuse. Data trusts are also emerging as a socio-technical intervention for effectively sharing public and private sector data for research purposes.[28] Data trusts rely on third-party intermediaries storing and governing access to data based on researcher credentials. The data trust model is yet to be implemented at scale, but promising experiments such as the University of Washington's Transportation Data Collaborative—hosting rideshare, bikeshare, and transportation data from municipal bus service providers—are at early stages of development.[29] Additionally many data repositories are offering increased service to help researchers adhere to data-sharing requirements and simultaneously protect human participants. ICPSR, for example, offers a "researcher passport" that credentials users through a screening process that allows for graduated access to restricted data.[30] Similarly, the Qualitative Data Repository offers services and protocols for researchers managing privacy sensitive information about human subjects.[31]

While many challenges remain, each of these advances in technology and the curation of open data attempts to provide a way for access to be enhanced while minimizing risk to the rights and expectations of research subjects.

DATA RESPONSIBILITY

Increasingly data about vulnerable populations is used to advance policy agendas and advocacy positions. This data constitutes some of the most fraught and complicated resources that require strict safeguards and community protocols for responsible use. The US Indigenous Data Sovereignty Network, for example, is an organization dedicated to advancing the governance of indigenous data. US IDSN prompted indigenous data sovereignty, which is defined as "the right of a nation to govern the collection, ownership, and application of its own data."[32] Technological advances for respecting and promoting data sovereignty are emergent, but not without precedent. The Exchange for Local Observations and Knowledge of the Arctic (ELOKA) project is one of the earliest and most advanced examples of community-informed data collection policies and local data storage that respects indigenous communities' contributions to and ownership of data.[33] More conceptually, in 2020 D'Ignazio and Klein published *Data Feminism*, a work extolling the virtues of data protection through the lens of care work.[34] This book provides a logic for operating from and with primary concern for data subjects through the rejection of traditional collection paradigms, as well as analysis techniques that often gloss over the positionality of research subjects.

IMPLICATIONS FOR INFORMATION PROFESSIONALS

Information professionals should keep data ethics at the core of their research data management services. There is never a bad time to remind community members to be thinking about the ethics of their research! Ethical data collection, storage, and access should be integrated into scholarly communication and data curation instruction. Developing strong working relationships and open lines of communication with subject librarians (particularly in areas with a lot of sensitive or personally identifiable information like health and social science) can also help to integrate ethical research and data practices throughout the institution. Data management consultations are another good time to discuss ethics with researchers—while discussing data management plans, information professionals can help to create ethical data practices at the start of a research project. Of course, not all researchers prioritize ethics or consult early on data management, so information professionals who deposit or ingest research materials into an institutional repository can also serve as the final line of protection before sensitive material gets published.

One other space where data ethics comes into play for information professionals is in crafting data collection policies for their own institutions. Libraries are increasingly collecting and using data or are providing data to vendors through licensing and access agreements. While this is rarely *open* data, many large library vendors aggregate data from many different places to sell to third parties like marketing firms or law enforcement.[35] The Digital Library Federation's Privacy and Ethics in Technology Working Group is one notable group working to better understand how patron data is being used and to better equip librarians to protect patron privacy.[36] The group has produced a number of valuable resources, including "A Practical Guide to Performing a Library User Data Risk Assessment in Library-Built Systems" and "Ethics in Research Use of Library Patron Data: Glossary and Explainer."[37]

CONCLUSION

In this section we have reviewed three ethical positions from which data curators, scholarly communication librarians, and researchers often operate: virtue, consequential, and non-consequential (or deontological). In practice, these ethical decision-making frameworks often intersect—requiring careful attention to not just the moral imperative of protecting from harm but also attempting to build technologies and services that can create a greater research good. Through three case studies, we have attempted to make clear how ethical decisions complicate the way data is made accessible and is used for research purposes. By describing what is at stake when ethical decisions are faced by stewards of data, we believe there is an opportunity to continue improving not only the openness of data, but the moral grounds upon which such decisions are made by individuals and institutions engaged in promoting open research practices.

NOTES

1. Stuart A. Burns, "Different Kinds of Ethics," in Evolutionary Pragmatism, A Discourse on a Modern Philosophy for the 21st Century (website), 2012, http://www.evolutionary-pragmatism.com/pg0405.htm.
2. Rosalind Hursthouse and Glen Pettigrove, "Virtue Ethics," last upd. December 8, 2016, Stanford Encyclopedia of Philosophy Archive, Winter 2018 ed., ed. Edward N. Zalta, https://plato.stanford.edu/archives/win2018/entries/ethics-virtue/.
3. Walter Sinnott-Armstrong, "Consequentialism," last upd. June 3, 2019, Stanford Encyclopedia of Philosophy Archive, Summer 2019 ed., ed. Edward N. Zalta, https://plato.stanford.edu/archives/sum2019/entries/consequentialism.
4. Larry Alexander and Michael Moore, "Deontological Ethics," last upd. October 30. 2020, Stanford Encyclopedia of Philosophy Archive, Winter 2020 ed., ed. Edward N. Zalta, https://plato.stanford.edu/archives/win2020/entries/ethics-deontological.
5. Laure Perrier, Erik Blondal and Heather MacDonald, "The Views, Perspectives, and Experiences of Academic Researchers with Data Sharing and Reuse: A Meta-synthesis," *PLOS ONE* 15, no. 6 (2020): e0229182, https://doi.org/10.1371/journal.pone.0229182.
6. See, for example, Heather A. Piwowar and Todd J. Vision, "Data Reuse and the Open Data Citation Advantage," *PeerJ* 1 (2013): e175, https://doi.org/10.7717/peerj.175; Garret Christensen et al., "A Study of the Impact of Data Sharing on Article Citations Using Journal Policies as a Natural Experiment," *PLOS ONE* 14, no. 12 (December 18, 2019): e0225883, https://doi.org/10.1371/journal.pone.0225883; Giovanni Colavizza et al., "The Citation Advantage of Linking Publications to Research Data," *PLOS ONE* 15, no. 4 (April 22, 2020): e0230416, https://doi.org/10.1371/journal.pone.0230416.
7. Marijn Janssen, Yannis Charalabidis and Anneke Zuiderwijk, "Benefits, Adoption Barriers and Myths of Open Data and Open Government," *Information Systems Management* 29, no. 4 (2012): 258–68, https://doi.org/10.1080/10580530.2012.716740.
8. Tim Davies and Zainab Bawa, "The Promises and Perils of Open Government Data (OGD)," *Journal of Community Informatics* 8, no. 2 (2012), https://doi.org/10.15353/joci.v8i2.3035.
9. US Department of Health and Human Services, "Summary of the HIPAA Privacy Rule," HHS.gov, last reviewed October 19, 2022, https://www.hhs.gov/hipaa/for-professionals/privacy/laws-regulations/index.html.
10. For more on the impact of GDPR on research data, see Mark Phillips, and Bartha M. Knoppers, "Whose Commons? Data Protection as a Legal Limit of Open Science," *Journal of Law, Medicine and Ethics* 47, no. 1 (Spring 2019): 106–11, https://doi.org/10.1177/1073110519840489.
11. John P. Holdren, "Increasing Access to the Results of Federally Funded Research," memorandum for the heads of executive departments and agencies, Executive Office of the President, Office of Science and Technology Policy, February 22, 2013, https://obamawhitehouse.archives.gov/sites/default/files/microsites/ostp/ostp_public_access_memo_2013.pdf.
12. See, for example, Colin Elman and Diana Kapiszewski, "Data Access and Research Transparency in the Qualitative Tradition," *PS: Political Science & Politics*, Volume 47, Issue 1 (January 2014): 43-47, https://doi.org/10.1017/S1049096513001777.
13. Alice Goffman, *On the Run* (Chicago: University of Chicago Press, 2014).
14. Steven Lubet, *Interrogating Ethnography* (New York: Oxford University Press, 2018).
15. Victoria Reyes, "Three Models of Transparency in Ethnographic Research: Naming Places, Naming People, and Sharing Data," *Ethnography* 19, no. 2 (June 2018): 204–26, https://doi.org/10.1177/1466138117733754.
16. Jessica Mozersky et al., "Are We Ready to Share Qualitative Research Data? Knowledge and Preparedness among Qualitative Researchers, IRB Members, and Data Repository Curators," *IASSIST Quarterly* 43, no. 4 (2020), https://doi.org/10.29173/iq952.
17. Adam D. Kramer, Jamie E. Guillory, and Jeffrey T. Hancock, "Experimental Evidence of Massive-Scale Emotional Contagion through Social Networks," *Proceedings of the National Academy of Sciences* 111, no. 24 (2014): 8788–90, https://doi.org/10.1073/pnas.1320040111.
18. Timothy Recuber, "From Obedience to Contagion: Discourses of Power in Milgram, Zimbardo, and the Facebook Experiment," *Research Ethics* 12, no. 1 (January 2016): 44–54, https://doi.org/10.1177/1747016115579533.
19. Evan Selinger and Woodrow Hartzog, "Facebook's Emotional Contagion Study and the Ethical Problem of Co-opted Identity in Mediated Environments Where Users Lack Control," *Research Ethics* 12, no. 1 (January 2016): 35–43, https://doi.org/10.1177/1747016115579531.

20. Adrienne LaFrance, "Even the Editor of Facebook's Mood Study Thought It Was Creepy," *Atlantic*, June 28, 2014, https://www.theatlantic.com/technology/archive/2014/06/even-the-editor-of-facebooks-mood-study-thought-it-was-creepy/373649/.

21. Selinger and Hartzog, "Facebook's Emotional Contagion Study."

22. Blake Hallinan, Jed R Brubaker, and Casey Fiesler, "Unexpected Expectations: Public Reaction to the Facebook Emotional Contagion Study," *New Media and Society* 22, no. 6 (June 2020): 1076–94, https://doi.org/10.1177/1461444819876944.

23. Office of the Mayor, City of Seattle, "Executive Order 2016-01: Directing departments to comply with the new Open Data Policy, directing all City data to be open by preference," February 27, 2016, https://www.seattle.gov/documents/Departments/Tech/OpenData/EO_2016-01_Open_Data.pdf.

24. Future of Privacy Forum, *City of Seattle Open Data Risk Assessment* (Washington, DC: Future of Privacy Forum, January 2018), https://www.seattle.gov/Documents/Departments/SeattleIT/DigitalEngagement/OpenData/FPF-Open-Data-Risk-Assessment-for-City-of-Seattle.pdf.

25. Race and Social Justice Initiative (RSJI) webpage, city of Seattle, WA, https://www.seattle.gov/rsji.

26. There is a rapidly increasing body of work in this area, most notably Safiya Umoja Noble, *Algorithms of Oppression* (New York: NYU Press, 2018); Anna Lauren Hoffman, "Where Fairness Fails: Data Algorithms, and the Limits of Antidiscrimination Discourse," *Information, Communication and Society* 22, no. 7 (2019): 900-915, https://doi.org/10.1080/1369118X.2019.1573912; and Virginia Eubanks, *Automating Inequality* (New York: St. Martin's Press, 2017).

27. Alexandra Wood et al., "Differential Privacy: A Primer for a Non-technical Audience," *Vanderbilt Journal of Entertainment and Technology Law* 21, no. 1 (2018): 209–75, https://salil.seas.harvard.edu/publications/differential-privacy-primer-non-technical-audience.

28. Kieron O'Hara, *Data Trusts*, WSI white paper 1 (Southampton, UK: Web Science Institute, 2019), https://eprints.soton.ac.uk/428276/1/WSI_White_Paper_1.pdf.

29. UW Transportation Data Collaborative, home page, https://www.uwtdc.org/.

30. Margaret C. Levenstein, Allison R. B. Tyler, and Johanna Davidson Bleckman, *The Researcher Passport: Improving Data Access and Confidentiality Protection*, ICPSR white paper series no. 1 (Ann Arbor: University of Michigan Inter-university Consortium for Political and Social Research, 2018), http://hdl.handle.net/2027.42/143808.

31. Sebastian Karcher, Dessislava Kirilova, and Nicholas Weber, "Beyond the Matrix: Repository Services for Qualitative Data," *IFLA Journal* 42, no. 4 (December 2016): 292–302, https://doi.org/10.1177/0340035216672870.

32. University of Arizona Native Nations Institute, "Indigenous Data Sovereignty and Governance," https://nni.arizona.edu/our-work/research-policy-analysis/indigenous-data-sovereignty-governance.

33. Peter Pulsifer et al., "The Role of Data Management in Engaging Communities in Arctic Research: Overview of the Exchange for Local Observations and Knowledge of the Arctic (ELOKA)," *Polar Geography* 35, no. 3–4 (2012): 271–90, https://doi.org/10.1080/1088937X.2012.708364.

34. Catherine D'Ignazio and Lauren F. Klein, *Data Feminism* (Boston: MIT Press, 2020).

35. Sarah Lamdan," Librarianship at the Crossroads of ICE Surveillance," *In the Library with the Lead Pipe*, November 13, 2019, http://www.inthelibrarywiththeleadpipe.org/2019/ice-surveillance/; SPARC, "Addressing the Alarming Systems of Surveillance Built by Library Vendors," April 9, 2021, https://sparcopen.org/news/2021/addressing-the-alarming-systems-of-surveillance-built-by-library-vendors/.

36. DLF Wiki, "Privacy and Ethics in Technology," Digital Library Federation, last updated January 12, 2022, https://wiki.diglib.org/Privacy_and_Ethics_in_Technology.

37. Kristin Briney et al., "A Practical Guide to Performing a Library User Data Risk Assessment in Library-Built Systems," Digital Library Federation, March 2018, last updated May 2020, http://doi.org/10.17605/OSF.IO/V2C3M; Andrew Asher et al., "Ethics in Research Use of Library Patron Data: Glossary and Explainer," Digital Library Federation, October 2018, last updated December 2018, https://doi.org/10.17605/OSF.IO/XFKZ6.

BIBLIOGRAPHY

Alexander, Larry, and Michael Moore. "Deontological Ethics." Stanford Encyclopedia of Philosophy Archive, Winter 2020 ed., edited by Edward N. Zalta. Last updated October 30, 2020. https://plato.stanford.edu/archives/win2020/entries/ethics-deontological.

Asher, Andrew, Kristin Briney, Gabriel J. Gardner, Lisa Janicke Hinchliffe, Bethany Nowviskie, Dorothea Salo, and Yasmeen Shorish. "Ethics in Research Use of Library Patron Data: Glossary and Explainer." Digital Library Federation, October 2018, last updated December 2018. https://doi.org/10.17605/OSF.IO/XFKZ6.

Briney, Kristin, Becky Yoose, John Mark Ockerbloom, Shea Swauger, Charlie Harper, Jacob Levernier, and Yasmeen Shorish. "A Practical Guide to Performing a Library User Data Risk Assessment in Library-Built

Systems." Digital Library Federation, March 2018, last updated May 2020. http://doi.org/10.17605/OSF.IO/V2C3M.

Burns, Stuart A. "Different Kinds of Ethics." In Evolutionary Pragmatism: A Discourse on a Modern Philosophy for the 21st Century (website), 2012. http://www.evolutionary-pragmatism.com/pg0405.htm.

Christensen, Garret, Allan Dafoe, Edward Miguel, Don A. Moore, and Andrew K. Rose. "A Study of the Impact of Data Sharing on Article Citations Using Journal Policies as a Natural Experiment." *PLOS ONE* 14, no. 12 (December 18, 2019): e0225883. https://doi.org/10.1371/journal.pone.0225883.

Colavizza, Giovanni, Iain Hrynaszkiewicz, Isla Staden, Kirstie Whitaker, and Barbara McGillivray. "The Citation Advantage of Linking Publications to Research Data." *PLOS ONE* 15, no. 4 (April 22, 2020): e0230416. https://doi.org/10.1371/journal.pone.0230416.

Davies, Tim, and Zainab Bawa. "The Promises and Perils of Open Government Data (OGD)." *Journal of Community Informatics* 8, no. 2 (2012). https://doi.org/10.15353/joci.v8i2.3035.

D'Ignazio, Catherine, and Lauren F. Klein. *Data Feminism*. Boston: MIT Press, 2020.

DLF Wiki. "Privacy and Ethics in Technology." Digital Library Federation. Last updated January 12, 2022. https://wiki.diglib.org/Privacy_and_Ethics_in_Technology.

Elman, C. and Diana Kapiszewski, Data Access and Research Transparency in the Qualitative Tradition, PS: Political Science & Politics , Volume 47 , Issue 1 , January 2014 , pp. 43–47 DOI: https://doi.org/10.1017/S1049096513001777

Eubanks, Virginia. *Automating Inequality: How High-Tech Tools Profile, Police and Punish the Poor*. New York: St. Martin's Press, 2017.

Future of Privacy Forum. *City of Seattle Open Data Risk Assessment* Washington, DC: Future of Privacy Forum, January 2018. https://www.seattle.gov/Documents/Departments/SeattleIT/DigitalEngagement/OpenData/FPF-Open-Data-Risk-Assessment-for-City-of-Seattle.pdf.

Goffman, Alice. *On the Run: Fugitive Life in an American City*. Chicago: University of Chicago Press, 2014.

Hallinan, Blake, Jed R. Brubaker, and Casey Fiesler. "Unexpected Expectations: Public Reaction to the Facebook Emotional Contagion Study." *New Media and Society* 22, no. 6 (June 2020): 1076–94. https://doi.org/10.1177/1461444819876944.

Hoffman, Anna Lauren. "Where Fairness Fails: Data Algorithms, and the Limits of Antidiscrimination Discourse." *Information, Communication and Society* 22, no. 7 (2019): 900–915. https://doi.org/10.1080/1369118X.2019.1573912.

Holdren, John P. "Increasing Access to the Results of Federally Funded Research." Memorandum for the heads of executive departments and agencies. Executive Office of the President, Office of Science and Technology Policy. February 22, 2013. https://obamawhitehouse.archives.gov/sites/default/files/microsites/ostp/ostp_public_access_memo_2013.pdf.

Hursthouse, Rosalind, and Glen Pettigrove. "Virtue Ethics." Stanford Encyclopedia of Philosophy Archive, Winter 2018 ed., edited by Edward N. Zalta. Last updated December 8, 2016. https://plato.stanford.edu/archives/win2018/entries/ethics-virtue.

Janssen, Marijn, Yannis Charalabidis and Anneke Zuiderwijk. "Benefits, Adoption Barriers and Myths of Open Data and Open Government." *Information Systems Management* 29, no. 4 (2012): 258–68. https://doi.org/10.1080/10580530.2012.716740.

Karcher, Sebastian, Dessislava Kirilova, and Nicholas Weber. "Beyond the Matrix: Repository Services for Qualitative Data." *IFLA Journal* 42, no. 4 (December 2016): 292–302. https://doi.org/10.1177/0340035216672870.

Kramer, Adam D., Jamie E. Guillory, and Jeffrey T. Hancock. "Experimental Evidence of Massive-Scale Emotional Contagion through Social Networks." *Proceedings of the National Academy of Sciences* 111, no. 24 (2014): 8788–90. https://doi.org/10.1073/pnas.1320040111.

LaFrance, Adrienne. "Even the Editor of Facebook's Mood Study Thought It Was Creepy." *Atlantic*, June 28, 2014. https://www.theatlantic.com/technology/archive/2014/06/even-the-editor-of-facebooks-mood-study-thought-it-was-creepy/373649/.

Lamdan, Sarah. "Librarianship at the Crossroads of ICE Surveillance." *In the Library with the Lead Pipe*, November 13, 2019, http://www.inthelibrarywiththeleadpipe.org/2019/ice-surveillance/.

Levenstein, Margaret C., Allison R. B. Tyler, and Johanna Davidson Bleckman. *The Researcher Passport: Improving Data Access and Confidentiality Protection*. ICPSR white paper series no. 1. Ann Arbor: University of Michigan Inter-university Consortium for Political and Social Research, 2018. http://hdl.handle.net/2027.42/143808.

Lubet, Steven. *Interrogating Ethnography: Why Evidence Matters*. New York: Oxford University Press, 2018.

Mozersky, Jessica, Heidi Walsh, Meredith Parsons, Tristan McIntosh, Kari Baldwin, and James M. DuBois. "Are We Ready to Share Qualitative Research Data? Knowledge and Preparedness among Qualitative Researchers, IRB Members, and Data Repository Curators." *IASSIST Quarterly* 43, no. 4 (2020). https://doi.org/10.29173/iq952.

Noble, Safiya Umoja. *Algorithms of Oppression*. New York: NYU Press, 2018.

Office of the Mayor, City of Seattle. "Executive Order 2016-01: Directing departments to comply with the new Open Data Policy, directing all City data to be open by preference." February 27, 2016. https://www.seattle.gov/documents/Departments/Tech/OpenData/EO_2016-01_Open_Data.pdf.

O'Hara, Kieron. *Data Trusts: Ethics, Architecture and Governance for Trustworthy Data Stewardship*. WSI white paper 1. Southampton, UK: Web Science Institute, 2019. https://eprints.soton.ac.uk/428276/1/WSI_White_Paper_1.pdf.

Perrier, Laure, Erik Blondal and Heather MacDonald. "The Views, Perspectives, and Experiences of Academic Researchers with Data Sharing and Reuse: A Meta-synthesis." *PLOS ONE* 15, no. 6 (2020): e0229182. https://doi.org/10.1371/journal.pone.0229182.

Phillips, Mark, and Bartha M. Knoppers. "Whose Commons? Data Protection as a Legal Limit of Open Science." *Journal of Law, Medicine and Ethics* 47, no. 1 (Spring 2019): 106–11. https://doi.org/10.1177/1073110519840489.

Piwowar, Heather A., and Todd J. Vision. "Data Reuse and the Open Data Citation Advantage." *PeerJ* 1 (2013): e175. https://doi.org/10.7717/peerj.175

Pulsifer, Peter, Shari Gearheard, Henry P. Huntington, Mark A. Parsons, Christopher McNeave and Heidi S. McCann. "The Role of Data Management in Engaging Communities in Arctic Research: Overview of the Exchange for Local Observations and Knowledge of the Arctic (ELOKA)." *Polar Geography* 35, no. 3–4 (2012): 271–90, https://doi.org/10.1080/1088937X.2012.708364.

Race and Social Justice Initiative (RSJI) webpage. City of Seattle, WA. https://www.seattle.gov/rsji.

Recuber, Timothy. "From Obedience to Contagion: Discourses of Power in Milgram, Zimbardo, and the Facebook Experiment." *Research Ethics* 12, no. 1 (January 2016): 44–54. https://doi.org/10.1177/1747016115579533.

Reyes, Victoria. "Three Models of Transparency in Ethnographic Research: Naming Places, Naming People, and Sharing Data." *Ethnography* 19, no. 2 (June 2018): 204–26. https://doi.org/10.1177/1466138117733754.

Selinger, Evan, and Woodrow Hartzog. "Facebook's Emotional Contagion Study and the Ethical Problem of Co-opted Identity in Mediated Environments Where Users Lack Control." *Research Ethics* 12, no. 1 (January 2016): 35–43. https://doi.org/10.1177/1747016115579531.

Sinnott-Armstrong, Walter. "Consequentialism." Last updated June 3, 2019. Stanford Encyclopedia of Philosophy Archive, Summer 2019 ed., edited by Edward N. Zalta. https://plato.stanford.edu/archives/sum2019/entries/consequentialism.

SPARC. "Addressing the Alarming Systems of Surveillance Built by Library Vendors." April 9, 2021. https://sparcopen.org/news/2021/addressing-the-alarming-systems-of-surveillance-built-by-library-vendors/.

University of Arizona Native Nations Institute. "Indigenous Data Sovereignty and Governance." https://nni.arizona.edu/our-work/research-policy-analysis/indigenous-data-sovereignty-governance.

US Department of Health and Human Services. "Summary of the HIPAA Privacy Rule." HHS.gov. Last reviewed October 19, 2022. https://www.hhs.gov/hipaa/for-professionals/privacy/laws-regulations/index.html.

UW Transportation Data Collaborative. Home page. https://www.uwtdc.org/.

Wood, Alexandra, Micah Altman, Aaron Bembenek, Mark Bun, Marco Gaboardi, James Honaker, Kobbi Nissim, et al. "Differential Privacy: A Primer for a Non-technical Audience." *Vanderbilt Journal of Entertainment and Technology Law* 21, no. 1 (2018): 209–75. https://salil.seas.harvard.edu/publications/differential-privacy-primer-non-technical-audience.

OPEN EDUCATION

Edited by Lillian Hogendoorn

INTRODUCTION TO OPEN EDUCATION

WHAT IS OPEN EDUCATION?

Lillian Hogendoorn

Scholarly communication librarians have a broad responsibility for supporting the creation and dissemination of research outputs. In many positions, this includes supporting licensing queries and facilitating access to materials used or created in the classroom for or by learners. By way of the internet, learners can find information instantly, teachers can share their knowledge with students anywhere in the world, and educational materials can be disseminated to a worldwide audience at little to no cost. However, our systems for sharing information in education have not caught up with the potential of current technology.

Instead, the educational materials market is dominated by commercial publishing models that restrict dissemination and innovative use of resources. Textbook prices have risen rapidly for a sustained period of time, leaving too many students without access to their required material.[1] Digital offerings from traditional publishers come laced with access restrictions and expiration dates with little savings in return, while print editions are too often out of date by the time they hit the shelves, with little or no recourse available to instructors or students to update them. There's a lot of work to be done.

Open education seeks to close this gap. Open education "encompasses resources, tools and practices that are free of legal, financial, and technical barriers and can be fully used, shared, and adapted in the digital environment."[2] The foundation of open education is open educational resources (OER), which are teaching, learning, and research resources that are free of cost and access barriers, and which also carry legal permission for open use.

OER are learning, teaching, and research materials in any format and medium that reside in the public domain or are under copyright and have been released under an open license, which permit no-cost access, reuse, repurposing, adaptation and redistribution by others.[3] These two pieces of the definition—(1) that the object can be used in teaching and learning and (2) that the object is open for others to build upon—are central to the concept of OER.

FREE IS NOT THE SAME AS OPEN

It is important to understand the difference between *gratis*—without cost—and *libre*—with little or no restriction. OER are *libre*. Thus, if someone shares a lesson plan on their website and doesn't put a Creative Commons license on it, one could argue that it isn't an OER due to default copyright restrictions. The same goes for multiuser e-books available through the library that classes might use as textbooks—they save students money, but they are missing that license and, thus, are not OER.

So, the key features of OER are threefold:

1. resources that are free of cost,
2. resources that are free of barriers to access, and
3. resources which you have permission to use openly.

Generally, this permission is granted by use of an open license which allows anyone to freely use, adapt, and share the resource—anytime, anywhere.

CREATIVE COMMONS REFRESH

Creative Commons, or CC, licenses were introduced in part I, "What Is Scholarly Communication?" but because they are so important to OER, let's quickly remind ourselves of their basics. There are six primary Creative Commons licenses, each with a combination of one or more of four terms that represent conditions for sharing a work. The four terms are

- *Attribution (BY)*—Others can copy, distribute, display, perform, and remix the work as long as they give credit. The attribution term is present in all six licenses, ensuring that the original creator always receives credit for their work.
- *Non-commercial (NC)*—Others can copy, distribute, display, perform, and remix the work for noncommercial purposes, which CC interprets as not primarily intended for or directed toward commercial advantage or monetary compensation.
- *No Derivative Works (ND)*—Others can only copy, distribute, display, or perform copies of the work if no changes are made to the content.
- *Share Alike (SA)*—Others can create and distribute derivatives of the work only if they use the same license assigned to the source work.

The openness of OER is most often legally facilitated by the use of a Creative Commons license. However, works in the public domain or with other less-popular open licenses that permit reuse are also often considered OER.

THE FIVE *R*S

The full potential of OER, including how users can adapt existing OER to suit their purposes, is well captured by the five *R*s of openness.[4] In this model, OER are open in the sense that they may be retained, reused, revised, remixed, and redistributed:

- *Retain*—The right to make, own, and control copies of the content
- *Reuse*—The right to use the content in a wide range of ways
- *Revise*—The right to adapt, adjust, or modify the content itself
- *Remix*—The right to combine the original or revised content with other open content to create something new
- *Redistribute*—The right to share copies of the original content, revisions to it, or remixes with others

Together, the five *R*s mean that the openness of OER allows users to have more control over open educational material, enabling them to customize and share it in ways that make sense for an intended user, group, purpose, or context.

In other words, when a work is open, it can be updated, adapted, and improved by any user who can comply with the terms of the licensed work. It can also be expanded to include additional or new information. For example, smartphones are a remix of a phone, a calculator, a camera, a GPS, and much more. Open works may be customized and localized, be adapted to a particular teaching or learning style, and better meet the needs of students.

In this section, we're going to examine the history, theory, and practice of open education and OER, particularly as experienced by academic librarians.

NOTES

1. Melanie Hanson, "Average Cost of College Textbooks," EducationData.org, August 12, 2021, last updated July 15, 2022, https://educationdata.org/average-cost-of-college-textbooks; Cailyn Nagle and Kaitlyn Vitez, *Fixing the Broken Textbook Market*, 3rd ed. (Washington, DC: U.S. Public Interest Research Group, 2021), https://uspirg.org/sites/pirg/files/reports/Fixing%20the%20Broken%20Textbook%20Market%2C%20 3e%20February%202021.pdf.
2. SPARC, "Open Education," accessed November 8, 2021, https://sparcopen.org/open-education/.
3. UNESCO, *Recommendation on Open Educational Resources (OER)* (Paris: UNESCO, 2019), https://unesdoc.unesco.org/ark:/48223/pf0000373755/PDF/373755eng.pdf.multi.page=3.
4. David Wiley, "Defining the 'Open' in Open Content and Open Educational Resources," OpenContent.org, http://opencontent.org/definition/.

BIBLIOGRAPHY

Hanson, Melanie. "Average Cost of College Textbooks." EducationData.org, August 12, 2021, last updated July 15, 2022. https://educationdata.org/average-cost-of-college-textbooks.

Nagle, Cailyn, and Kaitlyn Vitez. *Fixing the Broken Textbook Market*, 3rd ed. Washington, DC: U.S. Public Interest Research Group, 2021. https://uspirg.org/sites/pirg/files/reports/Fixing%20the%20Broken%20 Textbook%20Market%2C%203e%20February%202021.pdf.

SPARC. "Open Education." Accessed November 8, 2021. https://sparcopen.org/open-education/.

UNESCO. *Recommendation on Open Educational Resources (OER)*. Paris: UNESCO, 2019. https://unesdoc. unesco.org/ark:/48223/pf0000373755/PDF/373755eng.pdf.multi.page=3.

Wiley, David. "Defining the 'Open' in Open Content and Open Educational Resources." OpenContent.org. http://opencontent.org/definition/.

A SHORT HISTORY OF OER

Emily Carlisle-Johnston

Beginning in 1999, Massachusetts Institute of Technology (MIT) faculty began to consider how they might use the internet to fulfill the school's mission of advancing knowledge. MIT OpenCourseWare (OCW) was proposed in 2000, and with original funding from the William and Flora Hewlett Foundation and the Andrew W. Mellon Foundation, was announced in the *New York Times* by April 2001.[1] In the announcement, author Carey Goldberg cited the project as a ten-year initiative to create public websites "for almost all of [MIT's] 2,000 courses," where materials like "lecture notes, problem sets, syllabuses, exams, simulations, even video lectures" could be made available for use and repurposing at no charge.[2]

OCW would "offer course materials as ingredients of learning that [could] then be combined with teacher-student interaction somewhere else—or simply explored by, say, professors in Chile or precocious high school students in Bangladesh."[3] Five hundred courses were published by OCW's 2003 launch, and since then materials from over 2,000 courses have been made openly available.[4]

Like many early open education projects, OCW embodies pillars of open education's history: the project originated out of motivation to make education more accessible and was made possible with evolving technologies and the growth of the internet. As Martin Weller writes in *The Battle for Open*:

> [Open education's] foundations lie in one of altruism, and the belief that education is a public good. It has undergone many interpretations and adaptations, moving from a model which had open entry to study as its primary focus, to one that emphasises openly available content and resources. This change in the definition of openness in education has largely been a result of the digital and network revolution. Changes in other sectors, most notably the open source model of software production, and values associated with the internet of free access and open approaches have influenced (and been influenced by) practitioners in higher education.[5]

Yet the history of OER long predates MIT OpenCourseWare. This chapter will cover key milestones in the history of OER, tracing the relationship between technology and human aspirations throughout. We will begin with the 1948 Universal Declaration of Human Rights.

PRE-INTERNET (1948–1987)

UNIVERSAL DECLARATION OF HUMAN RIGHTS (1948)

The Universal Declaration of Human Rights (UDHR) is a critical document in the history of human rights and in education. It was proclaimed by the United Nations General Assembly in Paris on December 10, 1948, and drafted by individuals from across the world. The document established for the first time a set of fundamental and universal human rights,[6] and was also the first document to recognize education as a fundamental human right. As noted in Article 26(1):

> Everyone has the right to education. Education shall be free, at least in the elementary and fundamental stages. Elementary education shall be compulsory. Technical and professional education shall be made generally available and higher education shall be equally accessible to all on the basis of merit.[7]

Although the UDHR is not a legally binding instrument, it has served (and continues to serve) as a political and moral force. The right to education, in particular, has been reaffirmed in declarations adopted by the United Nations, such as the United Nations Educational, Scientific and Cultural Organization (UNESCO) Convention against Discrimination in Education (1960) and the Convention on the Rights of the Child (1989).[8]

The fact that education is a fundamental human right is cited as the driving motivation behind open education's efforts to democratize education. Rooted in access, agency, ownership, and participation, open education and OER are part of a broader movement to democratize education by removing "the traditional barriers that people often face in obtaining knowledge, credits, and degrees—including but not limited to cost."[9]

OPEN UNIVERSITIES (1946–)

Efforts to increase access to education by removing traditional barriers to access began in earnest with the establishment of open universities. In 1946, the University of South Africa (UNISA) became the first university to teach exclusively via distance education. Because of its distance learning opportunities—which brought education to those who could not attend residential institutions—UNISA played a key role in providing quality tertiary education to disadvantaged groups during political tensions and the apartheid years. While institutionalized racism reigned in South and South West Africa from 1948 until the 1990s, UNISA "was perhaps the only university in South Africa to have provided all people with access to education, irrespective of race, colour or creed."[10]

Seventeen years after UNISA pioneered tertiary distance education, British Prime Minister Harold Wilson proposed the UK Open University (the OU). Like UNISA, the OU was imagined as an opportunity to use communications technology to bring "high quality degree-level learning" to those without the opportunity to attend campus. Officially established on April 23, 1969, the OU's origins are similarly rooted in altruism and social justice, along with a motivation to disprove the assumed link between exclusivity and excellence in education.[11]

Since the internet did not yet exist, early students of the OU received their education at a distance through printed course materials and science home experiment kits. As time and technology advanced, university staff adapted their teaching methods. In 1971, for example, the OU signed an agreement with BBC that allowed the OU to deliver courses, news, and information about the university on BBC 2 and Radio 4 for thirty hours per week. By the 1980s, students of the OU were sent broadcasts via videocassette and, in some cases, were also required to have home computers.[12]

Following UNISA and the OU, other universities around the world have been established exclusively as distance learning opportunities—including Athabasca University in Canada (1970) and Bangladesh Open University (1992).[13] Schools everywhere have come to embrace distance education, at least in part. However, while the mission of open universities reflects the long-standing tradition of access to education that is at the core of open education, Weller acknowledges that open entry to study was only the beginning.[14] Open education has potential to "create opportunities for shared meaning-making, collaborative activities, and creative participation"[15]—opportunities that became apparent with the influence of the open source software movement.

FREE AND OPEN SOURCE SOFTWARE (1983)

Although there are critical differences between open source software and OER, David Wiley established a connection between the two by way of analogy when he coined the term "open content" in 1998. While working at Marshall University and as a graduate student at Brigham Young University, Wiley realized that "the ideals and principles of open source software could be applied to the world of digital educational content."[16]

Before *open source software* was the widely recognized term, *free software* was used as a blanket term to capture similar meaning. Richard Stallman is credited with laying the foundation for both. In 1983 Stallman launched the GNU free software project, creating an operating system free from constraints to use of its source code.[17] By Stallman's definition, free software does not have to be free of cost, but does give people the freedom to

1. run the program for any purpose,
2. modify the program from the source code to suit needs,
3. redistribute copies gratis or at a cost, and
4. distribute modified versions of the program for the community's benefit.[18]

To protect free software from being used in proprietary packages, Stallman developed the concept of copyleft:

> To copyleft a program, we first state that it is copyrighted; then we add distribution terms, which are a legal instrument that gives everyone the rights to use, modify, and redistribute the program's code or any program derived from it but only if the distribution terms are unchanged. Thus, the code and the freedoms become legally inseparable.[19]

Stallman's copyleft terms offered a compromise between releasing the program into the public domain (at the risk of it being licensed as a proprietary product) and releasing it under restrictive copyright terms preventing modification.[20] *Free* and *open source software* refer to these same distribution licenses.

The term *open source*, however, was born out of motivation by Eric Raymond, author of "The Cathedral and the Bazaar" (997),[21] and others to rebrand free software as appealing to the commercial software industry. Recognizing that *free software* was often interpreted to mean free of cost, Raymond's "The Cathedral and the Bazaar" introduced the argument that "open source software communities develop software faster, produce software with fewer bugs, are more innovative, and offer a better fit for the end-users than do proprietary software production companies."[22] The paper prompted Netscape Communications Corporation to release its internet suite as free software, leading to the term *open source* being coined at a 1998 strategy session in Palo Alto, California.[23]

Where *free software* focuses on the acts that users are permitted to take with the software, *open source* focuses on opportunities enabled by licenses, like collaboration around software development. Regardless, Richard Stallman's free software and Eric Raymond's open source movements uncovered a series of values and ideas—like collaboration, innovation, modification, and redistribution—that David Wiley would later apply to educational materials.[24] Before Wiley would make this connection, however, the development of the World Wide Web and the internet laid the technical groundwork for these values to be realized in open education.

LAUNCH OF THE WORLD WIDE WEB (1991)

In 1991, the World Wide Web became publicly available as a series of documents interconnected via hypertext links, paving the way for the internet as we know it today. The World Wide Web, and by extension the internet, has made it possible to share and access information at will. While the internet is a global network of networks across which data travels, the World Wide Web "provides a uniform, user friendly interface to the Internet."[25] Together, they have provided the infrastructure through which educational materials can be made openly available and global communities of OER champions can become connected.

EARLY DAYS: MERLOT/MIT OPENCOURSEWARE

Introduced at the beginning of this subsection, MIT depended upon both the World Wide Web and the internet to make its course materials freely available and accessible to anyone via the MIT OpenCourseWare project. Owing to this technical infrastructure, this early OER project has grown to reach roughly five hundred million visitors from across the world as of 2020.[26]

Another early OER project, MERLOT (Multimedia Educational Resource for Learning and Online Teaching), provides "curated online learning and support materials and content creation tools, led by an international community of educators, learners, and researchers."[27] MERLOT was launched in 1997 under the leadership of Chuck Schneebeck, director of California State University's Center for Distributed Learning (CSU-CDL)—an academic service provider for the California State University system's twenty-three campuses. MERLOT was developed out of the need for a technology service to which users could contribute a collection of online resources.[28] Over time it has grown into an online digital resource library.*

In 1998, a State Higher Education Executives Organization/American Productivity and Quality Center study on faculty development and instructional technology selected CSU-CDL as one of six best practices centers in North America. This award resulted in institutions collaborating with CSU-CDL on the MERLOT project so that by July 2000 the project had grown into a cooperative of twenty-three institutional partners of MERLOT—each a higher education system or individual institution. Today, MERLOT serves as one of the largest online OER repositories and as a consortium composed of over thirty partner members that contribute annual fees to sustain MERLOT's activities. Key to MERLOT's activities is the fostering of community, as the community drives growth by contributing and reviewing resources and networking on behalf of MERLOT's mission.[29]

---

* The digital resource library is available at the MERLOT home page, https://www.merlot.org/merlot/.

MIT OpenCourseWare and MERLOT illustrate early efforts to share online learning materials across international borders, made possible because of the affordances of the internet. With the technology in place to support open sharing of educational material at scale, however, a need arose to conceptually and legally define the kinds of open sharing that were beginning to take shape.

OPEN LICENSING (2001–2002)

Creative Commons licenses are the default licenses for sharing OER. Founded in 2001 by Lawrence Lessig and others, Creative Commons (the nonprofit organization) grew out of inspiration from web publisher Eric Eldred and in response to a growing community of bloggers who were creating, sharing, and remixing online content. The Creative Commons (often referred to as CC) licenses were released in 2002 as a means to legally enable creators like the community of bloggers to retain their copyright while sharing their work in a way that was more flexible than "all rights reserved."[30]

As the internet expanded the ways in which people were able to share digital content, educational resources were increasingly born digital. Creative Commons licenses made it possible for creators to define the conditions under which others use their work and for users to interpret their rights to an item. Around the same time, UNESCO would come to provide the first ever definition of OER—both of which may be deemed contributing factors to the significant increase in OER in the early twenty-first century.

OPEN EDUCATION ADVOCACY (2002– PRESENT)

UNESCO COINS *OER*

UNESCO convened the Forum on the Impact of Open Courseware for Higher Education in Developing Countries in Paris on July 1–3, 2002. The forum was held in partnership with the William and Flora Hewlett Foundation and the Western Cooperative for Educational Telecommunications. Following MIT's high-profile push to release OpenCourseWare, a group of seventeen principal participants representing higher education from over ten countries came together to increase support and collaboration in this new area of education. (For a full list of participants and the countries/institutions represented, view the forum's final report.)[31]

Recognizing the need to rename the service that was until that point referred to as *open courseware*, a working group at the forum coined and defined the term *open educational resources* as "the open provision of educational resources, enabled by information and communication technologies, for consultation, use and adaptation by a community of users for non-commercial purposes."[32]

GLOBAL DECLARATIONS

In the years that followed the coining of the term *OER*, international efforts to grow open education increased, including the first Open Education Conference (held at Utah State University) in 2003, the development of the not-for-profit organization China Open Resources for Education in 2004, and the Cape Town meeting in 2007.[33]

Cape Town Declaration (2007)

Held in Cape Town in September 2007, the Cape Town meeting brought together twenty-nine leading proponents of open education from nations across the globe, including South Africa, Poland, Chile, and Canada.[34]

Convened by the Open Society Institute and the Shuttleworth Foundation, the Cape Town meeting was intended to accelerate efforts to promote open resources, technology, and teaching practices in education. As at the Forum on the Impact of Open Courseware for Higher Education in Developing Countries, participants discussed ways to expand OER initiatives through collaboration. The Cape Town Declaration—coauthored by meeting participants—was the outcome.[35]

Released publicly on January 22, 2008, the Cape Town Declaration is a statement of principle, strategy, and commitment. It recognizes open education not just as a means to increase access to education, but also as an opportunity to imagine "a new pedagogy where educators and learners create, shape and evolve knowledge together."[36] It presents three strategies to "increase the reach and impact of open educational resources":

1. "Educators and learners" are encouraged "to actively participate in the open education movement."
2. "Educators, authors, publishers, and institutions" are encouraged "to release their resources openly."
3. "Governments, school boards, colleges, and universities" are called upon "to make open education a ...priority."[37]

> **Read the full Cape Town Open Education Declaration and view its list of authors at https://www.capetowndeclaration.org/.**

As of 2022, the declaration has been signed by more than 3,227 individuals and 362 organizations, each committing to the declaration's three strategies.[38] The Cape Town Declaration remains part of the global movement toward open education.

Paris OER Declaration

Global advocacy for OER culminated at the first World OER Congress in Paris on June 20–22, 2012, led by UNESCO, Commonwealth of Learning, and other partners. The congress was held to showcase global best practices around OER, celebrate the tenth anniversary of UNESCO's 2002 forum, and release the 2012 Paris OER Declaration.[39]

Recalling previous OER declarations, such as the Cape Town Open Education Declaration, and global declarations declaring education a human right, such as the Universal Declaration of Human Rights, the Paris OER Declaration made ten recommendations to grow OER:

1. Foster awareness and use of OER.
2. Facilitate enabling environments for information communications technology to bridge the digital divide.
3. Reinforce the development of strategies of policies on OER.
4. Promote the understanding and use of open licensing frameworks.
5. Support capacity building for the sustainable development of materials—support institutions and teachers in building OER.
6. Foster strategic alliances for OER.

7. Encourage the development and adaptation of OER in a variety of languages and cultural contexts.
8. Encourage research on OER.
9. Facilitate finding, retrieving, and sharing OER.
10. Encourage the open licensing of educational materials produced with public funds.[40]

Read the full 2012 Paris OER declaration at https://unesdoc.unesco. org/ark:/48223/pf0000246687.

The Paris OER Declaration therefore reaffirmed previous advocacy efforts and actions made at national and international levels to support the expansion of OER creation and adoption. The importance of these efforts were further reaffirmed with the United Nations' 2030 Agenda for Sustainable Development.

UN Sustainable Development Goal 4 (2015)

In 2015, the United Nations member states adopted the 2030 Agenda for Sustainable Development, which featured seventeen development goals that together address global challenges, including poverty, climate change, inequality, and justice. Goal 4 calls for quality education; it articulates the necessity to "ensure inclusive and equitable quality education and promote lifelong learning opportunities for all."[41] In doing so, UN Sustainable Development Goal 4 brings to focus the statements from the 1948 Universal Declaration of Human Rights, in which equal access to higher education was formally recognized as a human right.

UN Sustainable Development Goal 4 has given further cause to advocate for open education as a means to achieve inclusive and equitable lifelong access to education. In 2017, global representatives from 111 countries convened for the second World OER Congress, this time in Ljubljana, Slovenia, and organized by UNESCO and the government of Slovenia. Here, the representatives adopted the 2017 Ljubljana OER Action Plan, which recommends forty-one actions to achieve the 2030 Sustainable Development Goal on quality education.[42]

The action plan grew out of broad consultation, including six regional OER consultations attended by experts from more than 100 countries, an online consultation on the draft that saw input from more than 100 individuals, and recommendations from sessions at the second World OER Congress. The wide consultation resulted in a plan addressing five key areas for government action:

1. Building the capacity of users to find, re-use, create and share OER
2. Language and cultural issues
3. Ensuring inclusive and equitable access to quality OER
4. Developing sustainability models
5. Developing supportive policy environments[43]

Read the full Ljubljana OER Action Plan at https://en.unesco.org/ sites/default/files/ljubljana_oer_action_plan_2017.pdf.

The widespread consultation, culminating in a 500-person world congress, is indicative of the global attention that OER have gained over the course of open education's history.

ON-THE-GROUND WORK

The global declarations and action plans can be thought of as strategic efforts to draw visibility to—and forge connections across—on-the-ground efforts in support of OER growth and development. Since the inception of the declarations and action plans, on-the-ground efforts have grown interest and awareness in OER at local, national, and global scales. In the United States, national organizations such as the Scholarly Publishing and Academic Resources Coalition (SPARC) have driven program and policy development in support of OER from the federal government. In 2011, for example, the US Department of Labor developed a Trade Adjustment Assistance Community College and Career Training (TAACCCT) grant program to expand postsecondary education and training capacity, with the requirement that grantees openly license all digital assets created with TAACCCT funds.[44] The program and its $1.9 billion investment continued through to 2018, with the openly licensed products still available in SkillsCommons (https://www.skillscommons.org/), an online repository.[45] Then in 2014, for example, the US government released new open government initiatives as part of its Second Open Government National Action Plan. The new initiatives focused on open education and specifically on (1) raising open education awareness and identifying new partnerships, (2) piloting new models for using OER to support learning, and (3) launching an online skills academy.[46] And in 2018, the US Department of Education launched the Open Textbook Pilot grant program to support institutions in creating and expanding use of open textbooks.[47]

State policy and programs have followed accordingly. For example, the Connecticut state legislature passed an act to create an open textbook pilot program in 2015,[48] California launched a statewide Zero Textbook Cost degree initiative in 2016,[49] and in spring 2017, New York State allocated an initial $8 million in funding—split evenly between the City University of New York and the State University of New York—to increase the use and development of OER.[50] Additional investments have followed in subsequent years. Governmental adoption of OER is moving quickly outside of the United States as well. According to the Organization of Economic Cooperation and Development (OECD):

> In August and September 2014, governments were asked to respond to a [Centre for Educational Research and Innovation]/OECD questionnaire on how they support and facilitate the development and use of OER in all education sectors. The survey collected the responses of 33 countries: 29 OECD member countries and 4 accession and key partner countries (Brazil, China, Indonesia and Latvia). The results indicate a clear policy support for OER, with 25 countries reporting having a government policy to support OER production and use.[51]

The sheer volume of OER that now exist also points to uptake in creation and use of OER, as well as investment in the infrastructure to disseminate them. There are now more than two billion works licensed with a Creative Commons license, while MERLOT has grown to hold more than 98,000 learning resources since its establishment in 1997.[52] At the same time, more repositories have since been developed to host and increase discoverability of OER; the Open Textbook Library, which developed with support from the Open Education Network and which celebrated its tenth birthday in 2022, has grown in size to a collection with over 1,000 open textbooks.[53] More localized consortia, such as Canada's eCampusOntario and BCcampus, have also developed repositories to serve their constituents and beyond, which in recent years have grown to hold more than 700 and 350 resources, respectively.[54]

Studies on OER awareness and use, however, show that while awareness of OER is steadily increasing, use remains comparatively low. A 2014 Bay View Analytics report showed awareness of OER among 20 percent of faculty respondents, as compared to 25 percent in 2015–16, and 46 percent in 2018.[55] While awareness of OER has been shown to increase likelihood that a faculty member will use OER, a 2020 Bay View Analytics report showed that only 15 percent of faculty respondents assigned OER as required course material.[56] Results from the 2020 report also suggest that despite the opportunity presented with the rapid shift to remote learning at the onset of COVID-19 in 2020, the pandemic did not significantly increase adoption of OER.

For all of the successes, then, the OER community—in which librarians have a strong role—still has work before it. There is room to continue advocacy and awareness building and to provide the education and support needed to increase uptake among those already aware of OER. Scholars and practitioners have also identified open pedagogy (which will be covered section 2.3.3) as an area for future growth and development. Where OER have come to be as a result of commitments to improve access to education and knowledge, open pedagogy goes further. "Open pedagogy instead represents a vision for education that replaces classrooms of control with communities of possibility.… Open pedagogy …is firmly and explicitly grounded in concerns about social justice."[57]

Research has also demonstrated that although declarations like the 2012 Paris OER Declaration have a clear social justice alignment, key texts and literature that have followed are missing a social justice orientation. Dominant discourse around OER has framed openness and OER as good, often conflating access with social justice, but "access is not a synonym for social justice."[58] And even with open education's access-oriented commitment, most open textbooks do not meet basic accessibility requirements, meaning that OER are not accessible to all.[59] There is still work to be done to more closely align OER with the social justice values out of which the open education movement emerged.

CONCLUSION

This subsection has identified highlights throughout the history of open education, which originated out of a human rights–motivated desire to increase access to lifelong education. Through advocacy and advances in technology, open education has expanded into a global effort in which values like collaboration, inclusivity, and equity are at the forefront. And yet there is still work to be done. Noted by SPARC:

> For too long, our educational systems have operated with a fundamental disconnect between practices left over from the analog world, and the vast potential of technology and the Internet to support more affordable, effective teaching and learning. The movement for Open Education seeks to close this gap.[60]

Librarians play a key role in building the capacity for OER to be normalized as a means to achieve affordable, effective teaching and learning. Our work, and the present state of the field, are detailed in the rest of chapter 2.3.

ADDITIONAL RESOURCES ON THE HISTORY OF OPEN EDUCATION

Bliss, T. J., and M. Smith. "A Brief History of Open Educational Resources." In *Open: The Philosophy and Practices That Are Revolutionizing Education and Science*, edited by Rajiv Jhangiani and Robert Biswas-Diener. London: Ubiquity Press, 2017. https://doi.org/10.5334/bbc.b.

Kernohan, David, and Amber Thomas. "OER—A Historical Perspective." Presentation, Open Education Conference, Vancouver, BC, October 16–18, 2012. https://repository.jisc.ac.uk/4915/.

Open Education Working Group. "History of Open Education." In *The Open Education Handbook*, 13–14. Open Education Working Group, 2014. https://drive.google.com/file/d/0B3v5eAZeR0ERWmo1aDdRVWtNUkU/view?resourcekey=0-VvjxKRQsiMR3-2wHXv-X7A.

———. "Timeline." https://education.okfn.org/timeline/.

Peter, Sandra, and Markus Deimann. "On the Role of Openness in Education: A Historical Reconstruction." *Open Praxis* 5, no., 1 (January–March 2013): 7–14. https://openpraxis.org/articles/abstract/10.5944/openpraxis.5.1.23/.

Plotkin, Hal. "A Short History of the OER Movement." In *Free to Learn*, 3. San Francisco: Creative Commons, 2010. https://wiki.creativecommons.org/images/6/67/FreetoLearn-Guide.pdf.

DISCUSSION QUESTIONS

1. Why is the Universal Declaration of Human Rights integral to the history of open education?
2. What values drove early efforts to create open universities? How have those values remained at the foreground of efforts driving OER use and development?
3. What impact have open licenses had on the ability to share online content?
4. What are some key similarities between the Cape Town Declaration, Paris OER Declaration, and Ljubljana OER Action Plan? Key differences?

NOTES

1. Massachusetts Institute of Technology, "Our History," MITOpenCourseware, accessed November 25, 2019, https://ocw.mit.edu/about/our-history/ (page discontinued).
2. Carey Goldberg, "Auditing Classes at M.I.T., on the Web and Free," *New York Times*, April 4, 2001, https://www.nytimes.com/2001/04/04/us/auditing-classes-at-mit-on-the-web-and-free.html.
3. Goldberg, "Auditing Classes."
4. Massachusetts Institute of Technology, "About OCW," MITOpenCourseware, accessed November 25, 2019, https://ocw.mit.edu/about/ (page content changed).
5. Martin Weller, "The Victory of Openness," in *The Battle for Open* (London: Ubiquity Press Ltd., 2014), 2.
6. United Nations, "Universal Declaration of Human Rights," Paris, 1948, https://www.un.org/en/universal-declaration-human-rights/.
7. United Nations, "Universal Declaration."
8. Right to Education Project, "International Instruments: Right to Education" (public document, London, 2014), 3, 10, https://www.right-to-education.org/sites/right-to-education.org/files/resource-attachments/RTE_International_Instruments_Right_to_Education_2014.pdf.

9. Patrick Blessinger and T.J. Bliss, "Introduction to Open Education: Towards a Human Rights Theory," in *Open Education: International Perspectives in Higher Education*, ed. Patrick Blessinger and T. J. Bliss (Cambridge: Open Book Publishers, 2016), 12.

10. UNISA, "The Leading ODL University," last modified June 14, 2019, https://www.unisa.ac.za/sites/corporate/default/About/The-leading-ODL-university.

11. Open University, "Exhibition: The OU Story," Open University Digital Archive, 2018, https://www.open.ac.uk/library/digital-archive/exhibition/53.

12. Open University, "Exhibition."

13. Athabasca Web Services—Advancement Office, "History," Athabasca University, last modified January 30, 2020, https://www.athabascau.ca/aboutau/history/; Bangladesh Open University, "About Bangladesh Open University," accessed February 24, 2020, https://www.bou.edu.bd/ (site discontinued).

14. Weller, "Victory of Openness," 2.

15. Blessinger and Bliss, "Introduction to Open Education," 18.

16. David Wiley, "David Wiley, 'Open Content: The First Decade,'" in *An Open Education Reader*, ed. David Wiley (EdTech Books, 2016), https://edtechbooks.org/openedreader/the-first-decade-wiley.

17. David Wiley, "'History of Free and Open Source Software" (online lesson, 2013), https://learn.canvas.net/courses/4/pages/history-of-free-and-open-source-software.

18. Richard Stallman, "The GNU Operating System and the Free Software Movement," in *Open Sources: Voices from the Open Source Revolution*, ed. Chris DiBona, Sam Ockman, and Mark Stone (Sebastopol, CA: O'Reilly & Associates, 1999), 56.

19. GNU Operating System, "What Is Copyleft?" Free Software Foundation, 2018, https://www.gnu.org/licenses/copyleft.en.html.

20. David Bretthauer, "Open Source Software: A History," OpenCommons@UConn, University of Connecticut Library, 2001, 6, https://opencommons.uconn.edu/cgi/viewcontent.cgi?article=1009&context=libr_pubs.

21. David Wiley, "Eric Raymond, 'The Cathedral and the Bazaar,'" in *An Open Education Reader*, ed. David Wiley (EdTech Books, 2016), https://edtechbooks.org/openedreader/the-cathedral-and-the-bazaar.

22. Wiley, "Eric Raymond."

23. Wiley, "History of Free and Open Source Software."

24. Wiley, "David Wiley."

25. Mark Pallen, "Guide to the Internet: The World Wide Web," *BMJ* 311 (1995): 1552, https://doi.org/10.1136/bmj.311.7019.1552.

26. Massachusetts Institute of Technology, "About OCW."

27. MERLOT, home page, California State University System, 2020, https://www.merlot.org/merlot/.

28. MERLOT, "MERLOT History," California State University System, 2019, http://info.merlot.org/merlothelp/topic.htm#t=Who_We_Are.htm%23MERLOT_History.

29. MERLOT, "MERLOT History."

30. Creative Commons, "The Story of Creative Commons" (online lesson, Creative Commons Certificate for Educators and Librarians, 2020), https://certificates.creativecommons.org/cccertedu/chapter/1-1-the-story-of-creative-commons/.

31. UNESCO, *Forum on the Impact of Open Courseware for Higher Education in Developing Countries, UNESCO, Paris, 1–3 July 2002: Final Report* (Paris: UNESCO, 2002), 8–9, https://unesdoc.unesco.org/ark:/48223/pf0000128515.

32. UNESCO, *Forum on the Impact*, 8–9.

33. Cape Town Open Education Declaration, "Related Initiatives: Open Education Initiatives," accessed January 14, 2019, https://www.capetowndeclaration.org/related-initiatives.

34. Cape Town Open Education Declaration, "View Signatures," accessed January 14, 2019, https://www.capetowndeclaration.org/list_signatures?author=1&indorg=ind (page discontinued).

35. Cape Town Open Education Declaration, home page, accessed January 14, 2019, https://www.capetowndeclaration.org/.

36. Cape Town Open Education Declaration, "Read the Declaration," accessed January 14, 2019, https://www.capetowndeclaration.org/read/.

37. Cape Town Open Education Declaration, "Read the Declaration."

38. Cape Town Open Education Declaration, "Read the Declaration."

39. Cable Green, "2012 Paris OER Declaration," *Creative Commons* (blog), June 29, 2012, https://creativecommons.org/2012/06/29/2012-paris-oer-declaration/.

40. The list of ten recommendations is adapted, with editorial changes, from UNESCO, "2012 Paris OER Declaration," in *An Open Education Reader*, ed. David Wiley (EdTech Books, 2016), https://edtechbooks.org/openedreader/open-educational-resources-2012-paris-declaration, which is licensed under a Creative Commons Attribution 4.0 International License, https://creativecommons.org/licenses/by/4.0/.

41. United Nations, "Sustainable Development Goals," Sustainable Development Goals Knowledge Platform, accessed March 2, 2020, https://sustainabledevelopment.un.org/?menu=1300 (page content changed).

42. Second World OER Congress, *Ljubljana OER Action Plan 2017* (Paris: UNESCO, 2017), https://en.unesco.org/sites/default/files/ljubljana_oer_action_plan_2017.pdf.

43. Cable Green, "2nd World OER Congress + 2017 Ljubljana OER Action Plan," *Creative Commons* (blog), October 2, 2017, https://creativecommons.org/2017/10/02/2nd-world-oer-congress-2017-ljubljana-oer-action-plan/.

44. US Department of Labor, "Notice of Availability of Funds and Solicitation for Grant Applications for Trade Adjustment Assistance Community College and Career Training Grants Program," Employment and Training Administration, 2011, 21, https://www.dol.gov/sites/dolgov/files/ETA/grants/pdfs/SGA-DFA-PY-10-03.pdf.

45. US Department of Labor, "Trade Adjustment Assistance Community College and Career Training," Employment and Training Administration, accessed June 17, 2022, https://www.dol.gov/agencies/eta/skills-training-grants/community-colleges.

46. White House, "The Open Government Partnership: Announcing New Open Government Initiatives as Part of the Second Open Government National Action Plan for the United States of America," September 2014, https://obamawhitehouse.archives.gov/sites/default/files/microsites/ostp/new_nap_commitments_report_092314.pdf.

47. SPARC, "Open Textbook Pilot Grant Program," February 5, 2019, https://sparcopen.org/our-work/open-textbook-pilot/.

48. SPARC, "List of North American OER Policies and Projects," accessed March 13, 2022, https://sparcopen.org/our-work/list-of-oer-policies-projects/.

49. SPARC, "California's Zero Textbook Cost Degree Program," accessed March 13, 2022, https://sparcopen.org/our-work/california-governors-zero-textbook-cost-degree-budget-proposal/.

50. Andrew McKinney and Ann Fiddler, "City University of New York," chapter 19 in *Marking Open and Affordable Courses: Best Practices and Case Studies*, ed. Sarah Hare, Jessica Kirschner, and Michelle Reed (Arlington, TX: Mavs Open Press, 2020), https://uta.pressbooks.pub/markingopenandaffordablecourses/chapter/city-university-of-new-york/.

51. Dominic Orr, Michele Rimini, and Dirk van Damme, *Open Educational Resources: A Catalyst for Innovation*, Educational Research and Innovation (Paris: OECD Publishing, 2015), 20.

52. MERLOT, home page.

53. Center for Open Education, "Open Textbook Library," accessed March 13, 2022, https://open.umn.edu/opentextbooks.

54. eCampusOntario, "Open Library," accessed March 13, 2022, https://openlibrary.ecampusontario.ca/; BCcampus, "Find Open Textbooks," accessed March 13, 2022, https://open.bccampus.ca/browse-our-collection/find-open-textbooks/.

55. I. Elaine Allen and Jeff Seaman, *Opening the Curriculum: Open Educational Resources in U.S. Higher Education, 2014* (Babson Park, MA: Babson Survey Research Group, 2014); I. Elaine Allen and Jeff Seaman, *Opening the Textbook: Educational Resources in U.S. Higher Education, 2015–2016* (Babson Park, MA: Babson Survey Research Group, 2016); Julia E. Seaman and Jeff Seaman, *Freeing the Textbook: Open Education Resources in U.S. Higher Education, 2018* (Babson Park: Babson Survey Research Group, 2018).

56. Julia E. Seaman and Jeff Seaman, *Digital Texts in the Time of COVID: Educational Resources in U.S. Higher Education, 2020,* (Oakland, CA: Bay View Analytics, 2021).

57. Rajiv S. Jhangiani and Arthur G. Green, "An Open Anthenaeum: Creating an Institutional Home for Open Pedagogy," chapter 7 in *OER: A Field Guide for Academic Librarians | Editor's Cut*, ed. Andrew Wesolek, Jonathan Lashley, and Anne Langley (Forest Grove, OR: Pacific University Press, 2019), https://boisestate.pressbooks.pub/oer-field-guide/chapter/an-open-athenaeum-creating-an-institutional-home-for-open-pedagogy/.

58. Sarah R. Lambert, "Changing Our (Dis)course: A Distinctive Social Justice Aligned Definition of Open Education," *Journal of Learning for Development* 5, no. 3 (2015): 231, https://doi.org/10.56059/jl4d.v5i3.290.

59. Elena Azadbakht, Teresa Schultz, and Jennifer Arellano, "Not Open for All: Accessibility of Open Textbooks," *Insights* 34 (2021), https://doi.org/10.1629/uksg.557.

60. SPARC, "Open Education," accessed December 12, 2019, https://sparcopen.org/open-education/.

BIBLIOGRAPHY

Allen, I. Elaine, and Jeff Seaman. *Opening the Curriculum: Open Educational Resources in U.S. Higher Education, 2014*. Babson Park, MA: Babson Survey Research Group, 2014.

———. *Opening the Textbook: Educational Resources in U.S. Higher Education, 2015–2016*. Babson Park, MA: Babson Survey Research Group, 2016.

Athabasca Web Services—Advancement Office. "History." Athabasca University. Last modified January 30, 2020. https://www.athabascau.ca/aboutau/history/.

Azadbakht, Elena, Teresa Schultz, and Jennifer Arellano. "Not Open for All: Accessibility of Open Textbooks." *Insights* 34 (2021). https://doi.org/10.1629/uksg.557.

Bangladesh Open University. "About Bangladesh Open University." Accessed February 24, 2020. https://www.bou.edu.bd/ (site discontinued).

BCcampus. "Find Open Textbooks." Accessed March 13, 2022. https://open.bccampus.ca/browse-our-collection/find-open-textbooks/.

Blessinger, Patrick, and T. J. Bliss. "Introduction to Open Education: Towards a Human Rights Theory." In *Open Education: International Perspectives in Higher Education*, edited by Patrick Blessinger and T. J. Bliss, 11–30. Cambridge: Open Book Publishers, 2016.

Bretthauer, David. "Open Source Software: A History." OpenCommons@UConn, University of Connecticut Library, 2001. https://opencommons.uconn.edu/cgi/viewcontent.cgi?article=1009&context=libr_pubs.

Cape Town Open Education Declaration. Home page. Accessed January 14, 2019. https://www.capetowndeclaration.org/.

———. "Read the Declaration." Accessed January 14, 2019. https://www.capetowndeclaration.org/read/.

———. "Related Initiatives: Open Education Initiatives." Accessed January 14, 2019. https://www.capetowndeclaration.org/related-initiatives.

———. "View Signatures." Accessed January 14, 2019. https://www.capetowndeclaration.org/list_signatures?author=1&indorg=ind (page discontinued).

Center for Open Education. "Open Textbook Library." Accessed March 13, 2022. https://open.umn.edu/opentextbooks.

Creative Commons. "The Story of Creative Commons." Online lesson, Creative Commons for Certificate for Educators and Librarians, 2020. https://certificates.creativecommons.org/cccertedu/chapter/1-1-the-story-of-creative-commons/.

eCampusOntario. "Open Library." Accessed March 13, 2022. https://openlibrary.ecampusontario.ca/.

GNU Operating System. "What Is Copyleft?" Free Software Foundation. 2018. https://www.gnu.org/licenses/copyleft.en.html.

Goldberg, Carey. "Auditing Classes at M.I.T., on the Web and Free." *New York Times*, April 4, 2001. https://www.nytimes.com/2001/04/04/us/auditing-classes-at-mit-on-the-web-and-free.html.

Green, Cable. "2012 Paris OER Declaration." *Creative Commons* (blog), June 29, 2012. https://creativecommons.org/2012/06/29/2012-paris-oer-declaration/.

———. "2nd World OER Congress + 2017 Ljubljana OER Action Plan." *Creative Commons* (blog), October 2, 2017. https://creativecommons.org/2017/10/02/2nd-world-oer-congress-2017-ljubljana-oer-action-plan/.

Jhangiani, Rajiv S., and Arthur G. Green. "An Open Anthenaeum: Creating an Institutional Home for Open Pedagogy." Chapter 7 in *OER: A Field Guide for Academic Librarians | Editor's Cut*, edited by Andrew Wesolek, Jonathan Lashley, and Anne Langley. Forest Grove, OR: Pacific University Press, 2019. https://boisestate.pressbooks.pub/oer-field-guide/chapter/an-open-athenaeum-creating-an-institutional-home-for-open-pedagogy/.

Kentnor, Hope E. "Distance Education and the Evolution of Online Learning in the United States." *Curriculum and Teaching Dialogue* 17, no. 1–2 (2015): 21–34. https://digitalcommons.du.edu/cgi/viewcontent.cgi?article=1026&context=law_facpub.

Lambert, Sarah R. "Changing Our (Dis)course: A Distinctive Social Justice Aligned Definition of Open Education." *Journal of Learning for Development* 5, no. 3 (2015): 225–44. https://doi.org/10.56059/jl4d.v5i3.290.

Massachusetts Institute of Technology. "About OCW." MITOpenCourseware. Accessed November 25, 2019. https://ocw.mit.edu/about/ (page content changed).

———. "Our History." MITOpenCourseware. Accessed November 25, 2019. https://ocw.mit.edu/about/our-history/ (page discontinued).

McKinney, Andrew, and Ann Fiddler. "City University of New York." Chapter 19 in *Marking Open and Affordable Courses: Best Practices and Case Studies*, edited by Sarah Hare, Jessica Kirschner, and Michelle Reed. Arlington, TX: Mavs Open Press, 2020. https://uta.pressbooks.pub/markingopenandaffordablecourses/chapter/city-university-of-new-york/.

MERLOT. Home page. California State University System. 2020. https://www.merlot.org/merlot/.

———. "MERLOT History." California State University System. 2019. https://info.merlot.org/merlothelp/topic.htm#t=Who_We_Are.htm%23MERLOT_History.

Open University. "Exhibition: The OU Story." Open University Digital Archive. 2018. https://www.open.ac.uk/library/digital-archive/exhibition/53.

Orr, Dominic, Michele Rimini, and Dirk van Damme. *Open Educational Resources: A Catalyst for Innovation*. Educational Research and Innovation. Paris: OECD Publishing, 2015.

Pallen, Mark. "Guide to the Internet: The World Wide Web." *BMJ* 311 (1995): 1552. https://doi.org/10.1136/bmj.311.7019.1552.

Right to Education Project. "International Instruments: Right to Education." Public document, London, 2014. https://www.right-to-education.org/sites/right-to-education.org/files/resource-attachments/RTE_International_Instruments_Right_to_Education_2014.pdf

Seaman, Julia E., and Jeff Seaman. *Digital Texts in the Time of COVID: Educational Resources in U.S. Higher Education, 2020*. Oakland, CA: Bay View Analytics, 2021.

———. *Freeing the Textbook: Open Education Resources in U.S. Higher Education, 2018*. Babson Park: Babson Survey Research Group, 2018.

Second World OER Congress. "Ljupljana OER Action Plan." UNESCO. 2017. https://en.unesco.org/sites/default/files/ljubljana_oer_action_plan_2017.pdf.

SPARC. "California's Zero Textbook Cost Degree Program." Accessed March 13, 2022. https://sparcopen.org/our-work/california-governors-zero-textbook-cost-degree-budget-proposal.

———. "List of North American OER Policies and Projects." Accessed March 13, 2022. https://sparcopen.org/our-work/list-of-oer-policies-projects/.

———. "Open Education." Accessed December 12, 2019. https://sparcopen.org/open-education/.

———. "Open Textbook Pilot Grant Program." February 5, 2019. https://sparcopen.org/our-work/open-textbook-pilot/.

Stallman, Richard. "The GNU Operating System and the Free Software Movement." In *Open Sources: Voices from the Open Source Revolution*, edited by Chris DiBona, Sam Ockman, and Mark Stone, 53-70. Sebastopol, CA: O'Reilly & Associates, 1999.

UNESCO. *Forum on the Impact of Open Courseware for Higher Education in Developing Countries, UNESCO, Paris, 1–3 July 2002: Final Report*. Paris: UNESCO, 2002. https://unesdoc.unesco.org/ark:/48223/pf0000128515.

———. "2012 Paris OER Declaration." In *An Open Education Reader*, edited by David Wiley. EdTech Books, 2016. https://edtechbooks.org/openedreader/open-educational-resources-2012-paris-declaration.

UNISA. "The Leading ODL University." Last modified June 14, 2019. https://www.unisa.ac.za/sites/corporate/default/About/The-leading-ODL-university.

United Nations. "Sustainable Development Goals." Sustainable Development Goals Knowledge Platform. Accessed March 2, 2020. https://sustainabledevelopment.un.org/?menu=1300 (page content changed).

———. "Universal Declaration of Human Rights." Paris, 1948. https://www.un.org/en/universal-declaration-human-rights/.

US Department of Labor. "Notice of Availability of Funds and Solicitation for Grant Applications for Trade Adjustment Assistance Community College and Career Training Grants Program." Employment and Training Administration, 2011. https://www.dol.gov/sites/dolgov/files/ETA/grants/pdfs/SGA-DFA-PY-10-03.pdf.

———. "Trade Adjustment Assistance Community College and Career Training." Employment and Training Administration. Accessed June 17, 2022. https://www.dol.gov/agencies/eta/skills-training-grants/community-colleges.

Weller, Martin. "The Victory of Openness." In *The Battle for Open: How Openness Won and Why It Doesn't Feel like Victory*, 1–25. London: Ubiquity Press, 2014.

White House. "The Open Government Partnership: Announcing New Open Government Initiatives as Part of the Second Open Government National Action Plan for the United States of America." September 2014. https://obamawhitehouse.archives.gov/sites/default/files/microsites/ostp/new_nap_commitments_report_092314.pdf.

Wiley, David, ed. *An Open Education Reader*. EdTech Books, 2016. https://edtechbooks.org/openedreader.

World Open Educational Resources (OER) Congress. "Paris OER Declaration." UNESDOC Digital Library. 2012. https://unesdoc.unesco.org/ark:/48223/pf0000246687.

BENEFITS, BARRIERS, AND MYTHS

Camille Thomas, Ariana Santiago, and Laura Miller

Learning about OER and their history can raise a lot of questions. While the history of open education is relatively long and the advocacy movement is well established, for many it is new and may differ from previous methods of teaching and learning. This subsection will address common questions by discussing the benefits of OER, barriers faced when changing culture around course materials, and myths and misconceptions about OER. Understanding the benefits, barriers, and myths of OER can help open education advocates develop and sustain successful open education initiatives.

BENEFITS OF OPEN EDUCATION

Like open access and open data, which are discussed in detail in chapters 2.2 and 2.3, the day-to-day work for OER involves advocating by raising awareness about their benefits. OER are new to many instructors, students, and other education professionals, so it is important to provide evidence about the ways these resources can help address rising educational costs for students, updated information, engaged learning, student success, and broader impact on education.

FINANCIAL BENEFITS

The high and rising costs of course materials in higher education are a hindrance to student learning and success. Over several decades, college textbook prices increased more than three times the rate of inflation.[1] The recommended undergraduate student budget for books and supplies was an average of $1,240 per year in 2018, compared to an average of $900 just three years earlier.[2] In a survey of more than 150 university campuses, 65 percent of students reported that they decided not to purchase a textbook because it was too expensive, even though they were concerned their grades would suffer as a result.[3] This financial barrier causes many students to go without required course materials, putting them at an academic disadvantage when compared to peers who have the financial resources to purchase them. When compared to courses that use commercial textbooks, courses that use OER see lower student withdrawal rates.[4] Additionally, in courses that use OER, student learning outcomes are the same or better as in courses that use commercial textbooks.[5] OER provide a financial benefit to students without negatively affecting learning.

Because OER are free for anyone to access, they offer a solution to the problem of rising textbook prices. When costly course materials are replaced with OER, the cost and access barriers for students are removed. Not only are OER free to access, they are available online, are affordable in print, and can be retained by students forever.[6] When OER are assigned as required course materials, all students have free and immediate access on the first day of class, and no one is put at a disadvantage due to not being able to afford or access an expensive textbook.

Institutions often track OER adoptions and estimate the amount saved by students as a result of eliminating textbook costs (see table 2.7). Estimating student savings is one way to assess and communicate the impact of OER, particularly for institutions where OER initiatives are strongly motivated by textbook affordability concerns.

There are multiple methods used to estimate student savings. Table 2.7 shows the most commonly used methods. Estimates are often derived from institutional mini grant programs, campus bookstore textbook adoption data, and sometimes sources outside the institution (OER publishers, OER repositories, etc.). *Estimates* are common because it is difficult to take into account used textbooks, varied editions, rentals, outdated adoption information, and student behavior related to these issues. Inaccurate data at the institutional level is a common issue for many advocates.

PEDAGOGICAL BENEFITS

OER enable many pedagogical benefits, as they allow instructors to have greater control over course content. Due to the open licenses inherent in OER, instructors have the permission and flexibility to adapt the content of OER so that materials can be better tailored to their particular courses and learning outcomes. Most traditional course materials, such as commercial textbooks, are released under "all rights reserved" copyright and thus severely limit or eliminate instructors' ability to adapt the content.

The freedom to adapt and curate resources allows instructors to customize content exactly to course learning objectives and students' needs, whereas in a traditional model they

TABLE 2.7

Methods for calculating student savings

Method	Description
$100 Threshold Method	Many institutions, including the Open Education Network and Open Oregon, use an estimate of $100 saved per student.[a]
SPARC Averaging Method	To calculate the average price of materials for each course, SPARC took the average of the highest available price and the lowest available price. This was a community-wide effort to see how much OER saved students in North America.[b]
Retail Price Method	This method usually calculates savings based on maximum retail prices for new textbooks because it is difficult to determine nuances—such as secondary markets like renting or used book prices—due to variation.[c]
Cumulative Method	Institutions with long-standing alternative textbook or other programs may calculate cumulative savings as OER continue to be used in courses.
Mixed Material Method	Some alternative textbook programs may include library-licensed material, but this method still creates an expense for library collections budgets. Some institutions include these materials in their savings calculations as zero-cost materials because there is no cost to students.

a. Amy Hofer, "Is the Average Cost of a Textbook $100?" Open Oregon Educational Resources, February 17, 2017, https://openoregon.org/is-the-average-cost-of-a-textbook-100/.

b. Mo Nyamweya, "A New Method for Estimating OER Savings," SPARC, December 20, 2018, https://sparcopen.org/news/2018/estimating-oer-student-savings/.

c. Amy Hofer, "Estimating Student Savings from No-Cost/Low-Cost Course Materials," Open Oregon Educational Resources, April 19, 2018, https://openoregon.org/estimating-student-savings-from-no-cost-low-cost-course-materials/.

may be encouraged to follow the textbook.[7] In a survey of more than 200 students enrolled in courses using open textbooks across a variety of disciplines, Ikahihifo and colleagues found that a majority of respondents perceived OER to be higher quality and more engaging than traditional textbooks.[8] In addition to believing the OER to be more interactive and engaging, students appreciated that "content was tailored specifically to the course" and benefitted from instructors drawing upon a variety of open resources.[9] In a focus group of biology faculty who used open textbooks for the first time, faculty noted that OER allowed flexibility to reorganize course content and easily deliver a variety of resources to students.[10] Additionally, the ability to adapt OER allows for continuous quality improvement—instructors have permission to edit and make corrections to the material at any time, rather than alerting the publisher to a problem and waiting to see the correction in the next edition.[11]

The ability to adapt OER provides a unique benefit in allowing instructors to customize content to reflect the local environment, which can also increase diverse representation in course materials. For example, authors of an OER textbook for nutrition created at the University of Hawai'i at Mānoa intentionally designed the text to reflect the local food and culture of the region, a feature that appealed to many students.[12] An open textbook on American history could include the latest news from a recent election, or a math tutorial could incorporate local landmarks into word problems[13]—the possibilities are endless. Open license permissions also allow for open pedagogy, or teaching and learning practices that engage students in building upon or creating new OER, for example, though there are other models.[14]

Instructors can also enhance materials for various learners with disabilities according to universal design and inclusive design practices and then distribute those adaptations.[15] Unlike commercially published materials, OER that are adapted to meet accessibility requirements can be retained and freely shared with communities, reducing duplicative work at and across institutions. Typically, traditional proprietary materials allow adaptation for only one user (as required by law in the US), but not the distribution of the accessible derivative. Day-one access for students is a prominent benefit of OER, and even more so for students who may need to wait longer for course material enhancements based on self-reporting or to cover additional financial expenses. These benefits demonstrate how well suited OER can be for providing perpetual, immediate access for students with a diverse range of learning needs and systematic improvements to the overall design of course materials.

OER'S IMPACT ON HIGHER EDUCATION

STUDENT SUCCESS

It is common for colleges and universities to include student success as a strategic priority, for good reason. If students aren't succeeding, it reflects poorly on the institution and suggests a failure of the fundamental mission. Efforts to promote student success can include but is not limited to initiatives for retention; financial support; experiential learning; diversity, equity, and inclusion; and engagement with STEM. Affordable course materials have a clear alignment with these administrative initiatives due to correlating increases in enrollment, retention, and academic performance.

A large-scale study on the academic impact of OER found that OER improved end-of-course grades and decreased rates of D, F, and Withdrawal letter grades (DFW) for all students in comparison to non-OER courses; the improved grades and decreased DFW rates were even greater for Pell Grant recipient students, students of color, and part-time students.[16] Students and faculty both perceive OER to have positive impacts on learning goals,[17] and faculty agree that use of OER benefits students by improving grades, increasing engagement with lesson content, increasing participation in class discussions, better accommodating diverse needs of students, and more.[18]

Z DEGREES, COURSE MARKING, AND AFFORDABLE COURSE FEES

OER are generally adopted at the instructor or academic department level, but some institutions have gone above and beyond to create entire degree programs with no textbook costs for students. These zero-materials-cost degrees, or Z-Degrees, are more common at community colleges and are included in the institution's marketing to potential students. Tidewater Community College in Virginia is an innovator in this area. In a study on its Z-Degree, it used OER for twenty-one courses, providing a pathway for students to earn an associate of science degree in business administration. The investigators found that using OER significantly reduced the number of students who dropped or withdrew from courses, resulting in increased retention and sustainable use of tuition funds.[19] Universities have taken note and may see growth of Z-Degrees in the future—Kwantlen Polytechnic University, for example, offers several degree programs with zero textbook costs.[20]

Some universities that are not able to provide full zero-materials-cost degrees have made courses with OER or other affordable course materials more visible to students through course marking[21] Course marking is "the process of assigning specific, searchable attributes to courses."[22] These attributes may be letters, numbers, or visual indicators in course catalogs and registration systems that highlight courses with open, free, or affordable materials, as defined by the institution. Course marking can help students budget for classes in advance based on their program requirements.

OER RESEARCH

In addition to savings and student success based on OER adoptions, research about OER has increased. More research positively impacts teaching and learning by providing empirical evidence that addresses frequently asked questions about OER's legitimacy, sustainability, and impact. Continual advancements are being made in research around OER, with many such advancements being driven by the Open Education Group, an interdisciplinary group based primarily out of Brigham Young University. The Open Education Group developed the COUP Framework as an approach to studying the impact of OER, identifying cost, outcome, usage, and perception as research areas for measuring the impact of OER adoption.[23] Many studies on OER focus on efficacy and perceptions, though the body of research is growing to explore intersections with open pedagogy and social justice.[24]

POLICY AND GRANTS

Open education policy has seen success in a number of US states with the introduction of legislation related to researching textbook affordability for students, providing funding for OER, implementing course-marking programs, and other directives that support OER initiatives.[25] According to the SPARC *OER State Policy Playbook*, "nearly half of all states and the U.S. Congress have passed legislation leveraging OER as a solution to higher education challenges."[26] New bills are introduced every session in state legislatures across the country, and SPARC offers an OER State Policy Tracker to monitor developments in these state OER policies and pending legislation.[27]

The US Department of Education introduced the Open Textbook Pilot program in 2018 to help fund the development of open textbooks at higher education institutions, exemplifying the growing national demand for affordable textbook alternatives for students. Congress continued the program and funding into 2021, 2022, and 2023. According to SPARC, as of summer 2022, sixteen projects have been funded at a total of $35 million, with an estimated savings of $200 million since the start of the program in 2018.[28] Internationally, OER policies are developed with different contexts and motivations than in the US—for example, to contribute to the academic commons, rather than primarily decrease the cost of higher education, in countries where higher education tuition is not as prohibitively costly.[29] Countries are also working collaboratively to support international open education policy, evidenced by the adoption of UNESCO's Recommendation for Future International Collaboration in the field of OER by 195 members.[30] Open education has also been argued as a key avenue to reach the United Nations' Sustainable Development Goal 4: Equitable Access to Education.[31] International policy around open education broadens the scope of the movement and advances affordable and accessible education globally.

EXPANDING AFFORDABLE OPTIONS

Many commercial publishers have begun to offer products at varying price points that compete with the free open course materials, as well as the robust rental and resale markets for textbooks. Sources such as Inside Higher Ed and *Wired* magazine capture recent changes in commercial products.[32] In Inside Higher Ed's 2018 article, "Are Etextbooks Affordable Now?" e-book platforms VitalSource and RedShelf noted publishers cut prices by 30 to 50 percent between 2015 and 2018 due to secondary markets (e.g., renting, used books, print retail) and OER.[33] Other options offered by publishers such as Pearson and Macmillan, often in collaboration with campus bookstores, are Inclusive Access and OER accompanied by proprietary software.[34] Inclusive Access programs—"a textbook sales model that adds the cost of digital course content into students' tuition and fees"[35]—are discussed in further detail in section 2.3.4, "Current Issues in the Field." Some examples of OER accompanied by low-cost supplemental resources provided by publishers and vendors like OpenStax, panOpen, and Lumen Learning. While these are not open, they do demonstrate that OER's impact has influenced commercial publishers to respond to the evolving landscape of course material offerings.

BARRIERS TO OPEN EDUCATION

While many may support the ethos of open education and recognize the financial and pedagogical benefits of OER, a number of logistical and professional barriers limit instructors' ability to create and adopt OER in their courses. Understanding these barriers can help librarians, instructors, and institutions prepare more effective textbook affordability initiatives.

LACK OF AWARENESS

For instructors, it can be challenging to work with OER when they do not fully understand the concept. In 2019, only 37 percent of faculty reported being "Aware" or "Very Aware" of OER.[36] Misconceptions about what OER are and how they can be used limit faculty's ability to effectively implement open resources in their courses. Some resources like library-licensed journal articles are an attractive alternative to commercial textbooks, but paywalled journal articles are not OER because they are neither free nor reusable. OER advocates must share clear and concise information to instructors to ensure equal understanding.

Navigating fair use (in the US) or fair dealing (in the UK and other Commonwealth nations) and open licenses may also deter instructors who are unfamiliar with these concepts. Adopting OER can be daunting for instructors if they do not have adequate understanding or support for fair use/dealing and Creative Commons licensing.[37] The *Code of Best Practices in Fair Use for Open Educational Resources* aims to guide instructors in applying fair use principles when developing open course materials.[38] In short, the authors (one of whom, Cross, is an editor of this book), demonstrate that OER and fair use are compatible. Additional resources to help instructors demystify Creative Commons and fair use are discussed in "Myths and Misconceptions" later in this subsection. Instructors may wish to consult their library or curriculum center on campus for one-on-one copyright and licensing support to combat misinformation and copyright infringement.

DISCOVERY ISSUES

Instructors who understand and are interested in adopting open course materials may experience difficulty finding suitable open materials. Traditional publishers promote course-related textbooks directly to faculty and departments, which takes the burden of finding course materials off of instructors. Publishers spend a large amount of resources on this method of marketing, such as funding, personnel, and royalties for the department, that are not available to libraries at the same scale. OER are not marketed directly to instructors like traditional textbooks and don't have the brand recognition of large publishers, so faculty must dedicate time to seeking out and evaluating open resources.

There are several notable OER repositories, aggregators, or search engines, such as OER Commons, MERLOT, the Open Textbook Library, Openly Available Sources Integrated Search (OASIS), and the Mason OER Metafinder. Atenas and Havemann reviewed repositories of OER for quality indicators (including the use of metadata standards),[39] but until recently, little work was done to streamline discovery for OER across repositories. Recent collaborations show broad efforts to improve interoperability of metadata as well as usability. For example, the Institute for the Study of Knowledge Management in Education (ISKME), along with several library consortia, created personas based on user interviews with faculty instructors and librarians to further study discovery needs.[40] Resources with incomplete records may not appear in searches, and some subjects may be cataloged too narrowly for broad discovery.

In addition to repositories and discovery systems, OER librarians and subject liaisons can provide expertise to help instructors find content suitable for their courses. Open education e-mail discussion lists, such as the SPARC Libraries and OER Forum, exist for librarians and instructors who are seeking help from OER communities, including assistance with finding specific materials.[41] Libraries may license products like EBSCO's Faculty Select to help instructors find open course material and open access books.[42] Some libraries are adding OER to their local catalogs with MARC records including open license information and course reserve status to help faculty discover and access a range of educational resources.[43]

While OER discovery sees continuous improvement, there is room for future research and expansion in this area. Beyond cataloging and mega repositories, advocates can expand to more semantic and machine-readable retrieval, which reflects the dynamic nature of OER and common information-seeking behavior online.[44] OER advocates can also broaden emphasis from metadata to other aspects of discovery such as ease of use. User-centered design supports lifelong learning and availability of the materials.[45] However, it is important to note there is a prevalent assumption that all users of OER have the same access to technology, creating further barriers to true access and discovery. Therefore, improving metadata and usability of OER could potentially increase their adoption and use going forward.

TIME

Perhaps the largest barrier to broad OER adoption is the time investment in finding, evaluating, creating, implementing, and maintaining open materials. Textbooks and learning materials take considerable time to create, and instructors often do not have time to create custom materials alongside research, teaching, and service responsibilities. Labor is often centralized in OER creation so one person is creating the bulk of the content (with notable exceptions like collaborative wikis and blogs), and this centralized labor increases the amount of time instructors must dedicate to developing OER. The time needed to alter courses to incorporate OER and the labor needed to author new open course materials can be a barrier for busy faculty, especially when course releases are not available. Even once an OER is published, there is often maintenance work to be done to keep the material up-to-date with emerging research and evolving landscapes and topical issues.

Instructors must also budget time to ensure their OER are accessible for all learners. Accessibility is key to creating OER that benefit all students. Accessibility must be "'baked in' rather than 'bolted on'" to ensure inclusivity for all learners.[46] Creating accessible digital materials requires time to generate and review Optical Character Recognition (OCR) for digitized documents, code websites to Web Content Accessibility Guidelines (WCAG) standards, and create captioning for video and audio recordings. This work may be completed by student workers and research assistants (with proper credit given) to help distribute the labor, if funding permits. OER authors can work with campus disability resource centers and use existing resources like BCcampus's *Accessibility Toolkit* to help create accessible resources.[47]

LABOR ISSUES AND PROMOTION AND TENURE

Given the extensive time required to create or adopt OER, open resources should be appropriately taken into account in promotion and tenure (P&T) evaluations, but this is often not the case. The labor to produce and adopt OER is not consistently incentivized across institutions. According to the American Association of University Professors, 70 percent of instructors hold contingent positions.[48] Those in temporary, adjunct, and graduate teaching roles have little time or incentive to incorporate open education into their pedagogy. Without proper awareness and incentive to seek out OER, contingent instructors may continue to rely on commercial teaching materials, even when they may be interested in OER. On the other hand, contingent and non-tenure-track instructors may be more interested in adopting OER because tenure pressures are not a factor. If OER are not favored for P&T, contingent faculty may be best positioned to champion OER within their department. If the labor of OER creation is delegated to contingent faculty, institutions must properly compensate these instructors for their work to avoid perpetuating invisible labor in open education.[49] The culture around these issues can differ from institution to institution, department to department, and over time as chairpersons and committee membership (curriculum committees and P&T committees, for example) change.

The lack of incentives for contingent faculty to produce OER extends to tenure-track faculty, whose open educational resources may not be considered for P&T or valued as highly as materials from commercial publishers. Research and publications are weighed heavily for P&T, but peer-reviewed scholarship in high-impact journals is typically given more weight percent of faculty perceive that their institution recognizes or rewards instructor engagement with OER.[50] This perception is supported by the language of P&T guidelines. Ninety-one percent of university administrators reported that no language about open publications is included in their P&T guidelines, and only 17 percent have discussed adding OA and OER recognition to their P&T policies.[51] Lack of institutional support and incentives may understandably limit faculty's willingness to adopt or create OER.

McLaughlin, Versluis, and Hare outline these issues further in section 2.3.4, "Current Issues in the Field."

MYTHS AND MISCONCEPTIONS

The new and open nature of OER means that instructors, learners, and advocates learn about it through different pathways. They may not use the term *OER* or be familiar with all the details. They may conflate OER with other types of digital or emerging resources. This can turn the facts and messaging about OER into a game of telephone, with the associated level of distortion making its way in. Often, those new to OER will ask the same kind of questions or have perceptions based on traditional materials. While it is important to create a dialogue with instructors and learners that values their perspectives, those who advocate for OER, such as librarians or instructional designers, can work to stop the spread of misinformation. The ten myths discussed below are adapted from SPARC's *OER Mythbusting*.[52]

MYTH 1: *OPEN* SIMPLY MEANS FREE

Fact: *Open* means the permission to freely download, edit, and share materials to better serve all students.

Every day we encounter online resources that are free to read, watch, or listen to. However, there's a lot more to *open* than just being able to view something without cost. *Open* means that users have the permission to freely download, edit, and share educational resources to better serve all learners. Students can save copies of their assigned resources forever, and educators can tailor and update the content to meet course needs. While making resources free is a good first step, making them open taps into a world of expanded possibility.

Here are several examples of how students and educators have benefitted from the permissions that come with OER:
- Students and faculty at Brigham Young University took an openly licensed project management textbook and revised and remixed it as part of the course assignment.[53] This not only enhanced students' knowledge of the material, but also created an improved textbook for the next group of students in the course.
- A team of Canadian professors created a Canadian version of an American open sociology textbook, replacing content and examples with those that are relevant in a Canadian context.[54]
- Students who have completed any of the Textbook-Free courses at Tidewater Community College retain access to all of the course materials used during their studies.[55] These students are able to refer back to these materials in their future studies and are therefore better supported on their path of lifelong learning.

MYTH 2: ALL OER ARE DIGITAL

Fact: OER can be any format, whether digital or print.

Most modern educational resources—from textbooks to lectures—start out as digital files before being converted into other formats including (but not limited to) print and audio. The same goes for OER. Most OER start out as digital, but can be used in a wide variety of formats for many different devices. For example, an open textbook can be printed, read on a screen, or heard through text-to-speech technology. The difference between OER and traditional resources is that students and educators do not have to choose between formats. With traditional materials, students often need to purchase print books and e-books separately, and digital materials often carry an expiration date.

Here are a few examples of how OER exist in a variety of formats:

- Many open textbooks can be purchased through print-on-demand services made available by campus bookstores.
- OER are device-agnostic—students can simultaneously keep a printed copy at home, a mobile version to read on the bus on the way to school, and a browser-based version to use during class.
- OER can be legally converted from one format to another. This is especially helpful for campus disability services, who can create—and share—large-print, braille, or audio versions of OER text without seeking any additional permissions or navigating complex ADA-compliance systems.

MYTH 3: IF OER ARE FREE, THEY MUST BE LOW QUALITY

Fact: Whether resources are open or closed, faculty are the best judges of quality because they know their students' needs and are experts in the subject matter.

In this increasingly digital and internet-connected world, the old adage "You get what you pay for" is growing outdated. New models are developing across all aspects of society that dramatically reduce or eliminate costs to users, and this kind of innovation has spread to educational resources.

OER are created by experts in the field, instructors, and sometimes students. OER creators and publishers work to ensure the quality of their resources. Many open textbooks are created within rigorous editorial and peer-review guidelines, and many OER repositories allow faculty to review (and see others' reviews of) the material. There is also a growing body of evidence that demonstrates that OER can be both free of cost and high-quality—and more importantly, support positive student learning outcomes.

Here is evidence supporting the quality of OER:

- OpenStax—one of the most recognized open textbook publishers—created a library of seventy-three peer-reviewed, professional-grade open textbooks for college and high school courses, replicating a commercial production process. These books are kept up-to-date through a centrally controlled errata process.[56]
- The Open Textbook Library is a collection of over 1,000 open textbooks. Prospective users can read public reviews of the books written by disciplinary faculty, which assess the text through a star rating system and a ten-point rubric. While different from in-depth peer review, these ratings and reviews help instructors evaluate the suitability of OER for adoption.[57]
- *Blueprint for Success in College and Career*, an OER by Dave Dillon published by the Rebus Community, won a 2019 Textbook Excellence Award from the Textbook and Academic Authors Association, alongside traditionally published books.[58]

MYTH 4: COPYRIGHT FOR OER IS TOO COMPLICATED

Fact: Open licenses are often used in everyday life online. It makes OER easier to freely and legally use.

While copyright can be complex, all course materials carry some kind of copyright to consider when teaching. OER carry permissions for users to freely download, edit, and share content to better serve all students. These permissions are granted by the creator of an OER through an open license—a legal document that informs users of their right to retain, reuse, revise, remix, and redistribute the work (assuming the licensor applied a 5R compatible license). Open licensing is a simple, legal way for authors to keep their copyright and share their work under the terms and conditions they choose. We often see open licensing, such as Creative Commons, in everyday use online with many kinds of media (e.g., images, video, etc.).

Creative Commons (CC) licenses are a set of standard open licenses that are routinely used in the vast majority of OER. Compared to traditional copyright, CC licenses are easy to identify and provide clear instructions for reuse, and CC-licensed materials don't require any additional permission to use or adapt. To add an open license to a work, an author simply needs to include a copyright statement indicating that the resources carry a CC license and include a link to the specific license. It can be easier to get started by finding the right license to fit specific goals for using OER in a course and learn about other copyright aspects over time.

Here are some ways to learn about and provide support for CC licenses:

- Seek out the copyright specialist at your library or institution for help.
- Become familiar with the various CC license definitions[59] and the compatibility of licenses (see the Creative Commons license compatibility chart in subsection 2.3.2.3, "Day-to-Day OER Work," by Amanda Larson).
- To apply a CC license to a work, use the Creative Commons License Chooser tool.[60]
- When using CC-licensed content, tools such as the Washington State's Open Attribution Builder and the Creative Commons "Best Practices for Attribution" can help ensure proper attribution is given.[61]
- CC licenses can be compatible with non-CC-licensed content. The *Code of Best Practices in Fair Use for Open Educational Resources* is a great framework for exploring the role of fair use in OER.[62]

MYTH 5: OER ARE NOT SUSTAINABLE

Fact: Models are evolving to support the sustainability and continuous improvement of OER.

It takes time, expertise, and effort to develop high-quality educational resources, and there must be incentives and support models in place for OER to be sustainable in the long term. Incentives take many forms. Nonmonetary incentives include course release time or recognizing OER as a contribution toward tenure and promotion. Funding models include grants and up-front payments to authors to develop open resources. Commercial models are developing around important value-added services, such as professional development, curation, and customization. In fact, virtually all of the largest traditional publishing companies have launched services branded as OER.

Examples of models that support the sustainability and continuous improvement of OER include the following:

- Institutions such as UMass Amherst and North Carolina State University have developed OER grant programs where faculty can apply for funding to adopt, adapt, or create free or low-cost alternatives to expensive textbooks.[63] However, these funds are often not permanent or recurring.
- There is a move toward broader institutional commitments to supporting the sustainability of OER. For example, the administration at the University of Texas at Arlington

invested $500,000 to fund OER initiatives at UTA Libraries,[64] and the University of British Columbia invested $750,000 in the UBC OER program.[65]

- The OER Lab at Ontario Tech University employs undergraduate students to help develop course materials for Ontario Tech curriculum.[66] The OER Lab provides an opportunity for students to gain content development and project management skills while growing the collection of open course materials on their campus.
- The University of British Columbia formally recognizes OER as a contribution toward tenure and promotion as part of its Educational Leadership Stream.[67]

MYTH 6: OPEN TEXTBOOKS LACK ANCILLARIES, SUCH AS VIDEOS, LABS, LECTURES, AND SUPPLEMENTARY MATERIALS

Fact: Open textbooks often come with ancillaries, and when they do not, other existing OER can provide additional support.

Open textbooks may be the most recognizable form of OER, but, as OER are "materials in any format and medium,"[68] there are many other formats of educational resources that are openly licensed and can be adopted and remixed. OER can include video demonstrations, recorded lectures, lecture notes, lab activities, and many other supplementary materials. Some open textbooks are even designed with ancillary materials like homework packs and quizzes to support a full range of instructional needs.

Instructors increasingly expect commercial publishers to provide ancillary materials with textbooks, including lecture slides, images, videos, and homework platforms. This demand for ancillary materials is beginning to be met directly by open textbook publishers and commercial learning software companies that offer products complementary to open textbooks. There are also many repositories that hold openly licensed materials that can serve as ancillaries, including PowerPoint slides, videos, and simulations. Library staff can work with professors to help find these resources or share resources that other professors have already created. Teaching and learning staff on campus can also help with creating new ancillary resources, which themselves can be openly licensed and contributed to the commons.

Here are some examples of OER ancillary materials:

- OpenStax provides a free core set of ancillary resources available through its website for every book it publishes. OpenStax also offers a free OER Community Hub via OER Commons that includes user-created videos, homework assignments, student learning guides, and course syllabi.[69]
- The *Fundamentals of Business* User Group, hosted on OER Commons, facilitates sharing of openly licensed ancillary materials designed for use with the *Fundamentals of Business* (2016) textbook.[70]
- Traditional publishers have increasingly begun to offer software homework systems, particularly in STEM fields. MyOpenMath provides an open source alternative used by hundreds of campuses.[71]
- MIT OpenCourseWare is a popular source of openly available curricular resources, including ancillaries such as lecture notes, PowerPoint slides, and assessments from MIT course content.[72]

MYTH 7: MY INSTITUTION IS NOT READY FOR OER

Fact: Any institution can start with small steps toward OER that make an impact for students.

Changing institutional culture to support OER can start small. A single faculty member can exercise their academic freedom by choosing to replace traditional resources with OER—whether it's a set of supplementary simulations or an entire textbook. In some cases, faculty members may be using OER without even knowing it. For example, many YouTube videos and Flickr images are openly licensed, and textbooks published by projects like OpenStax are used at thousands of institutions.

If it seems like an institutional culture is not ready, seek individuals who have already taken steps toward OER or have expressed an interest in it, or who do work that is naturally aligned, such as general affordability advocates or those interested in innovative pedagogy. Colleagues within the library, teaching and learning centers, instructional design staff, faculty departments, student government, administrators, and campus stores can be great partners when starting an OER task force or campus program. Together, your group of open advocates can meet and exchange ideas for organizing larger efforts on campus. Every OER program started somewhere and learned along the way.

Check out these resources to learn what other campuses are doing on OER:

- Connect OER is a platform facilitated by SPARC to share and discover information about OER activities at campuses across North America.[73]
- Community College Consortium for OER (CCCOER) is a growing consortium of community and technical colleges committed to expanding access to education and increasing student success through adoption of open educational policy, practices, and resources.[74]
- Many institutions participate in the annual Open Education Week, hosted by Open Education Global, and share their OE Week events, resources, and highlights with the community.[75]

MYTH 8: OER HARM ACADEMIC FREEDOM

Fact: Open education supports true academic freedom.

If the use of OER (or any other type of content or practice) were mandated, this myth would be true, but that's generally not happening and would be opposed by open education advocates as a threat to academic freedom. Open education advocates aren't dogmatically committed to OER, but rather to the belief that OER constitute a vehicle toward better outcomes. The ability to adapt, update, and remix OER enables a new way of practicing academic freedom for faculty and instructional staff of all disciplines. Open licenses put the control of education back in the hands of faculty, researchers, instructional designers, and students. Open licensing allows for a community to grow: faculty can engage a broader spectrum of their peers in the creation, review, and revision process.

MYTH 9: AFFORDABLE RESOURCES ARE THE SAME AS OER

Fact: The 5 Rs are the crucial distinction between OER and other affordable resources such as library-licensed materials, inclusive access materials, or openwashed or faux-pen materials (e.g., an open textbook packaged with inseparable proprietary supplements, requiring the OER to be accessed at cost).

Affordable course materials exist on a spectrum. While increasingly affordable course materials are offered by publishers, campus bookstores, and libraries, these options may lack the flexibility of open materials. Only true OER afford instructors the ability to retain, reuse, revise, remix, and redistribute course materials. Figure 2.13 illustrates the range of materials on the spectrum of affordable resources.

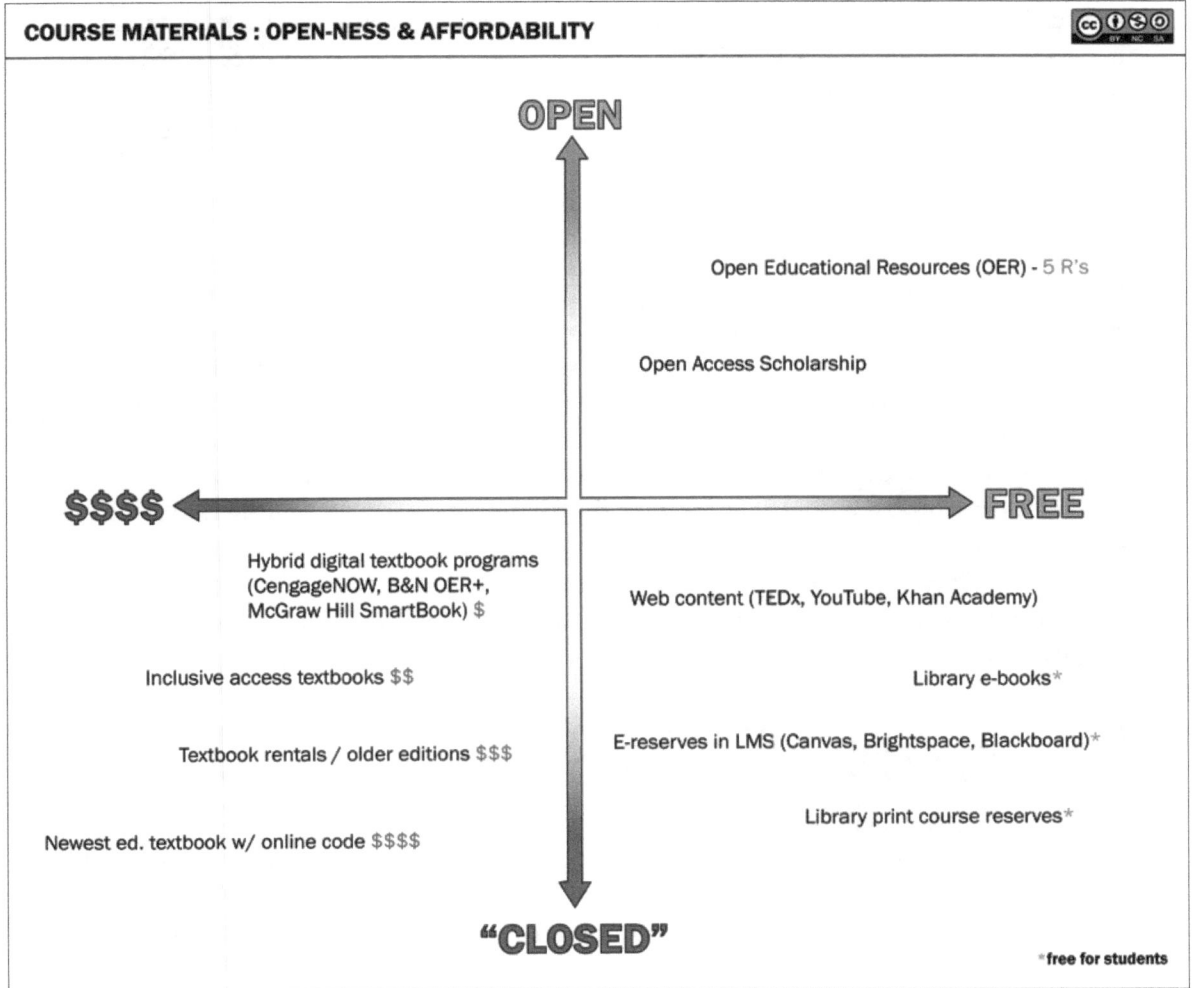

Figure 2.13
Course Materials: Open-ness and Affordability plots various types of course materials according to openness (on the y-axis) and cost (on the x-axis). In this model, OER are both open and free. Image from https://librarynews.lmu.edu/2020/03/jamie-hazlitt-on-the-open-and-affordable-textbook-initiative/, licensed CC-BY-NC-SA 4.0.

MYTH 10: ALL OUR STUDENTS ARE PRIVILEGED AND CAN AFFORD THE TEXTBOOK

Facts: Students come from diverse economic backgrounds.

This is a common misconception at private and public institutions alike. This myth assumes the majority of students have a privileged background, when in fact the student body in education is more economically diverse than ever before. Studies show that not only are students from low-income backgrounds disproportionately impacted by the cost of textbooks, they also perform better in courses when using OER or affordable alternatives.[76]

There is also a belief that any student savings would go toward frivolous spending. However, interviews conducted with college and university students about textbook afford-ability reveal that they are often choosing between textbook costs and critical living expenses such as food, housing, and transportation.[77] In some cases, students may be sending money home to their families or loved ones. While some may compare their experiences with budget-ing for higher education in the past eras to present day, it is not a fair comparison due to an unprecedented rise in course material and education expenses in general. This is especially true in the United States.

CONCLUSION

As OER gain popularity, students are benefitting from reduced expenses on textbooks and course materials, and institutions are seeing a rise in student success and retention in courses taught with OER. Instructors benefit from increased pedagogical freedom and flexibility in their courses. Despite these benefits, instructors still face barriers to creating and adopting OER, like lack of time and professional incentives and confusion about licenses and copyright. OER advocates on campus must be aware of the barriers to creating, adopting, and remixing open material in order to combat misinformation and argue for proper compensation for instructors' efforts to develop open and equitable educational resources. The open education movement is still growing, and dispelling myths about OER can help instructors and admin-istrators see the benefits of OER.

DISCUSSION QUESTIONS

1. What are the key benefits of OER?
2. What are the most significant barriers to the use of OER, and how might they be addressed?
3. What copyright and licensing resources are available to help instructors navigate open materials?
4. Where should instructors look for OER, and how do discovery systems impact finding OER?

NOTES

1. US Government Accountability Office, "College Textbooks: Students Have Greater Access to Textbook Information," June 6, 2013, https://www.gao.gov/products/GAO-13-368.
2. College Board, *Trends in College Pricing 2018*, Trends in Higher Education Series (New York: College Board, 2018), 10, https://trends.collegeboard.org/college-pricing/figures-tables/average-estimated-under-graduate-budgets-2018-19 (page discontinued).
3. Ethan Senack, *Fixing the Broken Textbook Market: How Students Respond to High Textbook Costs and Demand Alternatives* (USPIRG and the Student PIRGs, January 2014), https://uspirg.org/reports/usp/fixing-broken-textbook-market.
4. Virginia Clinton and Shafiq Khan, "Efficacy of Open Textbook Adoption on Learning Performance and Course Withdrawal Rates: A Meta-analysis," *AERA Open* 5, no. 3 (2019): 1–20, https://doi.org/10.1177/2332858419872212.
5. John Hilton III, "Open Educational Resources, Student Efficacy, and User Perceptions: A Synthesis of Research Published between 2015 and 2018," *Educational Technology Research and Development* 68 (2020): 853–76, https://doi.org/10.1007/s11423-019-09700-4.

6. SPARC, *Open Education Primer: An Introduction to Open Educational Resources, Practices and Policy for Academic Libraries*, ver. 1.0 (Washington, DC: SPARC, 2018), https://docs.google.com/document/d/1Shzgk23fO9MYUNWR38iga5o2Krzu95Uv_xpYCser_eE/edit.

7. SPARC, *Open Education Primer*, 8.

8. Tarah K. Ikahihifo et al., "Assessing the Savings from Open Educational Resources on Student Academic Goals," *International Review of Research in Open and Distributed Learning* 18, no. 7 (November 2017), http://www.irrodl.org/index.php/irrodl/article/view/2754/4442.

9. Ikahihifo et al., "Assessing the Savings."

10. C. Edward Watson, Denise P. Domizi, and Sherry A. Clouser, "Student and Faculty Perceptions of Open-stax in High Enrollment Courses," *International Review of Research in Open and Distributed Learning* 18, no. 5 (August 2017), http://www.irrodl.org/index.php/irrodl/article/view/2462/4299.

11. SPARC, *Open Education Primer*, 8.

12. Marie K. Fialkowski et al., "Open Educational Resource Textbook Impact on Students in an Introductory Nutrition Course," *Journal of Nutrition and Education Behavior* 52, no. 4 (2020): 359–68, https://doi.org/10.1016/j.jneb.2019.08.006.

13. SPARC, *Open Education Primer*, 8.

14. David Wiley and John Levi Hilton III, "Defining OER-Enabled Pedagogy," *International Review of Research in Open and Distributed Learning* 19, no. 4 (2018): 134–47, https://doi.org/10.19173/irrodl.v19i4.3601.

15. Dana Ayotte et al., "Personalizing Interfaces Using an Inclusive Design Approach," in *Universal Access in Human-Computer Interaction: Design and Development Methods for Universal Access*, ed. Constantine Stephanidis and Margherita Antona (Cham, Switzerland: Springer, 2014), 191–202; Jeff Gallant, "Even More Open: Inclusive Design in Open Educational Resources," Georgia Library Association Carterette Series Webinars, presented on October 27, 2021, https://gla.georgialibraries.org/carterette-series-webinars-archives/.

16. Nicholas B. Colvard, C. Edward Watson, and Hyojin Park, "The Impact of Open Educational Resources on Various Student Success Metrics," *International Journal of Teaching and Learning in Higher Education* 30, no. 2 (2018): 262–76, https://www.isetl.org/ijtlhe/pdf/IJTLHE3386.pdf.

17. Samuel Abramovich and Mark McBride, "Open Education Resources and Perceptions of Financial Value," *Internet and Higher Education* 39 (October 2018): 33–38, https://doi.org/10.1016/j.iheduc.2018.06.002.

18. Rajiv S. Jhangiani et al., *Exploring Faculty Use of Open Educational Resources at British Columbia Post-secondary Institutions*, BCcampus Research Report (Victoria, BC: BCcampus, 2016), https://bccampus.ca/wp-content/uploads/2016/01/BCFacultyUseOfOER_final.pdf.

19. David Wiley et al., "The Tidewater Z-Degree and the INTRO Model for Sustaining OER Adoption," *Education Policy Analysis Archives* 24, no. 41 (2016): 1–15, https://doi.org/10.14507/epaa.24.1828.

20. Kwantlen Polytechnic University, "Zero Textbook Cost," accessed June 29, 2022, https://www.kpu.ca/open/ztc.

21. Rebel Cummings-Sauls and Brian Lindshield, "Kansas State University," chapter 21 in *Marking Open and Affordable Courses: Best Practices and Case Studies*, ed. Sarah Hare, Jessica Kirschner, and Michelle Reed (Arlington, TX: Mavs Open Press, 2020), https://uta.pressbooks.pub/markingopenandaffordablecourses/chapter/kansas-state-university/.

22. Sarah Hare, Jessica Kirschner, and Michelle Reed, "Introduction," in *Marking Open and Affordable Courses: Best Practices and Case Studies*, ed. Sarah Hare, Jessica Kirschner, and Michelle Reed (Arlington, TX: Mavs Open Press, 2020), https://uta.pressbooks.pub/markingopenandaffordablecourses/front-matter/introduction/.

23. Open Education Group, "The COUP Framework," accessed June 23, 2022, https://openedgroup.org/coup.

24. Colvard, Watson, and Park, "Impact of Open Educational Resources"; John Hilton, Shawna Brandle, and Kathryn Suk, "Recent Research on OER" (presentation, Open Education Conference, Phoenix, AZ, October 30–November 1, 2019), https://opened19.exordo.com/programme/presentation/45; Ian McDermott, "Open to What? A Critical Evaluation of OER Efficacy Studies," *In the Library with the Lead Pipe*, February 19, 2020, http://www.inthelibrarywiththeleadpipe.org/2020/open-to-what/.

25. Sarah Hare, Jessica Kirschner, and Michelle Reed, "State and Federal Legislation," chapter 1 in *Marking Open and Affordable Courses: Best Practices and Case Studies*, ed. Sarah Hare, Jessica Kirschner, and Michelle Reed (Arlington, TX: Mavs Open Press, 2020), https://uta.pressbooks.pub/markingopenandaffordablecourses/chapter/state-and-federal-legislation/.

26. SPARC, *OER State Policy Playbook: 2021–22 Edition* (Washington, DC: SPARC, 2021), 2, https://sparcopen.org/our-work/oer-state-policy-playbook/.

27. SPARC, "OER State Policy Tracker," accessed June 23, 2022, https://sparcopen.org/our-work/state-policy-tracking/.

28. SPARC, "Open Textbook Pilot Grant Program," February 5, 2019, https://sparcopen.org/our-work/open-textbook-pilot/.

29. Fengchun Miao, Sanjaya Mishra, and Rory McGreal, *Open Educational Resources: Policy, Costs, Transformation* (Paris: UNESCO and Commonwealth of Learning, 2016), https://unesdoc.unesco.org/ark:/48223/pf0000244365.

30. Susan Huggins, "Coalition Formed to Support Implementation of UNESCO Open Educational Resources (OER) Recommendation," Open Education Consortium, November 28, 2019, https://www.oeconsortium.org/2019/11/coalition-formed-to-support-implementation-of-unesco-open-educational-resources-oer-recommendation/.

31. Rajiv Jhangiani, "Open Educational Practices in Service of the Sustainable Development Goals," Rajiv Jhangiani, Ph.D., website, October 18, 2018, https://thatpsychprof.com/open-educational-practices-in-service-of-the-sustainable-development-goals/.

32. Lindsay McKenzie, "Are Etextbooks Affordable Now?" Inside Higher Ed, May 1, 2018, https://www.insidehighered.com/digital-learning/article/2018/05/01/publishers-race-reduce-costs-digital-textbooks; Lindsay McKenzie, "Pearson's Next Chapter," Inside Higher Ed, July 16, 2019, https://www.insidehighered.com/digital-learning/article/2019/07/16/pearson-goes-all-digital-first-strategy-textbooks; Brian Barrett, "The Radical Transformation of the Textbook," *Wired*, August 4, 2019, https://www.wired.com/story/digital-textbooks-radical-transformation/.

33. McKenzie, "Are Etextbooks Affordable Now?"

34. Pearson, "Inclusive Access," accessed June 29, 2022, https://www.pearson.com/us/higher-education/products-services-institutions/inclusive-access/for-faculty.html; Macmillan Learning, "Macmillan Learning Inclusive Access," accessed June 29, 2022, https://www.macmillanlearning.com/college/us/solutions/inclusive-access.

35. InclusiveAccess.org, "What is Inclusive Access?" accessed August 15, 2022, https://www.inclusiveaccess.org/resources/what-is-inclusive-access.

36. Julia E. Seaman and Jeff Seaman, *Inflection Point: Educational Resources in U.S. Higher Education, 2019* (Oakland, CA: Bay View Analytics 2019), 25, https://www.onlinelearningsurvey.com/reports/2019inflectionpoint.pdf.

37. Seaman and Seaman, *Inflection Point.*

38. Center for Media and Social Impact, *Code of Best Practices in Fair Use for Open Educational Resources* (Center for Media and Social Impact, February 17, 2021), https://www.wcl.american.edu/impact/initiatives-programs/pijip/documents/code-of-best-practices-in-fair-use-for-open-educational-resources/.

39. Javier Atenas and Leo Havemann, "Questions of Quality in Repositories of Open Educational Resources: A Literature Review," *Research in Learning Technology* 22 (2014), https://doi.org/10.3402/rlt.v22.20889.

40. Melinda Boland et al., "OER Discovery Research: Librarian and Faculty Curation Personas" (adapted from presentation, Open Education Conference, virtual, October 18–22, 2021), https://www.oercommons.org/courseware/lesson/87668.

41. SPARC, "SPARC Libraries and OER Forum," accessed August 15, 2022, https://sparcopen.org/our-work/sparc-library-oer-forum/.

42. EBSCO, "EBSCO Faculty Select," accessed August 15, 2022, https://www.ebsco.com/products/ebsco-faculty-select.

43. Clare Sobotka, Holly Wheeler, and Heather White, "Leveraging Cataloging and Collection Development Expertise to Improve OER Discovery," *OLA Quarterly* 25, no. 1 (2019): 17–24, https://doi.org/10.7710/1093-7374.1971.

44. Christopher Brooks and Gord McCalla, "Towards Flexible Learning Object Metadata," *International Journal of Continuing Engineering Education and Life-Long Learning* 16, no. 1/2 (2006): 50–63, https://doi.org/10.1504/IJCEELL.2006.008917; Vivien Rolfe, "Web Strategies for the Curation and Discovery of Open Educational Resources," *Open Praxis* 8, no. 4 (October–December 2016): 297–312, https://doi.org/10.5944/openpraxis.8.4.305.

45. Carles Garcia-Lopez, Enric Mor, and Susanna Tesconi, "Human-Centered Design as an Approach to Create Open Educational Resources," *Sustainability* 12, no. 18 (2020): 7397, https://doi.org/10.3390/su12187397.

46. SPARC, *Open Education Primer*, 61.

47. Amanda Coolidge et al., *Accessibility Toolkit*, 2nd ed (BCcampus Open Education, 2018), https://opentextbc.ca/accessibilitytoolkit/.

48. American Association of University Professors, "Background Facts on Contingent Faculty Positions," accessed June 21, 2022, https://www.aaup.org/issues/contingency/background-facts.

49. Sarah Crissinger, "A Critical Take on OER Practices: Interrogating Commercialization, Colonialism, and Content," *In the Library with the Lead Pipe* , October 21, 2015, http://www.inthelibrarywiththeleadpipe.org/2015/a-critical-take-on-oer-practices-interrogating-commercialization-colonialism-and-content/.

50. Melissa Blankstein and Christine Wolff-Eisenberg, *Ithaka S+R US Faculty Survey 2018* (New York: Ithaka S+R, 2019), 48, https://doi.org/10.18665/sr.311199.

51. Becky Thoms, Dylan Burns, and Joshua Thoms, "Investigating Open Education and Promotion and Tenure in the United States" (presentation, Open Education Conference, Niagara Falls, NY, October 10–12, 2018), https://digitalcommons.usu.edu/lib_present/128/.

52. SPARC, *OER Mythbusting* (Washington, DC: SPARC, 2017), https://sparcopen.org/our-work/oer-mythbusting.

53. David Wiley et al., *Project Management for Instructional Designers* (EdTech Books, 2018), https://pm4id.org/.

54. William Little, *Introduction to Sociology*, 2nd Canadian ed. (BCcampus Open Education, 2016), https://opentextbc.ca/introductiontosociology2ndedition/.

55. Tidewater Community College, "Textbook-Free Courses," accessed August 15, 2022, https://www.tcc.edu/programs/specialty-programs/textbook-free/.

56. OpenStax, "Improving Educational Access and Learning for Everyone," accessed August 15, 2022, https://openstax.org/impact (page content changed).

57. Open Education Network, "Open Textbook Library," accessed August 15, 2022, https://open.umn.edu/opentextbooks/.

58. Textbook and Academic Authors Association, "Past TAA Textbook Award Winners," accessed August 15, 2022, https://www.taaonline.net/past-textbook-award-recipients.

59. Creative Commons, "About the Licenses," accessed August 15, 2022, https://creativecommons.org/licenses/.

60. Creative Commons, "License Chooser," accessed August 15, 2022, https://creativecommons.org/choose/.

61. Washington State Community and Technical Colleges, "Open Attribution Builder," accessed August 15, 2022, http://www.openwa.org/open-attrib-builder/; Creative Commons, "Best Practices for Attribution," last edited July 9, 2018, https://wiki.creativecommons.org/wiki/best_practices_for_attribution.

62. Center for Media and Social Impact, *Code of Best Practices*.

63. University of Massachusetts Amherst Libraries, "Open Educational Resources," accessed August 24, 2022, https://www.library.umass.edu/open-educational-resources/; North Carolina State University Libraries, "Alt-Textbook Project," accessed August 24, 2022, https://www.lib.ncsu.edu/alttextbook.

64. Alexandra Pirkle, "Transforming the Student Experience," news release, University of Texas Arlington, October 1, 2019, https://www.uta.edu/news/news-releases/2019/10/01/library-oer.

65. Sarah Zhao, "AMS Pushes for Millions of Dollars in Excellence Fund Allocation toward Student Priorities," Ubyssey, University of British Columbia, February 11, 2019, https://www.ubyssey.ca/news/ams-pushes-for-excellence-fund-allocation/.

66. Ontario Tech University, "OER Lab for Students," accessed August 24, 2022, https://learninginnovation.ontariotechu.ca/oer/creating/students.php.

67. Brady Yano, "Recognizing 'Open' in Tenure and Promotion at UBC," SPARC, April 14, 2017, https://sparcopen.org/news/2017/recognizing-open-tenure-promotion-ubc/.

68. UNESCO, *Recommendation on Open Educational Resources (OER)* (Paris: UNESCO, 2019), 5, https://unesdoc.unesco.org/ark:/48223/pf0000373755/PDF/373755eng.pdf.multi.page=3.

69. OER Commons, "OpenStax Hubs," accessed August 24, 2022, https://www.oercommons.org/hubs/OpenStax.

70. OER Commons, "*Fundamentals of Business*—User Group," accessed August 24, 2022, https://www.oercommons.org/groups/fundamentals-of-business-user-group/1379/.

71. MyOpenMath, "About Us," accessed August 24, 2022, https://www.myopenmath.com/info/aboutus.php.

72. Massachusetts Institute of Technology, "About MIT OpenCourseWare," accessed August 24, 2022, https://ocw.mit.edu/about/.

73. SPARC, "Connect OER," accessed August 24, 2022, https://sparcopen.org/our-work/connect-oer/.

74. Community College Consortium for OER, "About Us," accessed August 24, 2022, https://www.cccoer.org/about/about-cccoer/.

75. Open Education Global, "About OE Week," accessed August 24, 2022, https://www.oeglobal.org/activities/about-oe-week/.

76. Colvard, Watson, and Park, "Impact of Open Educational Resources."

77. Santa Ana College, "SAC Student Panel OpenEd 2017—Cost Factor," November 16, 2017, YouTube video, 7:03, https://www.youtube.com/watch?v=sZ6mTgQxG7A; Emma Whitman, "Textbook Trade-Offs," Inside Higher Ed, July 26, 2018, https://www.insidehighered.com/news/2018/07/26/students-sacrifice-meals-and-trips-home-pay-textbooks.

BIBLIOGRAPHY

Abramovich, Samuel, and Mark McBride. "Open Education Resources and Perceptions of Financial Value." *Internet and Higher Education* 39 (October 2018): 33–38. https://doi.org/10.1016/j.iheduc.2018.06.002.

American Association of University Professors. "Background Facts on Contingent Faculty Positions." Accessed June 21, 2022. https://www.aaup.org/issues/contingency/background-facts.

Atenas, Javier, and Leo Havemann. "Questions of Quality in Repositories of Open Educational Resources: A Literature Review." *Research in Learning Technology*, 22 (2014). https://doi.org/10.3402/rlt.v22.20889.

Ayotte, Dana, Joanna Vass, Jess Mitchell, and Jutta Treviranus. "Personalizing Interfaces Using an Inclusive Design Approach." In *Universal Access in Human-Computer Interaction: Design and Development Methods for Universal Access*, edited by Constantine Stephanidis and Margherita Antona, 191–202. Cham, Switzerland: Springer, 2014.

Barrett, Brian. "The Radical Transformation of the Textbook." *Wired*, August 4, 2019. https://www.wired.com/story/digital-textbooks-radical-transformation/.

Blankstein, Melissa, and Christine Wolff-Eisenberg. *Ithaka S+R US Faculty Survey 2018*. New York: Ithaka S+R, 2019. https://doi.org/10.18665/sr.311199.

Boland, Melinda, Sophie Rondeau, Cynthia Jimes, and Michelle Brennan. "OER Discovery Research: Librarian and Faculty Curation Personas." Adapted from presentation, Open Education Conference, virtual, October 18–22, 2021. https://www.oercommons.org/courseware/lesson/87668.

Brooks, Christopher, and Gord McCalla. "Towards Flexible Learning Object Metadata." *International Journal of Continuing Engineering Education and Life-Long Learning* 16, no. 1/2 (2006): 50–63. https://doi.org/10.1504/IJCEELL.2006.008917.

Center for Media and Social Impact. *Code of Best Practices in Fair Use for Open Educational Resources: A Guide For Authors, Adapters and Adopters of Openly Licensed Teaching and Learning Materials*. Center for Media and Social Impact, February 17, 2021. https://www.wcl.american.edu/impact/initiatives-programs/pijip/documents/code-of-best-practices-in-fair-use-for-open-educational-resources/.

Clinton, Virginia, and Shafiq Khan. "Efficacy of Open Textbook Adoption on Learning Performance and Course Withdrawal Rates: A Meta-analysis." *AERA Open* 5, no. 3 (2019): 1–20. https://doi.org/10.1177/2332858419872212.

College Board. *Trends in College Pricing 2018*. Trends in Higher Education Series. New York: College Board, 2018. https://trends.collegeboard.org/college-pricing/figures-tables/average-estimated-undergraduate-budgets-2018-19 (page discontinued).

Colvard, Nicholas B., C. Edward Watson, and Hyojin Park. "The Impact of Open Educational Resources on Various Student Success Metrics." *International Journal of Teaching and Learning in Higher Education* 30, no. 2 (2018): 262–76. https://www.isetl.org/ijtlhe/pdf/IJTLHE3386.pdf.

Community College Consortium for OER. "About Us." Accessed August 24, 2022. https://www.cccoer.org/about/about-cccoer/.

Coolidge, Amanda, Sue Doner, Tara Robertson, and Josie Gray. *Accessibility Toolkit*, 2nd ed. BCcampus Open Education, 2018. https://opentextbc.ca/accessibilitytoolkit/.

Creative Commons. "About the Licenses." Accessed August 15, 2022. https://creativecommons.org/licenses/.

———. "Best Practices for Attribution." Last edited July 9, 2018. https://wiki.creativecommons.org/wiki/best_practices_for_attribution.

———. "License Chooser." Accessed August 15, 2022. https://creativecommons.org/choose/.

Crissinger, Sarah. "A Critical Take on OER Practices: Interrogating Commercialization, Colonialism, and Content." *In the Library with the Lead Pipe*, October 21, 2015. http://www.inthelibrarywiththeleadpipe.org/2015/a-critical-take-on-oer-practices-interrogating-commercialization-colonialism-and-content/.

Cummings-Sauls, Rebel, and Brian Lindshield. "Kansas State University." Chapter 21 in *Marking Open and Affordable Courses: Best Practices and Case Studies*, edited by Sarah Hare, Jessica Kirschner, and Michelle Reed. Arlington, TX: Mavs Open Press, 2020. https://uta.pressbooks.pub/markingopenandaffordablecourses/chapter/kansas-state-university/.

EBSCO. "EBSCO Faculty Select." Accessed August 15, 2022. https://www.ebsco.com/products/ebsco-faculty-select.

Elder, Abbey. "An Introduction to Open Educational Resources." In *The OER Starter Kit*. Ames: Iowa State University Digital Press, 2019. https://iastate.pressbooks.pub/oerstarterkit/chapter/introduction/.

Fialkowski, Marie K., Allison Calabrese, Beth Tilinghast, Alan Titchenal, William Meinke, Jinan C. Banna, and Jennifer Draper. "Open Educational Resource Textbook Impact on Students in an Introductory Nutrition Course." *Journal of Nutrition and Education Behavior* 52, no. 4 (2020): 359–68. https://doi.org/10.1016/j.jneb.2019.08.006.

Gallant, Jeff. "Even More Open: Inclusive Design in Open Educational Resources." Georgia Library Association Carterette Series Webinars, presented on October 27, 2021. https://gla.georgialibraries.org/carterette-series-webinars-archives/

Garcia-Lopez, Carles, Enric Mor, and Susanna Tesconi. "Human-Centered Design as an Approach to Create Open Educational Resources." *Sustainability* 12, no. 18 (2020): 7397. https://doi.org/10.3390/su12187397.

Hare, Sarah, Jessica Kirschner, and Michelle Reed. "Introduction." In *Marking Open and Affordable Courses: Best Practices and Case Studies*, edited by Sarah Hare, Jessica Kirschner, and Michelle Reed. Arlington, TX: Mavs Open Press, 2020. https://uta.pressbooks.pub/markingopenandaffordablecourses/front-matter/introduction/.

———. "State and Federal Legislation." Chapter 1 in *Marking Open and Affordable Courses: Best Practices and Case Studies*, edited by Sarah Hare, Jessica Kirschner, and Michelle Reed. Mavs Open Press, 2020. https://uta.pressbooks.pub/markingopenandaffordablecourses/chapter/state-and-federal-legislation/.

Hilton, John, III. "Open Educational Resources, Student Efficacy, and User Perceptions: A Synthesis of Research Published between 2015 and 2018." *Educational Technology Research and Development* 68 (2020): 853–76. https://doi.org/10.1007/s11423-019-09700-4.

Hilton, John, Shawna Brandle, and Kathryn Suk. "Recent Research on OER." Presentation, Open Education Conference, Phoenix, AZ, October 30–November 1, 2019. https://opened19.exordo.com/programme/presentation/45

Hofer, Amy. "Estimating Student Savings from No-Cost/Low-Cost Course Materials." Open Oregon Educational Resources, April 19, 2018. https://openoregon.org/estimating-student-savings-from-no-cost-low-cost-course-materials/.

———. "Is the Average Cost of a Textbook $100?" Open Oregon Educational Resources, February 17, 2017. https://openoregon.org/is-the-average-cost-of-a-textbook-100/.

Huggins, Susan. "Coalition Formed to Support Implementation of UNESCO Open Educational Resources (OER) Recommendation." Open Education Consortium, November 28, 2019. https://www.oeconsortium.org/2019/11/coalition-formed-to-support-implementation-of-unesco-open-educational-resources-oer-recommendation/.

Ikahihifo, Tarah K., Kristian J. Spring, Jane Rosecrans, and Josh Watson. "Assessing the Savings from Open Educational Resources on Student Academic Goals." *International Review of Research in Open and Distributed Learning* 18, no. 7 (November 2017). http://www.irrodl.org/index.php/irrodl/article/view/2754/4442.

InclusiveAccess.org. "What Is Inclusive Access?" Accessed August 15, 2022. https://www.inclusiveaccess.org/resources/what-is-inclusive-access.

Jhangiani, Rajiv. "Open Educational Practices in Service of the Sustainable Development Goals." Rajiv Jhangiani, Ph.D., website, October 18, 2018. https://thatpsychprof.com/open-educational-practices-in-service-of-the-sustainable-development-goals/.

Jhangiani, Rajiv S., Rebecca Pitt, Christina Hendricks, Jessica Key, and Clint Lalonde. *Exploring Faculty Use of Open Educational Resources at British Columbia Postsecondary Institutions*. BCcampus Research Report. Victoria, BC: BCcampus, 2016. https://bccampus.ca/wp-content/uploads/2016/01/BCFacultyUseOfOER_final.pdf.

Kwantlen Polytechnic University. "Zero Textbook Cost." Accessed June 29, 2022. https://www.kpu.ca/open/ztc.

Little, William. *Introduction to Sociology*, 2nd Canadian ed. BCcampus Open Education, 2016. https://opentextbc.ca/introductiontosociology2ndedition/.

Macmillan Learning. "Macmillan Learning Inclusive Access." Accessed June 29, 2022. https://www.macmillanlearning.com/college/us/solutions/inclusive-access.

Massachusetts Institute of Technology. "About MIT OpenCourseWare." Accessed August 24, 2022. https://ocw.mit.edu/about/.

McDermott, Ian. "Open to What? A Critical Evaluation of OER Efficacy Studies." *In the Library with the Lead Pipe*, February 19, 2020. http://www.inthelibrarywiththeleadpipe.org/2020/open-to-what/.

McKenzie, Lindsay. "Are Etextbooks Affordable Now?" Inside Higher Ed, May 1, 2018. https://www.insidehighered.com/digital-learning/article/2018/05/01/publishers-race-reduce-costs-digital-textbooks.

———. "Pearson's Next Chapter." Inside Higher Ed. July 16, 2019. https://www.insidehighered.com/digital-learning/article/2019/07/16/pearson-goes-all-digital-first-strategy-textbooks.

Miao, Fengchun, Sanjaya Mishra, and Rory McGreal. *Open Educational Resources: Policy, Costs, Transformation*. Paris: UNESCO and Commonwealth of Learning, 2016. https://unesdoc.unesco.org/ark:/48223/pf0000244365.

MyOpenMath. "About Us." Accessed August 24, 2022. https://www.myopenmath.com/info/aboutus.php.

North Carolina State University Libraries. "Alt-Textbook Project." Accessed August 24, 2022. https://www.lib.ncsu.edu/alttextbook.

Nyamweya, Mo. "A New Method for Estimating OER Savings." SPARC. December 20, 2018. https://sparcopen.org/news/2018/estimating-oer-student-savings/.

OER Commons. "Fundamentals of Business—User Group." Accessed August 24, 2022. https://www.oercommons.org/groups/fundamentals-of-business-user-group/1379/.

———. "OpenStax Hubs." Accessed August 24, 2022. https://www.oercommons.org/hubs/OpenStax.

Ontario Tech University. "OER Lab for Students." Accessed August 24, 2022. https://learninginnovation.ontariotechu.ca/oer/creating/students.php.

Open Education Global. "About OE Week." Accessed August 24, 2022. https://www.oeglobal.org/activities/about-oe-week/.

Open Education Group. "The COUP Framework." Accessed June 23, 2022. https://openedgroup.org/coup.

Open Education Network. "Open Textbook Library." Accessed August 15, 2022. https://open.umn.edu/opentextbooks/.

OpenStax. "Improving Educational Access and Learning for Everyone." Accessed August 15, 2022. https://openstax.org/impact (page content changed).

Pearson. "Inclusive Access." Accessed June 29, 2022. https://www.pearson.com/us/higher-education/products-services-institutions/inclusive-access/for-faculty.html.

Pirkle, Alexandra. "Transforming the Student Experience." News release. University of Texas Arlington, October 1, 2019. https://www.uta.edu/news/news-releases/2019/10/01/library-oer.

Rolfe, Vivien. "Web Strategies for the Curation and Discovery of Open Educational Resources." *Open Praxis* 8, no. 4 (October–December 2016): 297–312. https://doi.org/10.5944/openpraxis.8.4.305.

Santa Ana College. "SAC Student Panel OpenEd 2017—Cost Factor." November 16, 2017. YouTube video, 7:03. https://www.youtube.com/watch?v=sZ6mTgQxG7A.

Seaman, Julia E., and Jeff Seaman. *Inflection Point: Educational Resources in U.S. Higher Education, 2019.* Oakland, CA: Bay View Analytics, 2019. https://www.onlinelearningsurvey.com/reports/2019inflectionpoint.pdf.

Senack, Ethan. *Fixing the Broken Textbook Market: How Students Respond to High Textbook Costs and Demand Alternatives.* USPIRG and the Student PIRGs, January 2014. https://uspirg.org/reports/usp/fixing-broken-textbook-market.

Sobotka, Clare, Holly Wheeler, and Heather White. "Leveraging Cataloging and Collection Development Expertise to Improve OER Discovery." *OLA Quarterly* 25, no. 1 (2019): 17–24. https://doi.org/10.7710/1093-7374.1971.

SPARC. "Connect OER." Accessed August 24, 2022. https://sparcopen.org/our-work/connect-oer/.

———. *OER Mythbusting.* Washington, DC: SPARC, 2017. https://sparcopen.org/our-work/oer-mythbusting.

———. *OER State Policy Playbook: 2021–22 Edition.* Washington, DC: SPARC, 2021. https://sparcopen.org/our-work/oer-state-policy-playbook/.

———. "OER State Policy Tracker." Accessed June 23, 2022. https://sparcopen.org/our-work/state-policy-tracking/.

———. *Open Education Primer: An Introduction to Open Educational Resources, Practices and Policy for Academic Libraries,* ver. 1.0. Washington, DC: SPARC, 2018. https://docs.google.com/document/d/1Shzgk23fO9MYUNWR38iga5o2Krzu95Uv_xpYCser_eE/edit.

———. "Open Textbook Pilot Grant Program." February 5, 2019. https://sparcopen.org/our-work/open-textbook-pilot/.

———. "SPARC Libraries and OER Forum." Accessed August 15, 2022. https://sparcopen.org/our-work/sparc-library-oer-forum/.

Textbook and Academic Authors Association. "Past TAA Textbook Award Winners." Accessed August 15, 2022. https://www.taaonline.net/past-textbook-award-recipients.

Thoms, Becky, Dylan Burns, and Joshua Thoms. "Investigating Open Education and Promotion and Tenure in the United States." Presentation, Open Education Conference, Niagara Falls, NY, October 10–12, 2018. https://digitalcommons.usu.edu/lib_present/128/.

Tidewater Community College. "Textbook-Free Courses." Accessed August 15, 2022. https://www.tcc.edu/programs/specialty-programs/textbook-free/.

UNESCO. *Recommendation on Open Educational Resources (OER).* Paris: UNESCO, 2019. https://unesdoc.unesco.org/ark:/48223/pf0000373755/PDF/373755eng.pdf.multi.page=3.

University of Massachusetts Amherst Libraries. "Open Educational Resources." Accessed August 24, 2022. https://www.library.umass.edu/open-educational-resources/.

US Government Accountability Office. "College Textbooks: Students Have Greater Access to Textbook Information." June 6, 2013. https://www.gao.gov/products/GAO-13-368.

Washington State Community and Technical Colleges. "Open Attribution Builder." Accessed August 15, 2022. http://www.openwa.org/open-attrib-builder/.

Watson, C. Edward, Denise P. Domizi, and Sherry A. Clouser. "Student and Faculty Perceptions of Openstax in High Enrollment Courses." *International Review of Research in Open and Distributed Learning* 18, no. 5 (August 2017). https://www.irrodl.org/index.php/irrodl/article/view/2462/4299.

Whitford, Emma. "Textbook Trade-Offs." Inside Higher Ed, July 26, 2018. https://www.insidehighered.com/news/2018/07/26/students-sacrifice-meals-and-trips-home-pay-textbooks.

Wiley, David, M. Amado, K. Ashton, S. Ashton, J. Bostwick, G. Clements, J. Drysdale, J. Francis, B. Harrison, V. Nan, et al. *Project Management for Instructional Designers.* EdTech Books, 2018. https://pm4id.org/.

Wiley, David, and John Levi Hilton III. "Defining OER-Enabled Pedagogy." *International Review of Research in Open and Distributed Learning* 19, no. 4 (2018): 134–47. https://doi.org/10.19173/irrodl.v19i4.3601.

Wiley, David, Linda Williams, Daniel DeMarte, and John Hilton. "The Tidewater Z-Degree and the INTRO Model for Sustaining OER Adoption." *Education Policy Analysis Archives* 24, no. 41 (2016): 1–15. https://doi.org/10.14507/epaa.24.1828.

Yano, Brady. "Recognizing "Open" in Tenure and Promotion at UBC." SPARC, April 14, 2017. https://sparcopen.org/news/2017/recognizing-open-tenure-promotion-ubc/.

Zhao, Sarah. "AMS Pushes for Millions of Dollars in Excellence Fund Allocation toward Student Priorities." Ubyssey, University of British Columbia, February 11, 2019. https://www.ubyssey.ca/news/ams-pushes-for-excellence-fund-allocation/.

LIBRARIES AND OPEN EDUCATIONAL RESOURCES

WHY LIBRARIES? WHY LIBRARIANS?

Regina Gong

As you learned in subsection 2.3.1.1, "Introduction to Open Education," open education is part of the broader movement to democratize education.[1] With its underlying values based on the principles of "access, agency, ownership, participation, and experience, open education has the potential to become a great global equalizer."[2] Similarly, open educational resources (OER) have the potential to provide broader access to higher education and to significantly improve the learning experience of students and globally diverse learners. In this section, you will learn the vital role that libraries and librarians play in leading an OER initiative and why it is imperative that we get institutional support and buy-in to advance the goals of open education.

At their very core, academic libraries are diverse knowledge ecosystems that provide a wide range of services and resources to the university writ large. Because of this, libraries play a significant role in supporting the teaching, learning, research, and outreach mission of their institutions. Engaging in open education initiatives is a natural fit because of the alignment between the library's core values of providing free and equitable access to information and its fundamental principles of access, agency, ownership, and the affordability benefits inherent in OER. An advocate for access to information and a key campus player in student learning, academic libraries are an essential partner in OER initiatives and a potentially powerful voice for more affordable learning resources.[3] Libraries and OER share commonalities because both emphasize removing barriers to knowledge and resources. Kleymeer, Kleinman, and Hanss make a case for their synergy:

> Academic OER initiatives and university libraries share a determination to improve access to all kinds of scholarly and educational materials, both on their campuses and throughout the world. Given those dovetailing values, partnerships between OER initiatives and libraries seem not just logistically convenient but philosophically obvious.[4]

In addition to this philosophical convergence, there are two key advantages that many academic libraries can offer, which an OER initiative needs: infrastructure and relationships. When we talk about library infrastructures, these refer to existing assets that could potentially benefit OER initiatives, which include search and discovery capabilities, copyright expertise, data storage, metadata and indexing, institutional repositories, and preservation.[5] Since OER adoptions take place in academic departments, OER initiatives that are acting as stand-alone units without library involvement might be duplicating infrastructure and consequently may be missing opportunities to use the library's existing and proven systems.[6] With regard to relationships, libraries have "a central and trusted position in the lives of faculty, students, and administrators on their campuses."[7] And despite the changes brought by technology and the broader and unmediated access to scholarly and educational content online, libraries are still as relevant as ever. Librarians can offer their skills and expertise in outreach and education, curriculum development, and instructional support, all of which could benefit OER programs.

LIBRARIES AS LEADERS IN OER

We have so far discussed the alignment between the core principles of open education and the library's values. Bell also mentions the alignment between the open access (OA) movement and OER, which both put "academic libraries on a trajectory to build cultures of openness at their institutions."[8] The institutional-level leadership in open education that libraries provide to support the strategic goals of affordability, access, equity, and student success makes them ideally suited to spearhead OER programs on college campuses. We can see the crucial position and transformative influence of OER on the future of academic libraries in reports published by professional and educational organizations. An example is the biennial report by the Association of College and Research Libraries (ACRL) "Top Trends in Academic Libraries,"[9] which reviews the top trends in higher education as they relate to academic libraries. Due in large part to the proliferation of OER programs in college campuses and the libraries' leadership in these initiatives, textbook affordability and OER made the list both in the 2016 and 2018 reports. In addition, the *2020 EDUCAUSE Horizon Report* has named OER as one of the emerging technologies and practices shaping higher education.[10]

The proliferation of OER is a "disruptive innovation that many instructors embrace for ethical, practical, and financial reasons, with the financial reasons often spearheading such experiments."[11] Due to a strong connection between the benefits of open education and the mission of libraries, it is not surprising that libraries are involved in a wide range of OER and other textbook affordability initiatives. Most OER programs initially start with the goal of eliminating barriers to cost and improving access to educational materials as a way to address the textbook affordability crisis that college students have been facing for decades. Removing the cost and access barriers associated with traditional course materials has been the primary drivers for implementing an OER or affordable textbook programs on many campuses. Library strategies toward achieving these goals usually combine the use of open textbooks, freely available online materials, library-subscribed or purchased e-books, and textbooks on course reserves. This strategy leverages the investment libraries make in their collections and allows faculty to redesign courses based on free or more affordable options if open textbooks are not available. However, as you have learned in section 2.3.1, "Introduction to Open Education," the benefits of OER extend beyond affordability and access. Because of the flexible nature of OER enabled through the freedoms brought about by open licenses, these materials can be modified and adapted to meet students' unique learning needs.

Library-led OER projects have focused on making content that supports existing traditional forms of instruction openly and freely available. In these projects, the power of the internet is used to overcome barriers to access by serving as a medium for freely distributing content. Making existing content available in this way is based on the revolutionary idea that education and discovery are best advanced when knowledge is shared openly. These OER projects have enabled a great leap forward in democratizing access to educational materials.[12]

It is also important to note that academic libraries are not just leading OER programs in their own institutions. Several libraries have assumed leadership roles at state and national levels to promote OER, providing support and professional development to faculty and making business case arguments for the use of OER in improving college affordability and student success. These are essential activities for libraries, both for the successful proliferation of OER use and for demonstrating the value of libraries to their institutions.[13]

Examples of state OER programs led by libraries:

- *OpenOregon Educational Resources* (https://openoregon.org/about/)—Provides training, webinars, consultations, and technical infrastructure needed to help educators in the state to engage in the adoption and creation of openly licensed materials.
- *Private Academic Library Network of Indiana* (https://www.palni.org/about-palni/)— Provides training and professional development to the member institutions of PALNI to raise awareness on scholarly communication issues including open access and OER.
- *Affordable Learning Georgia* (https://www.affordablelearninggeorgia.org/)—An initiative that promotes the development and use of OER through statewide grant funding and professional development and training resources that are open to all.
- *Affordable Learning PA* (https://www.affordablelearningpa.org/)—Supports a robust OER community among campuses in Pennsylvania for the creation and use of open textbooks and other related educational resources. It is a grant-funded project made possible in part by Library Services and Technology Act (LSTA) funds from the US Institute of Museum and Library Services and the Office of Commonwealth Libraries, Department of Education, Commonwealth of Pennsylvania.

It's clear that librarians and libraries are essential leaders and partners in promoting and supporting OER.

THE EVOLVING ROLE OF LIBRARIANS

As libraries continue to engage and support open education initiatives, the nature and scope of our work have changed and evolved in response to the unique context of our institutions. Discussions about how librarians might engage in OER have their beginnings in the 2009 ACRL/SPARC forum at the ALA Midwinter meeting, where leading experts convened to talk about what might be some opportunities for librarians in this area.[14] In summarizing the recommendations of the panel, Belliston states that "Librarians can help by contributing their own OER to the commons; screening for, indexing, and archiving quality OER; using OER in their own teaching; and participating in discussions leading toward responsible intellectual property policies and useful standards."[15]

As a growing number of librarians become heavily involved in OER initiatives, their roles have expanded in areas such as advocacy, promotion, and discovery; evaluation, collection, and preservation; curation and facilitation; and funding.[16] Other areas where the library might be involved are in resource description, classification, management, dissemination, intellectual property and licensing rights, use, creation or repurposing of OER, search engine optimization, e-learning, and content management tools.[17] And as libraries increasingly engage in OER publishing efforts, librarians have also become an invaluable source of support for open textbook publishing, project management, instructional design, and user experience, and as a resource to enable faculty to engage in open educational practices.

We will discuss in more detail the work involved in each of these areas, the various OER services that libraries provide, and the day-to-day work of librarians in the next two subsections. But for now, we will look at the expertise we bring to an OER initiative so we can make a case for librarians as not only allies but as partners and leaders in building and sustaining an OER program.

LIBRARIAN EXPERTISE

One of the distinctive strengths that librarians bring to any organization is our "broad and deep knowledge of the ecosystems of research and scholarship."[18] This comes from our expertise honed from our LIS education, ongoing professional development, plus our practical experience working with library colleagues, faculty, students, and other academic staff on our campuses. Not only is our professional training and expertise an ideal fit for open education leadership, but more importantly, our work directly supports the teaching and learning missions of our institutions. Many librarians have liaison responsibilities that enable us to collaborate with faculty from different academic departments. We can certainly capitalize on these existing connections and relationships in our role as open education advocates. The report from the Library as Open Education Leader (LOEL) project makes a compelling case for librarians and why we are particularly suited to do this work:

> To be an academic librarian is to be a leader in instruction, a student advocate, a faculty advocate, and a generalist with the ability to specialize enough to serve the needs of the student or faculty member when needed. Librarians can help to locate and organize OER, but they can also navigate copyright concerns, advise on open licensing, and support instructional design around the use of open materials. Librarians are natural open education advocates because they are most often trusted by the majority of people. The role of the advocate is to support the overall goals of exemplary learning experiences and equity of access to education. As a librarian, you are particularly suited to this work because you have probably been doing it for your entire career.[19]

The excerpt above suggests that we can leverage our existing skills and competencies in support of open education. Given that OER work is always a team-based approach, there is a range of expertise each librarian can bring to the table that intersects with our job responsibilities and roles. Cross identifies the librarian expertise and roles for building and developing an OER,[20] and though not exhaustive, table 2.8 might provide us with a general sense of what it entails.

So far, we have seen how library involvement, support, and participation are crucial to the success of any open education initiative. Indeed, librarians are not just allies and advocates but critical partners and collaborators in advancing education that is accessible, equitable, and more open for all.

TABLE 2.8
Librarian roles and expertise.

Type of Librarian	Expertise	Role
Collections, acquisitions, and subject specialist	Acquisition, collection development Table, relationship building	Content licensing, negotiating usage, customizing materials
Reference and instruction	Identifying materials, instructional design, information and digital literacy	Course design, content discovery, teaching and pedagogy support
Special collections	Preservation, rare materials, exhibits	Locating unique materials, sustainability
Digital management/digital curation	Web design, hosting, streaming media, learning management platforms, user experience	Creating digital materials, web hosting, open textbook publishing, authoring and annotation tools
Scholarly communication	Open licensing, fair use, copyright, data management, institutional repositories	Using 3rd-party systems, incorporating open materials into courses, accessibility

ADDITIONAL RESOURCES AND FURTHER READING

Association of College and Research Libraries. "Top Trends in Academic Libraries: A Review of the Trends and Issues Affecting Academic Libraries in Higher Education."

———. 2020—*College and Research Libraries News* 81, no. 6. https://crln.acrl.org/index.php/crlnews/article/view/24478.

———. 2016—*College and Research Libraries News* 77, no. 6. https://crln.acrl.org/index.php/crlnews/article/view/9505/10798.

Iiyoshi, Toru, and M. S. Vijay Kumar, eds. *Opening Up Education: The Collective Advancement of Open Education through Open Technology, Open Content, and Open Knowledge.* Cambridge, MA: MIT Press, 2008. https://library.oapen.org/bitstream/handle/20.500.12657/26069/1004016.pdf?sequence=1

McKernan, Rowena, Tria Skirko, Quill West, and Library as Open Education Leader. *Librarians as Open Education Advocates: Readings on Being an Open Advocate.* https://openedadvocates.pressbooks.com/.

Pelletier, Kathe, Malcolm Brown, D. Christopher Brooks, Mark McCormack, Jamie Reeves, and Nichole Arbino, with Aras Bozkurt, Steven Crawford, Laura Czerniewicz, Rob Gibson, Katie Linder, Jon Mason, and Victoria Mondelli. *2021 EDUCAUSE Horizon Report, Teaching and Learning Edition.* Boulder, CO: EDUCAUSE, 2021. https://www.educause.edu/horizon-report-2021.

Wesolek, Andrew, Jonathan Lashley, and Anne Langley. *OER: A Field Guide for Academic Librarians.* Forest Grove, OR: Pacific University Press, 2018. https://open.umn.edu/opentextbooks/textbooks/652

NOTES

1. Patrick Blessinger and T. J. Bliss. "Introduction to Open Education: Towards a Human Rights Theory," in *Open Education: International Perspectives in Higher Education*, ed. Patrick Blessinger and T. J. Bliss, (Cambridge: Open Book Publishers, 2016), 11.
2. David Kahle, "Designing Open Educational Technology," in *Opening Up Education: The Collective Advancement of Open Education through Open Technology, Open Content, and Open Knowledge*, ed. Toru Iiyoshi and M.S. Vijay Kumar (Cambridge, MA: MIT Press, 2008), 30.
3. Karen Okamoto, "Making Higher Education More Affordable, One Course Reading at a Time: Academic Libraries as Key Advocates for Open Access Textbooks and Educational Resources," *Public Services Quarterly* 9, no. 4 (2013): 270, https://doi.org/10.1080/15228959.2013.842397.
4. Pieter Kleymeer, Molly Kleinman, and Ted Hanss, "Reaching the Heart of the University: Libraries and the Future of OER" (paper, 7th Annual Open Education Conference, Barcelona, Spain, November 2–4, 2010), 3, https://deepblue.lib.umich.edu/bitstream/handle/2027.42/78006/ReachingtheHeartoftheUniversity-KleymeerKleinmanHanss.pdf?sequence=1&isAllowed=y.
5. Kleymeer, Kleinman, and Hanss, "Reaching the Heart," 4.
6. Gema Bueno-de-la-Fuente, Robert J. Robertson, and Stuart Boon, "The roles of libraries and information professionals in Open Educational Resources (OER) initiatives," (2012).
7. Kleymeer, Kleinman, and Hanss, "Reaching the Heart," 5.
8. Steven Bell, *Course Materials Adoption: A Faculty Survey and Outlook for the OER Landscape*, white paper (Chicago: ACRL/Choice, 2018), 6, https://www.choice360.org/research/course-materials-adoption-a-faculty-survey-and-outlook-for-the-oer-landscape/.
9. ACRL Research Planning and Review Committee, "2018 Top Trends in Academic Libraries," *College and Research Libraries News* 79, no. 6 (2018): 286–300, https://crln.acrl.org/index.php/crlnews/article/view/17001/18750.
10. Malcolm Brown et al., *2020 EDUCAUSE Horizon Report: Teaching and Learning Edition* (Louisville, CO: EDUCAUSE, 2020), https://www.educause.edu/horizon-report-2020.
11. Linda Vanasupa et al., "What Does it Mean to Open Education? Perspectives on Using Open Educational Resources at a US Public University," in *Open Education: International Perspectives in Higher Education*, ed. Patrick Blessinger and T. J. Bliss (Cambridge: Open Book Publishers, 2016), 200.
12. Candace Thille, "Building Open Learning as a Community-Based Research Activity," in *Opening Up Education: The Collective Advancement of Open Education through Open Technology, Open Content, and Open Knowledge*, ed. Toru Iiyoshi and M. S. Vijay Kumar (Cambridge, MA: MIT Press, 2008), 165, https://library.oapen.org/bitstream/handle/20.500.12657/26069/1004016.pdf?sequence=1.
13. Robin Colson, Elijah Scott, and Robin Donaldson, "Supporting Librarians in Making the Business Case for OER," *Reference Librarian* 58, no. 4 (2017): 278–87, https://doi.org/10.1080/02763877.2017.1377665.
14. Carmen Kazakoff-Lane, *Environmental Scan and Assessment of OERs, MOOCs, and Libraries*, white paper (Chicago: Association of College and Research Libraries, 2014), http://www.ala.org/acrl/sites/ala.org.acrl/files/content/publications/whitepapers/Environmental%20Scan%20and%20Assessment.pdf.
15. C. Jeffrey Belliston, "Open Educational Resources: Creating the Instruction Commons," *College and Research Libraries News* 70, no. 5 (2009): 284-303, https://doi.org/10.5860/crln.70.5.8183.
16. Okamoto, "Making Higher Education More Affordable," 271.
17. Bueno-de-la-Fuente, Robertson, and Boon, *Roles of Libraries*, 7.
18. Nancy Sims, "'Protecting' Our Works—From What?" in *Open Access and the Future of Scholarly Communication: Implementation*, ed. Kevin L. Smith and Katherine A. Dickson (Lanham, MA: Rowman & Littlefield, 2017), 11.
19. Rowena McKernan, Tria Skirko, Quill West, and Library as Open Education Leader, *Librarians as Open Education Advocates: Readings on Being an Open Education Advocate*, 2015, https://openedadvocates.pressbooks.com/.
20. William M. Cross, "Library Expertise Driving OER Innovations: The Role of Libraries in Bringing 'Open' to the Classroom and to the World," in *Open Access and the Future of Scholarly Communication: Implementation*, ed. Kevin L. Smith and Katherine A. Dickson (Lanham, MA: Rowman & Littlefield, 2017), 87.

BIBLIOGRAPHY

ACRL Research Planning and Review Committee. "2018 Top Trends in Academic Libraries." *College and Research Libraries News* 79, no. 6 (2018): 286–300, https://crln.acrl.org/index.php/crlnews/article/view/17001/18750.

Bell, Steven. *Course Materials Adoption: A Faculty Survey and Outlook for the OER Land-scape*. White paper. Chicago: ACRL/Choice, 2018. https://www.choice360.org/research/course-materials-adoption-a-faculty-survey-and-outlook-for-the-oer-landscape/.

Belliston, C. Jeffrey. "Open Educational Resources: Creating the Instruction Commons." *College and Research Libraries News* 70, no. 5 (2009): 284–303. https://doi.org/10.5860/crln.70.5.8183.

Blessinger, Patrick, and T. J. Bliss. "Introduction to Open Education: Towards a Human Rights Theory." In *Open Education: International Perspectives in Higher Education*, edited by Patrick Blessinger and T. J. Bliss, 11–30. Cambridge: Open Book Publishers, 2016.

Brown, Malcolm, Mark McCormack, Jamie Reeves, D. Christopher Brooks, and Susan Grajek, with Bryan Alexander, Maha Bali, et al. *2020 EDUCAUSE Horizon Report, Teaching and Learning Edition*. Louisville, CO: EDUCAUSE, 2020. https://www.educause.edu/horizon-report-2020.

Bueno-de-la-Fuente, Gema, R. John Robertson, and Stuart Boon. *The Roles of Libraries and Information Professionals in Open Educational Resources (OER) Initiatives: Survey Report*. London: JISC, 2012.

Colson, Robin, Elijah Scott, and Robin Donaldson. "Supporting Librarians in Making the Business Case for OER." *Reference Librarian* 58, no. 4 (2017): 278–87. https://doi.org/10.1080/02763877.2017.1377665.

Cross, William M. "Library Expertise Driving OER Innovations: The Role of Libraries in Bringing 'Open' to the Classroom and to the World." In *Open Access and the Future of Scholarly Communication: Implementation*, edited by Kevin L. Smith and Katherine A. Dickson, 71–96. Lanham, MA: Rowman & Littlefield, 2017.

Kahle, David. "Designing Open Educational Technology." In *Opening Up Education: The Collective Advancement of Open Education through Open Technology, Open Content, and Open Knowledge*, edited by Toru Iiyoshi and M.S. Vijay Kumar, 27–46. Cambridge, MA: MIT Press, 2008.

Kazakoff-Lane, Carmen. *Environmental Scan and Assessment of OERs, MOOCs, and Libraries: What Effectiveness and Sustainability Means for Libraries' Impact on Open Education*. White paper. Chicago: Association of College and Research Libraries, 2014. https://www.ala.org/acrl/sites/ala.org.acrl/files/content/publications/whitepapers/Environmental%20Scan%20and%20Assessment.pdf.

Kleymeer, Pieter, Molly Kleinman, and Ted Hanss. "Reaching the Heart of the University: Libraries and the Future of OER." Paper, 7th Annual Open Education Conference, Barcelona, Spain, November 2–4, 2010. https://deepblue.lib.umich.edu/bitstream/handle/2027.42/78006/ReachingtheHeartoftheUniversity-KleymeerKleinmanHanss.pdf?sequence=1&isAllowed=y.

McKernan, Rowena, Tria Skirko, Quill West, and Library as Open Education Leader. *Librarians as Open Education Advocates: Readings on Being an Open Advocate*. 2015. https://openedadvocates.pressbooks.com/.

Okamoto, Karen. "Making Higher Education More Affordable, One Course Reading at a Time: Academic Libraries as Key Advocates for Open Access Textbooks and Educational Resources." *Public Services Quarterly* 9, no. 4 (2013): 267–83. https://doi.org/10.1080/15228959.2013.842397.

Sims, Nancy. "'Protecting' Our Works—From What?" In *Open Access and the Future of Scholarly Communication: Implementation*, edited by Kevin L. Smith and Katherine A. Dickson, 11–30. Lanham, MA: Rowman & Littlefield, 2017.

Thille, Candace. "Building Open Learning as a Community-Based Research Activity." In *Opening Up Education: The Collective Advancement of Open Education through Open Technology, Open Content, and Open Knowledge*, edited by Toru Iiyoshi and M. S. Vijay Kumar, 165–80. Cambridge, MA: MIT Press, 2008. https://library.oapen.org/bitstream/handle/20.500.12657/26069/1004016.pdf?sequence=1.

Vanasupa, Linda, Amy Wiley, Lizabeth Schlemer, Dana Ospina, Peter Schwartz, Deborah Wilhelm, Catherine Waitings, and Kellie Hall. "What Does It Mean to Open Education? Perspectives on Using Open Educational Resources at a US Public University." In *Open Education: International Perspectives in Higher Education*, edited by Patrick Blessinger and T. J. Bliss, 199–220. Cambridge: Open Book Publishers, 2016.

HOW LIBRARIES SUPPORT OPEN EDUCATIONAL RESOURCES

Abbey K. Elder

The services that OER initiatives provide are broad and include general advocacy, publishing, and instructional design support, among other offerings.[1] This variation largely stems from the initiatives' differing capacities. Some academic libraries can afford to invest in extensive programs with a team of full-time staff dedicated to supporting OER, but many cannot. In this section, we'll be exploring the types of OER support regularly offered through libraries.

> [Instructional design] is a systematic process that is employed to develop education and training programs in a consistent and reliable fashion and …requires ongoing evaluation and feedback.
>
> —Reiser and Dempsey[2]

DEDICATED STAFF

As the demand for OER services continues to grow in higher education, so does the number of positions dedicated to supporting OER in libraries. In some cases, new positions are developed to support an initiative; however, these duties are more often folded into preexisting librarians' position responsibilities.[3] A case study about the Open Education Initiative at the University of Massachusetts Amherst describes the work starting with a department head who already had a plethora of existing responsibilities:

> The program was begun by the head of the Scholarly Communication department, who also managed the institutional repository, served on several internal and external committees, and was responsible for additional administrative tasks that did not allow the amount of time needed to administer an OER program.[4]

This is only a single example, but folding OER duties into other scholarly communication–related work is not uncommon in academic libraries.

Librarians who support OER do not need to be alone in their work, though. Whether they have OER in their job description or not, these support staff are regularly part of a larger group that oversees OER implementation at their institution, usually through a library-based or cross-campus committee.

WORKING GROUPS AND COMMITTEES

The presence of an OER committee can be incredibly useful for OER initiatives that lack a group of dedicated staff members who can coordinate OER-related work. As figure 2.14 shows, a report published by SPARC in 2019 found that 53 percent of the 129 higher education institutions surveyed had a committee or task force in place to support the institution's OER initiative.[5]

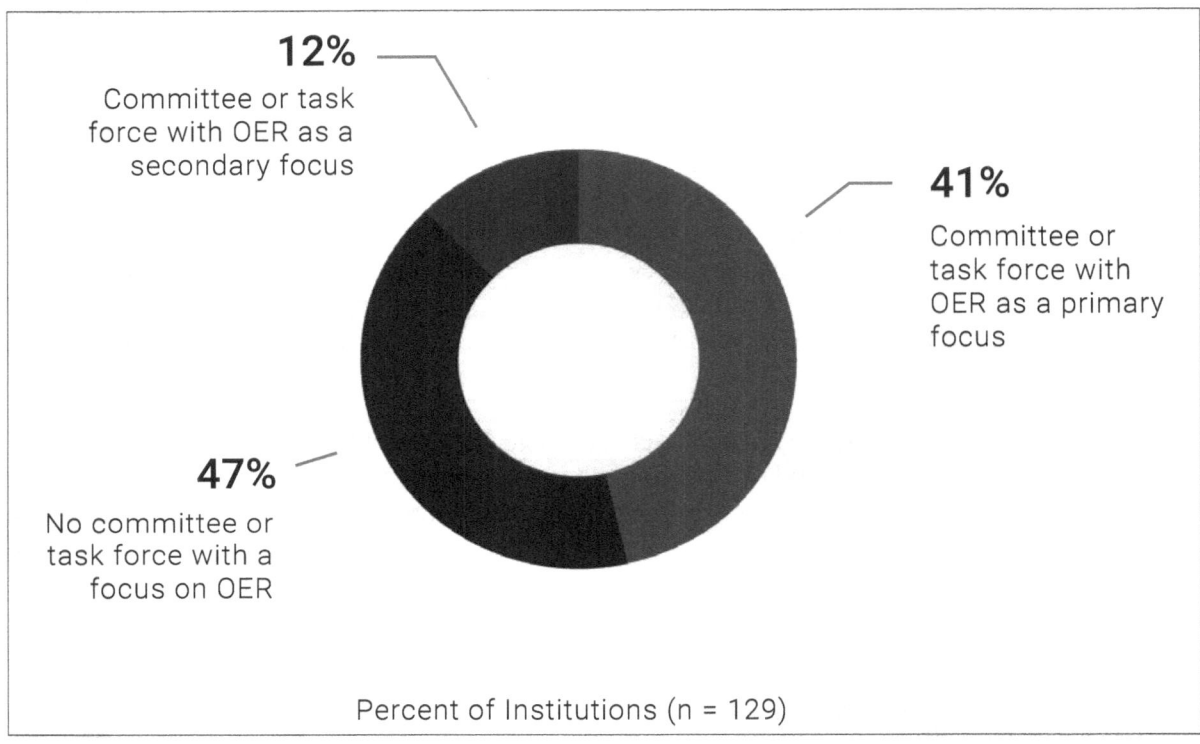

12%
Committee or task force with OER as a secondary focus

41%
Committee or task force with OER as a primary focus

47%
No committee or task force with a focus on OER

Percent of Institutions (n = 129)

Figure 2.14
Percent of institutions with an OER committee or task force. SPARC, 2018–2019 Connect OER Report (Washington, DC: SPARC, September 2019), 10, https://sparcopen.org/our-work/connect-oer/reports/.) Used under CC-BY 4.0.

The purpose of OER committees is to educate the community, interface with faculty about course material adoptions, and make the case for investing in OER to stakeholders who can support wider change across an institution. How a committee goes about this work, however, will depend on the scope of its team.

COMMITTEES IN THE LIBRARY

OER committees housed within an academic library usually become the first stepping stones to a wider, cross-campus committee structure. Whether they are mandated by a department head or created independently by librarians interested in open education, a library OER committee is often smaller in scope than its institutional counterparts and handles projects that can be integrated into a library's traditional work.

WORK DONE BY LIBRARY-BASED OER COMMITTEES

OER committees based in a library often prioritize work that can be folded into existing programs and support structures in the librarian representatives' work. For example, an OER committee based in a library might integrate OER workshops, faculty development, and outreach into they library's existing instruction workflows or work with course reserves to help faculty integrate library-licensed materials into their courses as an alternative to commercial textbooks, if an appropriate set of OER cannot be identified for their course.

At Iowa State University, Abbey Elder, the open access and scholarly communication librarian, holds "OER consultations," small interactions with instructors to talk about their courses and what they need to make the switch to OER. These conversations are structured very similarly to a traditional reference interview. As you will see in subsection 2.3.2.3, "Day to Day OER Work," consultations are a fairly common practice for OER librarians. However, it often starts as an implied service, one that comes about from e-mails and questions alone. The Iowa State University library did not make this an official consultation service that was promoted to faculty until after its OER committee came together and members mentioned that the service could benefit from more exposure across the institution. These are the sorts of things that committees can be particularly helpful for, even the small ones: bringing attention to small changes an OER librarian can make to strengthen their work.

One of the strengths of a library-based OER committee is the ability of staff to meet more regularly than larger and more dispersed groups and complete small projects relatively quickly. This is because library OER committees are made up of a group with similar work schedules and priorities (i.e., librarians). Just as with any type of committee, the larger and more complex a team is, the harder it becomes to get things done. When representatives from different institutional offices come together, they may have different expectations for what projects the committee should prioritize and how much control the library should hold over those projects. While it may be tempting to keep a group small to avoid these types of conflicts, there are also drawbacks to having an insular committee structure. Without representation from faculty, instructional design staff, or students, it can be difficult for library-led OER committees to innovate in their OER services or develop targeted outreach materials that can reach their audiences.

CROSS-CAMPUS COMMITTEES

In contrast with OER committees made up of librarians and library staff alone, cross-campus OER committees are often more representative of the institution as a whole. A case study from the University of Maryland states that the institution's OER committee began with staff from the library and IT departments, before soliciting additional members from "the Faculty Development Center, STEM and Humanities faculty, and [the] Division of Information Technology."[6] The diversity of representatives can be useful in many ways, both in expanding access to university resources and naturally spreading awareness of the institution's OER initiative. Faculty make particularly useful allies, both for their insight into the needs of their peers and as advocates embedded within departments themselves.[7]

WORK DONE BY CROSS-CAMPUS OER COMMITTEES

In addition to having a wider network of collaborators for outreach, cross-campus initiatives are also notable for their ability to reach out to administrators for support or funding. Whereas a library-housed committee might work with its dean or a departmental supervisor, a cross-campus committee can leverage the representatives of its group to get the attention of administrators. Because of their broader support system, cross-campus OER committees can develop more impactful programming. This might include the coordination of a course-marking initiative to denote which courses are using low- or no-cost course materials, a grant program to fund the adoption or creation of OER, or support for instruction using OER through awards or through recognition for open education work in tenure and promotion guidelines.

The benefits of a cross-campus OER committee are numerous, but concerns come along with this model as well. As we alluded to in the previous section, institutional committees are often harder to schedule and coordinate. This is particularly true of committees with faculty and student members, whose schedules are less flexible than those of staff. Nonetheless, these committees are useful for getting more diverse work in motion and reaching a wider audience.

STATE AND REGIONAL COMMITTEES

The final common type of OER committee is the least common, but the most impactful: the regional or statewide committee. These groups are often created by legislation or consortial interests in affordable education and may have a wider scope than OER alone. The strengths of statewide initiatives are easy to see: these groups are backed by large communities with funding available to support their needs, and they have a wide breadth of influence over their region.

However, statewide OER initiatives can also be incredibly fickle. Having funding from the state legislature might seem like a good idea, but what do you do if your state legislature has no interest in funding for higher education innovation? You could frame your work as a nonpartisan issue, focusing on advancing access to higher education and supporting students through college and into their careers. These are topics of interest to state governments generally, and you can adapt your language to the goals of your local legislature.

As Bell and Salem state in their pitch for a statewide OER initiative for Pennsylvania, "Funding for public education in Pennsylvania lags behind most states," continuing with, "Now we must catch up with other states to fund and support textbook affordability."[8] Nonetheless, their proposal eventually led to the development of Affordable Learning Pennsylvania, a statewide OER initiative managed by the Pennsylvania Academic Library Consortium (PALCI). This is much like Indiana's initiative, run by its own academic library consortium, PALNI. While not every statewide OER program is led by a consortium of libraries, librarians are clearly an integral part of many successful OER programs, whether they are a small team of like-minded peers or a regional group representing multiple institutions.

WORK DONE BY STATE AND REGIONAL OER COMMITTEES

Because of their reach, statewide and regional OER initiatives are more likely to coordinate high-impact grant programs, publishing programs, and training opportunities for faculty across institutional lines.[9] This sort of top-down support can help smaller institutions get access to publishing platforms and funding that they might otherwise have to do without. Because of their greater capacity for coordinating this work, partnering with a state or regional OER committee can be helpful for an institutional OER initiative, even if the institution already has a library or cross-campus OER committee in place.

MAKING AN OER COMMITTEE

In many cases, librarians are the ones not only heading their OER committees, but also finding members to run it. It can be difficult to know where to start when confronted with this task, so we have put together a list of potential institutional collaborators to help newcomers address this step in an OER initiative's development. More support can be found in subsection 2.3.2.3, "Day-to-Day OER Work," under "Framework for OER Outreach."

Common Partners

Before anything else, you should find those whose work aligns with your own. These partners often have extensive experience building a rapport with faculty and students alike, and they understand how OER can be of use in your community. Common partners for OER committees include

- student government
- faculty/faculty senate
- instructional designers
- communications/marketing
- IT/accessibility
- campus store
- dean of students/equal opportunity office
- admissions
- academic advisors
- graduate centers
- financial aid office

Each of these groups brings something valuable to the table for a cross-campus OER committee. Academic advisors are able to reach out to students and share news on a more personal scale than posters or other marketing campaigns allow, graduate centers can help gather information about whether TAs are using OER in their classrooms, and campus stores can make excellent partners for not only promoting OER but also making open materials easier to find in course schedules and student book lists.

Keep in mind that many of these individuals may be unaware of or uninterested in open education when you first contact them. Instead of assuming that everyone is interested in your work, an OER librarian should start soliciting team members by talking to potential partners about the OER work already underway at the university, how the experience and knowledge of your potential committee recruit could support your OER initiative's continued growth, and how their participation advances their own goals as well. For example, connecting with instructional designers can help your initiative do better work supporting instructors who want to incorporate OER into their courses, and connecting with your work can help the instructional designers at your institution find more ways of engaging with instructors who are interested in innovating in their teaching methods.

Find Your Champions

Some institutions may have an administration or campus store that is markedly against the ideals of open access and open education. In these cases, you would want to avoid addressing these groups until you have a stronger base of support at your institution. Instead, start where it's easy. Find the champions who are already embracing open textbooks or open pedagogy and ask them to join your group. Student government representatives can be excellent additions to an OER committee, both for their intrinsic understanding of the type of outreach most likely to reach students and for their personal investment in textbook affordability. In the same vein, faculty representatives can be a great addition to your team if they have experience creating or teaching with OER themselves.

OER SERVICES

The day-to-day work of a librarian with OER responsibilities can include a wide variety of support services, from one-on-one consultations with faculty to more official training programs and workshop management.[10] While we will cover these responsibilities and more in subsection 2.3.2.3, "Day-to-Day OER Work," here we will discuss larger programmatic responsibilities that an OER librarian might be tasked with as part of their work.

MARKETING AND OUTREACH

One of the first projects any librarian supporting OER will undertake is outreach. An initiative cannot support change if no one knows that it exists, after all. There are two major types of outreach that a librarian starting an OER initiative will want to cultivate: passive and active outreach.

Passive Outreach

Passive outreach includes things like library guides, websites, and promotional materials. These are passive because, once created, they do the work of informing others about OER and the support being offered through an OER initiative. However, because passive outreach is often encountered without context, a significant amount of work goes into the development and deployment of passive materials. For example, a handout about OER support available at an institution should also include a brief description of OER and the URLs for any websites available at your institution where the reader can learn more if they are interested.

Passive outreach projects are both one of the first and one of the last pieces that a librarian supporting OER will need to create. Often, an OER library guide is the first piece of content available about OER at an institution; however, as committees develop more programming and the scope of the OER initiative grows, it will become necessary for OER leads to think more holistically about the marketing for their initiative. This may lead to official branding for the OER initiative or a themed campaign structured around a particular service or program. For example, Oklahoma State University has branded its OER efforts as "Open OKState," with videos, marketing materials, and webpages[11] Open OKState is also the branding the institution has adopted for its Pressbooks instance, reinforcing the connection between the initiative and its individual pieces.[12]

Active Outreach

In contrast to passive outreach, active outreach requires one or more members of your team to periodically engage with members of the community to promote and assess the OER initiative in place. Active outreach includes things like surveys, meetings, and presentations to faculty and student groups. While this type of outreach can be exhausting for a single librarian to handle on top of their other duties, this work does not have to be handled by one team member alone. When presenting to student and faculty groups about your OER initiative, for example, librarians who support OER can lean on fellow OER committee members to present information about their work by leveraging a shared set of slides and presentation materials that can be reused in different venues or customized for a particular audience (e.g., emphasizing cost savings when presenting to student groups). In addition to helping promote your OER initiative, active outreach can help you gather data about the needs of students, instructors, and other staff to inform future projects that your team can undertake.

FACULTY RECOGNITION

One of the most impactful services an OER initiative can develop is a method for recognizing faculty members' open education work. This type of project can come in many types, from the low-stakes "champion profile" approach, wherein an instructor is highlighted on a website alongside a quote or information about their experience with OER, to the institutional policy approach, wherein open education work is acknowledged explicitly through an award program or through recognition from a department or institution according to formal promotion guidelines.

At Iowa State University, instructors who adopt OER are featured as OER Trailblazers, with a profile that includes information about the courses in which the instructors have adopted OER and a case study serving as a narrative description of the instructors' work.[13] The University of Kansas Libraries have a similar program called Textbook Heroes, who are described as "members of the KU community who've taken extraordinary initiative to increase access to and affordability of required course materials by implementing and advocating for OER and other low and no cost course materials."[14]

Providing a space for instructors to highlight their work can help legitimize an OER initiative while also providing passive outreach for instructors who are interested in learning more about how their peers have incorporated OER into their courses. Faculty recognition becomes even more impactful when it is incorporated into an institutional framework. This can be done on a small scale—for example, through an award program—or integrated into higher level documentation, such as a strategic plan or promotion and tenure guidelines. For an example of the former, you can look to the University of Tennessee, Knoxville, as its student government association helps sponsor an award "recognizing instructors who make use of OERs in the classroom."[15] On the other end of the spectrum, at the University of British Columbia, OER were incorporated into tenure and promotion evaluations for educational leadership in 2017, and this approach has gained wide acclaim as a model that can help incentivize the move toward OER.[16] Since 2020, more colleges have begun integrating language about OER into their promotion and tenure documents, and this trend will likely continue as OER initiatives continue to expand and report on the positive outcomes of open education work.[17]

Additional Resources on Faculty Recognition

Coolidge, Amanda, Andrew McKinney, and Deepak Shenoy. "The OER Contributions Matrix." DOERS3. https://www.doers3.org/tenure-and-promotion.html.
The DOERS3 matrix for OER in Tenure and Promotion provides a list of contributions that a staff or faculty member might develop in the course of their OER work and maps that work against traditional tenure and promotion categories (i.e., research, teaching, and service).
Open Education in Promotion, Tenure and Faculty Development. Home page. https://oept. pubpub.org/.
Open Education in Promotion, Tenure, and Faculty Development provides a narrative description for why an institution should support the addition of open education work in its promotion and tenure guidelines, tips for talking to stakeholders, a revised version of the DOERS3 matrix, and supplementary materials for OER initiatives.

TRACKING AND REPORTING DATA

It might not be the most glamorous part of the OER initiative, but collecting and reporting data is one of the most important tasks that librarians handle.[18] Two types of data can be analyzed for any research project: qualitative data and quantitative data. *Qualitative* describes something with words and ideas. This type of data can be particularly useful for perception studies, when you want to learn more about the opinions of faculty and students toward open content. In contrast, quantitative data measures concrete numbers and ratios. This type of data is best used for recording statistics of faculty who have used OER in their courses or, perhaps most importantly, for tracing students' savings from courses that have flipped from using a commercial textbook to an OER.

Whenever a team tries to track data about their work, an important consideration is what you will do with it. If you or your committee have not been tasked with finding data about OER, what do you do with the data you have? Using data effectively is just as important as collecting it well. Below are a few approaches an OER librarian can take to effectively use data about their institution to support their OER initiative.

Report the Data

The first and simplest use of data collected at your institution is to report the data to someone else. In these cases, data is typically reported to a supervisor, administrator, or even a legislator to whom you'd like to make the case for funding or otherwise supporting OER in your community (see figure 2.15).

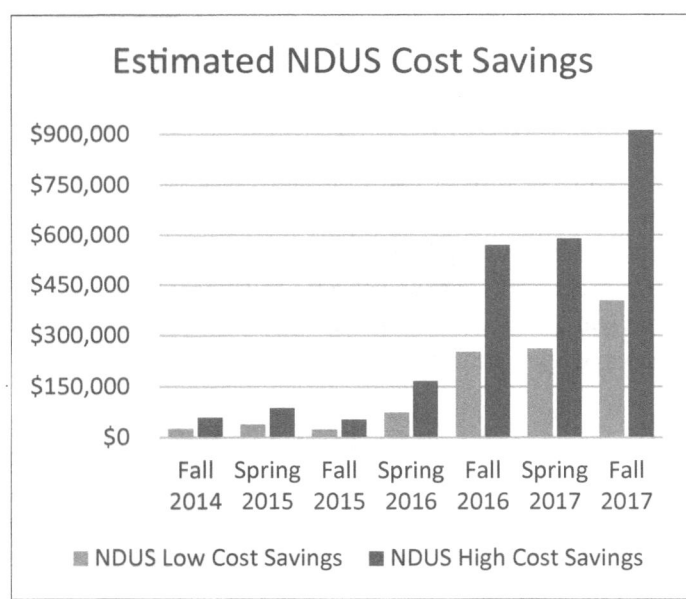
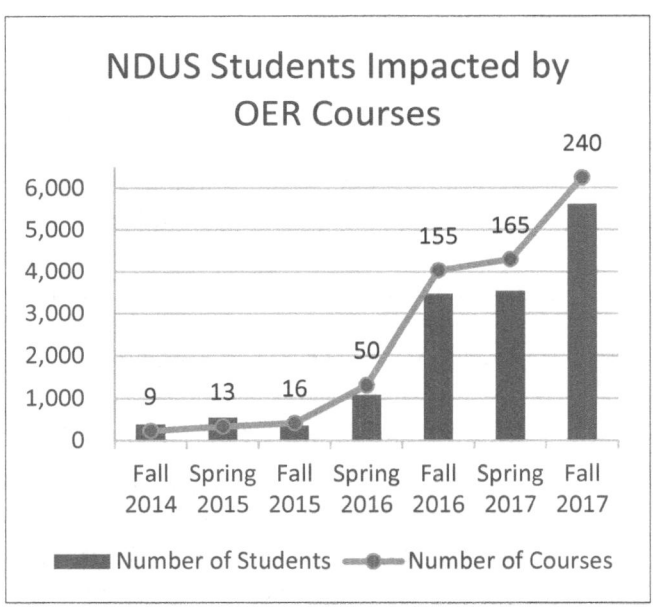

Figure 2.15

The North Dakota University System's 2018 audit shared this data about the impact of OER. North Dakota Office of the State Auditor, *2018 North Dakota University System—Open Educational Resources* (Bismarck, ND: Office of the State Auditor, November 14, 2018), https://www.nd.gov/auditor/2018-north-dakota-university-system-open-educational-resources.

Reporting data requires you to synthesize the main results of your work and to share the pieces that are most likely to be appreciated by your audience. For administrators and legislators, these data points are usually student savings and retention. At the academic level, it's important to understand how the use of OER can impact the learning outcomes of students. From a purely promotional standpoint, having a number that shows how big an impact the use of OER has had on student affordability can be especially useful. For this kind of data, it can be useful to track the use of OER across the institution through textbook adoption information.

Use the Data

Apart from simply taking the data you've pulled together and sending it to someone else, OER librarians can also use data gleaned from their institutions to drive the development and growth of OER programs. For example, if a survey of student perspectives on course materials found that the majority of your student body prefers print to electronic textbooks, you could invest in a collaborative printing program for OER with an institutional printing office or an affordable partner such as printMe1 (https://www.printme1.com).

Any type of data collected through an OER initiative can be used to inform future practices. OER usage data, while useful for calculating savings, can also be used to determine which departments have the most or least interest in open content. This information can be used when developing outreach materials and programming for faculty who may not know about open content available in their discipline. In the same vein, surveys can provide insight into faculty and student perceptions of both your initiative's programming and OER in general, which can help inform the types of programs that are being used and appreciated at your institution.

Share the Data

Finally, data can be public. Data like "dollars saved" or "number of courses using OER" is simple to track and requires very little interpretation. This makes the information particularly useful when broadcasting information to the institution in a live or regularly updated venue, like a website (see figure 2.16).

Institutions can create live data dashboards or static websites with regularly updated milestones to share information about the progress of their OER initiatives and to drive interest in their work.

FUNDING PROGRAMS

One of the most impactful investments in OER that an institution can make is to provide funding as incentives for instructors reviewing, adopting, or creating OER. Whether funding is limited to $100 stipends or as expansive as a $10,000 grant, funding faculty engagement with OER can drive an initiative to new heights.

Review incentive programs are the smallest of this type, through which a small stipend of $100 to $200 is given to faculty members for reviewing an open textbook that might be utilized in their course.[19] This method was pioneered by the Open Education Network, which encourages members to incentivize faculty to review textbooks in the Open Textbook Library (OTL) to encourage use of OER and to improve the usability of the OTL's catalog for users.[20] Below, larger incentives provided through grant programs are explored in more depth.

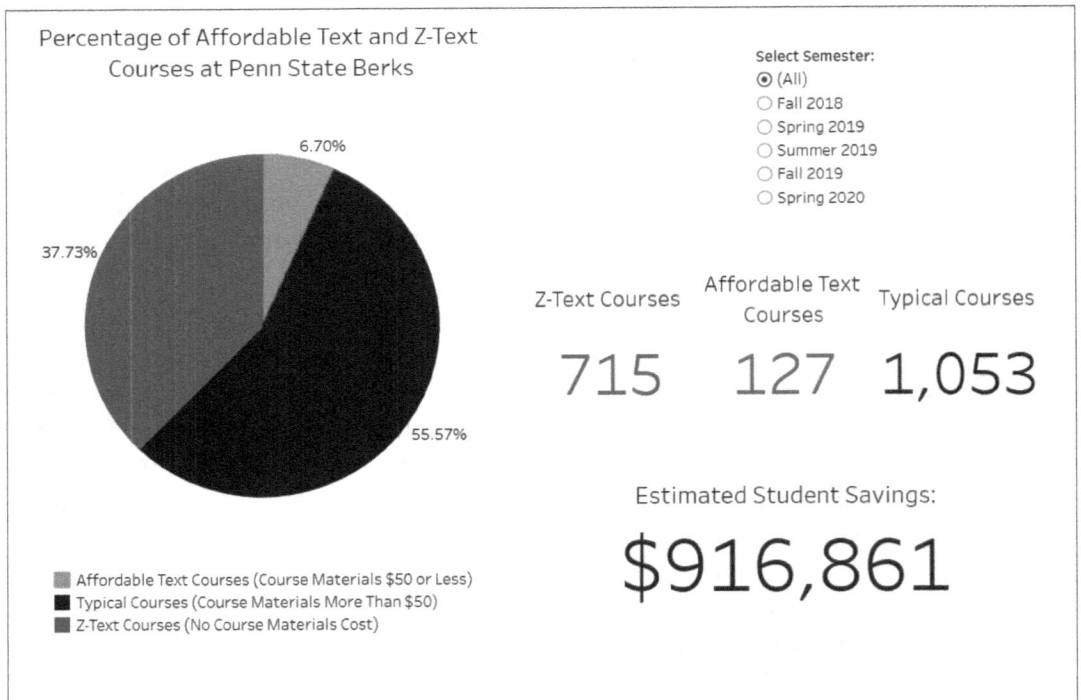

Figure 2.16
Penn State Berks OER, "Penn State Berks Textbook Affordability Dashboard," https://
sites.psu.edu/berksoer/. While access to this screen grab requires a login, the data
presented could be shared publicly..

Grant Programs

In addition to the small funds provided by institutions for OER reviews, some OER initiatives
oversee the management and dispersal of grants, larger pots of funding that can support the
adoption, adaptation, or creation of new OER. Grant support has become a fairly common
sight in well-funded OER initiatives, with forty-two of seventy-one institutions in SPARC's
Connect OER data stating that their initiative supports grants for faculty.[21]

The University of Texas at Arlington offers an expansive grant program, UTA CARES,
with multiple categories of grants available through the same program based on the scope
of a project. In addition to offering $800 adoption stipends for faculty who use OER in their
courses, this program also offers Scale Grants, which fund the adoption of OER across every
section of a course or program, and Innovation Grants for the creation of new open resources
that fill a particular niche.[22]

OER grant programs are usually managed jointly by an OER committee or other over-
seeing body at your institution, with funding supplied through an administrative body, such
as the president's or provost's office, or coming from the academic library's budget directly.[23]
When planning an OER grant program, librarians can make an impact by advocating for
additional funding from library administrators and academic departments to support projects
that cannot be covered by other pots of money available at your institution.

Running an OER Grant Program

Managing a grant program can be difficult, but we can look to existing initiatives as examples.
The University of Massachusetts Amherst offers the following advice about running a grant

program: Provide adequate funding for creation projects, provide faculty with release time to develop content, develop a campus-wide advisory group to support the grants, and allow flexibility in the funding structure for projects that do not fit into one of the traditional boxes of adopting, adapting, and creating content.[24] In addition to these administrative changes, librarians who manage OER work can also contribute to making grant programs more effective by coordinating publishing and project management support.

PUBLISHING PROGRAMS

Although publishing has not always had a natural place in the academic library, there are precedents for why librarians should help faculty navigate publishing their own OER. One reason ties directly into the previous section: grants. When funding the production of OER, it is incredibly useful for someone on the OER committee to be involved with the publication process, either at the project planning stage or throughout the project's development.

One way in which librarians support the publication of OER is through intellectual property assistance. Gumb calls out this topic in her article about OER publishing in the academic library, arguing that many librarians are not comfortable giving legal advice about navigating copyright licenses, despite this being an important part of the OER publication and adaptation process.[25] Nevertheless, intellectual property, and Creative Commons licensing in particular, are topics that should be addressed with faculty during the OER production process. Developing a base of knowledge on these topics can make a great OER librarian, or alternatively, you can rely on the experience of copyright librarians and lawyers at your institution to support these publication projects as well.

Managing OER publishing projects is not just a matter of giving advice, though. Project management is also an integral part of this process. Academic libraries can support OER publishing by collaborating with a university press, offering support through locally hosted software purchased for the sake of publishing OER such as Pressbooks or Manifold for open source book publishing, and utilizing existing infrastructures in the library such as institutional repositories. Depending on the funding available to the library and the programs already in place, some of these options will be more viable than others, but each can help to make publishing OER easier for faculty members who are interested in putting in the time to develop content. More information about the ins and outs of publishing open content can be found in subsection 2.3.2.3, "Day-to-Day OER Work," under "Tools and Platforms for Authoring and Remixing Content."

Additional Resources on Publishing Programs

Gold, Matthew K., Zach Davis, Susan Doerr, Kathleen Fitzpatrick, and John W. Maxwell. "Sustaining Open-Source Community Publishing Platforms." Panel presentation, Library Publishing Forum, online, May 4–8, 2020. YouTube video, 47:55. https://www.youtube.com/watch?v=RHpLAyt2nyE.

Meinke, Billy. "An OER Production Workflow for Faculty." *UH OER Blog*, University of Hawai'i, February 2017. https://oer.hawaii.edu/an-oer-production-workflow-for-faculty/.

Santiago, Ariana. "Developing OER Publishing Support: A Case Study." Poster presentation, Library Publishing Forum, online, May 4–8, 2020. https://docs.google.com/presentation/d/1j79AP85fVMV8CcuvVqqTPJWWXaJ5V8tZzKc4WttAogw/edit#slide=id.p.

MEMBERSHIPS AND NATIONAL NETWORKS

The final large-scale service that librarians manage for OER initiatives is membership in networks and support groups. This might seem underwhelming following grant programs and publishing support, but it is a notable aspect of an OER librarian's work. It is valuable to connect with groups that can offer support to your own initiative and to help fund national networks that are doing great things in the OER space. Academic libraries have been exploring ways to support open access publishing through networks and memberships for years, as evidenced through the wide-ranging support for the Open Library of the Humanities and similar projects.[26] The program highlighted here is one of the most popular among OER initiatives: the Open Education Network (OEN), previously the Open Textbook Network.[27]

The OEN began at the University of Minnesota in 2014 as a way of supporting colleges that want to band together to better support faculty at their institutions who were interested in OER.[28] Today, the network still serves that purpose, and membership in the network allows members to receive training on running a faculty workshop and utilizing the Open Textbook Library (a referatory of open textbooks) and supports the initiative's continued growth over time. Finding networks like these and advocating for them is another aspect of OER support offered by librarians, not simply because faculty will benefit from the support received through the network, but also because it supports the growth of a national network utilized by other OER librarians.

Additional Networks

Open Education Global, https://www.oeglobal.org/
Community College Consortium for OER (CCCOER), https://www.cccoer.org/
Library Publishing Coalition, https://librarypublishing.org/
Scholarly Publishing and Academic Resources Coalition (SPARC), https://sparcopen.org/

Now that we have explored the services offered by libraries to support OER on an institutional and regional scale, we can delve, in subsection 2.3.2.3, into the day-to-day duties of an OER librarian.

NOTES

1. Steven J. Bell and Joseph A. Salem Jr., "It's up to the Librarians: Establishing A Statewide OER Initiative," *Pennsylvania Libraries: Research and Practice* 5, no. 2 (Fall 2017): 77–82, https://doi.org/10.5195/palrap.2017.166.
2. Robert A. Reiser and John V. Dempsey, *Trends and Issues in Instructional Design and Technology* (Upper Saddle River, NJ: Pearson, 2006), 15.
3. Amanda Larson, "Open Education Librarianship: A Position Description Analysis of the Newly Emerging Role in Academic Libraries," *International Journal of Open Educational Resources* 3, no. 1 (2020), https://ijoer.scholasticahq.com/article/25044-open-education-librarianship-a-position-description-analysis-of-the-newly-emerging-role-in-academic-libraries.
4. Jeremy Smith, "Seeking Alternatives to High-Cost Textbooks: Six Years of the Open Education Initiative at the University of Massachusetts Amherst," chapter 16 in *OER: A Field Guide for Academic Librarians | Editor's Cut*, ed. Andrew Wesolek, Jonathan Lashley, and Anne Langley (Forest Grove, OR: Pacific University Press, 2019), https://boisestate.pressbooks.pub/oer-field-guide/.
5. SPARC, *2018–2019 Connect OER Report* (Washington, DC: SPARC, September 2019), https://sparcopen.org/our-work/connect-oer/reports/.
6. Erin Durham and Sheri Braxton, "Advancing an Open Educational Resource Initiative through Collaborative Leadership," *International Journal of Open*

Educational Resources 2, no. 1 (Fall 2019/Winter 2020): 49-77, https://ijoer.scholasticahq.com/article/25010-advancing-an-open-educational-resource-initiative-through-collaborative-leadership.

7. Rebel Cummings-Sauls et al., "Open Partnerships: Identifying and Recruiting Allies for Open Educational Resources Initiatives," in *OER: A Field Guide for Academic Librarians*, ed. Andrew Wesolek, Jonathan Lashley, and Anne Langley (Forest Grove, OR: Pacific University Press, 2018), 165–92, https://scholarworks.umass.edu/librarian_pubs/72.

8. Bell and Salem, "It's up to the Librarians," 77.

9. Affordable Learning Georgia, "Mission and Values," https://www.affordablelearninggeorgia.org/about-us/missions-values/.

10. Dr. Bradlee and Amy VanScoy, "Bridging the Chasm: Faculty Support Roles for Academic Librarians in the Adoption of Open Educational Resources," *College and Research Libraries* 80, no. 4 (2019): 426–49, https://crl.acrl.org/index.php/crl/article/view/17392/19519.

11. Oklahoma State University Library, "Open Textbooks/Open Educational Resources: Open OKState," last updated March 23, 2023, https://info.library.okstate.edu/open/.

12. Oklahoma State University Library, "Open OKState," https://open.library.okstate.edu/.

13. Iowa State University, "Trailblazers," Open Educational Resources, https://www.oer.iastate.edu/trailblazers.

14. KU Libraries, "Textbook Heroes," https://lib.ku.edu/textbook-heroes.

15. University of Tennessee Knoxville Libraries, "SGA Open Education Award," https://www.lib.utk.edu/scholar/services/scholarlycomm/sga-open-educator-award/.

16. Brady Yano, "Recognizing 'Open' in Tenure and Promotion at UBC," SPARC Open Education, April 14, 2017, https://sparcopen.org/news/2017/recognizing-open-tenure-promotion-ubc/.

17. Grand Valley State University Office of the Provost, "Faculty Responsibilities in the Area of Scholarly/Creative Activity," May 28, 2021, https://www.gvsu.edu/provost/faculty-responsibilities-in-the-area-of-scholarlycreative-activity-148.htm.

18. Smith, "Seeking Alternatives."

19. Jen Waller, Cody Taylor, and Stacy Zemke, "From Start-Up to Adolescence: University of Oklahoma's OER Efforts," chapter 17 in *OER: A Field Guide for Academic Librarians | Editor's Cut*, ed. Andrew Wesolek, Jonathan Lashley, and Anne Langley (Forest Grove, OR: Pacific University Press, 2019), https://boisestate.pressbooks.pub/oer-field-guide/chapter/from-start-up-to-adolescence-university-of-oklahomas-oer-efforts/; Karen Pikola, Dawn Lowe-Wincentsen, and Amanda Hurford, "Office Hours: Money, Money, Money—Paying OER Contributors," Rebus Community and Open Textbook Network Office Hours, October 29, 2019, YouTube video, 55:33, https://www.youtube.com/watch?v=NTY9bH2OjEo.

20. Open Textbook Network, "Local Workshops," https://open.umn.edu/otn/workshops/.

21. SPARC, *Connect OER Report*.

22. University of Texas Arlington Libraries, "UTA CARES Grant Program," LibGuide, last updated April 19, 2023, https://libguides.uta.edu/oergrants.

23. Smith, "Seeking Alternatives"; Waller, Taylor, and Zemke, "From Start-up to Adolescence."

24. Smith, "Seeking Alternatives."

25. Lindsey Gumb, "An Open Impediment: Navigating Copyright and OER Publishing in the Academic Library," *College and Research Libraries News* 80, no. 4 (2019): 202–15, https://crln.acrl.org/index.php/crlnews/article/view/17663/19477.

26. Open Library of the Humanities, "The OLH Model," https://www.openlibhums.org/site/about/the-olh-model/; Marcel LaFlamme et al., "Let's Do This Together: A Cooperative Vision for Open Access," *Anthro{dendum}* (blog), June 27, 2018, https://anthrodendum.org/2018/06/27/lets-do-this-together-a-cooperative-vision-for-open-access/.

27. Open Textbook Network, "6/15 Summit Kickoff: OTN's Vision with Dave," YouTube video, 56:28, June 17, 2020, https://www.youtube.com/watch?v=oc4zjr3vQnE.

28. Open Textbook Network, "About," https://open.umn.edu/otn/about/.

BIBLIOGRAPHY

Affordable Learning Georgia. "Mission and Values." https://www.affordablelearninggeorgia.org/about-us/missions-values/.

Bell, Steven J., and Joseph A. Salem Jr. "It's Up to the Librarians: Establishing A Statewide OER Initiative." *Pennsylvania Libraries: Research and Practice* 5, no. 2 (Fall 2017): 77–82. https://doi.org/10.5195/palrap.2017.166.

Bradlee, Dr., and Amy VanScoy. "Bridging the Chasm: Faculty Support Roles for Academic Librarians in the Adoption of Open Educational Resources." *College and Research Libraries* 80, no. 4 (2019): 426–49. https://crl.acrl.org/index.php/crl/article/view/17392/19519.

Coolidge, Amanda, Andrew McKinney, and Deepak Shenoy. "The OER Contributions Matrix." DOERS3. https://www.doers3.org/tenure-and-promotion.html.

Cummings-Sauls, Rebel, Matt Ruen, Sarah Beaubien, and Jeremy Smith. "Open Partnerships: Identifying and Recruiting Allies for Open Educational Resources Initiatives." In *OER: A Field Guide for Academic Librarians*, edited by Andrew Wesolek, Jonathan Lashley, and Anne Langley, 165–92. Forest Grove, OR: Pacific University Press, 2018. https://scholarworks.umass.edu/librarian_pubs/72.

Durham, Erin, and Sherri Braxton. "Advancing an Open Educational Resource Initiative through Collaborative Leadership." *International Journal of Open Educational Resources* 2, no. 1 (Fall 2019/Winter 2020): 49–78. https://ijoer.scholasticahq.com/article/25010-advancing-an-open-educational-resource-initiative-through-collaborative-leadership.

Grand Valley State University Office of the Provost. "Faculty Responsibilities in the Area of Scholarly/Creative Activity." May 28, 2021. https://www.gvsu.edu/provost/faculty-responsibilities-in-the-area-of-scholarlycreative-activity-148.htm.

Gumb, Lindsey. "An Open Impediment: Navigating Copyright and OER Publishing in the Academic Library." *College and Research Libraries News* 80, no. 4 (2019): 202–15. https://crln.acrl.org/index.php/crlnews/article/view/17663/19477.

Iowa State University. "Trailblazers." Open Educational Resources. https://www.oer.iastate.edu/trailblazers.

KU Libraries. "Textbook Heroes." https://lib.ku.edu/textbook-heroes.

LaFlamme, Marcel, Dominic Boyer, Kirsten Bell, Alberto Corsín Jiménez, Christopher Kelty, and John Willinsky. "Let's Do This Together: A Cooperative Vision for Open Access." *Anthro{dendum}* (blog), June 27, 2018. https://anthrodendum.org/2018/06/27/lets-do-this-together-a-cooperative-vision-for-open-access/.

Larson, Amanda. "Open Education Librarianship: A Position Description Analysis of the Newly Emerging Role in Academic Libraries." *International Journal of Open Educational Resources* 3, no. 1 (2020). https://ijoer.scholasticahq.com/article/25044-open-education-librarianship-a-position-description-analysis-of-the-newly-emerging-role-in-academic-libraries.

North Dakota Office of the State Auditor. *2018 North Dakota University System—Open Educational Resources*. Bismarck, ND: Office of the State Auditor, November 14, 2018. https://www.nd.gov/auditor/2018-north-dakota-university-system-open-educational-resources.

Oklahoma State University Library. "Open OKState." https://open.library.okstate.edu/.

———. "Open Textbooks/Open Educational Resources: Open OKState." Last updated March 23, 2023. https://info.library.okstate.edu/open/.

Open Education in Promotion, Tenure and Faculty Development. Home page. https://oept.pubpub.org/.

Open Library of the Humanities. "The OLH Model." https://www.openlibhums.org/site/about/the-olh-model/.

Open Textbook Network. "About." https://open.umn.edu/otn/about/.

———. "6/15 Summit Kickoff: OTN's Vision with Dave." YouTube video, 56:28. June 17, 2020. https://www.youtube.com/watch?v=oc4zjr3vQnE.

———. "Local Workshops." https://open.umn.edu/otn/workshops/.

Penn State Berks OER. "Penn State Berks Textbook Affordability Dashboard." https://sites.psu.edu/berksoer/ (requires login).

Pikola, Karen, Dawn Lowe-Wincentsen, and Amanda Hurford. "Office Hours: Money, Money, Money—Paying OER Contributors." Rebus Community and Open Textbook Network Office Hours, October 29, 2019. YouTube video, 55:33. https://www.youtube.com/watch?v=NTY9bH2OjEo&feature=youtu.be.

Reiser, Robert A., and John V. Dempsey. *Trends and Issues in Instructional Design and Technology*. Upper Saddle River, NJ: Pearson, 2006.

Smith, Jeremy. "Seeking Alternatives to High-Cost Textbooks: Six Years of the Open Education Initiative at the University of Massachusetts Amherst." Chapter 16 in *OER: A Field Guide for Academic Librarians | Editor's Cut*, edited by Andrew Wesolek, Jonathan Lashley, and Anne Langley. Forest Grove, OR: Pacific University Press, 2019. https://boisestate.pressbooks.pub/oer-field-guide/.

SPARC. *2018–2019 Connect OER Report*. Washington, DC: SPARC, September 2019. https://sparcopen.org/our-work/connect-oer/reports/.

University of Tennessee Knoxville Libraries. "SGA Open Education Award." https://www.lib.utk.edu/scholar/services/scholarlycomm/sga-open-educator-award/.

University of Texas Arlington Libraries. "UTA CARES Grant Program." LibGuide. Last updated April 19, 2023. https://libguides.uta.edu/oergrants.

Waller, Jen, Cody Taylor, and Stacy Zemke. "From Start-Up to Adolescence: University of Oklahoma's OER Efforts." Chapter 17 in *OER: A Field Guide for Academic Librarians | Editor's Cut*, edited by Andrew Wesolek, Jonathan Lashley, and Anne Langley. Forest Grove, OR: Pacific University Press, 2019. https://boisestate.pressbooks.pub/oer-field-guide/chapter/from-start-up-to-adolescence-university-of-oklahomas-oer-efforts/.

Yano, Brady. "Recognizing 'Open' in Tenure and Promotion at UBC." SPARC Open Education, April 14, 2017. https://sparcopen.org/news/2017/recognizing-open-tenure-promotion-ubc/.

DAY-TO-DAY OER WORK

Amanda C. Larson

As the role of the library grows to support instructors adopting, adapting, and authoring OER, so too have academic libraries started hiring librarians for positions to support that work. This subsection will look directly at the job landscape for these roles in libraries, what the day-to-day work may look like for these positions, and how librarians can build a community around OER both inside their institution and outside of it.

THE JOB LANDSCAPE*

For the most part, there are five readily identifiable categories of roles in the library doing work with OER:

- *Additional duties as assigned*—These are positions where librarians have had OER work added to their other duties. The percentage of OER-specific work they do can range based on the needs of their institution, but often is anywhere from 1 percent (they made a handout one time) to 30 percent (they are running workshops, starting an initiative, curating a LibGuide, etc.). It may also be referred to as doing OER work off the side of their desk.
- *Temporary*—Some libraries create temporary positions to try out this work at their institutions (for many reasons—for example, securing limited funding, such as one-time funding or donor funding). These positions are created with a finite time line ranging from one to five years typically.
- *Half and half*—A full-time position dedicated 50 percent to supporting OER. The other 50 percent of these positions often falls under scholarly communication (working with the institutional repository, open access, open publishing, etc.) or reference and instruction (time spent teaching undergraduate information literacy or working at a reference desk).
- *Full-time non-tenure-track*—A full-time position dedicated 100 percent to supporting OER.
- *Full-time tenure-track*—A full-time position with faculty ranking and additional research responsibilities.

---

* Caveat for this section: All of this may vary by institutional context. Librarianship supporting OER looks very different at community colleges versus large research institutions versus small liberal arts colleges, etc. There can also be overlap within one role between the categories listed. For example, a librarian could have a position that is half and half and have a tenure appointment, or they could have a full-time but temporary position.

The titles for these positions can vary quite a bit based on institutional position-naming practices, but try looking for open education librarian, open educational resources librarian, scholarly communication librarian, OER and emerging technology librarian, OER and textbook affordability librarian, or generic titles like librarian I, librarian II, or assistant librarian.

A lot of times these position descriptions take the kitchen-sink approach to job duties (as in everything but the kitchen sink is included!), so it can be hard to know what the scope of work looks like from the description alone. This can be frustrating to a job applicant. However, it may mean that the institution expects that the successful candidate will tailor the scope of work to fit their expertise.

Here are some kinds of work a librarian can anticipate doing in a role devoted to supporting OER:

Advocacy—Librarians in these roles should expect to be advocating for OER and open pedagogy to support their use with faculty and administrators. More often than not these roles will also include advocating for policy changes to accommodate a shift to OER in the classroom. These could be intellectual property policies, course material selection policies, open access policies, or tenure and promotion policies.

> **advocacy** Action taken by an organization, individual, or group of individuals to support *libraries* (3), especially action directed at securing funding for capital improvements and *library* (3) operations.
>
> —ALA Glossary[1]

Curation—A large portion of a librarian's work may be to curate OER for faculty to select from for their discipline. For more information on how to do this see "Finding Resources" under "Working with Resources" below.

Management—There are several ways that librarians may be in management roles while in these positions. Librarians may be asked to manage a textbook affordability or open textbook grant initiative. This can look like everything from fiscal stewardship of the grant, program management (for example, what does all the faculty development around running a grant program look like?), project management, and production management (actually doing the work to make the final product). This can also look like managing other folks who have roles doing some of the work (for example, are there instructional designers who could do the production of whatever the final product is?). They may also manage hourly-wage student workers.

Outreach—As with advocacy (outlined above), a large portion of a librarian's work in this role will be outreach. While Bay View Analytics (formerly the Babson Survey Research Group) reported that "more than half of faculty (53%) report some level of awareness of OER, up 19 percentage points from about a third (34%) in 2014–15" in the report *Inflection Point: Educational Resources in U.S. Higher Education* for 2019,[2] there is still a lot of work to do in most higher education institutions to raise faculty awareness that OER is an option for their courses. This can include doing large-scale outreach events like workshops, brown bags, and so on; speaking with faculty one-on-one or as departments; meeting with graduate students; running a #textbookbroke campaign with students; and more.

outreach program 1. A program that encourages *users* [1] to utilize *library* services. Sometimes referred to as a *marketing plan* or *public relations*. 2. A program designed for and targeted to an underserved or inadequately served *user group*.

—ALA Glossary[3]

Publishing—Depending on how the position is scoped, there may be the expectation that the librarian will do a lot of work in open publishing. For example, there may be a university grant program that allows faculty to adapt or author OER and the librarian is expected to assist. If publishing is one of their assigned duties, a librarian will want to figure out what capacity the publishing program has and set expectations with colleagues and authors early on.[4] The Open Education Network offers an openly licensed Publishing Curriculum that can help tackle this task.[5] There may also be some expectation that librarians will work in open publishing more broadly by including open journals and digital humanities projects in their workload.

Teaching—There may be an expectation that librarians provide undergraduate information literacy instruction along with other duties. Depending on the institution, this could be conducting one-shot sessions or teaching an entire course.

Training—No matter how the position is scoped, it is fair to expect that at the very least the librarian will provide training on Creative Commons licenses, open education, OER, and open pedagogy for various audiences. If they are responsible for a grant initiative that publishes OER, librarians may also be responsible for training users on the technology offered by the institution to deliver that content. For example, a lot of institutions use the WordPress-based publishing platform Pressbooks to author OER textbooks. To help authors, librarians might offer training on how to use the platform and select the appropriate license for the work. It may also be expected that, after settling into their role, the librarian will be responsible for cross-training on OER-related support or providing professional development opportunities for their library colleagues.

OTHER CONSIDERATIONS: EMOTIONAL AND INVISIBLE LABOR

In addition to being sometimes precarious, like a lot of roles in libraries, it is important to recognize that OER work may involve both emotional and invisible labor as part of the role.

[**Emotional labor** is] labor [that] requires one to induce or suppress feeling in order to sustain the outward countenance that produces the proper state of mind in others—in this case, the sense of being cared for in a convivial and safe place. This kind of labor calls for a coordination of mind and feeling, and it sometimes draws on a source of self that we honor as deep and integral to our individuality.

—Arlie Russell Hochschild, *The Managed Heart*[6]

[**Invisible labor**] includes the advising and mentoring of students, non-prestigious (often diversity-related) service work, and teaching preparation time.

—Social Sciences Feminist Network Research Interest Group[7]

Let's discuss invisible labor first. Librarians should anticipate doing a lot of support work that is not guaranteed to be seen, appreciated, or counted toward professional recognition when working on OER projects—whether that is building an advocacy effort to get an open education movement started at an institution, curating open content, running an OER grant program, or supporting production work for the adaptation or creation of OER. Therefore, it is important to figure out what metrics count at their library and make sure to build collecting those metrics into the work they do. All of this can be complicated by the category the librarian's role falls into. Are they tenure-track? How can this work build into a research agenda? How can a librarian balance it with the need to pursue tenure and promotion? Are they temporary? How can a librarian build an impact when they have to also look for another job three-quarters of the way through their contract? Are they doing this work off the side of their desk as other duties as assigned? How can they track this work to possibly argue for a position realignment or the hiring of another librarian, support staff, or a graduate assistant? For all the role categories, how much of the labor of these librarians in OER-related positions is spent educating their library colleagues about open education? How much is spent on service work and behind-the-scenes tasks? How much time is spent using their expertise to coach up their position line or administrators?

Moving onto emotional labor, librarians in OER-related roles should anticipate encountering it in their work. They will likely run into doing emotional labor when doing advocacy work, working with colleagues, and working with instructors. Librarians may have to suppress their feelings and opinions and create a veneer that is nonthreatening to generate buy-in on their campus. An OER-related librarian may also have to manage the feelings of their colleagues and administrators to do the work they were hired to do. They may have to bear the brunt of instructors who publicly denounce OER as a viable option without listening to the research on the topic or who want to continue to receive royalties for their self-authored course materials. Another way librarians in OER-related roles may suffer from emotional labor is by being the only person doing the work around OER. Sometimes, this can also involve carrying the mental load or being the de facto person responsible for an overwhelming number of tasks to make sure that the open education movement is successful on their campus—from planning and running the program to advocating, to advising administrators, to consulting one-on-one. This can lead to the librarian feeling overwhelmed. To counter this, librarians can try the following if possible: check in with a supervisor to discuss their workload or to decompress from a difficult interaction, do a capacity scan to see what is possible to do with the available resources, and try to set firm boundaries. It is also important to remember that both emotional labor and invisible labor can disproportionately affect librarians of color and others with less privileged identities.

ADDITIONAL RESOURCES: JOB LANDSCAPE

American Library Association. "Frontline Advocacy Toolkit." https://www.ala.org/advocacy/frontline-advocacy-toolkit.

Archives, Libraries, and Information Mentor Base (Alimb). Home page. https://www.
    alimb.ca/.
"Position Descriptions." https://drive.google.com/
    open?id=1242Az5rjiCz9FCMHXXC9ORMFRocWx4Gw.
Take a look at what position descriptions look like for these types of positions look in this
    curated Google Drive folder.
Wade, Carrie. "LIS Job Posting Red Flags." https://docs.google.com/
    document/d/16qz2s7_SsFIgRWU50cKiwoIvqolh9f53b4GAIuNO2f4/edit.

FURTHER READING ABOUT JOBS

Ettarh, Fobazi. "Vocational Awe and Librarianship: The Lies We Tell Ourselves." *In the
    Library with the Lead Pipe*, January 10, 2018. http://www.inthelibrarywiththeleadpipe.
    org/2018/vocational-awe/.
Keeran, Peggy, and Carrie Forbes. *Successful Campus Outreach for Academic Libraries:
    Building Community through Collaboration.* Lanham, MD: Rowman & Littlefield, 2018.
Larson, Amanda C. "Open Education Librarianship: A Position Description Analy-
    sis of the Newly Emerging Role in Academic Libraries." *International Journal of
    Open Educational Resources* 3, no. 1 (2020). https://ijoer.scholasticahq.com/arti-
    cle/25044-open-education-librarianship-a-position-description-analysis-of-the-new-
    ly-emerging-role-in-academic-libraries.
Welburn, William C., Janice Simmons-Welburn, and Beth McNeil, eds. *Advocacy,
    Outreach, and the Nation's Academic Libraries: A Call for Action.* Chicago: Association
    of College and Research Libraries, 2010.

WORKING WITH OER

A large portion of the work a librarian supporting OER does is working with resources. This can be helping instructors curate resources to adopt or adapt for their courses. This can also be vetting license compatibility, making sure resources are accessible, and demonstrating how instructors can use open pedagogy with open resources.

This section will walk through some strategies for searching for resources, evaluating resources, and the OER reference interview. It will also showcase some places to start searching for open resources.

FINDING OER

Librarians excel at finding resources! All the skills that a librarian would use to help patrons find articles, books, and media are completely transferable to finding OER. They'll just use a different search strategy. A lot of times when searching for library resources the goal is to get users to narrow down their topic to a more specific set of keywords to better match the controlled vocabulary of the database. The opposite is true of searching for OER—the goal is to start very broadly to see if there is content in that subject area because a lot of OER repositories don't feature a robust controlled vocabulary as vendor platforms do. For example, instead of searching for a very specific or niche topic like "conducting," broaden the search out to a subject area like "music" or "music appreciation" to find results.[8]

The OER Reference Interview

Another way to draw on the skills of librarianship when working to support instructors is through the reference interview modified for OER. An instructor seeking OER also has information needs that can be served through the same process. Some tips: ask open-ended questions, ask about the learning objectives and goals for their course, ask about whether they're looking for one resource or multiple resources, and ask how they plan to use the resource (as an assignment vs. a reading vs. a video vs. a lab, etc.).

> [The **reference interview**] is the interpersonal communication between a reference staff member and a library user to determine the precise information needs of the user.
>
> —ALA Glossary[9]

Quill West's templates and instructional videos on how to conduct an OER reference interview are a great resource to get started. Her series of templates and videos walks through the process step-by-step from pre-consultation to the end of the search.

The "Worksheet #1: Exploring OERs" template is a worksheet that the instructor fills out pre-consultation.[10] It collects information on their course objectives and the topics covered in their course. It also has places for them to explain what they think quality resources are and how they got interested in OER. Use these topics as the start of the keywords for the exploratory searches. West also provides a video that shows how the process works from the first contact to setting expectations to setting up the template.[11]

The "OER Search Template" shows what this looks like when the instructor has filled in their learning outcomes and the librarian does their first pass at searching for OER.[12] Notice that the librarian records the license of the material and the link of the item as well as any comments about the resource. Also note that there is a section for items that are freely available on the web, but not openly licensed.[13] The video for this template documents the first meeting between West and the instructor. It offers an excellent example of the kinds of questions to ask instructors when helping them search for OER and how to set expectations for what follow-up is going to look like with the instructor.[14] The completed "OER Search Template" demonstrates what the template looks like after the meeting with the instructor and a finished search for OER.[15] The video for this template covers the search process, using the template as a research notebook, and provides tips for searching.[16]

Strategies for Searching

The previous section ends with moving away from the OER reference interview and into searching for OER.

My strategy for searching starts very similarly to the OER reference interview outlined above.
- Start by identifying the learning object and goals for the course.
- Ask for a copy of the syllabus for the course the instructor wants to transition to OER.
  - Check for concepts and topics they teach.
- Ask the instructor to describe what they like about their textbook and what they don't.
  - Make a list of those features.
  - If they like their textbook but are choosing OER because the textbook has gone out of print or become unreasonably expensive, they might consider textbook mapping

to match the content of their current textbook. We'll talk about textbook mapping in more detail below.

– Make a list of the concepts they want to cover.
– Use that list as a set of starting keywords for the search.
– Start searching!

Textbook/Course Mapping

Textbook or course mapping is a process to systematically match content from an instructor's current textbook chapter by chapter or current course module by module.

For textbook mapping, start by reviewing the table of contents and then match content for each section. I recommend creating a spreadsheet with the following columns: chapter, concepts covered in the chapter, new open resources that match that content, links to the new resources, license information for the resources, and a column for the instructor to evaluate each resource.

Quill West also provides a great spreadsheet to help keep track of the progress made while course mapping and a video that explains how to use it and how open courses are built at Pierce College.[17] Her ancillary video also does a great job of talking about selecting assessments for the content and some considerations to keep in mind.[18]

Where to Search

There are a lot of places to search for OER! Inevitably, librarians develop a set of their favorite repositories and search tools. Because there is no one place to search for everything, it is best to start searching broadly.

It helps to think about the resource being replaced. Is it a full textbook? Then maybe start searching at the Open Textbook Library, MERLOT, or the Pressbooks Directory. Is it a module, chapter, or assignment? Then start searching in a federated search engine like OASIS, the Mason OER Metafinder, or the OER Commons. Looking for images or videos? Try CC Search or YouTube.

Table 2.9 lists common repositories and referatories where librarians can start searching for OER. For a more comprehensive list, be sure to check out the section "Repositories and Search Tools" in *The OER Starter Kit*, listed under "Further Reading" below. For tips on how to search each repository specifically, check out the "Searching for Resources Template" presentation, listed below under "Additional Resource." Not only does it walk through where and how to search, but it is openly licensed and can be adapted for future workshops.

[**Repositories**: Traditionally] 1. A place where archives (1), manuscripts (3), books, or other documents (1) are stored. [In this case, the platform stores the OER on their platform.]

—ALA Glossary[19]

Referatories: A searchable database of OER, but with links to files elsewhere instead of hosting the files directly on their platform.

—Affordable Learning Georgia[20]

TABLE 2.9

Recommended repositories and referatories.

Name	Location	Description	Considerations
SUNY Geneseo's Openly Available Sources Integrated Search (OASIS)	https://oasis.geneseo.edu/	"Openly Available Sources Integrated Search (OASIS) is a search tool that aims to make the discovery of open content easier."	This is a good option for introducing instructors to search because of its easy-to-use interface.
OER Commons	https://www.oercommons.org/	"OER Commons is a public digital library of open educational resources. Explore, create, and collaborate with educators around the world to improve curriculum."	It's important to filter by education level when building searches since it searches pre-K through 20.
Google Advanced Search	https://www.google.com/advanced_search	Enables search across sites indexed by Google, including by license type, to discover open content that is not indexed in repositories and referatories.	This way of searching is helpful for locating content in niche subject areas, but it is important to double-check that material is licensed openly.
MERLOT	https://www.merlot.org/merlot/	"MERLOT...provides access to curated online learning and support materials and content creation tools, led by an international community of educators, learners and researchers."	A good location to start looking to replace an entire textbook because of the ability to search by ISBN.
Open Textbook Library (OTL)	https://open.umn.edu/opentextbooks/	The OTL is a comprehensive referatory that points to over 1200 open textbooks by a variety of authors and publishers. It is a project of the Open Education Network.	Most of the textbooks in the OTL are licensed CC BY. The textbooks are reviewed through member institutions completing their advocacy workshops and then having instructors explore the library and review a textbook in their discipline using a rubric.[a]
Pressbooks Directory	https://pressbooks.directory/	Pressbooks Directory is a free, searchable catalog that includes over 5,000 open access books published by organizations and networks using Pressbooks. Many include interactive H5P learning activities to engage learners.	May include unfinished public content or content without an open license. Openly licensed content can be easily cloned for editing for users with Pressbooks accounts.

a.   Open Textbook Library, "Open Textbooks Review Criteria," https://open.umn.edu/opentextbooks/reviews/rubric.

TABLE 2.9
Recommended repositories and referatories.

Name	Location	Description	Considerations
Openverse	https://openverse.org	"An extensive library of free stock photos, images, and audio, available for free use." The place to start when searching for images and audio. Searches across "600 million items."[b] Openverse replaced CC Search.	Because it is searching for images and audio in aggregate, double-check that the content are licensed appropriately for intended use.
Old CC Search	https://search.creativecommons.org/	Enables keyword search for audio, video, and images from various sources of open content.	Largely superseded by Openverse. Always double-check the license of materials to make sure they are appropriately licensed.
ccMixter	https://ccmixter.org/	A community-focused music-remixing site that features music and music samples with Creative Commons licenses.	Most of the music is licensed with the CC-BY-NC designation, so it is important to make sure use cases are noncommercial.
YouTube	https://www.youtube.com/	Great place to start looking for videos due to the ability to filter search results by Creative Commons license.	Make sure to filter not only by license but also by Subtitles/CC so that the videos found are more accessible. Always double-check the license!

b.   Openverse, home page, https:// openverse.org.

Remember when searching for resources to always double-check that the items found are licensed in the way they appear to be and that those licenses are compatible with each other. Some resources like videos and images can be tricky to remix with other works! Figure 2.18 is a Creative Commons license compatibility chart.

Tips and Tricks

It may go without saying, but practice, practice, practice! The more time spent trying to search for different kinds of OER, the easier it will be to find it and the more familiar a librarian will be with what subjects and resources exist already. A large part of the skill set for a librarian in this role is to be a generalist. When there is a need for a deeper dive into a specific subject, be ready to bring in a subject matter expert for help.

Recommendation

Develop a standard practice search that will be used whenever a search is demonstrated for users. For example, a demo search could be for the keyword *kitten* because there will be resources, it's a safe search, and it's fun. Having fun can help build rapport with the user group learning to search for OER because it makes the task seem less daunting and more approachable.

ADDITIONAL RESOURCES: FINDING OER

Elder, Abbey. *The OER Starter Kit*. Ames: Iowa State University Digital Press, September 5, 2019. https://doi.org/10.31274/isudp.7.

Elder, Abbey K., Stefanie Buck, Jeff Gallant, Marco Seiferle-Valencia, and Apurva Ashok. *The OER Starter Kit for Program Managers*. Montreal, QC: Rebus Press, May 10, 2022. https://press.rebus.community/oerstarterkitpm/.

Larson, Amanda. "Searching for Resources Template." Google Slides, May 19, 2020. https://docs.google.com/presentation/d/1Wbd4NFOeUFo49ei44RUvaUU2XZ57F9QUUPaslMgBIrg/edit?usp.

Shank, John D. *Interactive Open Educational Resources: A Guide to Finding, Choosing, and Using What's Out There to Transform College Teaching*. San Francisco: Jossey-Bass, 2014.

USING OER: ATTRIBUTION

It's important to remember that every resource with a Creative Commons license needs to have an attribution unless the licensor has waived attribution, which is permitted by the licenses.

One of the best ways to remember what information is needed in an attribution is the acronym *TASL*—title, author, source, license. These best practices come from the legal code of the licenses themselves. For version 4.0 of Creative Commons licenses, the required information is author, source, and license, and title is optional.[21]

Looking for a tool to help build attributions? Check out Open Washington's Open Attribution Builder (https://www.openwa.org/attrib-builder; see figure 2.17)! This tool makes it easy to build an attribution. Just type in the title, author, and URL of the resource, and select a license from the list. It also offers options to customize the attribution with more information, such as organization, project, and whether the work is a derivative. It will generate an attribution that can be copied and pasted into the OER attributing the work.

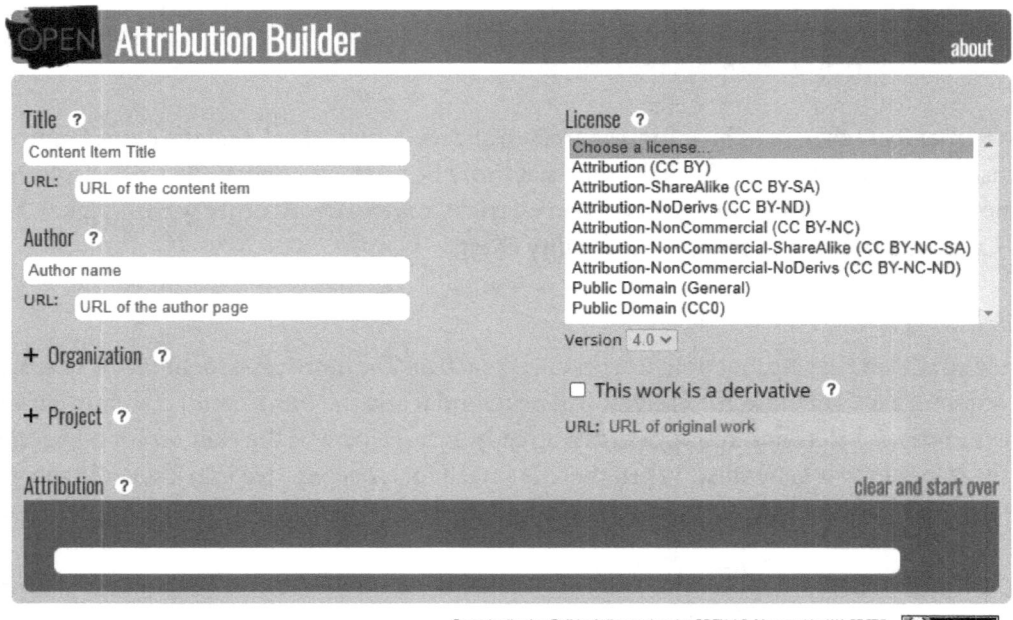

Figure 2.17

Screenshot of the Open Attribution Builder, which is licensed CC-BY 4.0

EVALUATING OER

Librarians doing this work should be prepared that, more often than not, they will be unfamiliar with the subject areas they're searching, so remember when thinking about evaluating OER that it isn't the librarian's role to evaluate quality or credibility of the resource. Leave that to the subject experts. Be prepared to train instructors in what to look for in an OER so they can evaluate it accurately.

Criteria instructors should be looking for when they evaluate OER:

- Is it accurate? Does it provide adequate coverage? Is it error-free (particularly for grammar and spelling)?
- Does it fit their course and pedagogical needs?
- Does it acknowledge its political and epistemological commitments? Does it show both sides of crucial issues? Does it have broad representations of different kinds of people? Does it interrogate its implicit biases?
- Does it have the appropriate license to meet their needs? Can it be modified?
- Is the material written in a way that will be easily understood by students?
- Does this material meet accessibility standards? Do the images within the text have alt text? Is the content structured correctly for a screen reader?

The OER librarian can help assess in a few of these areas. Be prepared to help assess if the license is adequate for how the instructor wants to use the material. Do they want to adopt the material, or do they want to adapt the resource to better fit their needs? If they want to remix several OER together, are the licenses compatible?

License Compatibility Chart

A great tool for a librarian to have in their toolkit for explaining how licenses work together and to refer back to when creating remixes of CC-licensed materials is the License Compatibility Chart created by Kennisland (see figure 2.18).[22] The chart uses green check marks to indicate compatibility with a license and black *x*s to indicate incompatibility with a license.

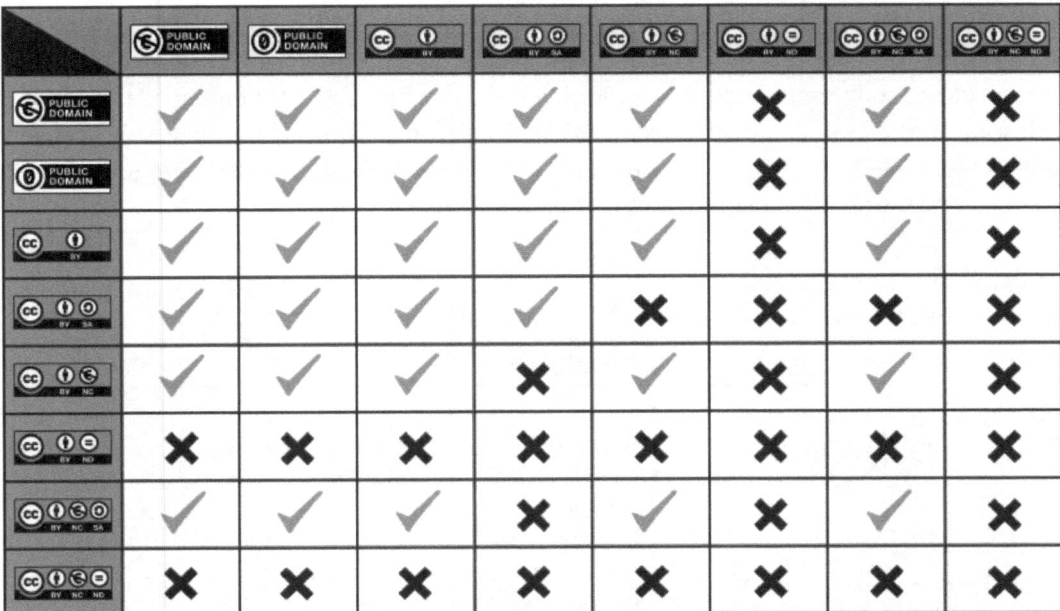

Figure 2.18

Creative Commons License Compatibility (CC-0).

Accessibility

Librarians should be prepared to help instructors assess whether the content is accessible and to teach some basic accessibility standards as well. This can be a great way to build a relationship with the folks working in accessibility services at their institution. This could be an office of disability services or student disability services. It's a good idea to bring them into programming for instructors adopting, adapting, and authoring OER to explain accessibility standards and how to comply with them.

Be prepared to point instructors to resources on evaluating OER. "Additional Resources: Evaluating OER" below includes some of the resources a librarian could share with instructors.

ADDITIONAL RESOURCES: EVALUATING OER

Achieve. "Rubrics for Evaluating Open Education Resource (OER) Objects," ver. 4. November 18, 2011. https://www.achieve.org/files/AchieveOERRubrics.pdf.

Affordable Learning Georgia. "Selection Criteria." https://www.affordablelearninggeorgia.org/oer/selection-criteria/.

mcbrarian. "iRubric: Evaluating OER." RCampus. https://www.rcampus.com/rubricshowc.cfm?code=L9WC6X&sp=yes.

Open UBC. "Faculty Guide for Evaluating Open Education Resources." University of British Columbia, April 15, 2022. https://open.bccampus.ca/files/2014/07/Faculty-Guide-22-Apr-15.pdf.

———. "OER Accessibility Toolkit." University of British Columbia. https://open.ubc.ca/oer-accessibility-toolkit/.

WAVE Web Accessibility Evaluation Tools. Home page. https://wave.webaim.org.

W3C. "Accessibility." https://www.w3.org/standards/webdesign/accessibility.

AUTHORING AND REMIXING CONTENT

Tools and Platforms for Authoring and Remixing Content

Once a librarian starts talking about OER and faculty take an interest, instructors will often want to author and remix content. As a result, it behooves a librarian to familiarize themselves with some of the tools and platforms that allow faculty to author and remix openly licensed content (see table 2.10). They are not the only options for making OER, but they are some of the most commonly used platforms to author and remix OER content.

TABLE 2.10

Tools and platforms for authoring and remixing openly licensed content.

Name	Location	Description	Considerations
Open Author by OER Commons	https://www.oercommons.org/	In addition to being a major discovery platform, OER Commons provides the ability to create OER through Open Author. The platform is a "basic rich text editor that allows authors to share text-based resources as well as embedded documents (such as downloadable worksheets) in an easy to use interface that also facilitates sharing."[a]	Requires registration, shares content directly on the OER Commons platform.

a. Abbey Elder, personal communication, June 12, 2020, 5:00 p.m.

TABLE 2.10
Tools and platforms for authoring and remixing openly licensed content.

Name	Location	Description	Considerations
Pressbooks (3rd party)	https://pressbooks.com/	An open source content management system, based on WordPress, designed for creating, editing, and publishing books. Can export content in many formats for e-books, web books, or print.[b] Pressbooks is a popular publishing solution for OER in higher ed. Its "What you see is what you get" editor makes it easy for authors to create open-content with robust metadata. Plug-ins for Hypothes.is and H5P allow annotation and interactive formative assessments, respectively.	Pressbooks.com is a third party service. Access to the authoring and editing capabilities is available to individuals and small teams through a subscription. Institutions may license the tool via the enterprise product, also known as PressbooksEDU. Can be confused with the Pressbooks.org, described below.
Pressbooks (self-hosted)	https://pressbooks.org/	The Pressbooks Open Source Project enables running Pressbooks on a local server rather than through a 3rd party. It's a great option where an institution doesn't have funding to invest in PressbooksEDU, but where technical hosting support may be provided.	Not as robust out of the box as Pressbooks.com, described above.[c] May be a good option when money is tight but technical support is available.
Manifold	https://manifoldapp.org/	This is an open-source platform for publishing networked, iterative, media-rich, and interactive monographs on the web.[d] A great resource for publishing content and connecting supplement materials to the monograph. The main difference between Manifold and Pressbooks is that Manifold is a publishing platform and not an authoring platform. This means that content must be authored outside of Man fold and then imported into the platform. Its robust theming and content organization make it a powerful publishing tool. It also has great reader features like annotation that are very helpful for the creation of OER textbooks.	Needs to be hosted (either by the institution or through Manifold) and is not an authoring platform.
LibreText Remixer	https://libretexts.org/	While not a stand-alone publishing platform, LibreTexts Remixer is a powerful tool that allows users to remix textbooks on their platform within a specific discipline. This allows users to create a custom version of the content they want their readers to have access to. It is really easy to use and build out content by dragging and dropping to create a remixed LibreText. It also has a robust selection of features such as embedded multimedia, dynamic figures, H5P, Jupyter, and Hypothes.is.[e]	Limited to remixing content on the LibreTexts platform.

b. Wikipedia, s.v. "Pressbooks," last updated December 4, 2019, https://en.wikipedia.org/wiki/Pressbooks.

c. Steel Wagstaff, personal communication, June 18, 2020, 11:52 a.m.

d. University of Minnesota Press, "About Manifold Scholarship," April 10, 2018, https://www.upress.umn.edu/about-us/about-manifold.

e. LibreTexts, "Advanced Features," https://libretexts.org/advanced.html.

Additional Resources: Authoring and Remixing Content

Elder, Abbey, and Stacy Katz. "Tools and Techniques for Creating OER." In *The OER Starter Kit Workbook.* CUNY Manifold, March 24, 2020. https://cuny.manifoldapp.org/read/the-oer-starter-kit-workbook/section/0a942a29-2d68-44a5-a2c5-a0d20d05808b.

LibreTexts Chemistry. "Remixing Existing Contents." Chapter 7 in in *LibreTexts Construction Guide.* https://chem.libretexts.org/Courses/Remixer_University/LibreTexts_Construction_Guide/07%3A_Remixing_Existing_Content.

LibreTexts Remixer Demo. https://chem.libretexts.org/Under_Construction/Development_Details/OER_Remixer.

OER and Accessibility. "Authoring Accessible OER." https://oeraccess.merlot.org/authoring_oer/index.html.

Pressbooks User Guide. https://guide.pressbooks.com.

University of Arizona. "Using the Free Version of Hypothes.is." June 19, 2020. https://digitallearning.arizona.edu/news/using-free-version-hypothesis

WORKING WITH PEOPLE

A large portion of the work of being an OER librarian is working with people and managing relationships. Whether a librarian is doing outreach or advocacy work, getting the message out will involve communicating to the right people at the right time as well as some blanket canvassing to general audiences.

FRAMEWORK FOR OER OUTREACH

Developed during the process of interviewing for open education librarian positions, the Framework for OER Outreach has been vital to building partnerships with stakeholders and explaining why the library is involved in this kind of work.[23] The framework consists of the following five steps:

1. *Identify stakeholders*—Who are they? Check out their mission statement.
2. *Research*—How can I help them? What would they recognize as something they want?
3. *Partnership*—Partnerships can look very different depending on who the stakeholders are. How will I make a solid connection with the stakeholder?
4. *Collaborate*—What is a mutually beneficial project? How can we work on it together?
5. *Frontline advocacy*—How can I turn solid connections into frontline advocates for OER?

Even when a librarian has a framework in their back pocket, laying the groundwork and making the right connections at their institution will take time. Expect to easily spend six months to one year making initial outreach connections. To get started, think about the strategic priorities of both the institution as a whole and the library to help identify those first stakeholders. Is it important to build connections with the teaching and learning units, or student government, or the faculty senate? What relationships does the library already have with other units on campus? How can those existing partnerships be leveraged in an outreach strategy? Does the institution have a mandated environment where guidance and support comes from the top down? Or does it have an environment where instructors guide from the bottom up? A combination of both?

Let's walk through the Framework for OER Outreach where Carmen, an open education librarian, identifies the student government as her stakeholders group:

1. *Identify stakeholders*—Who are they? Check out their mission statement.

   After exploring her options for groups to reach out to, Carmen identifies the student government as where she'd like to start making connections. She gets started by taking a look for a website for the student government. After finding its web presence, she looks to see if its has a mission statement information about what initiatives it is supporting currently. If the student government representatives are newly elected, she'll take a look at the issues they ran on. This information could be in a blog on the student government web page or in the student newspaper.

2. *Research*—How can I help them? What would they recognize as something they want? Now that Carmen found the web presence and looked at the initiatives, she's going to look for alignment. Are there any initiatives that match up with the kind of work she does? It is very common for students to run for office on affordability campaigns with goals of helping their fellow students save more money on textbooks and supplies or of making the cost of educational materials more transparent. In our example, the student government is interested in affordability measures. The president and vice president, Kamal and Tamara, ran on an affordability platform and have listed, on the student government website under Initiatives, that they want to help raise awareness of the cost of textbooks and supplies and the burden it can place on students. Carmen is thrilled to see that this is a goal she can help them with. She knows that the library can help out both through existing programs (like course reserves, interlibrary loan, subject specialists) and through an open education or affordability initiative.

3. *Partnership*—Partnerships can look very different depending on who the stakeholders are. How can I make a solid connection with the stakeholder?

   Carmen sends an e-mail to Kamal and Tamara and requests a meeting to chat about their affordability initiative and how the library might be able to help. They set up a meeting with Carmen, and they also invite along their academic affairs officer, who sits in the student seat on the faculty senate. In this initial meeting, Carmen asks them about their plans and what they've already started working on, and shares information about the services the library offers and suggests that they check out the Student PIRGs campaign on textbook affordability.

   Often the best people for a librarian to reach out to in student government are the president and vice president. They can choose to meet with the librarian themselves or redirect them to the appropriate student officer (maybe an academic affairs officer). The librarian can then invite them to meet, maybe for coffee, or virtually, because they have busy schedules. At that meeting, let them talk about their initiatives, the work they're doing with affordability, and identify places where the library can help out. Ask thoughtful questions about what work they've already done and where they see it going in the future. Provide space for them to ask questions, but also be prepared to answer questions about what the library is doing in this area.

4. *Collaborate*—What is a mutually beneficial project? How can we work on it together? During or after this initial meeting, the librarian may have identified a mutually beneficial project. In her meeting with representatives of the student government, Carmen learned that they were really interested in raising awareness about affordability and how their fellow students are struggling with textbook costs. She shared information with them about Student PIRGs and their campaign resources for making textbooks more affordable. Together, Carmen, Kamal, and Tamara decide to host a #textbookbroke

campaign. They decide to set up a space in the library with a whiteboard or Post-it Notes where students can write down the cost of what they spent on textbooks for that semester, what they could have used that money for, or something that fits the needs of a specific institutional context. They also use the campaign hashtag, #textbookbroke, on their social media to help crowdsource more answers. In our example, Carmen also sees this as an opportunity to get some great photos for later campaigns and important reports to upper-level administration to help tell the story of why open course materials matter and will make a difference in student success and retention.

5. *Frontline advocacy*—How can I turn solid connections into frontline advocates for OER? As a result of Carmen's partnership with the student government, more students know about OER as an option for course materials. They also are more educated about the open education movement and can help spread the word to faculty through the research they've done and talking points they've created. By providing them with the information they needed to be better advocates and warning them not to demonize their professors or the bookstore, Carmen has helped to create frontline advocates for OER on her campus. Faculty often say that their administration won't listen to them but that it will listen to students.

OUTREACH EVENTS

General Advice

Whenever the opportunity arises to talk to a target audience about OER, it's a good idea to avoid making claims that all OER are high-quality resources. There are plenty out there that are not or do not meet the high standards of a particular instructor, although librarians should feel free to mention that there is plenty of research that found OER is as good or better than publisher materials—or that a lot of commercial vendors are trying to sell OER within their proprietary platforms, which is often just openwashing but speaks to the fact the publishers think it is good enough to sell.[24] It is also best to avoid demonizing stakeholders (the bookstore, faculty, administration, students, etc.) and avoid talking about mandates (unless there is an actual mandate handed down). Do instead talk about the way OER increase academic freedom, the cost savings to students, the potential increases to student retention and student success, the research about OER, and open pedagogy. Think about what gets the target stakeholder audience excited about OER, meet them where they're at, and be OK with starting small and scaling up efforts over time.

Workshops

A workshop can be both informational and instructional. Ideally, a librarian will be introducing different stakeholders to OER and OER-adjacent topics. This can include an informational portion along with some active-learning activities for participants, or it can be largely informational with time for a Q&A session.

A typical workshop for an OER librarian might include the following: Creative Commons licenses, OER, open pedagogy, adoption, adaptation, authoring, publishing initiatives, creating OER with students, OER and accessibility, and so on.

It's important to note that a workshop with even one attendee can be a success! Instead of seeing this as an outreach failure, reframe it as providing an in-depth consultation. In addition, keep track of the attendance at workshops to have on hand to report up or include in an annual review.

Training

A training will be minimally informational, just enough to cover the topic of instruction and allow participants to try the skill they are learning.

A typical training for an OER librarian might include the following: applying Creative Commons licenses; searching for OER; making OER accessible; how to use (insert publishing platform here); how to use common tools like H5P (an HTML5 interactive activity builder) or Hypothes.is (a social annotation tool);[25] creating renewable assignments; and so on.

As with workshops, be sure to track the attendance of participants to add to the collection of outreach stats.

OFFICE HOURS

Depending on the institutional context a librarian is working in, holding regular office hours where people can drop in and ask questions could be a great opportunity to meet instructors who might not attend workshops. If a librarian hosts office hours, remember—location, location, location! It is important to meet folks where they are at. Try to find a location that is convenient for instructors, like a common space in their building or space dedicated to teaching and learning support, or even consider holding virtual office hours. Regardless of the type of office hours a librarian chooses to hold, consider the best way to advertise and get the word out at your institution.

CONSULTATIONS

In addition to outreach events, a lot of a librarian's time can be spent in one-on-one consultations with instructors. Whether an instructor is interested in replacing a textbook, exploring open pedagogy, or something else, it's a great idea to have a routine set of questions to use that will guide the conversation.

Examples: Can you tell me about the course you're teaching? Can you tell me about your current textbook? What do you like about it? What don't you like about it? If you could add something to it, what would that be? Are there particular features of the textbook that you can't live without? What kind of assignments do you have students do during the semester? Are you looking for supplemental content, like videos, podcasts, and so on? Are you looking for ancillary materials like slides, assessments, or study guides?

Another tip for one-on-one consultations is to demonstrate active listening. For example, as an instructor explains what they're looking for or wanted to talk about, a librarian can take notes in their favorite method and then repeat back what they heard. This makes sure that the instructor and librarian are on the same page, provides room to correct any misunderstandings, and gives the instructor the sense that they are really being heard and that their needs are understood.

Many libraries have employees track their reference statistics, so a librarian should also be sure to keep track of the open education consultations they have. There are multitudes of ways to do this! A librarian could use the software their library already has to keep track of these stats, they could use a separate spreadsheet for tracking with columns and rows that fit their consultation style, they could keep robust calendar notes by titling a consultation meeting with a specific subject line (for example: Consultation: Topic/Person) and then editing the notes field after the consultation is over with what was discussed. At the very least a librarian should keep track of how many consultations they have through the academic year to demonstrate a comparable value to reference consultations, to track growth and progress of their outreach for their annual review, and to include in progress reports up to administration about the open initiatives.

VENDOR RELATIONSHIPS

An unexpected side effect of taking on a role supporting open education is that librarians in these roles may have vendors reaching out to them with their affordable solutions, curated collections, or search systems. Often, the librarians won't have any decision-making power or a budget, but it might be worth listening to the vendor's pitch and passing it up the administrative chain if the product is a good fit for the library or institution. It is also a great way to stay up-to-date about what is out there in the marketplace. With that said, a librarian should also feel free to politely decline meetings with vendors because they're not a decision-maker at their institution and because these interactions can be time-consuming with minimal or no results.

REPORTING UP

Regardless of what outreach activities a librarian does at their institution, it's important for them to track stats from events and programs like attendance, adoptions, and cost savings, but also to gather stories to share up to the top that paint the picture of the impact those stats are having at the university. Getting quotes from the instructors or students impacted by the use of OER is a great way to collect information to share with administrators.

ADDITIONAL RESOURCES: WORKING WITH PEOPLE

"Consultation Tracking Spreadsheet Template." https://docs.google.com/spread-sheets/d/1DY8ULh7CYUcieFW8-YpgPn3OdVFxCGDzymHdsvqxSaM/edit?usp=sharing.

Student PIRGs. "Make Textbooks Affordable." https://studentpirgs.org/campaigns/make-textbooks-affordable/.

Open Textbook Alliance. Home page. https://opentextbookalliance.org/.

GETTING INVOLVED: COMMUNITIES OF PRACTICE

One of the most important ways a librarian can set themselves up for success is to actively work to join the open education community. Building these connections will help make the work easier because it opens up crowdsourcing of OER options for instructors, a place to ask questions, and a place to share resources. It is one of the best ways to stay up-to-date on OER news and what's happening in the community.

ONLINE COMMUNITY

Twitter*

The open education community is robustly active on Twitter. It is recommended that even if a librarian chooses not to post tweets themselves, they sign up for a Twitter account and make

---

* Editor's note: This section was written before Twitter was acquired by Elon Musk in October 2022 and subsequently renamed "X." Since those changes, a survey from Nature has found that about half of scientists who used to use Twitter have cut back or quit it entirely & half are using other platforms (https://www.nature.com/articles/d41586-023-02554-0). Some alternative metrics services have also dropped their coverage of tweet counts. The rapid erosion of what had been one of the most active and dynamic resources in scholarly communication offers a striking case study on the precarious nature of these platforms, particularly those exposed to commercial pressure and exploitation.

checking a few hashtags a priority. This allows them to keep up with the larger conversation happening in the open education community and to discover new OER as they are shared.

After lurking for a while, a librarian may feel more comfortable joining in the conversation. This will help increase their visibility with others working to support instruction using OER and, if they run an OER publishing program, to share out resources. It also provides a great networking opportunity—particularly during conferences that focus on open education where folks are live tweeting about the sessions they're attending.

One way a librarian can work checking Twitter into their workflow is to have a dedicated time, once or twice a day, where they scan their curated feed, engage if they have something to add to the conversation, and make note of anything important to follow up on. A good start to curating a feed around open education topics is to follow major OER organizations and these hashtags: #OER, #OpenEducation, #OpenEd, #OpenPedagogy, #GoOpen, #ZTC, #LeadOER, #OpenLeadership, #highered, #digiped.

It might also be helpful to access Twitter through TweetDeck, which provides more robust customization of the feed and allows tracking multiple hashtags at once. It also can help a librarian manage multiple Twitter feeds at once (for example, their personal Twitter feed and their institution's OER Twitter feed).

ADDITIONAL RESOURCES: GETTING INVOLVED

Eger, Courtney. "Open Education + Open Educational Resources (OERs): Twitter Accounts to Follow." https://t.co/cgIaei91oW.

Twitter Help Center. "How to Use TweetDeck." https://help.twitter.com/en/using-twitter/how-to-use-tweetdeck.

Networks
SPARC LIBRARIES AND OER FORUM

The SPARC Libraries and OER Forum (https://sparcopen.org/our-work/sparc-library-oer-forum/) is a community of practice for academic librarians and other stakeholders interested in OER. It offers an e-mail discussion list through Google Groups and a monthly community call. It has three goals: (1) to "enable library professionals and community members to share ideas, resources and best practices pertaining to open education"; (2) to "support coordination on librarian-focused events and educational programming about open education"; and (3) to disseminate important updates about policy, research, projects and other news from the broader open education movement."[26]

OER DIGEST

The OER Digest [https://oerdigest.org/] is a bi-weekly newsletter for open education updates, opportunities, and reminders. The primary audience is the OER community in the United States and Canada, although subscribers come from all around the world. New editions are published every other Thursday. The Digest is a joint project of Creative Commons USA, SPARC, and the Student PIRGs.[27]

Librarians can subscribe to the OER Digest and have it delivered directly to their inbox.

REBUS COMMUNITY

If part of the scope of a librarian's position is running an open textbook publishing initiative, this is a very important community of practice to know about. Rebus Community (http://about.rebus.community/) offers a platform for global collaboration for the creation of OER and partners with the Open Education Network to offer a monthly webinar series, which functions as a community of practice, for the open education community.

LOCAL COMMUNITY

The next community to explore is the local community. Are there other folks at the institution or neighboring institutions that are having conversations about OER? Does the library belong to a regional, statewide, or provincial consortium that has an OER group? If the answer to any of these questions is yes, a librarian can join those groups to stay up-to-date with what is happening locally. If the answer is no, maybe it's time to start a group? Even if a group just meets quarterly and spends the time sharing information about what is happening at everyone's institutions, it will be a worthwhile effort. This will also grow a librarian's local network and possibly their regional network. After building a network at the local and regional level, a librarian could start exploring the national and international networks that exist around OER.

BUILDING COMMUNITIES OF PRACTICE

A great way for a librarian to generate buy-in at their institution is to bring together like-minded individuals. Start by identifying instructors who have adopted, adapted, or even authored OER already. Then arrange a meeting so they can get together and talk about their experiences. This will allow them a way to interact with other instructors who they may never have had contact with before. It can lead to new collaborations. Ask them to give short talks about the OER they are using and how they build assignments around them. Ask what they want to learn about next, and then build informational sessions around the topics. If the program uses a specific tool for publishing, ask them where they're running into difficulty or what they found exciting or easy to do on it. After reaching all the early adopters of OER, ask them to bring a friend or peer to the next community of practice meeting to keep it growing.

This can also be formalized into a cohort model of programming and have instructors learn and create materials together. This can be called a learning circle, faculty learning community, community of practice, and so on. It can be instructor-led or librarian-led.

ADDITIONAL RESOURCES: COMMUNITIES

Larsen, Amanda. "Open Pedagogy Learning Circle Curriculum." https://drive.google.com/drive/folders/1UBqstcbEqxgcCQ8UHbdjaQs1j-QfX7BL.

Penn State. "Faculty Learning Communities Explore Educational Concepts and Technology." December 14, 2018. https://tlt.psu.edu/faculty-learning-communities/.

Pikula, Karen, moderator. "OER Learning Circles for Instructional Improvement." Panel presentation, June 30, 2020. YouTube video, 57:07. https://www.youtube.com/watch?v=jDAzdaF1v3w&list=PLWRE6ioG4vdZbJGUCc0XquZi23EHXXLK-M&index=6&t=0s.

PROFESSIONAL DEVELOPMENT

There are a lot of different ways to seek professional development as an OER librarian. A lot of this type of librarianship is learned on the job as there hasn't yet been much formal education in library schools around the topic. Below we take a look at informal training, formal training, and conferences.

INFORMAL TRAINING

Because there isn't a lot of formal education out there yet, informal training comprises all the learning that librarians do on their own to master this subject. That can range from watching webinars to reading resources and even completing training materials on their own without formal programming around the topic. For example, some of the certificates covered under "Formal Training" below have resources that are freely available with Creative Commons licenses so that they can be used asynchronously.

   As far as informal training goes, it's recommended that librarians start by learning the history of the open education movement, then move into the Creative Commons licenses and how they work, next learn about how best to search for OER, and finally tackle teaching with OER and open pedagogy.

ADDITIONAL RESOURCES: PROFESSIONAL DEVELOPMENT

Bliss, T. J., and M. Smith. "A Brief History of Open Educational Resources." In *Open: The Philosophy and Practices That Are Revolutionizing Education and Science*, edited by R. S. Jhangiani, and R. Biswas-Diener, 9–27. London: Ubiquity Press, 2017. https://doi.org/10.5334/bbc.b. License: CC-BY 4.0.

eLearning Infographics. "The History of Open Educational Resources Infographic." December 18, 2014. https://elearninginfographics.com/history-open-educational-resources-infographic/

FORMAL TRAINING

For more formal training there is a selection of programs, certificates, and fellowships that librarians might consider. It is important to note that most of these have a cost attached to participating. These can be a good use of professional development funds or grants offered by the library, and some even offer scholarships.

Certificates

"Creative Commons Certificate for Educators, Academic Librarians and GLAM," https://certificates.creativecommons.org/cccertedu/.

Open Education Network, "OEN Certificate in OER Librarianship PUBLIC," https://canvas.umn.edu/courses/178527.

Courses and Programs

Library Juice Academy, "Introduction to Open Educational Resources (OER)," https://libraryjuiceacademy.com/shop/course/312-introduction-to-open-educational-resources-oer/.

SPARC, "Open Education Leadership Program," https://sparcopen.org/our-work/ open-education-leadership-program/.

Fellowships

Open/Ed, "Open Education Research Fellowships," https://openedgroup.org/fellowship.
Designing with OER (DOER) https://openedgroup.org/ doer-fellows-renewable-assignments.

CONFERENCES

The conferences dedicated to OER range from local to regional, national, and international. Many of them, especially regional events, are free or affordable. Attending conferences is one of the primary ways that academic librarians participate in professional development. This is another instance where participating on Twitter is helpful to discover new conferences, and it allows librarians to follow live tweets from conferences they weren't able to attend.

ADDITIONAL RESOURCES: TRAINING

Casey, Cheryl (Cuillier). "OER Toolkit." Last updated March 22, 2023. https://www.google. com/url?q=https://drive.google.com/file/d/1kQdhTy8WMjoAD2SqKuB_quSZwkf-wVKHm/view&sa=D&ust=1593789725510000&usg=AFQjCNFhmSRBnMPde9CV-vqLXQctpV2VdNA.

Cheryl Casey pulled together an extensive OER Toolkit with lots of excellent places to get started with OER, including professional development opportunities.

CCCOER. "Open Education Conferences—2022." https://docs.google.com/ spreadsheets/d/1ALTdRKF1V7o_HgKOYEvHDIiBDXKYnB67Nk5MlHfAjFo/ edit#gid=0.

CCCOER tracks conferences that have OER-related content.

Open Education Network. "OER Action Plan Template with Examples." November 18, 2019. https://docs.google.com/ document/d/1Vhcdz6-HwNZN7t8Ka5u5HIun_H13_-LBjafC5UXDcrk/edit.

DISCUSSION QUESTIONS

After this exploration of ways to offer and receive professional development on OER-related topics, use the questions below to reflect on how a librarian might implement or explore these avenues.

1. What surprised you to learn throughout the chapter? How will this information inform your potential job searches in the future?
2. What strategies do you already use that you could adapt for supporting instructors interested in open education (for example, search methods, outreach, event planning)?
3. What's missing from your toolkit to support open education at an institution? How might you learn those skills?
4. What kind of professional development would you like to participate in to grow your expertise?

5. How might you support folks at an institution who are using OER or engaging in open pedagogy? How might you bring them together to start a conversation and share their experiences?

NOTES

1. Michael Levine-Clark and Toni M. Carter, eds., *ALA Glossary of Library and Information Science*, 4th ed. (Chicago: ALA Editions, 2013), s.v. "advocacy."
2. Nicole Allen, "Annual OER Survey: Momentum Continues to Grow as Landscape Evolves," SPARC, March 10, 2020, https://sparcopen.org/news/2020/annual-oer-survey-momentum-continues-to-grow-as-landscape-evolves/; Julia E. Seaman and Jeff Seaman, *Inflection Point* (Oakland, CA: Bay View Analytics, March 2020), https://www.bayviewanalytics.com/reports/2019inflectionpoint.pdf.
3. Levine-Clark and Carter, *ALA Glossary*, s.v. "outreach program."
4. Amanda C. Larson, "Individual and Organizational Capacity" (slides for presentation, Open Education Network, April 29, 2020), https://docs.google.com/presentation/d/1Ot7pq0QUYs7mJvpWZ9QlVcds5-cN9YaFrxYSkmCzFCI/edit?usp=sharing.
5. Open Education Network, "Open Textbook Publishing Orientation (PUB 101)," https://canvas.umn.edu/courses/377173.
6. Arlie Russell Hochschild, *The Managed Heart*, upd. (Berkeley: University of California Press, 2012), 7.
7. Social Sciences Feminist Network Research Interest Group, "The Burden of Invisible Work in Academia: Social Inequalities and Time Use in Five University Departments," *Humboldt Journal of Social Relations* 39 (2017): 236, https://www.jstor.org/stable/90007882.
8. OvercommittedJen (@jbkrich), "Music, specifically conducting. I managed to find a chapter in a music appreciation OER" Twitter, May 27, 2020, 12:12 a.m., https://twitter.com/jbkrich/status/1265496096371081218.
9. Levine-Clark and Carter, *ALA Glossary*, s.v. "reference interview."
10. Quill West, "Quill West Librarian-FacultyWorksheet#1," Google Docs, February 6, 2020, https://docs.google.com/document/d/1SG-MVcXC-kpERb7xHTS4L6VptbSankn1XOuTerUlwaw/edit?usp.
11. Quill West, "Searching for OER: A Tool for Librarians #1," April 10, 2015, YouTube video, 4:45, https://www.youtube.com/watch?v=mVhQErvuDlA.
12. Quill West, "Quill West EDUC 5173—Diversity in the Classroom, Faculty OER Collaboration Worksheet, OER Seearch Template," Google Docs, February 6, 2020, https://docs.google.com/document/d/1v8QuoNXl0rNznPJjJOICXn32HEsB9HbbsOXNy_fDP-g/edit.
13. Digital Media Law Project, "Linking to Copyrighted Materials," September 10, 2022, http://www.dmlp.org/legal-guide/linking-copyrighted-materials.
14. Quill West, "Searching for OER: A Tool for Librarians #2," April 10, 2015, YouTube video, 5:33, https://www.youtube.com/watch?v=Tm2bQHRmol8.
15. Quill West, "Quill West Librarian-Faculty OER Worksheet Example, OER Search Template," Google Docs, February 6, 2020, https://docs.google.com/document/d/1KsCJUm-HCEfuylocQCm5Qf3ihnTAfc0izB23jk_KLG8/edit?usp.
16. Quill West, "Searching for OER: A Tool for Librarians #3," April 10, 2015, YouTube video, 3:53, https://www.youtube.com/watch?v=CLM0St9qGzs.
17. Quill West, "Quill West Blank CourseMap," Google Sheets, February 6, 2020, https://docs.google.com/spreadsheets/d/14sSnKlcYWCdjn-vCt3V0YxHeZr4B1ZHoY0t6BDqH4EM/edit; Quill West, "OER Course Mapping Video," November 28, 2017, YouTube video, 4:16, https://www.youtube.com/watch?v=VM3Zk5E6MgI.
18. West, "OER Course Mapping Video."
19. Levine-Clark and Carter, *ALA Glossary*, s.v. "repository."
20. Affordable Learning Georgia, "Creating and Modifying Open Educational Resources: Module 6," accessed July 7, 2020, https://web.archive.org/web/20210413044112/https://www.affordablelearninggeorgia.org/help/creating-6.
21. Creative Commons Wiki, "Best Practices for Attribution," July 9, 2018, https://wiki.creativecommons.org/wiki/best_practices_for_attribution.
22. Wikimedia Commons, "CC License Compatibility Chart," May 31, 2013, https://commons.wikimedia.org/wiki/File:CC_License_Compatibility_Chart.png.
23. Amanda Larson, "Open Education Outreach," presentation, Pennsylvania State University, State College, PA, May 2017.
24. Openwashing, home page, https://openwashing.org/.
25. H5P, home page, https://h5p.org/; Hypothes.is, home page, https://web.hypothes.is/.

26. SPARC, "SPARC Libraries and OER Forum," https://sparcopen.org/our-work/sparc-library-oer-forum/.
27. *OER Digest*, "About the *OER Digest*," https://oerdigest.org/about/.

BIBLIOGRAPHY

Affordable Learning Georgia. "Creating and Modifying Open Educational Resources: Module 6." Accessed July 7, 2020. https://web.archive.org/web/20210413044112/https://www.affordablelearninggeorgia.org/help/creating-6.

Allen, Nicole. "Annual OER Survey: Momentum Continues to Grow as Landscape Evolves." SPARC, March 10, 2020. https://sparcopen.org/news/2020/annual-oer-survey-momentum-continues-to-grow-as-landscape-evolves/.

Creative Commons Wiki. "Best Practices for Attribution." July 9, 2018. https://wiki.creativecommons.org/wiki/best_practices_for_attribution.

Digital Media Law Project. "Linking to Copyrighted Materials." September 10, 2022. http://www.dmlp.org/legal-guide/linking-copyrighted-materials.

H5P. Home page. https://h5p.org/.

Hochschild, Arlie Russell. *The Managed Heart: Commercialization of Human Feeling*, upd. Berkeley: University of California Press, 2012.

Hypothes.is. Home page. https://web.hypothes.is/.

Larson, Amanda C. "Individual and Organizational Capacity." Slides for presentation, Open Education Network, April 29, 2020. https://docs.google.com/presentation/d/1Ot7pq0QUYs7mJvpWZ9QlVcds5-cN9YaFrxYSkmCzFCI/edit?usp=sharing.

———. "Open Education Outreach." Presentation. Pennsylvania State University. State College, PA: May 2017. https://www.canva.com/design/DACUmuxCSNE/kt5YfAUrRUrHEHg9AFJhYA/view?utm_content=-DACUmuxCSNE&utm_campaign=designshare&utm_medium=link&utm_source=viewer.

Levine-Clark, Michael, and Toni M. Carter, eds. *ALA Glossary of Library and Information Science*, 4th ed. Chicago: ALA Editions, 2013.

LibreTexts. "Advanced Features." https://libretexts.org/advanced.html.

OER Digest. "About the *OER Digest*." https://oerdigest.org/about/.

Open Textbook Library. "Open Textbooks Review Criteria." https://open.umn.edu/opentextbooks/reviews/rubric.

Open Education Network. "Open Textbook Publishing Orientation (PUB 101)." https://canvas.umn.edu/courses/377173.

Openverse. Home page. https:// openverse.org.

Openwashing. Home page. https://openwashing.org/.

OvercommittedJen (@jbkrich). "Music, specifically conducting. I managed to find a chapter in a music appreciation OER." Twitter, May 27, 2020, 12:12 a.m. https://twitter.com/jbkrich/status/1265496096371081218.

Seaman, Julia E., and Jeff Seaman. *Inflection Point: Educational Resources in U.S. Higher Education, 2019*. Oakland, CA: Bay View Analytics, March 2020. https://www.bayviewanalytics.com/reports/2019inflection-point.pdf.

Social Sciences Feminist Network Research Interest Group. "The Burden of Invisible Work in Academia: Social Inequalities and Time Use in Five University Departments." *Humboldt Journal of Social Relations* 39 (2017): 228–45. https://www.jstor.org/stable/90007882.

SPARC. "SPARC Libraries and OER Forum." https://sparcopen.org/our-work/sparc-library-oer-forum/.

University of Minnesota Press. "About Manifold Scholarship." April 10, 2018. https://www.upress.umn.edu/about-us/about-manifold.

West, Quill. "OER Course Mapping Video." November 28, 2017. YouTube video, 4:16. https://www.youtube.com/watch?v=VM3Zk5E6MgI.

———. "Quill West Blank CourseMap." Google Sheets, February 6, 2020. https://docs.google.com/spreadsheets/d/14sSnKlcYWCdjn-vCt3V0YxHeZr4B1ZHoY0t6BDqH4EM/edit.

———. "Quill West EDUC 5173—Diversity in the Classroom, Faculty OER Collaboration Worksheet, OER Seearch Template." Google Docs, February 6, 2020. https://docs.google.com/document/d/1v8QuoNXl0rNznPJjJOICXn32HEsB9HbbsOXNy_fDP-g/edit.

———. "Quill West Librarian-Faculty OER Worksheet Example, OER Search Template." Google Docs, February 6, 2020. https://docs.google.com/document/d/1KsCJUm-HCEfuylocQCm5Qf3ihnTAfc0izB23jk_KLG8/edit?usp.

———. "Quill West Librarian-Faculty Worksheet #1." Google Docs, February 6, 2020. https://docs.google.com/document/d/1SG-MVcXC-kpERb7xHTS4L6VptbSankn1XOuTerUlwaw/edit?usp.

———. "Searching for OER: A Tool for Librarians #1." April 10, 2015. YouTube video, 4:45. https://www.youtube.com/watch?v=mVhQErvuDlA.

———. "Searching for OER: A Tool for Librarians #2." April 10, 2015. YouTube video, 5:33. https://www.youtube.com/watch?v=Tm2bQHRmol8.

———. "Searching for OER: A Tool for Librarians #3." April 10, 2015. YouTube video, 3:53. https://www.youtube.com/watch?v=CLM0St9qGzs.

Wikimedia Commons. "CC License Compatibility Chart." May 31, 2013. https://commons.wikimedia.org/wiki/File:CC_License_Compatibility_Chart.png.

Wikipedia. S.v. "Pressbooks." Last updated December 4, 2019. https://en.wikipedia.org/wiki/Pressbooks.

OPEN PEDAGOGY

DEFINING OPEN AND OER-ENABLED PEDAGOGY

Robin DeRosa and Rajiv Jhangiani

The essay below by Dr. Robin DeRosa and Dr. Rajiv Jhangiani is adapted from their chapter, "Open Pedagogy," in *A Guide to Making Open Textbooks with Students*, a resource compiled and published under a Creative Commons Attribution 4.0 International License by the Rebus Community.[1] Robin and Rajiv are highly visible and accomplished advocates for open pedagogy and have helped that developing community consider its shape, benefits, risks, and practices. They wrote this for educators and allies, but it's a great introduction to the topic, so it is included here for that purpose.

There are many ways to begin a discussion of open pedagogy. Although providing a framing definition might be the obvious place to start, we want to resist that for just a moment to ask a set of related questions: What are your hopes for education, particularly for higher education? How do you see the roles of the learner and the teacher? What challenges do you face in your learning environments, and how does pedagogy address (or not address) them?

Open pedagogy, as we engage with it, is a site of praxis, a place where theories about learning, teaching, technology, and social justice enter into a conversation with each other and inform the development of educational practices and structures. This site is dynamic, contested, constantly under revision, and resists static definitional claims. But it is not a site vacant of meaning or political conviction. In this brief introduction, we offer a pathway for engaging with the current conversations around open pedagogy; some ideas about its philosophical foundation, investments, and its utility; and some concrete ways that students and teachers—all of us learners—can "open" education. We hope that this chapter will inspire those of us in education to focus our critical and aspirational lenses on larger questions about the ideology embedded within our educational systems and the ways in which pedagogy impacts these systems. At the same time we hope to provide some tools and techniques to those who want to build a more empowering, collaborative, and just architecture for learning.

Open pedagogy as a named approach to teaching is nothing new. Scholars such as Catherine Cronin, Katy Jordan, Vivien Rolfe, and Tannis Morgan have traced the term back to early etymologies.[2] Morgan cites a 1979 article by the Canadian Claude Paquette: "Paquette outlines three sets of foundational values of Open Pedagogy, namely: autonomy and interdependence; freedom and responsibility; democracy and participation."[3]

Many people who work with open pedagogy today have come into the conversations not only through an interest in the historical arc of the scholarship of teaching and learning, but also by way of open education, and specifically by way of open educational resources (OER). As conversations about teaching and learning developed around the experience of adopting and adapting OER, the phrase *open pedagogy* began to reemerge, this time crucially inflected with the same *open* that inflects the phrase *open license*.

In this way, we can think about *open pedagogy* as a term that is connected to many teaching and learning theories that predate open education, but also as a term that is newly energized by its relationship to OER and the broader ecosystem of open (open education, yes, but also open access, open science, open data, open source, open government, etc.). David Wiley wrote in 2013 about the tragedy of "disposable assignments" that "actually suck value out of the world,"[4] and he postulated not only that OER offer a free alternative to high-priced commercial textbooks, but also that the open license would allow students (and teaching faculty) to contribute to the knowledge commons, not just consume from it, in meaningful and lasting ways. Wiley has since revised his language to focus on "OER-enabled pedagogy," with an explicit commitment to foregrounding the 5R permissions and the ways that they transform teaching and learning.[5]

As Wiley has focused on students-as-contributors and the role of OER in education, other open pedagogues have widened the lens through which open pedagogy refracts. Mike Caulfield, for example, has argued that while OER have been driving the car for a while, open pedagogy is in the back seat ready to hop over into the front.[6] Caulfield sees the replacement of the proprietary textbook by OER as a necessary step in enabling widespread institutional open learning practice. In that post, Caulfield shorthands open pedagogy: "student blogs, wikis, etc." But beyond participating in the creation of OER via the 5 *R*s, what exactly does it mean to engage in open pedagogy

Open pedagogy sees access as fundamental to learning and to teaching and agency as an important way of broadening that access. Embedded in the social justice commitment to making education affordable for all students is a related belief that knowledge should not be an elite domain. Knowledge consumption and knowledge creation are not separate but parallel processes, as knowledge is co-constructed, contextualized, cumulative, iterative, and recursive. In this way, open pedagogy invites us to focus on how we can increase access to higher education and how we can increase access to knowledge—both its reception and its creation. This is, fundamentally, about the dream of a public learning commons, where learners are empowered to shape the world as they encounter it. With the open license at the heart of the work, open pedagogy seeks to engage both with "free" and about "freedom," with resources and practices, with access and about accessibility, with content and contribution.

To summarize, we might think about open pedagogy as an access-oriented commitment to learner-driven education AND as a process of designing architectures and using tools for learning that enable students to shape the public knowledge commons of which they are a part. We might insist on the centrality of the 5 *R*s to this work, and we might foreground the investments that open pedagogy shares with other learner-centered approaches to education. We might reconstitute open pedagogy continually, as our contexts shift and change and demand new, site-specific articulations. But if we want to begin "open" courses, programs, or institutions, what practical steps can we take to get started?

OEP, or open educational practices, can be defined as the set of practices that accompany either the use of OER or, more to our point, the adoption of open pedagogy. Here are some simple but profoundly transformative examples of OEP:

- Adapt or remix OER with students. Even the simple act of adding problem sets or discussion questions to an existing open textbook will help contribute to knowledge, to the quality of available OER, and to your students' sense of doing work that matters. The adaptation of the open textbook *Project Management for Instructional Designers* by successive cohorts of graduate students at Brigham Young University provides an excellent example of this approach.[7]

- Build OER with students. Though students may be beginners with most of the content in a course, they are often more adept than instructors at understanding what beginning students need in order to understand the material. Asking students to help reframe and re-present course content in new and inventive ways can add valuable OER to the commons while also allowing for the work that students do in courses to go on to have meaningful impact once the course ends. Consider the examples of the open textbook *Environmental ScienceBites* written by undergraduate students at the Ohio State University or the brief explainer videos created by psychology students around the world and curated by the Noba Project.[8]

- Teach students how to edit Wikipedia articles. By adding new content, revising existing content, adding citations, or adding images, students can (with the support of the Wiki Education Foundation) make direct contributions to one of the most popular public repositories for information.[9] Indeed, more than 22,000 students already have, including medical students at the University of California

San Francisco.[10] More than developing digital literacy and learning how to synthe-size, articulate, and share information, students engage with and understand the politics of editing, including how "truth" is negotiated by those who have access to the tools that shape it.

- Facilitate student-created and student-controlled learning environments. The learning management system (e.g., Canvas, Moodle, Blackboard, etc.) generally locks students into closed environments that prevent sharing and collaboration outside of the class unit; it perpetuates a surveillance model of education in which the instructor is able to consider metrics that students are not given access to; and it presupposes that all student work is disposable (as all of it will be deleted when the new course shell is imported for the next semester). Initiatives such as Domain of One's Own enable students to build "personal cyberinfrastructures"[11] where they can manage their own learning, control their own data, and design home ports that can serve as sites for collaboration and conversation about their work. Students can choose to openly license the work that they post on these sites, thereby contributing OER to the commons; they can also choose not to openly license their work, which is an exercising of their rights and perfectly in keeping with the ethos of open pedagogy. If students create their own learning architectures, they can (and should) control how public or private they wish to be, how and when to share or license their work, and what kinds of design, tools, and plug-ins will enhance their learning. It is important to point out here that open is not the opposite of private.

- Encourage students to apply their expertise to serve their community. Partner with nonprofit organizations to create opportunities for students to apply their research or marketing skills.[12] Or ask them to write (and submit for publication) op-ed pieces to share evidence-based approaches to tackling a local social problem.[13] Demonstrate the value of both knowledge application and service by scaffolding their entry into public scholarship.

- Engage students in public chats with authors or experts. Platforms such as Twitter can help engage students in scholarly and professional conversations with practitioners in their fields. This is another way that students can contribute to—not just consume—knowledge, and it shifts learning into a dialogic experience. In addition, if students are sharing work publicly, they can also use social media channels to drive mentors, teachers, peers, critics, experts, friends, family, and the public to their work for comment. Opening conversations about academic and transdisciplinary work—both student work and the work of established scholars and practitioners—is, like contributing to OER, a way to grow a thriving knowledge commons.

- Build course policies, outcomes, assignments, rubrics, and schedules of work collaboratively with students. Once we involve students in creating or revising OERs or in shaping learning architectures, we can begin to see the syllabus as more of a collaborative document, co-generated at least in part with our students. Can students help craft course policies that would support their learning, that they feel more ownership over? Can they add or revise course learning outcomes in order to ensure the relevancy of the course to their future paths? Can they develop assignments for themselves or their classmates and craft rubrics to accompany them to guide an evaluative process? Can they shape the course schedule according to rhythms that will help maximize their efforts and success?

- Let students curate course content. Your course is likely split into a predictable number of units (fourteen, for example) to conform to the academic calendar of the institution within which the course is offered. We would probably all agree that such segmenting of our fields is somewhat arbitrary; there is nothing ontological about Introduction to Psychology being fourteen weeks long (or spanning twenty-eight textbook chapters, etc.). And when we select a novel for a course on postcolonial literature or a lab exercise for Anatomy and Physiology, we are aware that there are a multitude of other good options for each that we could have chosen. We can involve students in the process of curating content for courses, either by offering them limited choices between different texts or by offering them solid time to curate a future unit more or less on their own (or in a group) as a research project. The content of a course may be somewhat prescribed by accreditation or field standards, but within those confines, we can involve students in the curation process, increasing the level of investment they have in the content while helping them acquire a key twenty-first-century skill.

- Ask critical questions about "open." When you develop new pathways based on open pedagogy, pay special attention to the barriers, challenges, and problems that emerge. Be explicit about them, honest about them, and share them widely with others working in open education so that we can work together to make improvements. Being an open educator in this fashion is especially crucial if we wish to avoid digital redlining, creating inequities (however unintentionally) through the use of technology.[14] Ask yourself: Do your students have access to broadband at home? Do they have the laptops or tablets they need to easily access and engage with OER? Do they have the support they need to experiment creatively, often for the first time, with technology tools? Do they have the digital literacies they need to ensure as much as is possible their safety and privacy online? Do you have a full understanding of the terms of service of the edtech tools you are using in your courses? As you work to increase the accessibility of your own course, are you also evaluating the tools and technologies you are using to ask how they help or hinder your larger vision for higher education?[15]

Open pedagogy is not a magical panacea for the crises that currently challenge higher ed. That being said, we both feel that open pedagogy offers a set of dynamic commitments that could help faculty and students articulate a sustainable, vibrant, and inclusive future for our educational institutions. By focusing on access, agency, and a commons-oriented approach to education, we can clarify our challenges and firmly assert a learner-centered vision for higher education.

As can be inferred from the essay above, open pedagogy is an actively evolving space that will continue to take shape and refine and challenge itself. In the subsection 2.3.3.2, "Critical Information Literacy and Open Pedagogy," we'll explore further the relationship between open pedagogy and librarianship and seek to unpack how and when scholarly communication librarians engage with faculty and students to support open and OER-enabled pedagogy.

NOTES

1. "Open Pedagogy," https://press.rebus.community/makingopentextbookswithstudents/chapter/open-peda-gogy/; *A Guide to Making Open Textbooks with Students*, https://press.rebus.community/makingopentext-bookswithstudents/; Creative Commons Attribution 4.0 International License, https://creativecommons.org/licenses/by/4.0/; Rebus Community, https://press.rebus.community/.
2. Catherine Cronin, "Opening Up Open Pedagogy," Catherine Cronin's professional website, April 24, 2017, http://catherinecronin.net/research/opening-up-open-pedagogy/; Katy Jordan, "The History of Open Education—A Timeline and Bibliography," *Dr Katy Jordan* (blog), June 19, 2017, https://shiftandrefresh.wordpress.com/2017/06/19/the-history-of-open-education-a-timeline-and-bibliography/; Dorey-Elias T, Morgan T, and Rolfe V, "Digging into the past – Historical branches of open," #OER18 Conference, April 18 and 19, 2018, https://oer18.oerconf.org/sessions/impact-of-the-uk-open-textbook-pilot-proj-ect-1897; Tannis Morgan, "Open Pedagogy and a Very Brief History of the Concept," *Explorations in the EdTech World* (blog), Tannis Morgan's professional website, December 21, 2016, https://homonym.ca/uncategorized/open-pedagogy-and-a-very-brief-history-of-the-concept/.
3. Claude Paquette, "Quelques fondements d'une pédagogie ouverte," *Québec français* 36 (1979): 20–21, quoted in Morgan, "Open Pedagogy."
4. David Wiley, "What Is Open Pedagogy?" *Improving Learning* (blog), October 21, 2013, https://opencon-tent.org/blog/archives/2975.
5. David Wiley, "OER-Enabled Pedagogy," *Improving Learning* (blog), May 2, 2017, https://opencontent.org/blog/archives/5009.
6. Mike Caulfield, "Putting Student-Produced OER at the Heart of the Institution," Hapgood, Mike Caulfield's professional website, September 7, 2016, https://hapgood.us/2016/09/07/putting-student-produced-oer-at-the-heart-of-the-institution/.
7. David Wiley et al., *Project Management for Instructional Designers* (EdTech Books, 2016). https://pm4id.org/.
8. Kylienne A. Clark, Travis R. Shaul, and Brian H. Lower, eds., *Environmental ScienceBites* (Columbus: Ohio State University, 2015); Noba, "2016–17 Noba + Psi Chi Student Video Award Recipients," https://nobaproject.com/student-video-award/winners.
9. WikiEdu, "Teach with Wikipedia," https://wikiedu.org/teach-with-wikipedia/.
10. Eryk Salvaggio, "For Wikipedia, the Doctor Is in …Class," WikiEdu, April 5, 2016, https://wikiedu.org/blog/2016/04/05/medical-students-wikipedia/.
11. University of Mary Washington, "Domain of One's Own," https://umw.domains/; Gardner Campbell, "A Personal Cyberinfrastructure," *EDUCAUSE Review* 44, no. 5 (September/October 2009): 58–59, https://er.educause.edu/articles/2009/9/a-personal-cyberinfrastructure.
12. Lori Rosenthal, "Mastering Research Methods with Community Projects," Action Teaching, https://www.actionteaching.org/award/community-action.
13. Kent State Online, "Assignment Type: Op-Ed," https://www-s3-live.kent.edu/s3fs-root/s3fs-public/file/OpEd_Handout.pdf.
14. Chris Gilliard, "Pedagogy and the Logic of Platforms," *EDUCAUSE Review* 52, no. 4 (July/August 2017): 64–65, https://er.educause.edu/articles/2017/7/pedagogy-and-the-logic-of-platforms.
15. Jesse Stommel, "Critically Evaluating Digital Tools," Digital Studies 101, Medium, January 21, 2016, https://dgst101.com/activity-critically-evaluating-digital-tools-3f60d468ce74.

BIBLIOGRAPHY

Campbell, Gardner. "A Personal Cyberinfrastructure." *EDUCAUSE Review* 44, no. 5 (September/October 2009): 58–59. https://er.educause.edu/articles/2009/9/a-personal-cyberinfrastructure.

Caulfield, Mike. "Putting Student-Produced OER at the Heart of the Institution." Hapgood, Mike Caulfield's professional website, September 7, 2016. https://hapgood.us/2016/09/07/putting-student-produced-oer-at-the-heart-of-the-institution/.

Clark, Kylienne A., Travis R. Shaul, and Brian H. Lower, eds. *Environmental ScienceBites*. Columbus: Ohio State University, 2015.

Cronin, Catherine. "Opening Up Open Pedagogy." Catherine Cronin's professional website, April 24, 2017. http://catherinecronin.net/research/opening-up-open-pedagogy/.

Dorey-Elias T, Morgan T and Rolfe V (2018). Digging into the past – Historical branches of open. #OER18 Conference, 18-19th April 2018. Available: https://oer18.oerconf.org/sessions/impact-of-the-uk-open-text-book-pilot-project-1897/ Slides: https://www.slideshare.net/VivRolfe/historical-branches-of-open

Gilliard, Chris. "Pedagogy and the Logic of Platforms." *EDUCAUSE Review* 52, no. 4 (July/August 2017): 64–65. https://er.educause.edu/articles/2017/7/pedagogy-and-the-logic-of-platforms.

Jordan, Katy. "The History of Open Education—A Timeline and Bibliography." *Dr Katy Jordan* (blog), June 19, 2017. https://shiftandrefresh.wordpress.com/2017/06/19/the-history-of-open-education-a-timeline-and-bibliography/.

Kent State Online. "Assignment Type: Op-Ed." https://www-s3-live.kent.edu/s3fs-root/s3fs-public/file/OpEd_Handout.pdf.

Morgan, Tannis. "Open Pedagogy and a Very Brief History of the Concept." *Explorations in the EdTech World* (blog), Tannis Morgan's professional website, December 21, 2016. https://homonym.ca/uncategorized/open-pedagogy-and-a-very-brief-history-of-the-concept/.

Noba. "2016–17 Noba + Psi Chi Student Video Award Recipients." https://nobaproject.com/student-video-award/winners.

Rosenthal, Lori. "Mastering Research Methods with Community Projects." Action Teaching. https://www.actionteaching.org/award/community-action.

Salvaggio, Eryk. "For Wikipedia, the Doctor Is in …Class." WikiEdu, April 5, 2016. https://wikiedu.org/blog/2016/04/05/medical-students-wikipedia/.

Stommel, Jesse. "Critically Evaluating Digital Tools." Digital Studies 101, Medium, January 21, 2016. https://dgst101.com/activity-critically-evaluating-digital-tools-3f60d468ce74.

University of Mary Washington. "Domain of One's Own." https://umw.domains/.

WikiEdu. "Teach with Wikipedia." https://wikiedu.org/teach-with-wikipedia/.

Wiley, David. "OER-Enabled Pedagogy." *Improving Learning* (blog), May 2, 2017. https://opencontent.org/blog/archives/5009.

———. "What Is Open Pedagogy?" *Improving Learning* (blog), October 21, 2013. https://opencontent.org/blog/archives/2975.

Wiley, David, et al. *Project Management for Instructional Designers*. EdTech Books, 2016. https://pm4id.org/.

CRITICAL INFORMATION LITERACY AND OPEN PEDAGOGY

Will Engle and Erin Fields

INTRODUCTION

Academic information literacy focuses on building students skills to engage in academic work which includes reading, evaluating, interpreting, and producing new knowledge. For librarianship, academic information literacy instruction initially focused on searching, accessing, and evaluating sources of information (e.g., book, journal article, etc.) within library systems as a means of supporting students' skill development. However, this approach ignored the more complex and critical skills needed to engage in academic work and simplified the cultural, political, and social aspects of information, making information literacy a set of neutral skills to be transferred from the librarian to the student.

Successful engagement in academic work means not only reading and understanding already existing research on a topic, but also engaging in critical evaluation of this research to create new knowledge. For students this means participating in the dialogue of the academy through criticizing and interpreting existing knowledge and creating new knowledge. This moves the conversation forward and brings students from outside academic engagement into the centre as collaborators and knowledge generators.

With new insights into instruction in academic libraries and the arrival of critical information literacy (CIL) within the professional research and governing organization documents (e.g., ACRL's *Framework for Information Literacy for Higher Education*), this critical form of academic engagement has become integral to the way in which librarianship perceives information literacy instruction. However, as with most discussions around information literacy and integration into academic environments, the question of how to engage faculty in incorporating this type of literacy instruction into coursework can be daunting. With the emergence of open education on academic campuses, the opportunity to align the values of CIL instruction with the pedagogical approaches to openness in the classroom provides librarians the opportunity to develop instruction addressing the critical aspects of information creation, dissemination, and interpretation.

This subsection will provide an overview of the fundamental differences between information literacy and CIL, outline how CIL and open pedagogy (OP) align, showcase examples of CIL-enabled OP and opportunities for librarians to engage in OP.

OVERVIEW OF CRITICAL INFORMATION LITERACY

The concept of information literacy was formalized in academic libraries through governing bodies like the American Library Association (ALA) and the Association of College and Research Libraries (ACRL). With the introduction of the *Information Literacy Competency Standards for Higher Education*, academic libraries engaged in integrating instructional practices into the profession and in the classrooms. The focus initially for information literacy instruction was on the development of measurable skills and competencies intricately connected to the practices of engaging in library information systems (e.g., library catalogue, article databases, etc.) to find and use information. This kind of instruction then was tied tightly to student success within academic coursework.

This initial focus on skills and standards for information literacy came under a lot of scrutiny as this approach to instruction did not address how information is constructed, shared, and given meaning by communities. This approach to information literacy instruction in librarianship standardizes the mechanical practices of finding, selecting, and using information but ignores the political, social, and cultural dynamics of information. This skills-based approach simplifies information and makes it a neutral entity by which students acquiring information skills can become productive at completing discrete information-seeking assignments but not critically engage in complex discussion such as who creates information and information systems; who is missing from the knowledge creation processes; who verifies what is considered knowledge; who has access to information; and what are we missing within the current information production.[1]

CIL instruction was in part a response to the competency-based model of information literacy in librarianship and intended to be an approach to information literacy instruction that addressed the complex systems of power that impact how information is created, distributed, and accessed. Drawing from critical pedagogy, this was a radical shift from skills-based instruction to instruction that facilitates students identifying the social construction and political dimensions of information and information systems. CIL makes visible the unequal power relations of people engaged in constructing and producing information and facilitates students building understanding of how information and knowledge are formed and reinforced within these systems. As students seek, examine, evaluate, and use information, they engage in critically questioning their role in these systems and their ability to enact change. The focus, then, of CIL is to facilitate this critical learning through student-centred instruction that prioritizes problem-posing and reflection. This shift in information literacy encourages instruction that focuses on elevating understanding of information inequity, privilege, authority, and power to engage students in action as critically aware citizens.[2]

Dig Deeper: Critical Pedagogy

Critical pedagogy is an education framework drawn from critical theory. In critical pedagogy the student and teacher engage in discussion and action that critically evaluate systems of power and seek to shift thinking toward critical consciousness—understanding the oppressive nature of social and political systems and personally engaging in taking action against them.

Theorists

Paolo Freire, Peter McLaren, Henry Giroux, bell hooks

With the ACRL *Framework for Information Literacy for Higher Education* (2016) replacing the *Information Literacy Competency Standards for Higher Education* (2000), information literacy was redefined as a social process by which learners engage in critique of the social and institutional information production and distribution processes. While the ACRL Information Literacy Framework was a step toward integrating a more critically focused pedagogy into information literacy and librarianship, criticisms of the Framework have noted the focus on growing expertise and the skills-based measurable approaches which remains at odds with the tenets of CIL—those of reflecting on information systems and participating in information communities. Readings on the criticisms of the Framework can be found under "Additional Resources" below.

OVERVIEW OF OPEN PEDAGOGY

Open scholarship is founded on the premise of barrier-free and equitable access to knowledge, with the understanding that the creation and dissemination of knowledge are best understood as social practices. Under this umbrella term, open education encompasses a set of practices directed at making the process and products of education more transparent, understandable, and available to all people. This effort includes not only the creation and use of open access learning materials but also the application of open scholarship to the practices of teaching and learning (i.e., the pedagogy). OP is therefore situated at the intersection of teaching and learning, technologies, and social connectivism.

Dig Deeper: Connectivism

Connectivism is an educational framework that posits that learning is part of a knowledge creation process facilitated by information sharing across connected learning communities, often assisted through networked technology. In connectivism, knowledge resides in a diversity of opinions and nodes, and growing and maintaining connections is important for the cyclical nature of learning. Learners will connect to a network to share knowledge they have learned, they will acquire new information or beliefs through sharing and dialogue within the network, and they will then share these new understandings, thus continuing the cycle of learning.[3]

Theorists
George Siemens, Stephan Downes

The core values for OP include teaching and learning practices that reduce barriers that prevent equitable access to education, including economic, technical, social, cultural, and political factors. OP facilitates connections across the boundaries of learning experiences that occur within classrooms, on campuses, and in communities by critically engaging with tools and practices that mediate learning, knowledge building, and sharing. OP protects the agency and ownership of one's own learning experiences, choices of expression, and degrees of participation and resists the treatment of open as neutral by providing space for critical evaluation and reflection while engaging in open practices.[4]

OP applies much of the earlier work of critical pedagogy to the modern teaching contexts. At its core, it encompasses a social justice approach to the collaborative and transparent construction of knowledge made openly available through networked technologies. While open scholarship focuses on equitable access to knowledge, the focus of OP is equitable participation in the *creation* of knowledge. In this way, OP often transforms the student experience within the classroom. It can help students begin to see themselves as scholars and it decentres the instructor from the information expert to a facilitation role that supports student negotiation of ideas and transforms the efforts of their learning into open knowledge resources. Thus, in this model, the university's approaches to teaching and learning and research are more closely aligned, and students are collaborators with faculty in the production of knowledge and meaning.[5]

If a core goal of scholarship is research, dissemination, and dialogue to further the knowledge base and growth of fields of study, then OP engages students in this very same process within their courses. In contrast to traditional learning assessments such as multiple-choice quizzes or essays, student work in OP is seen as having value beyond just informing the learner or instructor. As a result, students are asked to create new knowledge and given a degree of agency, autonomy, and control over their work. More so and fundamental to most OP projects, students are encouraged and given the opportunity to openly share their work with authentic audiences and not just with their immediate instructor or adviser. The projects can require a shift in the way students engage with their learning environment and communities. OP assignments can involve students engaging with communities other than their peers in a classroom, opening their ideas up to public scrutiny, and creating and communicating in new ways. When students openly publish their work through online platforms such blogs, wikis, open textbooks, social media, and so on, they are not necessarily using the same format or skills that they would in writing a research paper or persuasive essay; instead they are applying new strategies to the information and knowledge they have to produce something people will use.

ALIGNMENTS OF OPEN PEDAGOGY AND CRITICAL INFORMATION LITERACY

Transforming the classroom to engage students in constructing and sharing knowledge for authentic audiences represents an opportunity for information professionals to teach CIL. The creation process has the potential for students to engage in critically thinking about not only the information they find but also the tools that they use to find, create, and share information. This provides librarianship the opportunity to engage in instruction on the values and authority reinforced in information systems and processes. The unequal power relations of people engaged in constructing and producing information, the gaps and exclusions in existing academic publishing practices, the barriers for communities to participate or share in knowledge, can be brought to the forefront of the learning experiences of students as they negotiate intellectual property, author rights, copyright, metadata and description, and information access. This deeper engagement provides a natural opportunity to critically question their own practice and participate in actively resisting the inequities mentioned above while they create and openly share their work.[6]

CASE STUDIES OF CIL AND OP

While CIL and OP have obvious alignments, how are they enabled inside of the classroom? The following are examples of librarian and faculty OP and CIL course collaborations.

SOCIAL JUSTICE ZINE CREATION

In collaboration with the Gender, Race, Sexuality, and Social Justice Institute course GRSJ 102: Global Issues in Social Justice at the University of British Columbia (UBC), teams of seven to ten students were assigned to create a zine based on a self-chosen social justice theme (see figure 2.19). Zines are a self-published medium that are often created by collaging existing materials (e.g., images, text, etc.) with self-created content and published in simple photocopied formats for open sharing. For the assignment students were asked to pick a zine theme, research and write on specific related topics, cite resources, find and use visual elements, develop a copyright/reproduction statement for their finished work, and openly share their zines in a community fair and with public and special library collections. A number of common information tasks found in traditional course assignments (e.g., research papers) can be identified in the zine assignment: searching, accessing, reading, translating, and citing information sources. However, with the open nature of the assignment and the nontraditional form of publication, the students had to engage in thinking about information literacy elements in a more critical way through the introduction of more complex issues of copyright and intellectual property, open publishing and sharing, and knowledge creation and cultural appropriation.

Figure 2.19
1970s fanzines by Jake from Wikimedia Commons is licensed under CC-BY 2.0. Image available at https://commons.wikimedia.org/wiki/File:1970s_fanzines_(21224199545).jpg

SAMPLE ACTIVITY—COPYRIGHT, CULTURAL APPROPRIATION, AND CREATING CONTENT

Students were introduced to Canadian copyright as it pertains to creating, owning, and sharing intellectual property. In Canadian copyright law, intellectual property is protected when the idea is tangibly fixed (e.g., written, drawn, recorded, etc.) by the creator and lasts for fifty years after the death of the author. Once students learned these details around Canadian copyright, they were asked to analyze the example of an Inuit sacred shaman robe design and its use by a UK-based fashion label, KTZ, for the creation of "shaman towelling sweatshirt."[7] Students were asked to discuss this question: Does Canadian copyright apply to protect the intellectual property rights of the original creator in this example? This discussion led to students identifying the ways intellectual property and copyright fail to address traditional knowledge and the ways copyright protects financial benefits of property rather than the significance of the items to the cultural, spiritual, and communal health of the people who created them. With this new awareness, students were asked to think about their zine creation and how the themes and topics they chose might lead them to want to use culturally significant sources (e.g., images, texts, etc.). This led to discussion of cultural appropriation, representation, and the development of a list of considerations and practices when using cultural objects in their zines.

GAP ANALYSIS AND EDITING WIKIPEDIA

In collaboration with the First Nations and Indigenous Studies (FNIS) program at UBC, a Wikipedia-based assignment was incorporated into FNIS 220: Representation and Indigenous Cultural Politics. The assignment involved an analysis of a Wikipedia article on an Indigenous subject to identify errors, omissions, and possible improvements. Upon completion of the gap analysis, students were put into thematic groups to identify a single article to edit in real time. To perform the analysis, students needed to think not only about the information in the articles but also about how the articles are constructed within the Wikipedia editorial system, which may contribute to the gaps in the article. To engage students in thinking about their assignments, a workshop from the library was designed to address the differences in publishing and descriptive practices in open and closed systems and a critical overview of Wikipedia's neutral point of view, categorization, consensus, and reliable source guidelines (see figure 2.20).

Figure 2.20
The 5 Pillars of Wikipedia by Giulia Forsythe is licensed CC-BY 2.0.
Available at https://www.flickr.com/photos/gforsythe/21684596874

SAMPLE ACTIVITY—WIKIPEDIA CATEGORIZATION AND LIBRARY SUBJECT HEADINGS

Students were introduced to the Wikipedia guidelines on categorization. Categories are used in Wikipedia to make links between both individual pages and topic-based lists of pages. The guidelines, while focusing mostly on grammar and structure, do address the use of terminology. Students were also introduced to the concept of subject headings in library systems with a specific focus on how they are created, structured, and used systematically. Students were asked to analyze the categories in the article for Aaron Nelson Moody, a Sḵwx̱wú7mesh artist. Students were also asked to review the subject headings in the UBC Library catalogue for *Continuum: Vision and Creativity on the Northwest Coast*, a book containing Aaron Nelson Moody's artwork. The students were prompted with the following question: How do the categories and subject headings identify and describe Aaron Nelson Moody's artwork and identity? This prompt led students to identify missing and problematic descriptions of Aaron Nelson Moody and his work (e.g., use of subject heading "Indian Art" and the lack of his identified nation). Students further delved into issues of content organization and how inaccurate, misrepresented, and omitted descriptive language impacts the visibility of information sources but also reinforces dominant ideologies (i.e., values and beliefs of the majority) about Indigenous peoples.

DISCUSSION QUESTIONS

Using the sample activities discussed above, reflect on the following:

1. What elements of these activities address CIL development?
2. What elements of these activities address open pedagogical elements?
3. What impacts could the engagement from the activity have on the students in their zine creation?
4. What impacts could the engagement from the activity have on the students' gap analysis and Wikipedia editing?
5. What potential impact do these activities have on the growth of critical consciousness in the students?

OPPORTUNITIES FOR LIBRARIANS TO ENGAGE AND SUPPORT OPEN PEDAGOGY

Librarians and information professionals are uniquely situated to support both instructors and students engaging in OP projects. A key service area for many academic libraries is supporting the creation and sharing of knowledge, and OP extends the application of this service need from research to course curriculum.

Key support needs for OP include the following:

- *Research and information seeking*—Most knowledge creation projects start with research. Information professionals are experts at helping to identify relevant databases, journals, and library collections, as well as instructing on effective and efficient search strategies.
- *Copyright and intellectual property*—In Canada, students own the copyright to their work. Information professionals are often situated to help instructors and students

understand both their rights as copyright holders and their obligations when using other people's copyrighted materials. Relatedly, many OP projects are grounded upon the use of open copyright licenses, such as Creative Commons, and information professionals are also positioned to help instruct on identifying and applying open licenses.

- *Open educational resource/repository locating and evaluation*—OP projects can often involve adapting, modifying, or creating open resources. Information professionals are also well situated in helping instructors and students find open resources they can use, as well as in providing guidelines or suggestions for the evaluation of such repositories and resources.
- *Open tools/technologies*—Many traditional learning technologies do not support open publishing of open projects, and information professions are often knowledgeable about evaluating open technologies as well as often being responsible for directly managing open publishing systems.
- *Open publishing workflows and project management*—Often OP projects involve long-term, iterative processes similar to many projects in which informational professionals have experience. Providing workflow or project management suggestions and support can help make those projects viable and sustainable.
- *Dissemination and sharing strategies*—Many OP projects seek to share their outputs with authentic audiences through disciplinary and academic websites, community platforms, journals, and social media.

KEY TAKEAWAYS

Library and information professionals' approach to supporting information literacy have shifted from a skills-based practice connected to seeking and using information to a more critical approach that engages with how complex systems of power impact how knowledge is constructed, accessed, and shared. In OP, student or learner work is often seen as having value beyond the classroom, and OP assignments engage learners in knowledge construction as a social practice as part of their learning process. Library and information professionals are ideally situated to provide support for OP projects; core library services such research, copyright, and scholarly dissemination support can enhance such projects and help them succeed. More so, the ability to provide support for CIL helps elevate such projects from being solely about creating resources to facilitating students' learning about, and critically engaging with, the power structures and social processes inherent in information systems and in knowledge construction, access, and sharing.

ADDITIONAL RESOURCES

INFORMATION LITERACY FRAMEWORK DEBATES

Association of College and Research Libraries. *Framework for Information Literacy for Higher Education*. Chicago: Association of College and Research Libraries, 2016. https://www.ala.org/acrl/standards/ilframework.

Beilin, Ian. "Beyond the Threshold: Conformity, Resistance, and the ACRL Information Literacy Framework for Higher Education." *In the Library with the Lead Pipe*, February 25, 2015. http://www.inthelibrarywiththeleadpipe.org/2015/beyond-the-threshold-conformity-resistance-and-the-aclr-information-literacy-framework-for-higher-education/.

Fister, Barbara. "Crossing Thresholds and Learning in Libraries." *Library Babel Fish* (blog), Inside Higher Ed, May 22, 2014. https://www.insidehighered.com/blogs/ library-babel-fish/crossing-thresholds-and-learning-libraries.

Seale, Maura. "Enlightenment, Neoliberalism, and Information Literacy." *Canadian Journal of Academic Librarianship* 1 (2016): 80–91. https://doi.org/10.33137/cjal-rcbu.v1.24308.

OPEN PEDAGOGY

DeRosa, Robin, and Rajiv Jhangiani. "Open Pedagogy." Open Pedagogy Notebook. Chapter 1 in *A Guide to Making Open Textbooks with Students*, edited by Elizabeth Mays. Montreal, QC: Rebus Press, 2017. http://openpedagogy.org/open-pedagogy/.

Open UBC Working Group. "Toolkits: Education." Open UBC, University of British Columbia. Accessed July 17, 2020. https://open.ubc.ca/education/toolkits-education/.

NOTES

1. Cushla Kapitzke, "Information Literacy: A Review and Poststructural Critique." *Australian Journal of Language and Literacy* 26, no. 1 (2003): 53–66; Christine Pawley, "Information Literacy: A Contradictory Coupling," *Library Quarterly* 73, no. 4 (2003): 422–52.
2. Eamon Tewell, "A Decade of Critical Information Literacy: A Review of the Literature," *Communications in Information Literacy* 9, no. 1 (2015): 24–43; James Elmborg, "Critical Information Literacy: Implications for Instructional Practice," *Journal of Academic Librarianship* 32, no. 2 (2006): 192–99; James Elmborg, "Critical Information Literacy: Definitions and Challenges," in *Transforming Information Literacy Programs: Intersecting Frontiers of Self, Library Culture, and Campus Community*, ed. Carroll Wetzel Wilkinson and Courtney Bruch (Chicago: Association of College and Research Libraries, 2012), 75–95.
3. George Siemens, "Connectivism: A Learning Theory for the Digital Age," *International Journal of Instructional Technology and Distance Learning* 2 (2005): 3–10.
4. Caroline Sinkinson, "The Values of Open Pedagogy," *EDUCAUSE Review* (blog), November 14, 2018, https://er.educause.edu/blogs/2018/11/the-values-of-open-pedagogy.
5. Mike Neary and Joss Winn, "The Student as Producer: Reinventing the Student Experience in Higher Education," in *The Future of Higher Education: Policy, Pedagogy and the Student Experience*, ed. Les Bell, Howard Stevenson, and Mike Neary (London: Continuum, 2009), 192–210.
6. Erin Fields and Adair Harper, "Intersections of Open Pedagogy and Critical Information Literacy—A Case Study," *BCcampus*, November 27, 2018, https://bccampus.ca/2018/11/27/ intersections-of-open-pedagogy-and-critical-information-literacy-a-case-study/.
7. Sima Sahar Zerehi, "KTZ Fashion under Fire for Using Inuit Design without Family's Consent," CBC News, November 25, 2015, https://www.cbc.ca/news/canada/north/ktz-fashion-inuit-design-1.3337047.

BIBLIOGRAPHY

Elmborg, James. "Critical Information Literacy: Implications for Instructional Practice." *Journal of Academic Librarianship* 32, no. 2 (2006): 192–99.

———. " Critical Information Literacy: Definitions and Challenges." In *Transforming Information Literacy Programs: Intersecting Frontiers of Self, Library Culture, and Campus Community*, edited by Carroll Wetzel Wilkinson and Courtney Bruch, 75–95. Chicago: Association of College and Research Libraries, 2012.

Fields, Erin, and Adair Harper. "Intersections of Open Pedagogy and Critical Information Literacy—A Case Study." BCcampus, November 27, 2018. https://bccampus.ca/2018/11/27/ intersections-of-open-pedagogy-and-critical-information-literacy-a-case-study/.

Kapitzke, Cushla. "Information Literacy: A Review and Poststructural Critique." *Australian Journal of Language and Literacy* 26, no. 1 (2003): 53–66.

Neary, Mike, and Joss Winn. "The Student as Producer: Reinventing the Student Experience in Higher Education." In *The Future of Higher Education: Policy, Pedagogy and the Student Experience*, edited by Les Bell, Howard Stevenson, and Mike Neary, 192–210. London: Continuum, 2009.

Pawley, Christine. "Information Literacy: A Contradictory Coupling." *Library Quarterly* 73, no. 4 (2003): 422–52.

Siemens, George. "Connectivism: A Learning Theory for the Digital Age." *International Journal of Instructional Technology and Distance Learning* 2 (2005): 3–10.

Sinkinson, Caroline. "The Values of Open Pedagogy." *EDUCAUSE Review* (blog), November 14, 2018. https://er.educause.edu/blogs/2018/11/the-values-of-open-pedagogy.

Tewell, Eamon. "A Decade of Critical Information Literacy: A Review of the Literature." *Communications in Information Literacy* 9, no. 1 (2015): 24–43.

Zerehi, Sima Sahar. "KTZ Fashion under Fire for Using Inuit Design without Family's Consent." CBC News, November 25, 2015. https://www.cbc.ca/news/canada/north/ktz-fashion-inuit-design-1.3337047.

CURRENT ISSUES IN THE FIELD

Margaret McLaughlin, Ali Versluis, and Sarah Hare

INTRODUCTION

As the field of open education has grown and OER adoption has become more widespread, discussion about related critical issues has also developed, particularly in the discipline of library and information science (LIS). This section explores current issues that are often less visible or present in the literature but are paramount to librarians interested in furthering OER and representing the complexities of OER creation and adoption in their outreach.

OER provide an important solution to the access disparities caused by high costs for course materials, but they are not a panacea for the complicated issues that plague higher education. We believe that this stance can and should shape librarians' practice: we can balance presenting OER as an important tool for furthering access while still adequately representing the numerous barriers and constraints involved in adopting, sharing, accessing, and creating OER.

Our section begins by grounding OER usage within the larger publisher landscape, discussing trends in the delivery of OER and publisher attempts at openwashing, or co-opting open to further financial gains. We then address the unsustainable labor practices inherent in the open education movement, including the trend of temporary and part-time positions in leading OER work, limited compensation, overreliance on grant funding, and a lack of recognition of collaborators. Finally, we discuss how technocracy is embedded in open education discourse by addressing barriers students and educators face when adopting or using OER. Throughout the section, we present practical tips and resources, ultimately providing open advocates with a conceptual overview of critical issues as well as tangible actions they can undertake.

Remember, critique is an act of care, and OER are valuable and worthy of investment. Our critique serves not to dismantle ideas or movements, but to improve them. Only with critical engagement will librarians move the discourse about OER forward and make our practices more nuanced and accessible.

CURRENT PUBLISHER LANDSCAPE

Recently, publishing companies like McGraw-Hill Education, Pearson, Wiley, and Cengage have seen decreased revenues on print course material sales as students use a variety of strategies to save money.[1] The Scholarly Publishing and Academic Resources Coalition (SPARC) has conducted an in-depth analysis of the factors driving publishers' decline in revenue, which include decreasing national student enrollment, pricing challenges, and declining rates of student purchasing. In order to address their shrinking revenue, publishing companies have had to pursue and implement creative strategies for product development, often shifting their focus to digital learning or online-only course material and assessment products.[2] These trends have resulted in publishing companies entering the OER and data collection space.

At the same time, North American higher education as a whole is increasingly concerned with creating efficiencies while maximizing student retention. In order to reduce teaching costs, many institutions have opted to hire increasing numbers of sessional or untenured instructors, leading to widespread adjunctification and large course loads for instructors. This emphasis on efficiency has fostered an overreliance on using quantitative data to evaluate instructor effectiveness and student learning.

This emphasis on demonstrable success enables a technocratic audit culture that relies almost exclusively on statistical data to measure progress. Quantifiable statistics, such as higher test scores, lower course costs, and increased graduation rates, become synonymous with improved teaching and learning, which ultimately risks placing erudition and memorization entirely over critical engagement and transferable skills.[3] These technocratic higher education systems view their students less as students and more as human capital used to justify and measure an institution's success and prestige. This is compounded by the material conditions of teaching at the postsecondary level, where widespread adjunctification and large course loads have become the norm. Insecure faculty employment, coupled with higher education's predilection for asserting efficiency above all has fostered an overreliance on quantitative data to evaluate both instructor effectiveness and student learning.

OPENWASHING

Sometimes called *faux-pen*, openwashing intentionally co-opts the language of open for proprietary means without investment in the commons.[4] Publishing companies openwash when they call content that is not openly licensed "OER" or "open." There have been a number of recent examples of companies marketing new open or OER products that simply are not open.[5] This strategy capitalizes on the fact that instructors have been told that open is inherently good without a thorough explanation of open licensing or *why* open matters.

Openwashing is taken a step further when companies fetter OER as part of their products or platforms. Billy Meinke-Lau, OER technologist at the University of Hawai'i, notes that to fetter means "to restrain from motion, from action, from progress."[6] In the case of OER, fettering packages free and openly licensed materials into for-profit products, essentially rendering the 5R permissions that characterize OER untenable and limiting future adaptations and revisions. There are several models companies use to sell products that use OER. One is "openwrapping," which Scott Robison, Portland State University's associate director of digital learning and design describes as publishers wrapping services around OER.[7] These services can include "ancillary teaching materials, adaptive/personalized learning tools, data analytics, [and] customer support."[8] Another model is the freemium model, where instructors are given access to one of these services temporarily or until they reach a particular threshold, at which point they are asked to pay or are prompted to encourage their institution to purchase the product. Both of these models are designed to provide a seamless, value-added option for instructors, as they often make searching for OER more straightforward and robust by aggregating repositories and cleaning metadata, providing ancillary materials like question banks, and offering easy-to-use assessment mechanisms. However, despite the platforms using free OER, students are asked to pay to access them, either through fees related to a particular course or by contributing a portion of their tuition dollars to purchase institutional use. While the labor that companies contribute to enhance OER should be compensated, these products inherently ignore the intent of the creator of the original OER: to enable others to build upon the work. Additionally, while the enhancements provided often center on instructors and administrators, they frequently result in students being charged.

In short, these tools exploit several gaps that the open education movement has not yet been able to address: discoverability, the availability of ancillary materials, metadata consistency, the ability to pay instructors to develop content in areas where there are not many options, and the resources needed to continually maintain content. In a recent blog post, Jhangiani noted that sellers of these tools even purposefully present OER adoption as difficult, sometimes impossible, arguing that their product is the only mechanism instructors can use to manage this feat.[9] Despite their characterization as a magic-bullet solution, these platforms are problematic in that they utilize openly licensed content and the labor of OER creators, but none of this additional work benefits the commons. OER repositories are not improved, and related ancillary materials are not shared broadly or openly licensed as a result of publisher participation.

The revision of content is even stymied, as publisher platforms often limit the permissions that were originally inherent in the OER content they use. For example, one platform may use an OpenStax textbook that was originally licensed CC BY. When the OER is shared on the OpenStax site, the 5R permissions—often used a litmus test for evaluating if something is an OER—are intact. Educators can distribute the text, edit and remix it, and then re-share their adapted OER under any license they choose. When this same openly licensed text is locked in a commercial platform, there is often no mechanism for educators interested in remixing content. The platform makes it difficult to export an entire file in order to make changes. Beyond co-opting OER, for-profit publisher tools impede the development of the OER, often using the term *open* to convince instructors that these tools are inherently good or valuable.

STRATEGIES FOR LIBRARIANS AND OTHER OER ADVOCATES

- Utilize overviews of publisher products that incorporate OER. For example, open access and scholarly communication librarian Abbey Elder has created a spreadsheet that catalogs commercial tools that integrate OER into their platforms, which may be a good starting point for librarians considering a particular tool for their campus.[10]
- Use the ALMS framework to assess how specific tools limit or further open.[11] The ALMS framework assesses the technical decisions that impede or allow the 5R permissions, holding that if creators do not consider subsequent adaptations of the OER, other educators will not be able to enact the 5R permissions even if they are legally allowed to do so.
- Develop litmus tests similar to the ALMS framework that can be used to evaluate tools and publishers. One example of an existing litmus test is the CARE Framework, created by Petrides, Levin, and Watson.[12] The CARE Framework holds that thoughtful OER stewards should ensure that the content they create or adapt can be released widely and intentionally and explicitly empower minority voices in OER creation and adoption. This framework could be used to evaluate publisher platforms. Librarians should also consider developing other checklists or frameworks to analyze how platforms license the content they create, their business and sustainability model, and how they encourage or inhibit adaptations.
- Avoid using *open* as a proxy for *good* or *ethical*, and instead clearly define *open* so that instructors understand differences between open and affordable course materials.

Librarians might discuss the potential for corporate co-optation with instructors and provide guidance on appropriate licenses for avoiding it, namely licenses with noncommercial terms.

INCLUSIVE ACCESS

OER offer several benefits that affordable course material does not. For example, OER are completely free to students, students can access them after graduation, and there are no digital rights management (DRM) barriers (see figure 2.21 for additional details). Still, instructors will likely need to use a variety of strategies, including utilizing affordable content solutions or library-licensed resources, in order to move away from traditional course materials. This is particularly true for specialized courses where OER have not yet been developed.

"Can I Do That?" Affordable Course Material Options

	Inclusive Access	"OER" Courseware Platforms	Open Educational Resources	Library Licensed Materials	Websites and © online materials
	Digital course packs produced by publishers available online at a reduced subscription cost.	Subscription, digital course packs that may include a mix of open and proprietary content.	Free course content that is openly licensed to enable use and reuse.	Materials available freely to students and staff through the Library.	Content that is free to access online, but permissions for users may vary.
Can I get a print copy?	No	No	Yes	No	No
Can I download and keep a copy?	No	No	Yes	?	?
Can I import it into our LMS?	Yes	?	Yes	?	No
Can my students use it after my course ends?	No	No	Yes	?	?
Can I edit & revise it?	?	?	Yes	No	No
Can I share a copy of the version I edited?	No	?	Yes	No	No
Can I find ancillary materials optimized for the book?	Yes	?	?	No	?
Price	Typically <$100	Typically <$40	FREE	FREE*	FREE

■ Requires a subscription to rent digital content.
■ Some or all content is openly licensed (you can reuse & edit).
■ Content is free to read, but not to edit.

*Library-licensed e-books may be free for students to access, but they require users to log in and the library must pay fees to keep access.

"Can I do that?" by Abbey Elder, Helen McManus, and Jamie Hazlitt (2020) is licensed CC BY 4.0
[V.1.0 last updated January 28, 2020]

Figure 2.21
"Can I Do That?" Affordable Course Material Options by Abbey Elder, used under a CC-BY 4.0 License.

Inclusive access programs, sometimes called "automatic textbook billing," are one affordable course material solution. In exchange for every student in a particular course paying for access to a digital-only textbook (usually as part of their fees for the course), publishing companies discount course materials for all students. Institutions with these programs are usually directly involved in negotiating with publishers, liaising with them to troubleshoot issues, promoting the program to instructors, and processing student payments. While it may appear that inclusive access programs provide a vehicle both for institutions to intervene in the rising cost of course materials and for students to save money, there are several issues with this model. Rajiv Jhangiani, associate vice provost of open education at Kwantlen Polytechnic University, notes that students are essentially leasing content, as they will not have perpetual access to the course materials provided through inclusive access programs.[13] Students will also often experience DRM restrictions that limit how they can view and print the text. Additionally, the e-books in inclusive access packages are still essentially traditionally copyrighted textbooks, with no mechanism for instructors to revise or remix content based on context, audience, or learning objectives.

Perhaps most concerningly, the process for students to opt out of inclusive access programs is notoriously difficult, raising questions about student agency and autonomy. While an opt-out mechanism is required by US federal regulations under 34 C.F.R. Sec. 668.164(c),[14] Jhangiani notes that publishers have a "vested interest" in reducing the number of opt outs.[15] This often means that opt-out processes are not visible to students, the deadline for opting out is unattainable, and opting out can be attached to punitive measures for institutions or students. Citing an example at Trident Technical College, SPARC notes that this "pits the financial interests of the institution against the financial interests of the students" because the institution might lose money if it does not reach a quota or if too many students opt out.[16] A recent report from the U.S. Public Interest Research Group (PIRG) found that more than a third (68%) of the fifty-two inclusive access contracts they analyzed required institutions to meet a quota for the number of students automatically billed in order to secure discounts.[17]

Publishers' endeavors to emphasize affordable, digital-only course material programs are to be understood as diversifying revenue streams rather than altruism. SPARC notes that a digital-only strategy allows publishers to "lower their wholesale prices to reflect lower costs such as the savings on printing, binding, shipping and warehousing costs."[18] Inclusive access programs also allow publishers to eliminate print books that feed the used book market and cut out the markup generated by bookstores that sell print books to students, making discounted rates still profitable. Inclusive access programs' emphasis on publisher profit, as well as the constraints students face when using them, are considerations that librarians can introduce to instructors in order to complicate the narrative around inclusive access programs. Indeed, librarians may find that inclusive access models are presented as *the* answer to the problem of course material costs on their campus. An important response to this sentiment is to help instructors untangle the stakeholders involved in inclusive access models (including publishers and institutions themselves) and both the risks and benefits students face.

STRATEGIES FOR LIBRARIANS AND OTHER OER ADVOCATES

- Attempt to strike a balance between being open to other affordable course material solutions, giving voice to student concerns, and articulating the ethical concerns inherent in some models.
- Incorporate clear explanations of the differences between open and affordable course material solutions into all outreach.
- Prioritize the creation of OER where there is a lack of developed materials in order to ensure that there are OER options for every course, resulting in less need for affordable course material solutions. This may entail prioritizing more specialized or niche courses when reviewing OER creation stipend applications or deciding where to devote library staff time and expertise.

- Stay current with conversations on publishing company models and digital learning tools in order to dispel myths about specific products or approaches. Michael Feldstein's *eLiterate* blog often provides in-depth analyses of educational technology tools and is a useful resource for LIS students and librarians alike.[19]
- Take a historical approach to outreach in order to help instructors understand that there is "no mechanism preventing publishers from resuming their historical rate of price increases once [the inclusive access model] becomes widespread."[20] The Student PIRG report found that most contracts do not specify restrictions on price increases, for example.[21] Comparing inclusive access deals to journal Big Deals may be an effective approach for illustrating that this model makes controlling long-term prices close to impossible.

PRIVACY

Both of these trends have created a host of related issues that are important to librarians. Perhaps the most important trend is related to student privacy, as inclusive access programs and commercial platforms that incorporate OER both generally collect and sometimes even sell student data back to the institution for decision-making purposes. This data may include students' physical location when using course materials, study and reading habits, and overall performance.[22] The data may also be connected to the student information system (SIS), which includes demographic information about students, including their name, birth date, grades, and registration status.[23] Understanding privacy implications is complex and requires an awareness of how data is collected, stored, and shared between systems. Understanding how federal policies like the Family Educational Rights and Privacy Act (FERPA) interact with local agreements like end user license agreements is also a challenge.

A common retort to concerns about student privacy is that students are fine with data collection. Librarians should refute this erroneous assertion strongly and regularly, bringing data into the conversation as necessary. For example, research done as part of the Data Doubles Project illustrated that students "looked negatively upon" providing data to entities outside of their institution.[24]

While legislation like the Family Educational Rights and Privacy Act (FERPA) should protect students, SPARC notes that it has not been updated in decades and does not cover all use cases.[25] Meinke reinforces this, stating that data collected by these platforms is often exempt from FERPA protections for students, as many companies are defined as actors with an educational purpose.[26] This means that librarians should rely on other frameworks for understanding data collection practices and advocating for students. While the discussion is focused on library data collection, assessment librarian Andrew Asher presents one framework that could be of value for privacy advocates. The framework uses three guiding principles first outlined in the Belmont Report and often used by institutional research boards (IRBs):

> respect for persons, which establishes the requirements of disclosure of the data being collected and informed consent, beneficence, which asserts the research should first do no harm ...and justice, which states that the selection of research subjects should be equitable.[27]

While the data collection inherent in many educational technology tools and course material platforms is not required to be approved by IRB, this sort of framework may help librarians ask the right questions of companies and push back on unethical practices. For example, student consent to data collection is often inherent in the use of the learning management system (LMS)—which is embedded in many universities' core processes, including grading—and thus students' ability to opt out is often nonexistent. Asher's framework advocates for informed consent as well as student education on the types of data being collected.

LABOR

Although for-profit publishers make explicit their contributions to the open and affordable course content ecosystem by marketing additional features, robust metadata, and other "value-added" services, a nuanced understanding of the labor that goes into OER and OE-related efforts is still not widely appreciated. Many of these issues—sustainable funding models, academic status, reward and recognition, workload—are made infinitely more complex by the fact that they are largely structural and require the attention and intervention of administrators.

While open education work should be not solely in the purview of the library, libraries often provide the bulk of the resources to make this work a reality. While open education librarian positions are established and gaining prominence in academic libraries,[28] support is also being provided in the form of OER incentive programs. For example, the University of Massachusetts Amherst offers instructors $2,000 to replace traditional course materials with OER. Other incentive programs might offer a smaller stipend in order to encourage instructors to simply review an OER. While these programs may provide a wide range of professional development experiences and technical or instructional support structures, instructors are likely pursue them because they offer some sort of financial grant or award for using or creating OER.[29]

Though incentive programs are not without merit, offering a tacit acknowledgment of labor, visibility to boost nascent OE efforts, and a stipend that may offset lost revenue for text-book-authoring royalties, they should be undertaken only after substantial reflection. Many libraries have yet to successfully address the myriad of challenges posed by incentive programs, such as lack of clarity around maintenance of materials, long-term preservation, and how to sustainably scale up resource-intensive adaptations or creations. Sustainability concerns are often most acute in nascent incentive programs, where funding is often tied to grants, special use, one-time-only funds, or other short-term funding mechanisms.

Incentive programs can be increasingly challenging when considering the material conditions that are characteristic of adjunct faculty,[30] namely overwork, lack of office space or professional development funds, and precarity.* As more complex OER adaptations or creations are more time-consuming and require various levels of project management, facilitating a course buyout† may be desirable. However, as these buyouts are often made possible by hiring a sessional instructor, the structures that facilitate this release time further reinforces the adjunctification of the postsecondary education system. Even if release time or financial compensation is made possible through an incentive program, it is often provided only to the instructor, regardless of how much time or support the project requires from colleagues within the library and teaching support unit. Lastly and perhaps most importantly, if the use or

---

* *Precarity* in this context refers to "informal, temporary, or contingent work being a predominant mode of livelihood" (Sharryn Kasmir, "Precarity," *Open Encyclopedia of Anthropology*, March 13, 2018, https://doi.org/10.29164/18precarity). While precarity is not exclusive to the academy, it is certainly well-established within it: a report from 2016 shows that the majority (70%) of academic positions are both nontenured and part-time (American Association of University Professors, "Higher Education at a Crossroads: The Economic Value of Tenure and the Security of the Profession," *Academe* 102, no. 2 [March–April 2016]: 9–23, https://www.aaup.org/sites/default/files/2015-16EconomicStatusReport.pdf).

† Whereby a faculty member is offered a break from teaching a regularly scheduled course.

creation of OER is not formally encouraged in tenure and promotion guidelines, it risks being an endeavor that only faculty who have tenure or institutional status will opt in to, missing out on voices from a larger, potentially more diverse junior faculty population.

Complicating these discussions around OER incentive programs is the history of academic libraries providing open access funds. Originally envisioned as an incentive for faculty to select open access publishing venues, these funds often covered the article processing charges (APCs) associated with high-impact journals. This model has not worked out as anticipated. Rather than hastening a move to open access publishing, these funds have allowed commercial publishers to pursue a new and fruitful income stream to supplement their more traditional subscription-based model. While these funds were created with the best of intentions, they have now resulted in an unsustainable "library as bank" model, where the costs of covering open access publication are coming exclusively from the library, rather than other campus units, individual departments, or the institution as a whole. Thus, it should come as no surprise that some of these funds are currently paused, phased out, or terminated completely by many academic libraries.[31]

While incentive programs for the use or creation of OER offer a valuable transitionary model to foster faculty and institutional support, if they live solely within the library, they risk duplicating the same issues as open access funds before them. It would be more advantageous to consider support for open education initiatives as a holistic enterprise that draws on expertise both within and outside of the library. This would require not only the reallocation of funding away from a grant program toward the hiring of full or part-time staff, but also the rescoping of job responsibilities to note an increased emphasis on OER and their situation within existing workflows and services. If done thoughtfully, this will make the adaptation and creation processes as lightweight and frictionless as possible for faculty, offering greater sustainability and scalability for future efforts.

Indeed, institutional support for open education–related activities is crucial. However, OER work resides in a liminal space: it is not service, not teaching, not scholarship. One well-known example of OER-related language in tenure and promotion guidelines is at the University of British Columbia (UBC), where candidates are evaluated on "activity taken at UBC and elsewhere to advance innovation in teaching and learning with impact beyond one's classroom," of which the creation of OER is one such listed example.[32] While the inclusion of OER into institutional tenure and promotion guidelines is an accomplishment to aspire to, it is worth noting this language exists only in the "educational leadership" stream (a position that sees its distribution of effort [DOE] centered on teaching), not the "professoriate" stream (a position that has a more traditional DOE that is equally centered on research and teaching). While UBC is merely one example, its positioning of OER reveals how tenuous their position in the academy really is: it is important for teaching-focused faculty, but not for traditional faculty (despite the fact that a typical distribution of effort often weighs teaching and scholarship equally). Indeed, having teaching stream and more traditional faculty appointments coexist within the academy has created a two-tiered system, whereby "those that focus solely on teaching are considered less worthy or valuable."[33] This, when coupled with institutional misunderstandings around the definition of *open*,[34] may result in junior faculty—who may potentially already feel less respected or valued based on their positionality within a particular appointment type or within the academy more generally—proceeding through a tenure and promotion structure that largely does not understand or appreciate their open-related efforts. This elicits some of the more uncomfortable tensions around OER and faculty labor: while the academy values it in principle, it often does not in practice.

Issues around OER and labor are not limited to faculty members. The multifaceted nature of OER—which, depending on the project, may require expertise in copyright, accessibility, publishing, instructional design, and educational technology—means that compensation* and attribution of labor on these projects remain challenging and complex. Academic librarians and instructional designers can be classified as either staff or faculty, depending on how an institution has historically valued their skill sets and training. Both have specialized expertise acquired through terminal degrees but often do not possess a PhD, meaning that they are often denied the respect, prestige, and authority that accompanies "true" or "real" academics. Thus, even though they are crucial collaborators on open education–based projects, both librarians and instructional designers are often doing so in a limited capacity, in addition to several other responsibilities.

These contributions may be further marginalized within the structures of the contemporary university. Librarians and instructional designers are largely contributing service-based labor (providing guidance on tools, resources, and technology), while faculty are contributing scholarship-based labor (writing, editing, utilizing subject expertise to evaluate resources), perpetuating a hierarchical system of labor within open education projects. Librarian or instructional designer contributions to open education projects may not be formally acknowledged through funding, scholarship opportunities, or even attribution on the final resource or output itself. Even if these collaborators are given credit, it is often provided through an acknowledgment rather than a byline, signaling that this work is less important than subject expertise. Moreover, this labor is not formally accounted for in the grant programs described above, with librarians and instructional designers being expected to take potentially laborious adaptation and creation work without additional compensation or a relief in their other duties. Despite the absence of their labor being reflected, both instructional designers and librarians are asked to continuously contribute to OER projects because the work is important and admirable—ultimately harkening to professional or institutional values around access and equity—even if the material working conditions in which that work happens are challenging or problematic. This mirrors increased expectations of faculty to undertake OER work because they love it, regardless of whether their formalized evaluation structures support that work or not.

The issue of attribution or compensation is not exclusive to staff members. Open education work that involves students—whether they are sourcing materials for the creation of an OER or providing authorship to a book chapter in an open pedagogy class experience—is an even more challenging concept to explore. This is due to the inherent imbalance of power relations of the classroom and the transitory nature of the student experience: their participation in that classroom or on that project is contingent upon enrollment or employment (if they are undertaking such work as a research assistant or work-study student). Since students are involved for only a finite period of time, a shared understanding of rights and responsibilities must be fostered between them and their instructor/employer. While open pedagogy is by and large considered a worthwhile endeavor, giving students agency over their learning and providing them with opportunities to exercise their creativity, if assignments or final projects require the sharing of student-generated materials in a digital, public (or open) manner, conversations about attribution and intellectual property are crucial.[35] Moreover, as Tara Robertson, diversity and inclusion lead at Mozilla, points out, not everyone is comfortable with being open by default, with their names or identities being digitally accessible.[36] In

---

* When we refer to compensation here, it should be noted that we are not strictly referring to monetary compensation, but also to other types of compensation as well: grades, honoraria, authorship, and the myriad forms of acknowledgement of labor.

situations where a final grade is the compensation in exchange for student labor, the potential for coercion is great. Students must have an option for anonymization or to opt out of the public-facing component of the assignment completely.

STRATEGIES FOR LIBRARIANS AND OTHER OER ADVOCATES

- Take stock of your institutional context. Investigate tenure and promotion, collective agreements, and job description documentation to develop a fuller understanding of how labor operates and is valued within different roles.
- Seek out opportunities to highlight the contributions of others. Invite students, staff, early career professionals, and precarious workers to collaborate on conference presentations, papers, projects, and grants. Acknowledge their name and expertise in annual reviews, reports, and workflows.
- Advocate for permanent staffing to support OER work on campus. Use statistics and concrete examples to demonstrate this multifaceted, complex work so that decision-makers understand why additional resources and expertise are required.
- Understand the implications of incentive or grant programs before you begin one. Talk to others who have been involved in similar initiatives at different institutions to get context around logistics, resources, and sustainability. Make sure you understand the politics and values of your own institution so that you can be sure you are creating a program with support structures and objectives that resonate with your community.
- Reflect on your positionality. What does your role look like in terms of autonomy, responsibility, power, and privilege? Now reflect on the positionality of others. Is their positionality different? How so? How will this affect how you collaborate and support each other?

TECHNOCRACY

At least part of the reason OER work is prioritized, even when adequate resources are not available, is that the open aspect of OER carries with it many positive preconceived assumptions about accessibility, usability, and inclusivity. However, several scholars, such as Jeremy Knox and Jess Mitchell, caution that openness does not necessarily increase access and inclusion.[37] Nora Almeida notes that the popularity of openness in recent educational and pedagogical discourse renders the term "dangerously at risk of being appropriated, misused, and emptied."[38] She warns in particular of the conflation between the terms *open*, *access*, and *ethics*. Openness, Almeida argues, does not automatically equate to access, which does not consequently increase inclusion and equality. While openness and OER certainly have the potential to alleviate barriers to education, OER users and advocates can risk overestimating their efficacy.[39] The larger structures within which OER operate often render them less accessible than the way they are originally marketed.

One significant barrier to the discoverability, accessibility, and efficacy of OER is the way in which technocracy has been embedded in open education discourse. Technocracy refers to "a system of governance in which technically trained experts rule by virtue of their specialized knowledge and position in dominant political and economic institutions."[40] Technocratic societies assert technical expertise as the highest form of knowledge, often viewing technology as a panacea for inequality. Justin Cruickshank and Ross Abbinnett argue that technocracy coincides with and perpetuates a global sociocultural shift that emphasizes constant individual improvement, which can best be achieved through technological developments.[41] In higher education, these technocratic ideals are reinforced through the widespread use of data and uncritical acceptance of assessment culture, both of which are undertaken with the purpose of finding presumed efficiencies.

OER are often characterized as low-cost, easily accessible alternatives to traditional course materials, yet they are intertwined within technocratic higher education systems in many ways. Similar to the economic ideology technocracy imposes on higher education systems, OER are embedded in consumerist discourses. The language surrounding OER and their respective literature, Knox argues, exists "distinctly in terms of the marketisation and commodification of higher education and its subjects."[42] In addition to the ways in which OER have been presented and discussed in consumerist terms, their very creation and dissemination are intertwined with technocracy.

Those with technical expertise are the most likely creators and disseminators of OER, which creates a cyclical process of creation and dissemination by and among a privileged, homogeneous demographic. These creators are most often from well-funded Western institutions, which perpetuates their control over education standards.[43] OER and technocracy often assume a single type of user: an able-bodied and digitally competent individual with regular access to high-speed internet. The assumption that all current college students are digitally literate and prefer to access digital learning tools often oversimplifies the problems that OER attempt to alleviate, as this relies on the archetypical college student and overlooks those from marginalized communities, especially those with learning disabilities or without regular access to the internet. As Hylén and dos Santos argue, the tendency for OER and technocracy to assume a single type of user further perpetuates biases and does little to actually decrease educational barriers.[44] Technocracy informs not only the creation and dissemination but also the use and adaptation of OER as learning tools. This relationship in turn hinders users not traditionally valued in technocratic higher education systems from discovering, accessing, and benefiting from OER.

DISCOVERABILITY AND ACCESS

Discovering and accessing OER are recursive processes that largely depend on one another. Educators have the potential to either choose from already made OER, edit existing OER, or create new OER. In theory (and at their best) OER are more readily discovered and accessed than traditional educational resources. Tools such as the Mason OER Metafinder (MOM), a search engine for open textbooks and other educational resources, facilitate the discoverability of OER. Moreover, OER can be accessed anywhere as long as users have internet access and a device with a broadband connection. However, despite this positive potential, the dynamic nature of OER and assumptions about user identity can create barriers to both discoverability and access.

Despite the many ways in which instructors and other users can find pertinent OER, the format of the resources themselves can hinder their discoverability. The average lifespan of an OER repository is less than three years.[45] Most explanations for this brevity can be linked to the pedagogical structures of higher education. Friesen explains that paucity of funding for projects has hindered both the creation and maintenance of OER,[46] and Crissinger notes that the tenure system's failure to reward or recognize OER discourages many instructors from incorporating them into their pedagogy.[47]

Even if an OER has a longer lifespan than average, Kortemeyer claims that current metadata standards are unsuited for OER and their discoverability.[48] Not only is the metadata for OER often incomplete or incorrect, Kortemeyer argues, but the static nature of many metadata schemata (such as Dublin Core) is not suited to the dynamic nature of OER. As contributors and content regularly change, metadata elements are frequently either not updated or are left blank entirely, in turn rendering the OER less discoverable than resources with static metadata, such as a traditional textbook. In higher education, systems of evaluation that equate quantifiable metrics (such as a scholar's h index) with success and promotion often deter potential users from both creating and maintaining OER, which inhibits discoverability. These constraints, combined with the technological nature of OER, do not create barriers just to discoverability, but also to access.

The tendency for OER to assume user homogeneity risks overlooking barriers to access. Many students, especially in developing countries, lack adequate technology resources and a reliable internet connection. The high cost of broadband limits internet access and, even if an instructor is able to find pertinent OER, many students are unable to access them. This not only perpetuates use by a homogeneous demographic, but also exacerbates the digital divide between the Global North and the Global South. Monika dos Santos, a psychology professor at the University of South Africa, argues that technocracy does more to enable the subjectification of the Global South than to alleviate inequalities.[49] This claim is reflected through patterns of OER use and access. When analyzing access to MIT OpenCourseWare, Haßler and Jackson found that 41 percent of users were from North America, while only 5 percent of users were from South America and only 1 percent were from Sub-Saharan Africa.[50] Despite their openness, OER are not equally accessible.

Assumptions about user identity further perpetuate these inequalities. Even if students do have reliable internet access, a personal device with a broadband connection, or access to public devices, that does not mean that they can all equally access OER. As Reed and Turner argue, many OER are created for users without any physical or learning disabilities.[51] The lack of accessibility considerations, such as screen reader and smartphone compatibility, often render OER accessible only to fully able-bodied students with regular access to a desktop or laptop computer. Commuter students, students with a visual or hearing impairment, and students without regular and reliable access to a device with an internet connection all face barriers to accessing OER. These barriers can be alleviated by more thoughtful creation and maintenance of OER.

STRATEGIES FOR LIBRARIANS AND OTHER OER ADVOCATES

- At early stages, OER creators and content editors should maintain accurate and updated metadata to facilitate discovery. As metadata experts, librarians can suggest existing schemata and provide creators with ideas for enhancing these schemata to provide as much context as possible.
- Creators should also make sure that their OER adhere to web content accessibility guidelines as closely as possible.[52] The BCcampus Open Education *Accessibility Toolkit* provides resources for making an open textbook.[53] It includes an overview of universal design as well as best practices for accessibility, such as clearly organizing content, adding alternative text, and including captions.
- Creators can also ensure that a variety of formats are available, such as a downloadable PDF and smartphone compatibility options.
- OER advocates should consider the variety of possible users and think through the different ways in which OER might be discovered and accessed. Assumptions about user identity hinder the discoverability and accessibility of OER, and only once these preconceptions are eliminated can the resources be shared more conscientiously and equally.

EFFICACY

Even if barriers to access are eliminated or reduced, that does not automatically render OER effective learning tools for all audiences. One reason for the ineffectiveness of OER is their tendency to perpetuate privilege among already privileged peoples. Jhangiani addresses this issue, claiming that OER facilitate a kind of "digital redlining" that exacerbates, rather than alleviating, existing inequities.[54] He addresses the creation of OER in particular, arguing that current creation practices perpetuate "an implicit form of creative redlining, one that reserves the capacity to create or adapt OER for those who already enjoy positions of privilege, such as the tenured or those who do not need the income."[55] As technocratic systems of higher education rarely reward adopting OER, their creation largely depends on voluntary labor from those who can afford, either financially or academically, to create them. This limits OER creators to the privileged academic elite, in turn creating a certain amount of homogeneity among the resources themselves. Although by nature OER can be regularly reworked and adapted, these changes are largely made by the same type of user, usually one from a wealthy Western institution.[56] This type of creation often overlooks users who do not belong to these types of institutions or who have not been previously active in the creation of and contribution to OER and other educational tools. While OER are accessed and used by a wide array of institutions and users, traditions of homogeneous creation and subsequent dissemination hinder their efficacy as learning tools.

OER do not easily translate across socio-academic cultural contexts. This becomes particularly problematic as the differentiation across cultures increases. OER are inherently sharable resources, but sharing a resource does not grant it efficacy, and much is often lost in the dissemination of OER across cultures. Dos Santos notes that foreign knowledge and expertise is not impartial, and remnants of the original contexts are always present.[57] Considering OER as neutral resources that can be adapted to any context inhibits their effectiveness. In fact, when OER are decontextualized from the community in which they were created, they are less effective educational tools.[58] OER often fail to adapt to local contexts in general, a trend that is particularly prominent among non-Western peoples.[59] The inability for non-Western societies to access and effectively use OER to an equivalent extent as well-funded Western institutions perpetuates the homogeneous creation and use of OER.

NOTES

1. Claudio Aspesi et al., *SPARC* Landscape Analysis: The Changing Academic Publishing Industry* (Washington, DC: SPARC, 2019).
2. Aspesi et al., *SPARC* Landscape Analysis*.
3. Scot Danforth, "Social Justice and Technocracy: Tracing the Narratives of Inclusive Education in the USA," *Discourse: Studies in the Cultural Politics of Education* 37, no. 4 (2016): 582–99, https://doi.org/10.1080/01596306.2015.1073022.
4. Audrey Watters, "From 'Open' to Justice #OpenCon2014" (presentation, OpenCon 2014, Washington, DC, November 16, 2014), https://hackeducation.com/2014/11/16/from-open-to-justice.
5. Abbey Elder, "Commercial Platforms That Utilize Open Educational Resources," Google Doc, November 7, 2018, https://docs.google.com/spreadsheets/d/1xDGIKZ7T5fIho7yrTs8Lpu4zpqPbeqQn76aY6qEnAUg/edit#gid=941689191.
6. Billy Meinke-Lau, "The Business of Fettering OER: fOER and Lumen Learning's Identity Crisis," billy-meinke.com, May 28, 2019, http://billymeinke.com/2019/05/28/fettering-oer/.
7. Scott Robison, "A Not So Direct #OpenEd17 Reflection: Openwrapping," *Scott Robison* (blog), October 18, 2017. https://scottrobison.net/blog/2017/10/18/a-not-so-direct-opened17-reflection-openwrapping/ (site discontinued).
8. Robison, "Openwrapping," par. 1.

9. Rajiv Sunil Jhangiani, "For-Profit, Faux-Pen, and Critical Conversations about the Future of Learning Materials," *Rajiv Jhangiani, Ph.D.* (blog), October 15, 2019, https://thatpsychprof.com/for-profit-faux-pen-and-critical-conversations/.

10. Elder, "Commercial Platforms."

11. John Hilton III et al., "The Four 'R's of Openness and ALMS Analysis: Frameworks for Open Educational Resources," *Open Learning: The Journal of Open, Distance and e-Learning* 25, no. 1 (2010): 37–44, https://doi.org/10.1080/02680510903482132.

12. Lisa Petrides, Douglas Levin, and C. Edward Watson, "Toward a Sustainable OER Ecosystem: The Case for OER Stewardship," CARE Framework, March 4, 2018, https://careframework.org/.

13. Rajiv Sunil Jhangiani, "Pragmatism vs. Idealism and the Identity Crisis of OER Advocacy," *Open Praxis* 9, no. 2 (2017): 141–50, https://doi.org/10.5944/openpraxis.9.2.569.

14. Aspesi et al., *SPARC* Landscape Analysis.*

15. Jhangiani, "Pragmatism vs. Idealism," par. 3.

16. Aspesi et al., *SPARC* Landscape Analysis*, 40.

17. Kaitlyn Vitez, *Automatic Textbooks Billing: An Offer Students Can't Refuse?* (Washington, DC: U.S. PIRG Education Fund, February 2020), https://uspirg.org/sites/pirg/files/reports/Automatic-Textbook-Billing/USPIRG_Textbook-Automatic-Billing_Feb2020_v3.pdf.

18. Aspesi et al., *SPARC* Landscape Analysis*, 36.

19. Michael Feldstein, *eLiterate* (blog), https://eliterate.us/.

20. Aspesi et al., *SPARC* Landscape Analysis*, 40.

21. Vitez, *Automatic Textbooks Billing.*

22. Aspesi et al., *SPARC* Landscape Analysis.*

23. Meinke-Lau, "Business of Fettering OER."

24. Data Doubles, "Project," http://datadoubles.org/project/.

25. Aspesi et al., *SPARC* Landscape Analysis.*

26. Billy Meinke, "Student Data Harvested by Education Publishers," billymeinke.com, March 21, 2018, http://billymeinke.com/2018/03/21/student-data-grabbers/.

27. Andrew D. Asher, "Risk, Benefits, and User Privacy: Evaluating the Ethics of Library Data," in *Protecting Patron Privacy: A LITA Guide*, ed. Bobbi Newman and Bonnie Tijerina (Lanham, MD: Rowman & Littlefield, 2017), 45.

28. Amanda Larson, "What Is an Open Education Librarian, Even?" Google Slides, October 30, 2019, https://docs.google.com/presentation/d/13djsn1-Hbh3kMY1vzldZNRZbZ3U4kuNxEtV2LZOr9Uo/.

29. SPARC, *2018–2019 Connect OER Report* (Washington, DC: SPARC, 2019).

30. Karen Foster and Louise Birdsell Bauer, *Out of the Shadows* (Ottawa, ON: Canadian Association of University Teachers, 2019), https://www.caut.ca/sites/default/files/cas_report.pdf.

31. SPARC, *Open Access Funds in Action* (Washington, DC: SPARC, 2019).

32. University of British Columbia, *Guide to Reappointment, Promotion and Tenure Procedures at UBC* (Vancouver: University of British Columbia, 2019, upd. 2020), 18.

33. Susan Vajoczki et al., *Teaching-Stream Faculty in Ontario Universities* (Toronto: Higher Education Quality Council of Ontario, 2011), 6.

34. Juan P. Alperin et al., "Meta-research: How Significant Are the Public Dimensions of Faculty Work in Review, Promotion and Tenure Documents?" *eLife*, February 12, 2019, https://doi.org/10.7554/eLife.42254.

35. Heather Miceli, "Non-majors Science Students as Content Creators," Open Pedagogy Notebook, January 9, 2020, http://openpedagogy.org/course-level/non-majors-science-students-as-content-creators/; Simon Bates, "From Consumer to Creator: Students as Producers of Content," Flexible Learning, University of British Columbia, February 18, 2015, https://flexible.learning.ubc.ca/case-studies/simon-bates/.

36. Tara Robertson, "Not All Information Wants to Be Free" (keynote address, LITA Forum, Fort Worth, TX, November 20, 2016), http://tararobertson.ca/2016/lita-keynote/.

37. Jeremy Knox, "Five Critiques of the Open Educational Resources Movement," *Teaching in Higher Education* 18, no. 8 (2013): 821–32, https://doi.org/10.1080/13562517.2013.774354; Jess Mitchell, "'Open' and 'Inclusive': What the Heck Are They?" Medium, July 3, 2019, https://medium.com/@jesshmitchell/open-and-inclusive-what-the-heck-are-they-7b0960c1c05a.

38. Nora Almeida, "Open Educational Resources and Rhetorical Paradox in the Neoliberal Univers(ity)," *Journal of Critical Library and Information Studies* 1, no. 1 (2017): 2, https://doi.org/10.24242/jclis.v1i1.16.

39. Sarah Crissinger, "A Critical Take on OER Practices: Interrogating Commercialization, Colonialism, and Content," *In the Library with The Lead Pipe*, October 21, 2015, http://www.inthelibrarywiththeleadpipe.org/2015/a-critical-take-on-oer-practices-interrogating-commercialization-colonialism-and-content/.

40. Frank Fischer, *Technocracy and the Politics of Expertise* (Newbury Park, CA: Sage, 1990), 17.

41. Justin Cruickshank and Ross Abbinnett, "Neoliberalism, Technocracy and Higher Education: Editors' Introduction," *Social Epistemology* 33, no. 4 (2019): 273–79, https://doi.org/10.1080/02691728.2019.1638983.

42. Knox, "Five Critiques," 828.
43. Crissinger, "Critical Take on OER Practices."
44. Jan Hylén, "Open Educational Resources: Opportunities and Challenges," *Proceedings of Open Education*, 2006: 49–63; Monika dos Santos, "Power, Rights, Freedom, Technocracy and Postcolonialism in Sub-Saharan Africa," *Acta Academica* 50, no. 3 (2018): 88–101, https://doi.org/10.18820/24150479/aa50i3.4.
45. Norm Friesen, "Open Educational Resources: New Possibilities for Change and Sustainability," *International Review of Research in Open and Distance Learning* 10, no. 5 (2009): 1–13.
46. Friesen, "Open Educational Resources."
47. Crissinger, "Critical Take on OER Practices."
48. Gerd Kortemeyer, "Ten Years Later: Why Open Educational Resources Have Not Noticeably Affected Higher Education, and Why We Should Care," *EDUCAUSE Review Online*, February 26, 2013, https://er.educause.edu/articles/2013/2/ten-years-later-why-open-educational-resources-have-not-noticeably-affected-higher-education-and-why-we-should-care.
49. dos Santos, "Power, Rights, Freedom."
50. Bjorn Haßler and Alan McNeil Jackson, "Bridging the Bandwidth Gap: Open Educational Resources and the Digital Divide," *IEEE Transactions on Learning Technologies* 3, no. 2 (April–June 2010): 110–15, https://doi.org/10.1109/TLT.2010.8.
51. Michelle Reed and Ciara Turner, "Experiential Learning and Open Education: Partnering with Students to Evaluate OER Accessibility," chapter 5 in *OER: A Field Guide for Academic Librarians*, ed. Andrew Wesolek, Jonathan Lashley, and Anne Langley (Minneapolis: Open Textbook Library, University of Minnesota, 2018).
52. W3C Web Accessibility Initiative, "WCAG 2 Overview," July 2005, last updated March 21, 2023, https://www.w3.org/WAI/standards-guidelines/wcag/.
53. Amanda Coolidge et al., *Accessibility Toolkit*, 2nd ed. (Vancouver: BCcampus, University of British Columbia, 2018), https://opentextbc.ca/accessibilitytoolkit/.
54. Rajiv Sunil Jhangiani, "Delivering on the Promise of Open Educational Resources: Pitfalls and Strategies," in *MOOCs and Open Education across Emerging Economies: Challenges, Successes, and Opportunities*, ed. Ke Zhang, Curtis J. Bonk, Thomas C. Reeves, and Thomas H. Reynolds (New York: Taylor & Francis, 2020), 56-62.
55. Jhangiani, "Pitfalls and Strategies," 5.
56. Jhangiani, "Pragmatism vs. Idealism."
57. dos Santos, "Power, Rights, Freedom."
58. Almeida, "Open Educational Resources."
59. Knox, "Five Critiques."

BIBLIOGRAPHY

Almeida, Nora. "Open Educational Resources and Rhetorical Paradox in the Neoliberal Univers(ity)." *Journal of Critical Library and Information Studies* 1, no. 1 (2017): 1–19. https://doi.org/10.24242/jclis.v1i1.16.

Alperin, Juan P., Carol Muñoz Nieves, Lesley A. Schimanski, Gustavo E. Fischman, Meredith T. Niles, and Erin C. McKiernan. "Meta-research: How Significant Are the Public Dimensions of Faculty Work in Review, Promotion and Tenure Documents?" *eLife*, February 12, 2019. https://doi.org/10.7554/eLife.42254.

American Association of University Professors. "Higher Education at a Crossroads: The Economic Value of Tenure and the Security of the Profession." *Academe* 102, no. 2 (March–April 2016): 9–23. https://www.aaup.org/sites/default/files/2015-16EconomicStatusReport.pdf.

Asher, Andrew D. "Risk, Benefits, and User Privacy: Evaluating the Ethics of Library Data." In *Protecting Patron Privacy: A LITA Guide*, edited by Bobbi Newman and Bonnie Tijerina, 43–56. Lanham, MD: Rowman & Littlefield, 2017.

Aspesi, Claudio, Nicole Allen, Raym Crow, Shawn Daugherty, Heather Joseph, Joseph McArthur, and Nick Shockey . *SPARC* Landscape Analysis: The Changing Academic Publishing Industry—Implications for Academic Institutions*. Washington, DC: SPARC, 2019.

Bates, Simon. "From Consumer to Creator: Students as Producers of Content." Flexible Learning, University of British Columbia, February 18, 2015. https://flexible.learning.ubc.ca/case-studies/simon-bates/.

Coolidge, Amanda, Sue Donner, Tara Robertson, and Josie Gray. *Accessibility Toolkit*, 2nd ed. Vancouver: BCcampus, University of British Columbia, 2018. https://opentextbc.ca/accessibilitytoolkit/.

Crissinger, Sarah. "A Critical Take on OER Practices: Interrogating Commercialization, Colonialism, and Content." *In the Library with The Lead Pipe*, October 21, 2015. http://www.inthelibrarywiththeleadpipe.org/2015/a-critical-take-on-oer-practices-interrogating-commercialization-colonialism-and-content/.

Cruickshank, Justin, and Ross Abbinnett. "Neoliberalism, Technocracy and Higher Education: Editors' Introduction." *Social Epistemology* 33, no. 4 (2019): 273–79. https://doi.org/10.1080/02691728.2019.1638983.

Danforth, Scot. "Social Justice and Technocracy: Tracing the Narratives of Inclusive Education in the USA." *Discourse: Studies in the Cultural Politics of Education* 37, no. 4 (2016): 582–99. https://doi.org/10.1080/01596306.2015.1073022.

Data Doubles. "Project." http://datadoubles.org/project/.

dos Santos, Monika. "Power, Rights, Freedom, Technocracy and Postcolonialism in Sub-Saharan Africa." *Acta Academica* 50, no. 3 (2018): 88–101. https://doi.org/10.18820/24150479/aa50i3.4.

Elder, Abbey. "Commercial Platforms That Utilize Open Educational Resources." Google Doc, November 7, 2018. https://docs.google.com/spreadsheets/d/1xDGIKZ7T5fIho7yrTs8Lpu4zpqPbeqQn76aY6qEnAUg/edit#gid=941689191.

Feldstein, Michael. *eLiterate* (blog). https://eliterate.us/.

Fischer, Frank. *Technocracy and the Politics of Expertise*. Newbury Park, CA: Sage, 1990.

Foster, Karen, and Louise Birdsell Bauer. *Out of the Shadows: Experiences of Contract Academic Staff*. Ottawa, ON: Canadian Association of University Teachers, 2019. https://www.caut.ca/sites/default/files/cas_report.pdf.

Friesen, Norm. "Open Educational Resources: New Possibilities for Change and Sustainability." *International Review of Research in Open and Distance Learning* 10, no. 5 (2009): 1–13.

Haßler, Bjorn, and Alan McNeil Jackson. "Bridging the Bandwidth Gap: Open Educational Resources and the Digital Divide." *IEEE Transactions on Learning Technologies* 3, no. 2 (April–June 2010): 110–15. https://doi.org/10.1109/TLT.2010.8.

Hilton, John, III, David Wiley, Jared Stein and Aaron Johnson. "The Four 'R's of Openness and ALMS Analysis: Frameworks for Open Educational Resources." *Open Learning: The Journal of Open, Distance and e-Learning* 25, no. 1 (2010): 37–44. https://doi.org/10.1080/02680510903482132.

Hylén, Jan. "Open Educational Resources: Opportunities and Challenges." *Proceedings of Open Education*, 2006: 49–63.

Jhangiani, Rajiv Sunil. "Delivering on the Promise of Open Educational Resources: Pitfalls and Strategies." In *MOOCs and Open Education across Emerging Economies: Challenges, Successes, and Opportunities*, edited by Ke Zhang, Curtis J. Bonk, Thomas C. Reeves, and Thomas H. Reynolds, 56-62. New York: Taylor & Francis, 2020.

———. "For-Profit, Faux-Pen, and Critical Conversations about the Future of Learning Materials." *Rajiv Jhangiani, Ph.D.* (blog), October 15, 2019. https://thatpsychprof.com/for-profit-faux-pen-and-critical-conversations/.

———. "Pragmatism vs. Idealism and the Identity Crisis of OER Advocacy." *Open Praxis* 9, no. 2 (2017): 141–50. https://doi.org/10.5944/openpraxis.9.2.569.

Jones, Kyle M. L., Michael R. Perry, Abigail Goben, Andrew Asher, Kristin A. Briney, M. Brooke Robertshaw, and Dorothea Salo. "In Their Own Words: Student Perspectives on Privacy and Library Participation in Learning Analytics Initiatives." In *Recasting the Narrative: The Proceedings of the ACRL 2019 Conference*, edited by Dawn M. Mueller, 262–74. Chicago: Association of College and Research Libraries, 2019.

Kasmir, Sharryn. "Precarity." Open Encyclopedia of Anthropology, March 13, 2018. https://doi.org/10.29164/18precarity.

Knox, Jeremy. "Five Critiques of the Open Educational Resources Movement." *Teaching in Higher Education* 18, no. 8 (2013): 821–32. https://doi.org/10.1080/13562517.2013.774354.

Kortemeyer, Gerd. "Ten Years Later: Why Open Educational Resources Have Not Noticeably Affected Higher Education, and Why We Should Care." *EDUCAUSE Review Online*, February 26, 2013. https://er.educause.edu/articles/2013/2/ten-years-later-why-open-educational-resources-have-not-noticeably-affected-higher-education-and-why-we-should-care.

Larson, Amanda. "What Is an Open Education Librarian, Even?" Google Slides, October 30, 2019. https://docs.google.com/presentation/d/13djsn1-Hbh3kMY1vzldZNRZbZ3U4kuNxEtV2LZOr9Uo/.

Meinke, Billy. "Student Data Harvested by Education Publishers." billymeinke.com, March 21, 2018. http://billymeinke.com/2018/03/21/student-data-grabbers/.

Meinke-Lau, Billy. "The Business of Fettering OER: fOER and Lumen Learning's Identity Crisis." billymeinke.com, May 28, 2019. http://billymeinke.com/2019/05/28/fettering-oer/.

Miceli, Heather. "Non-majors Science Students as Content Creators." Open Pedagogy Notebook, January 9, 2020. http://openpedagogy.org/course-level/non-majors-science-students-as-content-creators/.

Mitchell, Jess. "'Open' and 'Inclusive': What the Heck Are They?" Medium, July 3, 2019. https://medium.com/@jesshmitchell/open-and-inclusive-what-the-heck-are-they-7b0960c1c05a.

Petrides, Lisa, Douglas Levin, and C. Edward Watson. "Toward a Sustainable OER Ecosystem: The Case for OER Stewardship." CARE Framework, March 4, 2018. https://careframework.org/.

Reed, Michelle, and Ciara Turner. "Experiential Learning and Open Education: Partnering with Students to Evaluate OER Accessibility." Chapter 5 in *OER: A Field Guide for Academic Librarians*, edited by Andrew Wesolek, Jonathan Lashley, and Anne Langley. Minneapolis: Open Textbook Library, University of Minnesota 2018.

Robertson, Tara. "Not All Information Wants to Be Free." Keynote address, LITA Forum, Fort Worth, TX, November 20, 2016. http://tararobertson.ca/2016/lita-keynote/.

Robison, Scott. "A Not So Direct #OpenEd17 Reflection: Openwrapping." *Scott Robison* (blog), October 18, 2017. https://scottrobison.net/blog/2017/10/18/a-not-so-direct-opened17-reflection-openwrapping/ (site discontinued).

SPARC. *Open Access Funds in Action*. Washington, DC: SPARC, 2019.

———. *2018–2019 Connect OER Report*. Washington, DC: SPARC, 2019.

University of British Columbia. *Guide to Reappointment, Promotion and Tenure Procedures at UBC*. Vancouver: University of British Columbia, 2019, upd. 2020.

Vajoczki, Susan, Nancy Fenton, Karen Menard, and Dawn Pollon. *Teaching-Stream Faculty in Ontario Universities*. Toronto: Higher Education Quality Council of Ontario, 2011.

Vitez, Kaitlyn. *Automatic Textbooks Billing: An Offer Students Can't Refuse?* Washington, DC: U.S. PIRG Education Fund, February 2020. https://uspirg.org/sites/pirg/files/reports/Automatic-Textbook-Billing/USPIRG_Textbook-Automatic-Billing_Feb2020_v3.pdf.

Watters, Audrey. "From 'Open' to Justice #OpenCon2014." Presentation, OpenCon 2014, Washington, DC, November 16, 2014. https://hackeducation.com/2014/11/16/from-open-to-justice.

W3C Web Accessibility Initiative. "WCAG 2 Overview." July 2005, last updated March 21, 2023. https://www.w3.org/WAI/standards-guidelines/wcag/.

OPEN SCIENCE AND INFRASTRUCTURE

DEFINING OPEN SCIENCE

Micah Vandegrift

Author's note: Many of the words, diagrams, and ideas in this chapter make generous use of Creative Commons–licensed materials. The basic framing and many words and sentences are borrowed directly from Bosman and Kramer's "Defining Open Science Definitions."[1] The chapter was then developed by Micah Vandegrift, with some rewrites, edits, updates, and contextualization. Humble gratitude is offered to Esther Plomp and Adrienne Mueller for helpful comments in the open peer-review process.

Keywords: open science, open knowledge, open source, open scholarship, open research

INTRODUCTION

This chapter lays out some definitional landscape for *open science*. It offers a brief overview of key points, core topics, and common discussions in this area.

Open science encompasses a multitude of assumptions about the future of knowledge creation and dissemination. Defining this term is important because it is picking up momentum in practical use as a shorthand umbrella term for a variety of activities that stem from a variety of principles on university campuses, across higher education, and in affiliated industries. As global scholarship continues to be more deeply intertwined, concerns about the unequal availability of participation in human knowledge are being unearthed. Open science is one of a few movements that are responding to the injustice of information access that tends to privilege the Anglo-Euro Western culture and northern hemisphere.

Because openness in higher education and research has been a public policy topic in Europe for years, many of the core definitions, ideas, and concepts of open science come from the European Union, member states, and organizations in Europe. Only recently has the United States begun to utilize the language of open science, due in part to the distributed nature of our higher education and research industry (we don't have a Department of Higher Education, Science, and Technology, for example), and also based on deeply entrenched ideals about American individualism and boostrapism that can often be resistant to a communal, share-alike orientation, which open science represents.

> [Open science is] ongoing transitions in the way research is performed, researchers collaborate, knowledge is shared, and science is organised.
>
> —EU Directorate-General for Research and Innovation[2]

In the broadest spectrum, open science is related to open access (how academic publications are shared), open data (sharing raw materials of research), open source software (reuse and adaptation encouraged), open educational resources (barrier-free teaching and learning), open participation (citizen science, inclusivity), and many subcategories of each of these. Additionally, open science bumps up against science and technology policy and the challenges and opportunities in the public policy sphere. To state it bluntly, a broad literacy in open science means to dabble a bit in each of these areas and to pull good ideas and aspects from all of them into a way of doing or supporting research (see figure 2.22).

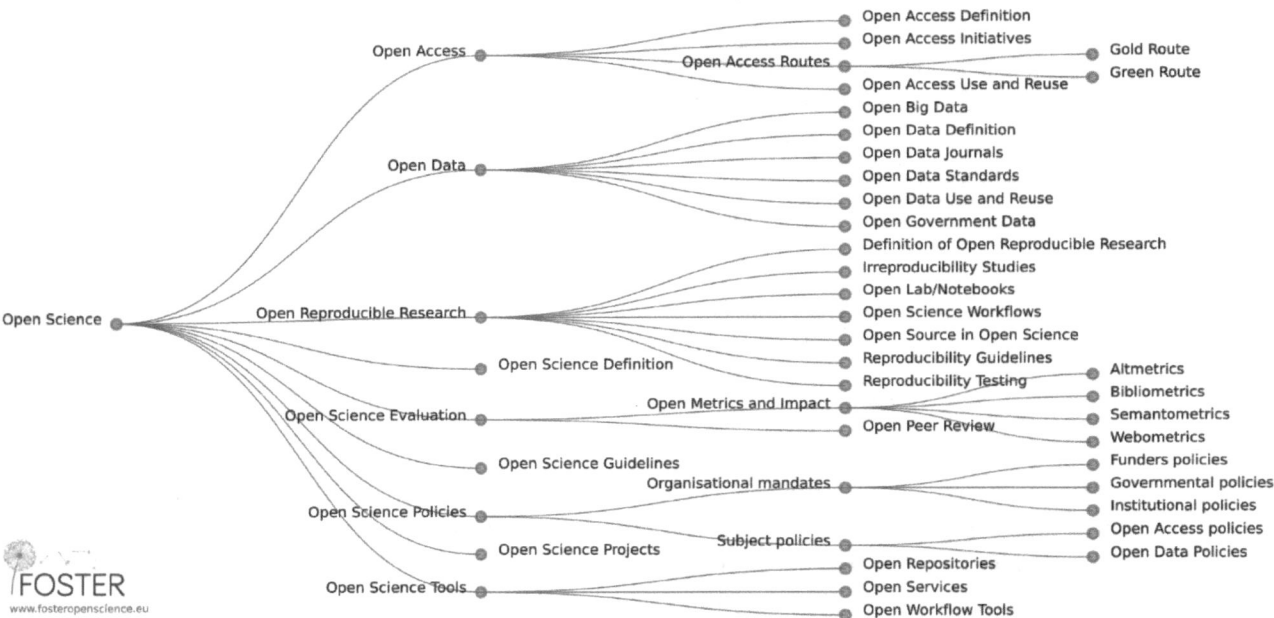

Figure 2.22
The EU's FOSTER Open Science Taxonomy is an essential tool for visualizing the connections between these areas, and also referencing basic definitions for the related terms. Infographic used under CC-BY 4.0 license, available at https://figshare.com/articles/figure/Open_Science_Taxonomy/1508606.

Danielle Robinson and the Open Source Alliance helpfully define *open* as "Transparent and freely available for use, reuse, remixing, and sharing …modif[ying] another term such as open source or open access, implying a difference from a conventional, closed or non-transparent approach."[3] Open science in their estimation is a new way of doing research and scholarship, where the goal is the advancement of knowledge through gracious giving to the common pool of resource from which anyone with an internet connection can pull.[4] As

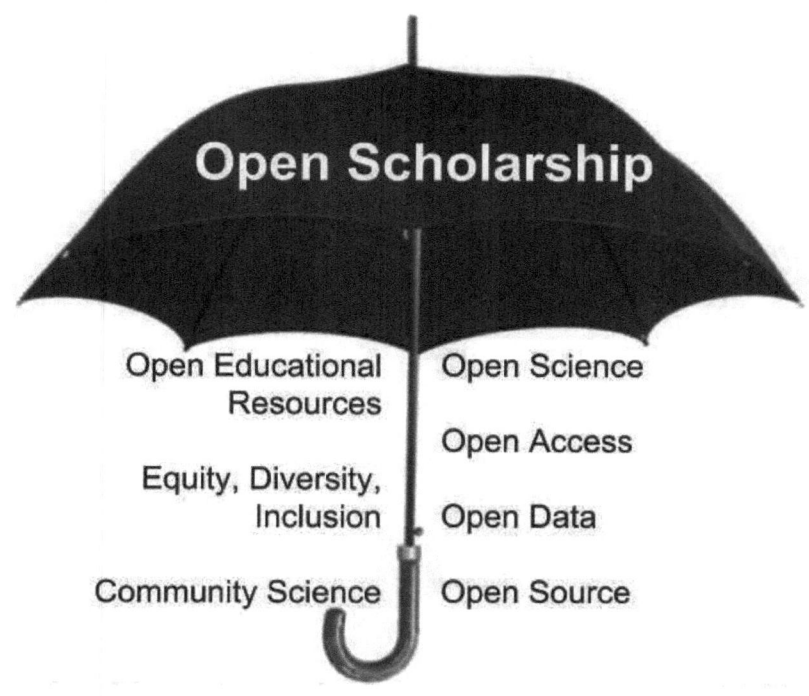

Figure 2.23

Open scholarship as an umbrella term. Image licensed CC-0. Adapted from: https://www.meetup.com/Berlin-Open-Science-Meetup/ by Robin Champieux and Danielle Robinson.

outlined in their umbrella diagram (figure 2.23), all the opens participate in creating a more just, equitable, diverse, and welcoming system of knowledge.

The broad scope of open science makes it unrealistic and counterproductive to expect there to be one unifying definition of open science that fits all. While there are common descriptors, the concept is evolving, so a helpful way to approach defining open science is to talk about what it does and to what it applies, rather than what it IS.

So, what does open science do? Open science, according to the National Academies report *Open Science by Design*, aspires to "increase transparency and reliability, facilitates more effective collaboration, accelerates the pace of discovery, and fosters broader and more equitable access to scientific knowledge and to the research process itself."[5]

Mirrored in the National Academies report and in the European Union's FOSTER *Open Science Training Handbook*,[6] the phrase *open science* applies to principles as well as practices (figure 2.24). For example, a researcher might believe in open access in principle and make judicious decisions about how to make their own work open. Open science is a spectrum rather than an on-off switch. Another helpful phrase from European open advocates is that research should be "as open as possible, as closed as necessary."*

We also need to be aware that some challenges of defining open science come from an English-language focus and Eurocentric perspective. The German word *Wissenscaft*

---

* This phrase first began to appear in relation to privacy and data use as the EU adopted open research data policies and has been adopted more widely in and across open science language. It is especially helpful when discussing sensitive research data about human subjects or endangered or marginalized populations. Referenced in EU policy at Publications Office of the European Union, *Open Data and the Reuse of Public-Sector Information* (Luxembourg: Publications Office of the European Union, February 21, 2023), https://op.europa.eu/s/oHuo.

Figure 2.24
The Open Science logo by Julien Colomb depicts the ideological roots, disciplinary trunk, and practice-based branches of open science. Image used under CC-BY-SA 4.0 license, available at https://github.com/open-science-promoters/opensciencelogo.

"incorporates scientific and non-scientific inquiry, learning, knowledge, scholarship and implies that knowledge is a dynamic process discoverable for oneself, rather than something that is handed down"[7] and is helpful for broadening open beyond just STEM (science, technology, engineering, and math). More recently, phrases like *open scholarship* and *open knowledge* are being employed for wider utility.

This chapter will default to the term *open science* in an effort to align with global efforts and established literature in this area. Practically in the United States, a phrase like *open research and scholarship* would probably best represent the fullest variety of activities, methods, and principles and also explicitly include, welcome, and make space for the social sciences and humanities in the conversation.

FRAMEWORKS

Much like *digital scholarship* or *digital humanities*, *open science* resists a monolithic definition, as outlined above. Even so, it is a helpful umbrella (figure 2.25) for situating lots of related concepts, ideas, services, technologies, and projects. We tend to talk about these umbrellas as "frameworks," which can encompass workflows (processes and procedures that are not always explicit), best practices, or just theoretical models. The idea of frameworks is helpful in shaping the concept of open science that is explored here.

Fecher and Friesike compiled a five "schools of thought" framework (figure 2.25) through which open science is approached:

- *Infrastructure School*—concerned with technological architecture
- *Public School*—concerned with accessibility or invitational qualities of knowledge
- *Measurement School*—concerned with evolving impact measurement
- *Democratic School*—concerned with free access to knowledge
- *Pragmatic School*—concerned with efficiency of collaborative research[8]

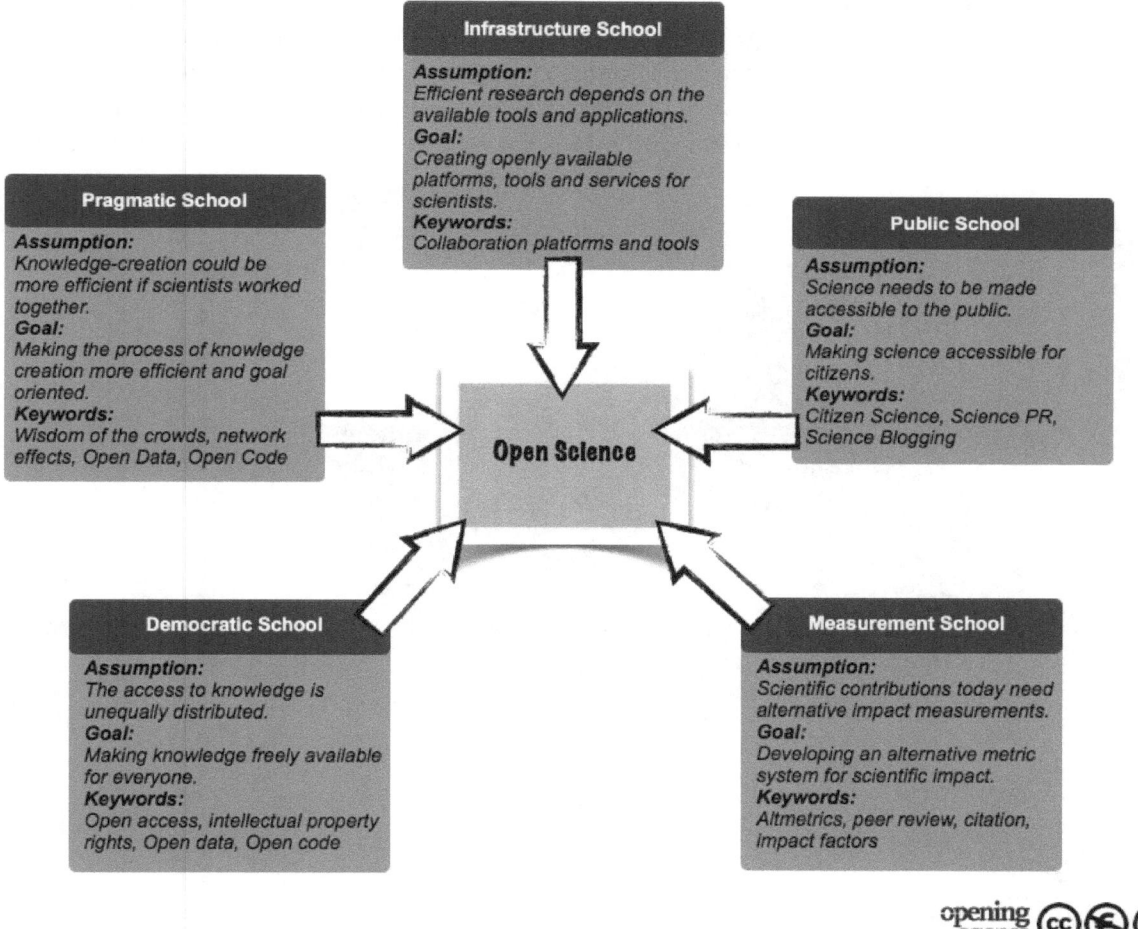

Figure 2.25

The EU's FOSTER Open Science Taxonomy is an essential tool for visualizing the connections between these areas, and also referencing basic definitions for the related terms. Infographic used under CC-BY-NC 4.0 license, available at https://doi.org/10.1007/978-3-319-00026-8_2.

Fecher and Friesike's framework proposes that these five approaches encompass most of the aspirations of open science. Libraries working in this area tend to lean toward one or maybe two of these schools, often based on the character of the university they are attached to and the specific strengths of the librarians employed there. For example, NC State University, a land-grant, STEM-focused university with deep connections to the state of North Carolina through our cooperative agriculture extension program, fits squarely in the Pragmatic School, invested in efficient and collaborative work. Florida State University, my alma mater and former place of employment, would fit much more comfortably in the Democratic School, as etched in stone above Dodd Hall, "The half of knowledge is to know where to find knowledge." The five schools model offers a flexible suite of definitions for understanding what open science does and where it applies.

The Knowledge Exchange, a think tank of European researchers, developed an "open scholarship framework," proposing that any open activity could be situated in between three dimensions: Arena, Research Phase, and Level (figure 2.26).[9] For example, a postdoc's software development project could be technological and focused on dissemination at a micro level while simultaneously being part of a larger research group's work that is challenging the social fabric of discovery across their discipline. While feeling a bit sterile and conceptual, this model is helpful for visualizing another important aspect of what open science does, as alluded to above; open science is a spectrum, effecting change in many ways concurrently, changing how researchers perform daily work, how universities value new forms of scholarly outputs, and also how governments invest in and extract value from higher education as an industry.

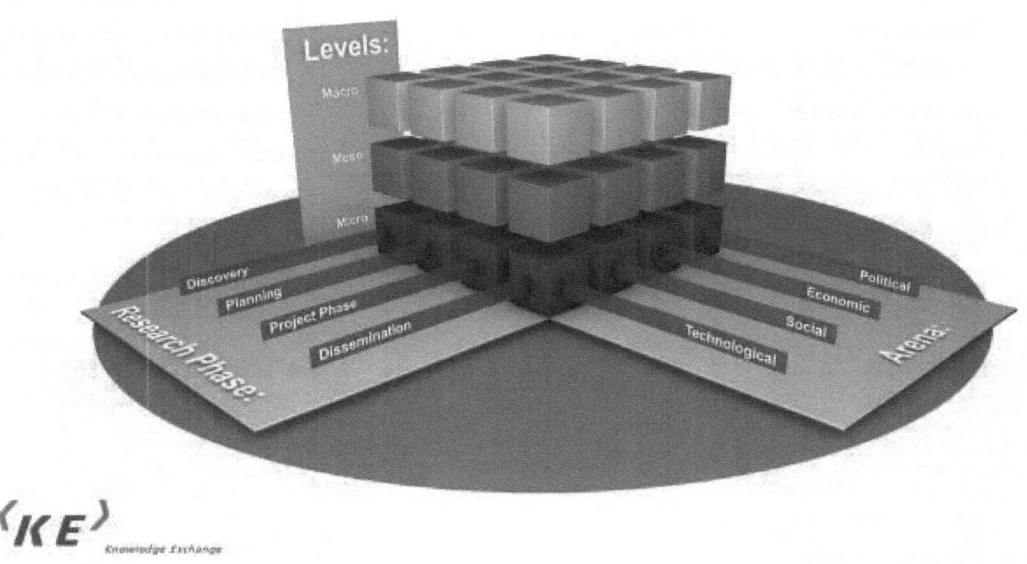

Figure 2.26
The Knowledge Exchange Open Scholarship Framework is licensed CC-BY 4.0, available with more detail at https://www.knowledge-exchange.info/event/os-framework.

Another important framework for understanding what open science does and applies to is the history of other "open" movements. A valuable trait in this history is that the predecessors of open science took care to document and refine their definitions over time, leading to a nice building-block approach using common terms and ideas across the years.

The precepts of open science arose from a few "open" movements that had several established framing definitions:

- *Free software (1986)*[10]—"Free software" means software that respects users' freedom and community. Roughly, it means that the users have the freedom to run, copy, distribute, study, change, and improve the software. Thus, free software is a matter of liberty, not price.

- *Open source definition (1998)*[11]—Lists qualities and characteristics for something to be called open source, including free redistribution, access to the source code, allowing and encouraging modified and derivative works, some progressive claims about anti-discrimination practices.

- *Open access (2002–2003)*—Refers primarily to scholarly literature that is "digital, online, free of charge, and free of most copyright and licensing restrictions. What makes it possible is the internet and the consent of the author or copyright-holder."[12]

- *Open definition (2005)*—"Open means anyone can freely access, use, modify, and share for any purpose (subject, at most, to requirements that preserve provenance and openness)."[13]

Building from this history, UNESCO issued a first draft of recommendations on open science in late 2020, following a six-month-long period of global comments and discussion including 2,900 participants from 133 countries,[14] underlining and responding to the need for a worldwide open science defining framework. Helpfully, that recommendation offered a mega-definition, affirming that open science is

> an umbrella concept that combines various movements and practices aiming to make scientific knowledge, methods, data and evidence freely available and accessible for everyone, increase scientific collaborations and sharing of information for the benefits of science and society, and open the process of scientific knowledge creation and circulation to societal actors beyond the institutionalized scientific community.[15]

Gesturing backward to history again, the UNESCO authors hedge their bets and say that open science is "a complex of at least the following elements," listing out lengthy definitions for *open access, open data, open source hardware/software, open science infrastructures, open evaluation, open educational resources, open engagement* of societal actors, and *openness* to diversity of knowledge.

Approaching open science through these frameworks, or others like them, has allowed a breadth of people to claim ownership in the term and utilize it as is helpful in describing their innovations in how they work, why they chose one perspective over another, and in what ways they distribute and invite others into their work. Teased in the introduction discussion of open knowledge and open research above and aligning with the trajectory toward a more equitable and inclusive research environment, a remaining barrier for open science is the *science* part of that phrase. If the distilled version of open science is an evolutionary movement in the culture and behaviors of how academic ideas are created, shared, and used, it's clear that many other people who do not identify as scientists also have purchase in that movement. What we can best glean from the five schools, the three dimensions, and the mega-inclusive global concept is that open science is changing things, rapidly, and hopefully toward a more equitable data, information, and knowledge future.

CHARACTERISTICS

The principles of open science, according to the National Academies report mentioned earlier, work together to "increase transparency and reliability, facilitate more effective collaboration, accelerate the pace of discovery, and foster broader and more equitable access to scientific knowledge and to the research process itself."[16] Taken individually, these principles in practice provide a loose set of qualities (not all-encompassing) that we can look for in a research project or a scholar's portfolio. While not a win-lose checklist, these characteristics can be helpful in identifying open interventions that one could encourage in partnerships, consultations, or collaborative projects. Open science is greater than what it is, and being aware of core principles can help us get closer to describing more clearly what it does.

Deepening the list the National Academies proposed, the Open and Collaborative Science in Development Network (OCSDNet) proposed in its Open Science Manifesto[17] that open science

- enables a **knowledge commons** where every individual has the means to decide how their knowledge is *governed and managed* to address their needs
- recognizes **cognitive justice**, the need for *diverse* understandings of knowledge making to co-exist in scientific production
- practices **situated openness** by addressing the ways in which *context, power and inequality* condition scientific research
- advocates for every individual's **right to research** and enables different forms of *participation* at all stages of the research process
- fosters **equitable collaboration** between scientists and social actors and cultivates *co-creation* and social innovation in society
- incentivizes **inclusive infrastructures** that empower people of *all abilities* to make, and use accessible open-source technologies
- strives to use knowledge as a pathway to **sustainable development**, equipping every individual to improve the *well-being* of our society and planet

Practically then, table 2.11 attempts to pair some open science practices to open science principles in an effort to show what open might look like in action.

TABLE 2.11
Open science practices and principles.

Practice	Principle
Documenting data workflows	increases transparency by allowing the process of research to be more visible.
Equitably apportioning credit across a research project	advocates for every individual's right to research and enables different forms of participation at all stages of the research process.
Sharing research ideas through preprints or video abstracts early in the research process	accelerates the pace of discovery by circulating new knowledge.
Producing nontechnical, non-technological things (art works, community events, translations/interpretations, etc.)	recognizes cognitive justice, the need for diverse understandings of knowledge making to coexist in scientific production.

TABLE 2.11
Open science practices and principles.

Practice	Principle
Clearly indicating copyright and licenses for the things you produce (data, articles, posters, graphics, software) and advocating for author-favored licensing in publishing	facilitates more effective collaboration by allowing anyone who encounters your work to immediately understand how they can use, build on, and re-share it.
Advocating for revised tenure and promotion guidelines	practices situated openness by addressing the ways in which context, power, and inequality condition scientific research.
Resisting corporate monopolization of academic tools and systems (like major publishing companies owning open access repository software)	enables a knowledge commons where every individual has the means to decide how their knowledge is governed and managed to address their needs.
Promoting inclusive environments that allow for diverse perspectives	will improve the quality and equity of knowledge production.

These characteristics, and the many not detailed in this section, are a snapshot of the kinds of actions a researcher or research collective might take to illustrate their commitment to open science. There is no shortage of articles, blog posts, conference presentations, or listicles on how to be an open researcher, indicating a growing shift in behavior. However, the culture of research production, steeped in the traditions of pre-digital higher education, is slower to recognize, value, and provide credit for many open practices. As open science practices become more commonplace, the expectation is that systems like tenure and promotion will adapt to take it into account. Looking ahead to that time, statements like the Vienna Principles (figure 2.27) or the San Francisco Declaration on Research Assessment offer a vision of "cornerstones of the future scholarly communication system" and "the need to improve the ways in which researchers and the outputs of scholarly research are evaluated."[18]

Figure 2.27
The Vienna Principles "is a set of twelve principles that represent the cornerstones of the future scholarly communication system." Image used under the CC-BY 4.0 license, available at https://viennaprinciples.org/.

The characteristic practices of open science are not confined to the empirical research that is often stereotyped as the only kind of research conducted in the physical or life sciences. Advancements in applied fields like education, sociology, public history, and fine arts can also connect and reaffirm goals and principles like those outlined above. A modern and progressive researcher might then talk about their work using familiar disciplinary terms (e.g., cultural heritage artifact) while also connecting to the increasingly common language of open science (e.g., FAIR data), effectively tying their work to this next phase of how we produce new knowledge.

HORIZON(S)

In the end it's perhaps more important to point to the increasing speed of developments toward open science, than worry about the exact definition of it. Returning to the transatlantic perspective that opened this chapter, the latter years of the 2010s have produced a groundswell of open science advancements, from individuals and communities building and aligning, to full-scale university programs and, perhaps most impactful, governmental and research funder policies shifting to full-throated support.[19] Concurrently, the global connectivity of research, riding the waves of open access and open educational resources thanks in large part to the maturity of the internet, has solidified the realization that an open science for North America and Europe is not open at all.

In an essay for *The Geopolitics of Open*, Chen, Mewa, Albornoz, and Huang urge caution in the spread of open science from the northern to the southern hemisphere, writing that, if it is not respectful and inclusive of local and diverse knowledge systems, "we will continue to witness the strengthening of systems that seek to be global and 'open' research infrastructures, yet continue to limit wider and equitable participations from researchers in less powerful regions and institutions."[20] A

> an uncritical uptake of 'openness' that does not actively work to redress power imbalances in the current system of academic knowledge production—such as the primacy of knowledge written in colonial languages in historically dominant institutions and validated by international academic journals (Chan 2011; Czerniewicz 2015; Canagarajah 2002)—threatens to replicate and amplify them.[21]

Knowing this, there is an implicit responsibility in open science to be aware of defining porous boundaries.

Bosman and Kramer rightly point out that open science does not develop in a vacuum and is part of a broader movement toward open knowledge. They refine this further, writing that open knowledge and the practices aligned with open knowledge, such as those loosely defined as open science, should be "open to the world, ...offering translations, plain language explanations, outreach beyond academia, open[ness] to questions from outside academia, curation and annotation of non-scholarly information, actionable formats, [and] participation in public debate."[22] The near horizon is to think globally and act locally; the distant horizon is to erase the barriers between the academy and the public. A broadly defined, principled, action-oriented open science movement may be part of realizing that vision for a more equitable, open knowledge environment.

DISCUSSION QUESTIONS

1. Micah resists defining open science, for good reason. How would you define open science, and what are the strengths and weaknesses of your definition?

2. This chapter observes that American individualism and bootstrapism may be slowing or deterring the advancement of open science practices. How does individualism delay the growth of open science, and what might be done about it?

3. The term *open science* suggests STEM disciplines, though Micah makes clear that broader terms like *open knowledge* or *open research and scholarship* are more inclusive. What aspects of open science as discussed in this section are applicable beyond STEM disciplines, to social science and humanities disciplines?

4. What is lost if open science methods and practices aren't applied beyond STEM fields? How might those disciplines and open practices suffer if openness is primarily practiced in STEM?

5. Fecher and Friesike propose five "schools" of open science as a framework for approaches to open science: infrastructure, public, measurement, democratic, and pragmatic (figure 2.25). Choose an institution and review the available resources related to open science that it provides and the language used. What schools are most present, and how? What is gained or lost by focusing on certain schools over others?

NOTES

1. Jeroen Bosman and Bianca Kramer, "Defining Open Science Definitions," *I&M / I&O 2.0* (blog), March 26, 2017, https://im2punt0.wordpress.com/2017/03/27/defining-open-science-definitions/.

2. Directorate-General for Research and Innovation (European Commission), *Open Innovation, Open Science, Open to the World* (Luxembourg: Publications Office of the European Union, 2016), https://doi.org/10.2777/061652.

3. Open Source Alliance and Danielle Robinson, "What Is Open?" *OSAOS Handbook* (blog), https://osaos.codeforscience.org/what-is-open/.

4. Cribbing Elinor Ostrom via Lucy Montgomery et al.. "Open Knowledge Institutions." Works in Progress, MIT Press, July 9, 2018, https://doi.org/10.21428/99f89a34.

5. National Academies of Sciences, Engineering, and Medicine, *Open Science by Design: Realizing a Vision for 21ˢᵗ Century Research* (Washington, DC: National Academies Press, 2018), https://doi.org/10.17226/25116.

6. Sonja Bezjak et al., *The Open Science Training Handbook* (FOSTER, 2018), https://book.fosteropenscience.eu/en/01Introduction/.

7. Wikipedia, s.v. "*Wissenschaft*," last updated February 4, 2023, https://en.wikipedia.org/wiki/Wissenschaft.

8. Benedikt Fecher and Sascha Friesike, "Open Science: One Term, Five Schools of Thought," in *Opening Science: The Evolving Guide on How the Internet Is Changing Research, Collaboration and Scholarly Publishing*, ed. Sönke Bartling and Sascha Friesike (Cham, Switzerland: Springer, 2014), 17–47, https://doi.org/10.1007/978-3-319-00026-8_2.

9. Knowledge Exchange, "Open Scholarship Framework," August 31, 2017, https://www.knowledge-exchange.info/event/os-framework.

10. Wikipedia, s.v. "The Free Software Definition," last updated April 2, 2023, https://en.wikipedia.org/wiki/The_Free_Software_Definition.

11. Open Source Initiative, "The Open Source Definition (Annotated)," ver. 1.9, last modified March 22, 2007, https://opensource.org/osd-annotated.

12. Peter Suber, "A Very Brief Introduction to Open Access," https://dash.harvard.edu/bitstream/handle/1/4727454/suber_verybriefintro.htm.

13. Open Knowledge Foundation, "Open Definition," https://opendefinition.org/.

14. UNESCO, *Towards a Global Consensus on Open Science* (Paris: UNESCO, 2020), https://en.unesco.org/science-sustainable-future/open-science/consultation.

15. UNESCO, "Preliminary Report on the First Draft of the Recommendation on Open Science," 2020, https://unesdoc.unesco.org/ark:/48223/pf0000374409.locale=en.

16. National Academies of Sciences, Engineering and Medicine, *Open Science by Design*, https://nap.nationalacademies.org/read/25116/chapter/3.
17. OCSDNet, "Open Science Manifesto," https://ocsdnet.org/manifesto/open-science-manifesto/.
18. Vienna Principles, home page, https://viennaprinciples.org/; DORA, home page, https://sfdora.org/.
19. See: Global Young Academy, "Open Science (GYA)," https://globalyoungacademy.net/activities/open-science/; Utrecht University, "Open Science," https://www.uu.nl/en/research/open-science; Plan S, home page, https://www.coalition-s.org/; Open Research Funders Group, home page, https://www.orfg.org/.
20. George (Zhiwen) Chen et al., "Geopolitical Inequalities behind 'Open' Infrastructures for Academic Knowledge Production," in *The Geopolitics of Open*, edited by Denisse Albornoz, George (Zhiwen) Chen, Maggie Huang, Tasneem Mewa, Gabriela Méndez Cota, and Ángel Octavio Álvarez Solís (Coventry, UK: Post Office Press, Rope Press and Culture Machine, 2018), 13, https://doi.org/10.17613/M65717N1C.
21. Chen et al., "Geopolitical Inequalities," 6.
22. Bosman and Kramer, "Defining Open Science Definitions."

BIBLIOGRAPHY

Bezjak, Sonja, April Clyburne-Sherin, Philipp Conzett, Pedro Fernandes, Edit Görögh, Kerstin Helbig, Bianca Kramer, et al. *The Open Science Training Handbook*. FOSTER, 2018. https://book.fosteropenscience.eu/en/01Introduction/.

Bosman, Jeroen, and Bianca Kramer. "Defining Open Science Definitions." *I&M / I&O 2.0* (blog), March 26, 2017. https://im2punt0.wordpress.com/2017/03/27/defining-open-science-definitions/.

Chen, George (Zhiwen), Tasneem Mewa, Denisse Albornoz, and Maggie Huang. "Geopolitical Inequalities behind 'Open' Infrastructures for Academic Knowledge Production." In *The Geopolitics of Open*, edited by Denisse Albornoz, George (Zhiwen) Chen, Maggie Huang, Tasneem Mewa, Gabriela Méndez Cota, and Ángel Octavio Álvarez Solís, 6–15. Coventry, UK: Post Office Press, Rope Press and Culture Machine, 2018. https://doi.org/10.17613/M65717N1C.

Directorate-General for Research and Innovation (European Commission). *Open Innovation, Open Science, Open to the World: A Vision for Europe*. Luxembourg: Publications Office of the European Union, 2016. https://doi.org/10.2777/061652.

DORA. Home page. https://sfdora.org/.

Fecher, Benedikt, and Sascha Friesike. "Open Science: One Term, Five Schools of Thought." In *Opening Science: The Evolving Guide on How the Internet Is Changing Research, Collaboration and Scholarly Publishing*, edited by Sönke Bartling and Sascha Friesike, 17–47. Cham, Switzerland: Springer, 2014. https://doi.org/10.1007/978-3-319-00026-8_2.

FOSTER. "Open Science Taxonomy." Infographic. https://www.fosteropenscience.eu/themes/fosterstrap/images/taxonomies/os_taxonomy.png.

Global Young Academy. "Open Science (GYA)." https://globalyoungacademy.net/activities/open-science/.

Knowledge Exchange. "Open Scholarship Framework." August 31, 2017. https://www.knowledge-exchange.info/event/os-framework.

Montgomery, Lucy, John Hartley, Cameron Neylon, Malcolm Gillies, Eve Gray, Carsten Herrmann-Pillath, Chun-Kai (Karl) Huang, et al. "Open Knowledge Institutions." Works in Progress, MIT Press, July 9, 2018. https://doi.org/10.21428/99f89a34.

National Academies of Sciences, Engineering and Medicine. *Open Science by Design: Realizing a Vision for 21st Century Research*. Washington, DC: National Academies Press, 2018. https://doi.org/10.17226/25116.

OCSDNet. "Open Science Manifesto." https://ocsdnet.org/manifesto/open-science-manifesto/.

Open Knowledge Foundation. "Open Definition." https://opendefinition.org/.

Open Research Funders Group. Home page. https://www.orfg.org/.

Open-science-promoters/Opensciencelogo, flower150.png. GitHub, May 23, 2019, https://github.com/open-science-promoters/opensciencelogo.

Open Source Alliance and Danielle Robinson. "What Is Open?" *OSAOS Handbook* (blog). https://osaos.codeforscience.org/what-is-open/.

Open Source Initiative. "The Open Source Definition (Annotated)," ver. 1.9. Last modified March 22, 2007. https://opensource.org/osd-annotated.

Plan S. Home page. https://www.coalition-s.org/.

Publications Office of the European Union. *Open Data and the Reuse of Public-Sector Information*. Luxembourg: Publications Office of the European Union, February 21, 2023. https://op.europa.eu/s/oHuo.

Suber, Peter. "A Very Brief Introduction to Open Access." https://dash.harvard.edu/bitstream/handle/1/4727454/suber_verybriefintro.htm.

UNESCO. "Preliminary Report on the First Draft of the Recommendation on Open Science." 2020. https://unesdoc.unesco.org/ark:/48223/pf0000374409.locale=en.

———. *Towards a Global Consensus on Open Science: Report on UNESCO's Global Online Consultation on Open Science*. Paris: UNESCO, 2020. https://en.unesco.org/science-sustainable-future/open-science/consultation.

Utrecht University. "Open Science." https://www.uu.nl/en/research/open-science.

Vienna Principles. Home page. https://viennaprinciples.org/.

Wikipedia. S.v. "The Free Software Definition." Last updated April 2, 2023. https://en.wikipedia.org/wiki/The_Free_Software_Definition.

Wikipedia. S.v. "*Wissenschaft*." Last updated February 4, 2023. https://en.wikipedia.org/wiki/Wissenschaft.

GENERATION OPEN

Sam Teplitzky

INTRODUCTION

Written in 2019, this essay summarizes some key stakeholder groups of open science and infrastructure. It lays out structural barriers, but also highlights examples of changing attitudes. More importantly, this essay addresses the European/North American–centric focus of open science and points to some encouraging movements to break that stalemate. Finally, this section features a discussion about authorship and contributorship as an example of the open evolution in progress, with effects at the social and technical layer of research.

THE ROLE AND POWER OF EARLY CAREER RESEARCHERS

Early career researchers (ECRs) face both benefits and challenges as they participate in open science. As the label implies, ECRs* are at the beginning of their careers, in the perfect place to question traditional practices at their institutions and in their disciplines more broadly.

BENEFITS AND INCENTIVES

How well open science works in action depends heavily on a researcher's field, but many benefits are not bound by discipline, falling under the umbrella of *exposure* and *acknowledgment*. Participation in open science results in *greater visibility and reach*, *reputational gains*, more opportunities for *networking and collaboration*, and ultimately both more informal coverage and formal *citations*.[1] When their work is openly available, ECRs are more likely to be acknowledged, to be invited to discuss their work, and to have their work shared through media channels.[2]

As ECRs establish their preferred practices, products, and workflows, they are well positioned to *learn best practices* and be rewarded by the *increased efficiencies* that come with open science.[3] As they establish individual research programs, ECRs benefit from the

---

* Definitions of early career researchers vary, but generally include researchers within eight to ten years of completing their PhD and within six years of their first academic appointment (UK Research and Innovation, "Early Career Researchers: Career and Skills Development," accessed May 25, 2022, https://www.ukri.org/councils/ahrc/career-and-skills-development/early-career-researchers-career-and-skills-development/.)

funder-friendly approach of open science as well as the *broader increase in the reliability of their research*.[4] Key to this is the integration of open practices through the research life cycle.

> Making research results openly available is not an afterthought when the project is over, but, rather, it is an effective way of doing the research itself. That is, in this way of doing science, making research results open is a by-product of the research process, and not a task that needs to be done when the researcher has already turned to the next project.[5]

Although not specific to ECRs, these final benefits exemplify the movement of science away from the work of a lone individual to a collaborative effort with a public reach. Open science adoption supports *science as a conversation*, the ability of science to meaningfully build on itself, rather than act as isolated case studies, and highlights the *public benefit* of research to democratize access to information and to allow the public to see the details of the scientific process.[6]

CHALLENGES AND DISINCENTIVES

Adopting open science practices as a new researcher is not without its challenges. The first among them is a general *lack of awareness*. Depending on where they have trained, ECRs may lack an awareness of the benefits and importance of opening up their research.[7] The *nebulous definition* of open science may also breed uncertainty. Many scientists already share their work, but may not consider those efforts as qualifying as open science.[8]

No one-size-fits-all approach applies to open science. Researchers from different disciplines may need to take diverse approaches,[9] and there can be an overwhelming *learning curve* involved in evaluating and incorporating new tools, software, and processes, particularly if it contradicts current lab, advisor, or disciplinary practices. At the outset, it can be difficult to assess which products or practices are good fits, which will be sustainable long-term, and whether the effort will be worth the reward.[10] Archiving, documenting, and quality control of code and data take time, but ideally these *time costs* are borne at the onset of a project and save time later. Nonetheless, many ECRs consider it an activity that is too time- and effort-consuming to add to their existing workloads.[11]

ECRs working in the current incentive system may hesitate to adopt open practices as an open science–friendly *incentive structure is not in place yet*. In the current incentive structure, quantity is often rewarded over quality, and innovation over collaboration, so that "as long as open science efforts are not formally recognised, it seems ECRs who pursue open science are put at a disadvantage compared with ECRs who have not invested in open science."[12] ECRs show the strongest support for open science reforms,[13] but at the same time, they have concerns about their careers as "research practices may change faster than incentive structures"[14] (see figure 2.28). Despite the growth of preprint options and both general and discipline-focused open access journals, the *pressure to publish in traditionally prestigious, high-impact journals* is felt acutely by early career researchers whose tenure decisions may rest on their publication records. According to the National Academies of Sciences' *Reproducibility and Replicability in Science*, the top five ranked drivers of change in the research system for ERCs are the importance of collaborating with other academic researchers, the importance of collaborating globally with other academic researches, focus on multidisciplinary research, changes in how research is assessed, and open science (listed as the least significant driver; see figure 2.28).[15]

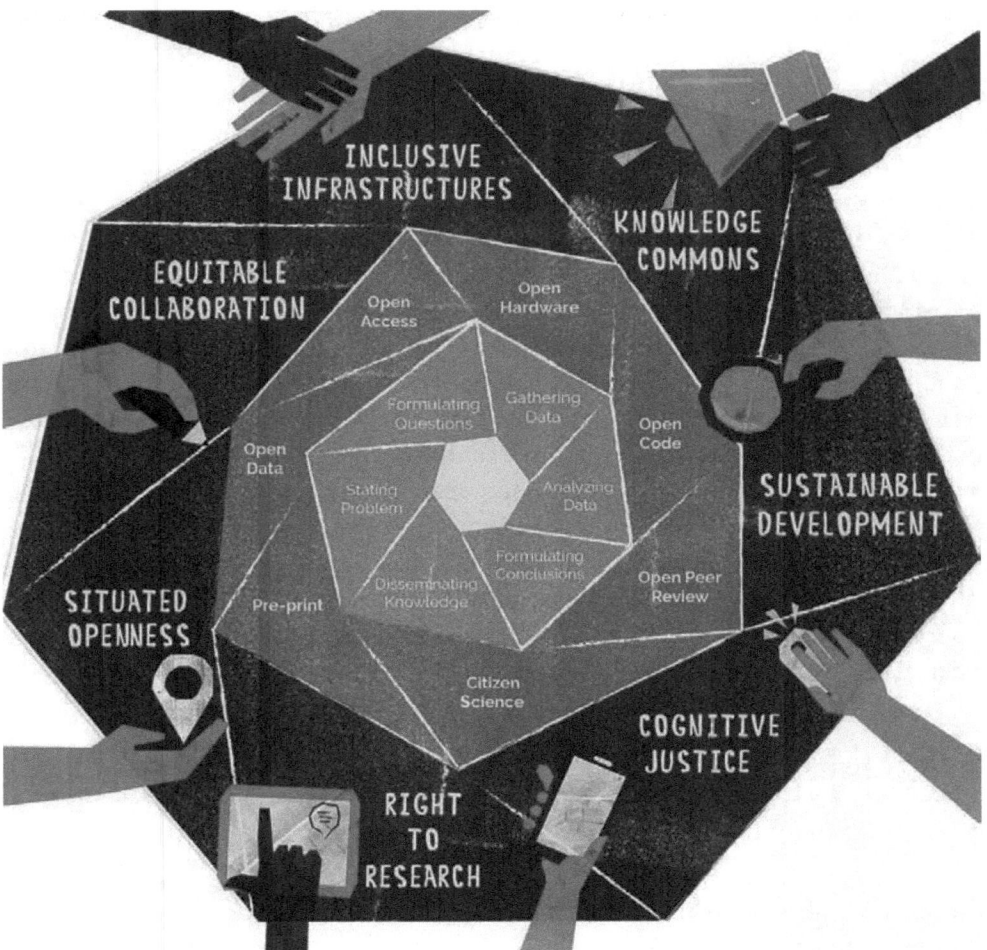

Figure 2.28
The OCSDNet Manifesto infographic identifies seven values and principles that they believe constitute a more open and inclusive science in development. Infographic is used under a CC-BY 3.0 license, available at https://ocsdnet.org/manifesto/open-science-manifesto/.

EVOLVING ATTITUDES

We have focused on ECRs who do not yet have sunk costs, but how do established or tenured researchers adopt open science goals? Established researchers may have the benefit of stature, name recognition, stable funding in place, but also bring skepticism, some reluctance to change, and an embeddedness in current systems. Established researchers have come up in a system that rewards *novelty* and *innovation*. The very novelty and innovation of open science are in its collaboration, connection, and shared contributions, but established researchers or reviewers do not always see the transformative nature of open science work, particularly when that work may focus on replication, processes, or collaborative workflows or perhaps diminish the role of the lone PI.[16]

Traditional researchers may also have concerns about being scooped or not being credited, and some are just unwilling to share their data. They may harbor *biases about preprints* or sow confusion about the *reputation of open access journals*.[17] However, there is growing support for *small steps toward reproducibility* and *good-enough practices* to encourage changes in attitude and overcome these concerns around adopting open science. Reproducibility entails an acceptance of good-enough practices (it's more important for code to be shared than to be perfect).[18] Scientists can focus on acquiring accessible skills for scientific computing, a minimum set of tools and techniques that can drive their work toward open practices and reproducibility.[19] Broman's initial steps toward reproducible research are also a great way to start.[20] This gradual approach also gets away from virtue signaling that can accompany open science. Individual scientists may face barriers and should not be penalized for failing to check all of the boxes for a project to be considered open.[21]

Established researchers can contribute in two other key areas: *prioritizing open science in hiring* and contributing to an inclusive *peer-review* culture. Open science statements are beginning to be required from job candidates, and many academic jobs highlight the importance if not the requirement of open science practices.[22] Established researchers can add their support by providing training for their graduate students and postdocs in the necessary skills, pushing for changes to incentive structures by valuing transparency in hiring and promotion and expecting transparency, not just from new hires, but from established colleagues and collaborators as well. They can also help their chosen journals improve the diversity of their reviewer pools by listing women, young scientists, and members of other underrepresented groups when asked for suggested peer reviewers.[23]

INCLUSION, DIVERSITY AND GEOPOLITICS OF OPEN

Does open science replicate existing structural barriers, biases, and power structures? It isn't enough to open up personal workflows; we also must consider who is included and who is left out more broadly in the drive toward open. Making science truly open requires not just opening up methods and software, but also questioning the foundation and priorities of modern science itself so that open science does not inherit the same structural barriers that already exist in mainstream science.[24] Questioning traditional definitions of scientific objectivity, discovery, and research excellence requires us to reconsider power structures in place and how those structures have reduced diversity and excluded many participants from the scientific process.[25]

The Open and Collaborative Science in Development Network's seven principles for open and collaborative science (figure 2.28) provide guidance for a true open approach to science that honors local and culturally embedded knowledge, engages with the question of how and for whom science is produced, and supports populations in their work to cocreate an agenda for their science.[26]

The seven principles are that open and collaborative science in development

1. Enables a knowledge commons where all individuals have the means to decide how their knowledge is governed and managed to address their needs;

2. Recognizes cognitive justice and the need for diverse understandings of knowledge making to co-exist in scientific production;

3. Practices situated openness by addressing the ways in which context, power, and inequality condition scientific research;

4. Advocates for each individual's right to research and enables different forms of participation at all stages of the research process;

5. Fosters equitable collaboration between scientists and social actors, and cultivates co-creation and social innovation in society;

6. Incentivizes inclusive infrastructures that empower people of all abilities to make and use accessible open-source technologies; and

7. Uses knowledge as a pathway to sustainable development, equipping every individual to improve the well-being of our society and planet.

These principles address the realities of diverse collaborations (citizen science, indigenous communities, etc.) where there is a "need to balance [a] reliable mechanism of validation of knowledge with the need to include a wider diversity of actors in the production of scientific knowledge."[27] Collaborations founded on open sharing of indigenous knowledge should result in research products that are made open and shared back with those communities,[28] and not every experience needs to be goal- and outcome-oriented. Workshops and collaborations that allow participants to "build tools and other equipment while discussing and integrating these implements in their communities" are important as well.[29] Open goals and a horizontal structure of interaction help make science part of everyday life, and not solely a benefit to traditional institutions.

The work of Woodley and Pratt is also helpful in understanding how power balances influence the interactions within open science communities. Applying their terminology (*convey, contribute, collaborate, cocreate*), we can better anticipate how expertise will be shared or communicated beyond individual workshops or sessions and expanded to change accepted norms in scientific research. When an organization conveys information, participants absorb established knowledge and standards. This may be necessary to welcome participants and introduce procedures, grant requirements, or other mandated practices, but moving toward *contribute* mode, where researchers share input about their research practices and *collaborate*, or *cocreate* mode, which distribute power to participants so that they may continue conversations and connections beyond the series, is a preferable goal in open science settings.[30]

MOVING FROM AUTHORSHIP TO CONTRIBUTORSHIP

As open science strives toward inclusion, traditional notions of authorship are increasingly limited. For many researchers, authorship is the primary means through which they are evaluated for employment, promotion, and tenure. Authorship implies a certain level of intellectual contribution to the completion of a work, but practices vary by discipline. Authorship may encompass experimental design, data analysis, and programming, with some authors playing a small or no role in writing the actual text of a published work.[31] But as collaboration becomes the norm in many disciplines, "Accepted research success for all collaborative research participants should extend beyond traditional metrics such as primary authorship or project leadership and should include credit for co-authorship, data production, outreach, education, and ongoing mentoring and administrative activities."[32]

Contributorship addresses some of the limitations of traditional authorship. CRediT (Contributor Roles Taxonomy) enables the formal attribution credit through roles that describe each contributor's specific contribution to the scholarly output.[33] The contributor model still requires researchers to be intellectually honest about their roles and has some limitations,[34] but it does resolve some fundamental omissions of authorship, enabling visibility and recognition for authors across all aspects of the research being reported (including data curation, statistical analyses, and software development).[35]

At the level of individual research groups or projects, authorship policies (written documents that describe policies for a research group, lab, or hybrid collaborative effort) can provide key guidance for those involved, particularly when power dynamics are at play. Authorship policies are living documents that should be revisited throughout the life of a project and should include a codification of discussions that occurred around author order. Authorship practices are very discipline-dependent, but that doesn't mean change is not possible.[36]

CONCLUSION

Understanding the *who* behind open science requires us to reconsider accepted norms of research output and participation and replace them with a model that strives toward inclusivity and collaboration. ECRs are poised to reject some of these outmoded practices and implement new approaches, but the onus cannot fall solely on them. Established researchers have the power and position to alter current promotion and reward structures that limit both what can be shared and how and who has the ability to participate in science at all levels. Open science has room to embrace these multiple approaches, from practical measures like implementing contributor roles to larger goals of challenging established power structures in order to broaden who belongs and what is valued in scientific research.

DISCUSSION QUESTIONS

1. How can librarians help ECRs face the challenges of embracing open science practices in ways that acknowledge their vulnerability?
2. How are open science practices as described in this chapter related to important tenets of librarianship like the ACRL *Framework for Information Literacy in Higher Education* (https://www.ala.org/acrl/standards/ilframework)?
3. Why are ECRs in a position to advance open science? How might the fact of their support shape the direction of open science in the next 10 years?

NOTES

1. OpenAIRE, "What Is Open Science?" Frequently Asked Questions, 2019, https://www.openaire.eu/faqs; *PeerJ*, "Early Career Researcher Benefits," 2019, https://peerj.com/benefits/early-career-researchers/.
2. Christopher Allen and David M. A. Mehler, "Open Science Challenges, Benefits and Tips in Early Career and Beyond," *PLOS Biology* 17, no. 5 (2019): e3000246, https://doi.org/10.1371/journal.pbio.3000246.
3. OpenAIRE, "What Is Open Science?"; *PeerJ*, "Early Career Researcher Benefits."
4. Allen and Mehler, "Open Science Challenges."
5. National Academies of Sciences, Engineering, and Medicine, *Open Science by Design* (Washington, DC: National Academies Press, 2018), 108, https://doi.org/10.17226/25116.
6. Christie Bahlai, "Baby Steps for the Open-Curious," *Practical Data Management for Bug Counters* (blog), October 23, 2014, https://practicaldatamanagement.wordpress.com/2014/10/23/baby-steps-for-the-open-curious/.

7. G. Bueno de la Fuente, "Challenges and Strategies for the Success of Open Science," FOSTER Facilitate Open Science Training for European Research, 2016, https://web.archive.org/web/20221102212405/https://www.fosteropenscience.eu/content/challenges-and-strategies-success-open-science.

8. Sarah E. Ali-Khan, Liam W. Harris, and E Richard Gold, "Point of View: Motivating Participation in Open Science by Examining Researcher Incentives," *eLife* 6 (2017): e29319, https://doi.org/10.7554/eLife.29319.

9. National Academies of Sciences, Engineering, and Medicine. *Open Science by Design*, 57.

10. Bueno de la Fuente, "Challenges and Strategies."

11. Allen and Mehler, "Open Science Challenges"; Bueno de la Fuente, "Challenges and Strategies."

12. Allen and Mehler, "Open Science Challenges"

13. Sarah Parks et al., *The Changing Research Landscape and Reflections on National Research Assessment in the Future* (Cambridge: RAND Corporation, 2019), https://doi.org/10.7249/RR3200.

14. Felix Schönbrodt, "Training Students for the Open Science Future," *Nature Human Behaviour* 3, no. 1031 (2019), https://doi.org/10.1038/s41562-019-0726-z.

15. National Academies of Sciences, Engineering, and Medicine, *Reproducibility and Replicability in Science* (Washington, DC: National Academies Press, 2019), https://doi.org/10.17226/25303.

16. B. A. Nosek et al., "Promoting an Open Research Culture," *Science* 348, no. 6242 (2015): 1422–25, https://doi.org/10.1126/science.aab2374.

17. Bahlai, "Baby Steps."

18. J. Leek, "Science-wise False Discovery Rate and Proportion of True Null Hypotheses Estimation" (presentation, AAAS Annual Meeting, Washington, DC, February 17, 2019).

19. Greg Wilson et al., "Good Enough Practices in Scientific Computing," *PLOS Computational Biology* 13, no. 6 (2017): e1005510, https://doi.org/10.1371/journal.pcbi.1005510.

20. Karl Broman, "Initial Steps toward Reproducible Research," Karl Broman professional website, accessed November 20, 2019, https://kbroman.org/steps2rr/.

21. Christie Bahlai et al., "Open Science Isn't Always Open to All Scientists," *American Scientist* 107, no. 2 (March–April 2019), https://doi.org/10.1511/2019.107.2.78.

22. Felix Schönbrodt et al., "Academic Job Offers That Mentioned Open Science," OSF, January 18, 2018, last updated April 5, 2023, https://doi.org/10.17605/OSF.IO/7JBNT.

23. IOP Publishing, *Diversity and Inclusion in Peer Review at IOP Publishing*," IOP Publishing, 2018, http://ioppublishing.org/wp-content/uploads/2018/09/J-VAR-BK-0818-PRW-report-final.pdf.; Thomas Gaston, "Gender Diversity in Peer Review," Wiley, January 10, 2019, https://www.wiley.com/network/journaleditors/editors/gender-diversity-in-peer-review; Brooks Hanson and J. Lerback, "Diversifying the Reviewer Pool," *Eos* 98 (October 4, 2017), https://doi.org/10.1029/2017EO083837.

24. Bahlai et al., "Open Science Isn't Always Open."

25. Cameron Neylon, "Research Excellence Is a Neo-colonial Agenda (and What Might Be Done about It)," in *Transforming Research Excellence: New Ideas from the Global South*, ed. Erika Kraemer-Mbula, Robert Tijssen, Matthew L. Wallace and Robert McLean (Cape Town: African Minds, 2020), 92–116, https://doi.org/10.17613/bta3-6g96; Paola Masuzzo, "From Open Science to Inclusive Science," Zenodo, October 25, 2019, https://doi.org/10.5281/zenodo.3518951; Antoinette Foster, "What Remains Invisible Controls Us the Most: What Really Drives Research?" *My Blog*, International Open Access Week, October 24, 2019, http://legacy.openaccessweek.org/profiles/blogs/what-remains-invisible-controls-us-the-most-what-really-drives; Jack Stilgoe, "Against Excellence," *Guardian*, December 19, 2014, https://www.theguardian.com/science/political-science/2014/dec/19/against-excellence.

26. OCSDNet, "Open Science Manifesto," https://ocsdnet.org/manifesto/open-science-manifesto/.

27. Mariano Fressoli and Valeria Arza, "Actualizing the Promise of a More Democratic Science: Three Challenges for Open Science," OCSDNet, October 12, 2017, https://ocsdnet.org/actualizing-the-promise-of-a-more-democratic-science-three-challenges-for-open-science/.

28. Edmond Sanganyado, "Addressing Climate Change through Indigenous Knowledge Systems," in *The Global Benefits of Open Research: The 2018 MDPI Writing Prize*, vol. 1, ed. Martyn Rittman (Basel, Switzerland: MDPI Books, 2018), 1–3, https://www.mdpi.com/books/edition/914-the-global-benefits-of-open-research.

29. Denisa Kera et al., "Open Science Hardware (OSH) for Development: Transnational Networks and Local Tinkering in Southeast Asia," in *Contextualizing Openness: Situating Open Science*, ed. by Leslie Chan, Angela Okune, Rebecca Hillyer, Denisse Albornoz, and Alejandro Posada (Ottawa: University of Ottawa Press, 2019), 69.

30. Lou Woodley and Katie Pratt, "The CSCCE Community Participation Model – A framework to describe member engagement and information flow in STEM communities," Zenodo. (2020). https://doi.org/10.5281/zenodo.3997802.

31. Wikipedia, s.v. "Academic authorship," last updated February 18, 2023, https://en.wikipedia.org/wiki/Academic_authorship.

32. Simon J. Goring et al., "Improving the Culture of Interdisciplinary Collaboration in Ecology by Expanding Measures of Success," *Frontiers in Ecology and the Environment* 12, no. 1 (February 2014): 39, https://doi.org/10.1890/120370.

33. National Information Standards Organization, "Contributor Roles Taxonomy," https://credit.niso.org/.

34. Jason Borenstein and Adil E. Shamoo, "Rethinking Authorship in the Era of Collaborative Research," *Accountability in Research* 22, no. 5 (2015): 267–83, https://doi.org/10.1080/08989621.2014.968277; Valerie Matarese and Karen Shashok, "Transparent Attribution of Contributions to Research: Aligning Guidelines to Real-Life Practices," *Publications* 7, no. 2 (2019): article 24, https://doi.org/10.3390/publications7020024.

35. Nicole A. Vasilevsky, et al. "Is authorship sufficient for today's collaborative research? A call for contributor roles." *Accountability in Research*, 28, no. 1 (2021): 23-43. https://www.tandfonline.com/doi/full/10.1080/08989621.2020.1779591.

36. Kendra S. Cheruvelil et al., "Creating and Maintaining High-Performing Collaborative Research Teams: The Importance of Diversity and Interpersonal Skills," *Frontiers in Ecology and the Environment* 12, no. 1 (February 2014): 31–38, https://doi.org/10.1890/130001.

BIBLIOGRAPHY

Ali-Khan, Sarah E., Liam W. Harris, and E. Richard Gold. "Point of View: Motivating Participation in Open Science by Examining Researcher Incentives." *eLife* 6 (2017): e29319. https://doi.org/10.7554/eLife.29319.

Allen, Christopher, and David M. A. Mehler. "Open Science Challenges, Benefits and Tips in Early Career and Beyond." *PLOS Biology* 17, no. 5 (2019): e3000246. https://doi.org/10.1371/journal.pbio.3000246.

Bahlai, Christie. "Baby Steps for the Open-Curious." *Practical Data Management for Bug Counters* (blog), October 23, 2014. https://practicaldatamanagement.wordpress.com/2014/10/23/baby-steps-for-the-open-curious/.

Bahlai, Christie, Lewis J. Bartlett, Kevin R. Burgio, Auriel M. V. Fournier, Carl N. Keiser, Timothée Poisot, and Kaitlin Stack Whitney. "Open Science Isn't Always Open to All Scientists." *American Scientist* 107, no. 2 (March–April 2019). https://doi.org/10.1511/2019.107.2.78.

Borenstein, Jason, and Adil E. Shamoo. "Rethinking Authorship in the Era of Collaborative Research." *Accountability in Research* 22, no. 5 (2015): 267–83. https://doi.org/10.1080/08989621.2014.968277.

Broman, Karl. "Initial Steps toward Reproducible Research." Karl Broman professional website. Accessed November 20, 2019. https://kbroman.org/steps2rr/.

Bueno de la Fuente, G. "Challenges and Strategies for the Success of Open Science." FOSTER Facilitate Open Science Training for European Research, 2016. https://web.archive.org/web/20221102212405/https://www.fosteropenscience.eu/content/challenges-and-strategies-success-open-science.

Chan, Leslie, Angela Okune, Rebecca Hillyer, Denisse Albornoz, and Alejandro Posada, eds. *Contextualizing Openness: Situating Open Science*. Ottawa: University of Ottawa Press, 2019. https://www.idrc.ca/sites/default/files/openebooks/Contextualizing-Openness/9781552506110.html.

Cheruvelil, Kendra S., Patricia A. Soranno, Kathleen C. Weathers, Paul C. Hanson, Simon J. Goring, Christopher T. Filstrup, and Emily K. Read. "Creating and Maintaining High-Performing Collaborative Research Teams: The Importance of Diversity and Interpersonal Skills." *Frontiers in Ecology and the Environment* 12, no. 1 (February 2014): 31–38. https://doi.org/10.1890/130001.

Foster, Antoinette. "What Remains Invisible Controls Us the Most: What Really Drives Research?" *My Blog*, International Open Access Week, October 24, 2019. http://legacy.openaccessweek.org/profiles/blogs/what-remains-invisible-controls-us-the-most-what-really-drives.

Fressoli, Mariano, and Valeria Arza. "Actualizing the Promise of a More Democratic Science: Three Challenges for Open Science." OCSDNet, October 12, 2017. https://ocsdnet.org/actualizing-the-promise-of-a-more-democratic-science-three-challenges-for-open-science/.

Gaston, Thomas. "Gender Diversity in Peer Review." Wiley, January 10, 2019. https://www.wiley.com/network/journaleditors/editors/gender-diversity-in-peer-review.

Goring, Simon J., Kathleen C. Weathers, Walter K. Dodds, Patricia A. Soranno, Lynn C. Sweet, Kendra S. Cheruvelil, John S. Kominoski, Janine Rüegg, Alexandra M. Thorn, and Ryan M. Utz. "Improving the Culture of Interdisciplinary Collaboration in Ecology by Expanding Measures of Success." *Frontiers in Ecology and the Environment* 12, no. 1 (February 2014): 39–47. https://doi.org/10.1890/120370.

Hanson, Brooks, and J. Lerback. "Diversifying the Reviewer Pool." *Eos* 98 (October 4, 2017). https://doi.org/10.1029/2017EO083837.

IOP Publishing. *Diversity and Inclusion in Peer Review at IOP Publishing*. Bristol, UK: IOP Publishing, 2018.

Kera, Denisa, Hermes Huang, Irene Agrivine, and Tommy Surya. "Open Science Hardware (OSH) for Development: Transnational Networks and Local Tinkering in Southeast Asia." In *Contextualizing Openness: Situating Open Science*, edited by Leslie Chan, Angela Okune, Rebecca Hillyer, Denisse Albornoz, and Alejandro Posada, 59–85. Ottawa: University of Ottawa Press, 2019.

Leek, J. "Science-wise False Discovery Rate and Proportion of True Null Hypotheses Estimation." Presentation, AAAS Annual Meeting, Washington, DC, February 17, 2019.

Masuzzo, Paola. "From Open Science to Inclusive Science." Zenodo, October 25, 2019. https://doi.org/10.5281/zenodo.3518951.

Matarese, Valerie, and Karen Shashok. "Transparent Attribution of Contributions to Research: Aligning Guidelines to Real-Life Practices." *Publications* 7, no. 2 (2019): article 24. https://doi.org/10.3390/publications7020024.

National Academies of Sciences, Engineering, and Medicine. *Open Science by Design: Realizing a Vision for 21st Century Research*. Washington, DC: National Academies Press, 2018. https://doi.org/10.17226/25116.

———. *Reproducibility and Replicability in Science*. Washington, DC: National Academies Press, 2019. https://doi.org/10.17226/25303.

Neylon, Cameron. "Research Excellence Is a Neo-colonial Agenda (and What Might Be Done about It)." In *Transforming Research Excellence: New Ideas from the Global South*, edited by Erika Kraemer-Mbula, Robert Tijssen, Matthew L. Wallace and Robert McLean, 92–116. Cape Town: African Minds, 2020. https://doi.org/10.17613/bta3-6g96.

National Information Standards Organization. "Contributor Roles Taxonomy." https://credit.niso.org/.

Nosek, B. A., G. Alter, G. C. Banks, D. Borsboom, S. D. Bowman, S. J. Breckler, S. Buck, et al. "Promoting an Open Research Culture." *Science* 348, no. 6242 (2015): 1422–25. https://doi.org/10.1126/science.aab2374.

OCSDNet. "Open Science Manifesto." https://ocsdnet.org/manifesto/open-science-manifesto/.

OpenAIRE. "What Is Open Science?" 2017. https://www.openaire.eu/what-is-open-science.

Parks, Sarah, Daniela Rodriguez-Rincon, Sarah Parkinson, and Catriona Manville. *The Changing Research Landscape and Reflections on National Research Assessment in the Future*. Cambridge: RAND Corporation, 2019. https://doi.org/10.7249/RR3200.

PeerJ. "Early Career Researcher Benefits." 2019. https://peerj.com/benefits/early-career-researchers/.

Sanganyado, Edmond. "Addressing Climate Change through Indigenous Knowledge Systems." In *The Global Benefits of Open Research: The 2018 MDPI Writing Prize*, vol. 1, edited by Martyn Rittman, 1–3. Basel, Switzerland: MDPI Books, 2018. https://www.mdpi.com/books/edition/914-the-global-benefits-of-open-research.

Schönbrodt, Felix. "Training Students for the Open Science Future." *Nature Human Behaviour* 3, no. 1031 (2019). https://doi.org/10.1038/s41562-019-0726-z.

Schönbrodt, Felix, Leonhard Falk Florentin Schramm, Franka Tabitha Etzel, Christina Bergmann, David Thomas Mellor, Antonio Schettino, Bianca Weber, et al. "Academic Job Offers That Mentioned Open Science." OSF, January 18, 2018, last updated April 5, 2023. https://doi.org/10.17605/OSF.IO/7JBNT.

Stilgoe, Jack. "Against Excellence." *Guardian*, December 19, 2014. https://www.theguardian.com/science/political-science/2014/dec/19/against-excellence.

UK Research and Innovation. "Early Career Researchers: Career and Skills Development." Accessed May 25, 2022. https://www.ukri.org/councils/ahrc/career-and-skills-development/early-career-researchers-career-and-skills-development/.

Vasilevsky, Nicole A., Mohammad Hosseini, Samantha Teplitzky, Violeta Ilik, Ehsan Mohammadi, Juliane Schneider, Barbara Kern, Julien Colomb, Scott C. Edmunds, Karen Gutzman, Daniel S. Himmelstein, Marijane White, Britton Smith, Lisa O'Keefe, Melissa Haendel, and Kristi L. Holmes. "Is authorship sufficient for today's collaborative research? A call for contributor roles." *Accountability in Research*, 28, no. 1 (2021): 23-43. https://www.tandfonline.com/doi/full/10.1080/08989621.2020.1779591.

Wilson, Greg, Jennifer Bryan, Karen Cranston, Justin Kitzes, Lex Nederbragt, and Tracy K. Teal. "Good Enough Practices in Scientific Computing." *PLOS Computational Biology* 13, no. 6 (2017): e1005510. https://doi.org/10.1371/journal.pcbi.1005510.

Woodley, Lou, and Katie Pratt. "The CSCCE Community Participation Model – A framework to describe member engagement and information flow in STEM communities." Zenodo. (2020). https://doi.org/10.5281/zenodo.3997802.

HOW OPEN BECAME INFRASTRUCTURE

Micah Vandegrift and Kaitlin Thaney

INTRODUCTION

This section provides a snapshot into the dynamic area of open infrastructure. Due to this topic developing rapidly over several years, the foundational literature and research were being written while relying heavily on ideas presented in section 2.4.1. The editors chose to frame this section with an introduction followed by a lightly edited interview with Kaitlin Thaney, the first executive director of the Invest in Open Infrastructure initiative. Thaney's position, vision, and perspective are a key driver and focal point of open research infrastructure, and including her voice here felt necessary and helpful.

The early pillars of scholarly communication were open access, open education, and open data, with libraries building teams around those service areas as well as investing financial resources and reputational bonus points in software products to support each of those initiatives. Bepress's Digital Commons was one such platform, functionally an institutional repository paired with a journal-publishing platform, and was adopted widely in the North American library market. Often, Digital Commons was the core of a library's open strategy, including the foundation of faculty-affirmed open access policies. In August 2017, surprising many, the publishing company Elsevier announced that it was acquiring Bepress and with it the contracts with many libraries as well as the user profiles and data each campus had developed. The responses varied from shock to despair. Barbara Fister, a leading voice in scholarly communication, remarked for Inside Higher Ed, "Libraries have invested time and dollars into institutional repositories and library-supported publishing because of the behavior of highly profitable publishers like Elsevier, so all of that effort abruptly becoming the property of Elsevier is especially vexing."[1]

In the wake of this singular moment, several threads came together: first, that further consolidation of the research workflow should be expected; second, that libraries should carefully and strategically reposition themselves as a coalition; third, that the service-level silos between open access, open data, and OER are undergirded by common technical and policy needs; and fourth, that clarifying shared values and principles around the broad world of scholarly communication would provide a solid foundation on which to build.

Recognizing this, organizations like SPARC increased their illumination of the business practices behind the curtain, with SPARC releasing an important landscape analysis in early 2019 that outlined market positions as well as concrete actions.[2] On a similar time line, the Joint Roadmap for Open Science Tools (JROST) convened an informal coalition aimed at piecing together an agenda for intentional investment in open infrastructure. This volunteer coalition grew in importance and impact, picking up incredible energy and activity with the hiring of Kaitlin Thaney in early 2020. Thaney's background in open internet advocacy, program development, and fundraising with stalwarts like Creative Commons and the Wikimedia Foundation matched well with the need for leadership in the burgeoning discussion about open infrastructure.

Micah Vandegrift spoke with Kaitlin on April 5, 2022. Their conversation is paired with some of Kaitlin's original writing below.

Q: WHAT IS OPEN INFRASTRUCTURE?

A: We define *infrastructure* as the sets of services, protocols, standards, and software that the academic ecosystem needs in order to perform its functions throughout the research life cycle—from the earliest phases of research, collaboration, and experimentation through data collection and storage, data organization, data analysis and computation, authorship, submission, review and annotation, copyediting, publishing, archiving, citation, discovery and more.[3] *Open infrastructure* represents the narrower sets of services, protocols, standards, and software that can empower communities to collectively build the systems and infrastructures that deliver new, improved collective benefits without restrictions to participation, engagement, or usage.

I want to underscore that we are being purposeful in saying that open infrastructure is something that is relied on, like roads, bridges, water, utilities—you notice when there is a disruption in the system. That is one of the key things that has evolved; we have to think about the underlying systems and the criticality of that reliance in terms of how the technology serves a given community, research area, or group. We also want to advance a definition that is not just about open source in terms of content, data, and licensing, but also about systems that help facilitate the dissemination and creation of open knowledge.

The need for shared, open infrastructure transcends disciplinary boundaries through, as examples, shared content repositories, digital preservation services, knowledge discovery tools, and platforms. The call for open infrastructure also empowers specific tools and platforms needed for more specialized research and scholarship (e.g., computational notebooks, capture and archiving of digital art and images, publishing workflow tools, etc.). The European Science Foundation's Standing Committee on the Humanities in 2011 issued a policy brief *"Research Infrastructure in the Digital Humanities"* that stated for some humanists

an infrastructure is the technical and operational framework that allows them to collaborate and share data and results; for some it is the content to which access is offered rather than the facilities around it; and for some it is both.[4]

In the last decade, the challenges to maintaining a robust scholarly open digital infrastructure have become clear.[5] At the core of our work around open infrastructure are platforms, tools, and services that enable knowledge creation and sharing, as well as the places for scholarship and learning to occur, to build an understanding of the societal context in which open knowledge sits.

Q: WHY DO WE NEED OPEN INFRASTRUCTURE(S) NOW?

A: The push for open infrastructure comes from an increased commercialization and acquisition of both for-profit and nonprofit services in recent years, such as Bepress, Social Science Research Network, and Mendeley, creating a more concentrated—and powerful—series of commercial players like Elsevier and Clarivate.[6]

As Katherine Skinner, executive director of Educopia Institute wrote in July 2019 after surveying forty-five key infrastructure programs and organizations as part of the Mellon-funded Mapping Scholarly Communication Infrastructure project, "academy-owned" and "academy-governed" (terms used by Skinner in her analysis) tools, platforms, and services have been well trained to run on as little funding as possible; are rewarded for building new tools, platforms, and services (rather than maintaining a solid base for existing work); and are set up to compete with each other for increasingly scarce resources.[7] She further states that we are missing key information to explore the power of the scholarly communication sector. Without knowing how much money is currently spent on scholarly communication as a field, the community is unable to measure, grow, or leverage its own market power.

Alongside this consolidation within scholarly publishing, we should be aware of the rise of data trails as economic objects across the web. Especially during the COVID-19 pandemic years, when an astounding percentage of professional and personal life was experienced in online spaces, the obscuring of the financial and capitalistic impulses of technology we relied on was concerning. A case for open infrastructure comes also from a place of resisting surveillance and advancing the cause of privacy online.[8]

In noting how infrastructure has come to light, the pandemic and other crises helped produce a call for openness in the broader public consciousness, bigger than we've seen inside higher education, scholarly communication, and research; we saw it in the fight for lifesaving solutions to address a global health crisis. That increased the awareness around the need for openness and frictionless access to information outside universities and into the broader public. The other element is that we started thinking about digital infrastructure as a banner for equity, change, and opportunity, including from national governments like here in the US. There is building momentum in industry, like OpenStack launching the OpenInfra Foundation. There is a lot of energy and conversion around this topic, and it is up to us to take that opportunity and move it forward.

Q: HOW DO SHARED VALUES OR PRINCIPLES RELATE TO INFRASTRUCTURE?

A: In recent years, there has been increased attention paid to the commercialization of key infrastructures and technologies relied on for research, scholarship, and civil society. Particularly in research and scholarship, there has been an active drumbeat building calling for more values-aligned investments and adoption of open infrastructure to combat the increasing commercialization of core tools and technologies, selling of user data, and misaligned motives of for-profit enterprises when it comes to open knowledge.

A series of projects, initiatives, and convenings, inspired in part by the Bepress acquisition, produced a set of resources that are helping shape many of the ideas around principles-aligned research infrastructure. Without rewriting them all, a few highlights are listed below with brief summaries.

- *Principles of Open Scholarly Infrastructures*—Under the headings *Governance*, *Sustainability*, and *Insurance*, the authors propose a series of ideals like "Revenue based on services, not data" that next-generation scholarly tools and systems could aim toward.[9]
- *Values and principles work (Educopia)*—A meta-analysis of various statements of principles, especially in and of higher education, the authors

propose a methodology for auditing publishing service providers to ensure adherence to agreed-upon academic values and principles, with the dual goals of helping to guide values-informed decision making by academic stakeholders and encouraging values alignment efforts by infrastructure providers.[10]

Paired with Educopia's Assessment Checklist from its Next Generation Library Publishing project,[11] this is a best-in-class resource to tease out the how and why of principles-based scholarly communication.

- *HuMetricsHSS Values Framework*—Designed from a humanities-informed approach to scholarly metrics, this project and the framework it proposes offer a set of "humane metrics" like Collegiality:Generosity, which "takes the approach that if our metrics are not shaped by our core values, our values will be distorted by our metrics."[12]
- COAR-SPARC Good Practice Principles for Scholarly Communication Services—A dual statement from a repository-based coalition and a US-based advocacy organization, these seven principles are expressly meant "to be used by users/clients to make decisions about which services they will contract with, and by service providers to improve their practices and governance."[13]

Other principle frameworks to consider:
- Scholarly Commons framework (FORCE11)[14]
- An open approach for developing infrastructure for open science (Paul Peters, Hindawi)[15]
- Ouvrir La Science!—French Open Science Committee criteria (Marin Dacos)[16]
- Design Justice Network Principles[17]
- STAR (Scholarly Transformation Advice and Review) Team Criteria Summary[18]

Q: WHO ARE SOME OF THE STAKEHOLDERS IN THE CONVERSATION ABOUT OPEN INFRASTRUCTURE AND HOW ARE THEY CONNECTED (OR NOT)?

A: There are a wide variety of stakeholders, some that make open infrastructure work, and some that are involved for a good business case. Obvious examples to start with are the providers of open infrastructure—services like CrossRef's Metadata Retrieval, protocols like ORCID (Open Research Contributor ID), standards like the DOI system, and software like Open Journal Systems. These kinds of providers are the bedrock of open infrastructure, and they are key stakeholders in driving the conversation about what an open scholarly research ecosystem could look like.

Supporting these providers are the various levels of human or social infrastructure—the library IT departments and developers who customize the software or fix bugs, the chief technology officers at a university that signs off on a budget item to commit funding, or the frontline support teams or ambassadors who advocate, train, and troubleshoot between the systems and a researcher, for instance. The human and social infrastructure is connected to institutional homes, another stakeholder, like universities and research performing institutions like CERN, or national labs or research groups. Of course, there are also many stakeholders outside academia like former researchers who launch related start-ups or work at tech companies like Red Hat or GitHub.

Those groups—the infrastructure providers and support teams—are closely connected by the nature of the work. Stakeholders that are less visible, which we are working to illuminate more, are the funders, consortia, and professional associations that play a significant role in bolstering the stability of the platforms. For example, fiscal sponsors like Code for Science and Society or Community Initiatives can provide strategic, administrative, and financial support to allow an infrastructure tool to grow and focus on effective service provision. A consortium or not-for-profit, something like Lyrasis as an example, can pool resources, convene a wider stakeholder group into a community, or even host and manage an infrastructure itself, like Lyrasis does for the SCOAP3 physics open access initiative and the US ORCID hub.

Finally, this attention paid to the characteristics of not just a software tool, but also the team that built it and their core principles, or the organization that hosts it and where its funding derives from, has to lead us to an increased awareness that there are entities in the space that may have different parts of their portfolios that you may or may not agree with. They are still present in terms of being key stakeholders and have organizational divisions or areas where partnerships can be quite fruitful in adding new revenue streams to support open infrastructure projects. There are a number of for-profit players that control significant amounts of not only activity and ownership but also revenue and profits that have contributed or are contributing more to developing, supporting, and yes, funding open infrastructure.

Q: WHAT ARE SOME FIRST STEPS THAT SOMEONE ENCOUNTERING OPEN INFRASTRUCTURE MIGHT TAKE?

A: I wish I had a better understanding of the tools that exist currently and where to get started learning about them. Luckily, because of attention being paid here, that is much easier to do now than in years past. I already mentioned Educopia's Mapping the Scholarly Communication Infrastructure, which is one of a few incredibly helpful wide-view takes on how all these pieces fit together. In addition to that, I'd add the Scholarly Communication Technology Catalogue (SComCat), the list of "OA Publishing Tools" from the Radical Open Access collective, the report from SPARC Europe on "Scoping the Open Science Infrastructure Landscape in Europe," and the "400+ Tools and Innovations in Scholarly Communication" compiled by Jeroen Bosman and Bianca Kramer of Utrecht University Library.[19] Marshall Breeding's guide to the history of mergers and acquisitions in the library technology industry and Posada and Chen's "Inequality in Knowledge Production: The Integration of Academic Infrastructure by Big Publishers" provide really helpful visuals to illustrate the consolidation of research infrastructure.[20] Developing a concept of the open infrastructure ecosystem is a great introductory action that can lead to different kinds of engagement.

Another practical tip is simply to ask lots of questions. These may uncover tension points in organizations, so some situational awareness will be wise, but these are the kinds of questions that are being asked in various industries as we learn more about aligning technologies with human experiences and values. For example, one could ask

- What parameters exist for infrastructure decisions at your institution?
- Do we have a responsibility to select members or users or to ensuring broader access to the global community?
- What history does this organization have with decisions of this kind?
- Are we bound to a mission or set of pre-subscribed guiding principles like a land-grant university mission or FAIR data (findable, accessible, interoperable, reusable)?
- Where do key decision-makers sit in relation to power? How might those structures enable this work or create additional friction?
- Where might organizational values or principles be at odds with those of institutional leadership? What steps can be taken to address that tension?
- How does your organization balance immediacy versus long-term change?
- Who is enabled to participate by this decision? Who may be excluded or negatively impacted?
- What does a worst-case scenario look like for the decision you're making? Could this decision or trade-off be used to negatively impact the community or users or lead to misuse?

Q: WHAT MIGHT OPEN INFRASTRUCTURE LOOK LIKE FIVE OR TEN YEARS IN THE FUTURE?

A: I find optimism in thinking about what we can do to help shift not only the adoption of the tools but also the broader investment in these tools. My frustration with the status quo is what continues to drive my optimism, and the fact that there are a number of examples of people and communities making progress on moving these things forward. There are people all around the world who are innovating without access to the tools and systems we enjoy, and amplifying their stories, finding opportunities to work alongside them, and looking outside the situation in North America and Western Europe provides a lot more space to work toward open infrastructure that benefits the actual global system of research and knowledge sharing.

My hope is that there are a set of openly and freely available technology solutions for those who are participating in research and knowledge creation that are accessible and it is not only an affordable option for institutions but is as prevalent as institutional Wi-Fi. That set of tools might not solve all the problems, but it will provide a baseline foundation to even the playing field and be available to every student of higher learning around the world. It would be subsidized by a mix of different funding sources but be made available for the most lucrative institutions and also all across to the other side of the spectrum.

DISCUSSION QUESTIONS

1. Why is commercial acquisition of research infrastructure a problem? What risks does it pose?
2. This chapter mentions a number of tools, platforms, and services; pick one you are not familiar with and research it. What does it do, for whom, why, and how? How would you explain it to a colleague or researcher?
3. Kaitlin mentions frustration with status quo as a driver of optimisma and action. What is something presently accepted or common that you find frustrating and how might you channel your frustration into action and hope?

NOTES

1. Barbara Fister, quoted in Lindsay McKenzie, "Elsevier Expands Footprint in Scholarly Work-flow," Inside Higher Ed, March 3, 2017, https://www.insidehighered.com/news/2017/08/03/elsevier-makes-move-institutional-repositories-acquisition-bepress.
2. Claudio Aspesi et al., *SPARC* Landscape Analysis: The Changing Academic Publishing Industry—Implications for Academic Institutions* (Washington, DC: Scholarly Publishing and Academic Resources Coalition, March 28, 2019), https://doi.org/10.31229/osf.io/58yhb.
3. Invest in Open Infrastructure, "About IOI," https://investinopen.org/about/.
4. European Science Foundation, *Research Infrastructure in the Digital Humanities*, policy briefing document (Strasbourg, France: European Science Foundation, September 2011), quoted in Karen Wulf, "Humanities Research Infrastructure Is Great ROI—Will We Sell It Short?" *Scholarly Kitchen* (blog), June 3, 2020, https://scholarlykitchen.sspnet.org/2020/06/03/humanities-research-infrastructure-is-great-roi-will-we-sell-it-short/.
5. G. Bilder, J. Lin, and Cameron Neylon, "Where Are the Pipes? Building Foundational Infrastructures for Future Services," *Science in the Open* (blog), 2016, http://cameronneylon.net/blog/where-are-the-pipes-building-foundational-infrastructures-for-future-services/.
6. Elsevier, "Elsevier Acquires Bepress, a Leading Service Provider Used by Academic Institutions to Showcase Their Research," news release, August 2, 2017, https://www.elsevier.com/about/press-releases/corporate/elsevier-acquires-bepress,-a-leading-service-provider-used-by-academic-institutions-to-showcase-their-research; George H. Pike, "Elsevier Buys SSRN.com: What It Means for Scholarly Publication,"

SSRN, written July 1, 2016, posted May 6, 2017, https://papers.ssrn.com/sol3/papers.cfm?abstract_id=2963709; Claire Shaw, "Elsevier Buys Mendeley: Your Reaction," *Universities* (blog), *Guardian*, April 10, 2013, https://www.theguardian.com/higher-education-network/blog/2013/apr/10/elsevier-buys-mendeley-academic-reaction; Elsevier, home page, https://www.elsevier.com/; Clarivate, home page, https://clarivate.com/.

7. Katherine Skinner, "Why Are So Many Scholarly Communication Infrastructure Providers Running a Red Queen's Race?" Educopia Institute, July 23, 2019, https://educopia.org/red-queens-race/; Educopia Institute, "Mapping the Scholarly Communication Infrastructure," 2018–2020, https://educopia.org/mapping-scholarly-communications-infrastructure/.

8. Zoom censoring academic conferences: Colleen Flaherty, "Zoom Faces More Allegations of Censorship," Inside Higher Ed, October 27, 2020, https://www.insidehighered.com/quicktakes/2020/10/27/zoom-faces-more-allegations-censorship; Privacy and surveillance issues // Proctorio: Naaman Zhou, "CEO of Exam Monitoring Software Proctorio Apologises for Posting Student's Chat Logs on Reddit," *Guardian*, July 1, 2020, https://www.theguardian.com/australia-news/2020/jul/01/ceo-of-exam-monitoring-software-proctorio-apologises-for-posting-students-chat-logs-on-reddit; Surveillance in higher ed: John Warner, "Choose Cooperation and Collaboration, Rather Than Surveillance," *Just Visiting* (blog), Inside Higher Ed, May 21, 2020, https://www.insidehighered.com/blogs/just-visiting/choose-cooperation-and-collaboration-rather-surveillance.

9. Principles of Open Scholarly Infrastructure, home page, https://openscholarlyinfrastructure.org/.

10. Educopia Institute, "Living Our Values and Principles: Exploring Assessment Strategies for the Scholarly Communication Field," October 21, 2020, https://educopia.org/living-our-values-and-principles/.

11. Katherine Skinner and Sarah Lippincott, "Assessment Checklist," June, 2020. https://commonplace.knowledgefutures.org/pub/i0pndjk9/release/1.

12. HuMetricsHSS, "Values Framework," https://humetricshss.org/our-work/values/.

13. SPARC, "Good Practice Principles for Scholarly Communication Services," https://sparcopen.org/our-work/good-practice-principles-for-scholarly-communication-services/.

14. Jeroen Bosman et al., "The Scholarly Commons—Principles and Practices to Guide Research Communication," OSF Preprints, September 15, 2017, https://doi.org/10.31219/osf.io/6c2xt.

15. Paul Peters, "An Open Approach to Developing Infrastructure for Open Science," *Hindawi* (blog), October 23, 2017, https://www.hindawi.com/post/a-radically-open-approach-to-developing-infrastructure-for-open-science/.

16. Open Science Steering Committee, "Examplarity Criteria for Funding from the National Open Science Fund through Platforms, Infrastructures and Editorial Content," trans. Richard Dickinson, Ourvrir la science! Ministère de l'Enseignement Supérieur et de la Recherche, April 17, 2019, https://www.ouvrirlascience.fr/examplarity-criteria-for-funding-from-the-national-open-science-fund/.

17. Design Justice Network, "Design Justice Network Principles," last updated summer 2018, https://designjustice.org/read-the-principles.

18. Bernie Hurley, "Charge to the RLF Persistence Task Force," memo, UC Libraries, December 18, 2004, https://libraries.universityofcalifornia.edu/sclg/star/charge.

19. SComCat: Scholarly Communication Technology Catalogue, home page, https://www.scomcat.net/; Radical Open Access, "OA Publishing Tools," last updated May 2019, https://radicaloa.disruptivemedia.org.uk/resources/publishing-tools/; Radical Open Access, home page, https://radicaloa.disruptivemedia.org.uk/; Victoria Ficarra et al., "Scoping the Open Science Infrastructure Landscape in Europe," Zenodo, October 30, 2020, https://doi.org/10.5281/zenodo.4159838; Jeroen Bosman and Bianca Kramer, comps., "400+ Tools and Innovations in Scholarly Communication—Data Collection Forms," Google Sheet, February 28, 2015, https://docs.google.com/spreadsheets/d/1KUMSeq_Pzp4KveZ7pb5rddcssk1XBTiLHniD0d3nDqo/edit; Bianca Kramer and Jeroen Bosman, "Innovations in Scholarly Communication: Changing Research Workflows," Universiteit Utrecht, https://101innovations.wordpress.com/.

20. Marshall Breeding, "History of Mergers and Acquisitions in the Library Technology Industry," Library Technology Guides, https://librarytechnology.org/mergers/; Alejandro Posada and George Chen, "Inequality in Knowledge Production: The Integration of Academic Infrastructure by Big Publishers" (presentation, ELPUB: International Conference on Electronic Publishing, Toronto, Canada, June 22–24, 2018), https://hal.science/hal-01816707.

BIBLIOGRAPHY

Aspesi, Claudio, Nicole Starr Allen, Raym Crow, Shawn Daugherty, Heather Joseph, Joseph McArthur, and Nick Shockey. *SPARC Landscape Analysis: The Changing Academic Publishing Industry—Implications for Academic Institutions*. Washington, DC: Scholarly Publishing and Academic Resources Coalition, March 28, 2019. https://doi.org/10.31229/osf.io/58yhb.

Bilder, G., J. Lin, and Cameron Neylon. "Where Are the Pipes? Building Foundational Infrastructures for Future Services." *Science in the Open* (blog), 2016. http://cameronneylon.net/blog/where-are-the-pipes-building-foundational-infrastructures-for-future-services/.

Bosman, Jeroen, Ian Bruno, Chris Chapman, Bastian Greshake Tzovaras, Nate Jacobs, Bianca Kramer, Maryann Martone, et al. "The Scholarly Commons—Principles and Practices to Guide Research Communication." OSF Preprints, September 15, 2017. https://doi.org/10.31219/osf.io/6c2xt.

Bosman, Jeroen, and Bianca Kramer, comps. "400+ Tools and Innovations in Scholarly Communication—Data Collection Forms." Google Sheet, February 28, 2015. https://docs.google.com/spreadsheets/d/1KUMSeq_Pzp4KveZ7pb5rddcssk1XBTiLHniD0d3nDqo/edit.

Breeding, Marshall. "History of Mergers and Acquisitions in the Library Technology Industry." Library Technology Guides. https://librarytechnology.org/mergers/.

Clarivate. Home page. https://clarivate.com/.

Design Justice Network. "Design Justice Network Principles." Last updated summer 2018. https://designjustice.org/read-the-principles.

Educopia Institute. "Living Our Values and Principles: Exploring Assessment Strategies for the Scholarly Communication Field." October 21, 2020. https://educopia.org/living-our-values-and-principles/.

———. "Mapping the Scholarly Communication Infrastructure." 2018–2020. https://educopia.org/mapping-scholarly-communications-infrastructure/.

Elsevier. "Elsevier Acquires Bepress, a Leading Service Provider Used by Academic Institutions to Showcase Their Research." News release, August 2, 2017. https://www.elsevier.com/about/press-releases/corporate/elsevier-acquires-bepress,-a-leading-service-provider-used-by-academic-institutions-to-showcase-their-research.

———. Home page. https://www.elsevier.com/.

Ficarra, Victoria, Mattia Fosci, Andrea Chiarelli, Bianca Kramer, and Vanessa Proudman. "Scoping the Open Science Infrastructure Landscape in Europe." Zenodo, October 30, 2020. https://doi.org/10.5281/zenodo.4159838.

Flaherty, Colleen. "Zoom Faces More Allegations of Censorship." Inside Higher Ed, October 27, 2020. https://www.insidehighered.com/quicktakes/2020/10/27/zoom-faces-more-allegations-censorship.

HuMetricsHSS. "Values Framework." https://humetricshss.org/our-work/values/.

Hurley, Bernie. "Charge to the RLF Persistence Task Force." Memo. UC Libraries, December 18, 2004. https://libraries.universityofcalifornia.edu/sclg/star/charge.

Invest in Open Infrastructure. "About IOI." https://investinopen.org/about/.

Kramer, Bianca, and Jeroen Bosman. "Innovations in Scholarly Communication: Changing Research Workflows." Universiteit Utrecht. https://101innovations.wordpress.com/.

McKenzie, Lindsay. "Elsevier Expands Footprint in Scholarly Workflow." Inside Higher Ed, March 3, 2017. https://www.insidehighered.com/news/2017/08/03/elsevier-makes-move-institutional-repositories-acquisition-bepress.

Open Science Steering Committee. "Examplarity Criteria for Funding from the National Open Science Fund through Platforms, Infrastructures and Editorial Content," trans. Richard Dickinson. Ourvrir la science! Ministère de l'Enseignement Supérieur et de la Recherche, April 17, 2019. https://www.ouvrirlascience.fr/examplarity-criteria-for-funding-from-the-national-open-science-fund/.

Peters, Paul. "An Open Approach to Developing Infrastructure for Open Science." *Hindawi* (blog), October 23, 2017. https://www.hindawi.com/post/a-radically-open-approach-to-developing-infrastructure-for-open-science/.

Pike, George H. "Elsevier Buys SSRN.com: What It Means for Scholarly Publication." SSRN, written July 1, 2016, posted May 6, 2017. https://papers.ssrn.com/sol3/papers.cfm?abstract_id=2963709.

Posada, Alejandro, and George Chen. "Inequality in Knowledge Production: The Integration of Academic Infrastructure by Big Publishers." Presentation, ELPUB: International Conference on Electronic Publishing, Toronto, Canada, June 22–24, 2018. https://hal.science/hal-01816707.

Principles of Open Scholarly Infrastructure. Home page. https://openscholarlyinfrastructure.org/.

Radical Open Access. Home page. https://radicaloa.disruptivemedia.org.uk/.

———. "OA Publishing Tools." Last updated May 2019. https://radicaloa.disruptivemedia.org.uk/resources/publishing-tools/.

SComCat: Scholarly Communication Technology Catalogue. Home page. https://www.scomcat.net/.

Shaw, Claire. "Elsevier Buys Mendeley: Your Reaction." *Universities* (blog), *Guardian*, April 10, 2013. https://www.theguardian.com/higher-education-network/blog/2013/apr/10/elsevier-buys-mendeley-academic-reaction.

Skinner, Katherine, and Sarah Lippincott. "Assessment Checklist." June, 2020. https://commonplace.knowledge-futures.org/pub/i0pndjk9/release/1.

Skinner, Katherine. "Why Are So Many Scholarly Communication Infrastructure Providers Running a Red Queen's Race?" Educopia Institute, July 23, 2019. https://educopia.org/red-queens-race/.

SPARC. "Good Practice Principles for Scholarly Communication Services." https://sparcopen.org/our-work/good-practice-principles-for-scholarly-communication-services/.

Warner, John. "Choose Cooperation and Collaboration, Rather Than Surveillance." *Just Visiting* (blog), Inside Higher Ed, May 21, 2020. https://www.insidehighered.com/blogs/just-visiting/choose-cooperation-and-collaboration-rather-surveillance.

Wulf, Karen. "Humanities Research Infrastructure Is Great ROI—Will We Sell It Short?" *Scholarly Kitchen* (blog), June 3, 2020. https://scholarlykitchen.sspnet.org/2020/06/03/humanities-research-infrastructure-is-great-roi-will-we-sell-it-short/.

Zhou, Naaman. "CEO of Exam Monitoring Software Proctorio Apologises for Posting Student's Chat Logs on Reddit." *Guardian*, July 1, 2020. https://www.theguardian.com/australia-news/2020/jul/01/ceo-of-exam-monitoring-software-proctorio-apologises-for-posting-students-chat-logs-on-reddit.

PART III

VOICES FROM THE FIELD:
PERSPECTIVES, INTERSECTIONS, AND CASE STUDIES

3

CHAPTER 3.0

INTRODUCTION

Maria Bonn with Will Cross and Josh Bolick

The earlier parts of this book are intended to lay a strong theoretical foundation for understanding the work of scholarly communication, especially as it is carried out in libraries and by librarians. The test of theory is often practice. How do the concepts that you have learned apply to actual practice? Once you leave the classroom and enter the workplace, will the big-picture ideas and contexts laid out so far help with your everyday work? Some of the people best prepared to help think about the application of theory to practice are those working in the field, people who spend their work lives engaged with scholars and scholarship, helping the scholars to navigate the wide world of choices in sharing the results of their work and helping the scholarship to realize its full potential as a contribution to its discipline and to the world. So that students learning about this work could hear from people in practice, we invited contributions that we call "voices from the field" to this book. You can hear thirty-seven of those voices in this part of the book, voices telling stories about successful work and work that failed, voices explaining how the work of scholarly communication is never isolated but intersects with many other areas of the profession, and voices that express wonderfully informative opinions about what's at stake in the work of scholarly communication.

Indeed, scholarly communication work almost inevitably leads to engagement with issues upon which opinions vary, as do the courses of action that address those issues. Personal and professional experience, as well as institutional context and personal and community identity inform and shape the opinions and the approaches of scholarly communication professionals. The *perspectives* included in this part offer situated and self-reflective discussions of topics of importance in scholarly communication and the ways in which libraries respond to those topics.

At its core, the work of the academic library is to collect, preserve, provide access to, and support the use of the scholarly record. Almost all work in academic libraries is in service of scholarly communication. While libraries increasingly designate scholarly communication specialists, those specialists often call upon colleagues from all over their organizations to provide their expertise in addressing scholarly communication opportunities and challenges. Conversely, any area of library work might turn to a scholarly communication specialist for an informed perspective and expertise. These *intersections* share examples and reflections upon such crossing of organizational boundaries in the context of scholarly communication and upon the work that takes place at these crossroads.

The *case study* chapter of the text presents stories drawn from experience. These stories are intended to provide specific, contextualized examples of the kinds of tasks and questions librarians working in scholarly communication encounter and strategies for response. The case studies describe and evaluate a case, reflecting upon the issues involved and their implications for scholars and scholarship. They suggest possible responses to the cases and evaluate the effectiveness and possible challenges of those strategies.

PERSPECTIVES

HOW VOCATIONAL AWE AND SERVICE-ORIENTED NEUTRALITY BRING BULLSHIT WORK TO SCHOLARLY COMMUNICATION LIBRARIANSHIP

Ian Harmon

INTRODUCTION

Scholarly communication librarians are charged with being advocates for change, but too often, our efforts are hamstrung by a reluctance to disrupt the status quo. Our work suffers from an inadequately examined sense of vocational awe and an ingrained belief that librarians are merely service providers, neutral non-agents lacking full membership within academia.[1] Left unchecked, these factors pose the danger of transforming our profession into a so-called bullshit job.[2]

While this predicament is not entirely of our own making, the path toward remediation begins at home. Why do we tolerate dismissive attitudes and unreasonable requests? How can we act as service professionals without presenting ourselves as subordinates? Why do we allow others to dictate the terms of our interactions?

I don't have the answers to these questions, but I do hope to offer some insight into our collective self-conception and suggest that working through its accompanying assumptions will make headway toward reframing power dynamics on campus. Rather than self-presenting as neutral service providers and downplaying our expertise, we can, and must, assert our status as full colleagues with equal standing.[3]

VOCATIONAL AWE AND BULLSHIT WORK

Librarianship's status as a service profession is often seen as a virtue, but it can be a vice when it results in vocational awe. Vocational awe, as introduced by Fobazi Ettarh, is "the set of ideas, values, and assumptions librarians have about themselves and the profession that result in notions that libraries as institutions are inherently good, sacred notions, and therefore beyond critique."[4] Vocational awe occurs in all areas of librarianship, and scholarly communication, with its associated causes, is no exception. We aim to make research available to everyone. We advocate for authors' rights. We educate students about information privilege.[5] But left unchecked, vocational awe prevents us from critically examining the efficacy of our daily work with respect to these aims. More provocatively, vocational awe threatens to transform scholarly communication librarianship into a bullshit job.

The concept of the bullshit job has been popularized by David Graeber, who describes it as

> a form of paid employment that is so completely pointless, unnecessary, or pernicious that even the employee cannot justify its existence even though, as a part of the conditions of employment, the employee feels obligated to pretend that this is not the case.[6]

In the context of academic libraries, Jane Schmidt describes a feeling of having "totally lost sight of what your work actually means to the wider world."[7]

For scholarly communication librarians, the danger of bullshit work results from a disconnect between our professed aims and our day-to-day practices. Our daily tasks include things like developing complex workflows to accommodate publishers' policies while populating our institutional repositories (IRs) with post-prints to which we rarely have access (largely due to authors' poor version-retention practices). Or creating authors' rights resources while faculty continue signing away their copyrights. Or developing programming for open access week without any indication of its having a tangible impact.

We view these tasks through the lens of vocational awe and complacently assume they are worthwhile. But too rarely do we ask whether they actually support our larger goals. This enables us to avoid confronting our fear of questioning the status quo or being otherwise disruptive.

This aversion is shared by many librarians, and it fits naturally within the mold of the neutral librarian.[8] It extends beyond the walls of the library and underlies our reluctance to question the norms of faculty and their disciplines. Instead, we resign ourselves to tasks that won't risk running afoul of their expectations. Indeed, many librarians live in fear of upsetting faculty, performing substantial emotional labor in order to avoid jeopardizing relationships or thwarting expectations.[9]

This fear of upsetting faculty makes sense, but only within the unbalanced relationship that we implicitly endorse when we present ourselves as mere service providers. I suggest we explore ways of withdrawing this endorsement.

DISRUPTIVE LIBRARIANSHIP

What might withdrawing this endorsement look like? I'll conclude by considering a common challenge faced in our field, the fact that faculty are rarely interested in self-depositing in institutional repositories.[10]

From the neutral-librarian perspective, we might reason that faculty are too busy to bother with repositories, and so it falls to us to deposit for them, bothering them as little as possible along the way and expressing profuse gratitude for any cooperation we may receive. This is an easy enough way to go (a way I've gone myself many times). But what good does it do? What does it suggest about the importance of librarians or the value of our time and skills as compared to those of our colleagues? In a profession preoccupied with demonstrating its value, it seems ill-advised to market ourselves by taking on the work that seems unimportant to those we aim to impress.

So how might we approach this situation from the paradigm of the disruptive librarian? There's no single right answer, but it's important that we understand our primary objective. Is it to increase the numbers in the repository as an end in itself? Is it to force researchers to confront their contributions to an unsustainable scholarly communication system? Or are we just following our understanding of what scholarly communication librarians are supposed to do?

No matter what your goal, if faculty don't care about repositories, then talking to them about repositories probably isn't the best way to assert our value. Instead, I suggest we identify points of overlap between their concerns and our expertise. What are they doing wrong, and how can we show them that they're doing it wrong? What kinds of evidence or arguments will they respond to?

This is one example, but I hope the point extrapolates to other areas of our work. We must find the points at which our expertise will allow us to be maximally disruptive, and doing so requires thinking both pragmatically and philosophically. But if our work is truly valuable, we shouldn't have to spend so much time convincing others, not to mention ourselves, of its worth. So spend more time doing, and less time defending what you're doing. Let your results speak for themselves, and disseminate them with the confidence your expertise warrants.

DISCUSSION QUESTIONS

1. Is the common understanding of librarianship as a service profession correct? Is scholarly communication librarianship a service profession? If so, how is this to be balanced with the advocacy mission of the role?
2. How should scholarly communication librarians balance principles and practical realities when interacting with faculty? Should we engage in emotional labor if it will help us accomplish our larger aims?
3. What are some specific ways in which scholarly communication librarians can practice disruptive librarianship? Is this an appropriate perspective to adopt, or would we be better suited to operate under a more traditional, neutral perspective? Are there other options?

NOTES

1. Fobazi Ettarh, "Vocational Awe and Librarianship: The Lies We Tell Ourselves." *In the Library with the Lead Pipe*, January 10, 2018, http://www.inthelibrarywiththeleadpipe.org/2018/vocational-awe/; Sandy Iverson, "Librarianship and Resistance," in *Questioning Library Neutrality: Essays from Progressive Librarian*, ed. Alison Lewis (Duluth, MN: Library Juice Press, 2008), 26.
2. David Graeber, David. *Bullshit Jobs* (New York: Simon & Schuster, 2018); David Graeber, "On the Phenomenon of Bullshit Jobs: A Work Rant," *STRIKE! Magazine*, no. 3 (August 2013), https://strikemag.org/bullshit-jobs/.

3. Kevin Seeber, "Colleagues," *KevinSeeber.com* (blog), December 16, 2019, https://kevinseeber.com/blog/colleagues/.
4. Ettarh, "Vocational Awe."
5. Char Booth, "On Information Privilege," *Info-Mational* (blog). December 1, 2014, https://infomational.com/2014/12/01/on-information-privilege/; Sarah Hare and Cara Evanson, "Information Privilege Outreach for Undergraduate Students," *College and Research Libraries* 79, no. 6 (September 2018): 726–36, https://doi.org/10.5860/crl.79.6.726.
6. Graeber, *Bullshit Jobs*, 9–10.
7. Jane Schmidt, "Innovate This! Bullshit in Academic Libraries and What We Can Do About It," Toronto Metropolitan University, May 21, 2021. https://doi.org/10.32920/ryerson.14639826.v1.
8. Nina Clements, "'Nothing More Than a Gear in Your Car': Neutrality and Feminist Reference in the Academic Library," in *The Feminist Reference Desk: Concepts, Critiques, and Conversations*, ed. Maria T. Accardi (Berkeley, CA: Library Juice Press, 2017), 47-60.
9. Celia Emmelhainz, Erin Pappas, and Maura Seale, "Behavioral Expectations for the Mommy Librarian: The Successful Reference Transaction as Emotional Labor," in *The Feminist Reference Desk: Concepts, Critiques, and Conversations*, ed. Maria T. Accardi (Berkeley, CA: Library Juice Press, 2017), 27-46.
10. Ruth Kitchin Tillman, "Where Are We Now? Survey on Rates of Faculty Self-Deposit in Institutional Repositories," *Journal of Librarianship and Scholarly Communication* 5, no. 1 (2017): eP2203, https://doi.org/10.7710/2162-3309.2203.

BIBLIOGRAPHY

Booth, Char. "On Information Privilege." *Info-Mational* (blog). December 1, 2014. https://infomational.com/2014/12/01/on-information-privilege/.

Clements, Nina. "'Nothing More Than a Gear in Your Car': Neutrality and Feminist Reference in the Academic Library." In *The Feminist Reference Desk: Concepts, Critiques, and Conversations*, edited by Maria T. Accardi, 47-60. Berkeley, CA: Library Juice Press, 2017.

Emmelhainz, Celia, Erin Pappas, and Maura Seale. "Behavioral Expectations for the Mommy Librarian: The Successful Reference Transaction as Emotional Labor." In *The Feminist Reference Desk: Concepts, Critiques, and Conversations*, edited by Maria T. Accardi, 27-46. Berkeley, CA: Library Juice Press, 2017.

Ettarh, Fobazi. "Vocational Awe and Librarianship: The Lies We Tell Ourselves." *In the Library with the Lead Pipe*, January 10, 2018. http://www.inthelibrarywiththeleadpipe.org/2018/vocational-awe/.

Graeber, David. *Bullshit Jobs: A Theory*. New York: Simon & Schuster, 2018.

———. "On the Phenomenon of Bullshit Jobs: A Work Rant." *STRIKE! Magazine*, no. 3 (August 2013). https://strikemag.org/bullshit-jobs/.

Hare, Sarah, and Cara Evanson. "Information Privilege Outreach for Undergraduate Students." *College and Research Libraries* 79, no. 6 (September 2018): 726–36. https://doi.org/10.5860/crl.79.6.726.

Iverson, Sandy. "Librarianship and Resistance." In *Questioning Library Neutrality: Essays from Progressive Librarian*, edited by Alison Lewis, 25–32. Duluth, MN: Library Juice Press, 2008.

Schmidt, Jane. "Innovate This! Bullshit in Academic Libraries and What We Can Do About It." Toronto Metropolitan University, May 21, 2021. https://doi.org/10.32920/ryerson.14639826.v1.

Seeber, Kevin. "Colleagues." *KevinSeeber.com* (blog), December 16, 2019. https://kevinseeber.com/blog/colleagues/.

Tillman, Ruth Kitchin. "Where Are We Now? Survey on Rates of Faculty Self-Deposit in Institutional Repositories." *Journal of Librarianship and Scholarly Communication* 5, no. 1 (2017): eP2203. https://doi.org/10.7710/2162-3309.2203.

SCHOLARLY COMMUNICATION SERVICES

FROM AN ISLAND, YOU CAN BUILD BRIDGES

Julia Rodriguez

In 2012, my library reorganized to align with a new strategic plan. As a result, my position changed and I needed a new job title. My dean suggested *scholarly communication librarian*, to which I had a strong reaction. "What on earth does scholarly communication even mean?" After some discussion, we settled on *faculty research support librarian*, agreeing that it more clearly communicated my role to campus. I was tasked with developing services for assisting faculty throughout the research life cycle. I didn't have a department or even a group of other librarians who also embraced this work. It was just me on my island, and it wasn't a sunny tropical island but a medium-sized Midwest public university library with not enough librarians (thirteen) to serve the growing student population (now 20,000), let alone over 500 faculty. My acquired competencies for this position at this point included some basic expertise in copyright, I had recently served as open access track lead for a regional teaching conference where I also presented on institutional repositories, and I was the author of two peer-reviewed articles. I thought back to four years earlier when I was assigned to support the School of Nursing and the School of Health Sciences with no corresponding experience beyond having been a patient. To alleviate my sense of impostor syndrome, I completed every continuing education course I could find on evidence-based medicine, PubMed, and systematic reviews. Fortunately, many courses were free and my administration financed the cost when there was a fee.

With my new title in hand, I set forth, sometimes deliberately and sometimes fortuitously, to develop my skills and knowledge. Reflecting on this eight-year journey, the following themes emerge.

BUILD COMPETENCIES

Seek out and immerse yourself in professional development opportunities. Be creative in finding funding, ask your administration for support, apply for scholarships, ask if registration fees may be waived. Many webinars are free and allow you to gain a deeper understanding of topics such as copyright, altmetrics, data sharing, open education, and myriad related and other topics. Identify and attend conferences that will provide opportunities to enhance your competencies and professional connections. I argued that these events directly contributed to building my skills and should be financed from administrative travel funds rather than my limited faculty travel budget. There is also an abundance of literature to read, and a growing amount of it is freely and openly available.

FIND COMMUNITY

As members of a service-oriented profession, librarians are characteristically welcoming and supportive. Introduce yourself to others doing scholarly communication work, either by chatting at poster sessions or after a presentation or even over e-mail. A game changer for increasing my professional opportunities and expert network was convincing my dean (the third in ten years) to join the Scholarly Publishing and Academic Resources Coalition (SPARC). SPARC is a leader and driving force for the open access, open data, and open education movements. Social media is another great way to tap into these communities. I had long resisted Twitter.* Now I can't imagine not having this network to connect and stay up-to-date with the open community (see #opened, #openaccess, #OER, #copyright, #ScholComm). The American Library Association (ALA) e-mail discussion list SCHOLCOMM and others also remain vital connections to communities of experts. Whatever your focal areas, find and connect with that network!

BORROW

You rarely need to start from scratch to develop a presentation or guide. Most librarians are more than happy to share their materials. My first presentation on copyright was borrowed almost completely, and I hoped no one would ask questions because I was so unsure of my abilities. Years later, the attribution on the presentation remains, but I'm pretty sure none of the original slides are still included and I very much welcome questions. Consider openly licensing your own work to participate in this culture of sharing.

BUILD BRIDGES

Find collaborators even if you have to grow your own. Provide professional development opportunities for your library colleagues to build their competencies. This will also help offset the load when faculty start requesting assistance. Forge relationships with faculty members throughout campus. Seniority often brings influence; find and befriend those who have longevity on campus, those whose values align with yours, and those who can help you influence the ones that don't.

NETWORK

Attend every campus event that presents itself, such as open forums, research office workshops, and graduate student presentations. Engage with presenters and other attendees, ask questions, learn more about their work and interests. Insert information about the library into these conversations. Sit with people you don't know at events, tell them what you do, and learn

---

* Twitter's acquisition in late 2022 by Elon Musk and subsequent controversies led many people, including librarians, to reconsider their use of the platform. The main point stands: Social media can be a helpful tool for developing professional communities.

about what they do. Expanding your connections beyond the academic faculty by meeting staff and administrators can be really valuable for future collaborations and initiatives.

BE VISIBLE

Seek opportunities to speak at department meetings, host events, and offer workshops on scholarly communication topics. Even if only a few people come, which happens to all of us, every conversation has value. Build a scholarly communication services web page that you can point to as a reference and as evidence of the library's engagement with these issues.

SERVICE

Seek service roles that intersect with your work. For me, this included the university research committee, e-learning and instruction support advisory board, academic computing committee, and responsible conduct of research faculty advisory committee. Librarians are often overloaded with service, but I've found it has always benefited me in some way. It's common that the most engaged people on campus tend to be of the same small group; meeting and connecting with these people is essential.

PUBLISH

Participate in the publication life cycle in whatever way you can. Be a peer reviewer. Serve on an editorial board. Write and submit articles and book chapters for publication. What you learn from these experiences will enhance your understanding of the research process and aid your growth as a professional in ways no other experience can.

BECOME YOUR TITLE

Have a thirty-second elevator pitch ready. You will frequently need to explain what you do in relatable terms. Consider how to adjust for different disciplines or career status. Practice explaining your job to your parents and nonlibrarian friends. If they get it, then you're ready.

In 2016, after five years of doing the work in the capacity of faculty research support librarian, I had my title officially changed to scholarly communications librarian. I requested and embraced this change. I finally connected with my role and found my professional community. The library was ready, the campus was ready, and many more people now understood what this work entailed. Through persistence, I am no longer alone on an island. I am recognized in the library and on campus as an expert, and I have built bridges with my library faculty colleagues, the research office, graduate school, e-learning, center for teaching, academic departments, and a national network of colleagues.

ADDITIONAL RESOURCES

Oakland University Libraries. "Kresge Library Open Access Fund." https://library.oakland.edu/services/scholarly-communication/OAFund.html.

———. "Kresge Library Open Access Resolution." https://library.oakland.edu/services/scholarly-communication/OULibrariesOpenAccessResolution%20FINAL_ACCEPTEDVERISON_LOGO.pdf.

———. "Scholarly Communications." https://library.oakland.edu/services/scholarly-communication/.

———. "Workshop Menu. https://library.oakland.edu/services/scholarly-communication/FacultyWorkshopMenuupdate%202018_19New%20format.pdf.

Scholarly Communication Presentations folder, Google Drive, https://drive.google.com/drive/folders/1oxodYMNv1HwhdEXuidTmpGocGLdccPg9?usp=sharing

DISCUSSION QUESTIONS

1. Why are community and a network of peers important to your developing professional practice?

2. How might authoring and presenting scholarship increase an academic librarian's credibility and professional performance?

3. Given your interests, identify a topical conference you might attend, a journal you might submit an article to, a relevant social media hashtag, and an e-mail discussion list (LISTSERV). For each, how would these resources advance your goals, and what are the ways you might engage with them?

OPEN ACCESS DOESN'T EQUAL ACCESSIBLE

SERVING PEOPLE WITH DISABILITIES

Teresa Schultz and Elena Azadbakht

INTRODUCTION

Open access (OA) and open educational resources (OER) break down financial and legal barriers to accessing, adapting, and using scholarly research and educational material, but other obstacles remain. Simply making information open fails to take into account individuals with disabilities who rely on screen readers and other accessibility aids. Steps must be taken to ensure that information is truly accessible to all. By accessibility, we mean ensuring content is usable for people with disabilities, including visual, auditory, cognitive, and physical disabilities, among others. This is both an ethical issue, as the American Library Association's Bill of Rights calls for making information available to all people,[1] and a legal issue, in that the Americans with Disabilities Act and Section 508 of the Rehabilitation Act of 1973 prohibit discrimination against those with disabilities and require online material to be accessible.[2]

This issue affects all librarians, including those focusing in scholarly communication, as more universities face lawsuits claiming discrimination in the online learning environment. Public material must meet certain accessibility requirements.[3] If open material is not accessible, many libraries will not be able to include it in their collections. We'll discuss what scholarly communication librarians need to know about accessibility, including best practices, challenges, and how they can incorporate accessibility into their work.

WHAT TO KNOW ABOUT ACCESSIBILITY

EMERGING ISSUES

Accessibility is the responsibility of individual instructors as well as their institutions. However, addressing accessibility can be both time-consuming and costly. Institutions produce a huge amount of online content, and the faculty content creators are often not familiar with accessibility best practices and tools. Meanwhile, staff who do possess this knowledge comprise a fraction of any given institution's population.[4] While automated accessibility checkers (e.g., Siteimprove, Ally, UDOIT, etc.) are rapidly being developed and enhanced, they are not able to identify or remedy complex or more nuanced accessibility errors.[5] For example, a website accessibility checker like Siteimprove can tell if there is alternative text for an image, but it can't tell if the text is just the file name or an actual description of the image. Moreover, some information, like mathematical equations, reference lists, and musical scores, are difficult to make accessible to screen readers.

EVOLVING BEST PRACTICES

Accessibility best practices are continually evolving, as is the supporting technology. The newest Web Content Accessibility Guidelines (WCAG 2.1) endorsed by the World Wide Web Consortium (W3C) in 2018, however, remain the gold standard.[6] Various organizations have developed their own guidelines and checklists that present WCAG in a digestible form, including the National Center on Accessible Educational Materials and EDUCAUSE.[7]

Some formats (e.g., Microsoft Word) are easier than others for novice content creators to make accessible and check for accessibility issues. Ensuring that certain content, such as web pages, is accessible requires more advanced knowledge and (coding) skills. OER authors should use built-in accessibility tools, such as those available in Microsoft Office and Adobe Acrobat Pro, whenever possible. Completed works should be evaluated first using a reputable automated accessibility checker like Siteimprove or WAVE, but be sure to follow their prompts for items that need a manual check.

Librarians can also look to the principles outlined in the Universal Design for Learning (UDL) framework when developing open material. UDL urges instructors to present information in a variety of ways so that learners have multiple means of acquiring and engaging with it.[8] For example, providing descriptive alternative text for any images or visual representations of information ensures that students of all abilities can comprehend their meaning.

CHALLENGES

Complex Tools

Although some programs like Adobe Acrobat Pro DC allow users to make files accessible, the process is not always easy. For example, you can use Adobe Acrobat Pro DC to correctly tag all parts of a PDF file (as headings, paragraphs, images, tables, lists, etc.) and order them in a way that makes sense (e.g., screen readers know to read a subheading before the paragraph it precedes). While it is fairly easy to run an accessibility check and perform auto-tagging in Adobe Acrobat Pro DC, you will quickly realize that this is not a complete solution. The process is imperfect and requires manual editing, especially for adding and checking alternative text for images. However, this is not a simple process in Adobe Acrobat, and you will likely need additional training if you do not have anyone on your campus who can assist with this. We recommend several tutorials in "Additional Resources" below. And while programs like Microsoft Word make it easy to tag documents, these tags do not always carry over when converting a document to a PDF file (figure 3.1).

Reliance on Platforms

For web content, the hosting platform needs to be accessible as well, and this often means relying on others to make them accessible. Platforms that host open material, such as Digital Commons, Open Journal Systems, Pressbooks, and more, are not always accessible. Some platforms, for instance, use images as links to advance through the books or access other parts of their sites; the links often do not have alternative text describing the link, however, so

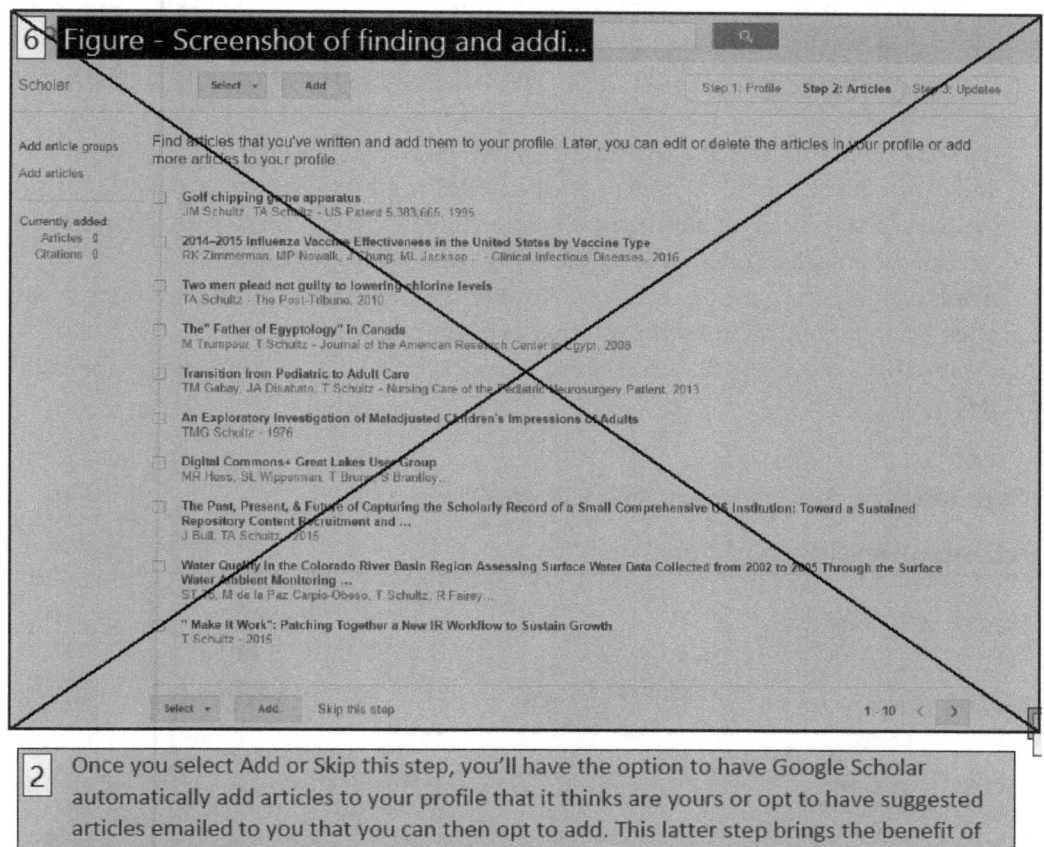

Figure 3.1

This screenshot shows a section of an accessible Word document that has been saved as a PDF file. An image in the document precedes a paragraph of text. However, Adobe Acrobat has labeled the paragraph with a 2, meaning it will be read after the text rather than before by a screen reader, thus potentially confusing the user.

someone relying on a screen reader would not know what the link is for. Unless your institution is able to run its own instance of an open source platform and can adapt it as needed to make it accessible, you are at the mercy of others.

ADVOCATING FOR ACCESSIBILITY

The most important work you can do to incorporate accessibility into your work as a scholarly communication librarian is to learn more about it (see "Additional Resources"). The more you learn and start making your own work accessible, the better able you will be to help others. Some simple steps anyone can take immediately include

- Use the preset text style formats for paragraphs, headings, subheadings, and more.
- As part of the above, use the heading styles for anything meant as a header or subheader (instead of bolding it) and keep the headers in the correct order (i.e., Header 1 should always precede Header 2, which should always precede Header 3, etc.).
- Provide alternative text that fully describes an image so that someone using a screen reader understands what a sighted reader sees. Do not use file names for this.

- Avoid images of text as much as possible (figure 3.2). If there is text in an image that a user needs to read, provide a full transcript of that text in the alt text.
- Do not include long hyperlinks in the text but instead create text links that describe where the link goes (i.e., not "Click here." For example, instead of typing *www.cnn.com*, type *CNN* and link it to the website.
- Table formatting should be used only when making an actual table, not to help format the overall text for visual aesthetics. If you do create a table, make sure to have a row marked as a header and to have a description of the table if needed.
- Avoid copying and pasting text from Word into a text-editing box for websites. It can often bring odd formatting that interferes with preset text formats.

For more tips, check out the *Accessibility Toolkit* by Coolidge and colleagues in "Additional Resources."

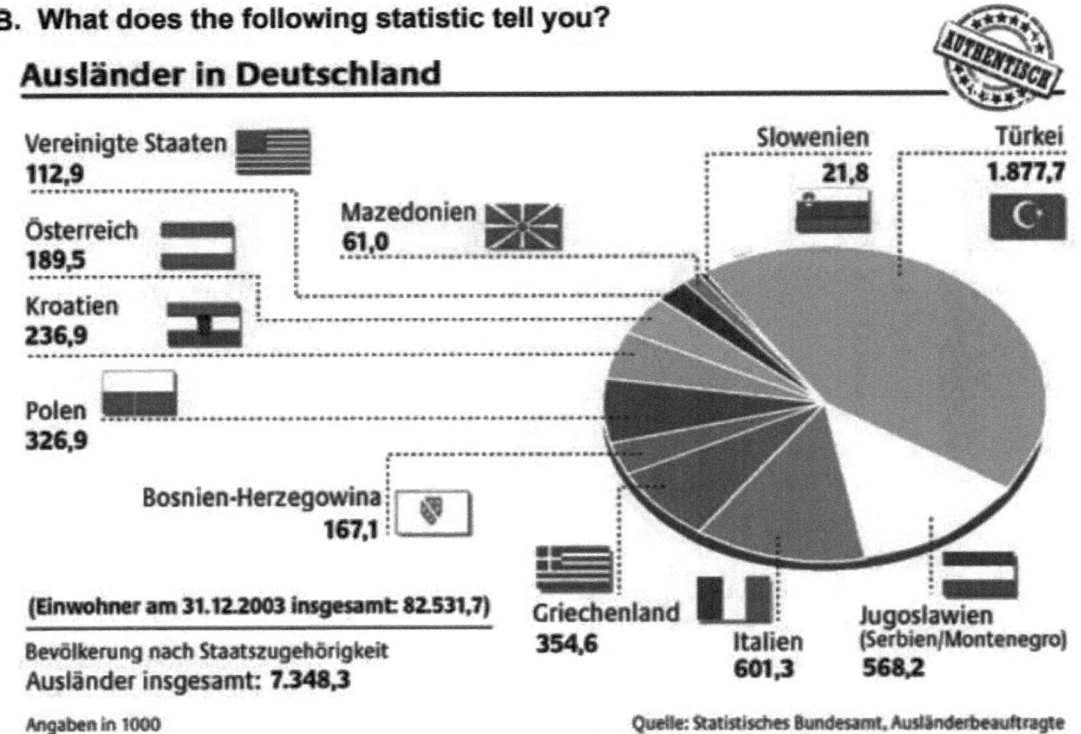

Figure 3.2

This screenshot shows an image of a pie chart in an open textbook. Students using the book are supposed to use the pie chart to answer a question about immigrants in Germany, but without a transcription of the text in the pie chart, a student using a screen reader would not be able to answer.

It's also important to educate those you work with. Your institution may have a large accessibility push, but for those whose institution doesn't have such an effort, it's important to add your voice. We also need more librarians advocating for accessible platforms. We need the groups behind the platforms to know that they can't ignore accessibility. If a large enough group of users calls for accessibility as a requirement, then we might bring about the change we need for all our patrons.

ADDITIONAL RESOURCES

GENERAL

DAISY Consortium. "Guidance and Training." Accessed March 23, 2020. https://daisy.org/info-help/guidance-training/.
This site provides various help on accessibility, including how to make content accessible, how to convert to more accessible formats, and various standards.

———. "Accessible Publishing Knowledge Base." Accessed June 19, 2023. https://kb.daisy.org/publishing/docs/
This site is a guide to accessible production practices for the creation of digital publications.

Liebler, Raizel, and Gregory Cunningham. "Can Accessibility Liberate The 'Lost Ark' of Scholarly Work? University Library Institutional Repositories Are 'Places of Public Accommodation.'" *UIC John Marshall Law Review* 52, no. 2 (2019): article 2. https://repository.law.uic.edu/lawreview/vol52/iss2/2.
This article discusses the need for content in institutional repositories to be accessible.

MERLOT. "OER and Accessibility." Accessed March 23, 2020. https://oeraccess.merlot.org/.
This site provides a connection to accessible content in MERLOT as well as other tools and resources for accessibility.

Mulliken, Adina. "Eighteen Blind Library Users' Experiences with Library Websites and Search Tools in U.S. Academic Libraries: A Qualitative Study." *College and Research Libraries* 80, no. 2 (2019): 152–67. https://doi.org/10.5860/crl.80.2.152.
This research article discusses the experience that blind library users have with academic library websites.

Wolfe, Amy. "Accessibility Toolkit for Open Educational Resources (OER)." CUNY Office of Library Services, March 9, 2020. https://guides.cuny.edu/accessibility/home.
This guide provides help related to OERs and accessibility.

Zhang, Xiangling, Ahmed Tlili, Fabio Nascimbeni, Daniel Burgos, Ronghuai Huang, Ting-Wen Chang, Mohamed Jemni, and Mohamed Koutheair Khribi. "Accessibility within Open Educational Resources and Practices for Disabled Learners: A Systematic Literature Review." *Smart Learning Environments* 7, no. 1 (January 3, 2020): article 1. https://doi.org/10.1186/s40561-019-0113-2.
This article provides an overview of research conducted in accessibility and OERs.

MAKING CONTENT ACCESSIBLE

These resources provide tips on how to make sure OA and OER works are also accessible.
Accessible Technology. "Creating Accessible Documents." University of Washington. Accessed March 23, 2020. https://www.washington.edu/accessibility/documents/.
———. "Checking PDFs for Accessibility." University of Washington. Accessed June 19, 2023. https://www.washington.edu/accesstech/documents/check-pdfs/.
Coolidge, Amanda, Sue Doner, Tara Robertson, and Josie Gray. *Accessibility Toolkit*, 2nd ed. Vancouver: BCcampus, University of British Columbia, 2018. https://opentextbc.ca/accessibilitytoolkit/.
US General Services Administration. "Create Accessible Products." Section 508.gov. Accessed March 23, 2020. https://www.section508.gov/create.

EVALUATING ACCESSIBILITY

These resources provide tools and what to look for when evaluating an item to see if it is acceptable.

PDF/UA Foundation. "PAC 2021 – The Free PDF Accessibility Checker." Accessed June 19, 2023. https://pdfua.foundation/en/pdf-accessibility-checker-pac/.

US General Services Administration. "Test for Accessibility." Section 508.gov. Accessed March 23, 2020. https://www.section508.gov/test.

Web Accessibility Initiative. "Easy Checks—A First Review of Web Accessibility." W3C Web Accessibility Initiative. Accessed March 23, 2020. https://www.w3.org/WAI/test-evaluate/preliminary/.

DISCUSSION QUESTIONS

1. Why is accessibility an important consideration for scholarly communication librarians?
2. Of the challenges authors might face as they try and make their content accessible, which are libraries and librarians best situated to address? Why?
3. What are some other ways in which librarians could advocate for accessibility at their institutions?
4. What accessibility policies, guidelines, or best practices does your institution promote or engage in? Can you identify any gaps or areas for improvement?

NOTES

1. American Library Association, "Library Bill of Rights," last updated January 29, 2019, http://www.ala.org/advocacy/intfreedom/librarybill.
2. Americans with Disabilities Act of 1990, AS AMENDED with ADA Amendments Act of 2008, Pub. L. No. 101–336, § 12101, 42 U.S. (1990), https://www.ada.gov/pubs/adastatute08.htm; Wikipedia, s.v. "Section 508 Amendment to the Rehabilitation Act of 1973," January 22, 2020, https://en.wikipedia.org/w/index.php?title=Section_508_Amendment_to_the_Rehabilitation_Act_of_1973&oldid=936954716.
3. Lindsay McKenzie, "50 Colleges Hit with ADA Lawsuits," Inside Higher Ed, December 10, 2018, https://www.insidehighered.com/news/2018/12/10/fifty-colleges-sued-barrage-ada-lawsuits-over-web-accessibility.
4. Lindsay McKenzie, "Feds Prod Universities to Address Website Accessibility Complaints," Inside Higher Ed, November 6, 2018, https://www.insidehighered.com/news/2018/11/06/universities-still-struggle-make-websites-accessible-all.
5. Mark Lieberman, "Technology Can Address Digital Accessibility—to an Extent," Inside Higher Ed, May 2, 2018, https://www.insidehighered.com/digital-learning/article/2018/05/02/technology-can-help-address-accessibility-challenges-many-say.
6. W3C Web Accessibility Initiative, "WCAG 2 Overview," July 2005, last updated March 21, 2023, https://www.w3.org/WAI/standards-guidelines/wcag/; Andrew Kirkpatrick et al., eds., "Web Content Accessibility Guidelines (WCAG) 2.1," W3C Recommendation, June 5, 2018, https://www.w3.org/TR/WCAG21/.
7. National Center on Accessible Educational Materials, "Communicating Digital Accessibility Requirements," http://aem.cast.org/creating/accessibility-standards-specifications-guidelines.html; EDUCAUSE, "Digital and Web Accessibility," https://library.educause.edu/topics/policy-and-law/web-accessibility.
8. Clark Nall, "Academic Libraries and the Principles of Universal Design for Learning: Representation beyond Courses," College and Research Libraries News 75, no. 7 (2015): 374–75, https://doi.org/10.5860/crln.76.7.9345.

BIBLIOGRAPHY

American Library Association. "Library Bill of Rights." Last updated January 29, 2019. https://www.ala.org/advocacy/intfreedom/librarybill.

Americans with Disabilities Act of 1990, AS AMENDED with ADA Amendments Act of 2008, Pub. L. No. 101–336, § 12101, 42 U.S. (1990). https://www.ada.gov/pubs/adastatute08.htm.

EDUCAUSE. "Digital and Web Accessibility." https://library.educause.edu/topics/policy-and-law/web-accessibility.

Kirkpatrick, Andrew, Joshue O'Connor, Alastair Campbell, and Michael Cooper, eds. "Web Content Accessibility Guidelines (WCAG) 2.1." W3C Recommendation, June 5, 2018. https://www.w3.org/TR/WCAG21/.

Lieberman, Mark. "Technology Can Address Digital Accessibility—to an Extent." Inside Higher Ed, May 2, 2018. https://www.insidehighered.com/digital-learning/article/2018/05/02/technology-can-help-address-accessibility-challenges-many-say.

McKenzie, Lindsay. "Feds Prod Universities to Address Website Accessibility Complaints." Inside Higher Ed, November 6, 2018. https://www.insidehighered.com/news/2018/11/06/universities-still-struggle-make-websites-accessible-all.

———. "50 Colleges Hit with ADA Lawsuits." Inside Higher Ed, December 10, 2018. https://www.insidehighered.com/news/2018/12/10/fifty-colleges-sued-barrage-ada-lawsuits-over-web-accessibility.

Nall, Clark. "Academic Libraries and the Principles of Universal Design for Learning: Representation beyond Courses." College and Research Libraries News 76, no. 7(2015): 374–75. https://doi.org/10.5860/crln.76.7.9345.

National Center on Accessible Educational Materials. "Communicating Digital Accessibility Requirements." http://aem.cast.org/creating/accessibility-standards-specifications-guidelines.html.

Wikipedia. S.v. "Section 508 Amendment to the Rehabilitation Act of 1973." January 22, 2020. https://en.wikipedia.org/w/index.php?title=Section_508_Amendment_to_the_Rehabilitation_Act_of_1973&oldid=936954716.

W3C Web Accessibility Initiative. "WCAG 2 Overview." July 2005, last updated March 21, 2023. https://www.w3.org/WAI/standards-guidelines/wcag/.

OTHER DUTIES AS ASSIGNED

Arthur J. Boston

The working day of any two scholarly communication librarians may bear little resemblance to each other. There is a wide range of topic areas (e.g., accessibility, bibliometrics, copyright, data management, digital humanities, open education, and open access advocacy) that practitioners might be working in to best serve their institutions. The field itself is swiftly moving, and to keep afloat, the latitude to flexibly interpret scholcomm librarian roles is an upside. However, such flexibility may also lead some administrators and colleagues across campus to have an ambiguous understanding of the role. While it may generally be understood that the history professor teaches history and the football coach leads the football team, scholcomm librarians cannot so readily depend on a descriptive title. Sometimes, it just so happens, as was the case for me, a scholcomm librarian ends up performing many *other duties as assigned*.

My employer institution is a regional comprehensive public university with enrollment just under 10,000 (mostly undergraduate) students. As I was being interviewed in 2016 to become the first person to hold a dedicated scholarly communication position there, the position details were still being defined. During a phone interview, I was informed that the position was being updated to include tasks previously handled by a departing personnel from outside the library. This meant the eventual scholcomm librarian would coordinate the Office of Research and Creative Activity (ORCA), which runs initiatives supporting faculty-mentored scholarly, creative, and research opportunities for undergraduate and graduate students in all disciplines (i.e., student conferences, grants, a journal).

The work that I presently put into coordinating ORCA and sitting on other university committees takes up the majority of my working year. But recently, I have figured out how to wield these other duties as a tool for constructing effective scholcomm conversations.

The terms *just in case* and *just in time* sometimes come to mind when I consider how to distribute my services as a scholcomm librarian to campus. These are terms technical service librarians use to describe acquisition models: where resources are acquired based on the potential for usage (just in case) and where resources are acquired based on a user request (just in time). For me, I might offer a campus workshop just in case it will be of interest to local faculty with an hour to spare. Doing research, either in preparation for a workshop or for my personal writing, also means I am better prepared to deliver a well-placed bit of information off the cuff, in any setting, just in time.

Below, I share examples where information about scholcomm was delivered just in time while performing my other duties.

COORDINATING A STUDENT SCHOLARSHIP OFFICE

The main student programs offered through ORCA are a statewide poster conference, twice-a-year campus conferences, research and travel grants, and a scholarly journal. Students who participate in these programs are mentored by a faculty member. Journals, conferences, and grants are among the things I'd hoped to have conversations about with my faculty, and coordinating these activities for students has put me into more conversations with faculty than I originally imagined.

One student who received a grant from our office decided she wanted to publish her results in our journal. Every part of her paper was written, from literature review to study design, but her IRB application would not be approved in time for her to collect data before graduation. When she and her faculty mentor approached me with their conflict, I recommended we publish, or *preregister*,* the hypothesis and methodology portions of her draft in the spirit of the Open Science Foundation.[1]

After a few conversations, the student and faculty member became convinced and we proceeded. We also recorded a conversation about the process. The student was accepted to her graduate program shortly after, based in part on having this scholarship in her portfolio. The faculty member was not only introduced to the concept of preregistration, but also witnessed it help gain professional traction for his student. This established a common ground between the faculty member and me, and we have corresponded and collaborated on projects since.

I have trouble imagining that this would have occurred had I advertised a workshop about preregistration. Frankly, it is hard for me to imagine that I would have half my present number of faculty relationships if I relied on cold-calling faculty to attend workshops. Rather, discovering specific research-based needs, just in time, while performing my other duties, has helped me to organically cultivate productive faculty relationships, even in the driest of settings, like campus committees.

SERVING ON CAMPUS COMMITTEES

The Undergraduate Studies Committee reviews proposals for new course offerings and modifications to existing courses. When I sat on this committee, I would review packets of syllabi. Then at our weekly meetings, departmental representatives would answer the committee's questions. Just after my first year of committee membership, I attended the Open Education Southern Symposium in Arkansas, where OER advocates gathered to share ideas. Coming back from that, I made it a point to look at the recommended textbooks in each proposed class and, when applicable, recommend that the representative consider an open textbook instead. I've repeatedly kicked myself for not tracking the data on whether there was any effect.

Similar opportunities have arisen for me as the elected chair for the university's Research Policy Committee, which reviews annual faculty research applications and selects awardees. Serving as the chair involves a lot of paperwork, but one valuable bit of this bureaucracy is in

---

* Preregistration is defined by Nosek and colleagues as an "effective solution is to define the research questions and analysis plan before observing the research outcomes," which helps overcome hindsight bias. Brian A. Nosek et al., "The Preregistration Revolution," *Proceedings of the National Academy of Sciences* 115, no. 11 (March 12, 2018): 2600.

the ability to set the agenda. Leading the discussion of our candidates this past year provided me the perfect platform to discuss the San Francisco Declaration on Research Assessment (SFDORA) and HuMetricsHSS (the Humane Metrics Initiative), which allowed me to address some of the problematic features of research evaluation with my faculty peers.

CONCLUSION

Embedding scholcomm work into my other campus duties has proved to be an effective work-around for reaching faculty where they are. In conclusion, I want to be clear that it is not my recommendation for administrators crafting new scholcomm positions to look at this example as a model for replication. The lemonade is nice, but it's not an invitation to start passing around lemons. It should also be noted that I do not mean to suggest in any way that other practitioners are not having spectacular success with their dedicated workshops; they are. Rather, my hope is that new scholcomm librarians understand the value of the elevator pitch, whatever form that elevator takes. The successful scholcomm librarian is the one who remains open and flexible to swiftly moving subject matter and creative in approaching their delivery to an audience, on campus or off.

DISCUSSION QUESTIONS

1. Think of some of the highest goals you have for your campus community. Try to think of the committees on your campus that might be your best partner in seeing those goals enacted. Would you have better luck presenting to that committee or being part of the committee itself?
2. If you are on a committee or engaged in some other campus service, list out which scholcomm topics are most relevant.
3. If you are not yet employed by an institution of higher education, try to imagine what percentage of your working year would provide the ideal balance for your scholcomm goals. Conversely, if you are in such a position, think of the percentage of your time devoted to other duties. If that number went down to zero, what would it allow you to do? What would you miss most?

NOTE

1.   OSF, home page, https://osf.io.

BIBLIOGRAPHY

Nosek, Brian A., Charles R. Ebersole, Alexander C. DeHaven, and David T. Mellor. "The Preregistration Revolution." *Proceedings of the National Academy of Sciences* 115, no. 11 (March 12, 2018): 2600–2606.
OSF. Home page. https://osf.io.

OPPOSING FORCES

NAVIGATING THE DUALITY OF SCHOLARLY COMMUNICATION WORK

Elisabeth Shook

INTRODUCTION

They go by many names and wear many hats, but a core function of a scholarly communication librarian (SCL) is upholding the rights of publishers while simultaneously supporting alternative methods of publication and dissemination. Simply put, as these positions are often currently implemented, SCLs strive toward two competing goals, creating a duality in the work. This duality requires a breadth of knowledge that is impossible to acquire without extensive experience and a patient mentor. In fact, the 2017 "NASIG Core Competencies for Scholarly Communication Librarians" report acknowledges the complexity of the job: "responsibility for the full suite of competencies is beyond the reach of even the most accomplished librarian."[1]

THE PROBLEM

Nevertheless, many universities and colleges are hiring SCLs or modifying existing positions to include these responsibilities. Often, these librarians are alone in their duties, with little understanding of the work they do by their colleagues or administrators, and the job description often highlights the duality of the work. For example, the SCL is generally expected to recruit content for the institutional repository and to comply with publisher policies on sharing. Simultaneously, many are expected to actively advocate for open access (OA) models. These conflicting and abstract job duties may create a frustrating work environment.

Unclear expectations and duality inherent in the position often lead to what Dorothea Salo identifies as "fundamental attribution error," which is "the human tendency to personalize error and failure by blaming them on an individual and his/her distinctive traits rather than the system in which the individual is embedded." Salo explains, "Encouraging the fundamental attribution error in everyone who interacts with the new initiative both savages the initiative and absolves everyone but the initiative's staff members of responsibility for any difficulties associated with it."[2] Essentially, SCLs are presented with not only a position of competing interests (duality), but also possible frustration by colleagues or supervisors when they are unable to solve the nebulous problems they were hired to address.

Why does this tension exist? A 2015 study concerning burnout in academic librarianship showed "that librarians in a variety of positions experience stress, resulting in part from uncertainty about expectations, the pace of the changing roles, and other role-related problems."[3] Unclear responsibilities, coupled with the intangible or ambiguous expectations of SCLs, are a recipe for failure. Indeed, most of those even peripherally engaged with scholarly communication know that library/publisher relationships are outdated and hurt readers and authors worldwide, but concerns such as fear of lost access, accreditation issues, and potential backlash by campus stakeholders may hold many SCLs back from advocating for or implementing inventive (possibly extreme) change. Without support of colleagues, library administration, and the university as whole, SCLs may find themselves losing traction, causing an initiative to suffer, and leading the librarian to burnout.

Despite the sometimes dire state of working in scholarly communication, there are positive changes on the horizon. These changes, coupled with tangible steps taken by individuals to protect their mental health, can make working in a scholarly communication role sustainable and satisfying.

STAYING HEALTHY

Self-care is of utmost importance when working in scholarly communication (or any role, anytime, anywhere). Librarianship is rife with rhetoric of being a calling, suggesting librarianship as a saintly profession. This rhetoric may be emotionally damaging, as one could believe one is inadequate if overwhelmed or dissatisfied by the work. "Vocational awe," as Ettarh explains, is "easily weaponized against the worker, allowing anyone to deploy a vocational purity test in which the worker can be accused of not being devout or passionate enough to serve without complaint."[4] Considering the duality and related conditions SCLs may confront, it is helpful to work each day with these principles in mind: have purpose, take baby steps, and focus work on university values and goals.

SCLs should start each day with a clear goal in mind, whether the lofty goal of free and open access for all or the less lofty, but equally important goal of earning a living. It is important to approach each day with purpose in order to not let vocational awe, fundamental attribution error, or the competing interests of the work get one down.

While working on those goals, achievable baby steps should be built into the process. For example, one path toward OA could be advocating for an OA policy, but passing such a policy requires a significant amount of groundwork. Each step within that extensive groundwork, though small, is extremely valuable. Beginning conversations locally within the library, collecting and understanding the arguments supporting and opposing OA policies, and identifying OA champions on campus are important steps toward the goal. Though these are small steps, their accumulation is invaluable to the realization of an OA policy.

Finally, SCLs should concentrate energy predominantly on the work the institution is willing to invest in to enact changes in the publishing life cycle. Assessment of the values and goals of an institution should be undertaken to inform the trajectory of work to produce the greatest results. By focusing the majority of one's energy on activities meaningful to the institution, the librarian is building trust with the campus, ensuring a healthy relationship that opens up the possibility of taking scholarly communication work further in the future. Institutional support is vital to the health and success of the SCL. If buy-in isn't present, the librarian should consider programmatic adjustments to align with institutional needs.

POSITIVE CHANGES IN THE SCHOLARLY COMMUNICATION LANDSCAPE

The years 2018 and 2019 were evolutionary for scholarly communication through the reveal of Plan S in Europe, as well as Big Deal cancellations by world-renowned research institutions. Under Plan S, all researchers conducting state-funded research must make their work accessible in "compliant Open Access journals or platforms"[5] by 2021. The cancellation of the Elsevier Big Deal by the University of California system made waves in the North American scholarly communication communities, as did cancellations by several other universities. These cancellations, carried out with support from the faculty and administration of these institutions, are instilling university libraries with greater confidence to confront the crisis in scholarly communication.

CONCLUSION

SCLs are often charged with publisher sharing policy compliance, while also investigating and instigating methods of moving away from the traditional publishing system. This duality, along with the fact that they may be acting alone with little support in a profession that thrives on vocational awe as a tool for undervaluing workers, can lead to burnout of SCLs. Through centering goals, valuing baby steps toward progress, and aligning efforts with institutional goals and values, scholarly communication librarians can stay healthy and enact the change for which they were hired.

DISCUSSION QUESTIONS

1. Can you identify ways in which vocational awe has impacted your work? How could you overcome vocational awe to better perform your job?
2. Do you think scholarly communication librarians are any more or less prone to burnout than other specializations in the profession? Why or why not?
3. In addition to the steps suggested by the author, what additional self-care strategies might you consider to avoid burnout and maintain wellness and health?

NOTES

1. Michael Rodriguez, "NASIG Core Competencies for Scholarly Communication Librarians," *Technical Services Quarterly* 35, no. 3 (2018): 307, https://doi.org/10.1080/07317131.2018.1456869.
2. Dorothea Salo, "How to Scuttle a Scholarly Communication Initiative," *Journal of Librarianship and Scholarly Communication* 1, no. 4 (2013): eP1075–7, https://doi.org/10.7710/2162-3309.1075.
3. Ellen I. Shupe, Stephanie K. Wambaugh, and Reed J. Bramble, "Role-Related Stress Experienced by Academic Librarians," *Journal of Academic Librarianship* 41, no. 3 (May 2015): 265, https://doi.org/10.1016/j.acalib.2015.03.016.
4. Fobazi Ettarh, "Vocational Awe and Librarianship: The Lies We Tell Ourselves," *In the Library with the Lead Pipe*, January 10, 2018, https://www.inthelibrarywiththeleadpipe.org/2018/vocational-awe/.
5. Plan S and COAlition S, home page, accessed March 3, 2020, https://www.coalition-s.org/.

BIBLIOGRAPHY

Ettarh, Fobazi. "Vocational Awe and Librarianship: The Lies We Tell Ourselves." *In the Library with the Lead Pipe*, January 10, 2018. https://www.inthelibrarywiththeleadpipe.org/2018/vocational-awe/.

Plan S and COAlition S. Home page. Accessed March 3, 2020. https://www.coalition-s.org/.

Rodriguez, Michael. "NASIG Core Competencies for Scholarly Communication Librarians." *Technical Services Quarterly* 35, no. 3 (2018): 306–8. https://doi.org/10.1080/07317131.2018.1456869.

Salo, Dorothea. "How to Scuttle a Scholarly Communication Initiative." *Journal of Librarianship and Scholarly Communication* 1, no. 4 (2013): eP1075. https://doi.org/10.7710/2162-3309.1075.

Shupe, Ellen I., Stephanie K. Wambaugh, and Reed J. Bramble. "Role-Related Stress Experienced by Academic Librarians." *Journal of Academic Librarianship* 41, no. 3 (May 2015): 264–69. https://doi.org/10.1016/j.acalib.2015.03.016.

IT'S UP TO US

OPEN ACCESS IN THE HUMANITIES

Jennie Rose Halperin

As I write this in spring 2020, the mainstream scholarly access conversation is focused on solving the challenges posed by the COVID-19 virus, and scientific communities are coming together to share data and discoveries. The rapidly changing situation is making the conversation around access to science feel present for people who are normally disconnected from the work of the lab or the work of scholars more generally.

While science is, as usual, front of mind in open access debates, something curious is happening in parallel within scholarly communication in the humanities. Suddenly, JSTOR is opening journals to the public and Jill Lepore is writing glowing pieces in the *New Yorker* about the Internet Archive's "National Emergency Library."[1*] A circulating Google Doc called "Vendor Love in the Time of COVID-19" contains dozens of examples of vendors loosening restrictions, rethinking e-book limits, and offering free access to students around the country.[2] In the words of copyright and fair use expert Kyle Courtney, the "safety valve of fair use" has been released. However, in his words, this is an "exigent circumstance with a limited timeline," meaning that eventually we will likely have to return to knowledge lockdown by vendors and publishers.[3]

Will students, teachers, librarians, and the general public now more willingly battle those who would withhold knowledge from them? Will organizations that purport to protect the rights of authors but actually protect entrenched rights holders be unmasked? Will scholarly communication ever look the same?

The answer to all these questions, for better or worse, is likely no. The humanities, which make up 1 percent of all research funding,[4] has been continuously devalued within the neoliberal university. In 2015, less than 12 percent of all awarded bachelor's degrees were humanities degrees, and writing skills among high school students have consistently fallen since 2006.[5,6] One need look no further than the tenure, mental health, and funding crises within universities to realize that humanities scholars are consistently underpaid and undervalued, with a few large platforms or publishers holding the lion's share of North American humanities research.

Without high-quality scholarly resources available for students, practitioners, and learners, North American hegemony becomes more entrenched, teaching and learning are cut off, and scholarly communication is needlessly hampered and undervalued. A measure of a healthy society is access to knowledge, necessary for a deliberative practice of democracy and

---

* Revisiting this in 2023, we now know how that turned out. Hachette Book Grp. v. Internet Archive, 20-cv-4160 (JGK), (S.D.N.Y. Mar. 24, 2023).

engagement in society, yet research is prohibitive for most scholars and learners, particularly those without institutional access. Curriculum is moving increasingly online, but a large subset of scholarly research is too expensive for students, even as those students are being expected to evaluate sources and article quality.

In terms of impact, Humanities Commons founder Kathleen Fitzpatrick and K|N Consultants Principal Rebecca Kennison's 2017 study of *Altmetrics in Humanities and Social Sciences* confirms that traditional bibliometrics do not serve the humanities due to the diversity within the field.[7] In addition, they write that analytics can disadvantage humanities research because of the qualitative use of metrics within humanities networks beyond counting citations. This takes the emphasis away from more generative modes of assessment. Metrics, as they write, are less about impact and more about money, as they utilize data that are not objective or based in discipline.

Professor and Open Library of the Humanities founder Martin Paul Eve writes that a significant aspect of open humanities access hinges on the difference between research and scholarship.[8] At its core, the humanities is based on inquiry, equity, and collaboration, or, as Eve puts it, "the discovery or communication of new findings or interpretations," which should be divorced from the "problematic rhetoric of utility."[9] However, this split between research in the sciences and scholarship in the humanities privileges the independent scholar and researcher, one whose career is defined by the publication of one idea or manuscript, often at the cost of a more integrative or collaborative approach.

The monograph, or single subject/author book, is the predominant mode of scholarly dissemination in the humanities.[10] This fact has long been called a crisis due to the issues of ownership, lack of diversity, and the culture of monetization that it creates in the field. However, Eve describes the reliance of the monograph in the humanities as more of a "chronic illness" than a crisis. The dominance of the monograph, compounded with funding, has created an untenable situation in the humanities, with the publication of scholarship created largely independent of lab or collaborative structures that are often key to scientific research. This method of publication and knowledge creation makes it more difficult to create consensus on the value of sharing. In North America, the monograph affects hiring, tenure, and promotion; limits more widely circulated forms of dissemination; and shapes how graduate students are trained. In important ways, reliance on the monograph is a fundamental obstacle to changing the way North American humanities are organized. This situation can be contrasted with that in the European Union, where collaborative grants and publications are much more amenable to being made available in repositories and Plan S includes the humanities in its structure. In addition, a lack of funding interventions for the humanities, like the Bayh-Dole Act in the sciences, has disincentivized author ownership of intellectual property.

The APC model, predatory journals, and hyper-specification, combined with an unspoken prestige factor and lack of economic interest, further discourage collaborative scholarship across the humanities, though alternative models, such as compensated or collaborative peer review and overlay journals, hold great promise. While a wide-scale embrace of collaborative scholarship sometimes feels far away, open access policies proliferate at individual institutions. High-profile funders and art collections, archives, and libraries have begun to favor open access as an online collection standard. Preprint servers are proliferating, and humanities scholars are no longer accepting the hegemony of the monograph and the traditional scholarship model, with alternative tenure considerations a possibility. At the same time, the pace of change feels glacial due to the overwhelming focus on scientific research at both the institutional level and the funding level.

As demonstrated in the sciences, better funding means more attention is paid to issues of access. A combination of decreasing public funding and a lack of collective action has locked away scholarship in journals owned by large corporations like Taylor and Francis or Elsevier or in overpriced monographs. A lack of consensus in evaluation of digital or alternative scholarship further depresses the situation. New institutional norms and a collective consensus could create consumer advocacy for ethical humanities access, but the future remains uncertain, and institutional precarity necessarily creates scholarly and human precarity. In a world of scholarly abundance, humanities scholars are creating false scarcity and replicating the worst parts of capitalism through lack of action.

In 2013, programmer and activist Aaron Swartz took his life while facing a thirteen-count indictment for mass downloading from JSTOR, the pricey scholarly database that in some ways most exemplifies the hypocrisy within humanities scholarship. In 2008, he wrote in the *Guerilla Open Access Manifesto*,[11] "With enough of us, around the world, we'll not just send a strong message opposing the privatization of knowledge—we'll make it a thing of the past."[12] Twelve years later, it took a global pandemic for vendors to do the right thing for a short time. From now on, it is up to us.

DISCUSSION QUESTIONS

1. What are some steps you can take to encourage open access in the humanities in your institution? How do these strategies help, and what are possible weaknesses of these strategies?

2. Find some examples of scholarship within the humanities that are taking alternative approaches to publication, such as preprints or digital scholarship. Are they successful? What makes them successful? What is challenging about their approach? Is this approach as one you would adopt or encourage? Why?

3. If you were to list metrics or altmetrics that would be applicable to humanities research, what would you put on the list? Why?

4. What would collaborative, scholar-driven scholarship look like in the humanities? What does collective action look like for you in this context?

NOTES

1. Jill Lepore, "The National Emergency Library Is a Gift to Readers Everywhere," *New Yorker*, March 26, 2020, https://www.newyorker.com/books/page-turner/the-national-emergency-library-is-a-gift-to-readers-everywhere.

2. University Information Policy Officers, "Vendor Love in the Time of COVID-19," Google Doc, April 15, 2020, https://docs.google.com/document/u/2/d/e/2PACX-1vT3pF6oX93Ok-0GqSvQuqOhQRTVF7lgxzq5GS3alUZsWyz2Q6SS3fl3wyMc1-XBhcjMQFoOXGhRZzGRT/pub.

3. Kyle Courtney, "Fair Use and Exigent Circumstances," *Kyle Courtney* (blog), March 11, 2020, https://kyle-courtney.com/2020/03/11/covid-19-copyright-library-superpowers-part-i/.

4. Peter Suber, "Why Is Open Access Moving So Slowly in the Humanities?," *Blog of the APA*, June 8, 2017. https://blog.apaonline.org/2017/06/08/open-access-in-the-humanities-part-2/.

5. American Academy of Arts & Sciences, "The State of the Humanities: Higher Education 2015," March 2015. https://www.amacad.org/sites/default/files/publication/downloads/HI_HigherEd2015.pdf.

6. Carnegie Mellon University, "Poorly prepared: How writing instruction influences college-readiness," https://www.cmu.edu/teaching/designteach/teach/instructionalstrategies/writing/poorlyprepared.html

7. Kathleen Fitzpatrick and Rebecca Kennison, "Altmetrics in Humanities and Social Sciences," Perspectives. K|N Consultants, October 30, 2017. http://knconsultants.org/altmetrics-in-humanities-and-social-sciences/.

8. Martin Paul Eve, "Innovations," in *Open Access and the Humanities: Contexts, Controversies and the Future* (Cambridge: Cambridge University Press, 2014), 137–51, https://doi.org/10.1017/CBO9781316161012.007.
9. Eve, "Introduction, or why open access?" in *Open Access and the Humanities: Contexts, Controversies and the Future* (Cambridge: Cambridge University Press, 2014), 26, https://doi.org/10.1017/CBO9781316161012.003.
10. Suber, "Why Is Open Access Moving So Slowly in the Humanities?"
11. Aaron Schwartz, "Guerilla Open Access Manifesto," July 2008, https://archive.org/details/GuerillaOpenAccessManifesto.
12. Ibid.

BIBLIOGRAPHY

American Academy of Arts and Sciences. "The State of the Humanities: Higher Education 2015." Report. March 2015. https://www.amacad.org/sites/default/files/publication/downloads/HI_HigherEd2015.pdf.

Courtney, Kyle. "Fair Use and Exigent Circumstances." *Blog*, March 11, 2020. https://kylecourtney.com/2020/03/11/covid-19-copyright-library-superpowers-part-i/.

Eve, Martin Paul. "Innovations." In *Open Access and the Humanities: Contexts, Controversies and the Future*, 137–51. Cambridge: Cambridge University Press, 2014. https://doi.org/10.1017/CBO9781316161012.007.

———. "Introduction, or why open access?" In *Open Access and the Humanities: Contexts, Controversies and the Future*, 1-42. Cambridge: Cambridge University Press, 2014. https://doi.org/10.1017/CBO9781316161012.003

Fitzpatrick, Kathleen, and Rebecca Kennison. "Altmetrics in Humanities and Social Sciences." Perspectives. K|N Consultants, October 30, 2017. http://knconsultants.org/altmetrics-in-humanities-and-social-sciences/.

Lepore, Jill. "The National Emergency Library Is a Gift to Readers Everywhere." *New Yorker*, March 26, 2020. https://www.newyorker.com/books/page-turner/the-national-emergency-library-is-a-gift-to-readers-everywhere.

Schwartz, Aaron. "Guerilla Open Access Manifesto." July 2008. https://archive.org/details/GuerillaOpenAccessManifesto

Suber, Peter. "Why Is Open Access Moving So Slowly in the Humanities?" *Blog of the APA*, June 8, 2017. https://blog.apaonline.org/2017/06/08/open-access-in-the-humanities-part-2/.

University Information Policy Officers. "Vendor Love in the Time of COVID-19." Google Doc, April 15, 2020. https://docs.google.com/document/u/2/d/e/2PACX-1vT3pF6oX93Ok0Gq-SvQuqOhQRTVF7lgxzq5GS3alUZsWyz2Q6SS3fl3wyMc1-XBhcjMQFoOXGhRZzGRT/pub.

REFLECTIONS ON MOVING ON AND SCALING UP

ADAPTING PAST EXPERIENCE TO EMERGING SCHOLARLY COMMUNICATION PROGRAMS

Emily Kilcer, Julia Lovett, and Mark Clemente

INTRODUCTION

Scholarly communication librarianship is always evolving. It is inherently malleable and context-dependent. Relevant skills can be challenging to learn in most LIS programs.

As a result, the experiences that shaped our early careers in scholarly communication were essential. Time at institutions with well-resourced, well-established, and highly visible scholarly communication programs, at MIT, Harvard, and the University of Michigan, showed us what was possible with a team working toward shared goals: where to look for opportunities, how to engage in strategic decision-making, when to keep nudging, and when to back-burner an effort.

An interesting shift we have each navigated is what happens when you move from where this sort of work is woven into an institution's structure and culture to somewhere that is just beginning to build a scholarly communication program.

Gaining experience in a well-established program and then having the opportunity to build a new program elsewhere seems to be a common juncture in many careers. Interestingly, the challenges we have faced and continue to navigate have striking parallels, despite the differences in our institutions and roles. Our discussion here offers what we hope are some practical takeaways distilled from our collective experiences.

OUR STORIES

Before we share some of our impressions from these shifts in our professional environment, what follows are brief snapshots of our experiences with scholarly communication work.

EMILY KILCER, FROM HARVARD TO THE UNIVERSITY AT ALBANY

Coming to librarianship as a second career, I was helped by internships and part-time positions to navigate my understanding of the profession. An internship at MIT with

Ellen Finnie soon after its open access (OA) policy passed crystalized my interest in OA and introduced me to scholarly communication work. When a position at Harvard's Office for Scholarly Communication opened, I found myself in the right place at the right time. My role there evolved over time, and I learned an incredible amount from the amazing team of people with whom I worked, which is a wildly insufficient characterization of that experience. One of the greatest lessons I learned is that high-functioning teams of people with different strengths build successful, impactful projects. After several years and life changes, I left to see if I could help build a new scholcomm program at UAlbany (part of the SUNY system). As I still work to adjust to this role, I remind myself regularly that while each organization has different resources and cultures, by the very nature of this work and with patience and persistence, there are always opportunities for progress.

JULIA LOVETT, FROM THE UNIVERSITY OF MICHIGAN TO THE UNIVERSITY OF RHODE ISLAND

In 2012, I was hired by the University of Rhode Island Libraries as the first digital initiatives librarian. Previously, I had worked for John Wilkin at the University of Michigan, managing parts of the university's Google Books project and the HathiTrust Digital Library. I learned so much in a short time while working with a large, experienced team, surrounded by seemingly unlimited knowledge and resources. The opportunity to start a new initiative at URI and transition into a leadership role was both exciting and intimidating. URI offered increased autonomy, flexibility, and the freedom to set priorities, but there were significant resource challenges, and I especially struggled with a lack of IT infrastructure at the time. Gradually, I made progress by setting realistic incremental goals, finding like-minded colleagues within the institution and through professional organizations, crafting projects to fit the setting, and benefiting from copious support from my colleagues and the administration.

MARK CLEMENTE, FROM MIT TO CASE WESTERN RESERVE UNIVERSITY

I began working in scholarly communication in 2012 as the library fellow for scholarly publishing and licensing in the MIT Libraries, part of a program for early career librarians. Within a highly structured and supportive environment, and with abundant networks of mentors to learn from—like Emily, I also benefited from Ellen Finnie's generous mentorship—I could not have anticipated a more immersive experience for learning the core areas of this field. In 2016, seeing an opportunity to return to my home city of Cleveland, I accepted a new role to build a scholarly communication program at CWRU. The transition was difficult. Moving from a supporting role within a well-established program to a new one, where the priorities and scope of the position were primarily up to me to identify and communicate, forced me to make the mental and emotional shift from early career to midcareer much sooner than I felt ready. Once I accepted this shift, however, I found ways to thrive that enabled me to take more ownership of my own role as an expert. Building peer-mentoring networks at multiple levels—within my immediate team, as well as in local, regional, and national communities—was crucial, as was identifying collaborative programs that I could build with my colleagues.

CHALLENGE, ACCEPTED

FIND YOUR COMMUNITY

One of the biggest shifts when arriving at a new institution is the loss of an established community.

In our former roles, we all worked with leaders in their domains who continue to shape the direction of this field. The conversations, connections, and projects we experienced attuned our ears to a strategic vision and organizational presence that continue to guide our work. Mentors and colleagues, both within our organizations and beyond, helped shape how we developed professionally.

When shifting from one institution to another, we have all found it important to maintain previous connections and establish new networks of peer support.

ESTABLISH AND NURTURE STAKEHOLDER RELATIONSHIPS

Nurturing a culture of openness first in the libraries is critical to building an effective scholarly communication presence, as well as a shared understanding of the value of this sort of work both within the libraries and outside. To this end, building cross-departmental allies can make the difference between a successful effort and one that fails to gain traction. Partnership can be built on deliberate conversations as well as serendipitous encounters. Being open and curious, asking questions, and finding the people who are the connectors on campus is a good start. When you are still trying to build energy within the library, having support from another unit or a trusted voice can help make the case for the legitimacy of an effort.

SCALE YOUR EXPECTATIONS

Setting a different pace, level of expectation, and measurement of success can be key to adjusting to a new institution and getting a new initiative off the ground. Even when progress on an effort seems frustratingly slow, look for quality over quantity. Scholcomm work is often touted as global in scope, especially OA initiatives that aim for global access to scholarship, but this work can also be transformative at a local level. Do not underestimate your program just because it is new or modest in size. There may be certain aspects of your program that are very successful—even more so than the known leaders in the field—that others would want to hear about.

TAKE TIME; BE DELIBERATE AND STRATEGIC

Another obvious benefit of building an emerging program is the flexibility and freedom to shape priorities. We have each experienced increased autonomy and agency in our new positions. It takes time to identify strategic priorities that cohere and make sense within an institution based on culture, staffing, and resources.

Relatedly, scholcomm roles are often responsible for work of high strategic importance to the library and institution and often do not come with the authority or level of influence to shape discussions. Navigating this tension is often part of a scholcomm role. Providing information and reasoning to help inform decision-making will often be an iterative process with fits and starts.

YOU CANNOT DO IT ALL. AND THAT'S OK.

Because this work is always changing, expanding your own expertise as a scholcomm librarian is part and parcel of the role. Deep expertise in all areas of scholarly communication is difficult and time-consuming at best, if not impossible. As a result, it is possible that your strengths may not match the requirements of your new institution. Understanding that you may need to tool up and explore new communities and practices should be a welcome challenge. Your expertise may help inform other efforts down the road. Again, there's opportunity everywhere!

CONSIDER YOUR AUDIENCE

Another expectation of a scholarly communication librarian is the ability to contribute to the knowledge of the profession through publications, presentations, or other means. When your vantage point is from a library with a robust program, your scholarship will reflect that stature. Coming from an emerging program, there will be fewer opportunities to speak from a leadership role. Remember, however, there are many scholarly communication librarians in the same boat, working with limited resources, who need information pertaining to their own situations. Hearing how a similar library tackled a problem will be more valuable than hearing what an elite institution is doing with its latest large grant.

CLOSING THOUGHTS

From taking the time to understand your new organization and build new communities of support to setting reasonable priorities and finding time to continue to grow professionally, navigating this sort of professional shift has the potential to be remarkably challenging, rewarding, and impactful. As you make this leap, try to maintain relationships with your mentors, remember that local impact is powerful, and be patient with the process and kind to yourself.

ADDITIONAL RESOURCES

Bonn, Maria. "Tooling Up: Scholarly Communication Education and Training." *College and Research Libraries News* 75, no. 3 (2014): 132–35. https://doi.org/10.5860/crln.75.3.9087.

Radom, Rachel, Melanie Feltner-Reichert, and kynita stringer-stanback. *Organization of Scholarly Communication Services*. SPEC Kit 332. Washington, DC: Association of Research Libraries, November 2012. https://doi.org/10.29242/spec.332.

Thomas, Camille. "Reaction to Scrappy Strategies #OpenPros Webcast." SPARC, July13, 2017. https://sparcopen.org/openpros/reaction-scrappy-strategies-openpros-webcast/.

Xia, Jingfeng, and Yue Li. "Changed Responsibilities in Scholarly Communication Services: An Analysis of Job Descriptions." *Serials Review* 41, no. 1 (2015): 15–22. https://doi.org/10.1080/00987913.2014.998980.

DISCUSSION QUESTIONS

1. After identifying the variables that you can control and those you can't, how might you be able to best direct the trajectory of the scholcomm efforts at your institution?

2. Since partnerships critical to this work take time to build, where can you best spend energy as those efforts develop?

3. As you map out and build upon your program, how will you advocate efforts to your leadership? What assessment measures will you need to have in place? How will you demonstrate impact? What language resonates with which communities on campus?

4. Each of these authors discusses how previous experience informed next jobs. How have your experiences, whatever they are, prepared you for your current or next role?

DRAWING FROM COMMUNITY ARCHIVES

APPROACHES FOR A MORE INCLUSIVE OPEN ACCESS MOVEMENT

Jennifer Patiño

Something that the community archives movement and the open access (OA) movement have in common is that they have grown out of a need to address disparities and barriers. Community-based archives as defined by archival scholars are "collections of material gathered primarily by members of a given community and over whose use community members exercise some level of control."[1] Often these archiving efforts are undertaken by members of marginalized communities to counter symbolic annihilation in mainstream archival collections.[2] Symbolic annihilation "describes what happens to members of marginalized groups when they are absent, grossly under-represented, maligned, or trivialized" or treated as if they don't exist,[3] and in the context of archives, this has "far-reaching consequences for both how communities see themselves and how history is written for decades to come."[4] The OA movement gained momentum because of a "dramatic increase in cost of access to the traditional scholarly literature, as well as the need for more equitable access to scholarly literature."[5] Financial barriers to access favor well-funded institutions both in the United States and globally while leaving others in "information-starved locations" or what Bonaccorso and colleagues term "information deserts."[6] While the OA movement seeks the elimination of financial barriers to research, scholarly communication demonstrates a tenacious cultural and racial hegemony. The lack of diversity throughout the scholarly enterprise, including publishers, librarians, and college and university faculty, can potentially create "a feedback loop that privileges and publishes the majority voice, which is often white and male."[7] In order to create a just OA movement, we must make an intentional and proactive effort to address barriers to inclusivity so that we are not recreating the disparities of the systems we wish to leave behind. I suggest that in looking to community archives, which have a tradition of building inclusive spaces, being accountable to the communities they represent, and working to overcome the symbolic annihilation of hegemonic institutions, we can find new approaches to help us reflect on and shift our practices.

Before joining the University of Wisconsin–Madison Libraries, I worked for Sixty Inches from Center, a community arts archiving project, for nine years. This effort grew out of a need identified by a group of local arts practitioners to support and document the work of artists from marginalized communities in Chicago. In critiquing the lack of diversity among artists covered in the popular press, exhibited in museums and galleries, or preserved in local archives, we were often told that the writers, curators, or archivists either hadn't been able to find artists from more diverse backgrounds or that there simply weren't any. This form of erasure is one of the outcomes of the kind of feedback loop among institutions described by Roh;[8] in other words, homogeneity among journalists, curators, and archivists was replicated in their practice. We partnered with the Harold Washington Library's Chicago Artist Files, an open archives collection of over 11,000 artists dating back to the nineteenth century, to contribute interviews with local artists that we would publish online and to organize Get Archived events where we encouraged artists to contribute their materials. The archives were open to donations from any artist in the city, but this did not prevent there being barriers to even knowing about the collection to begin with. "Inclusive isn't just creating opportunities. It's reaching out and encouraging those who are 'on the outside' to participate," according to a respondent in ACRL's Open and Equitable Scholarly Communications report.[9] It is this proactive approach, of purposefully bringing in those on the outside, that can help interrupt the feedback loops and barriers that privilege both wealthy and majority voices. In my own approach to supporting community archives and OA initiatives, I have often found it helpful to (1) stop and ask what's missing, (2) work to build community, and (3) empower individuals.

In asking what's missing, we challenge the passivity and status quo that allow symbolic annihilation to be perpetuated. Asking whose voice is missing is the first step in taking action to remedy erasure and increase representation and inclusion. Who is missing from our projects, libraries, and networks? If we don't make the effort to include those who are missing, or worse, assume they don't exist, we are engaging in erasure. In addition to the symbolic annihilation discussion, Caswell talks about her work cofounding the South Asian American Digital Archive and coming across the story of Anandibai Joshee, the first Indian woman to earn her medical degree in the US in 1883.[10] While commonly absent from university archives collections, publishers, scholars, and librarians of color and other marginalized identities have a long history on US campuses. They have often navigated spaces hostile to their presence by creating networks. What affinity-based groups or professional networks exist on your campus? How can you connect with them to ensure their visibility and representation within your organization's work?

One of the ways that we built community at Sixty Inches from Center was to use our platform to raise the visibility of other community archives and projects through something my colleagues Tempestt Hazel and Kate Hadley Toftness called the Archive Roll Call. At our Chicago Archives + Artists Festival, we asked community archives to share their work with us in a roll call format. This approach, which is in line with community archives' goals of countering erasure through documentation and increasing visibility also helped us increase the diversity of participation in our events and projects. Building community takes respect and requires us to treat others as equals, so in order to create inclusive and welcoming environments, we need to challenge ideas that we may hold of belonging and whose knowledge is worth centering. Building on Ettarh's "vocational awe" and Ahmed's "affective economy," Santamaria points out that "library awe circulates and in doing so, constitutes which bodies belong and those that do not belong in library spaces" effectively concealing structural white supremacy through a fantasy of egalitarianism.[11] In "The Democratisation Myth," Knöchelmann points out how by focusing on a narrower accessibility problem, that of increasing readership mainly for the results of Western scholarship, our discourse misses wider accessibility issues in terms of "who is allowed to publish where, for what reasons, and what are their non-materialist premises."[12] In a just OA movement, we must think more broadly about what we mean by access and for whom and strive for "an inclusive engagement of local particularities in a global context" rather than an expansion of Western ideals and metrics.[13]

For those of us from marginalized backgrounds, underrepresentation in publishing, libraries, or college and university faculty can feel disempowering. Circulated assumptions of belonging have an impact on us that colleagues who don't experience them may not understand or won't always feel safe to talk about for the marginalized.[14] The gaps and silences in institutional archives, spaces, journals, and databases are reminders of academia's history of erasure, hostility, and what Knöchelmann terms "epistemic objectification," the silencing of a person (or social group) that is "treated as an informant while being undermined in [one's] (or their) capacity of being an enquirer."[15] Mboa Nkoudou defines epistemic alienation as "the distortion of one's native way of thinking, and of seeing and speaking of one's own reality."[16] In attempting to describe what exactly I mean when I say "empower individuals," I realized I was experiencing epistemic alienation myself. What I really meant, but had difficulty saying, was that it is important to find or create spaces where you can *volver a tu ser*, or come back to yourself, and allow others to do so as well. This is something I learned from my grandmother, Emiliana Rico Terrazas, who was a curandera and would hold healing rituals for me and my sisters to cure us of *susto* and call our souls back to us. That is the best way for me to describe that what is needed is a healing space for us to be able to see ourselves, to bring our whole selves to our work, and experience what Mboa Nkoudou calls epistemic freedom. He describes this as

> the right to think, to theorize, and to interpret the world; to develop one's own methodologies, and to write from where one is located, unencumbered by Eurocentrism: to democratize "knowledge" from its current rendition in the singular into its plural known as "knowledges."[17]

So for me, part of the work of encouraging diversity of participation in an empowering way entails emphasizing the power of choice we have in our work to interrupt existing feedback loops and create space for historically excluded knowledges.

We must examine ourselves for library awe, or in this case OA awe, and question the ways in which it can obscure colonial legacies between the so-called Global North and South (and East/West). Coming from a Mexican immigrant background myself, discussions of "bad English" being seen as a sign that a journal from a non-English-speaking country might belong on a list of predatory journals makes me cringe at the linguistic imperialism and the expectation that our colleagues around the world be perfectly bilingual to be worthy of inclusion. While the US and Western Europe face challenges from dominant voices in commercial publishing, in Latin America, the dominant voices come from universities and research centers, meaning that whether or not it is called open access, "OA and its related technologies were rapidly embraced and had fewer voices opposing their adoption."[18] Instead, the major barrier in Latin America is editorial racism in the North, which manifests in a lack of OA national journals in international databases, a lack of inclusion on editorial boards of important international journals, and an overrepresentation of OA journals from non-English-speaking or minority populations in lists that conflate low quality with being predatory.[19] A just OA movement must break down other barriers to access beyond wealth disparities and create a more inclusive global community for institutions and scholars who have been historically marginalized.

DISCUSSION QUESTIONS

1. What can we learn from community organizations, and how can we implement those lessons or ideas in library and scholarly communication work?
2. What is lost when we fail to include perspectives different from dominant ones? How is that loss detrimental to erased communities, and to the collective?
3. In addition to the questions proposed throughout this piece, how can we create spaces where people can bring their whole selves to their work?

ADDITIONAL RESOURCES

Curry, Mary Jane, and Theresa Lillis. "The Dangers of English as Lingua Franca of Journals." Inside Higher Ed, March 13, 2018. https://www.insidehighered.com/views/2018/03/13/domination-english-language-journal-publishing-hurting-scholarship-many-countries.

Roh, Charlotte. "Reflections on the Intersection of Publishing and Librarianship: The Experiences of Women of Color." In *Pushing the Margins: Women of Color and Intersectionality in LIS* , edited by Rose L. Chou and Annie Pho, 427–44. Sacramento, CA: Library Juice Press, 2018.

NOTES

1. Andrew Flinn, Mary Stevens, and Elizabeth Shepherd, "Whose Memories, Whose Archives? Independent Community Archives, Autonomy and the Mainstream," *Archival Science* 9 (2009): 73, https://doi.org/10.1007/s10502-009-9105-2.
2. Michelle Caswell, "Seeing Yourself in History: Community Archives and the Fight against Symbolic Annihilation," *Public Historian* 36, no. 4 (November 2014): 26–34, https://doi.org/10.1525/tph.2014.36.4.26.
3. Caswell, "Seeing Yourself," 27.
4. Caswell, "Seeing Yourself," 36.
5. Elisa Bonaccorso et al., "Bottlenecks in the Open-Access System: Voices from around the Globe," *Journal of Librarianship and Scholarly Communication* 2, no. 2 (2014): 4, https://doi.org/10.7710/2162-3309.1126.
6. Bonaccorso et al., "Bottlenecks," 5.
7. Charlotte Roh, "Library Publishing and Diversity Values: Changing Scholarly Publishing through Policy and Scholarly Communication Education," *College and Research Libraries News* 77, no. 2 (February 2016): 82, https://doi.org/10.5860/crln.77.2.9446.
8. Roh, "Library Publishing and Diversity Values."
9. Association of College and Research Libraries, *Open and Equitable Scholarly Communications*, prepared by Nancy Maron and Rebecca Kennison with Paul Bracke, Nathan Hall, Isaac Gilman, Kara Malenfant, Charlotte Roh, and Yasmeen Shorish (Chicago: Association of College and Research Libraries, 2019), 3, https://doi.org/10.5860/acrl.1.
10. Caswell, "Seeing Yourself," 27.
11. Michele R. Santamaria, "Concealing White Supremacy through Fantasies of the Library: Economies of Affect at Work," *Library Trends* 68, no. 3 (Winter 2020): 437, https://doi.org/10.1353/lib.2020.0000.
12. Marcel Knöchelmann, "The Democratisation Myth: Open Access and the Solidification of Epistemic Injustices," preprint, SocArXiv, last edited February 19, 2021, p. 2, https://doi.org/10.31235/osf.io/hw7at.
13. Knöchelmann, "Democratisation Myth," 2.
14. *Scholarly Kitchen*, "On Being Excluded: Testimonies by People of Color in Scholarly Publishing," *Scholarly Kitchen* (blog), April 4, 2018, https://scholarlykitchen.sspnet.org/2018/04/04/excluded-testimonies-people-color-scholarly-publishing/.
15. Knöchelmann, "Democratisation Myth," 14.
16. Thomas Hervé Mboa Nkoudou, "Epistemic Alienation in African Scholarly Communications: Open Access as a *Pharmakon*," in *Reassembling Scholarly Communications: Histories, Infrastructures, and Global Politics of Open Access*, ed. Martin Paul Eve and Jonathan Gray (Cambridge, MA: MIT Press, 2020), 32, https://doi.org/10.7551/mitpress/11885.003.0006.
17. Mboa Nkoudou, "Epistemic Alienation," 36.

18. Juan Pablo Alperin, Gustavo E. Fischman, and John Willinsky, "Scholarly Communication Strategies in Latin America's Research-Intensive Universities," *Revista Educación Superior Y Sociedad* 16, no. 2 (2011):23. https://iesalc.unesco.org/ess/index.php/ess3/article/view/v16i2-6.
19. Cesar G. Victora and Carmen B. Moreira, "Publicações científicas e as relações Norte-Sul: racismo editorial?" [North-South relations in scientific publications: editorial racism?] *Revista de Saúde Pública* 40 (August 2006), https://doi.org/10.1590/s0034-89102006000400006; Ryan Regier, "The Institutionalized Racism of Scholarly Publishing," *A Way of Happening* (blog), June 9, 2018, https://awayofhappening.wordpress.com/2018/06/09/the-institutionalized-racism-of-scholarly-publishing/.

BIBLIOGRAPHY

Alperin, Juan Pablo, Gustavo E. Fischman, and John Willinsky. "Scholarly Communication Strategies in Latin America's Research-Intensive Universities." *Revista Educación Superior Y Sociedad* 16, no. 2 (2011). https://iesalc.unesco.org/ess/index.php/ess3/article/view/v16i2-6.

Association of College and Research Libraries. *Open and Equitable Scholarly Communications: Creating a More Inclusive Future.* Prepared by Nancy Maron and Rebecca Kennison with Paul Bracke, Nathan Hall, Isaac Gilman, Kara Malenfant, Charlotte Roh, and Yasmeen Shorish. Chicago: Association of College and Research Libraries, 2019. https://doi.org/10.5860/acrl.1.

Bonaccorso, Elisa, Renata Bozhankova, Carlos Daniel Cadena, Veronika Čapská, Laura Czerniewicz, Ada Emmett, Natalia Glukhova, et al. "Bottlenecks in the Open-Access System: Voices from around the Globe." *Journal of Librarianship and Scholarly Communication* 2, no. 2 (2014): eP1126. https://doi.org/10.7710/2162-3309.1126.

Caswell, Michelle. "Seeing Yourself in History: Community Archives and the Fight against Symbolic Annihilation." *Public Historian* 36, no. 4 (November 2014): 26–37. https://doi.org/10.1525/tph.2014.36.4.26.

Flinn, Andrew, Mary Stevens, and Elizabeth Shepherd. "Whose Memories, Whose Archives? Independent Community Archives, Autonomy and the Mainstream." *Archival Science* 9 (2009): 71–86. https://doi.org/10.1007/s10502-009-9105-2.

Knöchelmann, Marcel. "The Democratisation Myth: Open Access and the Solidification of Epistemic Injustices." Preprint. SocArXiv, last edited February 19, 2021. https://doi.org/10.31235/osf.io/hw7at.

Mboa Nkoudou, Thomas Hervé. "Epistemic Alienation in African Scholarly Communications: Open Access as a *Pharmakon*." In *Reassembling Scholarly Communications: Histories, Infrastructures, and Global Politics of Open Access,* edited by Martin Paul Eve and Jonathan Gray, 25–40. Cambridge, MA: MIT Press, 2020. https://doi.org/10.7551/mitpress/11885.003.0006.

Regier, Ryan. "The Institutionalized Racism of Scholarly Publishing." *A Way of Happening* (blog), June 9, 2018. https://awayofhappening.wordpress.com/2018/06/09/the-institutionalized-racism-of-scholarly-publishing/.

Roh, Charlotte. "Library Publishing and Diversity Values: Changing Scholarly Publishing through Policy and Scholarly Communication Education." *College and Research Libraries News* 77, no. 2 (February 2016): 82–85. https://doi.org/10.5860/crln.77.2.9446.

Santamaria, Michele R. "Concealing White Supremacy through Fantasies of the Library: Economies of Affect at Work." *Library Trends* 68, no. 3 (Winter 2020): 431–49. https://doi.org/10.1353/lib.2020.0000.

Scholarly Kitchen. "On Being Excluded: Testimonies by People of Color in Scholarly Publishing." *Scholarly Kitchen* (blog), April 4, 2018. https://scholarlykitchen.sspnet.org/2018/04/04/excluded-testimonies-people-color-scholarly-publishing/.

Victora, Cesar G., and Carmen B. Moreira. "Publicações científicas e as relações Norte-Sul: racismo editorial?" [North-South relations in scientific publications: editorial racism?] *Revista de Saúde Pública* 40 (August 2006): 36–42. https://doi.org/10.1590/s0034-89102006000400006.

NOTES FROM THE UNDERGROUND

ON BEING A SCHOLARLY COMMUNICATION LIBRARIAN WITHOUT EVER APPLYING

Brian Quinn and Innocent Awasom Afuh

Over the past decade, many of the most important issues in academic librarianship fall within the purview of scholarly communication: open access, digital repositories, data management, copyright and fair use, altmetrics, and predatory publishing, to name a few. The emerging role of the scholarly communication librarian is situated at the center of this activity. Librarians who want to be on the cutting edge of the discipline may find the scholcomm librarian an enviable figure: someone who is actively involved with many of the most critical issues in the field, who potentially has the ability to bring about enormous change in the way that scholarship is conducted and how libraries operate.

While many may aspire to these influential and important positions, the reality is that relatively few librarians are in a formal scholarly communication position. For every dedicated position, there may be many who wish they were in the role because of its exciting and pivotal potential. In contrast, traditional positions, such as subject or liaison librarian, may feel relatively peripheral, predictable, or routine. Liaison work, such as answering reference questions, teaching library instruction sessions, and ordering materials for the collection, may pale by comparison to the limelight surrounding many aspects of scholcomm work.

Core operational work is important, of course, but may feel less exciting or engaging and may lack the potential to transform scholarly practices and library operations in a similar way to scholarly communication work. Librarians who want to work with the interesting and important issues of scholarly communication may find their current positions less appealing. They may find themselves drawn to scholarly communication even if it lies outside their formal position.

Those interested in scholcomm librarian work may have reservations about formally applying for dedicated positions. While the role of the scholcomm librarian is important and exciting, it can also seem difficult and perilous. Scholcomm positions can be ill-defined, can lack support or clear expectations, and can be saddled with unrealistic demands or time frames. The scholarly communication librarian often must work with a variety of constituents who may be unsupportive, apathetic, distracted, disengaged, or, worse, resistant or even hostile to new initiatives and proposals. Not only may faculty and students be unwilling to change, but library colleagues may be reluctant as well.[1]

Librarians attracted to scholarly communication work cannot help but observe this and may feel ambivalent about serving in the formal role.[2] To some, it may seem simultaneously seductive and off-putting. As subject librarians with a strong interest in scholarly communication, we found ourselves in this position, fascinated by the work but at the same time realizing the formal role could be fraught with challenges: organizational politics, territoriality, pressure for results, and colleagues and patrons who seem indifferent to the work and its importance.

Our response was to pursue our passion for scholarly communication work by involving ourselves as much as possible in anything and everything in our library related to scholarly communication. This includes activities like volunteering to serve on the scholarly communication team, offering workshops on scholarly communication issues, taking an active role in promoting Open Access Week and Open Education Week—anything that we could conceive of that would advance scholarly communication goals within the library and on campus. By immersing ourselves in these activities, we stay engaged with scholcomm issues and get to collaborate with colleagues with similar interests to impact the community.

We did not think of it at the time as doing anything other than "following our bliss," as Joseph Campbell might say.[3] Yet, without holding the position or having the title, we are performing the work and serving in the role of scholarly communication librarian as much as our existing positions allow. It makes sense to create our own roles and grow our positions in this way because it enables us to do the work we love while at the same time not having to contend with all the organizational strings that can be attached to the formal position. For us, it's the best of both worlds, being able to enjoy the work without the organizational and positional baggage some scholarly communication librarians experience.

If you cannot be in the formal role or do not want to be in it, you can harness the power of enthusiasm and engagement to create your own role, serving as a scholarly communication librarian in all but name. In the organizational literature, this is sometimes referred to as growing a role or job crafting.[4] Positions are often more flexible than people realize, especially in newly emerging areas like scholarly communication, enabling librarians to exercise initiative and agency to adjust their positions to some degree in order to reflect their interests. When you are doing the work you love, you perform better and are of more value to the library. Many librarians do scholcomm work outside of dedicated positions, and many of those in dedicated positions got into them by crafting their jobs around their interests.

It can be challenging to juggle traditional responsibilities with activities of one's own choosing, but it is energizing and empowering to feel that you can make a contribution in areas that you feel are important even though they may not appear in your position description. When you feel like you are doing the most important work in the library (whatever that work may be), it affects your identity in a positive way. You feel needed and valued and that you are playing an active part in taking the library in a new direction. Rather than living vicariously and experiencing the envy or regret that comes from coveting someone else's position, you can own the work and experience a deep sense of fulfillment and meaning, without ever applying.

DISCUSSION QUESTIONS

1. If scholarly communication is so important to libraries, why do they have so few positions?
2. Why aren't positions more fluid in academic libraries to allow librarians to do the work that interests them?
3. Why is the role of the scholarly communication librarian not better defined and supported?

4. Is the authors' strategy of creating their own role within the organization a good one?

NOTES

1. Dorothea Salo, "How to Scuttle a Scholarly Communication Initiative," *Journal of Librarianship and Scholarly Communication* 1, no. 4 (August 2013): 5, https://doi.org/10.7710/2162-3309.1075.
2. Sarah Hillcoat-Nalletamby and Judith E. Phillips, "Sociological Ambivalence Revisited," *Sociology* 45, no. 2 (April 2011): 203, https://doi.org/10.1177/0038038510394018.
3. Joseph Campbell, *Joseph Campbell and the Power of Myth with Bill Moyers*, ed. Betty Sue Flowers (New York: Doubleday and Co., 1988), 113.
4. Bogdan Teodor Oprea et al., "Effectiveness of Job Crafting Interventions: A Meta-analysis and Utility Analysis," *European Journal of Work and Organizational Psychology* 28, no. 6 (December 2019): 724, https://doi.org/10.1080/1359432X.2019.1646728.

BIBLIOGRAPHY

Campbell, Joseph. *Joseph Campbell and the Power of Myth with Bill Moyers*, edited by Betty Sue Flowers. New York: Doubleday and Co., 1988.

Hillcoat-Nalletamby, Sarah, and Judith E. Phillips. "Sociological Ambivalence Revisited." *Sociology* 45, no. 2 (April 2011): 202-17. https://doi.org/10.1177/0038038510394018.

Oprea, Bogdan Teodor, Liubiţa Barzin, Delia Vîrgă, Dragoş Iliescu, and Andrei Rusu. "Effectiveness of Job Crafting Interventions: A Meta-analysis and Utility Analysis." *European Journal of Work and Organizational Psychology* 28, no. 6 (December 2019): 723–41. https://doi.org/10.1080/1359432X.2019.1646728.

Salo, Dorothea. "How to Scuttle a Scholarly Communication Initiative." *Journal of Librarianship and Scholarly Communication* 1, no. 4 (August 2014): eP1075. https://doi.org/10.7710/2162-3309.1075.

TEACHING SCHOLARLY COMMUNICATION

Dick Kawooya

I was supposed to write this piece in the late winter and early spring of 2020. However, life in academia happened! And it turns out I am glad I am writing it now, at the end of the 2020 spring semester, as opposed to several months earlier. If I had written it prior to COVID-19, most likely I would be referencing general trends in higher education and the much-anticipated slump in undergraduate admissions. COVID-19 has changed all that in the space of about 4 months.

Looking back through the history of higher education in the United States, nothing has changed the sector in as short a period of time as COVID-19 has in the first half of 2020. As I write, we are still in the middle of the COVID-19 crisis, but evidence already shows that some institutions of higher learning will not survive. COVID-19 represents an existential threat to many institutions, large and small, public and private. The COVID-19 crisis struck at the very vulnerable financial model most institutions have relied upon in the last few decades. That financial model largely depends on tuition revenue of mostly on-campus residential undergraduate students. Over-dependency on tuition revenue has gotten worse as state appropriations for higher education dwindled in the last few decades. What does all this mean for academic libraries that serve higher education communities? How can LIS programs best prepare future librarians that will serve in the academic libraries struggling to cope with these changes?

In the last few years, I have taught a survey course on academic libraries where the first module focused on the state of higher education in general and academic libraries in particular. The rest of the semester we focus on opportunities afforded to academic librarianship by emerging trends in scholarly communication. I focus on scholarly communication at the expense of "traditional" areas like technical services, leadership, and reference because this training prepares future academic librarians for both traditional services as well as emerging areas. "Traditional areas" are typically covered in other courses in our curriculum. I would also like to specifically prepare LIS students for the tenure requirements they may face as librarians, as well as areas that enhance the important contributions of academic libraries to student learning and faculty research.

After careful reflection and review of trends in academic librarianship, I decided to have students demonstratively show skills and competences in three areas: librarian scholarship, faculty support, and student support. These three practical activities focus on the research or scholarly support aspect of the library's core functions. Academic librarians are often expected to be part of research teams, a role that may entail participating in the entire lifecycle of a student or faculty research project. For librarians to make meaningful contributions to the research team and processes they must be excellent researchers themselves; hence the requirement for scholarship for librarian's tenure. In my class, the three areas are compiled into a planning portfolio project, which is a semester-long project aimed at enabling them to put together a portfolio of activities in the three areas. The portfolio is a tangible product students can, and many have, showcased at job interviews for positions in scholarly communication or academic librarianship in general. What are the three areas and what do they entail?

1. **Librarian scholarship.** What do librarians need to get tenure at a top tier research institution?

This activity requires students to identify the research-related activities, deliverables, or resources they will need to meet the research portion of the tenure and promotion requirements at two research-intensive institutions. Students obtain the tenure and promotion policies for the two institutions and identify the kind of evidence needed to support excellent or acceptable research or scholarship for tenure and promotion. They list and explain at least five areas of evidence for research or scholarship. Using a comparative table, they show the similarities and differences in the description of each evidence between the two institutions. For instance, are journal articles part of the evidence needed for scholarship? How do the two institutions describe the nature of such articles? Peer-reviewed, professional, published in a "recognizable journal"? Preference for a format (print versus digital) or no preference? Finally, they identify everything related to research or scholarship they would need to successfully gain tenure and promotion at both institutions.

2. **Faculty support.** What kind of scholarly support activities do librarians provide to faculty at all levels to advance their scholarly endeavors?

The faculty research component requires students to prepare instructional materials to support at least **three areas** of research support they will extend to faculty at a research-intensive university. Below is the list of some areas of faculty research support. It is not an exhaustive list, so students are free to find other scholarly communication areas of interest to them. It is also not mutually exclusive. Some areas necessarily overlap with others.

- Research data management plans
- Authorship, licensing, and licensing negotiations
- Dissemination and preservation of research output
  - Institutional repositories
  - Libraries as publishers
- Research reputation management
- Scholarly impact management and measurement (citation analysis and alternative metrics)
- Research grants—writing, funders' mandate (research data, etc.)
- Ethical and legal issues—intellectual property issues (copyright, patents, etc.), institution ethical reviews

For the three (or more) areas of faculty research support, students develop brief lesson plans and other materials to help them design and deliver effective instruction to faculty and other researchers. For each area, students provide:

1. A brief description of the area, what it entails, and outline of key issues under each
2. Three to five learning outcomes
3. Two to three practical and theoretical learning activities they would include in their instruction materials, such as a copyright quiz, http://www.csus.edu/indiv/p/peachj/edte230/copyright/quiz.htm

4. Tools faculty need for each research area, such as licensing guides, grant writing tools, data management plan tools such as DMPTool, https://dmptool.org, scholarly databases, etc.

5. Instruction resources for each area, such as two to three scholarly articles and proceedings of past ACRL's conferences, http://www.ala.org/acrl/conferences/past

6. Delivery method of instruction: face-to-face, online, blended, flipped

To complete this assignment, students are encouraged to visit academic library websites and specifically seek out the LibGuides on topics for the areas in question: citation analysis or research impact management, research reputation management, research data management/research data management plans, etc. ACRL has plenty of resources on this topic that students are also encouraged to explore, such as the Scholarly Communication Toolkit, https://acrl.libguides.com/scholcomm/toolkit.

   3. Student support. What kind of scholarly activities do librarians provide to students at all levels to advance their scholarly endeavors?

For this component, students are required to design research process or workflow activities to support a hypothetical graduate or undergraduate student in an area, major, or discipline of their choice. The goal is to identify ways in which they would support the student at every stage of the research process or workflow. This is a more involved relationship than simply helping to search for research or scholarly literature for students. Likewise, the research by the hypothetical student supported is much more than a term paper. The ideal research project involves the identification of a research problem/question and collection and analysis of primary or secondary data in the field of choice. For purposes of illustrating the process, figure 3.3 helps students understand the key stages of a research project, stages where they, as librarians, will provide support. This is helpful to students taking my class before the research methods class. If they have taken research methods, they will be intimately familiar with the research process.

Figure 3.3 illustrates the activities associated with the most common student (or faculty) research projects, be it a dissertation or thesis. Students can make it more detailed by adding stages that the librarian is in a unique position to support, such as bibliography creation and management. Students are encouraged not to limit

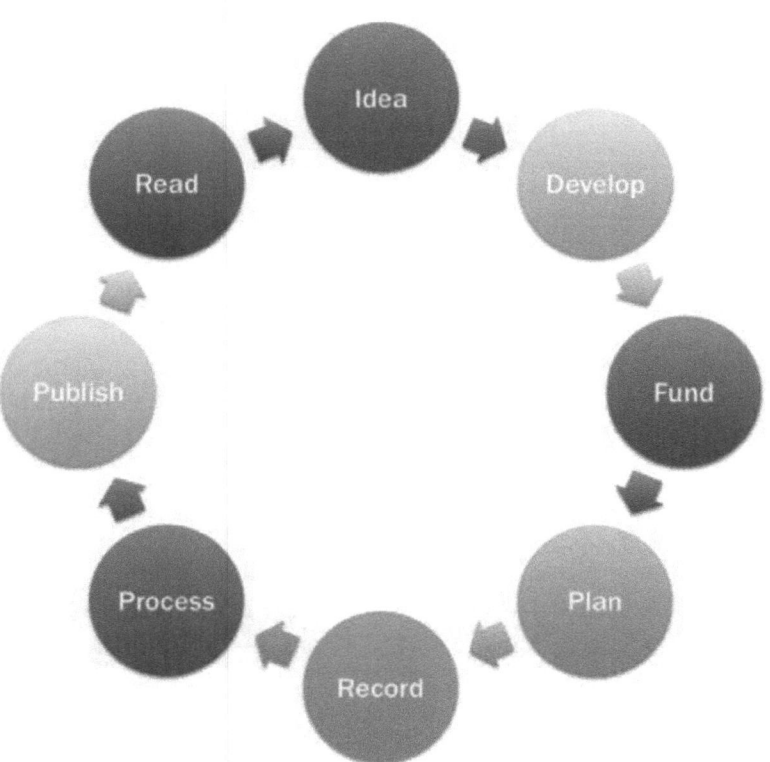

Figure 3.3

Typical elements of the scientific method, arranged in a cycle to emphasize the iterative nature of the research process. Image by Cameron Neylon is used under a CC-BY 2.0 license, available at https://commons.wikimedia.org/wiki/File:Research_cycle.png.

themselves to "traditional" services and to think of emerging areas of scholarly communication or academic librarianship where librarians can contribute to research.

Focusing on librarian scholarship, faculty support, and student support allows LIS students to have a complete understanding of the scholarly communication field within the academic librarianship domain. It gives them the grounding they need to succeed as academic or scholarly communication librarians and to effectively support research and learning communities. Equally important, the three areas give the library the visibility and presence on campus many academic libraries have lost with the shift to digital technology and services.

DISCUSSION QUESTIONS:

1. What would you need to gain tenure at an academic institution of your choice?
2. What kind of scholarly support activities would you provide to faculty at all levels to advance their scholarly endeavors?
3. What kind of scholarly activities would you provide to students at all levels to advance their scholarly endeavors?

INTERSECTIONS

THE RELATIONSHIP BETWEEN UNIVERSITY PRESSES AND ACADEMIC LIBRARIES

PAST, PRESENT, AND FUTURE

Annie Johnson

INTRODUCTION

University presses and academic libraries are two important pieces of the scholarly communication chain. Over the past twenty years, a number of university presses have started reporting to their university libraries, and we have seen a growing number of collaborative projects, mainly around digital and open access scholarship. At the same time, the perspectives of presses and libraries concerning the future of scholarly publishing can differ substantially. While the vast majority of scholarly communication librarians work at institutions without a university press, all librarians must understand the role of the university press and how that role intersects with the work they do around collections, open access, and library publishing. This intersection will primarily focus on university presses and academic libraries in the United States, although other countries will be mentioned.

FROM PARTNER TO CUSTOMER TO COLLABORATOR

From the earliest days of academic publishing, in the late nineteenth century, university presses and libraries were closely connected. The first director of Cornell University Press,

Daniel Williard Fiske, for example, was also the university librarian. As university presses professionalized in the mid-twentieth century, however, and began to publish more and more research from scholars outside of their home institution, this relationship shifted. Libraries were no longer just partners or affiliates with their home press, they were customers. Indeed, for many years, academic libraries were university presses' primary customers when it came to monographs. This started to change in the 1970s, when libraries were forced to devote more and more of their collections budget to purchasing expensive journals, primarily in the sciences, leaving less money for the purchase of monographs. This trend continued to accelerate in the 1980s and 1990s. Today, less than 25 percent of print books and 20 percent of e-books that libraries purchase come from university presses.[1]

Beginning in the 1990s, the digital revolution made it possible for libraries and presses to work together in new ways. Project MUSE, for example, began as a joint project between Johns Hopkins University Press and Johns Hopkins University Libraries in 1995.[2] Most recently, the Association of Research Libraries and AUPresses collaborated to launch the TOME (Toward an Open Monograph Ecosystem) initiative, where colleges and universities fund the costs of producing a monograph up front, and the monograph is then published open access. The idea behind TOME is to provide a path for sustainable open access publishing.[3] As more and more academic libraries have launched library publishing programs, this has opened up even more opportunities for presses and libraries to find joint projects to support the research output of their university. For example, a handful of university presses have started working with their university libraries to publish open access textbooks written by their faculty.[4]

PRESSES REPORTING TO LIBRARIES

Another way that the university press and library relationship has evolved is that a number of university presses now report to their library. Academic libraries now run the majority of the university presses in Germany and Australia. Purdue University was the first example of this in the United States, with the press reporting to the libraries in 1992. Penn State University and University of Michigan soon followed.[5] However, what this reporting relationship actually looks like varies from institution to institution, and presses and libraries face real challenges when trying to work together. Perhaps the biggest challenge is that both organizations operate under different financial constraints—the library is a budgeted service of the university, whereas most presses receive only a small stipend from their university and are generally expected to recover their costs.

Only a few institutions, including New York University, Northwestern University, and Temple University, have shared staff. At Northwestern, for example, Liz Hamilton is both the copyright librarian for the libraries and the intellectual property specialist for the press. At other institutions, press directors hold roles in the library as well. For example, the director of University of Michigan Press is also associate university librarian for publishing. Another example of a unique library/press relationship can be seen at the University of Cincinnati. There, instead of starting a library publishing program, the library launched a new university press that is based in the library.

With more university presses reporting to academic libraries than ever before, librarians should be mindful that the university press community often feels misunderstood by academic libraries. In fact, recently, some in the university press community have begun to question whether having presses report to libraries is actually a mistake. Wayne State University Press, for example, began reporting to the libraries in 2019. In 2020, three of the top employees of the press were fired without notice or explanation by the dean of libraries.

The press editorial board, authors, and members of the university press community mounted a campaign to reinstate these employees. The university eventually relented and hired back the employees. It also moved the reporting of the press back to the provost.[6] This event provoked outrage in the university press community. Although this is an extreme example, it is important to remember that libraries and university presses are not always on the same page when it comes to the future of scholarly publishing.

CONCLUSION

What is the future of the scholarly monograph? Should all monographs be open access? Should they be digital only? And how do we preserve them? These are questions that university presses and academic libraries should be tackling together, even if they do not always agree on the answer.

ADDITIONAL RESOURCES

Griffiths, Rebecca J., Matthew Rascoff, and Laura Brown. *University Publishing in Digital Age*. New York: Ithaka S+R, July 26, 2007. https://doi.org/10.18665/sr.22345.

Jagodzinski, Cecile M. "The University Press in North America: A Brief History." *Journal of Scholarly Publishing* 40, no. 1 (October 2008): 1–20. https://doi.org/10.1353/scp.0.0022.

Muccie, Mary Rose, Joe Lucia, Elliott Shore, Clifford Lynch, and Peter Berkery. *Across the Great Divide: Findings and Possibilities for Action from the 2016 Summit Meeting of Academic Librarians and University Presses with Administrative Relationships (P2L)*. Washington, DC: Association of Research Libraries, 2016. https://www.arl.org/resources/across-the-great-divide-findings-and-possibilities-for-action-from-the-2016-summit-meeting-of-academic-libraries-and-university-presses-with-administrative-relationships-p2l/.

DISCUSSION QUESTIONS

1. Which university presses do your faculty tend to publish with? What are these presses' policies when it comes to supporting open access?
2. Which university press books does your library order in print? Which are available only as e-books?
3. What are some new ways academic libraries and university presses could work together to advance scholarly communication?

NOTES

1. Katherine Daniel, Joseph J. Esposito, and Roger C. Schonfeld, *Library Acquisition Patterns* (New York: Ithaka S+R, January 29, 2019), https://doi.org/10.18665/sr.310937.
2. See Project MUSE, "The MUSE Story," https://about.muse.jhu.edu/about/story/.
3. See TOME, home page, https://www.openmonographs.org/.
4. See, for example, Shan C. Sutton and Faye Chadwell, "Open Textbooks at Oregon State University: A Case Study of New Opportunities for Academic Libraries and University Presses," *Journal of Librarianship and Scholarly Communication* 2, no. 4 (2014), https://doi.org/10.7710/2162-3309.1174.

5. See Charles Watkinson, "From Collaboration to Integration: University Presses and Libraries," *Getting the Word Out: Academic Libraries as Scholarly Publishers*, ed. Maria Bonn and Mike Furlough (Chicago: Association of College and Research Libraries, 2015), 83–112, http://hdl.handle.net/2027.42/113231.
6. See Claire Kirch, "Wayne State University Press Fires Three Senior Employees," *Publishers Weekly*, February 10, 2020, https://www.publishersweekly.com/pw/by-topic/industry-news/publisher-news/article/82387-wayne-state-university-press-fires-three-senior-employees.html; Claire Kirch, "Three Fired Employees Return to Work at Wayne State U Press," *Publishers Weekly*, February 24, 2020, https://www.publishersweekly.com/pw/by-topic/industry-news/publisher-news/article/82509-three-fired-employees-return-to-work-at-wayne-state-u-press.html.

BIBLIOGRAPHY

Daniel, Katherine, Joseph J. Esposito, and Roger C. Schonfeld. *Library Acquisition Patterns*. New York: Ithaka S+R, January 29, 2019. https://doi.org/10.18665/sr.310937.

Kirch, Claire. "Three Fired Employees Return to Work at Wayne State U Press." *Publishers Weekly*, February 24, 2020. https://www.publishersweekly.com/pw/by-topic/industry-news/publisher-news/article/82509-three-fired-employees-return-to-work-at-wayne-state-u-press.html.

———. "Wayne State University Press Fires Three Senior Employees." *Publishers Weekly*, February 10, 2020. https://www.publishersweekly.com/pw/by-topic/industry-news/publisher-news/article/82387-wayne-state-university-press-fires-three-senior-employees.html.

Project MUSE. "The MUSE Story." https://about.muse.jhu.edu/about/story/.

Sutton, Shan C., and Faye Chadwell. "Open Textbooks at Oregon State University: A Case Study of New Opportunities for Academic Libraries and University Presses." *Journal of Librarianship and Scholarly Communication* 2, no. 4 (2014). https://doi.org/10.7710/2162-3309.1174.

TOME. Home page, https://www.openmonographs.org/.

Watkinson, Charles. "From Collaboration to Integration: University Presses and Libraries." *Getting the Word Out: Academic Libraries as Scholarly Publishers*, edited by Maria Bonn and Mike Furlough, 83–112. Chicago: Association of College and Research Libraries, 2015. http://hdl.handle.net/2027.42/113231.

DEFINING COLLECTION DEVELOPMENT AS OPERATIONAL SCHOLARLY COMMUNICATION IN ACADEMIC LIBRARIES

Lindsay Cronk

INTRODUCTION: IT'S ABOUT MONEY

> Cash rules everything around me / CREAM, get the money / dollar dollar bill, y'all.
>
> —Wu-Tang Clan[1]

Let's begin here—collection strategy is about budgets and what they can accomplish.[2] Collection work is necessarily money work. We steward the collection by stewarding the budget—getting the best deals on access on behalf of our communities, based on their input and needs. We try to stretch that dollar as far as it will go. This is why, for many decades, cost savings was the central priority of any library worker negotiating any subscription.

But that needs to change. Collection work can and should be reframed to achieve a more open and equitable scholarly information ecosystem, to challenge the whiteness of collections, and to do more justice with our substantial resource investment. It can change by considering that work as operational scholarly communication.

As Matt Ruen was quoted earlier in this text, "We're alive during an ongoing revolution in the ways people create, share, and build upon information" (chapter 1.1, "Basics and Definitions"). That revolution has real costs, and those costs offer transformative opportunities for divestment in some established infrastructures and direct investment in creators and communities. The professionals best equipped to manage and collaborate in reframing library collections as a scholarly investment are the collection development and acquisitions professionals who have been managing this operational side of scholarly communication for the entire history of academic libraries.[3] Many of them are already doing so. To that end, this section explores the potential of this operational work of scholarly communication.

DEFINING OPERATIONAL SCHOLARLY COMMUNICATION IN ACADEMIC LIBRARIES

When we acknowledge collection development as operational scholarly communication, we embrace the power of that term's significant umbrella. In such an arrangement, collections are empowered to support nuanced investing that embraces considerations beyond cost. Integrating the work has transformative implications for connecting a beloved and well-understood foundational service, collection development, to directly supporting research and scholarship: scholarly communication. In making this connection, we move the entire organization of the library forward to a more aspirational and sustainable trajectory.

At the University of Rochester, we are developing a successful scholarly communication program by connecting libraries' established role of provisioning collections to our users as creators and consumers of knowledge. Library collections are engines for knowledge creation and access, and proactively expressing the connection of our work to the publication cycle is a practical and scalable means of building scholarly communication capacity in traditional library services.

This pivot has allowed us to invest in underserved and underrepresented scholarly communities—literally. We have used our collection budget to compensate and amplify previously overlooked voices. If having materials appear in a research library is a benchmark of scholarship—it is—then we can honor different ways of knowing and acknowledge their inherent value by bringing them into our collections. What if we acknowledged the tacit understanding that the presence of material in a library confers value? We have used our investment in collections as a proxy investment in scholars, but what if we actually directly invested in scholars? It will require such radical reinvestment to challenge the whiteness and homogeneity of scholarly publishing.[4]

EXAMPLE PROJECTS

The following three examples all constitute relatively inexpensive and straightforward efforts that move away from collecting what is published and toward seeking what is missing through commissioning materials that address absent resources, voices, and perspectives.[5]

PARTNERING WITH INDIGENOUS ARTISTS

As part of an effort to address a glaring gap of indigenous knowledge within our collections, particularly contributions from our neighbors, the Seneca people and the Turtle Clan of Western New York, we connected with them directly to support indigenous creators. The resulting commissions have so far included an original painting and an original performance, with all compensation going directly to the creators. We want to continue to expand this collaboration and collection.

Indigenous knowledge has traditionally been excluded from the scholarly record. By partnering with our community and seeking their knowledge in a respectful way that compensated them for their work, we avoided appropriation.

STUDENT CURATION PROJECTS

Representation within collections should be a primary consideration for acquisitions strategies. Who is in our collections and who does the collecting matters. We have partnered with student groups, including the Black Student Union, to empower them to actively select and curate collections. This shifts the collecting budget into community curation. Students even collected open resources, notably memes, adding an entirely new format to the collection.

DATA GRANTS

We established a small fund to support acquiring and creating data sets for undergraduate and graduate students. The students then add their work and data to open repositories. The scholarly record is expanding, and data is of increasing interdisciplinary value. By supporting data creation directly, we shifted our collection budget to embrace more than the traditional scholarly end product of a publication and the more traditional published scholar.

GUIDING QUESTIONS FOR OPERATIONAL SCHOLARLY COMMUNICATION EFFORTS

In approaching an integrated program, it helps to start with shared context and understanding. These questions can help ensure shared vocabulary and understanding that supports program success.

1. What collection initiatives supporting scholarly communication (including open access memberships and support) are already in place?
2. What processes in place within collections should be examined through a scholarly communication lens?
3. What latitude do the collection budget and process offer?
   a. Are there unrestricted endowments we can use?
   b. Are there unrestricted funds we can use?
   c. What caveats and reporting do we need to observe?
4. What are our immediate priorities for scholarly communication in this institution?
5. What are our long-term priorities?
6. What legacy collection processes should be evaluated and reframed in support of scholarly communication?

CONCLUSION: INVESTING IN A SUSTAINABLE FUTURE AND LIBRARY VALUES

Here's a question worth asking: Why aren't we further along in the revolution of scholarly communication? The barriers are simple and rooted in habit and tradition, established workflows, and expectations. Library budgets are under scrutiny, as is the content of our collections. These are the key challenges to reinvestment. Making allies, through a matrixed outreach and collection effort, is the only way to allow such changes to advance and be adopted as the norm.

With such integrated effort, operational scholarly communication efforts will prove successful and present a path forward for libraries that both honors our foundational strengths and aligns with a transformed future. We can create an essential link between what we have always done and where we hope to go. It is also the way we can finally put our money where our values are.

DISCUSSION QUESTIONS

1. Lindsay provides a great example of how scholarly communication is operationalized in roles that haven't always been considered scholarly communication roles (though that is changing). What other library roles might be similarly reconceived?
2. There have been some formal efforts to merge collections work into scholarly communication work, such as at MIT.[6] What are the costs and benefits of this model?
3. Lindsay asks, "Why aren't we further along in the revolution of scholarly communication?" What are the primary reasons, from your perspective?

NOTES

1. Wu-Tang Clan, "C.R.E.A.M." track 8 on *Enter the Wu-Tang (36 Chambers)*, Loud Records, 1994.
2. Peggy Johnson, *Fundamentals of Collection Development and Management*, 3rd ed. (London: Facet, 2014).
3. Alice Crawford, ed., *The Meaning of the Library* (Princeton, NJ: Princeton University Press, 2015).
4. April Hathcock and Susan Davis, "Racing to the Crossroads of Scholarly Communication: But Who Are We Leaving Behind?" *Serials Librarian* 74, no. 1–4 (2018): 49–53.
5. Hathcock and Davis, "Racing to the Crossroads."
6. Ellen Finnie, "Voting with Our Dollars: Making a New Home for the Collections Budget in the MIT Libraries," *Against the Grain* 28, no. 4 (September 2016): 90–92, https://dspace.mit.edu/handle/1721.1/105123.

BIBLIOGRAPHY

Crawford, Alice, ed. *The Meaning of the Library: A Cultural History*. Princeton, NJ: Princeton University Press, 2015.

Finnie, Ellen. "Voting with Our Dollars: Making a New Home for the Collections Budget in the MIT Libraries." *Against the Grain* 28, no. 4 (September 2016): 90–92. https://dspace.mit.edu/handle/1721.1/105123.

Hathcock, April, and Susan Davis. "Racing to the Crossroads of Scholarly Communication: But Who Are We Leaving Behind?" *Serials Librarian* 74, no. 1–4 (2018): 49–53.

Johnson, Peggy. *Fundamentals of Collection Development and Management*, 3rd ed. London: Facet, 2014.

Wu-Tang Clan. "C.R.E.A.M." Track 8 on *Enter the Wu-Tang (36 Chambers)*. Loud Records, 1994.

PARTNERSHIP BUILDING ACROSS SOCIAL MEDIA AND COPYRIGHT

AN EDITED CONVERSATION

Sarah Moczygemba and Perry Collins

Expertise in copyright and fair use informs a social media landscape dependent on reproduction and sharing; at the same time, social media itself offers channels to promote library services and resources around copyright. This edited conversation explores points of intersection in our work and emphasizes the ways in which we aim to model internal library partnerships that foster trust and mutual respect.

HOW DID WE COME TOGETHER? WHAT WERE OUR RESPECTIVE INTERESTS?

Perry: When I started my position, I was thinking about how I could build a brand around copyright literacy that would be engaging enough to capture attention at a large research university. I saw social media as one starting point to create content that could be repurposed multiple times for instruction and events.

Moxy: And I was really excited for you to get here because I'm more of a content creation person and needed help putting in place some guidelines and educating people working in our libraries about what we can and can't do on social media. There is a tendency to get what you need, post it, and go on. Libraries and librarians are good at thinking about copyright in an abstract sense or when talking to patrons. When library staff react to something or need something to post, they may not think through best practices.

Perry: Honestly, when I arrived, our social media program seemed like a well-oiled machine, and I was envisioning it primarily as a platform for outreach, but I began to think about it as a jumping-off point for conversations around copyright internally in our libraries, where almost everyone at some point will make use of social media. It helped me to have a hook to bring up challenges, such as understanding that just because images online are free doesn't mean they're open or reusable. We want to make sure our colleagues understand that without inflating the level of risk. Or when there is risk, how are we mitigating that by adding more context or referring to guidance from the field?

Moxy: I need to be the person who tells people no, but I always like to quickly pivot to a resource they can use instead. When we started working together, you really empowered me to say, "This option is better."

WHAT ARE SOME EXAMPLES OF SPECIFIC PROJECTS WE'VE WORKED ON TOGETHER?

Perry: Early on, you expressed interest in highlighting special events or weeks. It was helpful at the beginning of my job to say, "OK, everything is a little bit overwhelming, but I know I can target a specific week and come up with three posts." My goal is to reassure students but also to help them understand what might be different between applying copyright in a college classroom versus making material available online or in a job post-graduation.

Moxy: And also how to protect their own work. It goes both ways, because part of your job is to empower people to be creators who are able to intelligently put their materials online.

Perry: Yes, how can we remind students that they are not just users of content but also have their own copyrights? The real challenges come in trying to boil down something incredibly complex into a bite-sized snippet and in making copyright engaging and friendly. One idea we rolled out during Fair Use Week 2019 was Fair Use Gator (based on UF's mascot), which highlights what you actually *can* do with protected materials. This was a fun, simple example to illustrate fair use by taking tiny pieces of copyrighted material—magazine clippings—and quite literally transforming them into something new. I usually engage with social media through text and links, and I appreciated your expertise in developing a visual story from this behind-the-scenes creative process.

Moxy: I'm very pro showing behind-the-scenes. We're taking our audience into the kitchen of the libraries and sharing how things happen. We also codeveloped a copyright workshop internally, and that was a good example of bringing our colleagues into that kitchen and saying, "Here are the ingredients. These are the tools you have at your disposal. These are the things you probably should avoid, but when in doubt, these are some solid choices you can fall back on." Fewer issues have come up for library employees who create social media content since that workshop.

Perry: It was helpful for me to gather examples from our libraries where people have struggled, either where they are *not* showcasing our collections because they are afraid or where they are making higher risk choices. You gave some amazing examples—including memes—during this talk that were funny, which is an area where I struggle in my instruction.

Moxy: Meme culture is one of the most interesting parts of the internet, because you can see different cultures and trends captured in a brief moment. We did a meme contest last year, and you put together a great guide for students to help determine how fair use applies to their memes. One of the biggest challenges of my job is to take really serious topics that have a lot of depth and history and connect with people who are quickly scrolling through social media. Especially students, who we're trying to reach more than anyone else.

Perry: For the handout you mention, I had to sit down and think about what a meme really is and what makes for the best memes. As with traditional kinds of instruction or scholarship, the best examples are those that are taking a bit of material and transforming it in some way to add a different meaning. That's exactly the message I'm communicating to students about using images or quotations in a paper. Often, better practices around copyright go hand in hand with better pedagogical or scholarly practice.

Moxy: I put that handout everywhere as a starting point for those in my professional network to talk to their marketing teams or general counsel and ask, "Can we make this argument for fair use instead of being overly cautious?"

WHAT IS THE KEY TO A PRODUCTIVE COLLABORATION?

Perry: The biggest takeaway for me is making sure that anyone in this kind of partnership is really thinking about how to express respect, particularly around marketing and related areas that are sometimes undervalued.

Moxy: Part of what's made this partnership great is that we're both very curious and willing to talk through anything that comes up.

EXAMPLES OF OUR WORK

The University of Florida institutional repository offers access to an up-to-date collection of our collaborative work (https://hcommons.org/deposits/?tag=uf+copyright+and+social+media).

ADDITIONAL RESOURCES

These publications offer practical guidance in creating social media policies and in leveraging social media to promote a deeper understanding of copyright.

Burclaff, Natalie, and Catherine Johnson. "Developing a Social Media Strategy: Tweets, Pins, and Posts with a Purpose." *College and Research Libraries News* 75, no. 7 (July 2014): 366–69. https://doi.org/10.5860/crln.75.7.9156.

Thiede, Malina, and Jennifer Zerkee. "An Active Learning Approach to Teaching Copyright Essentials." In *Copyright Conversations: Rights Literacy in a Digital World*, edited by Sara R. Benson, 141–58. Chicago: Association of College and Research Libraries, 2019. https://summit.sfu.ca/item/18938.

DISCUSSION QUESTIONS

1. Brainstorm one example of how a student might apply fair use in a public, web-based project. How would you go about presenting this example in a social media post?
2. When using social media in a professional or educational context, who do you imagine as your intended audience?
3. Identify an item in a library or archive digital repository. Does it include copyright information? If it is in copyright, how might fair use apply if you were to use it in a social media post?

LIBRARY PUBLISHING AND COLLECTION DEVELOPMENT

ELIMINATING INFORMATION ASYMMETRY

Emma Molls

Keywords: collection development; publishing; economics; budgets

---

PAYING FOR MORE THAN ACCESS

Openly accessible information—specifically, the same type of information that libraries have, in the past, paid to access—has created the need for a high level of knowledge about open access in an area of librarianship that is not often considered within the realm of scholarly communication: collection development.[1] In recent years, libraries' collection development strategies have moved front and center in advancing open access goals, the most notable being the University of California's cancellation of the system's Elsevier subscription.[2]

California's Elsevier cancellation was not the result of the traditionally defined serials crisis,[3] in which the cost of the journal package was simply too high; the cancellation was a result of failed negotiations between the university and the publisher to reach a deal that would ultimately roll open access publishing charges for UC authors into the overall subscription costs paid by the university.[4]

Although California's would-be deal with Elsevier, referred to as *read-and-publish*, is still a novel arrangement between publishers and customers,[5] the strategy of using library collection dollars to directly pay for the publication of open access content is not. In 2010, SPARC published a guide for libraries and universities interested in designing and implementing funding sources to be used by campus researchers seeking to publish in open access journals.[6] These types of funds, sometimes called *open access* or *subvention funds*, rose in popularity in the five years that followed and often became a major part of the outreach message for scholarly communication librarians.[7] Read-and-publish deals and library-sponsored subvention funds pose the same question for library budgets: Can we use our dollars to pay for publishing rather than solely for access?

THE CHALLENGE OF APCS

For some academic journal publishers, *what* a library is paying for is less of a concern than *if* a library is paying. The current open access publishing environment is occupied by large, commercial publishers that have built empires on the subscription model. In 2017, Elsevier noted its role in open access as being "the second largest gold OA publisher" and that "our article publishing charges (APCs) remain at industry average."[8] Elsevier's place in open access publishing is a perfect illustration of what Dave Ghamandi describes as the "neoliberalization of open access,"[9] in short meaning that public goods (in this case, knowledge) have been sold off to private companies. Ghamandi directly addresses the use of article processing or publishing charges (APCs) as merely a market solution to a broken market, or says more specifically that the APC business model is simply a new name for the old subscription model.[10]

The rise of APCs, both in place of and alongside of subscription costs, has led to ongoing mathematical confusion around a very large question: What does it cost to publish an article? Elsevier's claim that the publisher's APCs are at industry average is backed by its own data putting the average Elsevier APC at $2,577.[11] Recognizing the role the free market plays in academic publishing, it is unlikely, even given the recent push from Europe-based Plan S to provide more transparency behind APC pricing,[12] that libraries will ever know a clear answer to "What does it cost to publish?" or even "How is our money spent?"

LEARNING FROM LIBRARY PUBLISHING

So what is a library to do? Open access journals are increasing in the portfolios of traditional publishers but depend on the APC business model, which compounds the price problems that subscription costs caused. Some libraries, in expanding their scholarly communication programs and in attempting to contribute to the creation of open access content, created library publishing programs. Ghamandi proposes a larger, cooperative approach to library publishing, one that would completely shift the resources and approach to scholarly publishing.[13] Library publishing programs are relatively new and are likely years away from shifting the academic publishing industry. However, these programs can provide libraries with an additional asset at the collection development negotiating table—actual information about the workings of the publishing industry.

For example, in the University of California's "Introductory Guide to the UC Model Transformative Agreement" (created after its high-profile negotiations with Elsevier in 2018–2019), UC lays out how to negotiate with publishers for what it calls the UC transformative model.[14] This model creates open access content authored by UC authors, the cost of which is a combination of a reading fee (a percentage of the former subscription fee) and a discounted APC. Both of these fees must be negotiated by the library with the publisher. The discounted APCs, UC notes, should be negotiated to a price that "protect[s] both the university and the publisher from undue economic risk."[15] In another portion of the toolkit, UC notes that data analytics play a large part in determining negotiation targets and that while using publisher-provided data, libraries should "perform …analyses to confirm or refute any data the publisher may provide."[16] Library publishers can assist in performing this type of analysis, ensuring that publisher-provided service prices match market price, thus helping reduce the current level of information asymmetry, which can hold libraries back from entering complicated negotiations as the University of California did.

Information asymmetry is the economic term for when one party has more information than the other party (typically, when the seller possesses greater knowledge than the buyer). Libraries do not know how much it costs to publish an article because libraries do not know what, specifically, is involved in publishing. Libraries with publishing programs are growing in-house knowledge of the digital publishing industry. For example, libraries publishing journals now have an understanding of costs associated with plagiarism-detection software, copyediting, and peer review management systems. Each of the costs is commonly paid for academic publishers and is, outside of library publishing programs, not a cost or service handled by the library. Library publishers, especially programs with modest budgets and staffing, also appreciate the labor that is involved in publishing, a perspective that is typically absent from libraries.

Figuring out what a fair APC ought to be should not be the single goal of involving library publishers in conversations of open access investments and collection development. However, as long as APCs continue to be a part of publishing models supported by academic publishers, libraries should be asking questions and making demands, just as is common practice when subscriptions are negotiated, and especially when libraries are signing read-and-publish deals. Library publishers can help.

PUTTING IT TOGETHER

Eliminating information asymmetry, to at least some extent, will help libraries navigate the confusing open access investment opportunities that are now commonplace in collection development. If the future of collection development is one of fewer subscriptions, it should also be one of more informed librarians when it comes to dollars spent.

ADDITIONAL RESOURCES

Copernicus Publications, JMIR Publications, MDPI, Ubiquity Press and Frontiers. "Current Transformative Agreements Are Not Transformative: Position Paper—For Full, Immediate and Transparent Open Access." In *Frontiers Science News* (blog), March 10, 2020. https://blog.frontiersin.org/2020/03/10/current-transformative-agreements-are-not-transformative/.

Farley, Ashley. "How Libraries and Funders Can Drive APC Transparency." *F1000* (blog), January 31, 2020. https://blog.f1000.com/2020/01/31/how-libraries-and-funders-can-drive-apc-transparency/.

Ghamandi, Dave, "Library Publishing for the 99%: Why Neoliberalism and Scholarly Publishing Need a Divorce." Presentation, Library Publishing Forum, Baltimore, MD, March 20–22, 2017. http://eprints.rclis.org/31122/.

Hinchliffe, Lisa Janicke. "Transformative Agreements: A Primer." *Scholarly Kitchen* (blog), April 23, 2019. https://scholarlykitchen.sspnet.org/2019/04/23/transformative-agreements/.

DISCUSSION QUESTIONS

1. What other insights could libraries gain from work being done with library publishing programs?

2. Elsevier is now a large open access publisher. What challenges might libraries encounter when negotiating for OA publishing with traditional subscription publishers?

3. Can you think of other examples of information asymmetry that libraries face?

4. Not all libraries agree that transformative agreements like the University of California's are the path forward for open access. What other ways might libraries contribute to creating more open access content?

NOTES

1. NASIG, "NASIG Core Competencies for Scholarly Communication Librarians," *NASIG Newsletter* 32, no. 5 (2017), https://tigerprints.clemson.edu/nasig/vol32/iss5/1.
2. Nisha Gaind, "Huge US University Cancels Subscription with Elsevier," *Nature*, February 28, 2019, upd. March 1, 2019, https://www.nature.com/articles/d41586-019-00758-x.
3. Judith M. Panitch and Sarah Michalak, "The Serials Crisis (A Whitepaper)" (Scholarly Communications Convocation, University of North Carolina at Chapel Hill, January 2005).
4. Gaind, "Huge US University."
5. Gaind, "Huge US University."
6. Greg Tananbaum, *Campus-Based Open-Access Publishing Funds*, ver. 1.0 (Washington, DC: SPARC, February 2010), https://sparcopen.org/wp-content/uploads/2016/01/oafunds-v1.pdf.
7. Greg Tananbaum, *North American Campus-Based Open Access Funds* (Washington, DC: SPARC, Fall 2014), https://sparcopen.org/wp-content/uploads/2016/01/OA-Fund-5-Year-Review.pdf.
8. Gemma Hersh, "Five Surprising Facts about Elsevier and Open Access," Elsevier, June 13, 2017, https://www.elsevier.com/connect/5-surprising-facts-about-elsevier-and-open-access.
9. Dave S. Ghamandi, "Liberation through Cooperation: How Library Publishing Can Save Scholarly Journals from Neoliberalism," *Journal of Librarianship and Scholarly Communication* 6, no. 2 (2018), https://doi.org/10.7710/2162-3309.2223.
10. Ghamandi, "Liberation through Cooperation."
11. Elsevier, "Pricing," accessed June 1, 2020, https://www.elsevier.com/about/policies/pricing.
12. European Science Foundation, "Price and Service Transparency Frameworks," archived content, accessed June 4, 2020, https://www.coalition-s.org/price-and-service-transparency-frameworks/.
13. Ghamandi, "Liberation through Cooperation."
14. University of California, "An Introductory Guide to the UC Model Transformative Agreement," Office of Scholarly Communication, accessed July 8, 2020, https://osc.universityofcalifornia.edu/uc-publisher-relationships/resources-for-negotiating-with-publishers/negotiating-with-scholarly-journal-publishers-a-toolkit/an-introductory-guide-to-the-uc-model-transformative-agreement/.
15. University of California, "Introductory Guide."
16. University of California, "The Role of Data Analytics," Office of Scholarly Communication, accessed July 9, 2020, https://osc.universityofcalifornia.edu/uc-publisher-relationships/resources-for-negotiating-with-publishers/negotiating-with-scholarly-journal-publishers-a-toolkit/the-role-of-data-analytics/.

BIBLIOGRAPHY

Elsevier. "Pricing." Accessed June 1, 2020. https://www.elsevier.com/about/policies/pricing.

European Science Foundation. "Price and Service Transparency Frameworks." Archived content. Accessed June 4, 2020. https://www.coalition-s.org/price-and-service-transparency-frameworks/.

Gaind, Nisha. "Huge US University Cancels Subscription with Elsevier." *Nature*, February 28, 2019, upd. March 1, 2019. https://www.nature.com/articles/d41586-019-00758-x.

Ghamandi, Dave S. "Liberation through Cooperation: How Library Publishing Can Save Scholarly Journals from Neoliberalism." *Journal of Librarianship and Scholarly Communication* 6, no. 2 (2018). https://doi.org/10.7710/2162-3309.2223.

Hersh, Gemma. "Five Surprising Facts about Elsevier and Open Access." Elsevier, June 13, 2017. https://www.elsevier.com/connect/5-surprising-facts-about-elsevier-and-open-access.

NASIG. "NASIG Core Competencies for Scholarly Communication Librarians." *NASIG Newsletter* 32, no. 5 (2017). https://tigerprints.clemson.edu/nasig/vol32/iss5/1.

Panitch, Judith M., and Sarah Michalak. "The Serials Crisis (A Whitepaper)." Scholarly Communications Convocation, University of North Carolina at Chapel Hill, January 2005.

Tananbaum, Greg. *Campus-Based Open-Access Publishing Funds: A Practical Guide to Design and Implementation*, ver. 1.0. Washington, DC: SPARC, February 2010. https://sparcopen.org/wp-content/uploads/2016/01/oafunds-v1.pdf.

———. *North American Campus-Based Open Access Funds: A Five-Year Progress Report*. Washington, DC: SPARC, Fall 2014. https://sparcopen.org/wp-content/uploads/2016/01/OA-Fund-5-Year-Review.pdf.

University of California. "An Introductory Guide to the UC Model Transformative Agreement." Office of Scholarly Communication. Accessed July 8, 2020. https://osc.universityofcalifornia.edu/uc-publisher-relationships/resources-for-negotiating-with-publishers/negotiating-with-scholarly-journal-publishers-a-toolkit/an-introductory-guide-to-the-uc-model-transformative-agreement/.

———. "The Role of Data Analytics." Office of Scholarly Communication. Accessed July 9, 2020. https://osc.universityofcalifornia.edu/uc-publisher-relationships/resources-for-negotiating-with-publishers/negotiating-with-scholarly-journal-publishers-a-toolkit/the-role-of-data-analytics/.

PUTTING COMMUNITY IN SCHOLARLY COMMUNICATION

PARTNERSHIPS WITH PUBLIC LIBRARIES

Anali Maughan Perry and Eric Prosser

INTRODUCTION

Although they have distinct missions, public libraries and academic libraries serve overlapping populations and can leverage their institutional strengths through collaboration. These diverse partnerships include sharing resources through consortia, joint-use libraries, and shared programming, such as introducing students to public library collections as resources for theses.[1] For the scholarly communication librarian, collaborating with public libraries provides opportunities to educate about the ethical and legal use of information, advocate for the promotion and use of open resources and pedagogies, and interact with communities, particularly in rural areas, that are traditionally underserved by academic libraries. We'll share two personal examples of the intersection between scholarly communication and public libraries.

SPEAKING TO LOCAL BUSINESSES

Durango, Colorado, is home to both Fort Lewis College and a patent and trademark resource center (PTRC) housed at the Durango Public Library.[2] In its rural location, Durango includes a number of traditionally underserved populations and is near the Southern Ute Reservation, the Ute Mountain Ute Reservation, and the Navajo Nation.

Partnerships between scholarly communication librarians and public patent and trademark librarians are naturally complementary. Scholarly communication librarians deal frequently with copyright questions, while the public librarians field questions about patent and trademark searching. While both are experienced in intellectual property research, neither provides legal advice to their patrons. Even in public libraries without PTRCs, many provide support for local businesses through a business librarian, who is often experienced in some level of patent and trademark searching.

Durango's PTRC librarian and I (Eric) were invited to speak about intellectual property issues to both the La Plata County Economic Development Alliance and the Durango

Chamber of Commerce. This required repackaging the standard academic presentation on copyright into language and examples appropriate for small business owners. The background discussion on copyright—definition, duration, bundle of rights—turned to asset management and how businesses create copyrighted material on a daily basis. Discussion of using copyrighted material legally and ethically—licensing, fair use, infringement, work-for-hire—morphed into talk about risk management strategies for businesses using copyrighted material, including examples of background music in restaurants, art and photos from the web being used for advertising, and work-for-hire issues with contractors hired by the businesses. By reshaping an academic copyright presentation into business terms, I was able to raise the awareness of copyright issues and provide outreach to a segment of the local community outside of the traditional realm of the scholarly communication librarian.

OPEN ACCESS 101 FOR STATE AND REGIONAL LIBRARY ASSOCIATION CONFERENCES

Public libraries serve as research centers for their communities, particularly serving K–12 students whose schools may not have libraries, media centers, or professional librarians on staff. In less densely populated areas of the country where there are fewer colleges and universities within a given geographic area, public libraries may also be the most available partners for broader scholarly communication initiatives.

In many states, the majority of attendees and presenters at local library association conferences are public library personnel simply because there are more public libraries than other types of libraries. While scholarly communication–related presentations are now common at academic library conferences, they are less so at conferences attended primarily by public libraries. As an active Arizona Library Association member who regularly attends the annual conference, I (Anali) can testify that no presentations had been given on any topic related to scholarly communication at any conference in the organization's history.

In order to address this gap, I submitted a presentation proposal entitled "Open Access 101" to the Arizona Library Association Annual Conference and indicated that it was intended for inclusion on the public library track. It was accepted, and the presentation was well received. That same year, I also copresented a slightly revised version of the same presentation to the Mountain Plains Library Association Annual Conference in South Dakota.

Both presentations provided a basic overview of open access: defining open access, types of open access content, current relevant legislative actions, searching for open access content, and ideas for advocacy. I gave examples of how open access to scholarly work would benefit specific user groups such as teachers, students, small businesses, patients, and hobby or citizen scientists. Finally, I suggested strategies for including open access content in public library collections and provided sample elevator pitches for different audiences. By adapting an open access presentation to a public library audience, I was able to raise awareness of the existence and usefulness of open access resources to library professionals across the state.

TAKEAWAYS

There are many possibilities for public libraries to benefit from open access and open education tools and resources. For example, public libraries can augment their collections and resources by

- including the Directory of Open Access Journals in database lists to increase the discovery of open journal resources;
- including open textbooks and other openly licensed works in public library catalogs;
- using Unpaywall or the Open Access button with ILL requests or on library computers to reduce access barriers for patrons; and
- incorporating journal quality indicators as part of information literacy or research instruction and reference assistance.

Similarly, academic libraries can incorporate scholarly communication issues into public services and programming by

- supporting community author groups (author rights outside of the context of academic publishing);
- educating business development groups on intellectual property issues and the legal and ethical use of information;
- empowering public/academic makerspace programming with copyright and intellectual property information; and
- intersecting with citizen science initiatives.[3]

While public libraries may not have the ability to have a scholarly communication expert on staff, partnering or consulting with their local university's or college's scholarly communication librarian for programming can benefit both parties. Partnering with public libraries can inspire academic librarians to think beyond serving their institutions to develop broader, inclusive goals of providing needed resources to everyone in their community. By leveraging public libraries' strong relationships with their communities, these partnerships allow us to expand the scholarly conversation to include more diverse experiences and viewpoints and truly promote the inclusiveness and egalitarianism that all libraries strive for.

ADDITIONAL RESOURCES

Carey, Elaine, and Raymond Pun. "Doing History: A Teaching Collaboration between St. John's University and the New York Public Library." *College and Research Libraries News* 73, no 3 (2012): 138–41. http://crln.acrl.org/index.php/crlnews/article/view/8721.

Engeszer, Robert J., William Olmstadt, Jan Daley, Monique Norfolk, Kara Krekeler, Monica Rogers, Graham Colditz, et al. "Evolution of an Academic–Public Library Partnership." *Journal of the Medical Library Association* 104, no. 1 (2016): 62–66. https://www.ncbi. nlm.nih.gov/pmc/articles/PMC4722645/.

Overfield, Daniel, and Coleen Roy. "Academic and Public Library Collaboration: Increasing Value by Sharing Space, Collections, and Services." Presentation, ACRL 16th National Conference, "Imagine, Innovate, Inspire," Indianapolis, IN, April 10–13, 2013. https://alair.ala.org/bitstream/handle/11213/18066/OverfieldRoy_Academic. pdf?sequence=1&isAllowed=y.

Richards, Maureen. "Stronger Together: Increasing Connections between Academic and Public Libraries." *Collaborative Librarianship* 9, no. 2 (2017): 135–58. https://digital-commons.du.edu/collaborativelibrarianship/vol9/iss2/10.

DISCUSSION QUESTIONS

1. Many times during presentations, audience members will ask for your opinion on specific situations. How does the audience for your presentation (public vs. academic) affect the opinions or advice that you give regarding intellectual property questions?
2. Can you think of a different example of a public library initiative that would benefit from scholarly communication–related advocacy?
3. What conflicting tensions or competing priorities exist between public libraries and academic libraries that might serve as obstacles to a partnership?
4. What do you think you could learn from partnering with your local public library?
5. What skills or knowledge could you provide that would benefit your local public library?

NOTES

1. Marmot Library Network, home page, https://www.marmot.org/; Phoenix Public Library, "South Mountain Community Library," https://www.phoenixpubliclibrary.org/locations/smcl.
2. US Patent and Trademark Office, "Patent and Trademark Resource Centers," https://www.uspto.gov/learning-and-resources/support-centers/patent-and-trademark-resource-centers-ptrcs.
3. Darlene Cavalier et al., eds. *The Librarian's Guide to Citizen Science* (Tempe: Arizona State University Library, February 2019), https://s3-us-west-2.amazonaws.com/orrery-media/misc/CitSci_Librarians_Guide_02_22_r1.pdf.

BIBLIOGRAPHY

Cavalier, Darlene, Caroline Nickerson, Robin Salthouse, and Dan Stanton, eds. *The Librarian's Guide to Citizen Science: Understanding, Planning, and Sustaining Ongoing Engagement in Citizen Science at Your Library*. Tempe: Arizona State University Library, February 2019. https://s3-us-west-2.amazonaws.com/orrery-media/misc/CitSci_Librarians_Guide_02_22_r1.pdf.

Marmot Library Network. Home page. https://www.marmot.org/.

Phoenix Public Library. "South Mountain Community Library." https://www.phoenixpubliclibrary.org/locations/smcl.

US Patent and Trademark Office. "Patent and Trademark Resource Centers." https://www.uspto.gov/learning-and-resources/support-centers/patent-and-trademark-resource-centers-ptrcs.

LIBRARIANS OPENING UP OPEN EDUCATION

A UNIVERSITY, COMMUNITY COLLEGE, AND PUBLIC LIBRARY PARTNERSHIP TO INCREASE OER USAGE IN TEXAS

Carrie Gits, Natalie Hill, and Colleen Lyon

BACKGROUND

UT Libraries (UTL) is uniquely positioned at the University of Texas at Austin to promote and assist with the adoption and usage of open educational resources (OER) by university students and faculty. However, UTL is not well situated to connect these resources to the broader public beyond the university campus. From a 2019 statewide survey, we know that 38 percent of responding academic libraries have an open education program.[1] As academic librarians, we wanted to find a way to partner with Austin Public Library (APL) and create an open education program with the potential to dramatically expand our reach, bridge the gap between academic and public libraries, and potentially save students thousands of dollars over their academic careers.

Building on our shared goal of increased information access, UTL partnered with APL in 2019 to promote the use of OER in the greater Austin community. Through this partnership, we have learned that the primary groups in greater Austin likely to use OER include teachers from Austin Independent School District (ISD) and Del Valle ISD, Austin Homeschool Network, and individuals who come to APL for workforce and economic development trainings. We have also identified gaps in our collective experience, primarily in terms of assisting with workforce and economic development, that have led to the extension of our partnership to include Austin Community College (ACC)—a leader in OER programs—in this important work. Going forward, we are excited to harness the talent and expertise that each library brings to the table to best serve our community.

GOALS

Goals for this pilot program have been driven primarily by the needs and desires of APL. These goals include increased awareness of OER among high school students and their families, as well as school librarians, guidance counselors, and teachers. APL's reference staff will be trained by UTL and ACC librarians to provide a working knowledge of open educational principles and resources for use in reference interactions, educator in-service training, and college readiness programming.

Early exposure to OER can broaden the understanding of how to take advantage of financial savings that increase access to higher education, especially for first-generation college students.[2] Working with APL college readiness staff, we want to expand this level of knowledge to first-generation applicants and their families, allowing these students to enter college already aware of affordable learning materials. That knowledge can help them advocate for greater use of OER by their instructors and at the very least can provide them with supplemental materials that they can use to enhance their learning.

For instructors, we aim to highlight the open licenses that make OER customizable for specific courses. School librarians and teachers are already using freely available resources in their instruction. A recent study by ISKME surveyed school librarians in several states and found that school librarians are also adapting, evaluating, and re-sharing those materials.[3] We hope our training helps Austin ISD and Del Valle ISD librarians and faculty be more intentional about their use of OER to supplement required curriculum.

IMPLEMENTATION AND EVALUATION

UTL received a grant in fall 2019 from the Tocker Foundation funding an open education librarian position at UTL for five years. The Tocker Foundation is an Austin-based philanthropic organization primarily focused on supporting and improving resources and services in rural Texas libraries.[4] The Tocker open education librarian will start in August 2020 and will take over the open education program at UTL, including serving as the lead facilitator of this collaboration with ACC and APL. Using the APL partnership as a pilot program, UTL hopes to expand this train-the-trainer model of OER education to public libraries across the wider state in line with the goals of the Tocker Foundation's grant.

One key aspect of the collaboration is training and awareness for public librarians. Together with ACC, UTL will colead workshops to train APL librarians on OER so they can start offering them in their list of resources and services. This training and information sharing has the potential to serve thousands in the Austin community who come to APL for research help. To further these efforts, UTL, APL, and ACC would colead additional targeted workshops for local school district staff.

The first workshop, Open Educational Resources: What's Your Role?, was held February 21, 2020, at APL as part of its systemwide staff development day.[5] Librarians from UTL and ACC provided a workshop and conversation that served as an introduction to OER.[6] The workshop not only defined OER and open licenses, but also provided a brief overview of the diversity of searching platforms and outlined the Texas legislative landscape surrounding OER. A significant piece of the presentation focused on the crucial roles librarians have in OER work, with an emphasis on a librarian's professional commitment to equitable access to information and resources for all users. The objective was to help public librarians identify their role in OER. It is the public librarians' strong relationships with various student and parent communities that positions them to become advocates, educators, curators, and creators of OER. Participants walked away from this initial workshop with a broader understanding of OER and the roles public libraries and librarians have in awareness and use of these resources.

Our intention was to offer more intensive training during the summer to help APL librarians ramp up for the start of the 2020–2021 academic year. The COVID-19 pandemic presents both a unique opportunity to promote OER and significant complications to outreach efforts. With all Austin area libraries closed, it's unlikely that in-person training will be possible. One idea to keep this collaboration moving forward is to adapt the ACC Learn OER resource for use by public and school librarians, allowing for an online option to learn more about OER.[7]

Our goal over the course of the Tocker Foundation grant is to reach all the reference librarians within APL and by extension the faculty and staff associated with local school districts and homeschool networks, as well as high schoolers and their families who come to APL for college readiness programming and FAFSA preparation.

FUTURE PLANS

To extend this cross-training to librarians across Texas and increase OER awareness and engagement among rural public libraries, we will seek out two or three annual conference presentation opportunities, in addition to exploring virtual learning opportunities. Lessons learned from the partnership among UTL, APL, and ACC will guide future public library programming and outreach efforts.

DISCUSSION QUESTIONS

1. How does the cross-institutional collaboration described above advance the goals of each participating organization?
2. The authors refer to the "Texas legislative landscape surrounding OER"; what is that landscape, and what does it mean for librarians working to advance OER in Texas?
3. How can collaboration across institutional or organizational boundaries result in better projects and outcomes?

NOTES

1. C. Jimes et al., *Open Educational Resources (OER) in Texas Higher Education* (Austin: Digital Higher Education Consortium of Texas and Texas Higher Education Coordinating Board; Half Moon Bay, CA: Institute for the Study of Knowledge Management in Education, 2019), https://reportcenter.thecb.state. tx.us/reports/reports-and-studies-non-fiscal/oer-texas/.
2. DeeAnn Ivie and Carolyn Ellis, "Advancing Access for First-Generation College Students: OER Advocacy at UT San Antonio," in *OER: A Field Guide for Academic Librarians*, ed. Andrew Wesolek, Jonathan Lashley, and Anne Langley (Forest Grove, OR: Pacific University Press, 2018), 213–38.
3. Institute for the Study of Knowledge Management in Education, "Exploring OER Curation and the Role of School Librarians," *ISKME* (blog), 2017, https://www.iskme.org/our-work/ exploring-oer-curation-and-role-school-librarians.
4. Tocker Foundation, "About the Tocker Foundation," https://tocker.org/about/.
5. Carrie Gits and Hannah Chapman Tripp, "Open Educational Resources: What's Your Role?" (presentation, Austin Public Library Staff Development Day, February 21, 2020), https://doi.org/10.26153/tsw/7110.
6. Gits and Tripp, "Open Educational Resources."
7. Carrie Gits, ACC Learn OER, online course, Austin Community College, https://sites.google.com/austincc. edu/acclearnoer.

BIBLIOGRAPHY

Gits, Carrie. "ACC Learn OER." Online course. Austin Community College. https://sites.google.com/austincc. edu/acclearnoer.

Gits, Carrie, and Hannah Chapman Tripp. "Open Educational Resources: What's Your Role?" Presentation, Austin Public Library Staff Development Day, February 21, 2020. https://doi.org/10.26153/tsw/7110.

Institute for the Study of Knowledge Management in Education. "Exploring OER Curation and the Role of School Librarians." ISKME (blog), 2017. https://www.iskme.org/our-work/exploring-oer-curation-and-role-school-librarians.

Ivie, DeeAnn, and Carolyn Ellis. "Advancing Access for First-Generation College Students: OER Advocacy at UT San Antonio." In *OER: A Field Guide for Academic Librarians*, edited by Andrew Wesolek, Jonathan Lashley, and Anne Langley, 213–38. Forest Grove, OR: Pacific University Press, 2018.

Jimes, C., A. Karaglani, L. Petrides, J. Rios, J. Sebesta, and K. Torre. *Open Educational Resources (OER) in Texas Higher Education. Austin: Digital Higher Education Consortium of Texas and Texas Higher Education Coordinating Board; Half Moon Bay, CA: Institute for the Study of Knowledge Management in Education, 2019.* https://reportcenter.thecb.state.tx.us/reports/reports-and-studies-non-fiscal/oer-texas/.

Tocker Foundation. "About the Tocker Foundation." https://tocker.org/about/.

BRIDGING SCHOLARLY COMMUNICATION AND DATA SERVICES

INTERSECTIONS IN OPENNESS AND SHARING

Erin Jerome and Thea Atwood

INTRODUCTION

Institutional repositories (IRs) play an important role in equitable access to scholarship and formed the early backbone of scholarly communication departments. As a result, IR managers are well aware of available repository platforms and their infrastructures (e.g., DSpace and Digital Commons), as well as best practices for sharing research openly (e.g., licensing, versioning, and metadata). These features are aspects of information management that facilitate end users' accessing and sharing of information. IR managers oversee what is often the institution's primary platform for sharing research outputs generated by its campus community.

Data librarians (a nascent category of librarians that includes titles such as *data librarian*, *data services librarian*, *data management librarian*, *reproducibility librarian*, and *data curator*, to name just a few; heretofore *data services* or *data services librarianship*) play an important role in managing research, with an end goal of improving stewardship of data. By working to improve management of research products (like data) at the beginning of a project, sharing those products at the end of a project can be streamlined. Data services librarianship has long focused on the foundational elements of born-digital research: file-naming conventions, file hierarchies, and nonproprietary data formats are important components of our educational platforms.

The push for open data by researchers, publishers, and governments has resulted in a unique overlapping, or intersection, of these two formerly distinct library disciplines. While the overlaps between scholarly communication and data services appear obvious to the authors, data issues are rarely mentioned on scholarly communication– and IR-focused e-mail discussion lists. Just as researchers are now presented with a plethora of unique platforms through which they can share their writing (discipline-specific preprint repositories, academically inclined social media sites like Academia.edu, university websites, etc.), the same can be said about data-sharing possibilities. IRs provide an opportunity for universities to showcase all of their scholarly content in one place, including data. Even if the IR is not the right fit for a campus's data, IR managers can provide data services librarians and departments with insight into best practices for making research objects openly available.

OPEN ACCESS PUBLISHING OF RESEARCH-RELATED MATERIALS AND INTERSECTIONS

For librarians, open access publishing has been widely accepted as the best possible means of breaking down the barriers to accessing current research, and, until recently, the focus has primarily been on the finished research objects (e.g., journal articles, book chapters, or entire monographs). Yet while many of the sciences have embraced open access publishing as a way of life for these research objects, the idea of sharing data is relatively recent. There is something really magical about reading an article and knowing that its supporting data is just one mouse click away, be that through a digital object identifier (DOI) or another URL.

Making data openly available is not without its own complexities, but in contrast to sharing manuscripts, data has experienced fewer barriers to sharing. This is likely due to data operating outside of the boundaries of traditional, manuscript-based metrics of scholarship. Publishers have, until recently, paid only passing attention to data, largely sequestering data in a supplemental section of an article. While supplemental data is one way of sharing data, lack of robust metadata, documentation, and licenses, and poor guidance on file formats* negatively impact the data's findability and reuse.

As open data and research-related materials gain momentum, IR managers can provide recommendations about metadata, controlled vocabulary, repository policies, and open licensing. This expertise can help bridge the gap in guidance. This includes changing the mentality of data management to something that occurs throughout the entirety of a project and not just at article submission or project closeout. Preparing data for deposit has largely occurred at the end of a project, after memory has decayed, and the contextual information required to appropriately interpret data is often locked in (and lost to) the memories of the researchers who collected the data.

Just as librarians want to help our researchers retain their rights to their published works, we want to ensure the same remains true for their data. By collaborating across departments to create local repositories, or referring researchers to already existing independent repositories (e.g., arXiv), we are ensuring that their work will not get scooped up by publishers or other vendors as part of the purchase of a particular tool or platform.

OPPORTUNITIES FOR COLLABORATIVE GROWTH

While institutional repositories are not the perfect fit for every single data set, IR managers also have insight into most basic repository platform infrastructures and, occasionally, their limitations. At the same time, data services librarians can inform repository managers about their platform-specific needs when it comes to sharing data.

When the authors collaborated to build a data repository within their institution's IR, ScholarWorks@UMass Amherst, they realized that they could learn a lot from one another. What did ScholarWorks, which runs on the Digital Commons platform, do out of the box that would support hosting data? What kind of requirements did open data have that differed

---

* E.g., *Blood* asks for supplementary data to be uploaded as a single PDF (*Blood*, "Supplemental Data," https://ashpublications.org/blood/pages/supplemental-data). PDFs are largely considered as a poor format for purposes of reuse because you cannot easily extract information from tables, for example.

from sharing finished research objects like theses, dissertations, journal articles, and so on? What metadata requirements did data have? Because data repositories are a relatively new tool when compared with print-based IRs, the authors worked together to build off of each other's areas of expertise to create a tool that best met their shared needs.

SHARED CHALLENGES IN IMPLEMENTING SERVICES

Scholarly communication and data services ask faculty to be vulnerable in unprecedented ways: we ask their papers and data to be made openly available to the public. While scholarly articles have long been made available to a small cohort of peers, data has largely been excluded from discourse or peer review, and both forms of scholarship have largely been unavailable en masse to the public. We see a critical intersection of opposition from faculty in terms of buy-in, misunderstanding and misinformation, fear, and reluctance to change promotion and tenure standards.

UNITED FRONT TO EFFECT CHANGE

A unified front between these two areas of librarianship can improve our research and the strength of our open access and open research agendas.

Collaborating across scholarly communications and research data services will have a greater impact on the entirety of the research life cycle and will allow us to touch on projects at their beginnings and ends, and as a result help facilitate the aims of scholarly inquiry—to better society through investigation.

ADDITIONAL RESOURCES

Digital Science. *The State of Open Data 2019*. London: Digital Science, 2019. https://doi.org/10.6084/m9.figshare.9980783.v2.

Fenner, Martin, Mercè Crosas, Jeffrey S. Grethe, David Kennedy, Henning Hermjakob, Phillippe Rocca-Serra, Gustavo Durand, et al. "A Data Citation Roadmap for Scholarly Data Repositories." *Scientific Data* 6 (2019): article 28. https://doi.org/10.1038/s41597-019-0031-8.

Johnston, Lisa R. "Data Discovery: The Role of Academic Institutional Data Repositories." Slides from presentation, "Establishing a FAIR Biomedical Data Ecosystem: The Role of Generalist and Institutional Repositories to Enhance Data Discoverability and Reuse," Bethesda, MD, February 11–12, 2020. https://conservancy.umn.edu/handle/11299/211664.

DISCUSSION QUESTIONS

1. How can librarians in data services and scholarly communication work with those outside of their subfield to improve their reach?
2. What are some issues that you see facing scholarly communication and data services?

3. How can be mitigated by librarians?
4. How do we help faculty, and others, be unafraid of change and the open access and open data movements?

CASE STUDIES

SO YOU HAVE AN OPEN ACCESS POLICY—NOW WHAT?

EVALUATING SIMON FRASER UNIVERSITY'S OPEN ACCESS POLICY

Alison Moore and Jennifer Zerkee

THE SFU CONTEXT

Simon Fraser University (SFU) is a comprehensive, doctoral-granting university in Burnaby, BC, Canada, with 23,000 FTE students. Simon Fraser University Library employs approximately thirty-five librarians in non-administrative, public service roles. Librarians are organized in divisions across three campus libraries and include subject specialists as well as functional specialists dedicated to activities such as data services, scholarly communication, the makerspace, and digital humanities.

THE SFU OPEN ACCESS POLICY

In January 2017, following sixteen months of campus-wide consultation, SFU Senate endorsed the SFU Open Access Policy (OA Policy). The OA Policy acknowledges the commitment of faculty, students, and postdoctoral fellows to sharing the products of their research with the broadest possible audience, including other scholars, practitioners, policy-makers, and the public at large.[1] The OA Policy calls upon SFU researchers to deposit their authored and co-authored scholarly articles in Summit, SFU's institutional research repository.

In late 2019, we were asked to conduct a three-year review of the OA Policy, with the intention of producing a three-page report. While we had both worked with open access initiatives and resources in the library for some time (including between us our institutional repository Summit, the SFU Open Access Fund, and copyright and digital scholarship support), neither of us was involved in the development or implementation of the OA Policy in 2017. We worked on this review in collaboration with our associate dean of libraries, collections, and scholarly communication.

OUR POLICY REVIEW PROCESS

When we were asked to review the policy, we thought we knew what that meant—but in hindsight we could have asked for more guidance on the expectations for this process. For example, was this a general update on the progress and outcomes of the policy, or were we expected to make recommendations of some kind? And if recommendations were expected, did that include the possibility of large-scale overhauls or even reconsideration of the policy itself, or just smaller suggestions such as changes to workflow or outreach activities?

We determined that this review was intended to be more reflective than evaluative, so we began from a position that took for granted that working toward openness is a valuable endeavor. This led us to adopt a SOAR approach, which considers the strengths, opportunities, aspirations, and results of an initiative. This approach is grounded in appreciative inquiry, a framework that "begins by identifying what is positive" in an organization.[2] SOAR is designed to be a "constructive and optimistic" framework, as opposed to the "negative and competitive" SWOT analysis.[3] To this end we reflected not only on the policy itself but also on supports such as our institutional repository Summit and our Open Access Fund (OA Fund), as well as the outreach and education that we do around open access generally. This approach helped us to identify a broader variety of strengths and successes than data specific to the OA Policy alone would have. For example, we consider it a key strength that open access–related support happens across library divisions and involves numerous librarians and staff members in areas including not only scholarly communication but also copyright, collections, data services, Summit, the Public Knowledge Project,[*] and liaisons to both academic departments and external communities.

We looked beyond SFU in order to situate our participation in open access more broadly: within Canada first, because SFU was one of the first of a small but growing number of Canadian institutions with an institution-wide open access policy,[†] and then of course within the international open access landscape.

We reviewed the communications and outreach activities that took place around the policy's implementation in 2017 and since and looked at responses to feedback mechanisms put in place in 2017. Hearing from our community and incorporating such qualitative data in our review was extremely important to us, so we also actively sought comments from SFU researchers about the policy and related supports and initiatives.

Because the OA Policy did not have an implementation plan or specific goals developed at implementation, we had to think about the best ways to assess its successes: How could we measure uptake of the policy without the capacity for a large-scale survey or interviews with researchers? We determined that using our OA Fund and repository deposit statistics as proxy measures would provide the closest related data points. We looked at the number of articles

---

[*] The Public Knowledge Project, https://pkp.sfu.ca/, supported by SFU, is a collaborative project across multiple universities which develops free open-source software for open publishing, including Open Journal Systems (OJS) and Open Monograph Press (OMP).

[†] As of May 6, 2020, the Coalition of Open Access Policy Institutions (COAPI), https://sparcopen.org/coapi/members/, lists only four Canadian institutions as full members.

funded by the OA Fund from one year before the policy was implemented through the most recent year and the number of articles and book chapters deposited to Summit for the same period. While these proxies are not perfect substitutes for data about compliance with (or awareness of) the policy itself, substantial increases in the use of both services satisfied us that, at the very least, general awareness of and engagement with open at SFU has increased in tandem with outreach efforts related to the policy.

Our resulting report went to the dean of libraries for review and then was presented at a meeting of the university's Senate Library Council, where we addressed questions and collected feedback from faculty representatives. Following this faculty input, we finalized the report, and it was presented to SFU Senate. The final report is now available on the library's website and SFU's institutional repository Summit.[4]

TAKE-AWAYS AND TIPS

Here are some things we wish we had determined before embarking upon our policy review and the take-aways we recommend for others engaging in a similar review:

- *Understand your role in the policy review.* Where do you have the opportunity to make decisions? When do you need to go to someone else (such as administrators) for decisions? Can you ask colleagues for support (e.g., assistance with retrieving statistics)?
- *Find out who the key stakeholders are.* Are they all located in the library, or across campus departments and offices? Will they be consulted in some way, asked for feedback, or just presented with the final report? Who will need to see the report and at what stages? Who will need to sign off on it before it is finalized?
- *Determine the purpose and expected outcomes of the policy review.* Are recommendations expected? Is the policy itself open for reconsideration? The outcomes may be up to you (e.g., if you are at a smaller institution) or may come from administrators or other stakeholders.
  - Was there an implementation plan? Can this guide the review?
  - Are there different expectations at different organizational levels (e.g., internal recommendations for the library separate from the public-facing report)?
- *Consider whether an existing framework would be useful (e.g., SOAR, SWOT).* Is there one that suits the goals of your review?
- *Determine what data is relevant and useful.*
  - Consider both the short term in the context of your review and the longer term to inform future initiatives related to the policy.
  - Consider quantitative as well as qualitative types of data.
  - If you collect or capture researcher testimonials, request permission to quote them in promotion, publication, and other potential additional uses.
- *Survey the landscape to situate the policy within the institution, the scholarly landscape, and the broader community.*

Addressing these questions will provide an outline to guide the policy review. These answers will also help to keep momentum going around promotion of the policy and related services and provide measures for assessment to identify successes and gaps going forward. This outline and the resulting review will provide continuity for staff assessing or updating the policy in the future and can provide evidence for increasing support or developing related services.

DISCUSSION QUESTIONS

1. What factors might influence a decision to use a framework and selection of an appropriate framework to guide a policy review?
2. What kinds of evidence (both quantitative and qualitative) might inform a policy review? How could these be planned for and collected in a proactive way?
3. Who might the stakeholders be for a similar policy review at a small, medium, or large institution? Who or what could help you determine who they are?

NOTES

1. Simon Fraser University Library, "SFU Open Access Policy," last modified October 2019, https://www.lib.sfu.ca/help/publish/scholarly-publishing/open-access/open-access-policy (requires SFU login).
2. David Cooperrider, Diana D. Whitney, and Jacqueline M. Stavros, *Appreciative Inquiry Handbook*, 2nd ed. (Brunswick, OH: Crown Custom Publishing, Inc., 2008), xv.
3. Jill Zarestky and Catherine S. Cole, "Strengths, Opportunities, Aspirations, and Results: An Emerging Approach to Organization Development," *New Horizons in Adult Education and Human Resource Development* 29, no. 1 (2017): 6, https://doi.org/10.1002/nha3.20166.
4. Patty Gallilee, Ali Moore, and Jennifer Zerkee, *Report on the SFU Open Access Policy* (Burnaby, BC: SFU Library, 2020), http://summit.sfu.ca/item/20041.

BIBLIOGRAPHY

Cooperrider, David, Diana D. Whitney, and Jacqueline M. Stavros. *The Appreciative Inquiry Handbook: For Leaders of Change*, 2nd ed. Brunswick, OH: Crown Custom Publishing, Inc., 2008.

Gallilee, Patty, Ali Moore, and Jennifer Zerkee. *Report on the SFU Open Access Policy*. Burnaby, BC: Simon Fraser University Library, 2020. https://summit.sfu.ca/item/20041.

Simon Fraser University Library. "SFU Open Access Policy." Last modified October 2019. https://www.lib.sfu.ca/help/publish/scholarly-publishing/open-access/open-access-policy (requires SFU login).

Zarestky, Jill, and Catherine S. Cole. "Strengths, Opportunities, Aspirations, and Results: An Emerging Approach to Organization Development." *New Horizons in Adult Education and Human Resource Development* 29, no. 1 (2017): 5–19. https://doi.org/10.1002/nha3.20166.

FAILURE IS AN OPTION!

WHAT WE CAN LEARN FROM UNSUCCESSFUL SCHOLARLY COMMUNICATION INITIATIVES

Carla Myers

Too often, the failure of a scholarly communication initiative is viewed as an unacceptable outcome, with negative personal and professional implications for those who were supporting it. Realistically, it is impossible for every initiative we pursue to be successful, and expectations placed upon a scholarly communication program that indicate otherwise are unrealistic, unachievable, and likely to inhibit the creativity and initiative of those who support this important work. We should be ashamed of failure only if it results from a true lack of effort, either as an individual or an institution, toward seeing an initiative succeed. Often, though, this is not the case. Many failures come about as a result of internal and external influences that were not properly identified, addressed, or resolved when planning and executing an initiative, and while these situations are frustrating, if viewed in the right context they provide an opportunity for reflection, change, and ensuring future successes.

WHAT WENT RIGHT?

It is rare for an initiative to produce no results whatsoever, and it is important to identify successes that did result from our efforts. For example, perhaps only three people may participate in a workshop offered on Creative Commons licensing, when least thirty participants were expected. The low attendance may be disappointing, but if the participants left with an understanding of what these licenses are and how they can be used—an understanding they put into practice by openly licensing works they create—then the effort should not be seen as a failure. Here, reframing perspective to focus on session outcomes rather than attendance numbers helps us identify what went right with the initiative.

WHAT WENT WRONG?

While celebrating small victories is important, staff do need to identify why a scholarly communication initiative failed to meet established goal or produce expected outcomes. This is especially important if a significant amount of resources invested in the initiative (e.g., staff time, money, space, supplies) did not provide a satisfactory return for the institution. Questions to ask include

- Was the initiative not properly tailored to meet the needs of the campus community? Too often, scholarly communication initiatives are pursued because they are on trend in the profession or because other institutions are having success with them, but what works well at one institution may not be a good fit for another. For example, research impact services may readily find traction at an R1 institution but not see much engagement at an institution that focuses more on teaching than research.
- Did the team supporting the initiative have access to adequate supplies, technology, and funding given the scope of the initiative? A lack of resources can make it difficult to effectively launch and administer any scholarly communication project or program.
- Was there a breakdown in communication or collaboration among the team supporting the initiative? This should not be seen as an exercise in assigning blame. Rather, team members should try to identify why they were unable to act as a cohesive unit in supporting the initiative.
- Was there a failure to effectively market the initiative to those it was intended to serve? If the target audience does not understand the scope and intent of an initiative, they are not likely to engage with it. For instance, a workshop on the Technology, Education and Copyright Harmonization (TEACH) Act may be useful for faculty teaching online classes, but if they are unfamiliar with the purpose of the statute and options it provides for sharing copyrighted works online with students, they are unlikely to attend.
- Did some key piece of information the team missed during the planning process result in gaps or redundancies in services that could have contributed to the failure? If the scholarly communication team launches a data analytics and visualization service, but it is narrow in scope or duplicates services offered by another department, the library's services are not likely to gain traction on campus.
- Was the timing right to launch the initiative? For example, was an initiative to get faculty to adopt OER (open educational resource) launched during the winter break, when their focus is on transitioning from the fall semester to the spring semester, rather than in early spring, when they might be thinking about what textbook they will use in the fall?

WHO WAS (AND WAS NOT) REPRESENTED?

It is also important to consider if the right people were involved in the planning process. For example, were other employees in the library, such as subject librarians, invited to get involved to provide input and promote the initiative to their faculty and students? Were there individuals or departments on campus who could have contributed knowledge and expertise to the initiative or been able to invest resources (e.g., time, staff, technology, or funding) to help ensure its success?

Team members should also ask who might have been left out of the planning process. Was the right audience targeted by the library in marketing the initiative? For example, was an instructional session on text and data mining offered to faculty, but not graduate students? Were members of marginalized or underrepresented communities, such as persons of color, LGBTQ individuals, those with a disability, and individuals from financially disadvantaged backgrounds, invited to participate in the planning process to help ensure their voices were heard and needs addressed?

SOURCES OF ADDITIONAL FEEDBACK

The scholarly communication team may wish to speak with members of the intended audience to find out why they did not engage with the initiative. Team members should also interview individuals who did engage with the initiative to identify what parts of it they found most useful and areas for improvement. For instance, a graduate student may say that they enjoyed participating in a workshop that explored opportunities for sharing and promoting their scholarship via the institutional repository but would have benefited from follow-up appointments with staff where they received one-on-one assistance in uploading their works.

At this stage, it can also be useful to discuss the situation with colleagues outside of the institution. External perspectives can be valuable in identifying where mistakes were made or considerations were overlooked. This should include people who have had successes or experienced frustrations with similar initiatives to see what insight and recommendations they might have.

IS THE INITIATIVE SALVAGEABLE?

Armed with all of the information and insights gathered in reviewing the initiative, members of the scholarly communication team should have frank and open discussion about its future. It may be decided that

- The initiative will be continued, but in a smaller capacity. For example, perhaps only one or two events will be planned to celebrate Open Access Week, rather than planning a different event each day.
- The service has potential, but needs to have more resources devoted to it in order to see it succeed, such as additional funds being provided to support an APC (article processing charge) fund that was drained too quickly.
- The service will be continued, but revised substantially. For instance, an OER publishing service that did not see much engagement might be revamped to support open access journal publishing.
- The initiative will be retired or phased out, with lessons learned about its successes and failures applied to future endeavors.

TIPS AND RECOMMENDATIONS

The following tips and recommendations will not ensure success in every undertaking, but when combined with lessons learned from other project failures can provide a solid foundation for launching new initiatives:

- Be open to new ideas, from your colleagues, constituents, and the profession.
- Be realistic about what resources you have available, including staff time and expertise, space, finances, and capacity.
- When in doubt, start small and grow the initiative based upon interest and engagement.
- Identify ways to effectively assess the initiative, and perform assessment often.
- Be adaptable and willing to shift in different directions based upon feedback received.
- Practice self-care! Ask for the resources you need, speak up when you need help, offer assistance when others seem to be struggling, and keep communication channels open, both internally and externally

Failures come in a variety of ways. A few are the result of an intentional or malicious action of a bad actor. Other times, someone (often unintentionally) makes an unwise move that derails an initiative. Frequently, failures come after honest and intense efforts put forward by a dedicated team that had high hopes of success. Occasionally, services that were once extremely popular need to be retired because they no longer see significant use or because resources are reprioritized in the library. When initiatives don't succeed, it is important to acknowledge that changes need to be made. However, failures can lead to future successes if viewed through the right lens and efforts are made not to repeat mistakes made in the past.

NAVIGATING OPEN ACCESS INITIATIVES IN A SEA OF MIXED SUPPORT

Kerry Sewell and Jeanne Hoover

East Carolina University (ECU) is a large, public doctoral institution with medical and dental schools, located in rural Greenville, North Carolina. ECU Libraries comprise a health sciences library and a main academic library with a separate music library. The libraries are institutionally separate but collaborate frequently, including their efforts to support open access (OA). ECU Libraries' OA efforts began around 2008 with the establishment of the institutional repository (IR). Since 2008, OA support has grown into a three-pronged approach that includes working with faculty to deposit the appropriate, publisher-permitted version of their article in our IR; providing funding for open access articles through an Open Access Publishing Support Fund (OAPSF); and offering recurring classes to faculty and graduate students on selecting and evaluating journals, with a focus on OA publishing. The three efforts were created to address the informational, financial, and infrastructural and procedural barriers to OA publishing identified through local conversations and in the literature.[1]

To date, we have taught at least one class per semester on evaluating publishers, supported over ninety OA articles through our OAPSF, and deposited 1,178 journal articles in our IR. Faculty members provide positive feedback about the libraries' OA efforts. The authors note increased awareness of OA publishing among faculty, annual depletion of the allotted OAPSF funds for both the health sciences and academic affairs campuses, and increased demand for classes on selecting and evaluating journals. While the quantitative and anecdotal observations indicate the fruitfulness of our efforts, our OA efforts have also revealed unforeseen challenges in convincing campus stakeholders of the value and legitimacy of OA publishing. Occasionally, our OA efforts have landed the libraries in the middle of campus politics.

Unsurprisingly, the omnipresence of predatory publishers underlies many of the challenges the libraries face in supporting OA. Despite nearly two decades of OA publishing and the rise of respected OA publishers like PLoS, many faculty still conflate OA with predatory publishers. This varies by department but problematically becomes evident in personnel decisions. ECU faculty report learning that departmental tenure committees will not favorably review faculty dossiers that include too many articles published in OA journals. Faculty also report unfavorable annual evaluations resulting from publication in OA journals, even when the OA journals are reputable.

ECU Libraries have a vested interest in remaining uninvolved in external evaluation or tenure and promotion decisions. However, one unintended effect of our advocacy and support for OA has been that faculty associate the libraries with all matters related to OA. While this is a welcome association, there have been instances where faculty members involved in unfavorable evaluation or tenure and promotion decisions related to OA publications looked to the library to provide support for these publications. Responding to such requests requires delicacy. When the libraries have decided to meet these requests, the response has involved carefully crafting requested documentation to avoid embroilment in personnel decisions. Typically, we preface our response with a statement that the libraries support OA, provided the publishing practices of an OA journal ensure meaningful peer review, discoverability of contents, adherence to publishing ethics, and long-term preservation of scholarship. The statement precedes an evaluation of a specific journal according to specified criteria. Even these measured responses cause anxiety among the librarians involved in crafting them; we reason, however, that we provide similar evaluations of journals for faculty members asking for journal assessment during reference interactions.

As more OA articles are included in dossiers, ECU personnel committees and chairs seek definitive journal quality criteria for OA publishers and journals. Faculty previously used Beall's List and desire a vetted replacement for it. ECU's institutional governance became involved in meeting the demand; the Faculty Senate, Faculty Senate Libraries Committee, and Scholarly Communication Committee were tasked with creating a set of general guidelines on publishing, subject to full Faculty Senate approval. Additionally, the Scholarly Communication Committee revised a checklist, developed at the University of Toronto, to fit our campuses' needs.[2] The guidelines are meant to provide institutionally approved criteria for assessing journal quality, equipping faculty to assess journal quality themselves or refer to librarians. Notably, departmental use of the guidelines is not mandatory and thus real adoption uncertain.

Our OAPSF has periodically been at the center of campus politics as well. The fund started during the 2014–2015 academic year and was initially entirely supported by ECU's Advancement Council, which includes high-ranking administrators. The Advancement Council provided $15,000–$20,000 per year until 2018, when the Advancement Council declined to continue support for the fund. The reasons for the loss of university-level funding are unknown, but likely result from budgetary decisions. In lieu of university-level funding, ECU Libraries provides $10,000 per year, with each campus receiving $5,000.

Under the previous Advancement Council funding model, navigating the OAPSF guidelines proved challenging. All applications were shared with representatives from upper administration, in addition to our ongoing practice of application review by a committee comprised of librarians and faculty representatives. We encountered disagreements among stakeholders about awards, with nonlibrarian members suggesting making OAPSF a competitive award, preferentially granted to faculty publishing in high-impact journals, refusing support for graduate student applications, and requiring departments to help fund article processing charges (APCs). ECU Libraries advocated for equity in awards, educating administrators about issues with impact metrics, including disciplinary variation in impact metrics. We compromised on graduate student support, accepting only student submissions with a faculty mentor as coauthor. ECU Libraries steadfastly declined becoming involved in impelling departments to help cover APCs; we asserted that requiring departments to allocate funds to support faculty publishing would necessitate broad, university-level mandates. We do, however, suggest to applicants that departments *may* be able to use facilities and administrative funding to assist with APCs.

The challenges we have experienced underline that OA support involves institutional cultural changes that must include addressing the mindset of administrators, who are critically placed to influence faculty publication choices. This is not always a comfortable effort for librarians, but an important one. Taking multiple approaches to OA and involving multiple librarians to provide OA support has also been critical, especially when difficulties arise.

DISCUSSION QUESTIONS

1. How would you handle a request to become involved in an evaluation decision related to open access? Should librarians be involved in these questions?
2. What type of funding is provided to support open access at your institution? How vulnerable are your funding sources to budgetary changes? In what ways do funding sources effectively constrain how you can use your funds?
3. Has your library identified administrators who may be resistant to open access publishing? What strategies might you employ to address their concerns?

NOTES

1. Nature Research, "Author Insights 2015 Survey," Figshare, 2015, https://doi.org/10.6084/m9.figshare.1425362.v7; Martin Duracinsky et al., "Barriers to Publishing in Biomedical Journals Perceived by a Sample of French Researchers: Results of the DIAzePAM Study," *BMC Medical Research Methodology* 17, no. 1 (December 2017): article 96, https://doi.org/10.1186/s12874-017-0371-z; Gareth J. Johnson, "Cultural, Ideological and Practical Barriers to Open Access Adoption within the UK Academy: An Ethnographically Framed Examination," *Insights* 31 (2018): article 22, https://doi.org/10.1629/uksg.400.
2. University of Toronto, "Identifying Deceptive Publishers: A Checklist," University of Toronto Libraries and Office of the Vice-President, Research and Innovation, 2018, https://onesearch.library.utoronto.ca/deceptivepublishing.

BIBLIOGRAPHY

Duracinsky, Martin, Christophe Lalanne, Laurence Rous, Aichata Fofana Dara, Lesya Baudoin, Claire Pellet, Alexandre Descamps, Fabienne Péretz, and Olivier Chassany. "Barriers to Publishing in Biomedical Journals Perceived by a Sample of French Researchers: Results of the DIAzePAM Study." *BMC Medical Research Methodology* 17, no. 1 (December 2017): article 96. https://doi.org/10.1186/s12874-017-0371-z.

Johnson, Gareth J. "Cultural, Ideological and Practical Barriers to Open Access Adoption within the UK Academy: An Ethnographically Framed Examination." *Insights* 31 (2018): article 22. https://doi.org/10.1629/uksg.400.

Nature Research. "Author Insights 2015 Survey." Figshare, 2015. https://doi.org/10.6084/m9.figshare.1425362.v7.

University of Toronto. "Identifying Deceptive Publishers: A Checklist." University of Toronto Libraries and Office of the Vice-President, Research and Innovation, 2018. https://onesearch.library.utoronto.ca/deceptivepublishing.

COPYRIGHT FIRST RESPONDERS
DECENTRALIZED EXPERTISE, CULTURAL INSTITUTIONS, AND RISK

Kyle Courtney and Emily Kilcer

INTRODUCTION

Today librarians and other information professionals regularly intersect with intellectual property law. As our work increasingly encompasses copyright-intensive programs and projects (e.g., digitization, scholarly publishing, open access, streaming media, MOOCs, and more), questions about fair use, public domain, and copyright law invariably emerge. Libraries occupy a liminal space, they both serve knowledge creation and information access and enjoy special privileges under copyright law.

Unfortunately, comprehensive copyright training is still not a pillar of LIS programs,[1] and while there are seminal resources to look to and professional development opportunities to explore (e.g., MOOCs, copyright bootcamps, or one-offs at conferences), this sort of support may feel ephemeral or once removed. In response, Copyright First Responders (CFR) training is designed to create a network of local copyright experts who can support each other in efforts to provide thoughtful and responsive copyright support to their community.

Over the last six years, the CFR program has extended from its origins at Harvard Library to Alaska, Arizona, California, Massachusetts, New Hampshire, Oregon, Rhode Island, and Washington. Does training copyright experts reasonably reduce risk for an institution? How does the CFR curriculum fill a well-documented gap in information professional training and help drive the learning experiences that become the backbone of local services? How does the CFR's decentralized hub-and-spoke model best serve the interest of these participating institutions?

Here we will explore the structure underpinning the CFR program and share how it aims to reduce risk and provide mission-critical expertise in libraries and archives.

PROBLEM

Library services have evolved over time, and so too has library education. As programs correct course to take into account the shifts required when trends become established practice, there are invariably gaps, which need to be filled through either on-the-job training or professional development. As noted above, to practice responsive, informed librarianship in the twenty-first century, librarians need to both understand and advocate for copyright law to provide effective service to their communities. A very small sampling of the literature on copyright training for librarians identifies the need for copyright expertise and documents the absence of training available to librarians to arm them to be well informed enough to be effective in their roles.[2]

One might argue that practitioners can find opportunities to scaffold their copyright learning; as a small subsampling, for example, Kenny Crews's and Peter Hirtle's essential resources, Coursera's and HarvardX's copyright-focused offerings, and the Kraemer Copyright Conference, the Library Copyright Institute, and the Miami University Libraries Copyright Conference for professional development and networking, do offer librarians a supply of tools for their copyright toolbox.[3]

Professional development and on-the-job training are a norm of librarianship. To remain relevant in an evolving ecosystem, it is imperative that we seek opportunities for learning and growth. And while available, these resources and learning opportunities are often stand-alone or singular opportunities, without the deep engagement afforded with an immersion experience or continual learning. As Reeves states, "Deciphering copyright law is no minor challenge.... It is not clear-cut or absolute."[4] The strength of copyright's flexibility and built-in balance presents great opportunity and also inherent challenges when offering support. Library professionals and their larger institutions have to consider risk aversion and be clear that they are not providing legal assistance. Making these sorts of decisions with limited training can be fear-inspiring.

As an antidote to all of these challenges, the strength of CFR training, which is missing from other professional development opportunities that seem available thus far, is creating a decentralized hub-and-spoke copyright learning community that can provide network-wide support in a trusted environment over time.

SOLUTION

With its start at Harvard Library, the CFR program was developed with one thing in mind: training librarians to be copyright experts in their roles on the front lines. While many colleges and universities may have a central copyright office or general counsel (who may or may not have the capacity to address these questions), a decentralized service operating out of the library offers the community more responsive, nimble support in answering many of these questions and fostering greater understanding of copyright across the university.

When engaging with copyright questions, a solid and practical understanding of copyright law is necessary. However, knowing the factual background of the question is equally as critical. This is often discipline-specific. Whatever the field of study, knowledge of the discipline's subject matter, norms, and so on, is relevant to a copyright question's framing:[5] How does the community approach and disseminate information? What databases and licenses are common in the field? Where are the materials located and accessed? Because librarians frequently have degrees or extensive work experience in the fields they serve, their practical, contextual knowledge makes for a solid ground on which to engage with copyright questions.

A librarian's subject-informed copyright expertise is powerful and can serve the institution's best interests. Coupling this expertise with a library-focused copyright curriculum, emphasizing the special nature of libraries under copyright law, is a cornerstone of the CFR program. A well-trained CFR can ease a patron's fears and present relevant legal alternatives grounded in well-established library law and policy. This reduces risk and serves to create an informed, empowered community.

The "how" of the CFR program has been equally important to its success. The hub-and-spoke model has proven utility in other spheres, such as health care, shipping, and education,[6] that are "immensely complex" and "characterized by perpetual change,"[7] much like copyright (which is complex and continues to evolve with new case law). As Elrod and Fortenberry note, "the hub-and-spoke model affords unique opportunities to maximize efficiencies and effectiveness …in a manner that fosters resource conservation, return on investment, service excellence, and enhanced market coverage."[8] This might not be language common to libraries, but the underlying principles are: we do not have a lot of capital or endless resources, but we are devoted to serving our communities as best as we are able.

With the CFRs, the distributed hub-and-spoke approach to teaching and learning relies initially on a copyright expert, or hub, for hands-on, case law–rooted foundational training. Once graduated from the CFR program, these new copyright experts, or spokes, serve as local hubs, grounding the program, training colleagues and staff, and serving as a liaison between the different constituents (e.g., users, other CFRs, and administration and institutional stakeholders). As spokes, they can also move higher-level questions upward to the expert hub. Trained local staff become spokes out to the community, providing information about copyright and a point of access to the local CFR hub.

This tiered level of support ensures the right resources are devoted to the community's questions. For example, FAQs (e.g., "Do I need to cite my own previously published work in my dissertation?") can be triaged by appropriately trained frontline staff (e.g., circulation or reference staff, etc.). Weightier questions (e.g., "I am doing a project on activism and social media. Can I scrape Facebook event pages?") should be addressed by the CFR, in partnership with the copyright expert as needed. In rare cases where the initial copyright expert hub needs administrative-level support, the institution's general counsel or copyright office is a key partner in the program. User needs are met with the appropriate level of resources at the right time.

Communication and collaboration between the hub and spokes are critical for a CFR program's success. As the program advances, eventually the hubs and spokes expand and build greater networks of hubs and spokes into the community. As more CFRs are added to the program, coverage in institutions, departments, and units develops. This can be the beginning of new and useful contact points through an institution that can aid in the creation of structures and workflows. With local hubs serving as data points, the institution will gain a better understanding of the copyright questions with which the community is struggling and the answers provided. With this information, administrators can develop appropriate, responsive copyright policies that aid the mission of the institution.

The beauty of this program is that it is scalable. Whether a CFR program exists within a library, institution, consortium, or region, the same principles apply: a copyright expert trains a cohort. The cohort become points of support for one another as they go out to serve their communities, with the hub serving as a touchstone for higher-level questions or providing updates and roundups.

Which brings us to the last and perhaps most important hallmark of the CFR program: in learning together, the cohort becomes a community. During their training, CFRs build a shared understanding, but also a trust, which fosters a willingness to raise questions and discuss potential solutions to copyright questions. Not only the training, but also the shared experience, creates a thoughtful network of engaged, empowered colleagues that understand copyright, continue to learn together, support each other, and thereby better serve their communities, their collections, their institutions, and the scholarly enterprise.

NOTES

1. William M. Cross and Phillip M. Edwards, "Preservice Legal Education for Academic Librarians within ALA-Accredited Degree Programs," *portal: Libraries and the Academy* 11, no. 1 (January 2011): 533–50, https://www.muse.jhu.edu/article/409892.
2. Deborah H. Charbonneau and Michael Priehs, "Copyright Awareness, Partnerships, and Training Issues in Academic Libraries," *Journal of Academic Librarianship* 40, no. 3–4 (2014): 228–33, http://digital-commons.wayne.edu/slisfrp/123; Rachel Reeves, "Understanding Copyright: Essential for Academic Librarianship," *Public Services Quarterly* 11, no. 1 (2015): 66–73, https://doi.org/10.1080/15228959.201 4.996274; Cross and Edwards, "Preservice Legal Education"; and later work by Maria Bonn, Will Cross, and Josh Bolick, "Finding Our Way: A Snapshot of Scholarly Communication Practitioners' Duties and Training," *Journal of Librarianship and Scholarly Communication* 8, no. 1 (2020): eP2328, https://doi.org/10.7710/2162-3309.2328.
3. Kenneth D. Crews, *Copyright Law for Librarians and Educators*, 4th ed. (Chicago: American Library Association, 2020); Peter B. Hirtle, "Copyright Term and the Public Domain," LibGuide, Cornell University Library Copyright Information Center, accessed March 2020, https://copyright.cornell.edu/publicdomain; Kevin Smith, Lisa Macklin, and Anne Gilliland, "Copyright for Educators and Librarians," Coursera, accessed March 2020, https://www.coursera.org/learn/copyright-for-education; William (Terry) Fisher III, CopyrightX, home page, accessed March 2020, http://copyx.org/; University of Colorado Colorado Springs, "Kraemer Copyright Conference," Kraemer Family Library and Kraemer Family Endowment, accessed March 2020, https://www.uccs.edu/copyright/; Library Copyright Institute, home page, Duke University, UNC-Chapel Hill, North Carolina Central University, and NC State University, accessed March 2020, http://library.copyright.institute/; Miami University Libraries Copyright Conference website, accessed March 2020. https://copyrightconference.lib.miamioh.edu/.
4. Reeves, "Understanding Copyright," 67.
5. See, e.g., the Center for Media and Social Impact's fair use best practices by field: Center for Media and Social Impact, "Codes of Best Practices," American University School of Communication, accessed April 2020, https://cmsimpact.org/codes-of-best-practices/.
6. Michael E. Porter and Thomas H. Lee, "The Strategy That Will Fix Health Care." *Harvard Business Review* 91, no. 11 (October 2013): 117–22, https://hbr.org/2013/10/the-strategy-that-will-fix-health-care; James K. Elrod and John L. Fortenberry Jr., "The Hub-and-Spoke Organization Design: An Avenue for Serving Patients Well," *BMC Health Services Research* 17, Suppl 1 (2017): 457, https://doi.org/10.1186/s12913-017-2341-x; SCRC SME, "Success with Hub and Spoke Distribution," Supply Chain Resource Cooperative, North Carolina State University, October 14, 2003, https://scm.ncsu.edu/scm-articles/article/success-with-hub-and-spoke-distribution; Laura Millar, "Use of Hub and Spoke Model in Nursing Students' Practice Learning," *Nursing Standards* 28, no. 49 (2014): 37–42, https://doi.org/10.7748/ns.28.49.37.e8616.
7. Elrod and Fortenberry, "Hub-and-Spoke Organization Design, 25.
8. Elrod and Fortenberry, "Hub-and-Spoke Organization Design," 25-26.

BIBLIOGRAPHY

Bonn, Maria, Will Cross, and Josh Bolick. "Finding Our Way: A Snapshot of Scholarly Communication Practitioners' Duties and Training." *Journal of Librarianship and Scholarly Communication* 8, no. 1 (2020): eP2328. https://doi.org/10.7710/2162-3309.2328.

Center for Media and Social Impact. "Codes of Best Practices." American University School of Communication. Accessed April 2020. https://cmsimpact.org/codes-of-best-practices/.

Charbonneau, Deborah H., and Michael Priehs. "Copyright Awareness, Partnerships, and Training Issues in Academic Libraries." *Journal of Academic Librarianship* 40, no. 3–4 (2014): 228–33. http://digitalcommons.wayne.edu/slisfrp/123.

Crews, Kenneth D. *Copyright Law for Librarians and Educators: Creative Strategies and Practical Solutions*, 4th ed. Chicago: American Library Association, 2020.

Cross, William M., and Phillip M. Edwards. "Preservice Legal Education for Academic Librarians within ALA-Accredited Degree Programs." *portal: Libraries and the Academy* 11, no. 1 (January 2011): 533–50. https://www.muse.jhu.edu/article/409892.

Elrod, James K., and John L. Fortenberry Jr. "The Hub-and-Spoke Organization Design: An Avenue for Serving Patients Well." *BMC Health Services Research* 17, Suppl 1 (2017): 457. https://doi.org/10.1186/s12913-017-2341-x.

Fisher, William (Terry), III and Ruth Okediji, "Courses on Intellectual Property Law," IPX, accessed April 8, 2023, http://ipxcourses.org.

Hirtle, Peter B. "Copyright Term and the Public Domain." LibGuide. Cornell University Library Copyright Information Center. Accessed March 2020. https://copyright.cornell.edu/publicdomain.

Library Copyright Institute. Home page. Duke University, UNC-Chapel Hill, North Carolina Central University, and NC State University. Accessed March 2020. http://library.copyright.institute/.

Miami University Libraries Copyright Conference website. Accessed March 2020. https://copyrightconference.lib.miamioh.edu/.

Millar, Laura. "Use of Hub and Spoke Model in Nursing Students' Practice Learning." *Nursing Standards* 28, no. 49 (2014): 37–42. https://doi.org/10.7748/ns.28.49.37.e8616.

Porter, Michael E., and Thomas H. Lee. "The Strategy That Will Fix Health Care." *Harvard Business Review* 91, no. 11 (October 2013): 117–22. https://hbr.org/2013/10/the-strategy-that-will-fix-health-care.

Reeves, Rachel. "Understanding Copyright: Essential for Academic Librarianship." *Public Services Quarterly* 11, no. 1 (2015): 66–73. https://doi.org/10.1080/15228959.2014.996274.

SCRC SME. "Success with Hub and Spoke Distribution." Supply Chain Resource Cooperative, North Carolina State University, October 14, 2003. https://scm.ncsu.edu/scm-articles/article/success-with-hub-and-spoke-distribution.

Smith, Kevin, Lisa Macklin, and Anne Gilliland. "Copyright for Educators and Librarians." Coursera. Accessed March 2020. https://www.coursera.org/learn/copyright-for-education.

University of Colorado Colorado Springs. "Kraemer Copyright Conference." Kraemer Family Library and Kraemer Family Endowment. Accessed March 2020. https://www.uccs.edu/copyright/.

MIND YOUR PS AND TS

PROMOTION, TENURE, AND THE CHALLENGE FOR OPEN ACCESS

Josh Cromwell

Over the past decade, faculty have shown increasingly favorable attitudes toward open access (OA), and to be sure, the efforts of scholarly communication librarians have contributed significantly to this shift. Yet this changing perception of OA has not tended to have a significant effect on where faculty choose to publish their research. What is the source of this disparity? The scholarly communication staff at the University of Southern Mississippi set out to understand faculty attitudes toward journal prestige and open access through a series of conversations and panel discussions with faculty across multiple disciplines in hopes of understanding why they choose to publish where they do and of conveying why they should consider publishing their scholarship openly.

While attitudes toward open access tend to vary across disciplines, a consistent concern from faculty during these discussions focused on the way open access publications are viewed in promotion and tenure (P&T) guidelines. In many cases, P&T guidelines emphasize publishing in highly cited prestige journals, which tend to be subscription-based. Thus, even if faculty prefer to publish in OA journals, they often feel pressured to publish in traditional outlets to maximize their likelihood of getting promoted or earning tenure. During one panel, a faculty member in the College of Business told us that they have a ranking of journals in their discipline, with A-ranked journals considered the most prestigious. In order to satisfy tenure requirements, faculty were required to publish in an A-ranked or B-ranked journal.[1] However, the faculty member said that they and their colleagues did not read these prestige journals because they found that the lower-ranked journals were publishing articles that were much more relevant to their teaching and research. These faculty can see that a journal's quality and a journal's reputation are not necessarily synonymous, but they still gravitate toward the journals with stronger reputations when choosing where to publish due to pressure from above.

Another topic that has often come up during faculty discussions is the question of audience. Are faculty primarily publishing for their peers or for a broader audience? A faculty member in the College of Nursing highlighted this tension during a panel. He pointed out that he strongly desires for his research to be readily available to practitioners because it has implications for the ways they care for patients and could potentially save lives.[2] So if given the choice, he prefers to publish his research in OA journals. On the other hand, OA journals in his discipline are not evaluated highly in his department's P&T document. So he faces a dilemma: publish in a prestigious journal with a paywall and limit his audience but ensure he keeps his job, or publish in an OA journal so the research is as widely available as possible while jeopardizing his chance to become tenured. It became clear that if we were going to encourage more faculty to embrace OA, we needed to have higher-level discussions about changing the way that faculty were evaluated, or at least the way in which journals are evaluated in the current P&T processes.

Before initiating these discussions,, we surveyed the available literature to see if there was evidence to support our anecdotal findings. In the 2018 Ithaka S+R faculty survey, almost 40 percent of faculty indicated that it is highly important to publish in journals where articles are freely available online with no cost to readers—a significant number, to be sure—while just under 80 percent noted that the reputation or impact factor of a journal was highly important.[3] This points to the fact that if presented with the choice, faculty are more likely to choose journals with higher reputations or better metrics over those with lower metrics that are OA. A 2019 survey of faculty research practices at Virginia Tech presented similar findings, noting that faculty tend to rely more on metrics they are expected to use (such as JIF and publication counts) rather than those that they find personally useful, such as expert peer reviews or altmetrics, when it comes to evaluating journals.[4] With regard to the benefit of OA for increasing citations, it has been difficult to identify an exact number because of citations over time, but a recent study by Piwowar and colleagues indicates that OA publications on average are cited 18 percent more often.[5] With this research to support our findings, we decided to include administrators in future discussions.

Obviously, recruiting administrators for events can be challenging. Thankfully, our dean of libraries was able to assist us in bringing in two fellow deans, along with the provost, for a panel discussion following a screening of Jason Schmidt's documentary, *Paywall: The Business of Scholarship*, during Open Access Week 2019. During that discussion, we asked the panelists about adding support for OA publications in P&T guidelines, and the provost stated that, while it was ultimately up to the individual academic units across campus to determine their P&T processes, the university administration would support any units that added support for OA publications.[6] Following that panel, a faculty member reached out to us to inquire about the process of developing such a policy for the university. Our goal is to build upon these conversations in hopes of encouraging faculty in all disciplines to encourage OA publications in their P&T criteria.

Another approach is to model what this process might look like within the libraries. The dean, in discussion with the librarians, who have faculty status, is discussing a revision to the libraries' P&T document that incentivizes OA publications. While the plan is still in development, the most likely options at this point are to either incentivize OA publications so that they are weighted more favorably than those in subscription journals or to lower the number of required publications if the articles are OA. Hopefully, the completed version of this plan will serve as an example for other units on campus considering similar changes.

ADDITIONAL RESOURCES

Bales, Stephen, David E. Hubbard, Wyoma vanDuinkerken, Laura Sare, and Joseph Olivarez. "The Use of Departmental Journal Lists in Promotion and Tenure Decisions at American Research Universities." *Journal of Academic Librarianship* 45, no. 2 (March 2019): 153–61. https://doi.org/10.1016/j.acalib.2019.02.005.

McKiernan, Erin C., Lesley A. Schimanski, Carol Muñoz Nieves, Lisa Matthias, Meredith T. Niles, and Juan P. Alperin. "Meta-research: Use of the Journal Impact Factor in Academic Review, Promotion, and Tenure Evaluations." *eLife* 8 (2019): 347338. https://doi.org/10.7554/eLife.47338.

Niles, Meredith T., Lesley A. Schimanski, Erin C. McKiernan, and Juan Pablo Alperin. "Why We Publish Where We Do: Faculty Publishing Values and Their Relationship to

Review, Promotion and Tenure Expectations." *PLOS ONE* 15, no. 3 (2020): e0228914. https://doi.org/10.1371/journal.pone.0228914.

Wical, Stephanie H., and Gregory J. Kocken. "Open Access and Promotion and Tenure Evaluation Plans at the University of Wisconsin–Eau Claire." *Serials Review* 43, no. 2 (2017): 111–19. https://doi.org/10.1080/00987913.2017.1313024.

DISCUSSION QUESTIONS

1. What are some strategies that scholarly communication librarians can use to encourage faculty to support open access in their promotion and tenure guidelines?
2. What advice would you give to a junior faculty member like the one in the case study who was torn between publishing openly for the benefit of practitioners or publishing in a prestige subscription journal to strengthen their dossier?
3. What are some other ways that librarians with faculty status can lead by example with their own promotion and tenure processes?
4. Why do you think that promotion and tenure guidelines have generally not kept pace with the changes in scholarly communication and academic publishing? How might the answer to this question inform your approach to advocating for change?

NOTES

1. Robert Doan et al., "The Alphabet Soup of Scholarly Communication: IRs, OA, T&P, and More" (panel discussion, Southern Miss Institutional Repository Conference, Hattiesburg, MS, April 12–13, 2017).
2. Doan et al., "Alphabet Soup."
3. Melissa Blankstein and Christine Wolff-Eisenberg, *Ithaka S+R US Faculty Survey 2018* (New York: Ithaka S+R, 2019), 38, https://doi.org/10.18665/sr.311199.
4. Rachel A. Miles et al., "What Do Faculty Think About Researcher Profiles, Metrics, and Fair Research Assessment? A Case Study from a Research University in the Southeastern United States" (PowerPoint presentation, Virginia Tech, 2019), https://vtechworks.lib.vt.edu/handle/10919/93360.
5. Heather Piwowar et al., "The State of OA: A Large-Scale Analysis of the Prevalence and Impact of Open Access Articles," *PeerJ* 6 (2018): e4375, p. 17. https://doi.org/10.7717/peerj.4375.
6. Sam Bruton et al., "Reactions and Responses to the Paywall Documentary" (panel discussion, Open Access Week 2019, Hattiesburg, MS, October 22, 2019), https://aquila.usm.edu/oaweek/2019/1/3/.

BIBLIOGRAPHY

Blankstein, Melissa, and Christine Wolff-Eisenberg. *Ithaka S+R US Faculty Survey 2018*. New York: Ithaka S+R, 2019. https://doi.org/10.18665/sr.311199.

Bruton, Sam, John Eye, Trent Gould, Douglas Masterson, Steven Moser, Teresa Welsh, and Chris Winstead. "Reactions and Responses to the Paywall Documentary." Panel discussion, Open Access Week 2019, Hattiesburg, MS, October 22, 2019. https://aquila.usm.edu/oaweek/2019/1/3/.

Doan, Robert, Leisa R. Flynn, Marcus M. Gaut, Jeanne Gillespie, Alisa Lowrey, and Douglas S. Masterson. "The Alphabet Soup of Scholarly Communication: IRs, OA, T&P, and More." Panel discussion, Southern Miss Institutional Repository Conference, Hattiesburg, MS, April 12–13, 2017.

Miles, Rachel A., Amanda B. MacDonald, Nathaniel D. Porter, Virginia Pannabecker, and Jim A. Kuypers. "What Do Faculty Think About Researcher Profiles, Metrics, and Fair Research Assessment? A Case Study from a Research University in the Southeastern United States." PowerPoint presentation. Virginia Tech, 2019. https://vtechworks.lib.vt.edu/handle/10919/93360.

Piwowar, Heather, Jason Priem, Vincent Larivière, Juan Pablo Alperin, Lisa Matthias, Bree Norlander, Ashley Farley, Jevin West, and Stefanie Haustein. "The State of OA: A Large-Scale Analysis of the Prevalence and Impact of Open Access Articles." *PeerJ* 6 (2018): e4375. https://doi.org/10.7717/peerj.4375.

PROFESSIONALIZING FOR NEW PERFORMANCE DUTIES

Gemmicka Piper

Frankly, I didn't have any guidance on leveraging my skills while I was a student, and this lack continued through my first position. Right after graduation, I landed a position as a resident/visiting assistant librarian at an institution that was exclusively focused on instruction. In this environment it was made abundantly clear that the chief function of a subject specialist was to provide instruction to lower level students. This translated to almost no professional development support. In this position I more or less functioned as the ethnic studies librarian. My subject fields were all interdisciplinary and treated as programs rather than a department with its own unique user needs. Realistically, I saw almost no instruction related specifically to my subject disciplines. Instead, creative and instructional opportunities emerged out of nonsubject partnerships that I had actively pursued with individuals and units across my campus. Any coordinated outreach efforts were at my discretion.

After a year and a half, I transitioned into a new role at a new institution. I was still a subject specialist, but now I was the humanities librarian. My situation was improved by the facts that (1) research support was also considered part of what librarians did, and (2) funding support for professional development was available via several mechanisms. I was highly encouraged to go places and to experiment. Because of the shift in environment and greater flexibility in how I was allowed to engage with my subject areas as a liaison, I felt comfortable attempting something that I thought was way outside of my discipline range. As part of an experimental process to get the necessary work completed, while still under budgetary constraints, my library decided to test a new hybrid functional liaisonship model. There were a couple of 20-percent-time positions, each dedicated for two years, that were created under this hybrid model, one of which was for a copyright liaison. I saw a position description that was interesting because it was looking for someone who could assist the university in growing a new service and develop training and education around copyright issues.

After I accepted the position I was told to come up with a service model, draft a copyright policy, and do a campus survey to better understand our user needs around copyright. But I was given no time line or other information. I was able to leverage previously developed analytical skills. First, I drafted a rough time line for the full two years of the position. Then I drafted a full-scale service model. I drew upon my experience with creating learner-centered educational assessments. I started with the learning objectives for each group of perspective customers for the service. Working backward, I was able to define what success looked like at each year of a potential program and to come up with a five-year service model. By reviewing the copyright policies of our peer and aspirational peer institutions, I was able to get a sense of the points they stressed. I created a synthesis grid noting key issues in their policy statements, as well as some sample language. Once I had this comprehensive understanding of user-focused issues in copyright policies, I was able to create a policy draft for my institution.

Let me stress, none of the above magically came together. I routinely keep up with broader trends in library instruction. I attended the 2019 ACRL preconference on Accessibility and Universal Design for Learning (UDL). This was how I learned about UDL, and in doing so saw its potential applications in creating a framework for this new service we were imagining. Because I was point person, it was left up to me to establish the vision and direction for my liaisonship. I had never created a new service before, and when I searched online for templates and models I wasn't finding anything ready-made. So I had to lean into the skills I already had with designing curriculum to create something new. The result is that we now have a new research support service model that is more outcome-focused and instruction-entwined. As this is a train-the-trainer model, the connection back to instruction is critical for getting other liaisons trained to a basic standard. I am in the process of developing new online training materials for everyone. This has included a recorded webinar in partnership with our Center for Teaching and Learning (CTL) and the creation of an open self-paced course in our Canvas LMS with a certificate at completion.

I more or less had the skills for designing and executing my task. What I did not have was content knowledge. I had never received any training in copyright prior to taking it on as a liaison. Almost from the moment of being assigned to be copyright lead, I was slammed with questions. I really had to get up to speed quickly. So before I attempted any of the design stuff above, I reached out to our general counsel and a few local copyright librarians and scheduled virtual meetings with them to get a sense of (1) what service models they deployed, (2) what support they had from their campuses, (3) the scope of their services, (4) how they drew the line between providing information and offering legal advice, and (5) when they referred the client to general counsel. I found it to be interesting and illustrative, and I think the associate dean for the project did as well. I made sure to schedule meetings when administration could come. I think that helped them think more about the role that they had tasked me with.

In addition to directly contacting individuals, I have done a lot of online training. Coursera's online course Copyright for Educators and Librarians, Library Juice Academy's Introduction to Scholarly Communication, and now the weekly CopyrightX program. Aside from these, I also attended the 2019 Miami University Library Copyright Conference. This past year has been a series of learning things in spurts but then having to apply this information during a real consultation context. I have had to be proactive in identifying training opportunities to acquire more copyright knowledge. This means checking out sections or topics posted at large conferences like ACRL. It also means looking locally for opportunities around specialty areas. For example, my state library hosted a workshop on copyright in context to digital preservation. I also receive forwarded messages from my colleagues who know about the work I am doing on copyright. It is impossible to attend every event, so do what is feasible in accordance with your time and your financial resources.

Things are always in flux, and change is a reality of this profession. My duties have changed twice in the two and a half years I have been at my current institution. Equally important as knowing how to go about new duties is also knowing (1) when you are overloaded, and (2) how to adapt to failure (because not everything you try will be an immediate success).

DISCUSSION QUESTIONS

1. What strategies did Gemmicka use to skill up to new duties?
2. What skills have you learned so far that would help you to skill up when tasked with new responsibilities?
3. Think of a time that you failed to achieve a desired goal or outcome; what did you learn from that experience? How might you approach new duties differently with that experience in mind?

A JOURNAL OF ONE'S OWN

DEVELOPING AN INNOVATIVE, VALUES-DRIVEN OPEN JOURNAL

Spencer D. C. Keralis and John Edward Martin

INTRODUCTION

Open journal publishing, as well as the broader internet publishing phenomenon, has the potential to advance innovation in scholarly communication. The past decade has seen a flourishing of independent, open access journals, but too often these journals replicate traditional models of scholarly communication, perpetuating the inequities, bias, cronyism, abusive peer-review processes, and disciplinary silos that have corrupted the scholarly publication ecosystem.[1] Institutional and for-profit barriers to access to the scholarly record amplify these problems and exacerbate misperceptions of scholarly work.

In 2019, the Digital Frontiers community founded the online journal *Unbound: A Journal of Digital Scholarship*.[2] Digital Frontiers was established in 2012 as an inclusive community for digital scholarship practitioners in a range of disciplines.[3] Inspired by the recent work of Kathleen Fitzpatrick, Roopika Risam, and others, our vision of values-driven scholarly communication addresses the needs of underserved and marginalized communities within the disciplines by building publication models based on open access, transparent peer review, inclusivity, interdisciplinarity, community, mentorship, and an ethic of care. In what follows, we'll offer a snapshot of our intentions in establishing a values-driven open journal and look at ways these values can be incorporated into the bones of a journal—from its mission statement and editorial policies to its peer-review and submission guidelines. *Unbound* serves as an example of how core humanistic values and open practices might be integrated into a scholarly journal while maintaining a commitment to intellectual rigor, quality writing, editorial best practices, and publishing ethics.

VALUES

When we talk about values in this context, we're describing a shared set of social, professional, and intellectual priorities. The Digital Frontiers community has long practiced intentional inclusion—moving beyond merely advocating for diversity to organizing the community in a way that establishes clear policies and practices that deliver on the promise implied in that advocacy. We follow labor organizer Jane F. McAlevey in drawing a sharp line between advocacy, which tends to be top-down and focused on policy, and organizing, which builds "the skills of organic leaders" for building and influencing communities and is most likely to result in systemic change.[4] In our experience, organizing is a process, not an event, and as individuals and a community we are continually learning and striving to bring our practice in line with our shared values.

When we talk of values, we aren't talking about morality, but at the same time, we are not *not* talking about morality. Citation politics are one example of this. Lauren Klein describes how he field of digital scholarship is reckoning with the legacy of a particular scholar who is one of the most prominent academic figures to be implicated in the #MeToo movement.[5] The decision whether to continue citing this individual or to seek alternative genealogies for digital scholarship is, we believe, a moral choice, and not merely academic. Ultimately we see decisions to respect students' and nonfaculty colleagues' labor and intellectual property rights, to make our work open, to implement inclusive practice that welcomes transgender people, to strive for racial and gender parity, and to support women, queer people, and people of color in our citations as choices between good and bad, right and wrong. Moral choices that are not merely trendy or expedient.

How, then, do we as individuals and as a community bring these values into focus in the context of scholarly communication?

IMPLEMENTATION

As we set out to establish *Unbound*, we considered what factors made the Digital Frontiers community attractive to its members. Over the years as the conference has evolved, we implemented transparent peer review for submissions, substantive documentation of our inclusion policy and code of conduct,[6] and provocative calls for proposals that explicitly addressed communities traditionally underserved by digital scholarship and that encode adherence to community standards for the use of the labor of students and nonfaculty collaborators as requirements for inclusion in the conference.[7] As an extension of this community, it was important to us that *Unbound* reflect these same practices.

In developing the journal, we chose an open source online platform, Open Journal Systems (OJS), hosted through the University of North Texas Libraries.[8] Library publishing offers an opportunity for innovation and self-direction that university or for-profit presses might not support and shares our mission of openness, access, diversity, and collaboration.[9] The UNT Libraries Scholarly Publishing Services likewise supports our goals of immediate public access, no fees to authors, compensation of student labor, and adherence to core principles of publication ethics.[10] The last includes transparent policies for submission, intellectual property, peer review, and data privacy.[11] In choosing to publish through a library and an open platform, we are embracing a shared goal of making scholarly communication available to a broader community without either the profit incentive or gatekeeping mentality that often accompanies academic publishing and its prestige economy.

Our values are also reinforced by the policies and practices that we have adopted for the journal. Principal among these is our transparent peer-review process, in which authors and reviewers know one another's names and engage in direct communication. This practice is intended to disrupt the bias and abuses that are endemic in traditional anonymous peer review and to move toward a practice of peer review grounded in a spirit of mentorship and an ethic of care. Ours is not the first journal to embrace such an approach. *The Public Philosophy Journal* at Michigan State University has elaborated a similar peer-review model that it calls "formative peer review."[12] In contrast to traditional peer review, which it feels "has become hostile to new ideas, composers, and audiences, and can even be traumatic for those involved," it proposes a process of mutual engagement "rooted in trust and a shared commitment to improving the work through candid and collegial feedback." Rather than seeing peer review as a method of gatekeeping or disciplinary homogeneity, we envision it as a method of improving both the content and the experience of scholarly publishing for all those involved. By approaching peer review from a spirit of mentorship, we hope to inculcate these same values in students and early career scholars and librarians so they can bring this model to other journals and other scholarly communities.

Likewise, our submission policies, content categories, and CFPs are designed to reflect the demographic and disciplinary diversity of the Digital Frontiers community and to encourage the work of "scholars and professionals at all stages of professional development in all fields," including students, early career scholars, nonacademic professionals, and creative artists— voices often excluded from scholarly conversations or the academic rewards system.[13] The inclusion of digital scholarship reviews, notes on practice, and artist portfolios allow these contributors to engage with the broader scholarly community and render their intellectual and creative work legible as scholarship to new audiences.

CONCLUSION

Unbound is, and perhaps always will be, a work in progress. For a journal to be shaped by the values of the community it serves, change will be an ongoing and inevitable characteristic of its business and editorial models. The protean nature of digital communications will necessarily inform decisions about platforms, circulation, and media support, but those technical realities must be informed by the founding values of the publication and the community that sustains it. We anticipate that this will make for a less homogenous body of work than is expected from more traditional scholarly journals, but the heterogeneity of content will reflect the diversity of our community and allow for growth and evolution over time as we learn and strive together.

DISCUSSION QUESTIONS

1. What ethos informs your scholarly communication program, and what are its central values?
2. What are the concrete ways that you embody or implement these values in your scholarly communication programs, services, resources, or policies?
3. Who within your communities is excluded from full participation in the scholarly communication system and how can you facilitate their inclusion?

NOTES

1. Kathleen Fitzpatrick, *Planned Obsolescence* (New York: NYU Press, 2011), 28–29.
2. *Unbound: A Journal of Digital Scholarship*, home page, https://journals.library.unt.edu/index.php/unbound.
3. Digital Frontiers, home page, https://dsco-op.org.
4. Jane F. McAlevey, *No Shortcuts* (New York: Oxford University Press, 2016), 10–13.
5. Lauren Klein, "Distant Reading after Moretti," Arcade: Literature, Humanities, and the World, Stanford Humanities Center, January 29, 2018, https://arcade.stanford.edu/blogs/distant-reading-after-moretti.
6. Digital Frontiers, "Statement of Inclusion and Accessibility," Accessed May 6, 2020, https://dcsco-op.org/inclusion/.

7. See Haley Di Pressi et al., "A Student Collaborators' Bill of Rights," UCLA HumTech, June 8, 2015, https://humtech.ucla.edu/news/a-student-collaborators-bill-of-rights/; Hannah Alpert-Abrams et al., "Postdoctoral Laborers Bill of Rights," Humanities Commons, 2019, https://doi.org/10.17613/7fz6-ra81; and Tanya Clement et al., "Collaborators' Bill of Rights," In *Off the Tracks—Laying New Lines for Digital Humanities Scholars* (Media Commons Press, 2011), 9, https://mcpress.media-commons.org/offthetracks/.
8. Public Knowledge Project, "Open Journal Systems," accessed May 6, 2020, https://pkp.sfu.ca/ojs/.
9. Library Publishing Coalition, "About Us," accessed May 6, 2020, https://librarypublishing.org/about/.
10. University of North Texas Libraries, "UNT Libraries Journal Hosting," accessed May 6, 2020, https://library.unt.edu/scholarly-communication/unt-libraries-journal-hosting/.
11. Committee on Publication Ethics (COPE), "Core Practices," accessed May 6, 2020, https://publicationethics.org/core-practices.
12. *Public Philosophy Journal*, "Formative Peer Review," accessed May 6, 2020, https://publicphilosophyjournal.org/about/review/ (page discontinued).
13. *Unbound: A Journal of Digital Scholarship*, "Call for Contributions," November 23, 2019, https://journals.library.unt.edu/index.php/unbound/announcement/view/3.

BIBLIOGRAPHY

Alpert-Abrams, Hannah, Heather Froehlich, Amanda Henrichs, Jim McGrath, and Kim Martin. "Postdoctoral Laborers Bill of Rights." Humanities Commons, 2019. https://hcommons.org/deposits/item/hc:26741/ https://doi.org/10.17613/7fz6-ra81.

Clement, Tanya, Brian Croxall, Julia Flanders, Neil Fraistat, Steve Jones, Suzanne Lodato, Laura Mandell, et al. "Collaborators' Bill of Rights." In *Off the Tracks—Laying New Lines for Digital Humanities Scholars*, 9. Media Commons Press, 2011. https://mcpress.media-commons.org/offthetracks/

Committee on Publication Ethics (COPE). "Core Practices." Accessed May 6, 2020. https://publicationethics.org/core-practices.

Digital Frontiers. Home page. https://digital-frontiers.org/ (site discontinued).

———. "Statement of Inclusion and Accessibility." Accessed May 6, 2020. https://dcsco-op.org/inclusion/.

Di Pressi, Haley, Stephanie Gorman, Miriam Posner, Raphael Sasayama, and Tori Schmitt, with contributions from Roderic Crooks, Megan Driscoll, et al. "A Student Collaborators' Bill of Rights." UCLA HumTech, June 8, 2015. https://humtech.ucla.edu/news/a-student-collaborators-bill-of-rights/.

Fitzpatrick, Kathleen. *Planned Obsolescence: Publishing, Technology, and the Future of the Academy*. New York: NYU Press, 2011.

Klein, Lauren. "Distant Reading after Moretti." Arcade: Literature, Humanities, and the World, Stanford Humanities Center. January 29, 2018. https://arcade.stanford.edu/blogs/distant-reading-after-moretti.

Library Publishing Coalition. "About Us." Accessed May 6, 2020. https://librarypublishing.org/about/.

McAlevey, Jane F. *No Shortcuts: Organizing for Power in the New Gilded Age*. New York: Oxford University Press, 2016.

Public Knowledge Project. "Open Journal Systems." Accessed May 6, 2020. https://pkp.sfu.ca/ojs/.

Public Philosophy Journal. "Formative Peer Review." Accessed May 6, 2020. https://publicphilosophyjournal.org/about/review/ (page discontinued).

Unbound: A Journal of Digital Scholarship. "Call for Contributions." November 23, 2019. https://journals.library.unt.edu/index.php/unbound/announcement/view/3.

———. Home page, https://journals.library.unt.edu/index.php/unbound.

University of North Texas Libraries. "UNT Libraries Journal Hosting." Accessed May 6, 2020. https://library.unt.edu/scholarly-communication/unt-libraries-journal-hosting/.

MENTORSHIP IS A THING

Marilyn S. Billings and Charlotte Roh

The University of Massachusetts Amherst Libraries began a scholarly communication librarian residency program in the late 2000s. After my 2005 sabbatical to investigate the role of institutional repositories, the libraries began conversations with faculty using a survey instrument and engaged with potential partners to sustain our efforts: Graduate School; Office of Research; Office of Outreach and Engagement. By 2007 we had built a robust relationship with all three partners, working closely with the Graduate School to automate the theses and dissertations workflows, creating opportunities for the Office of Research to highlight individual faculty and group research projects, and furthering the campus's outreach and engagement in preparation for the elective Carnegie Community Engagement classification application. Recognizing the need for additional support in these nascent efforts, the libraries shared the residency program concept with the partners, asking for financial support to fund a two-year scholarly communication resident librarian position. Each partner contributed one quarter of the salary; signed MOUs to ensure ongoing, sustainable funding; and agreed to library oversight of the position. These contracts were reviewed every two years until the program closed in 2016, when the position was reenvisioned as a permanent position in the Office of Scholarly Communication.

One of the residents, Charlotte Roh, had the following to say about the program:

> My previous career was in academic publishing, but I was brand new to librarianship in the fall of 2013, when I began my residency with Marilyn Billings at the Libraries. The residency was crucial in giving me experience in all the major scholarly communications topics: institutional repositories, open education, copyright advisory, and library publishing. The institutional repository was already one of the largest repositories in the country, so my role was really one of everyday maintenance and growth of its content, as well as leveraging its popularity to discuss (and eventually pass) an open access policy. The open education program was also well underway, but had not undergone a programmatic assessment. We were able to assess not just the one-time course savings, but savings over time (which were tremendous), as well as qualitative outcomes, such as a better relationship between educational technology and the library. The overwhelmingly positive outcomes of this assessment were an amazing professional development opportunity for me to present at workshops and conferences and teach on the topic at a very early point in my career. I want to note that these weren't opportunities that I sought out on my own—I wasn't yet aware of the open education community and its players, and would not have known how to leverage my new expertise on open education to leverage my career. I was fortunate that Marilyn Billings took the time to introduce me to people, ideas, and opportunities, even suggesting on several occasions that I speak on panels and workshops when people requested her as

a presenter. She also made sure I had an opportunity to build skills outside the scope of my job description to broaden my portfolio, such as data management in conjunction with the science librarians and copyright knowledge with the copyright lawyer/librarian. I learned more than scholarly communications in this residency, I learned how to be generous and thoughtful in building the careers of those around me, and to consider the whole person.

OTHER WAYS TO SHARE ONE'S MENTORING PASSION

- Create or participate in a mentorship program among staff at your library to engage them in scholarly communication topics.
- Engage in mentoring activities of professional organizations. Examples: ACRL's Instruction Section and Science and Technology Section; ACRL Spectrum Scholar Mentor Program; Library Publishing Coalition's (LPC) peer mentorship program; SPARC Open Education Leadership Program.

Willa Tavernier, open scholarship resident librarian at Indiana University, an LPC mentee, shared the following comments:

When LPC issued a call for the mentoring program, I was skeptical. My concept of a mentor was someone at my own institution who could guide me through the ins and outs of workplace culture. However, the experience far exceeded my expectations. Being able to talk to someone external to my institution actually allowed me to open up without the usual anxieties I felt as a new hire and diversity resident librarian communicating with senior colleagues. An unexpected bonus was that Marilyn had experience running the diversity residency program at her own institution. Her warm and easygoing manner made our monthly calls a pleasure, and Marilyn served as a valuable sounding board for my research interests. I benefited from the connections that she helped me to make as well as her practical advice, which dovetailed perfectly with specific priorities and opportunities I received within my own institution and in national organizations.

Stephanie Pierce, head of the Physics Library at the University of Arkansas Libraries, a SPARC Open Education Leadership Program mentee, made the following comments:

When Marilyn Billings was assigned as my mentor for SPARC's Open Education Leadership Fellows program, I knew was getting the opportunity to learn and be guided by one of the open education community's respected leaders and voices. The mentoring relationship Marilyn and I established proved to be invaluable as we worked through my capstone project's scale and purpose; content; and adaptability for our community's needs. One of Marilyn's greatest strengths as a mentor is listening and then connecting you with others in order to help you build a community of support and provide opportunities for collaborations or partnerships. These connections translated into service opportunities and collaborations with other institutions that align with my work to provide equitable professional development to those working within open education. Even when the formal mentorship period ends, support and guidance continues because when you're a mentee of Marilyn's, you're a mentee, colleague, and friend for life.

KEY TAKEAWAYS

- Ensure the need for a new librarian position by conducting a needs assessment using tools such as surveys, focus groups, and qualitative measures, and ensure that these lead to purposeful projects.
- Engage in new cross-campus partnerships wherever possible to address needs identified by the needs assessment and ensure their engagement with the resident in meaningful ways through work assignments.
- Embed resident in as many scholarly communication areas as possible for broad, substantive engagement in open scholarship topics.
- Provide professional development opportunities for the resident in committee assignments, visiting department hours, travel funds for conferences and workshops, time to create content for workshops and presentations to a wide array of audiences and to pursue other professional development opportunities.

The scholarly communication librarian residency program, along with other professional mentoring opportunities shared herein, is an excellent example of the influence that well-designed programs have in ensuring that new librarians have the skill sets needed in today's new, evolving open scholarship librarianship positions. We encourage other institutions to build upon case studies such as the one at UMA Libraries to provide additional options for new librarians.

DISCUSSION QUESTIONS

1. In summary, what are the benefits of receiving mentoring as described by Charlotte, Willa, and Stephanie?
2. How might you cultivate formal and informal mentors as an early career librarian and throughout your career?
3. Once you are in a position to mentor, what ideas do you take from this chapter that may inform your mentorship?

ADDING YOUR VOICE TO THE CONVERSATION

Congratulations, you have come to the end of this book. The good news is that you should now have an outstanding foundation in scholarly communication, especially as librarians engage with the topic. The bad (or not-so-bad, as we will see) news is that much of what you have just read is already out of date.

As your three editors are putting the finishing touches on these materials in the summer of 2023, we are tremendously proud of the materials provided by roughly eighty(!) leaders in the field. We are confident that this book provides a solid foundation for the work, that the topics covered sit at the heart of scholarly communication, and that the examples provided reflect a diverse and exciting cross-section of the state of the art today.

But, of course, you aren't reading this in the summer of 2023. Or, most likely, in 2024 or possibly even in 2025. Any book is necessarily reflective of the finite set of contributors who created it and specific moment when it was written and released (two distinct points in time that are often months or even years removed from one another). Because scholarly communication is an emergent and particularly fast-moving field, the gap between practices when we created this work and the practices you will find as you enter or find a new role in librarianship in 2024, 2025, and so on may seem stark.

Every day cool people do cool new things that make scholarly communication better. Innovative library programs are developed, ingenious scholars find new and better ways to share what they are doing and learning, and the field itself continues to evolve and expand. That's our job as librarians and scholarly communicators.

At the same time, every day many companies and not-so-great actors continue to pioneer new ways to exploit and monetize the work of scholars with an eye squarely trained on their fiduciary duties and quarterly earnings. That's their job as capitalists.

What *you* do as a professional will shape the future of the field. That's the really good news. The story of scholarly communication is not yet finished, and our guess is that we're still very much in the early chapters. We've got some plans to keep this book up-to-date over time, and hopefully you'll find communities of practice where you can share your own ideas and hear what others are up to. Those are constantly evolving too, from e-mail discussion lists a decade ago to social media hashtags or Discord channels in 2023, to wherever folks gather as you make your way through the profession.

With all of these changes in mind, we've also designed what we hope will be a bridge between the work you've been doing as you made your way through this book and the professional communities that will benefit from your passion and expertise. The Scholarly Communication Notebook (https://www.oercommons.org/hubs/SCN) is a place you can go to see the latest and greatest examples of work being done in the field. Scholars, practitioners, and librarians from every type of institution and at all levels of experience use the Notebook to share models, case studies, and documents from their own work and to build on the resources shared by others.

If you used this book in a formal educational setting, your professor may have already shared the Notebook with you. We are developing some crosswalks for finding materials and building assignments around the Notebook that we hope have been helpful. Likewise, if you've been learning on the job, the Notebook may already be on your radar. As a result, you may have already contributed your own work to the Notebook under the guidance of an instructor or at your own initiative. Whether or not you have already shared something with the SCN community, we hope you will do so early and often throughout your career.

There is no one-size-fits-all way to communicate scholarship or to support that work, so hearing from many different people at many types of institutions and building on the work they have done is critical to shaping more diverse and inclusive systems for scholarly communication. To be sure, there are core values: openness, inclusion, working for the public benefit. But the right way to support OA or OER at a large, publicly funded R1 institution might be a total disaster when applied at a small, wealthy liberal arts college. A compelling model for opening up history monographs may fall flat when applied to support for a student-facing psychology journal.

The flexible, evolving, and unfinished nature of scholarly communication is the thing that makes it so exciting. This is a book that will never really be finished because it supports an effort that is ongoing: leveraging the work of the academy to make the world a better place. We've laid a pretty solid foundation here and made space for you to share your own work as you write the next chapter. We're excited to see what you do.

BIOGRAPHIES

Thea Atwood (she/her) is currently the public and environmental health sciences librarian at Indiana University Bloomington and was formerly the data services librarian at the University of Massachusetts Amherst, where she established and led UMass Amherst's data services program. Dedicated to reproducibility, Thea is interested in incorporating reproducible research and data management concepts into her regular teaching. She currently leads the newly established systematic reviews service at Indiana University Bloomington.

Innocent Awasom Afuh, associate librarian at Texas Tech University Libraries, Lubbock, is a STEM reference librarian with research, instruction, and outreach liaison responsibilities to the Davis College of Agriculture, biological sciences, chemistry, and biochemistry. He holds a BSc and an MSC in zoology from the University of Ibdan and a MInfSc from the African Regional Center for Information Science (ARCIS). He is a 2022–23 Fulbright Scholar to the Bindura University of Science Education, Zimbabwe, researching science communication patterns.

Elena Azadbakht is health sciences librarian at the University of Nevada, Reno, where she provides information literacy and research support to students and faculty in public health, kinesiology, nutrition, and social work. She is also interested in library usability, accessibility, systematic reviews, and research data management. Elena received her master of science in information (MSI) from the University of Michigan.

Katie Barrick is currently a content specialist at Square, and previously she was the biosciences liaison librarian at the University of Minnesota. She holds a BA in English from Gonzaga University and an MLIS from the University of Washington.

Marilyn S. Billings, who retired in December 2021, formerly served as head of the Office of Scholarly Communication at the University of Massachusetts Amherst Libraries. Marilyn provided campus, regional, and national leadership in alternative scholarly communication strategies and presented on a variety of open scholarship topics as well as providing oversight to the digital repository ScholarWorks@UMass Amherst and the Open Education Initiative. She was an active member of the Library Publishing Coalition, the Open Education Network, and SPARC. She currently serves as the faculty advisor to the Massachusetts ROTEL (Remixing Open Textbooks through an Equity Lens) grant funded through the US Department of Education.

Josh Bolick is the head of the David Shulenburger Office of Scholarly Communication and Copyright at the University of Kansas and a colead editor of this book and related projects. He advocates for open access, authors' rights, open education, and issues related and is interested in OER as a vehicle for expanding scholarly communication knowledge and expertise. Josh holds a bachelor's degree from the University of North Carolina Wilmington and a master's in library and information studies from Florida State University.

Maria Bonn is an Associate Professor and Director of the MS in Library and Information Science program in the School of Information Sciences at the university of Illinois Urbana Champaign. Her research and teaching focuses on academic librarianship and the role of libraries in scholarly communication and publishing. She served as the associate university librarian for publishing at the University of Michigan Library, with responsibility for publishing and scholarly communications initiatives, including Michigan Publishing. She has also been an assistant professor of English at institutions both in the United States and abroad. She received a bachelor's degree from the University of Rochester, master's and doctoral degrees in American literature from SUNY Buffalo, and a master's in information and library science from the University of Michigan.

Arthur J. Boston is the scholarly communication librarian at Murray State University. Boston manages the institutional repository, plans programming around open knowledge practices, and coordinates the Office of Research and Creative Activity. ORCID: 0000-0001-8590-4663.

Amy Buckland is Head, Research and Scholarship at the University of Guelph. In her work at McGill University, the University of Chicago, and most recently the University of Guelph, Amy has worked to build scalable and sustainable services in libraries to support open scholarship. She has been involved in large-scale digitisation initiatives, developed library-based publishing programmes, coauthored research data management policies, partnered with digital humanities researchers to further their reach, and drafted more pilot projects than she cares to remember. Elle est très fière d'être Montréalaise.

Gillian Byrne is manager of the Toronto Reference Library (Ontario, Canada), the largest library in the Toronto Public Library system, and one of the only public research libraries in Canada. She's written and presented on topics around library management, OA, and library technology and was the 2018 leader-in-residence at the University of British Columbia Okanagan Library.

Emily Carlisle-Johnston is a research and scholarly communication librarian at the University of Western Ontario. In this role, she provides education and support to scholars at Western University in order to facilitate open scholarship practices. This includes working with researchers to choose open venues for their research articles, providing guidance to editors whose open access journals are hosted with Western Libraries, and engaging with instructors to create or use open educational resources in their teaching.

Mark Clemente is the open access publisher agreements manager at the California Digital Library of the University of California, where he is responsible for initiating, developing, and coordinating the implementation of open access publisher agreements across a broad spectrum of publishing partners in support of UC's transformative open access initiatives. Prior to CDL, Mark worked in research libraries at Case Western Reserve University, MIT, Boston College, Hampshire College, and Georgetown University supporting programs in scholarly communication, digital collections, archives, and public services. Open access advocacy and a commitment to diversity, equity, and inclusion have been guiding principles in his career. Mark holds a BA in philosophy from American University and an MS in library and information science from Simmons College.

Perry Collins is the copyright and open educational resources librarian at the University of Florida Libraries, where she manages initiatives promoting open access in education, copyright literacy, and ethical approaches to digital scholarship. Before joining UF in 2018, Collins held a similar position at the Ball State University Libraries in Muncie, Indiana, and worked for six years as a program officer in the Office of Digital Humanities at the National Endowment for the Humanities. Collins holds an MLIS from the University of Illinois at Urbana-Champaign and an MA in American studies from the University of Kansas.

Cameron Cook is the data and digital scholarship manager for the University of Wisconsin-Madison general library system. Her interests include building holistic research infrastructures, leadership, building strong organizations, digital scholarship, equity in data and emerging research, data sharing, and open research. She strives to take a people-centered approach to her work and aims to empower and be an advocate for her campus communities, a translator between stakeholders, an improver of systems, and a dreamer of opportunities.

Kyle K. Courtney is a lawyer and librarian, serving as the copyright advisor at Harvard University, working out of Harvard Library's Office for Scholarly Communication. His work frames the law as the foundation for advancing the mission of all libraries, archives, and cultural institutions to acquire, preserve, maintain, and share the world's culture. He serves on boards and legal advisory committees for various law, library, and open access institutions including the Buddhist Digital Resource Center, the American Law Institute's Restatement of Copyright project, EveryLibrary Institute, and Library Futures.

Josh Cromwell is the scholarly communications manager at the University of Southern Mississippi, where he oversees the institutional repository, Aquila, and administers the library's publishing initiatives. He chairs the OER Working Group and oversees the Open Textbook Initiative, a joint venture between the libraries and provost's office to promote OER adoption on campus. He is also the chair of the libraries' copyright task force.

Lindsay Cronk, dean of libraries at Tulane University, is covered in tattoos and full of strong opinions, arguably the strongest of which being that as scholarly communication operators, library workers are key leaders in reforming the research enterprise. You can find her at Howard Tilton Library or on Twitter @LindsOnMars.

Will Cross is a medium-sized pile of diplomas in a trench coat. He serves as the Director of the Open Knowledge Center at N.C. State University, an instructor at UNC Chapel Hill, and a Senior Policy Fellow at American University's Washington College of Law. His current research on harmonizing copyright literacy in open knowledge communities is supported by grants from the IMLS, the Hewlett Foundation, and LYRASIS. In 2023 he conducted research on copyright literacies in European open science communities as a Fulbright Schuman Innovation Fellow.

Dr. Robin DeRosa is a national leader in open pedagogy, and an advocate for public infrastructures and institutions for higher education. As an undergraduate, she majored in Women's Studies and English, and participated in campus activism around LGBTQ+ issues, race and financial aid, and sexual assault policies. After college, she taught high school English and Theater before returning to school to complete a PhD in English with a focus on early American history and literature. She is a professor at Plymouth State University in New Hampshire, where she was a faculty member in English, the chair of the Interdisciplinary Studies program, and the founder and director of the Open Learning & Teaching Collaborative before moving into her current role as director of Learning & Libraries.

Abbey K. Elder is the open access and scholarly communication librarian for Iowa State University, where she manages campus initiatives for open access and open education. Their work focuses on empowering community members to engage with theories of openness by broadening access points to the conversation. In addition to her institutional work, Elder serves as the statewide open education coordinator for the Iowa Open Education Action Team (Iowa OER), where she coordinates with peers to develop and assess programs that can assist colleges supporting open education across the state of Iowa.

Will Engle, open strategist at the Centre for Teaching and Learning at the University of British Columbia, engages with projects that leverage open technologies, approaches, and pedagogies to support open learning and scholarship. With a background in library science, he is interested in understanding and supporting the removal of barriers that limit access to, and participation in, education, information, and knowledge creation.

Erin Fields, open education and scholarly communications librarian at the University of British Columbia Library, supports open scholarly practice on the UBC campus, including making scholarly knowledge openly accessible to the public and supporting OER-enabled pedagogy in the classroom. Through her role, she works collaboratively on developing policies and procedures with students, faculty, and support units to see the university progress toward barrier-free access to information resources.

Carrie Gits is head librarian at Austin Community College, Highland Campus. As the library services open educational resources (OER) facilitator, Carrie supports faculty and librarians through training and information sharing on open education and OER. Carrie supports faculty in their discovery, adoption, evaluation, creation, and use of OER. She works closely with others across the college to advance ACC's Z-Degree pathways and the adoption of OER. She authored the OER LibGuide as a resource for ACC faculty.

Regina Gong is the associate dean for student success and diversity at the University of San Diego Copley Library. In this inaugural role, she works alongside campus partners to ensure that all USD students succeed in their academic and non-academic pursuits. Regina also advances diversity, equity, inclusion, and accessibility in programs, partnerships, and outreach while championing OER across campus. Regina is actively involved in the open education community and has done numerous presentations, webinars, and workshops on OER, open education, open educational practices, and Women of Color in OER (#WoCinOER). She obtained her master's in library and information science (MLIS) at Wayne State University and is currently a Ph.D candidate in the Higher, Adult, and Lifelong Education (HALE) program at Michigan State University.

Jennie Rose Halperin (she/her/hers) is a digital strategist, community builder, and librarian who serves as executive director of Library Futures. She is focused on growing the organization and its reach and fostering a culture of open, inclusive leadership to support equitable library policy, technology, and advocacy. In 2021, she was named a visionary by Public Knowledge—a "future leader who will drive tech policy in the public interest for the next 20 years." Jennie is on the community advisory board for Invest in Open Infrastructure and has completed the Coaching Fellowship, Outreachy, and the CBYX Exchange for Young Professionals.

Sarah Hare is currently the open education librarian at Indiana University Bloomington, where she leads several affordable course material initiatives. These include IU's Course Material Fellowship Program (CMFP), which supports and incentivizes instructors to adopt or create OER. Sarah has published, presented, and taught several courses on open education.

Dr. Ian Harmon is the former scholarly communications librarian at West Virginia University, where he led outreach and provided instruction in the areas of open access publishing, data management, and digital scholarship. He holds a PhD in philosophy and an MS in library and information science from the University of Illinois.

Dr. Gabriele Hayden is librarian for research data management and reproducibility at the University of Oregon Libraries, where she supports research data management, sourcing and sharing data, and computational reproducibility. She has worked for an enterprise database reporting company and taught African American poetry, literary translation, and Greek and Roman humanities at Reed College. She earned her PhD in English from Yale University.

Natalie Hill is currently Marlboro Institute librarian at Emerson College and previously was open education librarian and a diversity resident librarian with the University of Texas Libraries. She is committed to increasing representation of historically underrepresented groups in teaching, learning, and research materials and taking a feminist, equity-informed approach to her own disciplinary practices. She holds an MLIS from Drexel University and a BA in literary studies from the University of Texas at Dallas.

Lillian Hogendoorn (née Rigling) is curator of digital experience at the University of Toronto Libraries. Lillian is a trained librarian with a passion for universal design and equitable access. She provides strategic management of the University of Toronto Libraries' web spaces to help users to connect with their services, resources, people, and libraries. She earned her master of information in library and information science at the University of Toronto Faculty of Information in 2016.

Christopher Hollister is the head of scholarly communication with the University at Buffalo Libraries. A longtime advocate and activist for transforming the current system of scholarly communication into an open one, Chris is cofounder and coeditor of the award-winning open access journal *Communications in Information Literacy*. He also teaches the scholarly communication course for the university's Department of Information Science.

Jeanne Hoover is head of scholarly communication in academic library services at East Carolina University. She leads the scholarly communication team in supporting faculty and student scholarly communication needs on campus. In this role, she helps coordinate ECU's mini-grant textbook program, provides workshops on scholarly communication topics, and manages the institutional repository.

Susan Ivey is the director of the research facilitation service at North Carolina State University, where she provides vision and leadership for the service, partnering with colleagues across campus to support evolving research computing and data needs. She received an MS in information science from the University of North Carolina at Chapel Hill and an MA in English and a BA in communication media from North Carolina State University. She is active in national organizations advancing research computing and data in higher education and is currently co-chair of the EDUCAUSE Research Computing and Data Community Group.

Meredith Jacob is project director—copyright and open licensing at American University's Washington College of Law and public lead for Creative Commons USA. Jacob's work focuses on research and advocacy on open access to federally funded research, flexible limitations and exceptions to copyright, and the public interest in intellectual property law.

Erin Jerome is the library publishing and institutional repository librarian at the University of Massachusetts Amherst. She manages the campus's institutional repository, which includes an open data repository, and supports the libraries' open access journal and monograph publishing program. Beyond UMass, she is committed to building platform-agnostic communities within the world of institutional repository practitioners and is one of the cofounders of both the Northeast Institutional Repository Day (NIRD) and the IR Managers Forum.

Dr. Rajiv Jhangiani is the vice provost, Teaching and Learning at Brock University, where he holds faculty appointments in the Departments of Educational Studies and Psychology, directs the Inclusive Education Research Lab, and is affiliated with the Social Justice Research Institute and the Social Justice and Equity Studies MA program. The architect of Canada's first zero textbook cost degree programs, Rajiv's scholarship focuses on open educational practices, student-centered pedagogies, and ethical approaches to educational technology. A co-author of three open textbooks in Psychology, his books include *Open: The Philosophy and Practices that are Revolutionizing Education and Science* (2017) and *Open at the Margins: Critical Perspectives on Open Education* (2020). Together with Dr. Robin DeRosa, he is a co-founder of the Open Pedagogy Notebook.

Dr. Annie Johnson is the associate university librarian for publishing, preservation, research, and digital access at the University of Delaware Library, Museums and Press. She holds a PhD in history from the University of Southern California.

Dr. Dick Kawooya is an associate professor at the School of Information Science, University of South Carolina. Dick has eighteen years' experience of research, teaching, and advocacy work in the field of intellectual property (IP) with a special focus on IP and innovation, IP and the informal economy in Africa, and copyright and access to knowledge. He has been involved in several major international projects. He was lead researcher for the African Copyright and Access to Knowledge (ACA2K) project (2006–2010), and he participated in Open AIR, the African Innovation Research and Training Project (2010-2014), where he studied the role of IP in technology transfer in Africa's emerging informal economies, with a specific focus on the nascent electric vehicle industry. Currently, Dick is involved in the project Contributing to Public Interest Copyright Policy at WIPO: Promoting Access to Knowledge and the Right to Research (2021–2023).

Dr. Spencer D. C. Keralis, an independent scholar and educator, studies the ethics of collaboration in humanities research and critical digital pedagogy. Their work has appeared in Disrupting the Digital Humanities, Debates in Digital Humanities, and other collections and journals. They hold a PhD in English and American literature from NYU.

Emily Kilcer is the scholarly communication librarian at the University at Albany, where she works collaboratively to inform, support, and connect open practices on campus. In this role, she manages scholarly communication and data services initiatives, including outreach and education on open access, scholarly publishing, copyright, and research data management.

Sophia Lafferty-Hess is a senior research data management consultant at Duke University Libraries, where she provides instruction and guidance in data management, open science, and reproducible research practices and curates data for publication via data repositories. She obtained an MS in information science and a master of public administration from the University of North Carolina at Chapel Hill.

Marcel LaFlamme, open research manager at the Public Library of Science, is a qualitative researcher and scholarly communication professional committed to understanding the needs of diverse communities and designing solutions to meet them.

Amanda C. Larson is the affordable learning instructional consultant at the Ohio State University, where she creates professional development opportunities for staff, librarians, and instructors around open pedagogy and open educational practices. She also liaises with the Affordable Learning Exchange (ALX) to connect ALX grant winners to library resources, subject specialists, and affordable materials through project management and resource curation. Previously, she was the open education librarian at the Penn State University Libraries, where she coordinated affordable content initiatives across twenty-plus campuses and provided guidance on OER curation, Creative Commons licensing, and project management.

Brandon Locke is the Community Cultivation Program Officer at Educopia Institute. His work spans scholarly communication, digital scholarship, and data literacy. He received an MLIS from the University of Illinois at Urbana-Champaign and an MA in American History at the University of Nebraska–Lincoln.

Julia Lovett is an associate professor and the digital initiatives librarian at the University of Rhode Island Libraries. She manages digital and scholarly communication-related initiatives such as digitization projects, digital collections, the institutional repository, library-based publishing services, open access ETDs, and the URI open access policy. She recently wrapped up a 4-year term as reviews co-editor for the Journal of Librarianship and Scholarly Communication.

Colleen Lyon is the head of scholarly communications at the University of Texas at Austin and leads a team working on issues related to OER, open access, repositories, and copyright. She is broadly interested in supporting a more sustainable scholarly communication ecosystem and in improving copyright education.

Brianna Marshall is a library worker with research interests in digital scholarship and scholarly communication services, person-centered change strategies, and library administration. She is currently interim dean at Northern Kentucky University (NKU); previously, she was senior associate dean at NKU, director of research services at the University of California Riverside Library and digital curation coordinator and research data services lead at the University of Wisconsin-Madison Libraries. She is the editor of the book *The Complete Guide to Personal Digital Archiving*, published by the American Library Association Press; an author of the openly licensed *Fostering Change: A Team-Based Guide*, published by the Association of College and Research Libraries; and designer and facilitator for the Fostering Change cohort.

Dr. John Edward Martin, director of scholarly communication, coordinates scholarly communication outreach and education at the University of North Texas Libraries and oversees their open publishing, OER, scholarly impact, data management planning, and comics studies initiatives. He is a 2022 HumetricsHSS Community Fellow, for which he is developing workshops on values-based scholarly assessment. He holds a PhD in American literature from Northwestern University and an MS in library science from the University of North Texas.

Margaret McLaughlin (she/they) is currently an associate instructor and PhD student at Indiana University Bloomington. Her research focuses on open education, multilingual pedagogy, and translation and adaptation. She holds an MLS and an MA in comparative literature from Indiana University.

Tisha Mentnech is the research librarian for life sciences and research metrics at North Carolina State University Libraries, where she supports agriculture and life science disciplines, reproducibility, responsible metrics, and open science. Tisha received their MSLIS from Simmons University.

Laura Miller is currently a proposal specialist in the Office of Research at the University of Central Florida. She was formerly the visiting open publishing librarian at Florida State University, where she led open publishing programs for students and faculty. She holds an MSI from Florida State University.

Sarah "Moxy" Moczygemba is a digital communication professional who strives to blend current trends with best practices in the field. After spending six years at the University of Florida George A. Smathers Libraries as the social media specialist and the outreach and promotion assistant for the Florida and Puerto Rico Digital Newspaper Project, Moxy is now part of the E-Learning, Technology and Communications department in the UF College of Education. They hold an MA in religious studies from the University of Florida and a BA in political science from Trinity University.

Emma Molls is the director of the Open Research & Publishing Department at the University of Minnesota, which includes research data services, research impact and research information management, publishing services, and houses the Data Curation Network. Emma is an associate editor for Directory of Open Access Journals, president of Library Publishing Coalition, and past board chair of the *Journal of Librarianship and Scholarly Communication*. They hold a MLIS from University of Wisconsin-Milwaukee.

Alison Moore is digital scholarship librarian for the Digital Humanities Innovation Lab and manager of the SFU Knowledge Mobilization Hub at Simon Fraser University Library. Ali has an MLIS from McGill University, and since joining SFU Library in 2015, she has worked in a variety of roles, most recently as the assistant head of the Research Commons. Ali has expertise supporting student and faculty researchers with scholarly communication, knowledge mobilization, research impact, online presence, and data visualization. Ali's research interests include library assessment and scholarly publishing.

Dr. Samuel A. Moore is the scholarly communication specialist at Cambridge University Library and a research associate at Homerton College. His research explores the ethics and politics of academic knowledge production and research communication, specifically on topics relating to academic publishing, open research and community governance. He has a Ph.D in Digital Humanities from King's College London and over a decade's experience as a publisher, educator and researcher specialising in open access and academic publishing. He is also one of the organisers of the Radical Open Access Collective.

Carla Myers serves as associate professor and coordinator of scholarly communications for the Miami University Libraries. Her professional presentations and publications focus on fair use, copyright in the classroom, and library copyright issues.

Peace Ossom-Williamson, MLS, MS, AHIP, is associate director of the NNLM National Center for Data Services, NYU, Langone Health. She is a medical librarian and health educator with experience providing reference services and outreach, data services and scholarly communication, and back-end services in libraries. She is a recognized researcher, receiving the 2021 Texas Woman's University Hallmark Alumni award and the Eliot Prize from the Medical Library Association for a paper deemed most effective in furthering medical librarianship in 2020. As an active educator, she teaches courses on data services and public health informatics.

Jennifer Patiño is the data and digital scholarship librarian for the University of Wisconsin–Madison general library system. She works to support the institutional open access repository MINDS@UW, Research Data Services, and instruction in library-based tools for text and data mining and data visualization. Her interests include open access, digital humanities, data equity, and building communities of practice.

Anali Maughan Perry is the head of the Open Science and Scholarly Communication division at ASU Library at Arizona State University. In this role, she leads efforts to provide outreach and education to the ASU community regarding open science and scholarship, scholarly publishing, and copyright, with particular emphasis on fair use, open access to scholarly information, and open education.

Dr. Gemmicka Piper is the Humanities Librarian and an adjunct lecturer in Africana Studies at Indiana University–Purdue University Indianapolis. While engaging in public facing librarianship, Dr. Piper also leverages her educational background in 20th and 21st century African American literature and writing to offer specialized research support for BIPOC graduate students. She also uses her skillset to support the advancement of non-STEM focused research through intentional activities and collaborations with ethnic and humanities scholarship focused centers on her campus.

Eric Prosser is the STEM division head and engineering and entrepreneurship librarian at the Arizona State University Library. Eric provides research services for faculty, graduate students, and undergraduate students, along with instruction in critical analysis and information literacy, including the legal and ethical use of information.

Brian Quinn, graduate student services and social sciences librarian at Texas Tech University Libraries, is Barnie E. Rushing Jr. Outstanding Researcher and author of numerous peer-reviewed publications. A recipient of the Excellence in Librarianship Award from the American

Psychological Association, Brian has served on the editorial boards of *Library Resources and Technical Services* and other journals. He is interested in scholarly communication issues and serves on the scholarly publishing team at TTU.

Vicky Rampin (née Steeves), librarian for research data management and reproducibility at New York University, is a librarian who cares deeply about open and persistent access to knowledge. She works at the intersection of data management, reproducibility, and digital preservation.

Tara Robertson is a professional leadership coach and a diversity, equity and inclusion consultant. As a coach, she primarily serves women of color in corporate careers to go from being underestimated and overworked to being unapologetic and wildly successful. She is an intersectional feminist who uses data and research to advocate for equality and inclusion. She brings nearly fifteen years experience leading change in open source technology communities and corporate spaces, including three years leading Diversity and Inclusion at Mozilla. As a consultant she partners with corporate leaders to help drive systemic change. Once upon a time she was an academic librarian.

Julia E. Rodriguez is the scholarly communications and health sciences librarian at Oakland University in Rochester, Michigan. She is the team lead for the campus-wide Affordable Course Materials Initiative and coordinates OU Libraries' OER and open access initiatives and the institutional repository. Her scholarship has focused on open access, copyright, and library instruction pedagogy.

Charlotte Roh, publications manager for the California Digital Library, has an MLIS from the University of Illinois at Urbana-Champaign and has worked as a reference and instruction librarian at Cal State San Marcos, as scholarly communications librarian at the University of San Francisco, scholarly communication resident at the University of Massachusetts Amherst, and with publishers like Taylor & Francis and Oxford University Press. Her research and writing focuses on the intersection of scholarly communication and social justice, and she currently serves as a board member for the Society of Scholarly Publishing, community manager for We Here, and a member of the Library Publishing Coalition's Ethical Framework Task Force.

Dorothea Salo is an instructor at the University of Wisconsin iSchool (formerly School of Library and Information Studies). Salo is an academic librarian and library-school instructor whose interests include security and privacy, metadata and linked data, scholarly communication, research-data management, audiovisual digitization, and digital preservation.

Ariana Santiago is the head of open education services at the University of Houston Libraries. She is a graduate of the SPARC Open Education Leadership Program (2018–2019) and a curriculum designer and presenter for the ACRL RoadShow on OER and Affordability. Ariana holds an MA in applied learning and instruction from the University of Central Florida, an MA in library and information science from the University of South Florida, and a BA in anthropology from the University of Central Florida.

Franklin Sayre is the makerspace librarian and department cochair at Thompson Rivers University (TRU). Prior to coming to TRU, Franklin was a health science librarian at the University of Minnesota and the University of British Columbia, where he focused on advocating for open and reproducible methods, building collaborative research partnerships, and teaching evidence-based practice.

Teresa Schultz is an associate professor and the scholarly communications and social sciences librarian at the University of Nevada, Reno. Teresa educates the UNR community about new initiatives in scholarly communication, including open access, data sharing, and open educational resources, as well as answering questions about copyright. She received her MLS from Indiana University-Indianapolis.

Kerry Sewell serves as the research librarian within the William E. Laupus Health Sciences Library at East Carolina University. Within that role, Kerry supports Open Access publishing, data management and sharing, and responsible use of bibliometrics. She also leads the Laupus Library Systematic Review Service.

Elisabeth Shook is the data impact librarian for the Inter-university Consortium for Political and Social Research (ICPSR) at the University of Michigan where she contributes to the development of the Bibliography of Data-Related Literature. Prior to joining ICPSR, Elisabeth was the head of scholarly communications and data management for Albertsons Library at Boise State University. She oversaw the development of Boise State's institutional repository and assisted in the development of the university's data management and open educational resources services. Elisabeth earned her master of library and information studies from the University of Wisconsin–Madison and her bachelor of arts in history from Sterling College. Prior to Boise State, Elisabeth was the librarian for copyright and scholarly communications at Vanderbilt University. In addition, Elisabeth has held positions with Wright State University in Dayton, Ohio, and with the United States Forest Service.

Samantha Teplitzky is the open science librarian at the University of California, Berkeley, and the library's liaison to the Earth and Planetary Science department and the Lawrence Berkeley National Laboratory. Sam enjoys working on topics related to open science, data, reproducibility, transparency in research workflows, and inclusive science community building. She holds a BA in geology and art history from Williams College, an MA in geography from UC Berkeley, and an MLIS from San José State University.

Kaitlin Thaney is the Executive Director of Invest in Open Infrastructure, a nonprofit initiative dedicated to increasing investment, adoption, and sustainability of open infrastructure for research and scholarship. Her career has been centered around open infrastructure organizations; previously serving as the Endowment Director for the Wikimedia Foundation, where she led development of a fund to sustain the future of Wikipedia and free knowledge. Prior to joining Wikimedia, Thaney directed the program portfolio for the Mozilla Foundation, following her time building the Mozilla Science Lab, a program to serve the open research community. She was on the founding team for Digital Science, where she helped launch and advise programs to serve researchers worldwide, building on her time at Creative Commons, where she crafted legal, technical, and social infrastructure for sharing data on the web.

Camille Thomas is scholarly communication librarian at Florida State University (FSU), where she encourages the adoption of OER at FSU in addition to offering copyright, open publishing, and impact outreach. Camille is also a former SPARC Open Education Fellow for projects on public interest groups and OER discovery. She also served in several relevant editorial appointments, national and regional service groups, and research projects, such as

Perceptions of Open Access Publishing among Black, Indigenous, and People of Color Faculty. Camille received her MLIS from Florida State University in 2015 and a BA in English from the University of Central Florida in 2012.

Paul A. Thomas is a library specialist at the University of Kansas in Lawrence, KS. He holds a PhD in library and information management from Emporia State School of Library and Information Management in Emporia, KS. An avid Wikipedia editor, Thomas has authored several scholarly articles about Wikipedia, which have appeared in publications like *Transformative Works and Cultures*, the *Journal of Fandom Studies*, the *Journal of Information Literacy*, and *College & Research Libraries*.

Micah Vandegrift works at the intersection of community, policy, and technology through his role as a senior user experience strategist for the National Institutes of Health's All of Us Research Program. He spent a decade working as an academic librarian and was a Fulbright Scholar to the European Union in 2018, where he studied open science policy.

Ali Versluis (she/hers) is currently the acting head of the Research and Scholarship team at the University of Guelph, which resides on the ancestral lands of the Attawandaron people and the current treaty lands of the Mississaugas of the Credit. Prior to running point on strategic and operational matters for the R&S team, Ali was an open educational resources librarian. She tweets half-baked thoughts, organized labour wins, and vociferous appreciation for the Toronto Raptors @aliversluis.

Dr. Nic Weber is assistant professor in the Information School at the University of Washington, where he teaches and does research in the areas of systems analysis and design, software sustainability, and data curation. At the iSchool he has affiliations with the DataLab and the Technology and Social Change (TASCHA) group. Weber is the technical director of the Qualitative Data Repository, where he leads a small development team in building open source tools to facilitate transparent social science research. He has a PhD in information science from the University of Illinois.

Jennifer Zerkee is a copyright specialist in the Simon Fraser University Copyright Office, where she develops and delivers copyright information and education to instructors, researchers, students, and staff. Her research examines the parliamentary review of Canada's Copyright Act with the aim of using the findings to support future advocacy for copyright and user rights in higher education and libraries.